WALL STREET

Wall Street
A Cultural History

STEVE FRASER

faber and faber

First published in the USA in 2005
by HarperCollins
First published in the UK in 2005
by Faber and Faber Limited
3 Queen Square London WC1N 3AU
This paperback edition first published in 2006

Typeset by Faber and Faber Limited
Printed in England by Mackays of Chatham plc,
Chatham, Kent

A CIP record for this book
is available from the British Library

ISBN 978-0-571-21829-5
0-571-21829-6

2 4 6 8 10 9 7 5 3 1

For:
Jill, Max, Emma and Jonny
and Geggie and Figgie

In Memory of:
Hilshka, Yink, Cuddy, Vev, Babe, Eachy, Bucky, Ruth, Nimie,
Rivie, Suckie, Van, Hilda, Goose

Contents

Introduction

Daniel Drew[1] was a notorious speculator during Wall Street's early years, around the time of the Civil War. He was famed for his truly stunning feats of insider trading and book-cooking, and his ruthless disregard for the public interest. Today's Americans, who have just lived through the greatest series of Wall Street scandals since the Crash of 1929, would find him a familiar figure. So too might people around the world. Similar characters populate the pasts of cities like London, Paris, and Berlin. More recently, thanks to the global dispersion of financial markets, roguish operators like Drew have shown up in such unlikely places as Bangkok, Kuala Lumpur, and St Petersburg. The penumbra of mass delusion, appalling transgression, and financial panic hovering around infamous speculators like Jay Gould in the nineteenth century and Michael Milken in the twentieth is a universal, not uniquely American phenomenon. It infected Antwerp and Amsterdam even before the seventeenth-century Dutch colonials erected the wooden stockade in New Amsterdam from which Wall Street draws its name.

This book is about the multitude of ways in which Wall Street has infused everyday life and culture in America over the past two centuries. It is therefore in some irreducible sense an American history. But it is also a story with global ramifications. Capitalism, which Wall Street has come to stand for, is, and always has been, an international phenomenon. Naturally, American capitalism is different from British capitalism which in turn is not the same as what goes on in Thailand, Russia, or South Korea. Nonetheless, capitalism no matter where it arises incubates a distinctive set of cultural attitudes and behaviors. Or rather, it sets in motion protracted cultural warfare about what should matter most: God or Mammon, risk or social welfare, equality or hierarchy, work or wealth, democracy or elitism, individual freedom or communal integrity, imperial hegemony or national self-determination, prudent self-restraint or erotic self-expression. The financial system operates as a magnet around which heated emotions about these and other bedrock human concerns tend to collect. That's why the story of the way Americans have wrestled with these dilemmas – a tale of cultural combat played out on Wall Street since the founding of the Republic in the late eighteenth century – contains an inherent universality despite its peculiarly American features.

Drew, who came from humble beginnings, once reportedly said about his colorful career on the Street that 'It seems like a dream to me.' This book is about dreams, and nightmares too. It is not, however, so much about the reveries of people like Drew, those men (and they were almost exclusively men) who rose to fame and fortune or infamy and ruin by trafficking in the mysteries of the Street. There already exists a sizeable library of books about them. Though we will periodically come face to face with these men and their fantasies, this book is mainly about the rest of us: Americans and others around the world for whom the Street has long been an object of fascination, even if they never bought a single share in their lives. It tells the two-hundred-year-old story of how Wall Street has inspired dreams and nightmares deep inside American culture, leaving its imprint on people's lives. Those popular images and metaphors, those visions and anxieties and desires that have attached themselves to the Street, can reveal something fundamental about its history, about its place in the national saga. They can tell us something not only about the mind of Wall Street, but also, more intriguingly, about the Wall Streets of the American mind.

Examining how Wall Street has entered into the lives of generations past and present is both a probe into the American character and an inquiry into the way the character of America has changed. But this is tricky terrain. The idea that the nation in all its polymorphous diversity can nonetheless be assigned a distinctive and unitary character – a profile that captures a set of universally applicable traits, mental states, and behaviors – is an elusive and dubious one at best. The United States is a country whose profound heterogeneity has been in some sense its very reason for being. So there have always been multiple American 'characters', many Wall Streets of the mind. Still, all the satiric cartoons and magazine exposés, the occasional hit movies and Broadway plays, the highbrow novels along with the potboilers and the folk poetry, the political jeremiads and hellfire and brimstone sermons, all the Horatio Alger inspirational storybooks and hero-worshipping biographies, the memoirs of derring-do and irretrievable loss, the visions of imperial grandeur and masculine prowess, do make Wall Street a window into the souls of Americans. By traveling down those Wall Streets of the American mind we encounter more than the Street itself. It becomes the terrain on which people have wrestled with ancestral attitudes and beliefs about work and play, democracy and capitalism, wealth, freedom and equality, godliness and evil, heroes and villains, luck and sexuality, national purpose and economic well-being. And of course these basic preoccupations are hardly confined to the United States even if this book zeroes in on their distinctly American inflection.

What is all the more astonishing is that we can learn about all this even though until very recently most people had no active involvement in the daily life of the Street. The dissociation is still greater in Britain: John Maynard Keynes long ago observed that the American stock market was inherently more unstable than securities markets in Europe, because it invited the participation of rank amateurs on a mass scale and for frankly reckless, speculative purposes. But even the United States has only been a 'shareholder nation', with roughly half its families having some stake in the market, for the last quarter-century. And even that exaggerates the degree of real personal engagement. The crucial point, however, is that even when no more than a minuscule proportion of the population actually invested anything in the stock market, Wall Street nonetheless exerted an indisputable magnetism.

Wall Street's presence was already felt at the nation's founding. Veterans of the Revolution, vigilant guardians of its democratic achievements, worried about Wall Street as an incubator of counter-revolutionary conspiracies. Others, like Alexander Hamilton, already conceived of the Street as an engine of future national glory. The founding fathers fell out and became the bitterest of enemies, trading some of the most vitriolic accusations in American political history about the virtues and dangers of speculation.

The country then underwent half a century of extraordinary territorial expansion, with an explosion of commercial agriculture, new

settlements, and marvelous new means of transportation and communication. Jacksonian America dreamt of boundless opportunity for
Every Man. Some saw Wall Street as yet another arena in which those
plebeian fantasies might come true. Others grew anxious that the
Street might take advantage of the youthful nation's callow self-confidence, its benign cupidity, and become a breeding ground for confidence men. Still others remained convinced that Wall Street was what
their revolutionary ancestors had warned about: a monstrous house of
aristocrats whose inscrutable machinations would engorge the country's fortune, making it, like the Old World, a place of presumptuous
elites and dispossessed peoples.

After the Civil War, an industrial revolution remade the nation at
unimaginable speed. In a generation, America became more similar to
today's United States than to the nation of Lincoln. Wall Street figured
centrally in that great transformation. Its financiers dominated the
economic and political landscape, especially the railroads, which were
the cornerstone of the new economy and depended on a sympathetic
government for their creation. The men who choreographed their construction and lived lavishly off their proceeds were revered by some as
master-builders and Napoleonic conquerors. Writers marveled at their
Darwinian ferocity, but they were reviled by others as robber barons
and sinners. For the first time the Street became a spectacle, an object
of mass fascination. It seduced and repelled people – sometimes the
same people, all at once.

Fortunes amassed by titans like Commodore Vanderbilt and Jay
Gould were personal and dynastic. This was an age still marked by
family capitalism. By the turn of the century, however, the modern,
publicly traded corporation familiar today began to supplant the family firm. It was invented on Wall Street and once again the Street
revamped the economy, its innovation later emulated abroad. There
were those who hailed the new order as a progressive step and credited its creators, men like J. P. Morgan, with saving the nation from an
endless cycle of boom and bust, bringing panic, depression and severe
social upheaval. Even if they never came anywhere near the New York
Stock Exchange, new legions of the urban middle class shared vicari-
ously in the nation's rise as a prominent player in international affairs,
challenging Britain's pre-eminence – much of this due to Wall Street's
growing financial clout. Although it would take the profound
upheaval of World War I to re-order the pecking order permanently,

even by the turn of the century the European Great Powers were acutely aware of Morgan's global reach.

Millions of Americans, however, were less impressed with 'Morgan, the financial gorgon'. Prairie farmers, urban workers, middle-sized businessmen and others bitterly denounced him and waged a second civil war against the 'money trust'. Populists excoriated Wall Street as a 'devil fish' sucking away the life-blood of the country's agrarian heartland. Progressive reformers in the cities indicted the country's principal investment bank for misusing 'other people's money' and degrading the nation's democratic heritage. Patrician survivors of New England's Brahmin and New York's Knickerbocker elites issued Götterdämmerung judgments about how Morgan's ascendancy signaled the fall of western civilization. Working-class socialists welcomed the Street's trustification of the economy, but only because they were sure it was but a transit point on the way to the collective ownership of the means of production by an emancipated proletariat.

During its first century, Wall Street had very slowly widened the orbit of popular participation in its money-making, but the proportion of the population who were really involved remained tiny. That didn't stop people from regarding Wall Street from afar as a yellow brick road to instant wealth, admiring and envying those from modest backgrounds who'd ridden down the Street to fame and fortune. But it was only with the Jazz Age in the 1920s that the possibility of a democratized Wall Street became realistic. While the same process was only faintly visible abroad, Europeans were nevertheless fascinated with goings-on in America, mesmerized by Wall Street's zany and infectious exuberance.

Whether 'democratization' was real or not, the Street, along with the speakeasy and the Charleston, came to symbolize a landmark moment in American popular culture. For Wall Street, moreover, it was a moment of notable transgression. As the association with bootleg liquor, short skirts, and sexualized music suggests, the Street took on an erotic appeal. Actually, that had always been true in so far as the activities on Wall Street seemed to violate the precepts of the work ethic. But in earlier times, official society severely censured Wall Street's tendency to libidinal abandon. Others may have secretly enjoyed the way the Street seemed to thumb its nose at the strictures of Protestant morality, but they did so covertly, enjoying a sneaky thrill. In the 1920s, that underground Wall Street came to embody a new culture of play, and for a moment at least shed the moral stigma that had shadowed it for generations. Only a few die-hard Populists and left-wing bohemian intellectuals still remembered the dark side.

The Jazz Age lasted only a moment though. It was ended by the second of the two great ruptures in the fabric of national life, so fundamental that nothing would be the same afterwards. The first was the Civil War. The second was the Great Depression. The Crash of 1929 did more than end the national infatuation with the Street's sexiness. It implicated Wall Street in a crisis so grave it wouldn't recover its credibility for forty years. Moreover, Wall Street's implosion was felt all over the world. It ruined embryonic efforts at international commercial and financial cooperation undertaken during the 1920s, ignited a new round of ferocious mud-wrestling among the great powers to grab onto what was left of the world capitalist economy, and trailed in its wake an enduring skepticism about Wall Street's activities.

For a generation and more, since at least 1900, Wall Street had been a central gathering place for a genuine American ruling class – or at any rate, Wall Street's inner circle came as close to constituting one as was likely in a society as fissiparous and liquefied as America's. That class possessed enormous economic power of course, but also political influence, social cachet and cultural authority. All of that was vaporized by the Depression. For the first time, the Street's business was subjected to a real if flawed public supervision under the New Deal. Faith in the free market, the defining principle of the ancien regime, was at a steep discount. The whole tone of the country shifted, muting the traditional incantations of self-interest in favor of social welfare. Wall Street's most august figures were not merely exposed as cheaters or felons, but were widely ridiculed as incompetent.

Laughter is a punishing historical sentence. The public face of the Street, so conspicuous for so many years, subsided beneath its waves. By 1940, all those bright young graduates of Ivy League colleges who used to flock there were finding work elsewhere. For nearly a century, Wall Street had been an essential element of the country's cultural iconography, nearly as omnipresent as Uncle Sam or the Western cowboy. But for the next forty years, roughly from 1940 to 1980, it vanished from the front page and lived out its life in the business section of the daily newspaper.

There was something bizarre about this invisibility. After all, the post-war order that put the western world back together again after the carnage – that cluster of institutions including the International Monetary Fund, the World Bank, the Marshall Plan, and NATO – was designed and presided over by Wall Street's 'wise men', a group of self-effacing financier-statesmen who came to be known as the 'Establishment', proconsuls of the American Century. Because the 'Establishment' devoted itself almost exclusively to matters of foreign policy, it was ironically, a more palpable presence – at least until the Vietnam years – in the domestic politics of post-war Western Europe, the Middle East, and Asia than it was back home. Indeed, the political alliances and even the ideological accent of the 'Free World' were the creation of an American patriciate nurtured on Wall Street but more engaged by Anglo-European culture and the strategic calculation of America's global ambitions.

In the United States, these years of cultural silence and political pre-eminence were a strange interlude indeed. And they eventually set off even stranger reverberations. 'The Establishment' ended up getting attacked not only from the left, which one might expect, but from the right as well. For as long as anyone could remember Wall Street had been associated with the forces of concentrated wealth and power. However, from the time of Ronald Reagan's cheering news that it was 'morning in America' once again, the Street re-emerged as a site of revolutionary struggle; only this time it was Wall Street in the vanguard of the revolution, a revolution directed in part against itself. Under the banner of freedom and the free market, held aloft by President Reagan and Prime Minister Margaret Thatcher, Wall Street warriors promised to take on the ossified, strangulating bureaucracies of the government, the corporation, and Wall Street's old guard. Emancipation Wall Street-style was, in America at any rate, partly a counter-revolution against the New Deal, against all its irritating interference and egalitarian sentimentality. America's second gilded age during the 1980s vented those resentments, wore its new wealth and ostentatious self-indulgence like a badge of honor, and dismantled every piece of government regulatory apparatus it could lay its hands on. Compared with the first gilded age exactly a century earlier, there was much less opposition, although there was some: in Tom Wolfe's mocking send-ups of these new 'masters of the universe', and in Oliver Stone's memorable cinematic portrait of Wall Street sociopath Gordon Gekko, who preached the gospel that 'greed is good'. Novels like *The Bonfire of the Vanities* and movies like *Wall Street* became international cultural events, testimony to the Street's global presence and to a lingering antagonism.

By and large, however, resistance had weakened and lost its political sting. Apparently, the social and psychic revolution associated with Wall Street went deeper than the mere lionization of Michael Milken in his glory days. By the 1990s, if it wasn't quite fair to describe America as a 'shareholder nation', it was nonetheless true that the Street's aroma was no longer the infernal one so familiar from the days of Jefferson, Jackson, and Roosevelt. Every Man could feel at home there like never before.

Moreover, Wall Street led a 'financialization' of the world's economy whose consequences were felt everywhere from London to Tokyo, from Russia to East Asia. The 'Washington Consensus', so long as it lasted, was hardly received with universal acclaim. But neither was the assent skin-deep. The intermarriage of Wall Street and foreign investment banks and brokerages blurred national boundaries and relaxed old rivalries while generating new ones, de-localizing Wall Street while extending its reach. The capacity of the 'Washington Consensus' to reorder national economies, especially in the Third World and newly liberated Eastern Europe, was considerable. What remains far more doubtful is whether the liberationist esprit, the democratic excitement about Wall Street utopianism so exuberantly celebrated in America, would flourish in these very differently constituted societies. Even in Europe, where the kinship is closest, there persists an ethos of social solidarity that, however attenuated, is still far more robust than anything remaining from the New Deal era in America. In addition, Wall Street-driven globalization proceeds within a context of a constricted world market and worrying signs of internecine competition among nations and regional trading/political blocs.

The history of Wall Street, then, is one of deep ambivalence and chronic cultural warfare. The ambivalence has left its mark across American citizens' common and private lives. Is speculation a species of gambling or parasitism or both, and so a sin against the work ethic and the Protestant moral order; or is it on the contrary at the very heart of the American entrepreneurial genius, that audacious instinct to seek out the new, to cross frontiers, to place a bet on the future? Has Wall Street secured the nation's economic efficiency, innovation, and growth, or did it on the contrary convert potential material wherewithal into waste while choking off opportunity for those outside its charmed circle? Has the hero-worshiping of financiers degraded the manners and mores of American civilization; or do these men deserve credit for the nation's abundance at home and stature abroad? Has democracy suffered as power gravitated to domineering aggregations of concentrated wealth; or is the damage to democracy made worse by attempts to rein in that impulse to accumulate, to fetter the urge for self-aggrandizement nurtured by the free market? Has Wall Street destroyed the national faith in a classless America, the land of equal opportunity for all; or has Wall Street always opened itself up to the self-made man, as a place where a person from nowhere could become a somebody from somewhere? Is the ferocious and steely titan of finance a worthy model of masculinity; or merely the prototype for the 'rip their eyes out' primitivism of Gordon Gekko? Is Wall Street a Babylon on the Hudson, reeking of de-sublimated sex, a land of anarchic luck and reckless play; or is it a commercial City on a Hill, a zone of prudential calculation, deferred gratification, and sober rationality? And if it's both, which is to be preferred? Has Wall Street's growing pre-eminence in the global economy enhanced the nation; or nurtured delusions of grandeur and imperialist bullying?

Ambivalences like these – and many more one might name – make the history of Wall Street in American life an enigma. Or perhaps Wall Street's enigma is a purely American one: how could the United States turn out to be a deeply conservative country, yet irresistibly drawn to change? The collective instinct to resist the usurpations of presumptuous wealth runs up against the individual impulse to seize the main chance. Even those multitudes for whom market society has brought worrying insecurity remain tempted by the dream. For all its hustle and bustle, its faith in the next big thing, the nation's center of cultural gravity hovers in place. Again and again the country has headed back to the future – and at no time has that seemed truer than now.

For the moment at least, Wall Street has won the war for hearts and minds – in America at least. What an extraordinary reversal: while Americans have generally been divided about what they thought of Wall Street, the verdict has usually been negative, at least until about the end of World War II. If Wall Street was an arena of cultural warfare, then Lincoln's 'angels of our better nature' were for generations mobilized against the Street. Even as its power and cultural weight grew, those who applauded it and placed hope in its impressive if inscrutable undertakings found themselves on the defensive. Certainly this was true within the precincts of high culture: among novelists and playwrights, theologians and academics, jurists and highbrow magazine editors. Again and again the financial elite found itself indicted by the country's intellectual establishment: from Edith Wharton's first bestseller, *The House of Mirth*, to the patrician jeremiads of Henry Adams, to the future Supreme Court Justice Louis Brandeis's merciless dissection of the 'money trust' in *Other People's Money*. This was so in the realm of popular culture as well, where the grotesque caricatures of cartoonists like Thomas Nast, the silent movies targeting villainous bankers, and the sensationalist exposés of yellow journalists like Joseph Pulitzer and William Randolph Hearst returned to Wall Street again and again as a site of scandal and iniquity. It was even true in the political realm, notwithstanding the enormous influence over public policy wielded by the Street. No President until Calvin Coolidge found it strategically wise to lavish praise on the Street in public; no President after him dared do so until Ronald Reagan; no President since Reagan has failed to do so.

This striking trajectory of conventional political wisdom reflects something deeper: the sentimental re-education of the nation over these two hundred years. In living rooms all across America, where cultural wars ultimately get settled, the verdict about the Street has been revised. Even in the teeth of the most stunning Wall Street frauds since the Crash of '29, people remain enamored. The political fallout has been minimal. The wellsprings of opposition seem to have dried up; not only in the political world, but more intimately too: in what people think about the relationship between God and Mammon, in the way our literary and cinematic fictions and daily newspapers assume a stance of fateful inevitability about the reign of the free market. Crony capitalism so blatant it might have made Daniel Drew blush hardly arouses comment, much less condemnation. Delusional or not, for the moment at least Wall Street's promise of emancipation, of 'Every Man a Speculator', has taken hold. The old Wall Street is dead. Long live Wall Street!

How did this happen? At least some part of the answer may be found here.

PART ONE

Buccaneers and Confidence Men on the Financial Frontier

I

Revolution and Counter-Revolution

One of the strangest documents ever authored by a public official appeared in 1797. Soon to become known as 'The Reynolds Pamphlet', its formal title, so typical of eighteenth-century literature, amounted to a miniature essay in its own right: 'Observations on Certain Documents Contained in #s 5 & 6 of "The History of the United States for the Year 1796" in which Charges of Speculation Against Alexander Hamilton, Late Secretary of the Treasury, is Fully Refuted by Himself.' An accusation of financial malfeasance in office is, in itself, hardly an extraordinary occurrence, even when, as in this case, directed against a founding father. What makes 'The Reynolds Pamphlet' at the same time so titillating and so somber is the bizarre combination of circumstances that gave rise to its publication. Those circumstances touched on both private matters and international affairs of state. Charges of financial impropriety notwithstanding, what was really at issue in 'The Reynolds Pamphlet' was illicit sex on the one hand and global revolution and counter-revolution on the other.

Alexander Hamilton's refutation is first of all a deeply humiliating public confession. He acknowledges not any financial wrongdoing, but rather that he engaged in an adulterous affair some years before, during his tenure as Secretary of the Treasury, with the wife of one James Reynolds. This adultery, he further reveals, was carried on, perhaps from the very beginning and certainly later, with the full connivance of Mr Reynolds. The turning-point arrived, according to the Secretary, when James Reynolds confronted him with his knowledge of the relationship and a demand for $1,000. When Hamilton paid the money, Reynolds made it clear the adultery could continue, presum-

3

ably in return for future installments. The Secretary concludes the confessional part of his pamphlet by apologizing to his 'loving wife' for these inexcusable transgressions. And he explains, only his sense of honor, the need to clear his name of the graver charge of official misconduct, could have driven him to expose his wife to this embarrassing and shameful ordeal.

Most of 'The Reynolds Pamphlet', however, runs in a very different direction. The whole real issue is not, Hamilton contends, sex or even financial misconduct. Instead he blames everything on the riotous spirit of Jacobinism loose in the world. French revolutionaries, regicides and terrorists in Hamilton's eyes, had formed an alliance with the noisome rabble gathered around Thomas Jefferson, his bitter political rival. Conscienceless foes, these American Jacobins will resort to any kind of calumny, will even exploit Hamilton's moment of sexual weakness, to damage not only his reputation but those of all men of 'upright principles'.

Hamilton is determined to defeat this 'conspiracy of vice against virtue'. His pecuniary record remains 'unblemished', he avers, as during his whole term as Secretary of the Treasury he was indifferent to the acquisition of property. Yet his Jacobin enemies are so unscrupulous that they accuse him of sacrificing 'his duty and honor to the sinister accumulation of wealth', and promoting 'a stock-jobbing interest of myself and friends'. These charges, he notes, first surfaced in the earliest years of the new government, back in 1791, and when they did it was he, Hamilton, who demanded a formal Congressional inquiry. That investigation, conducted by a committee where his political opponents were in the majority, showed that rumors of public monies being made 'subservient to loans, discounts, and accommodations' for Hamilton and his friends were groundless. Yet, despite this complete exoneration, these slanders were being circulated again by those contaminated by Jacobinism, including such distinguished statesmen as Senator James Monroe, not to mention Hamilton's one-time co-revolutionists and now inveterate enemies, Thomas Jefferson and James Madison.

And what then might be the connection between Jacobinism and the Secretary's sexual adventure? It turns out, according to Hamilton, that it was James Reynolds, the cuckold, and an otherwise obscure, frustrated place-seeker, who first alleged that Hamilton had confided in him about a conspiracy to speculate in government bonds. It was that rumored conspiracy, purportedly conceived and captained by Hamilton, taking advantage of his unique position as the fledgling nation's chief financial officer, which made the disreputable Reynolds and his wife tools of the Jacobin menace. Men such as Madison and Jefferson were scarcely concerned with Hamilton's marital infidelities. Moreover, no matter how much they otherwise distrusted his motives, it is doubtful they ever took seriously the charge that the Secretary was lining his own pockets, given his impeccable reputation. What they feared was rather that Hamilton was responsible for implanting a system of finance that bred not only the kind of conspiracy of speculators he was rumored to belong to, but also, more fatally, a system of speculation that would elevate a 'moneyed aristocracy' intent on undoing the great democratic accomplishments of the Revolution. Not sex, not peculation, but the specter of counter-revolution turned Hamilton's tryst into an affair of state.[1]

How could this have happened? At least part of the answer lies in a vital detail of James Reynolds' concoction. Hamilton's chief co-conspirator, Reynolds claimed, was one William Duer. And it is in the career of William Duer that one can first glimpse how Wall Street found itself embroiled in controversy over the fate of the American Revolution.

By the time the 'Reynolds Pamphlet' was published, William Duer had been exposed as a bankrupt and a fraud and was languishing in debtors' prison where he would soon die in 1799. A decade earlier, no one would have predicted such a sorry end. Duer was bred to be a patrician. Born in England in 1747, the son of a wealthy West Indian planter, educated at Eton, he'd served in the British army in India before settling in New York where he began a lucrative business supplying masts and spars to the Royal Navy while serving as a colonel in the local militia. A man of enterprising vigor, Duer was soon enough running saw, grist, snuff, and powder mills and had opened up a thriving distillery.

When the revolution erupted, Duer sided with the rebels; formed, together with John Jay, a secret 'committee of correspondence' in British-occupied New York; was elected to the Continental Congress; and made a second fortune furnishing all sorts of supplies to the Continental Army, including timber for barracks and ships as well as ammunition, horses, cattle, and feed. He married the daughter of a wealthy American general, lived royally in a mansion on the Hudson staffed by liveried servants, served as a judge, and was appointed secretary of the Treasury Board under the Articles of Confederation. He seemed to have capped his career in 1789 when Hamilton made him an assistant secretary of the Treasury under the new constitution (thanks in part to the fact that Duer's wife was a cousin of Hamilton's wife). But it was then that William Duer suddenly emerged as a prototype of a new species that many in the infant nation were coming to fear and despise.[2]

William Duer became America's original Wall Street speculator. Trading on inside information, he tried to make a killing in government bonds. These were the same bonds that Hamilton had struggled mightily to get the new government to issue in order to make good the nation's revolutionary war debt and thereby establish its financial credibility abroad. Hamilton's plan incited fierce debate which became increasingly inflamed during the 1790s. The Secretary was therefore concerned to avoid the slightest hint of financial impropriety. He even cautioned his father-in-law, the New York grandee, General Phillip Schulyer, not to let the General's son speculate in government securities for fear it would taint Hamilton's reputation as Treasury Secretary. And when he became aware that William Duer was in over his head betting on a rise in government bonds, he told him bluntly that 'I have serious fears for you – for your purse and for your reputation.' But Duer, counting on whatever special information and insight he'd gleaned during his brief tenure in the Treasury Department, saw his main chance and took it.

Together with a secret circle of fellow grandees, Duer put together the 'Six Percent Club' to manipulate the price of the new national government's securities. The conspirators plotted as well to corner the stock of the new Bank of the United States and the Bank of New York; they spread gloomy stories designed to depress the price of the securities they were amassing and borrowed heavily to finance their schemes. Duer went so far as to sell a family estate in New Jersey and dipped into the funds of a state lottery for which he served as a trustee. Like so many to follow, Duer and his associates seized the moment, got caught, and crashed.

For those who suspected or were already convinced that Hamilton's financial schemes were venal and dangerous, William Duer became living proof. His revolutionary war record notwithstanding, Duer had for some time lived under a moral and political shadow. His reservations about the leveling tendencies of the Revolution were well known. Long before his final disgrace, people suspected him of caring more about enriching himself than serving the revolutionary cause; rumors circulated about his war profiteering, about his hoarding of precious supplies of rum, blankets, and lumber, even about some sub-rosa trading with the enemy. After the war, he was thought to belong to the anti-republican 'Aristocratic Faction'. This reputation was enhanced by his practice of buying up abandoned Tory estates in the Hudson valley. To finance these real-estate speculations, Duer used the 'continentals' and pay warrants he'd purchased from impoverished war veterans. He was part of an organized syndicate of such speculators who managed to corner the supply of this paper as well as the outstanding securities of hard-pressed state governments, especially in the South. By 1786, when Duer was serving on the Treasury Board of the Confederation government, he regularly passed on inside information to his agents on matters affecting the price of these securities. No doubt this elastic melding together of his private and public functions helped deafen him to Hamilton's urgent warnings.

All this helps explain why the democratic faction was so exercised when Duer's scheming fell apart in the spring of 1792. Jefferson gleefully recorded that 'the failure of Duer in New York brought on others, and these still more, like ninepins knocking one another down'. Melodramatically, he suggested that 'the credit and fate of the nation seem to hang on the desperate throws and plunges of gambling scoundrels'. Duer's collapse, along with his confederates, ignited a panic. Real-estate prices plummeted, credit tightened, and housing schemes were halted. Governor Clinton denounced 'adventurers' who 'swim on the fluctuating waves of speculation'. Business came to a standstill impoverishing not only an inner circle of merchant-financiers, but 'shopkeepers, Widows, orphans, Butchers, Cartmen, Gardeners, market women and even the noted Bawd, Mrs Macarty'. Mobs threatened to seize Duer and disembowel him. And so the Street made its first appearance on the dark side of the American imagination where it would remain for some long time to come.

Yet William Duer was a patrician as well as a financial intriguer: it was his lethal combination of aristocracy and money that most alarmed Jefferson, Madison, and all their fellow republicans. Moreover, Jefferson's flippant allusion to 'ninepins' was on the mark:

Duer was not alone in his plottings. His co-conspirators – all of whom suffered losses but without the additional ignominy that accompanied Duer to jail – included members of New York's great dynastic families: the Livingstons, the Roosevelts, the Macombs. Duer's scandalous career encapsulated Wall Street's inflammatory entry into American public life: the struggle between aristocracy and democracy, the sub-textual drama of 'The Reynolds Pamphlet', would haunt the Street for a century and more to come.[3]

Wall Street had long been the gathering place of a hybrid elite, one respectful of traditional order but open to the destabilizing currents of the Atlantic economy. Jefferson once described New York City as 'a cloacina of all the depravities of human nature'. Deserved or not, this reputation owed something to the city's origins as a remote outpost of the Dutch empire in the seventeenth century. The Dutch invented the rudiments of modern finance: commercial banking, credit, insurance, the stock market. Dealers set up the first exchange to trade in stocks on a bridge over the Amstel river in Amsterdam. There the shares of the United East India Company became a speculator's favorite. Indeed, such staples of Wall Street argot as 'short-selling', 'bear raids', 'pools', 'syndicates', and 'corners' were already standard practice on the Netherlands stock exchange before New Amsterdam even existed. Contracts to sell stocks one didn't own to people who didn't have the money to buy them quickly became standard practice and were known as 'windhandel' or 'trading air'.[4]

The Dutch colony, created by the East India Company, then the world's largest corporation, aped the mother country in its avidity for trade and lucre. Its settlers also nurtured a cosmopolitan indifference to the scriptural preoccupations of a more zealous Protestantism. Trading in a wide range of commodities, including lumber, slaves, fur, and flour, it was a most unprovincial Dutch province, its gaze trained on the whole world, not just Western Europe.

Wall Street itself was a Dutch construction, or at least the wall was. It was originally built to keep the cows in and the Indians out, but was rebuilt in sturdier fashion to discourage neighboring British colonists from casting covetous eyes on this frail Dutch colony with its mar-velous harbor and outlet to lucrative trans-Atlantic commerce. The wall, probably erected by slaves and native Americans, made of twelve-foot-high wooden posts running from the East River to the

Hudson, gun emplacements and all, faced northward as Peter Stuyvesant feared an attack by land from New England. But the British came by sea instead and overran Stuyvesant's bustling and commercially minded settlement easily and peacefully. Hints of Dutch and later French designs on New York kept the wall in place, although poorly maintained, until the 1690s, when it was paved over with cobblestones and a street appeared in its place.[5]

New Amsterdam was already rather cosmopolitan, and became even more so once the British took over and rechristened it as New York. Its mixture of several European nationalities, African slaves, free blacks, Jews, Quakers, and Anabaptists, speaking eighteen different languages, made it by far the most heterogeneous of all the American colonies. Wall Street and the surrounding neighborhood emerged as the arterial core of the city's social, residential, and political life.

Captain Kidd was one of Wall Street's best-known residents. He was, to begin with, a privateer protecting American slave-traders from pirates. 'Red Seamen' like Kidd were an integral part of the triangular transactions so enriching to merchants on both sides of the Atlantic, lubricating relationships between merchants and slavers. Kidd's house on Wall Street was an elegant structure that came equipped with a toll house, fluted chimneys, and scrolled dormers. Together with the pew he purchased in the neighborhood's exclusive Trinity Church, it marked Kidd's social ascendancy at the end of the seventeenth century. His stay on the Street turned out to be brief, however; after he crossed over the admittedly blurred line between privateering and piracy he was hung in London in 1701.

Trinity Church, standing at the western head of Wall Street, was the house of worship for the mayor, aldermen, and the rest of the city's social elite. Across the street was City Hall which contained a prison, pillory, stock, and dungeon as well as court and jury rooms and a meeting place for the Common Council. An active slave market conducted its business nearby well into the eighteenth century, shipping its human cargo South to Virginia and the Carolinas. It was dismantled only when it began to offend the sensibilities of the patricians who lived and socialized in the area, although they would not desist from the slave trade itself until the Revolution.

Wall Street became the city's most fashionable address, home to its flourishing mercantile aristocracy. By the time of the Revolution, the

Merchants Coffee House at the corner of Wall and Water was the preferred rendezvous point for the city's leading merchants and politicians. Money-making was already a preoccupation for the patriciate. One of its members, Codwallader Colden, observed that 'The only principle of life propagated among the young people is to get money, and men are only esteemed according to what they are worth – that is, the money they are possessed of.' In 1786, one apothecary, three auctioneers, one grocer, six merchants, two tailors, one clockmaker, one printer/bookseller, one snuff and tobacco manufacturer, one tavern keeper, one milliner, one school teacher, one upholsterer, and one quartermaster general worked and lived on Wall Street, servicing an elite clientele and lending the Street variety and vitality. [6]

Like all the chief seaboard cities of the colonial era, New York was swept up in the commercial expansion of the Atlantic economy in the eighteenth century, which meant it was immersed in the market, increasingly familiar with its instruments of credit and debt, and had come to expect, if not welcome, a certain economic arrhythmia and instability. This was far less true in the interior of the country. But in places like Boston, Philadelphia, and New York, taking advantage of the seemingly mysterious oscillations of the marketplace, behavior once stringently proscribed, now appeared culturally and morally permissible.

This adjustment did not come easily, however. Venerable traditions, sanctioned by religion as well as customary practice, had long viewed sudden and erratic fluctuations in the value of precious commodities with the gravest suspicion. Although speculation was widespread in the flourishing cities of Flanders in the sixteenth century, where great international market fairs were regularly conducted, condemnation was frequent and unforgiving. In Antwerp speculators had taken to wagering on changes in the rates of exchange, modeling their activity on the traditional 'parturas', or bets on whether a newborn baby would be a boy or a girl. They were chastened for this by the cleric Christoval de Villalon, whose tract observed that 'a horrible thing hath arisen, a kind of cruel tyranny which the merchants there have invented among themselves'. The culture of opposition ran deep. Speculation was often likened to gambling (the equation lives on into our own era) and gambling, in the eyes of the Church, was a sacrilege tantamount to divination – this was at least part of the reason why the Flemish viewed it as a 'public danger'. These illicit, even underworld associations led the mightiest Dutch magnates to keep their distance from the Amsterdam exchange while allowing agents or brokers to act on their behalf. Even at the end of the seventeenth century, when all of western Europe was inveigled in the commercial revolution, the word 'broker' was still an unsavory signifier for 'a procurer, pimp, bawd; a pander generally'. The first book written about the stock market described Amsterdam stock brokers as 'double-dealers'.[7]

An unmistakable air of the alien surrounded the enterprises of the new merchant capitalism. Savor, for example, the exotic formal title of the very first joint-stock company, colloquially known as the 'Russia Company': 'The Mysterie and Companie of the Merchants Adventurers for the Discoverie of Regions, Dominions, Islands, and Places Unknown'. Stocks did indeed threaten a leap into the unknown, and worse. Daniel Defoe, who was in other respects a proponent of British commercial development, and an investor in the notorious South Sea Bubble, considered stock-trading on the London exchange to be 'Knavish in its Private Practice and Treason in its Public'. The whole enterprise was 'founded in Fraud, born of Deceit, and nourished in Trick, Cheat, Wheedle'. Defoe dredged up a specter familiar to all of Christian Europe in describing a stock market that 'throngs with Jews, Jobbers, and Brokers, their Names are needless, their Characters as dirty as their Employment'.[8]

When in 1719 the roving Scottish gambler, John Law, lured thousands of Frenchmen into delusional speculations in the kingdom's New World province of Louisiana – alleged to be a cornucopia of precious metals – Defoe composed couplets to commemorate the foundering of Law's 'Mississippi Scheme'.

> Some in clandestine companies combine;
> Erect new stocks to trade beyond the line;
> And raise new credits first, then cry 'em down;
> Divide the empty nothing into shares;
> And set the crowd together by the ears.

Europe seemed particularly susceptible at this time to the new contagion of financial hallucination. Alexander Pope ridiculed his countrymen's credulity as they lost themselves in the madness of the 'South Sea Bubble', a seductive fantasy about a company granted royal license to exploit the imaginary El Dorado lying off the east coast of South America:

At length corruption like a general flood,
Did deluge all! and avarice creeping on,
Spread, like a low-born mist, and hid the sun.
Statesmen and patriots plied alike the stocks,
Peeress and butler shared alike the box;
And judges jobbed, and bishops bit the town.
And mighty duke packed cards for half-a-crown.
Britain was sunk in lucre's sordid charm.[9]

In the New World, Cotton Mather scathingly observed that 'gains of money or estate by games, be the games what they will, are a sinful violation of the laws of honesty and industry which God has given us'. Nearly a century later, a populist poet, calling himself 'An American', echoed Mather in decrying New England merchant princes who had strayed from the ways of their ancestors:

Oh Massachusetts, once my boast and pride,
The Nurse of Heroes and the Patriot's guide,
How hast thou fallen, all thy glory lost,
Damn'd by a speculating, stock-jobbing host.[10]

Protestant theologians and patriotic farmers didn't object to the simple amassing of wealth. After all, the spiritual calisthenics of disciplined work and delayed gratification so widely subscribed to were supposed to result in material accumulations, if only as tokens of an inner moral robustness. What grated and frightened were those newer, more shadowy forms of money-making: 'stock-jobbing', 'speculating', economic game-playing which promised wealth without visible signs of work, encouraged a dangerous release of animal passions, and pandered to men's baser desires.

Nonetheless, despite these hoary protests, a new economic morality fought for legitimacy. That cultural revolution had begun with the slow rehabilitation of usury in the thirteenth century, when it was rescued from hell and consigned to a kind of purgatory of temporal sufferings. The profits of money-lending escaped the stigma of theft, gradually emerging instead as a quasi-legitimate compensation for the labors of lending and the assumption of risk. Traders in commodities, even speculators, were reconceived, at least in some quarters, as producers of markets and prices. In the late eighteenth century – by which time the word 'speculation' began to take on its modern financial connotations – avarice, once treated as deadly sin, corrosive of all that supported virtue and good order, was still regarded as sulphurous, but no longer as deadly. It could mutate into a more benign interest that might even be usefully deployed to restrain more primitive and threatening instincts. Even so, a shadowy borderland, in which modern interests regressed all too easily into covetousness, separated the moral and economic certitudes of two warring cultures.[11]

This war was carried out throughout the 1790s, and the two armies were commanded by Jefferson and Hamilton. Wall Street, literally and figuratively, was again and again the terrain on which they fought.

A great American historian, Charles Beard, once argued that a principal force responsible for scrapping the Articles of Confederation and replacing it with the US Constitution was a wealthy circle of moneylenders and speculators. Their holdings of Revolutionary war debt – otherwise worthless bonds and securities issued both by the Continental Congress and the several states – could only be made secure through the creation of a strong central government empowered to generate revenue through taxation. Opposition to the proposed Federal government, Beard argued, drew its energy from suspicions about the mercenary and power-hungry motives of its advocates. The protracted negotiating at the Constitutional Convention over the form the new government was to take never seriously jeopardized the overriding interests of this elite circle of bondholders (and land speculators).[12]

Alexander Hamilton's first act as Secretary of the Treasury was the issuing of a 'Report on the Public Credit'. His plan called upon the Federal government to assume the Revolutionary war debts of the Continental Congress and the states. By purchasing these securities at face value in the open market in return for interest-bearing bonds of the new national government, and by levying new taxes to support that financial operation, Hamilton hoped to accomplish multiple and interrelated objectives. First of all he sought to bolster the credit and thereby the international credibility of the new nation. And a year after its adoption by the Congress in 1790, President Washington was able to report that 'Our public credit stands on that ground which three years ago it would have been considered as a species of madness to have foretold.' Moreover, by redeeming the Revolution's debt, creditors both foreign and domestic would be encouraged to furnish new

funds that might be directed toward the further economic development of the country. A natural alliance would then grow up between
these wealthy possessors of liquid capital and the government, an
alliance conceived to be in the national interest rather than that of any
individual. Hamilton's 'Report' was strategic in a double sense: it was
a means of incubating the rapid economic growth and modernization
of an otherwise underdeveloped country through the mobilizing of its
rare and precious capital resources, and a way of corralling a stable
and influential political constituency to support the daring experiment
in federalism.

Hamilton was hardly oblivious to the dangers of speculation. A thin
line separated the productive use of the funded debt from sheer financial
recklessness, and he was worried: 'There is at the present juncture a certain fermentation of mind, a certain activity of speculation and enterprise which if properly directed may be made subservient to useful
purposes; but which if left entirely to itself, may be attended with pernicious effects.' Responding to his critics, he acknowledged to Washington
that speculation and stock-jobbing 'fosters a spirit of gambling, and
diverts a certain number of individuals from other pursuits'.[13]

What Hamilton hated most of all, however, was inert capital. It
might be locked up by hidebound, anti-federalist agrarians habitually
averse to venturing into the unknown. Or it might be rendered sterile
by speculators who stayed away from manufacturing or other risky
forms of productive enterprise, seeking more purely and quickly to
make money out of money. Given the country's paucity of 'active
wealth', of 'moneyed capital', and the overriding importance of the
public credit to the life of any modern nation – to its military security,
its spirit of enterprise, its internal improvement, its commerce and
manufacturing – Hamilton was prepared to swallow his reservations
about the dangers of speculation and borrowed capital. Theorists of
economic history might characterize the Treasury Secretary's strategic
thinking as a classic case of 'finance-led modernization'. Profit-making
came a distant second in these calculations to what really mattered to
Hamilton: the future fame and power of the new American nation-
state.[14]

The criticism of Jefferson and others compelled President
Washington to ask Hamilton to defend his policy. Washington was
troubled by his own baleful memories from the Revolutionary war,
when 'speculation, peculation, engrossing, forestalling with all their

concomitants' had afforded 'too many melancholy proofs of the decay of public virtue'. Would not the new capital inevitably find its way into speculation, 'barren and useless, producing, like that on a gaming table, no accession to itself . . . withdrawn from Commerce and Agriculture where it would have produced addition to the common mass'? Would it not as well 'nourish in our citizens vice and idleness instead of industry and morality', aggravate dangers of political corruption, and ultimately pose a threat to republican government by 'a corrupt squadron of paper dealers'?[15]

Rather than drain the country of productive capital, Hamilton retorted, the debt, even that portion of it that would predictably end up in the hands of foreign investors, would flow instead into the ship-building industry, into home-building, canal and road construction, and new manufacturing enterprises. Although adopted by later generations as an avatar of the free market, Hamilton was actually a committed mercantilist. His strategic vision of national greatness included a potent dose of state-sponsored and subsidized economic development funneled through the Treasury. Moreover, he argued, speculation was 'the fault of the Revolution, not the Government'.

The Secretary was in some sense the ideal heir to the commercial cosmopolitanism that founded Nieuw Amsterdam. He was firmly convinced that the upper echelons of the merchant class were the country's truly dynamic element: they were bred to use capital to create more capital, which in turn would accelerate economic change – itself a good, not a bad thing. To aid that work, Hamilton sought to fashion a support structure of mobile capital, a stable currency, ready credit, and government encouragement of key enterprises. Liquid capital was the most important of these objectives: the fuel that would start the mercantile engine. Hamilton's 'Report on the Public Credit' was conceived first of all to concentrate that pool of government capital in the hands of the merchant-banker elite where it would do the most good for the nation as a whole. For this reason he made no attempt to conceal his desire to create a 'great moneyed interest'. But there was more at stake here than money or even economic development. As the Secretary openly declared in his 'Report', 'those who are most commonly creditors of a nation, are, generally speaking, enlightened men'. Commerce was the soil from which a new society would flower; it would be as urbane and cultured as anything Europe had to offer. For this reason, speculation, despite its potential evils, might become a positive good. Down that road, however, the Secretary's enemies were determined not to travel.[16]

In the summer of 1791, shortly after the adoption of Hamilton's funding plan but long enough for Wall Street's first speculative frenzy to have worked up a head of steam, a piece of telling doggerel appeared in the *New York Gazette*:

> What magic this among the people,
> That swell a maypole to a steeple?
> Touched by the word of speculation,
> A frenzy runs through all the nation,
> For soon or late, so truth advises,
> Things must assume their proper sizes -
> And sure as death all mortal trips
> Thousands will rue the name of SCRIPTS.[17]

Hamilton's funding plan fed the paranoia aroused by the campaign to scrap the old decentralized Confederation government. Suspicion was rife that there were designs against the Revolution's democratic accomplishments. A folk literature of novels, memoirs, plays, political tracts, and poems like this one expressed a spreading cultural anxiety. New kinds of economic behavior, like black magic, conjured up wealth without work. It might be sanctioned by revered figures, but speculation still struck many an astonished witness as intrinsically illicit, like forgery or counterfeiting. It suggested a moral epidemic and inspired the gloomiest rhymes:

> We thought when once our liberty was gain'd,
> And Peace had spread its influence thro' the land,
> That Learning soon would raise its cheerful head,
> And arts on arts would joyfully succeed;
> Till all Columbia's genius 'gain to blaze,
> And in true science more than rival's Greece:
> But Speculation, like a baleful pest,
> Has pour'd his dire contagion in the breast;
> That monster that would ev'rything devour.

Novels like *Dorval; or The Speculator*, delivered a similar prognosis. The villainous Dorval was a moral as well as an economic seducer, a man with a liquid identity, so depraved he turns even his romantic adventures into clever financial ruses. Trade, in stories like this one, might be legitimate enough, but only if sharply segregated from shadier practices like speculation in currency, land, and commodities. Anti-federalist ministers sermonized that 'bare-faced' speculation would undermine 'common honesty'. In his satiric 'Chronology of Facts' in the *National Gazette*, Philip Freneau pronounced 1791 'The Reign of the Speculators'. He invented a mock plan for an American aristocracy whose meticulously graded and serried ranks mirrored rising levels of speculative practice from 'the lower order of the Leech' to the middling 'Their Huckstership' on to the sublime 'Order of the Scrip'. In his 'Medical Inquiries and Observations Upon Diseases of the Mind', the nation's most eminent medical mind, Benjamin Rush, diagnosed the post-Revolutionary craze for speculation as a spreading insanity: 'In the United States, madness has increased since the year 1790 . . . The funding system and speculations in bank scrip, and new lands, have been fruitful sources of madness in our country.'[18]

The passions aroused by Hamilton's scheme clearly ran deep. Beneath its sophisticated approach to economic development something far more primitive was at work. Hamilton's 'enlightened' bondholders had arguably amassed their capital through a process of primitive accumulation; that is, they had bought up at rock-bottom prices the revolutionary war debt originally purchased by hard-pressed veterans and other desperately strapped smallholders who had seen the value of their patriotic holdings plummet throughout the Revolution and the interregnum that followed. Profits accruing to men like Duer, therefore, would derive not from any services they provided, but from prior forms of productive labor occurring outside the charmed circle of this mercantile elite.

This argument was taken up widely. Madison, Jefferson, and others, although they would ultimately endorse Hamilton's funding plan, at first demanded that current bondholders share the spoils with the original holders of the debt to reduce the inequity involved. Hamilton opposed this compromise on the grounds that it would subvert the sanctity of contract, thereby undermining confidence in the financial probity of the new government, which was the object of the entire plan. The Jefferson–Madison amendment died in Congress, but the censure it expressed lived on.[19]

Just as Hamilton's encouragement of financial activity implied a more capacious vision of what American society might become, so the

Jeffersonian opposition drew its energy from broader fears about the perils speculation might cause the new nation. These fears might be personal, as in Jefferson's rather Franklinesque advice to a friend's son to 'Never spend your money before you have it', a maxim no self-respecting speculator could abide by. They could just as easily be strategic and political, as when Jefferson wrote to his Virginia ally, George Mason, confiding his anxiety about Hamilton's plan to sponsor a National Bank: 'the only corrective of what is corrupt in our present form of government will be the augmentation of the number in the lower house, so as to get a more agricultural representation which may put that interest above that of stock-jobbers.'[20]

Even many years later, Jefferson could still conjure up the vitriol he once felt about the injustice caused by those who bought up the revolutionary war bonds and worthless 'continentals': 'Speculators had made a trade of cozzening them from the holders by the most fraudulent practices.' They were both stealthy and quick off the mark: 'couriers and relay horses by land, and swift sailing pilot boats by sea, were flying in all directions', buying up paper securities cheap before word got out that Congress was to redeem them at their original face value. 'Immense sums were thus filched from the poor and ignorant', and the dangers to honest government, Jefferson warned Washington, were alarming: people would be lured away from industrious labor 'to occupy themselves and their capitals in a species of gambling, destructive of morality, and which introduced its poison into the government itself', tempting legislators to feather their own nests.[21]

Jefferson was hardly alone in his concern about the antagonism between the embryonic mechanisms of modern finance and the more tangible and virtuous universe of productive labor. Whatever their personal religious affiliation, most Americans were faithful to the moral rigors of the work ethic. Some were committed pastoralists for whom only toiling in the earth constituted legitimate and spiritually enriching labor. Others were more broad-minded and admitted the crafts and more straightforward commercial businesses of the city into the sanctioned circle of honest effort. Moral skepticism, however, surrounded the insubstantial world of paper values.

John Adams, who found in Hamilton a sometimes useful ally, with his conservative acceptance of social class distinctions, nonetheless observed that 'paper wealth has been the source of aristocracy in this country, as well as landed wealth, with a vengeance. Witness the immense fortunes made per saltum by aristocratical speculations, both in land and paper.' The Revolutionary war hero, 'Light-Horse Harry Lee', a Virginia slave-owner typically insensitive to his own morally compromised position, starkly opposed the moral status of the two economies: 'What can be denominated the habit of supporting life, subsisting family and etc. by buying and selling in the funds, when contrasted with the habit of performing the same object by tilling the earth? Avarice, deception, falsehood, and constant overreaching belong to the first, while contentment, moderation, hospitality, frugality, and love to mankind result from the last.'[22]

When the speculative bubble that Duer and his compatriots had been floating on burst, popular revulsion was palpable. Speculators became derisively known as 'Hamilton's Rangers' and 'Paper Hunters'. Local news-sheets filled up with talk of 'scriptomania', 'scripponomy', and 'scriptophobia'. James Jackson, a Jeffersonian hot-head from Georgia, was driven to denounce these speculators as 'rapacious wolves seeking whom they may devour', and accused them of draining 'the gallant veteran' of the 'pittance which a grateful country had afforded him in reward for his bravery and toils.' Madison summed up his moral and political outrage: 'There must be something wrong, radically and morally and politically wrong, in a system which transfers the reward from those who paid the most valuable of all considerations, to those who scarcely paid any consideration at all.'[23]

The Jeffersonian antipathy to Wall Street, then, was far more moral and political than it was economic. Jefferson himself was a not untypical representative of a planter elite enmeshed in the intricacies of the world market and restricted by webs of strangulating credit and debt. Whatever the romantic myth of Jefferson's origins as a self-sufficient yeoman farmer, the smallholder agriculture he sought to encourage was in fact oriented to the marketplace, both at home and abroad. He was more than happy to make America the bread-basket of Europe, exporting its agricultural surplus in return for the Continent's manufactures. A man of the Enlightenment and a believer in progress, Jefferson accepted the widening division of labor and the inevitable spread of a trading society. He and his followers relished the cultural sophistication of Europe's great cosmopolitan centers, but they worried about its paradoxical social consequences: social progress could, they feared, entail moral rot. Commerce and the luxury it bred would be both civilizing and demoralizing, enlightening and cheapening, a source of advance in manners and morals and at the same time their corruption. The contagion was morally dangerous insofar as it rewarded idleness instead of truly useful labor. Jefferson's celebrated aphorism – 'those who labor in the earth are the chosen people of God' – implied its converse: that the people of the City, all those engaged in commerce, were more vulnerable to the seductions of the Devil. And this moral disease seemed to penetrate the healthy social organism most easily through those arteries of finance where 'trading air', living off the industry of others, epitomized a system of gross corruption. It was against this that the Revolution had been fought.[24]

Ultimately, then, it was the Revolution itself that seemed at stake. Jeffersonian republicans feared the loss of the wartime élan that had instilled the spirit of self-sacrifice and devotion to the commonweal. Unless this Spartan dedication was sustained, all the democratic and egalitarian achievements of 1776 were at risk. Jefferson envisioned a new social order, an 'empire of liberty' based on widespread land ownership, not the facsimile of British society Hamilton frankly admired. The real sin in Hamilton's design was that it would 'prepare the way for a change, from the present republican form of government to that of a monarchy of which the English constitution is to be the model'. For just that reason, the fusion of luxury, venality, and deception so luridly on display in the Duer affair seemed pregnant with counter-revolution. An anonymous patriot, writing in 1792, declared that speculators 'sap the foundation of republicanism' and paved the way for 'aristocracy and despotism'.[25]

A different specter terrified Hamilton and his federalist followers. The wholesale repudiation of lawful, contractual obligations, which the republicans seemed ready to entertain, was symptomatic of the Jacobin-inspired democratic excesses then overrunning France. Hamilton had harbored anxieties about 'mobocracy' for a long time. His proposals during the Constitutional convention to make the Presidency and the Senate lifetime posts were designed to keep the mob at bay. While these propositions died in Philadelphia, the Treasury Secretary clearly envisioned his funding scheme as part of a grander design to use the Federal government to incubate a national ruling class, a regime of 'the wise, the rich, and the good'.[26]

Such stark alternatives left emotions in a feverish state. Jefferson came to see Hamilton's funding plan, his promotion of a national bank, and other measures, as pieces of a larger plot to restore some form of monarchical government. And he told Washington so. By inundating the country with speculative paper, he argued to the President, the Treasury was in effect building up a war chest on behalf of a circle of counter-revolutionary mercenaries. If they weren't checked, a new aristocracy – one based on money rather than on hereditary titles to land, as in the Old World – would install itself between the people and their government, trampling on the rights of the latter while suborning the integrity of the former. Jefferson's good Virginia friend and agrarian ideologue, John Taylor, warned that this new aristocracy of liquid wealth, parasitical by nature, was grounded, like all previous aristocracies, in social theft.[27]

Talk of an aristocracy linked to money invoked a well-seasoned culture of opposition directed especially at a self-aggrandizing monarchy. The great executive powers of France and Great Britain, so the anti-monarchists believed, floated on a sea of public debt with which they financed their imperial wars. That funded debt had engendered in turn big banking institutions, well-oiled markets for money, new forms of investment, and a whole new class that traded in public securities and other paper. An alliance between this moneyed class and the Crown had supplanted independent sources of political authority, supplying the executive with the wherewithal to bribe whatever resistance might remain, through official appointments, honors, and other emoluments. Such an alliance might do the same damage in America.

The equation between Wall Street and counter-revolution was therefore a straightforward one. Madison reported to Jefferson that 'the licentiousness of the tongues of speculators and Tories far exceeded anything that was conceived'. When shares of Hamilton's Bank of the United States went on sale on Independence Day, 1791, they produced an instantaneous eruption in the market, infuriating Jefferson. 'Several merchants from Richmond were here lately,' he told Madison. 'I suspect it was to dabble in Federal filth.' Inevitably these doings perverted the political process, demoralized the legislature, and weakened the Constitution; a 'corrupt squadron', headquartered in the Treasury Department, plotted to end the republican experiment and replace it with a monarchy on the English model. Madison too worried about the political fall-out: 'The stock-jobbers will become the praetorian band of the Government, at once its tool and its tyrant; bribed by its largesse, and overawing it by clamours and combinations.'

By the mid-1790s, when hysteria over Jacobin and monarchical conspiracies was at its height, guilt by association was an accepted part of common conversation. A Philadelphian, writing to his local newspaper, described his efforts to find safe passage through the factional battlefield. Although averse to joining the local Jeffersonian Democratic Society, he still wanted to reassure his neighbors that he was certainly 'no tory, no British agent, no speculator'. In 1794, Massachusetts voters pondered whether to ban speculators from legislative office.[28]

In such a super-heated atmosphere it is hardly surprising that ill-founded rumors were given credence and cynically circulated to cause political damage. So it was that Hamilton had to face a formal Congressional inquiry into charges of peculation, even though James Monroe, who deliberately leaked news of these secret hearings, probably knew the charges to be unfounded. Indeed, Jefferson went so far as to introduce nine resolutions of censure against the Secretary that were drawn from these accusations of fiduciary wrongdoing. Designed to further stain Hamilton's reputation, they stood no chance of passage, but when they were defeated, Jefferson blamed it on 'the character of the present house, one-third of which is understood to be made up of bank directors and stock-jobbers who would be voting on the case of their chief'.[29]

A cottage industry of character assassination flourished in this environment. Rumors of Hamilton's marital transgressions circulated for years after the Treasury Secretary made a private confession of his lapses to Monroe and others. By admitting the truth of his infidelity he hoped to defuse the false accusations about official corruption to which James Reynolds implied they were linked. But resisting this strategy were men like James Callender and William Duane, and groupings of republican newspaper editors, publicists, and gossip-mongers with a political agenda. Callender, a Scotch-Irish radical forced to flee to the US in 1793, sought to impugn the motives and actions of political patricians like Hamilton for whom honor and reputation constituted their claim to political precedence and to their social status as gentlemen. It was Callender whose pamphleteering in 1797 made public the innuendos about Hamilton's insider trading in Federal securities.

Thus it became necessary for Hamilton publicly to reveal his affair with Maria Reynolds. Callender gloated that Hamilton had irreparably ruined his reputation. The irony, though, was that Maria's husband, James, was a creature of Hamilton's own system. Both his money-making aspirations and the dire financial predicament which drove him to blackmail Hamilton were fueled by the speculative mania unleashed by the Secretary's funded debt and national bank. Hamilton had envisioned enlightened men investing for the public good. Jefferson saw instead 'sharpers' and 'gambling scoundrels'. Both turned out to be right, as the sad career of William Duer – an 'enlightened scoundrel' if ever there was one – exemplified.

Duer was hardly alone. Speculation in government paper during the first years of the new republic was intense. And although seedier men of the James Reynolds sort got involved, respectable ones like William Duer dominated the action. Whatever their background and breeding, the scent of instant riches was intoxicating. Patrician New Yorker Robert R. Livingston, although sharing Jefferson's anxiety, nonetheless confided a hard truth: namely, that in New York City, 'hundreds have made fortunes by speculating in the funds and look forward to a great increase of them by the establishment of a bank, and have no idea of a more perfect government than that which enriches them in six months'.[30]

These were men of independent means, often with time on their hands, enough to gather regularly in the Merchants Coffee House (soon to be replaced by the more celebrated Tontine Coffee House, the informal site of the first stock exchange). Like coffee-houses throughout cosmopolitan Europe, it functioned as a multi-purpose public space for the bourgeoisie: a social club, a political meeting-house, an insurance brokerage, a commodity market, a post office, a city newsroom, and a place to gamble on just about everything, even who would and would not get guillotined in Paris. Not many years earlier, the Sons of Liberty had assembled in this same haven and some of these merchant-speculators, like Duer, were among them. These were genuine patriots who helped make the Revolution. Men of varied interests, they might dabble in land speculation, in commercial credit, in insurance and banking; many were not only, or even principally, businessmen. John Pintard, who became Duer's accomplice and only escaped debtors' prison by fleeing New York, was a blue-blood himself, a founder of the American Bible Society and the New York Historical Society, the editor of the *New York Daily Advertiser*, an author of works on medicine and topography and an expert on Indian cultures. Later, when tempers had cooled, he was able to return to the city and resume a lucrative career on the Street.[31]

During the Revolution the interests of such men had often suffered severely. New York was an occupied city through most of the war so its native commercial life withered. Two major fires made things worse, and the population dropped by half. But by the 1790s, its revival was well under way, and these same men were ready to take advantage of what Hamilton's funding and banking schemes offered. Momentum began building even earlier, in 1789, with the first rumors of what Hamilton had in mind. Once the 'Report' was issued, activity became truly feverish. Wall Street (and similar financial nodules in Philadelphia, Boston, and down South in Charleston) experienced its first speculative boom. Between 1789 and 1791, Federal securities quadrupled in value. As the boom inflated, instruments of debt became concentrated in fewer and fewer hands; seventy-two per cent of the North Carolina debt was held by a group small enough to sit together in an average-size living room. Like their predecessors and successors, these speculators – however enlightened, whatever their patrician lineage, no matter their revolutionary war credentials, and despite their devotion to the commonweal and bourgeois sobriety – became reckless and lost their heads. Thinking the market for government securities would continue to rise without limit, they borrowed heavily to enlarge their investment until those days of reckoning in March and April 1792 when Wall Street, along with similar communities in other eastern seaboard cities, suffered its first true panic.[32]

As panics go, this first one was brief and shallow. After all, the American economy operated, to a considerable degree, outside the networks of trans-Atlantic credit and debt; indeed, back-country subsistence agriculture was hardly monetized or subject to the vagaries of even local markets. Wall Street was one of a tiny handful of financial nerve centers headquartered on the East Coast. The intricate busyness of its brokers and jobbers was a mystery that most of the time could be safely left unsolved by their countrymen. Moreover, Hamilton responded quickly to the panic and had the Treasury act to shore up the declining value of Federal securities.

Shortly after the collapse, a group of brokers were alleged to have met under a buttonwood tree on Wall Street to enter into a formal agreement regarding the trading of securities, an agreement which over the years has become regarded as the founding moment of the New York Stock Exchange. While this is largely just a legend, there probably was some concerted effort at self-regulation on the part of this embryonic Wall Street community alarmed by the speculative extravagance and dire consequences of the boom and panic. In any event, for the rest of the 1790s the stock exchange, such as it was, became a quiet, even somnolent place. More importantly, the American economy boomed. But the conundrums linking Wall Street to the nature and fate of the American Revolution would continue to expose deep rifts in American culture for generations to come.[33]

Duer's panic, the subsequent economic recovery, and the ferocious name-calling between Hamiltonian Federalists and Jeffersonian Republicans that lasted all through the decade, signaled an underlying ambivalence about the import of an incipient commercial civilization. Wall Street seemed to epitomize that ambivalence. Was it a gambling den or a monastery of abstemious investors? Was it pimping for monarchy or incubating a rich and powerful republic? Did it pander to the basest instincts for instant gratification or, on the contrary, call for the patient pursuit of great undertakings? Was it a cockpit of counter-revolution or a modern engine of revolutionary progress?

Such an either/or state of warlike contradiction excluded the possibility of their co-existence. Both sides felt vindicated; both sides were disappointed. The prosperity and economic growth of the 1790s seemed to confirm Hamilton's strategic plan. But the good times were arguably also due to the wars in Europe catalyzed by the French Revolution, which generated an enormous demand for American goods. Moreover, while some of the newly created Federal debt no doubt found its way into useful enterprise and expanded trade, Hamilton could hardly deny that his enlightened men had proved capable of purely selfish and irrational economic behavior, thus damaging not only themselves, but everybody else too, by undermining precisely those habits of industry and frugality his plan had meant to cultivate. Most odd and ironic of all, this dark side of Wall Street, the side that produced what Hamilton called 'this present rage for speculation', seemed called into being, like some evil genie, by the very prospect of healthy and vigorous economic growth Hamilton so cherished. He hadn't counted on that.[34]

Jefferson, on the other side of the Revolutionary divide, reveled in the financial undoing of those Wall Street 'knaves' and especially in the routing of conspiratorial designs on republican government in which speculators, he believed, played such a loathsome part. But his own presidential administration devoted itself to protecting and fostering the commercial interests of the country, even while he shuddered at its moral and political implications. Jefferson's predicament was ironic: speculation, a species of gambling, of irreligious divination, turned out to be the demonic face of the New World's enterprising spirit, which, in a different light, seemed benign and filled with the virtues of honest labor. This sense of ambiguity about just where the moral, ethical, and political boundary line could be drawn between gambling and investment would distinguish the cultural war over Wall Street for many years to come.

2

Monsters, Aristocrats, and Confidence Men

In July 1849, the *New York Herald* published an extraordinary article about the arrest of a local confidence man. This particular con artist, one William Thompson, was a genteelly dressed character who would strike up a conversation with some unsuspecting 'mark' while discreetly flashing an impressive bundle of cash. He intended to invest the money in a sure-fire business deal, Thompson confided. He would do the same with the money belonging to the 'mark' – that is, if his new confidant showed sufficient trust in Thompson's promises. To test that 'confidence' Thompson asked the 'mark' for his gold watch, pledging to return the next day with the watch and much more besides. Thompson was obviously persuasive, as he'd succeeded on several previous occasions. But he was also lacking in imagination: the repetitiveness of his scheme led to his inevitable capture and incarceration in 'the Tombs', the city's aptly named jailhouse.

Despite its rather pedestrian circumstances, the case attracted vast attention not just from the *Herald* but from other papers within and beyond New York. Stories about underworld characters like Thompson were becoming standard newspaper fare, feeding a growing urban anxiety. Thompson himself was interviewed widely and became a minor celebrity, proud of his new moniker as the 'confidence man'. The *National Police Gazette* made the not-so-unusual observation that confidence men like Thompson succeeded thanks to the cupidity of their victims, that the confiding man is 'a knave wrong-side out'. More outlandish, even laughable, was the Pollyanna-ish conclusion drawn by the *Merchants' Ledger*, which applauded the success of the confidence man because it was the best proof that society remained fresh and uncynical, trusting, big-hearted, and optimistic about the future. But most striking was the editorial commentary in James Gordon Bennett's *New York Herald*. In wrapping up the Thompson case, the paper managed, and with considerable panache, to bring together the two great ogres of the Jacksonian imagination – the aristocrat and confidence man – revealing them to be cohabiting incestuously on Wall Street.

A flamboyant and sensationalist publisher, Bennett used William Thompson's arrest to triangulate the Street. His argument was vivid and direct. Thompson himself was just a petty swindler, but on the other hand:

> Those palazzas [sic], with all their costly furniture and all their splendid equipages, have been the product of the same genius in their proprietors, which has made the 'Confidence Man' immortal and a prisoner at 'the Tombs'. His genius has been employed on a small scale in Broadway. Theirs has been employed in Wall Street . . . He has obtained half a dozen watches. They have pocketed millions of dollars.

Then the journalist called into question the country's moral compass. Thompson 'is a swindler. They are exemplars of honesty. He is a rogue. They are financiers. He is collared by the police. They are cherished by society. He is a mean, beggarly, timid, narrow-minded wretch . . . They are respectable, princely, bold, high-soaring "operators", who are to be satisfied only with the plunder of a whole community.' Thompson ended up in jail and not some 'fashionable faubourg' only because he aimed too low. He should have gone to Albany instead and secured himself a railroad charter or issued 'a flaming prospectus of another grand scheme'. If only he'd manipulated some stock, secured secret control of the management of some company and sucked it into debt, 'he should have brought the stockholders into bankruptcy,' and then 'returned to a life of virtuous ease, the possessor of a clear conscience, and one million dollars!' But the hapless Thompson wasn't up to it – 'Let him rot, then, in "the Tombs".' Meanwhile:

> The genuine 'Confidence Man' stands one of the Corinthian Columns of society – heads the lists of benevolent institutions – sits in the grandest pew of the grandest temple – spreads new snares for new victims . . . Success, then, to the real 'Confidence Man'. Long life to the real 'Confidence Man' – the 'Confidence Man' of Wall Street – the 'Confidence Man' of the Palace uptown.[1]

Historians have argued for generations about the nature of ante-bellum society. Was it the age of the common man overrun with enthusiasm for democracy and egalitarian reform? Was it the age of the entrepreneur in feverish pursuit of the main chance? Was it both of these at the same time, or on the contrary, something distinctly more backward-looking than can be captured by modern notions of democracy and individualism? Whichever way the controversy twists and turns, however, all would agree that the country, especially north of the Mason–Dixon Line, was in a state of chronic economic heat. This was an agrarian economy undergoing a dizzying commercial revolution. People were on the move – settling new lands, founding towns, traveling faster and farther on extraordinary new means of transport, conducting monetary transactions on a scale their parents never imagined, amassing and losing fortunes at an astonishing rate, devising schemes, inventing machines, and trafficking in intangible dreams of the future.[2]

Ante-bellum middle-class Americans were deeply ambivalent about this spirit of enterprise. They believed in its promise, but recoiled from its consequences. They were fascinated by the prospect of new wealth, but suspicious of aristocrats. They were righteous upholders of Protestant self-restraint, but tempted by the gas-lit sensuality of the new urban demi-monde. They subscribed to the free market, but found the gravitational pull of government-subsidized enterprise irresistible. They were supremely self-confident, yet haunted by the specter of the confidence man.

In the grander scheme of things, Wall Street was still an unprepossessing place full of its local self-importance, but not exactly at the heart of the economy. Ante-bellum America remained overwhelmingly agrarian, supplying local and international markets, but largely innocent of the intricacies of high finance. Wall Street was still two generations away from emerging as the economy's center of gravity. After all, the nation's principal preoccupations were slavery, territorial expansion, national unity, and the future of republican government. Though the activities of Wall Street sometimes impinged on those concerns, they attracted attention more often because of their resonances with the transformation of everyday life happening far away from the exotic environs of Manhattan's 'golden toe'. Nonetheless, the Street's weightiness and visibility – and its elusive, shape-shifting role in the popular imagination – steadily grew as the country's commercial networks multiplied.

On the one hand, Wall Street seemed to epitomize the glamour of money-making in the enterprising free market. Yet throughout the nineteenth century, and especially leading up to the Civil War, Wall Street was tethered to the State, entirely dependent on government resources and government enterprise. It was a vital piece of machinery in a state-driven economy that was dedicated to erecting the essential infrastructure of a national marketplace. But in a culture inherently wary of political power this naturally cast suspicion on the Street.

While Wall Street was a site occupied by a native aristocracy, it was at the same time a boulevard of plebeian ambition, opening up to the socially nondescript, not to mention the socially disreputable. To the degree that one could identify a true American establishment – within the free states of the North, that is – which could be trusted to consider the general as well as its own self-interest, merchant bankers from Wall Street tracing their lineage back into the colonial era might qualify for membership. But the Street also loomed up in the popular mind as a monstrous apparition, the despoiler of a wiser, more humane and venerable order of things. The princes of Wall Street appeared to be men of indubitable wisdom and commercial virtue; yet the Street seemed periodically overcome with spasms of convulsive recklessness. Half the time the Street gloried in its wealth, probity, and public esteem; the other half it lived shadowed by danger, illicit gratification, and moral risk.

The Street lived in confidence. The Street lived in fear. During the two great trials of the Jacksonian era – the President's war on the 'Monster Bank' and the devastating Panic of 1837 – the figures of the financial prince and the confidence man congealed in the popular imagination to become something truly unnatural, something monstrous. An older, more sedentary Wall Street, one that moved to the stately rhythms of Knickerbocker New York, vanished in the conflagration.

Not long after Alexander Hamilton felt compelled to make a spectacle of himself by confessing his sexual transgressions, everything grew much calmer. With the election of Jefferson in 1800, the emotions set off by the French Revolution and the birth of the new American republic subsided. Wall Street, too, became more placid, almost becalmed.

Business was slow. Jefferson abhorred debt, both because he

believed it morally and politically corrupting, and because of his personal experience as an especially imprudent Virginia planter. His administration was parsimonious: determined to reduce the national debt, it succeeded. But of course it was trading in the national debt which first gave life to Wall Street. Without fresh supplies of gilt-edged government securities, the market languished. State and local governments made tentative forays into the capital markets to help finance their minimal needs, but it hardly amounted to much, certainly not enough to rekindle the fires of the mid-1790s. A dwindling supply of government bonds, shares in a small handful of banks and an insurance company or two, and that was it. Most businesses relied on family money with an occasional loan from a local bank. It would be nearly another century before industrial corporations raised capital on the stock exchange. The only major exception would be the railroads, and in 1800 they were still thirty years in the future.[3]

How to keep busy? Denizens of the Street were a close-knit group of bankers, merchants, and brokers whose activities transgressed the permeable boundaries of mercantile specialization. Until the war of 1812 and for some time after that, very few if any were exclusively occupied in brokering or speculating in the buying and selling of securities. They might have managed family trusts, dealt in urban real estate, insured marine property, lent money to importers, imported goods themselves, or combined these and other functions. They were a clubby bunch, dressed alike in swallow-tail coats and stove-pipe hats. If they were true Knickerbockers, they might attend churches where the preaching was still in Dutch, and afterwards, promenade on the Battery or attend a ball, formal dinner, or concert at the City Hotel. Accustomed to conducting their proceedings in secret, in code even, they enjoyed their local prominence, and spent their idle moments musing about how Wall Street might one day supplant Chestnut Street in Philadelphia as the young nation's financial capital. What they did not do, and could not have done had they wanted to, was spend each and every working day on the 'floor' of the exchange.[4]

To begin with there was no 'floor', nor any permanent indoor site that might be called an exchange. Groups of brokers and investors gathered irregularly, usually in the neighborhood's most prominent coffee houses. Those who'd caught the fever of speculation in the 1790s, betting on the rise and fall of Hamilton's debt, now sought other outlets. They might attend auctions at the foot of Wall Street, fronting the East River, where cotton, sugar, and West Indian spices were bartered. Wagering on the outcome of political controversies, elections, foreign upheavals, sporting events, even the weather, were not uncommon ways for these part-time brokers to pass the time. It's worth noting that the city's very first gambling house set up operations on Wall Street. One way or another, trading securities was part profession, part avocation. As late as the 1820s, by which time there was an actual 'stock exchange', an average day saw no more than a hundred shares change hands. Brokers, in the strictest sense, were marginal in this heavily agrarian world. An illustration of Wall Street in 1825 reveals a still semi-rustic 'financial district', not far from open fields and masticating cows, its modest wooden and brick buildings mixing residences with places of business, its skyline still dominated by the rebuilt and elegantly appointed Trinity church.[5]

But if Wall Street had not yet rematerialized as the Street in these early years of the nineteenth century, the economy surrounding it was lively beyond all previous experience. Annual sales of western lands soared from 100,000 acres in 1790 to half a million in 1800. The whole trans-Appalachian wilderness came alive, with commercial activity driven mainly by venturesome ordinary folk rather than Hamilton's investing elite.

The Napoleonic wars turned New York City into a major port, the value of its imports rising from $1.4 million to $7.6 million between the early 1790s and 1807, double the growth rate of its chief rival, Philadelphia. A third of the overseas trade and a quarter of the coastal trade of the nation went through New York harbor. Mercantile activity of all kinds flourished and the pool of liquid capital grew exponentially. A French traveler described the reigning commercial pandemonium during this first decade of the new century: 'Everything in the city is in motion.' New York reminded him of 'ancient Tyre, which contemporary authors called the queen of commerce and sovereign of the seas'. Amidst all this hustle and bustle, the exchange, such as it was, barely stirred.[6]

The war of 1812 roused the Street from its long siesta – and rekindled suspicions about its role as a breeder of loose morals and counter-revolution. President Madison was desperate for funds to fight the war. He and Treasury Secretary Albert Gallatin negotiated the nation's survival with the country's two principal financiers, Stephen Girard of

Philadelphia and John Jacob Astor of New York. Together with Baring Brothers and other European investment banks, a deal was struck to issue government bonds at a heavy discount and bearing a high rate of interest. At the same time, Madison agreed to establish a second Bank of the United States, the charter of the first Bank having been allowed to expire in 1811 thanks to the still simmering popular skepticism about banking in general.

Fresh supplies of bank stock and government bonds were sufficient to restart the engines of speculation. New York's legislature tried outlawing short-selling as a form of gambling, but the tide was running in the other direction. Business was brisk enough that in 1817, brokers felt the need to institutionalize and regulate their affairs by establishing the New York Stock and Exchange Board. They moved indoors and one could now truly speak of the floor of the exchange. While Astor and Girard were estimable prototypes of the prudent merchant-banker elite, less cautious plungers soon swarmed into the Wall Street and Chestnut Street marts, hot on the trail of government securities and commodities made precious by the conditions of war, now fluctuating widely in value.[7]

The Treaty of Utrecht ending the war rapidly deflated expectations. Depression followed. This panic of 1819 was important not so much because it wiped out the paper profits of wartime speculators, but as the country's first serious brush with economic collapse in the modern sense: that is, a crisis originating within the economic system itself and not from some exogenous natural or political disaster. Half a million were unemployed in the cities, and paupers roamed the streets. Towns were depopulated, homes and farms were auctioned off by the sheriff. In New York City, 13,000 people sought public relief. Jefferson nearly lost Monticello, southern planter/speculators like Andrew Jackson suffered financially in ways they wouldn't forget, and frontier entrepreneurs like Davey Crockett watched as their improbable schemes imploded along with the boom. Banks and businesses folded in waves, and eight states were compelled to repudiate their debts. Amidst the calamity, 'money-brokers' raced around the country buying up notes from far-flung state banks at unseemly discounts, hoping to make a killing.[8]

The fall-out from the panic recalled the paranoia of the 1790s. Jefferson hated the speculative mania that accompanied the wartime and post-war boom, treating it as a form of mass delusion that 'legerdemain tricks upon paper can produce solid wealth as hard labor in the earth'. John Adams was appalled at the devastation and condemned the banks for the injury they'd done to 'the religion, morality, tranquility, prosperity, and even the wealth of the nation'. He minced no words: 'Our whole banking system I ever abhorred, I continue to abhor, and shall die abhorring.' Out West, where the wreckage was extensive, fire-breathing Senator Thomas Hart Benton of Missouri voiced regional resentment of an eastern money power so voracious the whole country was caught in its jaws, like 'a lump of butter in the mouth of a dog! One gulp, one swallow, and all is gone!'

Back East a cry went up to abolish the newborn New York Stock and Exchange Board. A popular Broadway farce, *Wall Street – or Ten Minutes Before Three*, dramatized the moral dissipation of a newly visible Wall Street species. Characters called 'Hardrun', 'Easy', 'Shaves', 'Addlehead', and 'Broker' ran amuck in a miasma of bad debts, bank failures, and nerve-racking forced optimism. Once 'honest men lived here', according to 'Oldtimes', but now Wall and Pearl streets were invaded by a swarm of shavers and speculators, joking and drinking their way from one site of distress to the next. At ten to three each day their precarious, up-tempo scheming gave way to an after-hours spent in 'ruffled shirts' and visiting 'hotels and theaters to play billiards and cards and dice and ride, and walk Broadway, and drink brandy and water and hot whisky punch and so on'.[9]

The rise of a 'paper economy' was a strange and forbidding development for both Southern planters and middling farmers, North and South. Banknotes, bonds, mortgages, bills of exchange, and stocks together seemed to form a spider's web, snaring and devouring the hard-earned fruits of honest labor. Intangible yet powerful, this system of paper produced a nauseating social and even intellectual vertigo in some. Family lineages, ancient homesteads, honored occupations, long-established social positions, cherished beliefs about the natural sources of wealth and the springs of virtue – all that defined the natural moral and social order of things could be instantly disordered, deranged by the madness of an economy no more stable and enduring than the paper it chased after. The openness, fluidity and power of the market, so exhilarating for some, was for others a dreaded presentiment of social chaos. It is instructive to listen to the reverie of a man for whom Wall Street was once an ancient homestead.

In 1871, nearing the end of a prosperous and quietly distinguished life, Abram Dayton, a sober-minded Wall Street merchant, paused to reflect, and in part, to lament. The nostalgic title of Dayton's reminiscence, *The Last Days of Knickerbocker Life in New York*, captured his melancholy. The simple, stately life of 'Dutch Gotham with its noiseless, steady routine' had vaporized. Rising in its place, at a speed that Dayton found dumbfounding, appeared a new New York, the 'moneyed center of the continent', buzzing with a 'bustling, flighty excitement'.

Wall Street in the days of the Knickerbocker ascendancy, Dayton recalled, was the habitat of men of means, bankers, and a handful of brokers, who conducted their affairs with a kind of studied slowness and grace. Men spent hours and hours in consultation and 'considering' before a single share of stock changed hands. The 'Street' itself was only partly given over to financial affairs. Fashionable shops served an elite clientele whose imposing homes filled up the surrounding neighborhood. Wall Street's Presbyterian Church catered to their spiritual needs and exercised a chastening influence over the Street's commercial appetites. For Dayton, it was a transparent world – socially, and morally as well. Everybody's means of livelihood was known to his neighbors and the system for amassing fortunes 'without visible continuous labor' had not yet been discovered. Distinctions of social class were recognized by all, but without rancor: the pre-eminence of the Knickerbocker aristocracy rested on merit – on breeding, taste, sentiment, and education – and not on wealth. No 'mere golden key' could secure admission into the charmed circle of the Knickerbocker elect. 'The greed for speculation' had not yet infected the behavior of these businessmen still caught up in the mysteries of their peculiar callings: 'the railway and mining mania was unborn.'

'In the twinkling of an eye', this mercantile quadrille was overrun by a restless throng which coursed through the Street as if 'the day of doom' had arrived, as if each one 'had to hand in his chips' before the new Trinity Church 'strikes three'. Self-important bankers concealed behind plate-glass, ensconced in plush, 'revolving chairs' were guarded, 'Cerberus-like', by some 'stalwart darkey'. Wild swings in the prices of stocks and bonds 'make and unmake scores of desperate speculators'. In Dayton's eyes, men had gone mad in their unnatural desire to become instantly rich and Wall Street drew them like a 'magnet': 'honor, honesty, self-esteem – all the higher qualities which should attach to mankind were thrown aside in this wild chase after gain.' Wall Street had opened itself up to the world, a promiscuity Dayton found appalling: 'The shrewd Israelite, the cunning Yankee, the philosophic German, the mercurial Frenchman, the dignified Spaniard, the indolent Italian, the phlegmatic John Bull, even the spectacled blue stocking was present.' For this hybrid mob of arrivistes, everything not nailed down had become an object of speculation – urban as well as frontier real estate of course, but also gold and silver, lead and copper mines, oil deposits and stock in railroads whose tracks and carriages had yet to leave the round-house of their promoters' imagination. All sorts of simple, unassuming folk were caught up in a torrent of 'reckless gambling'; even the 'artizan' [sic] and the 'methodical bookkeeper was infected with this contagion'.

Dayton was as sad as he was astonished. The 'commemorative monuments' of his Knickerbocker Wall Street had been swept away by tidal waves of new wealth. Boulevards and avenues had 'swallowed its winding streets . . . Imposing structures of marble and granite have . . . displaced modest piles of homely brick . . . The comparison of the brilliant gas light to the glimmering taper fails to define the marvelous transition.'

Dayton had the advantage of hindsight, albeit one tinted with an elegiac Brahmin sentimentality. But in the aftermath of the very real trauma of 1819, who could have imagined that the unsettling passions conjured up by Wall Street would become so captivating for wider and wider circles of Americans. Most of them would never come anywhere near the hurly-burly of the Street, but found themselves moved by kindred desires. Abram Dayton's world was about to be submerged for ever in the waters of the Erie Canal.[10]

The construction of the Canal was a marvel of engineering, and the signature event in the commercialization of Midwestern agriculture. Its repercussions hurtled New York City beyond the jealous grasp of its urban rivals, and accelerated the state-subsidized jump-starting of the American free-enterprise economy. If Wall Street wasn't the midwife to this process, it was certainly a nurturing presence. And from that moment on, the Street's fate was bound up with the hard-wiring of the national marketplace. Without an extensive network of transportation and communication, there would be no industrial and commercial revolution. Without the promotional zeal of local, state, and national governments, there would be no arterial mesh of roads, turnpikes, canals, railroads, docks, piers, steamboats, gas-lights, street-cars, and telegraphs – without enterprising government, no Wall Street. Odd as it may sound to our contemporary ears, so full to over-flowing with paeans to the free market, the relationship between the Street and the state at that stage was organic. The consequences for American democracy were profound.

Some might argue the sequence ought to be reversed: without Wall Street, no pooling of the liquid capital essential for the country's eco-nomic take-off. There's much truth in that notion, once one presumes no alternative to the mechanisms of private finance. But given the dearth of private capital, the inherent riskiness of complex, long-ges-tating projects like the Canal, and the cautious inclinations of Dayton's Knickerbocker financiers, the case looks different. The great public works of early American economic development could never have been built without the state taking on the roles of innovator, guarantor, builder, subsidizer, leaser, owner, co-owner, and several others.

The Erie Canal is exemplary. It was built, owned, and operated by the state of New York. And it's noteworthy that the great merchant princes of Wall Street were not actually present at the moment of its creation; indeed, they were reluctant to participate. Instead, the Canal's bonds, which were to finance its construction, were initially subscribed to by orphans, widows, and others of less lordly station. The Bank for Savings in New York City was a key early investor. It was set up to encourage habits of thrift among the city's poor, its cap-ital drawn from the savings of laborers, seamstresses, cooks, boot cleaners, nurses, and members of the city's middling business classes.[11]

Quickly enough, however, the extraordinary success of the Canal in accelerating the commercial revolution of the agrarian hinterland impressed the doyens of the Street. It cut the cost of moving a ton of goods from Buffalo to Albany to a twelfth of the previous amount. A ton of flour could travel from Buffalo to New York in a third of the time it used to take. Eventually, thanks largely to the canal, New York City's imports and exports would exceed those of all other American ports combined. By 1821, big-time investors were convinced the state had the financial and administrative competence to make the project work. Distinguished brokerage houses dating back to the earliest years of the republic like Prime, Ward, and King, and financial nabobs like John Jacob Astor, eager after the panic of '19 to find outlets for their idle capital, raced to buy and trade the securities of the Canal.

Nathaniel Prime, the first president of the New York Stock and Exchange Board and leading 'loan contractor' in the city, bought Erie bonds wholesale and resold them at retail to individual investors. Foreign investment banks, especially the English, who were used to speculation in canal stocks, soon followed. The returns were lavishly pleasing.[12]

Canal fever reached epidemic proportions, spreading virtually to every region of the country. States and municipalities, sometimes in partnership with private promoters, often in fierce competition with nearby, like-minded developers, rushed to excavate watery ditches, still hazy about their final destination or purpose. Between 1815 and 1840 the Federal government made land grants of four million acres to canal projects in the Great Lakes states. Moreover, government invested its own funds subscribing to the stock issues of companies like the Chesapeake and Ohio Canal.[13]

The canal craze nurtured unrealistic dreams not only about the value of canal securities themselves, but about the limitless riches anticipated to arise from their construction. Visions of new towns and cities bustling with business and booming real estate, drawing into commercial production thousands of acres of once unexploited countryside, pregnant with food crops and precious metals – all of that and more animated the imaginations of the canal boosters, investors, and increasingly, the general public. Some of this came true; some remained a pipe dream; some passed into the lingua franca of the criminal confidence man.

Nor were canals the only artery facilitating this commercial coming of age. Roads and turnpikes and public waterworks, as well as the wharves, dikes, and piers of urban waterfronts, prompted like-minded schemes. Moreover, even more outsized expectations, would accompany the railroad boom that began in the early 1830s and resumed after the long depression that lasted from 1837 until the mid-1840s. Even by 1840, the United States had more miles of railroad track than any country in the world. Here too, government was the indispensable ally of promoters and investors, less often as outright owner, more often as shareholding partner, public creditor, guarantor of bonds, land grantor, franchise provider, construction subsidizer, and so on.

For much of rural America the railroad was an unmitigated moral as well as mechanical horror. The Lancaster, Ohio school board would not even make its building available to discuss the coming of the iron horse. Citizens, the board decided, might use the schoolhouse to debate 'all proper questions', but railroads and telegraphs were beyond the pale, examples of 'rank infidelity'. The board concluded that 'if God had designed that his intelligent creatures should travel at the frightful speed of 15 miles per hour, by steam,' he would have said so, or had one of his prophets approve it. Clearly, the railroad was 'a device of Satan to lead immortal souls down to Hell'.[14]

For the braver or more foolhardy, however, the railroads became carriers not only of goods and passengers, but of febrile illusions that excited the ambitions as well as the cupidity of more and more Americans fixated on the main chance. More than a century before it became an advertising commonplace, being 'bullish on America' was a way of life, even a philosophy.

Ante-bellum America ran a traveling school for amateur speculators. The elementary classrooms convened on the land; indeed, that was where most people received their first and often their last lesson in the mysterious arts of speculation. The opening up of the Ohio Valley encouraged familiarity with the idea of a fluctuating cash value attached to the land and its purely prospective uses. Land speculation had hitherto been a genteel vocation, practiced by many of the founding fathers, but rarely outside elite circles. But in the Age of Jackson, whose namesake was himself a great speculator in the land (as well as horses and slaves), betting on the rapid appreciation of real estate seemed as sure a thing as Progress itself.

Sales through the government's General Land Office, which amounted to $2.5 million for the whole year of 1832, were rocketing along at an average of $5 million per month by 1837. New York money followed the pioneers west into Indiana, Michigan, and Illinois, as well as down South. Eastern financiers invested heavily in frontier Chicago, for example, when it was still but a military and fur-trading village. But land speculation was an outdoor sport. It attracted all sorts.[15]

At the height of this national infatuation, Charles Dickens published his hilarious satire of American Mammon-worship. Martin Chuzzlewit, the hapless, ingénue hero of the novel of the same name, is seduced by the huckstering riffs of New York land promoters – an irresistible rhetorical blend of high-falutin democratic egalitarianism and unblinkered covetousness – even before he gets off the boat from

England. Soon enough, shown a map depicting 'banks, churches, cathedrals, market-places, factories, hotels, stores, mansions, wharves; an exchange, a theater; public buildings of all kinds', Martin invests his small capital in the Eden Land Corporation, only to discover, after schlepping out to some remote corner of Illinois, that Eden turns out to be nothing more than a hellish, deadly swamp where he nearly loses his life, not to mention his life savings.

Fatal fantasies tied to the land, featuring thriving towns, impeccably arranged just like this one, were typical of America's craftily constructed commercial utopianism. In fact, Dickens probably based his portrait on the real-life Cairo, Illinois, originally mapped out in 1818 by a merchant-developer, left barren for years, then 'founded' anew in 1837 by a land company hoping to lure settlers to this region that would soon be known by sardonic locals as 'the land of Egypt'. *Martin Chuzzlewit* was published a year or so after Dickens' visit to the United States in 1842, where he'd soured on the country's obsessive reverence for the dollar. He acidly described Wall Street in particular: a place where fortunes were won and lost overnight, where the 'very merchants you see hanging about here now have locked up money in their strong boxes, like the man in the Arabian Nights, and opening them again have found but withered leaves'. You didn't have to trek out to some fetid marsh on the frontier to be infected by the mania for speculation.[16]

Economic adventuring, often lawless, sometimes violent, always aggressive, greedy, and grasping, intruded itself into an older, more settled order of things. Dickens was only one of many European visitors struck by the American lust for money, and especially the desire 'to make a fortune out of nothing'. Native observers, too, fastened on this character trait. Frederick Jackson, an obscure scribbler, wrote his moralizing burlesque of Wall Street shenanigans – *A Week in Wall Street By One Who Knows* – shortly before Dickens arrived on the scene. Jackson peopled the Street with all sorts of colorful mountebanks, but what really concerned him was that the 'whirlwind' of gambling and speculation was sweeping innocent citizens into its vortex, people drawn by the allure of instant wealth but without an inkling of how this bizarre new economy functioned.[17]

Among ordinary people like Jeremiah Church, however, the belief was growing that 'Everyman is a speculator from a wood-sawyer to a President, as far as his means will go, and credit also.' Even Old

Hickory's most steadfast constituents could be tempted. When the President issued his controversial Maysville veto in 1830, the enterprising citizens of Kentucky were furious, as Jackson had effectively killed plans to finance a promising turnpike by authorizing the Federal government to subscribe to the company's stock. Jeremiah Church would hardly have defended the trickery that victimized Martin Chuzzlewit, but the line between legal and criminal forms of speculation was becoming a harder one to draw. After all, state banks were printing up new currency by the sheet. The explosion of speculative economic behavior was naturally enough accompanied by a steadily rising number of frauds, embezzlements, defalcations, and inspired forms of financial chicanery. 'Fancy stocks' appeared, designed for speculation and for no other purpose. Traders on the exchange connived to 'buy' and 'sell' securities at artificial prices without any shares actually changing hands. These 'wash sales' were calculated to gull the wider investing public into believing the action was hot when in fact there was no action at all. The arts and crafts of land speculation could be applied widely and devil take the hindmost.

If the whole American landscape became, for a season at least, a schoolroom for speculation, Wall Street was everywhere in attendance. But it was of two minds about what it was learning. Conservative by training and instinct, the great merchant banks gravitated to the security and modest returns of state-guaranteed bonds. Upstart new arrivals felt the lure of overnight gain. Most other people who didn't actually make their living on the Street either fell in love with this new culture of speculation, or damned it.[18]

The pace of the Street itself quickened as its presence in the public mind grew more formidable. Still trading as little as a hundred shares a day in the late 1820s, by the mid-1830s a 6,000-share day was not uncommon on the exchange. Railroads began to supplant canals as the chief source of new, tradable securities. The thirteen miles of railroad in 1830 grew to 3,328 by 1840. Orders for railroad bonds streamed in from all over the country. By 1835 trading in railroad securities outnumbered all other transactions on the New Stock and Exchange Board. Much of this business was handled by private bankers like Nathaniel Prime, acting in the capacity of underwriter or 'loan contractor', reselling bonds to investors seeking safe returns. A good deal of the capital was British.

A newer generation of Wall Street gambler rose up alongside Nathan Prime and the English banking house of Baring Brothers. Some were small-timers, their offices 'merely desk-rooms in upper lofts or murky basements. More generally, the flooring of their office is the sidewalk and its ceiling the firmament.' Others moved into the brokerage business from careers as ticket brokers and contractors for the numerous public lotteries that since colonial days had functioned as a principal way of raising capital for community projects. And then there were high-flying financial adventurers, men like Jacob Little, Wall Street's original 'bear'. Little's moniker originated in a familiar proverb – 'to sell the bear's skin before one has caught the bear' – and carried with it a reminder of Wall Street's intricate ties to the economics of rural America. Eager to participate in the new business of trading 'on margin', unafraid of the risks associated with the 'glamour stocks' of the day, especially railroads, Little, 'the Great Bear of Wall Street', was a full-time speculator, a man of legendary coolness under fire, shunned by the financial gentry who disapproved of his manipulation of canal and railroad shares.[19]

Already by the mid-1830s, Wall Street was winning a reputation not only as a money center, but as a hotbed of speculation, with its own distinctive life-cycle of booms and panics and its own dramaturgy of plots, counter-plots, and quasi-military campaigns complete with sieges and assaults, defenses and redoubts, skirmishes and wars to the death. Even those used to the Street's old 'noiseless routine', its stately circumspection, found it hard to resist the accelerated tempo. Nathan Prime himself became an immensely wealthy speculator in stocks, bonds, and real estate, but the mental habits of a lifetime continued to haunt him. In 1832, obsessed with the idea that he was actually becoming poorer, that his recklessness would land him in the poorhouse, he slashed his throat with a razor, thus avoiding the social disgrace he most feared.

No lessons were drawn, however, from Prime's fatal insanity. Instead, with the discovery of gold in California, twenty-seven new banks opened their doors in New York, doubling the number operating in 1849. Telegraph wires facilitated the first high-speed information economy in stocks and bonds, and more and more city papers began carrying daily price quotes from the Exchange. In addition to the railroads, horse-drawn streetcar lines and other public works provided new vehicles of stock-market speculation. A British businessman traveling in America hyperbolically described Wall Street as the most 'concentrated focus of commercial transactions in the world . . . The whole money-dealing of New York is brought here into a narrow corpus of ground, and is consequently transacted with peculiar quickness and facility.' Oliver Wendell Holmes, Sr, betraying the disdain and envy Boston Brahmins often felt for their flashier urban rival, noted that with the advent of the Erie Canal 'the brokers waxed strong as New York became the tip of the tongue that laps up the cream of the commerce of a continent'.[20]

The human face of Wall Street had also begun that transfiguration which so troubled Abram Dayton. In staccato prose that mimicked the recently invented telegraph, Walt Whitman recorded the distinctive physiognomy and body language of the new breed of Wall Street broker: 'Dress strictly respectable; hat well down on forehead; face thin, dry, close-shaven; mouth with a grip like a vice; eye sharp and quick; brows bent; forehead scowling; step jerky and bustling.' The more regal among them, merchants and money-traders, had become a conspicuous part of the Broadway pageant, and 'a grim and griping generation are they; some fat and sturdy; most lean and dried up . . . their brains full and throbbing with greedy hopes or bare fears about the almighty dollar, the only real god of their i-dollar-try.' They gathered to eat, gossip and do deals in the area's flourishing up-scale restaurants, Delmonicos, most famously. Downing's Oyster House catered to the city's fresh oyster craze. Below ground, it boasted plush appointments, including damask curtains and crystal chandeliers, and was owned by a free black, born to manumitted slaves from Virginia. Through his daily intercourse with the high and mighty, Mr Downing managed to make a small fortune speculating in railroad shares.[21]

In December 1835, a fire, ignited by a gas-pipe explosion and driven by frigid, seventeen-degrees-below-zero winds, ravaged the whole Wall Street area. Little of Abram Dayton's Knickerbocker neighborhood survived. Looters briefly filled the streets and were heard rejoicing that 'this will make the aristocracy haul in their horns'. Even as the fire burned, a cholera epidemic terrorized the city. Popular expectations that the Street would be forced to lower its public profile seemed entirely plausible – but turned out to be wrong.

Within a year of these multiple disasters, the financial district was restored, its lightning reconstruction driven by an appetite for commercial speculation that nothing seemed able to dampen. Philip Hone, the city's ex-Mayor, boasted after the fire that 'in no city of the globe does the recuperative principle exist in so great a degree as in our good city of Gotham.' Wall Street presented a strikingly new physical face. The original designs of the Street's banks and insurance companies were based on the architecture of Greek or Roman temples – appropriately, since a temple invoked a sacred trust to guard the public welfare and in ancient times had actually served as the repository of communal wealth. Greek facades in particular became ubiquitous at the turn of the nineteenth century, a suitable architectural gesture of appreciation from a nation in love with the notion of democracy and its Athenian beginnings. Greek forms venerated tradition and authority, while also allowing for the expression of more plebeian aspirations. But then seven hundred buildings were destroyed in the fire. When they were replaced, Wall Street gave up its residential face for ever and began to resemble the great financial district we are familiar with today. Its monumental splendor evoked real civic pride: 'Mammon here holds his court . . . Old Plutus never settled one of his sons in a better "stand for business" . . . There is probably no business street in the world – certainly not in the United States – that can exhibit so much architectural elegance. Wealth in Wall Street does not choose to dwell in humble mansions.' Soon enough, an aristocratic architectural style, modeled on the Renaissance palazzo of the Italian merchant prince, supplanted the democratic symbolism embodied in the Greek temple. Wood and brick gave way to costly brown sandstone and marble. Dense and stony, Wall Street was becoming a physical metaphor for power. By the mid-1850s, the Street could legitimately claim the status of a world financial center, attracting both domestic and foreign capital.

Yet this muscle-flexing induced a certain moral queasiness. Alexander McCay, the era's architect to the rich and powerful, noted the incongruity of Trinity Church, standing at the axial head of the Street, 'as if perpetually to remind the busy throngs that they cannot serve two masters'. Fire and plague had failed to halt the momentum of development, but the political and economic upheavals of the mid-1830s were more shaking. President Andrew Jackson's 'war' on the Bank of the United States, which began almost as soon as he assumed office in 1828, lobbed some heavy artillery in Wall Street's direction. And the panic of 1837 and the long depression that followed undermined not so much the confidence of the Street as the confidence of others in what the Street was doing.[22]

*

The second Bank of the US, created due to the exigencies of the war of 1812, was heir to all the fermenting Jeffersonian suspicions and animosities: that same post-revolutionary agrarian hostility to a 'moneyed aristocracy' and its alleged monarchist sympathies that had so inflamed the 1790s. A quasi-private institution, the Bank was endowed with enormous power over public finance. That was a deadly combination. Its capital resources dwarfed those of every other bank in the country, especially since it served as the depository of Federal revenues. By exercising its authority it could license an uninhibited expansion of currency and credit by local and regional banks, or do the opposite, sopping up the liquidity that sustained the speculative mania.

The Bank itself was located not on Wall Street but on Chestnut Street in Philadelphia, and was run by an unapologetic patrician, Nicholas Biddle, who was tactless enough to advertise his disdain for the popular will. He and the Bank were perfect foils for President Jackson's aristocrat-bashing: a financial monopoly run by a bewigged blue-blood in defiance of the people's elected representative. Jackson's successful crusade to terminate the Bank was the defining political issue of his era. All the anxieties about the new market economy – its unpredictability, its increasing reliance on paper transactions, the way it seemed to encourage non-productive, even parasitic forms of economic behavior and conspiracies to monopolize and manipulate the currency, its seductive appeal to luxury and excess – found expression in the Jacksonian rhetoric directed at the 'Monster Bank'. The fact that the Bank under Biddle was actually acting to restrain unbridled speculation and improvident state banks made no impression on a movement in search of a scapegoat.

Some of the tidal wave of presidential invective washed over Wall Street. Over and over again, the President's denunciations of the Bank embraced 'stockjobbers, brokers, and gamblers and would to God they were all swept from the land!' When a delegation of New Yorkers approached the President pleading for credit relief, his enraged response perfectly captured the stigma that indiscriminately attached to the whole financial apparatus and inflamed the war against the Bank: 'I tell you I am opposed to all banks and banking operations from the South Sea bubble to the present time.' He had no sympathy for 'brokers and stock speculators' and told a Philadelphia group that 'all such people ought to break'. Thundering on, the President warned that 'the people of this country shall yet be punished for their idolatry'. Jackson's farewell address cautioned against the 'spirit of speculation' which drained effort away from the 'sober pursuits of honest industry', and urged vigilance against the usurping designs of the 'organized money power'.

In his inaugural address, Jackson's successor, Martin Van Buren, in turn condemned 'the rapid growth among all classes, and especially in our great commercial towns, of luxurious habits founded too often on merely fancied wealth'. He cautioned that the vast over-extension of bank credit would 'seduce industry from its regular and salutary occupations by the hope of abundance without labor', that it would tempt 'all trades and professions into the vortex of speculation on remote contingencies'. Nor were the Jacksonians about to be intimidated by the nation's financial panic. Their Whig opponents tried counter-attacking by appealing to the universal thirst for property. The Democratic assault on 'monopoly', they cried, was really the crazed voice of the mob threatening all property, not just that tainted portion they denounced as 'fictitious'. But according to one Presidential adviser, these circles of Whig businessmen had miscalculated: 'They forgot that [while] Wall Street may be converted into a Bedlam nations seldom run mad except in war or revolution.'[23]

One hardly has to read between the lines here to recognize that the ogre frightening these two Presidents and so many others, was as much the unnatural instincts stirring among the people as it was the 'Monster Bank' itself or the suspect intrigues of Wall Street operators. The material grievances of ordinary working people, farmers, and small businessmen were real enough; the Bank could clamp down on credit, with all the ramifications on prices, wages and work that could entail, and did so when pressed. Still, drawn by a desire to seek out the main chance, sorely tempted by the idea of speculation, yet full of fear and guilt about abandoning the world of their fathers, people found in the Bank a psychologically consoling repository for all those illicit passions, long decried by their ancestors, that they now felt alive within themselves. At least that is the compelling argument of one historian: if the Bank was guilty, then the rest of society could maintain its innocence, remain chastely loyal to the old republican faith, gamely resisting the snares of speculation, self-promotion, and greed.[24]

All these emotions became still more intense when the panic of 1837 leveled the economy. The downward spiral began with the failure of the Ohio Life Insurance and Trust Company. In a pattern so often repeated as to suggest some underlying pathology inherent to the Street, the company had actually been founded by conservative New York financiers to redirect capital from the wildest speculations and into productive agricultural pursuits. But by 1836, no one could resist playing the game. When the Ohio Company suspended specie payments to its depositors, the orgy of land speculation and over-extended bank credits was over. Wall Street's collapse was the least of it. By September 1837, nine tenths of the nation's factories had closed. New York City witnessed 250 bankruptcies in two months. The winter of 1838 saw instances of starvation and death by exposure: the poorhouses were full, food stores were raided, and there were riots and angry demonstrations for relief in city streets. Emerson noted the 'Cold April; hard times; men breaking who ought not to break; banks bullied into the bolstering of desperate speculations.' And the misery went on for five long years. What more convincing evidence that speculation was lethal?[25]

It would be virtually impossible to exaggerate the level of vitriol directed at the Bank. And so it died an ignoble death. For the remainder of the nineteenth century, the idea that Federal government would regulate currency and credit would be treated as almost subversive. Yet even the Bank's harshest critics had carnal knowledge of the spirit of enterprise abroad in the land; after all, the Jacksonian credo of equal opportunity for all was a vital part of the bill of particulars used to indict the Bank. People might league together to level the ground, but only in order to set off on their own in pursuit of the main chance. Thinkers like Emerson could lament the 'hard times', yet remain romantically infatuated with the country's unparalleled prospects for self-discovery. American writers and intellectuals struggled to come to grips with this baffling new society while the one they'd grown up in melted before their eyes. Their community was divided down the middle. It would become more and more so in the next few generations, as Wall Street itself became the main battlefield in a nationwide cultural war.

Distinguished ante-bellum intellectuals, sometimes surprisingly, became articulate defenders of the new speculative order. Rip Van

Winkle's stunned awakening to a world he no longer recognized might be treated as a parable of Washington Irving's own experience. Identified with the Knickerbocker ascendancy, Irving had long deplored the new spirit of avaricious self-seeking. Nonetheless, by the late 1830s, he'd discovered its rationale: 'There are moral as well as physical phenomena incident to every state of things, which may at first appear evils but which are devised by an all-seeing Providence for some beneficial purpose. Such is the spirit of speculative enterprise which now and then rises to an extravagant height and sweeps throughout the land.' Mere trade might be grubby and pedestrian, but speculation was its 'romance': 'it renders the stock-jobber a magician and the [stock] exchange a region of enchantment.' Irving himself became a propagandist for the western imperial schemes of John Jacob Astor and a speculator in railroads and land, where he lost heavily. Despite his personal losses, and while acknowledging land speculation had ruined many, he argued that it helped force agriculture and civilization into the wilderness, establishing future towns and cities amidst 'savage solitudes', and that it strengthened the nation by building up its ports and commerce – 'all this has in great measure been affected by the extravagant schemes of land speculators.' And so, unlike Rip, Irving managed to reconnect himself to the new Jacksonian landscape.[26]

The great lexicographer, Noah Webster, struck a note that would echo down the generations, lending an air of inevitability as well as economic consolation to the growing powers of concentrated wealth. How could the poor get by without the rich, Webster asked. Who would employ them? 'Who can furnish the capital for canals, and railroads, and all other public improvements?' Michael Chevalier, the Frenchman whose *Letters on North America* were written during the height of the speculative mania of the mid-1830s, sprang to the defense of Wall Street. The exclusion of the brokers, merchants, and capitalists of Wall and Pearl streets from the body of the people, which was becoming a favorite refrain of Jacksonian critics, was, in Chevalier's view, grossly unfair. After all, 'consider what New York would be without them.' Numerically an insignificant minority, these denizens of the Street contributed mightily to the astounding growth of New York State.[27]

In his own way, Ralph Waldo Emerson agreed. He owned some stock himself, about $22,000 worth, a safe, non-speculative investment returning a six per cent dividend. But he was ambivalent. He resented the new tendency to defer to wealth and nothing else, yet he admired the new railroad promoters of New England such as John Murray Forbes, and approved what he regarded as the legitimate activities of the region's financial barons. While holding no brief for a small coterie of rich men, he recognized that the passion for quick gain was hardly confined to those circles. Indeed, this instinct might be interpreted as part of the American speculative genius for enterprise, innovation, and great projects. In the end, Emerson felt a revulsion for the unprincipled striving that seemed to inspire so many. Still, this kind of metaphysical speculation about speculation could, if carried far enough, turn Wall Street into an odd sort of breeding ground of democratic self-reliance.

Alexis de Tocqueville, that astute analyst of *Democracy in America*, also identified the acquisitive instinct (though without Emerson's transcendent rhetoric) as a dominating motive of the American character, and singled out rootlessness, the existential complement of an economy of speculative uncertainty, as the defining American trait. For Tocqueville, this constituted the tragic heroism of the American experiment. Even someone like Horace Greeley, who could turn apoplectic about the depravity of gambling, was nonetheless able to offer an apologia for speculation, as inherent in the national character and expressive of a democratic social order – it was a form of equal opportunity open to the bold. Richard Hildreth, one of the era's most prescient economists, attempted to naturalize and defuse the phenomenon. He noted, with ironic detachment, that when it succeeded, speculation was called enterprise; only when it failed was it described pejoratively as a 'bubble'. Hildreth considered such behavior a natural phenomenon, best left alone. Puritan intellectuals and Jacksonian publicists like Theodore Sedgwick and William Cullen Bryant shared the ambivalence: both welcomed the spirit of enterprise; both worried about the acquisitive excesses and speculative habits that seemed to follow in its wake.[28]

Many observers, however, felt no ambivalence. What went on in Wall Street was gambling, and gambling was sin. All the great western religions had condemned it as a form of pagan divination. In militantly Protestant America, gambling was treated as a kind of moral and psychological scourge, encouraging delusions of effortless gain, undermining the fragile armature of rational, deliberate, disciplined behavior upon which a virtuous soul and a virtuous society depended. Gamblers were dissolute, frivolous, addicted to extravagance and aristocratic pretense. The association with gambling would dog Wall Street throughout the nineteenth century, making its activities morally suspect to the pious. Young clerks on Wall Street were often identified as likely gamblers, and it was no surprise to the reform community that real gambling operations flourished on the fringes of the Street, frequented after hours by brokers grown accustomed to betting with other people's money during the daytime. John Pintard, one of the Street's Knickerbocker grandees, cautioned his daughter about *bon vivant* bank clerks and bookkeepers, too easily lured by gamblers and likely to end in ruin, defalcations, or even suicide. Henry Ward Beecher, the era's most celebrated minister, whose theology was otherwise as sunny as the nation's bumptious economic outlook, nevertheless worried about speculative earnings: 'Indeed, a Speculator on the exchange, and a Gambler at his table, follow one vocation, only with different instruments.' William Ellery Channing, a New England minister of great influence, likewise damned the spirit of 'feverish, insatiable cupidity' aroused by speculations in railroad stock. To the righteous, profits made on the exchange and winnings in the casinos seemed indistinguishable and equally ill-gotten.[29] Wall Street came to occupy a moral borderland, a twilight zone full of mutant passions, where healthy acquisitiveness dissolved back into its covetous precursor.

Comparisons between speculation and gambling were hardly confined to religious circles. Philip Hone noted during the panic of 1837 that the first Wall Street houses to fall were run by gambling types, not investors, a distinction he felt comfortable with but one that might have been tough to nail down on the Street. Wall Street insider, William Fowler, who published his *Revelations of Inside Life and Experience on Change*, raised the red flag for 'men and women of America who making haste to be rich, and taking evil counsel would enter Wall Street and put your money on the hazard of a die'. Those who opposed speculation often objected not to the market economy itself, but to the conversion of the marketplace into one vast casino where no law – natural, godly, or man-made – prevailed.[30]

Gamblers on the exchange, like gamblers everywhere, were supposed to be inherently dissolute. But the conventional gambler did not necessarily lack a sense of honor, even though the exigencies of gambling might lead him to commit dishonorable acts elsewhere. For many critics, however, those who plied their trade on Wall Street were morally suspect. Voices ranging up and down the social hierarchy, from the free North to the slave South, and from various points on the ideological compass, found something profoundly dishonorable and dissembling about the Street and the speculative behavior it nurtured.

Dickens was appalled by what he witnessed in America in general, but he viewed New York as the country's Gomorrah, compared to which 'the golden calf they worship at Boston is a pigmy'. Boston Brahmins at least had the good sense to make their sons beware Gotham's extravagance, which 'borders on insanity'. It was a city pregnant with 'mighty frauds, peculations, forgeries'. New England's patrician old guard, an amalgam of bankers, merchants, jurists, and literary intellectuals, translated Dickens' faint flattery into a regional conceit. For people like Charles Eliot Norton, the great classical scholar and educator, theologian Theodore Parker, and Oliver Wendell Holmes, Sr, Wall Street was as much the contemptible site of arriviste social climbing, as it was a hotbed of vulgarly democratic ambition run riot.[31]

Without the same elitist disdain, some of the country's most distinguished writers shared this deep estrangement from a society given over to money-making. The Pyncheon patriarchs, whose satanic Mammon-worship leaves an indelible curse on Nathaniel Hawthorne's *The House of Seven Gables*, are consumed by greed. While the original 'Colonel Pyncheon' concealed a decadent heart beneath an angular Puritanical grimness, his descendant, the 'Judge', who has invested diversely in land and various securities, displays a smoother exterior more suited to an economic order that rested increasingly on appearances, self-promotion, and the facsimile of trust.[32]

James Fenimore Cooper championed the Republic's 'Doric age'. Despite his upbringing as the son of a wealthy Federalist squire and friend of the Knickerbocker Jays and Rensselears, and despite his reservations about rule by the unruly, he became a committed Jacksonian Democrat. It was his way of combating the commercial nouveaux riches, the speculators and promoters who comprised 'Wall Street Whiggery'. In the 1820s, Cooper, an agrarian romantic, still believed America a place of decorous good order, of steady progress: lacking perhaps in education and taste, too susceptible to the demagogue, but holding fast to its simple, industrious virtues. For him the balance was upset in the uproarious '30s with their air of frenzied speculation, centered especially in the business district of New York populated by a 'race of cheating, lying, money-getting blockheads'. In *Homeward Bound* and *Home as Found*, novels of that period, Wall Street is offered as a kind of forensic exhibit of social suicide. It's an auctioneers' paradise, a place where virtually everything – farms, villas, estates, even towns – is up for grabs, turning over at ever escalating prices. This is true even of the most useless objects. The new art of hype makes crowds bid for rocks and worthless bags, all 'in the fearful delusion of growing rich by pushing a fancied value to a point still higher'.[33]

Southerners echoed, in their own accent, some of the sentiments of Cooper and the disaffected cultural elite of New England. Decrying speculation became a way of defending the mythos of the South. However commercially active they were in reality, Southern planters and their ideological defenders found Wall Street a perfect object to encapsulate their dislike of mean-spirited Northern capitalism. Their paternalism, their chivalry, their love of the land – the whole self-deluded romance that allowed the slavocracy to regard itself as superior to the money-grubbing North – would shield them against the commercial threat to the 'wholesome labors of the field and the enjoyment of moderate independence'. Brokers' profits were based on the 'increased suffering of labourers and the hardworking mass' – this last piety designed to win sympathy for the South among the Northern working classes.

When the stock market collapsed again in the panic of 1857, the *Louisville Courier* editorialized about Babylon on the Hudson: 'Their houses are dens of iniquity. Their aim is financial ruin. Their code of laws is that of the gambler, the sharper, the imposter, the cheat, and the swindler.' Senator John C. Calhoun of South Carolina, the South's leading ideological defender, chastised the Whig Party for mortgaging the people's inheritance to those who 'look to debts, stocks, banks, distributions, and taxes as the choicest of blessings. The greater the debt – the more abundantly the stock market is supplied.' For Southerners, it was naturally tempting to condemn the system outright. There was no escape from this charnel house of commerce and speculation; it bred demoralization and social insurrection, and was ultimately doomed. Not surprisingly, the 'only check on its diffusion is the existence of slavery; for this institution and the social system determined by it, have hitherto repelled its ravages, and even its extensive admission in the Southern States.'[34]

Elements of xenophobia and anti-Semitism found their way into the southern aversion to Wall Street, but were by no means confined to that region. The country depended heavily on infusions of foreign, especially British capital for its development. That money made up a good part of the trafficking in stocks and bonds and even land and other items of speculation. Such financial subordination naturally encouraged both groveling and resentment – the latter in particular when the market went bust and foreign funds fled the country. George Peabody, a Baltimore merchant banker and a major broker of American securities in London, boasted that there was 'nothing as good on earth' as these native stocks, and in the end his fellow citizens would pay for them, even if 'the rotten and tottering monarchies never will and never can'. Foreign investment banking houses like Baring Brothers and the Rothschilds were frequently singled out as 'dragons of finance', the prosperity of the nation depending on their 'caprice'. When wild-cat banks went under and numerous states defaulted on their bonds in the late 1830s, British investors condemned 'the dishonesty and bad faith of the American people' and called for a Parliamentary investigation. Predictably, this did not play well back in the States. James H. Hammond, senator from South Carolina and adamantine defender of slavery, bitterly complained of southern vassalage not only to New York, but to London, 'the great world center of exchanges in our age'.[35]

Seeking a plausible scapegoat for the financial trauma of 1837, the Governor of Mississippi, Alexander McNutt, lashed out at the Bank of the United States which had, he claimed, 'hypothecated these bonds and borrowed money upon them of the Baron Rothschild. The blood of Judas and Shylock runs in his veins.' Anti-Semites had fixated on the figure of the money-lender since at least the Middle Ages; their voices were heard at the creation of the first stock exchanges in the Netherlands. Part of the exoticism of 'Change Alley' in London derived from its promiscuous consorting with Jews, even when their social mobility was strictly circumscribed outside the 'Alley'. Jew-baiting of financiers was exported to the New World along with the Puritans and was a casually assumed part of even the most refined upbringing. John Quincy Adams, while representing the United States in the Netherlands during the War of 1812, complained about 'stock-jobbing and Jew-brokering tricks' which some dishonorable American speculators abroad had committed 'upon the Royal Exchange'.

The Mississippi Governor's remarks were therefore neither unusual nor characteristic only of the South. The Jacksonian Senator Silas Wright of New York was doleful about the panic but gleefully reported the failure of the Joseph brothers as the 'Jew brokers of New York'. Even before the panic, a satirical 'memoir', subtitled 'A Taste of the Dangers of Wall Street by a Late Merchant', described the brokers on the Exchange as a guild of thieves for whom honor applied only to themselves, 'like dogs or Jews'. A burlesque of life on the Street, published in 1841, featured a joint-stock company, the 'Wall Street Stock Company', whose raison d'être was to gull the inhabitants of New Amsterdam. Its two instigators were 'Mr Solomon Single-Eye' and 'Mr Jacob Broker', and every piece of chicanery that would later come to discolor the Street was implicitly attributed to their perversely fertile, Semitic intelligence.

It was August Belmont, however, who served as the first prototype of the satanic Wall Street Jew. He amalgamated everything that was hated: he was a major financier; he represented the Parisian Rothschilds, a foreign and Semitic financial dynasty, and was even rumored to be their illegitimate offspring; he was himself a foreigner, falsely alleged to have changed the family name from the Jewish 'Schoenberg'. Uncannily he arrived in New York, like some predatory bird, just as the 1837 panic took hold; he was fast becoming a figure of considerable political influence in the Democratic Party; and as if that were not enough, he was suave and reputedly a seducer of women. Belmont was an ideal foil not only for people like McNutt, but for all the McNutts that would follow, through Belmont's long life and beyond.[36]

William Gouge was neither a Southern planter nor an intellectual; nor was he a Senator or a minister – nor indeed an anti-Semite. He was, on the contrary, a self-taught mechanic and Philadelphia printer blessed with a remarkable technical grasp of the new paper economy and a desire to expose that system as 'the principal cause of social evil'. Gouge, who at the height of the Bank War went to work for the Treasury Department, authored a celebrated treatise, *A Short History of Paper Money and Banking in the US*. It served as the bible for circles of plebeian agitators who also disliked Wall Street, though less because it seemed a haven for gamblers, foreigners, and Jews, than because they were worried about aristocrats.

Protest was rife in Jacksonian America among the urban lower orders: apprentices, day-laborers, journeymen, skilled artisans, and small entrepreneurs from a vast range of occupations. They directed their ire at the Bank of the United States as well as those putative 'aristocrats' and 'monopolists' who might sometimes include their own employers. Most often, however, they condemned the paper-money 'parasites': bankers, money-lenders, and middlemen of all sorts. Wall Street brokers and speculators fell comfortably within this category.

The reasons for condemning Wall Street differed according to the class origins of those making the complaint. Gentrified planters and Brahmin intellectuals despised the whole commercial order and subsumed Wall Street within that generous hatred. Working-class publicists like Gouge or William Leggett, on the other hand, warmly embraced free enterprise as liberating, but condemned Wall Street because it threatened to derail the system, hoarding its advantages while fleecing everyone else. For Leggett, whose writings in the *New York Evening Post* fiercely defended Jackson's war on the Bank, Wall Street was becoming America's 'Street of Palaces', home to a 'script nobility', living off a corrupt government, intent on enslaving the rest of America. Though Leggett declared stock-exchange transactions perfectly legitimate in theory, as a useful way of encouraging trade and production, in the same breath he decried the inequities that seemed always to accompany those transactions.

Could they be separated? No one really knew. Populist critics objected to the 'artificial inequality of wealth', pointing to banks and other corporations that amassed their riches thanks to government charters and other favors often paid for in hard cash. But since they championed the competitive marketplace, it was really the political artificiality, not the inequality, that they sought to remedy.

For many, the notion of the capitalist signified not, as we might assume, the employer of wage labor, but rather Wall Street and the wider world of finance which seemed to live off the enterprise of others. Gouge pointed his finger at the 'accumulators' (a class distinct from the 'producers') who piled up great fortunes 'in stock and bonds and notes and mortgages – in claims upon the future products of the land and upon the future earnings of the industrious'. These were the folk responsible for fomenting a spirit of 'wild and daring speculation', or its opposite, a 'prostration of confidence, and a stagnation of business'. Far worse than a lottery – where at least all had a fair chance of winning or losing – this financial gambling was underpinned by secret rules, rigged prices, fake sales, and purchases among brokers: a circus of commercial trickery.

Gouge was far more than an agitator engaged in rhetorical overkill. He described, knowledgeably and with astonishing prescience, a mechanics of the Street that sounds familiar even today. Speculators, seeking control of an insurance company, he observed, borrowed from a variety of sources, using other people's money to buy up the stock:

> The original advance of the combination is thus small, and they are thence enabled to be operating on the stock of many companies at once, till, having acquired a control in several concerns, they turn out all the old administrators, put in their own men, and then go to work again . . . By artful management, assiduous puffing, magnificent predictions, and supplies of stock skillfully curtailed as the demand increases – any one of the stocks thus owned, may be blown up to an absurd rate – and spared as a favor to the public, until the Managers have sold all out, and realized their profits, leaving the new purchasers to come in and assist at the bursting of the bubble.

Gouge did more than pillory these moneyed aristocrats. As much a social psychologist as he was an economist, he touched another nerve, one closer to the conflicted heart of Jacksonian America. Gouge observed that this paper economy spread its contagion far and wide so that the 'visionary profits of one day stimulate extravagance, and the positive losses of another engender spleen, irritation, restlessness, a spirit of gambling, and domestic inquietude'. Paper currency, stocks, bonds, and other snares of the new order were 'Like the Syrens of the fable, they entice to destroy.'[37]

'The Syrens of Wall Street' could easily have been the name of a play, musical revue, or some other form of popular entertainment in Jacksonian New York. It wasn't. But the phrase suggests the vertiginous mixture of innocence and guilt, of self-seduction and the fear of seduction, of hope mingled with cupidity, that lent the Street the allure of the demi-monde. For all of their daily inculcation in the Protestant work ethic – indeed, perhaps in part thanks to that arduous regimen – many people were drawn to its sybaritic opposite.

A whole popular literature appeared which embodied this dilemma. Harry Franco, the hapless hero of *The Adventures of Harry Franco: A Tale of the Great Panic*, is a country boy who comes to New York to seek his fortune. America's first depression novel, the book was a great success in part because no matter how many times Harry gets taken in by the city's confidence men, he comes back for more, irrepressibly confident, indefatigably innocent. Above all, he can't resist the atmosphere of delirious speculation that follows the panic of 1837. Wall Street is alive with posters advertising every conceivable promotional scheme, buzzing with talk of rising stocks, 'lots' – gossamer towns and paper cities. It creates in Harry a voracious appetite to join in; yet through it all, he remains utterly credulous, a true believer in honesty, thrift, hard work, and democracy, notions which in the mouths of his shadier business associates have become pure cant, useful merely for making a buck.[38]

Harry experienced 'adventures'; protagonists of other fictions, which often masqueraded as memoirs, confronted 'dangers' or were swept away by the 'undercurrents' of Wall Street. In *Perils of Pearl Street*, Peter Funk, the story's anti-hero, is an imp of deception who hails from nowhere, a pandering phantasm. The authors of these potboilers – like Harry's creator, Charles Frederick Briggs, a well-known satirist and associate of Edgar Allen Poe's – intended their stories as cautionary tales, warnings against the folly of the desire to rise rapidly and without effort through the magic of speculation. Briggs himself had been forced to go to sea as a common sailor when his family's fortune was lost in the China trade. He and tale-tellers like him maintained a simmering anger about the economic injustice and poverty urban commercial life fostered.[39]

But they knew their readers well. To 'raise a wind' and hope it blew favorably lured those who chafed at the social limitations of small-town America. They might run up against Wall Street operators who 'shaved' their over-extended clients 'till the blood followed the razor'; they would soon enough learn that 'the more a man engages in speculation . . . the less tender his conscience grows on the subject of doing to others as he would have them do to him'; they could conceivably end up in jail or as suicides. Nonetheless, the sense of 'adventure', of 'danger', of mysterious 'undercurrents' drew them on. This underground Wall Street lived precariously, a breed apart from those Wall Street grandees who drove in 'fancy carriages', dined sumptuously, and finished their day at the opera house. The lives of the less privileged dealers were more transient: harried, under constant stress, one day sleeping in first-class hotels, the next their backs pressed to the wall. Disreputable as they might seem, however, these men had their own appeal. Measured against the typical ascetic banker, a man of impeccable honesty but also rigid and unfeeling – 'all justice, no mercy' – these Wall Street adventurers seemed like boon companions, generous and full of fun while the money lasted. Though they were psychic prisoners of the speculative mania, perhaps, they were also liberated from the treadmill of business. Some of them, at least, qualified as 'picturesque rascals'. Others, less savory and scrupulous, were depicted as 'adroit knaves'. It was a shadowy realm indeed.

The urban underworld exercised a compelling fascination for a people newly acquainted with its exoticism. Journalists began to include Wall Street in their perambulations. It might be 'the purse-string of America – the key of the Union', but it was also the site of 'a million deceits and degradations and hypocrisies and miseries played off there as if in some ghastly farce'. It was likened to the valley of riches described in *Sinbad the Sailor*, 'where millions of diamonds lay glistening like fiery snow, but which was guarded on all sides by poisonous serpents, whose bite was death and whose contact was pollution'. For the outsider, Wall Street appeared 'a place of deep and dangerous mystery; a region of dens and caves and labyrinths full of perils'. Here was not only duplicity, but conspicuous frivolity and dissipation which seemed to mock the abstemious axioms of commercial virtue. Here too, where New York's faux aristocracy dressed in purple and fine linen and imbibed vintage wines 'out of Bohemian glass', the social order seemed in a perpetual state of carnival-like upheaval: 'All classes and grades are represented here – rich and poor, gentle and simple, learned and illiterate.'[40]

Darker visions than this inspired George Foster, perhaps the most popular anatomist of New York's demi-monde. In his *New York by Gaslight*, a series of newspaper sketches of his wanderings, he depicted Wall Street as a dehumanizing place where puppet-like people cloaked their misery in deceptive gentility: 'Wall Street! Who shall fathom the depth and rottenness of thy mysteries? Has Gorgon passed through thy winding labyrinths, turning with his smile everything to stone – hearts as well as houses.' Foster's portrait was unforgiving. The Street was a 'crimson-canopied altar of Mammon', shrouded in secrecy, where a small coterie of men 'settle the question of whether the country is to be prosperous or unfortunate.' Their power lay in the 'over-reaching' of littler men, so that no matter how savagely they oppressed the poor, 'no matter how many lips may turn white with hunger', no matter 'how many milk-white virgin bosoms be given to the polluting touch of lust', they somehow retained their public eminence. Their reputation was made worse by the fact that the New York Stock Exchange conducted its proceedings in cryptic confidence, and cultivated an air of a secret brotherhood. For Foster and a host of other writers appalled and intrigued by this urban inferno, Wall Street was, above all, a boulevard of deceit.[41]

Jacksonian America was thus gripped by a crisis of confidence: despite unprecedented commercial opportunities, it was haunted by the figure of the Confidence Man – men such as William Thompson, who cynically exploited that credulous optimism. Wall Street was his natural, if not his only habitat.

Some versions of the Confidence Man were more benign. 'Yankee Jonathan' was a ubiquitous figure in ante-bellum popular culture. A roving pedlar, moving from village to village, he initially seemed a comic country bumpkin. But he usually turned out to be shrewder than that suggested: a clever, versatile bargainer adept at getting people to buy 'a pig in a poke'. He was a fast-talker, inventive and seductive, never totally honest, and sexually notorious: all in all, someone it was dangerous to be near but hard to stay away from. 'Uncle Sam' himself, with his lean, angular body, resembled this folkloric figure and in some incarnations celebrated this Yankee genius for heady optimism and sharp bargaining.

The Confidence Man proper, originally an English import, was much more malevolent. In America, he was a version of the *picaro*, relying not on his charm but on the country's social fluidity to ply his trade. He preyed upon the poor and vulnerable; he was a criminal and lived among criminals; he was a trickster, a man of masks, a 'character' without character who undermined that sense of trust essential to a commercial society. Popular perceptions of Wall Street oscillated between these two images. But as the country went through the panics of 1819 and especially 1837, the frightening visage of the Confidence Man supplanted the happier one of 'Yankee Jonathan'.[42]

James Gordon Bennett's acid excoriation of the Wall Street confidence man, occasioned by the William Thompson case, caught the popular antipathy to this darker figure. Bennett knew his audience: he was the William Randolph Hearst of ante-bellum America, an inventor of the penny press crafted to appeal to the sensationalist appetites of the city's non-genteel. His paper, the *New York Herald*, carried ads from prostitutes and ran long columns of salacious gossip about the city's leading citizens. Like Hearst, he was deliberately provocative. And like Hearst, he hated Wall Street. Shrewdly, however, Bennett also pioneered financial reportage, including a daily Wall Street column and listings of canal, railroad, and bank stock prices. At the same time, he fired verbal shots at the 'princes of "change"', as the Exchange was then known. His whole editorial and marketing strategy tended to the populist sensibilities of his readers. Labeling his upmarket, 'six penny' competitors the 'vehicles of mere stock-jobbers and speculators', Bennett pledged that 'We shall . . . deal justly, honestly, and fearlessly with every institution in Wall Street – every broker – every bank – every capitalist.'

A year after he opened the paper in 1835, he converted this antipathy into a notorious scandal. Bennett accused a rival publisher, Colonel James Watson Webb, of stock-market defalcations and of serving as a creature of Nicholas Biddle's Bank of the United States. Webb was editor of the *Courier and Enquirer*, a paper read by 'Society'. He was also a Wall Street 'bear', at this time betting against the fortunes of the Morris Canal, a favorite object of speculation in the early days of the Exchange. Bennett's accusations were bad enough, but they came laced with contempt and advice that Webb ought to be imprisoned or put in an asylum. Webb exploded. He attacked Bennett in broad daylight on the street with a club, cutting his head. Nursing his wounds, Bennett defiantly retorted that neither 'the assassin Webb', nor, for that matter, Wall Street would succeed in silencing the *Herald*.[43]

James Gordon Bennett traded in demagoguery. Herman Melville did not. But they shared a mordant fascination with a modern, commercial civilization which seemed fraudulent at its core. Melville's probes into the psychological, social, and even sexual interiors of that civilization run through many of his major novels and short stories. He was arguably the nineteenth century's profoundest seer into the spiritual malignancy caused by the young country's infatuation with the marketplace. Starbuck's terrifying confrontation with Ahab in the captain's cabin echoes even today for all those who, like the Pequod's first mate, trust to the inherent rationality, equality, and peacefulness of the capitalist order of things. Ahab answers Starbuck's plea on behalf of the ship's owners (in effect its shareholders) with implacable, minatory indifference. 'Let the owners stand on Nantucket beach and outyell the Typhoons. What cares Ahab? Owners, owners? Thou art prating to me, Starbuck, about those miserly owners, as if owners were my conscience. But look ye, the only real owner of anything is its commander.'[44]

Again and again Melville reveals the darkness his countrymen are too sun-blinded to see. 'Bartleby the Scrivener', perhaps the most famous of Melville's stories, was subtitled 'A Story of Wall Street'. Whatever else might be said about this enigmatic tale, it conveys an overpowering sense of the Street as the eerily dead center of a world lost in its own busyness. Bartleby's refusal unto death, his 'I prefer not to' to all claims on his labor and ineffable self-respect, stands as a reproach to his employer's 'snug business among rich men's bonds, and mortgages, and title-deeds'. The confines of his Wall Street office are as airless and viewless as 'the Tombs' in which Bartleby ultimately expires. The Street, which by day teems with life, nonetheless exudes a kind of inhuman coldness and social estrangement. One hears echoes here of George Foster's 'Gorgon' turning everything on Wall Street into stone, 'hearts as well as houses.' Even Bartleby's intransigence is tellingly inert.[45]

Melville's gaze was remorseless, finding chicanery wherever it looked in a society given over to the pursuit of money. That vision achieved a certain black density in what is certainly Melville's most allusive and recondite novel, *The Confidence-Man: His Masquerade*. It has been claimed that the novel was inspired by William Thompson's arrest. True or not, the book is a veritable black mass of confidence men: religious confidence men and philosophical confidence men, literary and political confidence men, crooked businessmen and crooked philanthropists, pedlars of nostrums and miracle cures for the ailments of body and soul, all masquerading together on the steamboat, *Fidele*, as it floats down the Mississippi River, the nation's principal artery.

Among them, predictably, is a speculator, experienced in the ways of the stock market. He encounters a younger man to whom he seeks to sell stock in the Black Rapids Coal Company. Negotiations proceed, shrouded in mystery; tempting allusions are made to the stock's unavailability, suggesting its preciousness. The young man turns out to be less callow than he seemed and inquires why the stock's price has of late been depressed. Our speculator/confidence man blames it on 'the growling, the hypocritical growling, of the bears'. Why 'hypocritical', the young man asks. Now the negotiation becomes a metaphysical jeremiad against speculation, delivered in the interests of speculation. It is a send-up of Emerson's pervasive cultural optimism:

> Why the most monstrous of all hypocrites are these bears: hypocrites by inversion; hypocrites in all the simulation of things dark instead of bright; souls that thrive, less upon depression, than the fiction of depression; professors of the wicked art of manufactured depressions; spurious Jeremiahs . . . who, the lugubrious day done, return, like sham Lazaruses among the beggars, to make merry over the gains got by their pretended sore heads – scoundrel bears!

Bears, like gloomy philosophers, are destroyers of confidence, avers our speculator: 'fellows who, whether in stocks, politics, bread-stuffs, morals, metaphysics, religion – be it what it may – trump up their black panics in the naturally-quiet brightness solely with a view to some sort of covert advantage.'

With this reasoning, our young man is in perfect emotional sympathy, as are, presumably, most of his countrymen in their quest, undertaken in guilty innocence, for the main chance. His confidence won – he naturally gravitates to 'fellows that talk comfortably and prosperously, like you' – the young man saunters off to conclude the transaction: not however, in the 'bright sunlight', but in 'a private little haven' hidden from view. And there the game continues as the speculator/confidence man, his thirst for mercenary deceit unquenchable, entices his young convert with talk of stock in a 'New Jerusalem, a new and thriving city, so called, in northern Minnesota'.[46]

The Confidence-Man was published in the spring of 1857, and was like a premonition. Just months later, panic and depression swept Wall Street and the country. In its wake, an amalgam of Bennett's 'Confidence Man of the Palace Uptown' and Melville's steamboat hustler would open up a fresh chapter in the saga of the Street.

3

From Confidence Man to Colossus

A monument, to be known as the Vanderbilt Memorial Bronze, was erected in 1869 at the depot of the Hudson River Railroad (later part of the New York Central) in St John's Park. This address, south of Canal Street near the Hudson River, had once been fashionable but was by then given over to commerce. The depot itself was a gigantic, ornate building, and its huge pediment was now capped by a twelve-foot-high statue of Cornelius Vanderbilt. The *New York Herald* noted that while it was perhaps 'not so prodigious as the Pyramid of Cheops, nor so lofty as the Colossus of Rhodes . . it will do'. The Commodore's fur-coated, stony likeness was surrounded by bas-reliefs depicting his fabled career on land and sea. A fifty-ton cyclorama included carvings of steamships and locomotives, of Neptune and a sea monster, of boilers, birds, machinery, and cows, pineapples, and railroad tracks.

The city of New York had contributed a half million dollars to this truly imperial monument in honor of 'old eighty millions'. People differed violently over whether that money had been well spent. *Harpers Weekly*, which as much as any magazine gave voice to prevailing middle-class opinion, found the statue wholly admirable; everything from the lushness of its panorama to the immensity of its construction struck the editors as appropriate to the formidable subject. The *Herald* – now run by James Gordon Bennett's son, who identified with the type of Wall Street tycoon his father had once chided – treated it as 'a monument of the greatest material inventions and enterprises of the nineteenth century'. It proclaimed the bronze 'beautiful', a granite memorial to the 'genius and progress of the age', given flesh and bone in the garlanded career of the Commodore. In florid rhetoric, the paper praised Vanderbilt's heroic rise, his energy, and his 'luminous sagacity', Above all, it expressed an oddly unquestioning conviction that his Napoleonic aura confirmed him as the epitome of the American self-made man.

Not everyone joined in this popular ovation. More genteel circles voiced a sophisticated disdain for the grandiose memorializing of great wealth. E. L. Godkin, editor of *The Nation* and the conscience of bourgeois rectitude, took note of a hilarious burlesque unveiling staged by some brokers of the New York Stock Exchange on Wall Street. At this mock ceremony, an actor posing as a statue of Vanderbilt held a watering can labeled '207' – the price of the railroad's stock established by the Commodore when he consolidated the system. The actor informed the audience that 'the use of water, not as a beverage, but as an element of wealth' constituted Vanderbilt's true achievement. 'We may say of him not only that he commenced life as a waterman' (the Commodore moniker came from his early career as a Staten Island ferryman carrying passengers across New York harbor) 'but that water has been the Central idea of his life'.

Like those who applauded the bronze, *The Nation* also found it appropriate to its subject, but perversely so. Its 'brute utilitarianism' failed to achieve a noble effect; instead it 'makes ridiculous what before was at worst only disagreeable'. It was a monumental mockery of everything about Vanderbilt: his lack of interest in the arts and education, his miserliness, his callous indifference to the public interest. Godkin made fun of the bronze's symbolism: the steamboat lines that were in fact unsafe and uncomfortable, the railroads which 'bought whole legislatures, debauched courts, crushed out rivals'. All in all, he concluded, what was being memorialized here were the 'trophies of the lineal successor of the medieval baron', an execrable character lacking in learning, grace, moral integrity, and manners, whose indifference to matters of civic honor was legendary. Furious that people like Horace Greeley and Bishop James had joined in the chorus of tribute, Godkin asked rhetorically why the city should honor these 'kings of the street', these 'giants of the stock exchange'.

Why indeed? Godkin implicitly condemned a whole culture. Why were people like Vanderbilt admired rather than stigmatized? Why did people tolerate these displays of 'unmitigated selfishness' and raise monuments to those 'peculiarly American virtues' such as 'audacity, push, unscrupulousness, and brazen disregard of others' rights'? Godkin was a study in self-righteousness, smugly ensconced in the certitudes of his Brahmin liberalism. But his question was a good one and he was not alone in asking it. It is an enigma that even during an era of legendary rapaciousness, Wall Street figures could elicit feelings of awe and reverence and come to exemplify national achievement.[1]

In the hustle and bustle of Jacksonian America, amidst all its striving and conniving, Wall Street had seemed an Oz in the confabulatory land of the confidence man. But in the era of the Civil War and the gilded years that followed, the Street fostered a peculiarly American form of idolatry. The confidence man had become a hero – or at least a heroic scoundrel. The mountebank had become king, though of an irregular and eccentric type. Free-booting, lawless, he was half aristocrat, half democrat – yet, like Napoleon, neither. His character was in keeping with the hybrid economy, part mercantilist, part laissez-faire. In a country obsessed with the infinite possibilities of uninhibited beginnings, he was a frontiersman and a mogul at the same time.

The four horsemen of this Gilded Age of finance included Vanderbilt himself along with Daniel Drew, James Fisk, and Jay Gould. Each had a distinctive part to play. 'The Commodore' took on an imperial absolutism. 'Uncl Dan'l' Drew assumed the plebeian position. Gould, the 'Mephistopheles of Wall Street', seemed utterly demonic. 'Jubilee Jim Fisk' played the ribald fool. Moreover, they and men like them were drawn to outlandish forms of sumptuary display that marked them as a kind of faux aristocracy. With the grime and slime of farms and fishing boats still clinging to them, they built grandiose palaces staffed by liveried servants and paraded in the finest equipage. But they fooled no one. Beneath that papery veneer they remained the ruffians they started out as – and that was part of their charm.

This odd conjoining of aristocratic and plebeian traits fascinated the generation that straddled the Civil War and left a legacy that still colors our sense of Wall Street. 'Diamond Jim' Brady, Charles Yerkes, Joseph Kennedy, Samuel Insull, and Michael Milken belong to a rogues' gallery of Wall Street Napoleons stretching from the Civil War to the dot.com era. All confirm a cultural stereotype of the free-booting financier as imperious, self-made, ambitious, and full of masculine audacity. They were and are perceived as outlanders: outside the law, outside established institutions, outside the conventions of normal social behavior. Indeed, it is precisely because they were not to the manor born that their rise carries associations of democratic adventure, turning roguishness into heroism.

Two cataclysmic events cleared the stage for the opening scene of this Napoleonic romance. The panic of 1857, the less momentous one, marked the end of Wall Street's dependency on the rhythms of commercial agriculture. It also disassembled the prevailing pecking order on the Street, opening up room for new men. Then of course there was the Civil War. Its idealism and blood sacrifice notwithstanding, the war presented undreamt-of opportunities for speculative money-making. And its aftermath left republican government at the mercy of financial gamesmen with imperial appetites.

Wall Street panicked once again in the fall of 1857 and the country quickly fell into depression. As severe hardship spread, public denunciations of the rich multiplied. Some of the newly wealthy found an odd way to express their remorse. At 'poverty parties' attended by New York's most affluent, guests dressed in calico and homespun imbibed cold water and bread and butter, and raised money for the relief of the poor. They sought to separate themselves from 'the annoyance of snobs who go only to guzzle champagne and to stuff themselves with oysters'. The panic and depression made everyone acutely sensitive to the presence of an aristocracy whose special breeding ground was Wall Street.

The collapse of '57 had its roots in the Crimean War and the decade's railroad boom. The 1850s had begun with rampant speculation in everything from guano to real estate, fed by the discovery of gold in California. Then the war in the Crimea, by shutting down the supply of Russian wheat, led to a sizeable expansion of American farming, which in turn fed the craze for new railroad lines to get the grain to market. A billion dollars was poured into railroad construction before the Civil War. The United States led the world in miles of track. A bull market in railroad shares naturally followed. While Boston had enjoyed a brief period as the center of railroad finance during the 1840s, by the 50s Wall Street clearly predominated. At least a quarter of the total active capital of the country was invested in railroads.[2]

When the Crimean war ended in 1856, the American wheat market was glutted, thanks to a bumper crop in the Midwest and the resumption of supplies from the Russian steppes. Farmers were caught short.

Banks couldn't collect their debts. Railroad shares plummeted and major lines stopped running. Bubbles of land speculation burst. Wall Street immediately felt the pain, as most of its business – government bonds, railroad securities, commodity trading, and speculation – was dependent on the land. Over-extended brokers broke into fist fights on the floor of the New York exchange. The whole mercantile economy imploded. Shipbuilding ground to a halt, merchants went under in droves, foundries and textile factories closed, railroads went bankrupt, construction sites stood deserted. Over 1,400 banks failed in the month of October alone. In New York, Fourth Street between Avenues A and B became known as 'Ragpickers Row', and ten thousand squatters settled above Forty-Second Street where they fed on pigs fattened on the carcasses of horses, dogs, cats, and rats, or worse still on the carcasses themselves. Homelessness and destitution spread throughout the country as mass prayer meetings pleaded for divine relief. As the crisis ricocheted from the United States to Europe and back to South America, Friedrich Engels confided to Karl Marx that he found the whole situation 'delicious', while his fellow members of the Manchester Exchange grew 'black in the face with rage at my suddenly rising good spirits'.[3]

Tempers flared and scapegoats were not hard to find. The South, which until then prided itself on immunity from the vicissitudes of Northern capitalism, was particularly enraged. The *New Orleans Crescent* decried New York as the 'center of reckless speculation, unflinching fraud and downright robbery', responsible for 'injuring almost every solvent community in the Union'. George Fitzhugh, impassioned ideologue of Southern extremism, denounced the 'fugitive' and 'cosmopolitan' capital of the North and especially stocks, which 'by means of the idleness and luxury which they beget, are the most alarming evil of modern times'. *De Bows Review*, a more sober Southern journal, blamed the crisis on 'the abstraction of a large amount of capital from the uses of commerce' into speculation in inflated railroad securities. The editors, like many of the region's journalists, held up the depression as Exhibit No. 1 in the case for Southern independence, at least from its 'commercial vassalage' to the North.[4]

Northern critics sounded similar themes. Like Fitzhugh, crusading journalist Horace Greeley laid out a causal chain that ended at the stock market. The country's imports had vastly exceeded its exports, due to the materialistic cravings of the new class of parvenus. This group, in turn, was rapidly expanding, thanks to the reckless boom in railroad and other securities, in 'paper bubbles of all descriptions'. Boston's mercantile elite deplored New York's financial irresponsibility. Newspapers around the country warned their readers, especially the commercially minded among them, not to become 'the football of Wall Street stock jobbers'. President Buchanan joined the chorus condemning 'wild speculations and gambling in stocks'. Even the *Journal of Commerce*, the voice of mercantile New York, advised people to 'steal a while away from Wall Street and every worldly care, and spend an hour about mid-day in humble, hopeful prayer'.

Frank Leslie's *Illustrated Newspaper*, one of the first to cater to the tastes of the new urban middle classes, normally adopted the prevailing optimism of its readers. When the panic hit, the editors expected it to blow over quickly, thanks to the country's wonderful 'recuperative powers'. But soon enough the magazine had to take stock of the darker side of the country's joie de vivre. So much 'youthful leaping of the blood in the hearts of our people' led to 'injudicious indulgence'. A cartoon depicted the Wall Street brokers and bankers as a band of inebriates reeling down the Street, empty liquor bottles labeled 'bull' and 'bear' trailing behind them. Fearing the return of '37, but persistently upbeat about the long-term future, Leslie's paper nonetheless singled out 'the moneyed aristocracy' in their 'brownstone and marble palaces' who 'strut their brief existence . . . From nothing they come, to nothing they return.'[5]

Criticism moved from the editorials onto the streets when 5,000 of the unemployed demonstrated in Wall Street, chanting 'We Want Work' and demanding that banks open up credit lines to businesses promising work. There was loose talk of storming the banks. When these 'hunger meetings' persisted, Federal troops under Mexican War hero General Winfield Scott were sent to guard the Customs House and Sub-Treasury. Populist Mayor Fernando Wood denounced Wall Street, claiming that 'those who produce everything get nothing, and those who produce nothing get everything'. He was instantly abandoned by his one-time conservative backers in the business community. The *New York Times* accused him of raising the banner of 'the most fiery communism'. Brokers and bankers congregated in Wall Street to rescue what they described as 'the worst governed city in Christendom'. When Wood was unceremoniously dumped from the Democratic Party ticket, his friends blamed it on 'Wall Street Democrats' who were willing for the government to bail out failing banks, but not destitute workers.

Despite the devastation, the crisis passed quickly, just as *Leslie's Illustrated* had predicted. But concern remained over Wall Street's moral as well as its economic impact on the country's well-being. Some saw the panic as a purgative ridding the economy of a cancerous growth. The prosperity fostered by the speculators had been delusory; thanks to the crash, 'much, very much, will be swept away that was rotten and unhealthy, but all that is worth preserving will remain.' The moral of the story was 'to live slower and be more respectable'.

For Henry Varnum Poor, the creator of the first investors' guide to railroad securities, the panic of '57 confirmed the need for reliable information about railroad operations and finance. Of New England stock, a transcendentalist and friend of Emerson, Poor placed his faith in industrial progress as the key to universal enlightenment. Railroads were the means to that happy end and Poor advised their management on how to raise money on the Street. Early rail-stock issues were often purchased by local merchants and farmers who hoped not only to profit personally, but felt themselves engaged in a communal undertaking. But the stock soon passed into the hands of speculators and its social usefulness was perverted, producing the calamity of '57 and sending Poor off to do the work that would make him famous.[6]

The 'story papers' that circulated widely among the working and lower-middle classes drew their own lessons from the panic. Asserting the essential egalitarianism of American society, they insisted that even a chimney sweep could be 'as independent and haughty, if need be, as the Wall Street shaver with his bonds and coupons'. The panic was a welcome astringent, reining in a deplorable tendency to extravagance and debt. A 'cheering fact' was that the violence of the crash had at least hit hardest at those most responsible: 'The overtraders [sic] and speculators must bear the scorch of the sirocco.' This was only just, as 'nine-tenths of all the hardship and sufferings have been caused by the men who gamble in stocks and railway shares'. Capital was controlled by 'a despicable party of rash, unprincipled speculators', who used part for their own aggrandizement while the rest was 'buried in worthless railroads, mining companies, banks and other dismal swamps'. Story-papers like *The New York Ledger* editorialized in favor of a system of moral and economic regulation and called for enforcement of the laws against gambling, defamation of character, and conspiracy to defraud.[7]

Whatever its social origins, criticism of Wall Street tended to reveal deep anxiety about the emergence of a presumptuous financial and social aristocracy. The very notion of aristocracy was in flux. It still signified pre-industrial concepts such as dynastic titles and estates, political privileges, sumptuary codes, strategic matrimonial alliances, and 'good breeding'. All that, however, was now diluted by money. A mercantile aristocracy, dressed in old-world costume and still a creature of the country's state-subsidized economy, was mutating into the industrial plutocracy that would lord it over Gilded Age America.

George Francis Train, whose series of extended 'letters' were published as *Young America in Wall Street,* acidly decried the 'silks and satins, laces and crinoline, hoops and diamonds, fast horses, clubs, and brandy smashes' which seemed to accompany 'the brandy of bubbling speculation' that had led the country into a sort of 'delirium tremens'. In Train's opinion New York's financial elite, try as it might, could not refute the charge that its 'luxurious living, extravagant dressing, splendid turn-outs, and fine horses, are the causes of distress to the nation'.[8]

New York's explosive growth since the completion of the Erie Canal had incubated this new aristocracy. Home to nearly a million people by 1860, the city was already displaying the early signs of its imperial career in its architectural presence, geographical expansion, commercial energy, and cultural diversity. Even by the 1840s, New York was handling half the country's imports and a third of its exports. Ships from 150 foreign countries entered New York harbor in 1835. Carried away, a British visitor described Wall Street, Manhattan's 'golden toe', as the most 'concentrated focus of commercial transactions in the world'. Bank capital doubled during the 1850s and Wall Street was emerging as second only to London as a world financial center.

Newly constructed commercial buildings on Wall Street, inspired by the style of the Italian Renaissance, exuded the swelling confidence of that world of fast horses and brandy smashes Train excoriated. The clean lines of the modest bourgeois style were abandoned in favor of gaudy ornamentation and sculpted flourishes. From inside these renaissance palazzos the Street's financiers exercised an influence that would extend well beyond the northeast region by the time of the Civil

War. Mobilizing domestic capital resources as well as serving as conduits for European, especially British investors, Wall Street houses affected not only trade but also agriculture, and through their railroad dealings, the rate of industrial development.[9]

'Millionaire' was a term coined in about 1845 to describe the wealth of John Jacob Astor and about ten others who qualified. By 1860, there were over a hundred people warranting the title. An 'upper tendom' or 'upper ten thousand', much of it quartered in Wall Street and defined by its boxes at the Opera and pricey pews at Grace Church, had become part of the spectacle of city life. Whatever reservations this engendered, there was also something undeniably bewitching about the Street's splendor. 'Wealth in Wall Street does not choose to dwell in humble mansions. There is little of log-cabinism in the tastes and habitudes of our merchant and banker princes,' editorialized the *New York Daily Mirror*, boasting that no business street anywhere in the country, perhaps in the world, could outshine Wall Street's 'architectural elegance.' [10]

August Belmont, who had arrived in New York as an agent of the Rothschilds on the eve of the Panic of 1837, became, thanks to his European background, a cultural missionary to the arrivistes: 'He taught New Yorkers how to eat, how to drink, how to dress, how to drive four-in-hands, how to furnish their houses, how to live generally according to the rules of the possibly somewhat effete, but unquestionably refined society of the Old World.' The results of this education were evident in architecture, as the brick and wood of Knickerbocker days gave way to costly marble and sandstone; to interiors of mahogany, rosewood, imported silk or satin draperies, gilt-edged furniture, and private libraries; and outdoors to carriages with heraldic crests and liveried footmen. The self-consciously private and studiously modest Knickerbocker ascendancy reluctantly began to dissolve into the newer, showier financial one. Belmont deftly combined old-world refinement with New World flash; he was an avid pioneer of the new sport of thoroughbred horse-racing and staged the sort of opulent balls that would have scandalized the city's old Anglo-Dutch patricians.[11]

Belmont's civilizing mission notwithstanding, beneath this veneer of heraldic pomp and clubby exclusivity there was something irreducibly fake that opened the nouveaux to ridicule. An artist's rendering of 'One of the Upper Ten Thousand', done in the mid-1840s, sketches a risible image of a strutting, pouting, pompous, top-hatted New York swell. This rising aristocracy was not only privileged and arrogant like the old one, but was also associated with the financial jobbery and reckless speculation identified with Wall Street. Referred to over and over again as a 'shoddy aristocracy' – the intention was to compare these parvenus to the cheap fabric made from reclaimed wool – it was a milieu whose bona fides were forever under inspection. Even those who'd trafficked in the Street themselves could be appalled. William Fowler's insider's exposé described the typical Wall Streeter dressed in purple and fine linen, gorging on delicacies and 'wines of the vintage of Waterloo'; a creature who 'produces nothing, he drives no plough, plies no hammer, sends no shuttle flashing through the loom'.[12]

This was a world not only to be gazed at but to be seen through. George Foster's revelations of urban mystery and exoticism made richly allegorical use of Wall Street. His tales of vice and virtue, of sin and redemption included 'true-to life' depictions of hypocritical and avaricious stockbrokers preying on the working poor. Here too was a mockery of an aristocracy, an 'old fogy class' or the 'shaving cream of our financial aristocracy. Heaven help those who are so unlucky as to be shaved by them.' This was typical anti-aristocratic melodrama, of the sort that American folk culture had been steeped in since the Revolution. But Foster noticed something more mysterious as well. Lamentably, he told his readers, no one dared dispute the new aristocrats' claims to social or aesthetic eminence: 'No one dares question them as they stride indecently through the temple of fashion and good society.' The people were overawed. They fawned in hope of a favoring smile from 'these misshapen images that the demon of snob democracy sets up in the beautiful and the great'. And so in the teeth of their many sins, notwithstanding their oppression of the poor, 'no matter how many they may have driven to hunger or into acts of criminal desperation', these soulless aristocrats retained their unblemished respectability.

A Viennese nobleman, Francis Grund, who took up US citizenship in 1827, was fascinated by this American flirtation with aristocracy. Mimicking de Tocqueville, he published *Aristocracy in America*, in which he sketched the strenuous and sometimes uproarious efforts of the newly rich to ape and curry favor with European nobility, acting as if their eminence was carried in the blood and not in their pocketbooks. What particularly struck Grund, a committed Jacksonian

Democrat, was the way the 'laboring classes', free for perhaps the first time in human history to 'legislate for themselves', were nevertheless found 'worshipping wealth in its most hideous colors'. Grund was deeply disturbed. It seemed to suggest that despite the egalitarian ambitiousness of American culture, there was an amazing tolerance, even adoration, for the amassing of great wealth, especially if those amassing it came from humble backgrounds. Resentment of the rich could be transformed in a moment into a burning desire to be as rich as the rich. Another European visitor to America, Harriet Martineau, observed that because of the cultural antipathy to ascriptions of status, the only kind of aristocracy the country could abide was one based solely on wealth.

The chance to get rich led to a peculiar version of egalitarianism. While Everyman's right to the main chance was prized, the instinct for social leveling was less often indulged. It was this ambivalence that would mark popular attitudes to Wall Street during the years after the panic of 1857. And it was the odd popular instinct to revere what it was bred to despise that would, in the years following the Civil War, transform unsavory financiers into Napoleonic heroes.[13]

Less than a year before the Civil War began, a piece of sentimental poetry appeared in an illustrated weekly magazine. Entitled 'The Lone Tree in Wall Street', it was an ode to the sycamore or buttonwood tree under which, so legend had it, the stock exchange was born. The poet lamented the vanished days of a bucolic New York, a city less single-mindedly intent on gain. All that was left was this one 'gray sycamore' standing silent vigil:

> How many runs upon the banks,
> Hast thou, old tree, beheld.

Forced and bathetic, the poet's sense of something having passed away was nonetheless shared by many.[14]

Insiders were particularly sensitive to the change. Daniel Drew scented the shift in the wind early on in the '57 panic which, he alleged, 'put old fogeyism out of date forever more . . . the think-of-the-other fellow methods . . . were swept away or at least so crippled that they didn't figure much in the world of affairs afterwards.' William Fowler's *Ten Years in Wall Street* was published in 1870 and took stock of what the decade had wrought. 'Titanic' figures had emerged, 'nimrods of the

market' like Cornelius Vanderbilt and Daniel Drew, who swept away
the Street's old guard and its cliquish exclusion of bolder if less polished
traders. Fowler exaggerated: the 'old guard', which itself was hardly
old, had certainly not vanished, even if some ruinations of former
'titans' like Jacob Little now haunted the exchange in pathetic penury.
But Fowler's sense that 'the ground shook' as a 'new race of financiers'
trod the earth hinted at what had been born amidst the chaos of the
war. Henry Clews, another insider but one who defended rather than
condemned the Street, echoed Fowler. Writing many years later, he
remembered the '57 panic as the 'western blizzard': bad news had
blown in from the agrarian West, where defaulting farmers brought
down eastern banks. It had sounded the death knell of the Wall Street
establishment, allowing room for a new breed of 'young Turks', more
innovative and less risk-averse than their elders, to take over.[15]

Less risk-averse indeed! At first Wall Street shuddered at the
prospect of war. Just before Lincoln's election, railroad shares and the
bonds of Southern state governments had collapsed. The mercantile
community of the North was worried about the disruption of its link
to Southern cotton. Union patriots looked on suspiciously as merchants and bankers cast about for some solution short of war. One
constituent wrote to Senator Washburn of Wisconsin worrying that
'artful politicians, rich merchants, and speculators whose god is
money will council peace regardless of principle.' Wall Street in particular was singled out as a haven of a pusillanimous 'Dry Goods
Party', conspiring at surrender to the slavocracy.[16]

The outbreak of war, however, put an end to the economics of peace
and incited instead a ghoulish speculation in death. As the carnage
spread over the land, enterprising Wall Street brokers sent agents to
accompany the clashing armies and even planted spies in military
headquarters, hoping to secure advance notice of battle plans that
would affect the trading floor. Often enough news of victories and
defeats would reach the exchange before even the President and the
press. Many were betting on Union defeats.

Substantial segments of Wall Street were in fact hostile to the
Lincoln government from the start. Even before the election of 1860
the Street's anxiety about the prospect of Republican victory sent
stocks plummeting by twenty per cent in two weeks, and the prices of
state and Federal bonds collapsed too. A great deal of Southern money
invested in the Street was instantly withdrawn on the outbreak of hos-

tilities. Moreover, a feverish speculation in gold soon developed; the fortunes of the metal rose and those of the Federal 'greenback' dollar fell with each actual or anticipated battlefield loss by the army in blue. The very creation of 'greenbacks' in 1862 was designed by leaders of the Republican Party to free the government of its dependency on the bond markets to finance the war. Later on Congress tried but failed to banish the bloody speculation in gold. The President found it horrific, writing to the Governor of Pennsylvania to say: 'What do you think of those fellows in Wall Street who are gambling in gold at such a time as this? For my part, I wish every one of them had his devilish head shot off.' The country's most distinguished and celebrated financier, Jay Cooke, who successfully marketed the Federal government's war bonds to a mass clientele of farmers and small town businessmen, was himself scandalized and called New York's gold traders 'General Lee's left flank'. Speculators were colloquially referred to as 'Jefferson Davis speculators'.

During the 1864 presidential campaign, unionist newspapers attacked General George McClellan, the Democratic candidate, by associating him with August Belmont, the Party's chairman. The general's candidacy was a 'sell-out to Wall Street and the Rothschild interests'; worse than that, his victory would only enrich 'the whole tribe of Jews, who have been buying up Confederate bonds'. Republican Party orators, including the crowd-pleaser Edward Everett, traveled the country in a cloud of anti-Semitic rhetoric, speaking in mock Yiddish accents about German Jewish money dishonoring the country. Generals Grant and Sherman engaged in casual accusations of Jewish war profiteering, and Senator Henry Wilson of Massachusetts reduced the bloody conflict to one between 'the curbstone Jew Broker' and the 'productive, toiling men of the country'. It made no difference that Belmont was entirely loyal to the Union cause, that he was an apostate to his ancestral Judaism, and that rumors about Jewish speculators buying up Confederate securities were groundless. When Atlanta fell to Sherman, one magazine expressed satisfaction that Wall Street's days of unpatriotic reveling were finally over.[17]

As the war-induced appetite for speculation grew, collateral exchanges sprang up to handle specialized business in mining or petroleum stocks. 'Bubble companies' with little or no real capital resources were magically floated on the market and then quickly burst. Trading on the stock exchange was no longer limited to two regularly scheduled daily episodes, but took place at all hours of the day and night. Part of the mystique of the Street has always derived from its frantic pace. It first earned that reputation, and the popular fascination that went with it, during these years of wartime and post-war abandon. E. C. Steadman, a broker and writer, described a scene where men no longer worked normal hours, but 'rushed into the arena from a hurriedly snatched breakfast and shouted and wrestled throughout the day, stealing a few moments to sustain vitality and encourage indigestion at a lunch counter or restaurant, and renewed the desperate tension in the evening, prolonging it till long past the hour when wearied bodies and shocked nerves demanded respite . . . It was a killing pace.'

The mood was contagious and infected improbable quarters. *Leslie's Illustrated,* which catered particularly to a female audience, took note that 'in fact the ladies have been the wildest speculators'. The magazine cautioned that more than one wife or daughter had gone to 'ruin' as a result, and included reproving sketches of the miser, the 'gold gambler in luck', and the ruined man to illustrate the dangerous consequences of all this 'vanity.'[18]

Alongside these cautionary words a more alluring prospect opened up. Magazines read by a prospering middle class pioneered an association between the Street and a budding culture of conspicuous consumption. For generations it would provide a form of mass entertainment, a spectacle first gazed at with awe and envy and later emulated. With some hyperbole a contemporary observer noted that:

> The entire population of the country entered the field. Offices were besieged by crowds of customers . . . Broadway was lined with carriages. The fashionable milliners, dress-makers, and jewelers reaped golden harvests. The pageant of Fifth Avenue on Sunday and of Central Park during the week-days was bizarre, gorgeous, wonderful! Never were such dinners, such receptions, such balls . . . Vanity Fair was no longer a dream.

The Street itself became more welcoming too. A sketch of 'A Broker's Office in the 1860s' displayed a real cross-section of clients in all states of dress, from the most lavishly attired dandy to the working man in overalls. Horace Greeley's *Tribune* commented that 'The intense desire to buy almost any kind of security amounted almost to insanity.'

All this luxury could arouse feelings of revulsion. *Harpers Weekly* scathingly noted that the price of a single act of gluttony at Delmonicos or La Maison Doree could support a soldier and his family for most of a year. It was also noted that rich women staked their jewels, clergymen their salaries, as the rage for speculation was the talk of the town: 'at clubs, in the streets, at the theaters, in drawing rooms'.

While it would be a mistake to conclude that dabbling in the Street had become a pastime of the masses – that wasn't even true in the 1920s and only became so well after World War II – this post-Civil War euphoria was nonetheless real. One observer noted that 'The war, which made us a great people, made us also a nation in whom speculative ideas are predominant.' And this air of psychological and moral abandonment provided the atmosphere in which the cult of the Wall Street titan would thrive once the war was over.[19]

When the country exhaled after Appomattox, Daniel Drew, always candid, summed up the prevailing mood. 'We fellows in Wall Street had the fortunes of war to speculate about and that always makes great doings on a stock exchange. It's good fishing in troubled waters.' It is always wise to take Drew's words with a grain of salt. But, after all, Wall Street was hardly the only commercial mercenary. Fortunes had been made by businessmen, some of great renown, who had supplied the Army with uniforms made of shoddy, shoes out of paper, meat from diseased cattle and hogs, guns unlikely to fire.[20]

If people had managed to gratify their more selfish appetites even during the war, then peace relaxed all remaining restraints among social circles affluent enough to indulge. The 'universal stock ticker', invented by Edward A. Colchin in 1867 and improved a few years later by Edison, excited investors and spectators alike. Stock-market slang found its way into refined drawing rooms where speculative ventures were avidly compared: 'Gold was the favorite of the ladies. Clergymen rather affected mining-stock and Petroleum. Lawyers had a penchant for Erie.' The lavishness of the social scene bordered on the bizarre. Mrs Hamilton Fish hosted a party for her friends' dogs where the 'guests' were presented with diamond necklace party favors and a place of honor at the table was reserved for an ape. Financier Leonard Jerome erected a palace on Madison Avenue equipped with a theater to seat six hundred and carpeted horse stables paneled in black walnut. The 'flash age' had arrived, its gaudy show presided over by Belmont and his Wall Street cronies.

Contemporary observers, sometimes mistaking the peculiar habits of the upper classes for the behavior of 'the whole population of the North', worried that 'salaried men' and 'small merchants' considered it safe to divert their small surplus to 'the chances of the market'. But they had reason to worry. All along the radiating railroad lines, local citizens bought up stocks and bonds and a world of dispersed, small-time speculators took shape: 'Villages whose names are scarcely known beyond the boundary of their counties have their own rustic Fisks and Vanderbilts.' A poem appearing in the *Atlantic Monthly*, 'Pan in Wall Street', announced that 'Pan is dead', the god's sweet music no longer able to silence 'the cries of greed and gain'. The Erie Railroad emerged, after the war, as the 'scarlet woman of Wall Street', because its stock price bore little if any connection to the value of the company but see-sawed erratically in response to the back-door manipulations. Drew was indubitably the master puppeteer, but what also struck observers was how many others from diverse walks of life responded to his promptings. Aghast, a British magazine observed that all the prudent financial principles of a lifetime had been thrown overboard: 'Professional men tired of their slow gains; clerks sick of starvation salaries; clergymen, dissatisfied with a niggardly stipend . . . even the fair sex, practically asserting women's rights under the cover of a broker, dabbled in Erie shares.'

The game might produce hundreds of 'human wrecks scattered through towns and cities, some shut up in asylums, others living out aimless lives – mental paralytics, dazed or crazed by the swift shock of ruin'. The market might be likened to a 'withered old harridan, enameled, painted, and decked in the latest mode which leers on the speculator and points to golden prizes, that, like the desert mirage, fades away and leaves him to his ruin.' But no matter the consequences, it was inspiring delusions of grandeur. In the over-heated imaginations of some, Wall Street was becoming the 'greatest money-making and money-losing spot on the globe'. [21]

In truth, Wall Street was still a generation removed from achieving such stature – but it was already more than just a money-making spot. It was also a lightning rod for the cultural crisis that gripped the country once the Civil War was over. Hopes that the war would act like a purgative, a great moral crusade cleansing the nation of its self-seeking materialism, were sorely disappointed. The avarice and shabby dealings that began during the war and worsened after it saw to that. Wall Street seemed to stand at the headwaters of this deluge. No aspect of the country's political, moral, social, and cultural life escaped unaffected.

Walt Whitman lamented the hypocrisy, crudity, and shallowness that seemed to characterize post-war American culture. The depravity of the business classes was 'infinitely greater' than supposed, and all levels of the government were 'saturated in corruption, bribery, false-hood, mal-administration . . . The best class we show is but a mob of fashionably dressed speculators and vulgarians.' Yet the poet was at the same time thrilled by the country's electric vitality, its material powers, its ingenuity, 'this many-threaded wealth and industry'.[22]

Whitman was a mystic democrat, his poetry often a beatification of the multitudes. But the urge to celebrate the nation's 'many-threaded wealth and industry' could also express an imperial instinct that was just as much in the American grain. Wall Street shared in the glory. It was so associated in the public mind with the country's industrial coming of age, with its growing economic independence from the Old World, that some people were more than willing to avert their gaze from the scandal and piracy that perpetually surrounded the Street.

Jefferson foresaw an 'empire of liberty' and had Cuba and Spanish Florida particularly in mind. Jacksonian publicists rallied to the nation's 'manifest destiny' in rolling waves of territorial expansion. New York's ante-bellum merchant elite, civic promoters, and literary luminaries were predicting the city would soon contend with London for commercial supremacy. Daniel Webster had anointed New York the 'Imperial city of the American continent' a generation before it emerged as the engine of the industrial explosion. Even people sensi-tive to its grievous faults credited Wall Street for this national coming of age.

Junius Henry Browne, for example, hailed from a distinguished banking family before becoming a war reporter. His *Great Metropolis: A Mirror of New York* was a widely read tale of the pastimes, priva-tions, and criminal misadventures of both the upper and lower class-es. His chapter on Wall Street called it the 'banking house of the continent', its power felt from Maine to San Francisco, 'even across the sea and round the sphere'. Despite all its transgressions Browne couldn't despise the Street, because it 'holds the levers that move the American world'. In his view the whole country benefited from Wall

Street's energy, enterprise, and financial derring-do: 'The North, the South, the East, and the West go there for aid to hew and build and mine.'

Native resentment of the Old World fed this pride in Wall Street's new muscularity. *The New York Herald* lost its sense of perspective, claiming decades before it became true that the Street was now the favored asylum for 'capital and substantial money interests. Paris has gone into total eclipse and London trembles toward her sunset. The westward story of empire is in the zenith of New York.' Spectators from all over the country came to view the Street as the battlefield where independence from European capital would be won or lost. Here was living proof of the nation's pluck and nerve, its inventiveness, stature, and power.[23]

Evidence to support this imperial chest-thumping was everywhere. The architectural transformation of lower Manhattan was a stunning case in point. Lithographs and other pictorial representations marked the receding of the city's waterfront as its geographical axis. Instead, steel massed in downtown skyscrapers – made possible by the invention of the elevator, new iron-shell framing, and improved load-bearing techniques – imparted a kind of physical bravado to the cityscape, Wall Street in particular. There men conducted their worldly affairs at altitudes far removed from ordinary life. Working in this airborne seclusion in buildings capped with watchtowers, ornamental pediments, statues, and domes, their labors took on a certain grandeur and mystery. Thanks especially to Wall Street, New York began to assume the unofficial title of the nation's other capital city.

The Street's material achievement was no less impressive than its architecture. Expansion of the national rail network was astonishing. Railroad mileage doubled in the eight years between 1865 and 1873. More track was laid in 1872 than in any other year of the nineteenth century. By 1893 there were 150,000 miles of track that hadn't been there at the time of the Civil War. As the iron horse crisscrossed the country, its appetite for coal, steel, and heavy machinery helped make those industries into world leaders in size and technical sophistication.[24]

Financier Jay Cooke's grandest undertaking, the creation of the Northern Pacific Railroad, which aimed to blaze through the wilderness of the American northwest, was exemplary. It promised to seal Cooke's reputation: already heralded as a special kind of patriot for keeping the Union solvent by single-handedly disposing of the government's war bonds, it would be hard to exaggerate the regard in which he was held at the end of the Civil War. When the rest of the New York banking world proved skittish about financing the Union's cause (and Europe's 'haute banques' were withdrawing their capital), Philadelphia's 'modern Midas' stepped forward and staged the first really successful effort to mass-market a financial security.

It was a spectacular campaign. Cooke took out full-page ads and deployed brass bands, top-draw orators, handbills, posters, and hundreds of thousands of flags. He inundated the editorial and financial pages with pre-packaged material that often masqueraded as legitimate news or independent editorial opinion. He hired 2,500 'minute man' agents, highly trained salesmen, to peddle the government's war bonds direct to the consumer.

Cooke was a war hero, a patriot-financier, whose sense of duty and fiduciary integrity were universally praised. Encomiums poured in from statesmen, religious leaders, and opinion-shapers. He became a confidant of the President and continued that role through the first Grant administration, in effect serving as an unofficial Secretary of the Treasury. During the gold panic of 1869, he denounced Fisk and Gould and called upon the government to intervene, because 'the business people of this land must have stability or we will become a nation of gamblers'. The public fascination with Cooke was fed by stories about his homes, his fishing expeditions, his art collection, his game parks, even wild rumors about the extravagant cost of his dental care. His fifty-two-room palace, Ogontz, with its theater, fountains, and vast collection of paintings, sculpture, and assorted European bric-a-brac, was perceived less as vulgar than as a fitting monument. Indeed, Cooke was compared favorably to Lincoln and Grant.[25]

War hero, railroad pathfinder, financial tycoon: Cooke embodied the genius of America – and of Wall Street, which showed no signs of slowing the pace. By the middle of the Gilded Age, ninety per cent of all securities transactions were conducted on the New York Stock Exchange. It was there that the nation's great undertakings – its coast-to-coast railroads and stupendous agricultural output, its gigantic steel, oil, and raw materials industries, its pioneering technologies in electricity and chemicals – were alchemized. Even men like Andrew Carnegie and Collis Huntington, whose steel and railroad enterprises were hundreds or thousands of miles away from the eastern metropolis nonetheless directed their affairs from Wall Street. Here the city's investment bankers and brokers turned the country's tangible wherewithal into its paper facsimile, a virtual economy which made possible the mobilizing of ever greater capital resources. New York was on its way to becoming the queen of American cities and would soon enough assume that position in the world.

Captains of industry and finance were the first beneficiaries of this transformation, but not the only ones. All sorts of people could admire the new system and its continental accomplishments, and although the era was marked by frequent panics and depressions real wages tended to rise and prices to fall. National income grew, as did the country's gross national product. To the degree that Wall Street was implicated in this ascension, it was applauded for it.

Silence could on occasion be a telling measure of popular acquiescence in the Street's elevation. The election of 1876 is a case in point. The country was in the third year of a severe economic contraction. Political scandals, many of them traceable to Wall Street operators, had riveted public attention for several years. New York Governor Samuel Tilden, the Democratic nominee and winner of the popular vote (the congressional compromise of 1876 gave the election to Republican Rutherford B. Hayes), was known as the 'Great Forecloser' of bankrupt railroads, a Wall Street insider and legal adviser to some of the most suspect characters on the Street, including Gould and Fisk. Yet the campaign proceeded with hardly a mention of the ravaged economy, nor of Wall Street's role in this or the corrupt schemes in which both parties were embroiled. In one sense this reveals the inherent limitations of the nation's two-party system and the other preoccupations of the electorate. But it also suggests public tolerance for the Street's misbehavior so long as the trade-off in material progress and national empowerment seemed sufficient.[26]

Henry Adams was far less tolerant, lamenting the election-year amnesia that found 'failure . . . to be the one unpardonable crime, success as the all redeeming virtue'. Not only did a deluded citizenry fail to stigmatize the four horsemen and their Wall Street confederates; they actually raised them as objects for emulation . . . or at least entertainment.[27]

Board games aimed at the Victorian middle classes proliferated in the 1870s and afterwards thanks to the perfection of chromolithography. These games went through their own moral evolution.

'Mansions of Happiness' (invented in 1843) rewarded small-town Christian virtues – piety, honesty, humility. Gilded Age games featured different settings and emphasized different talents. The Post Office game placed the player in the hustle and bustle of urban life and included Wall Street as a central locale, just a ferry ride away from a more sedate Brooklyn. Participants in these new games were encouraged to be enterprising. A popular game called 'Bulls and Bears: The Great Wall Street Game' starred two well turned-out bull- and bear-headed stockbrokers dressed like 'fancy men': slick, in the know, and enjoying themselves immensely. Promotional patter promised potential players that the game 'for the time being will make players feel like speculators, bankers, and brokers'. Gazing down at the board's playing area were Vanderbilt and Gould, sitting atop piles of Erie and Western Union stock.[28]

No legislation Adams might ever have dreamed of could address this vicarious identification with the Street. By the 1870s, Wall Street was a tourist destination, pointed out in all the town guides and even used as the mise-en-scene in thriller novels. Washington Fowler, Noah Webster's grandson, published *Ten Years in Wall Street* in 1870. It sold out its first printing of 40,000 copies and was reviewed everywhere. Accounts like Fowler's ostensibly offered to penetrate this occult financial arena, decipher its secret codes and its mathematical exotica. Invariably, however, they gave in to the irresistible spectacle of the Street's spasmodic metabolism, the violent emotions that colored its daily life.

The sight of people abandoning all decorum and flouting all etiquette could be an elixir to people already intoxicated with democratic enthusiasm. Young men found it especially fascinating, so much so that detectives were periodically sent in search of those (and young women too) who had 'decayed from service and from home by the glare and fascination of the place'. Crowds gathered to gape at the Street's helter-skelter motleyness, the promiscuous mixing together of 'women wringing their hands and crying in nervous excitement . . . old people scarcely able to totter . . . people who had risen from sick beds', Jew and gentile, lettered and illiterate, 'puritan and blackleg'.

The Street became a kind of zany replica of Whitman's democratic mix-master. One writer found this hurly-burly an emblem of the nation, a gathering in of 'men of every clime, of every nation, of every tongue, and of every religion'. The electricity, the social intermingling, the mesmerizing sense that one was at the vortex of the inscrutable mechanism that set in motion the whole world trading system was breathtaking, a kind of metaphysical thrill. There was plenty of bedrock sympathy and even adulation for these 'nimrods of the market' who Adams found so detestable.[29]

The public's ambivalent attitude was epitomized in its reaction to the four men who defined the 'Flash Age': Vanderbilt, Drew, Fisk, and Gould. All four earned their notoriety as well as a great deal of their fortune by looting and re-looting the Erie Railroad, yet their exploits inspired awe even as they were censured. It was a romance of industrial privateering. Starting out with little or nothing at all, they put together vast systems of daunting financial, engineering, and logistical complexity. Industries, towns, and cities, whole untracked regions were given life (or deprived of it) as they executed their grand calculations. Men of such boldness and reach, such encompassing practical intelligence, were inherently powerful.

Even as they went about their business of robbing the public treasury and piling up unprecedented personal fortunes, a certain mystique grew up around the 'four horsemen' and the luminaries who orbited in their shadow. *Great Fortunes and How They Were Made*, John D. McCabe's 1870 celebration of self-made American heroes, included portraits of Vanderbilt and Drew as exemplary 'capitalists': kingly yet humble, plain but hypnotic, specimens of men the Bard called 'born great'. While the four were very different, in the popular mind they shared a social genealogy and a general set of character traits that lent them a collective identity.[30]

Rising out of obscurity, all of these men were attributed with precocious audacity, raw aggressiveness, and a wolfish cunning that equipped them to thrive on the urban frontier. If they were coarse they were also perceived as irreverent in the best, democratic sense of the word. If they were moguls, they were of the uncut variety, without airs – relying, in the end, only on themselves. They were seen as Promethean, indefatigable, prepared like any frontiersman to do what had to be done. They seemed to reincarnate the English 'sea-dogs' of the sixteenth century, those romanticized avatars of a ruthless commercial ambition, who synthesized the greed for gold, the desire for adventure, and the love of exploration into an unquenchable spirit of early capitalist enterprise. If they were lionized as well as condemned, it was principally because they seemed to capture the raw triumphalism of the age, its creative, democratic, and adventurous spirit.

A distinctive vocabulary inscribed these men in urban-industrial legend. Contemporaries, even critical ones, described them as 'bold', and 'magnificent of view', full of 'verve', capable of absorbing a hard blow without flinching. Often treated as American Primitives, observers marked and often celebrated their lack of education and refinement; they were profane and uncouth but endowed with native frankness, self-confidence, and force of personality. Such language also hinted at their inspiring escape from unprepossessing origins. Vanderbilt left the modest family farm on Staten Island to run a small ferryboat to Manhattan. Fisk was the son of a Vermont pedlar and spent time in a traveling circus where he was educated in the art of the con and the easy mark. Drew also spent part of his youth in the circus, tended bar, drove cattle, and later in life deliberately cultivated his rustic airs, dressing shabbily, never seen without his old drover's hat. Gould sprang from marginal farming stock in upstate New York and ran a tannery before bilking its owner of his life's investment. Accounts of their doings often began with depictions of their youthful escapades. Cast adrift in a liquefied society, scarcely restrained by law or convention, they made their way and triumphed without apology. They may have started out as little more than confidence men, but in the imagination of the Gilded Age they played the role of the colossus. And that improbable trajectory was precisely the source of their cultural allure.[31]

In dozens of ways, no two men could have been more different than Drew and Vanderbilt. But according to one insider both men 'have the mind of crystal, the heart of adamant, the hand of steel, and the will of iron'. This is the language of Napoleonic myth-making and it saturated the media. Jacob Little was perhaps the first figure to be popularly christened as the 'Napoleon of Wall Street', but by the 1860s he was a spent figure. No time was lost transferring the title. Jay Cooke first assumed it, thanks to his financial patriotism during the Civil War. But before long even a paper like *The Herald*, which otherwise declaimed against the Erie debacle, acknowledged that the schemes devised by Gould and Fisk 'exhibit Napoleonic genius'.

Fisk in fact developed a reputation as an industrial Robin Hood. A big spender on wine, women, and flashy good times, he also made conspicuous charitable donations: coal and flour to the needy, funds to support a poor Negro church on 8th Avenue, and most spectacularly, Erie trainloads of food and provisions to the victims of the Chicago fire. When Fisk was assassinated in 1872 by the current paramour of his ex-mistress, he was lionized as that 'poor, toiling lad who had wrought his success out of hard, earnest effort', and one hundred thousand New Yorkers gathered 'Like a Black Restless Sea' at his funeral. One anonymous bar-room poet remembered Wall Street's Robin Hood:

> We all know he loved both women and wine,
> But his heart it was right I am sure;
> He lived like a prince in his palace so fine,
> Yet he never went back on the poor.

Newspapers that had held their noses in disgust when he was alive decided that 'there was a grandeur of conception about Fisk's rascality which helps to lift him above the vulgar herd of scoundrels'.

Vanderbilt was sent off in even grander style in 1877; flags flew at half-mast at City Hall, at the stock exchange and Grand Central Station, and all along the routes of his railroads. *The New York Times*, which had once labeled him a 'robber baron', called him an 'immense boon to the public.' Other obituaries memorialized his unaided rise from unlettered ferry-boat captain to 'one of the kings of the earth'. Senator Chauncey Depew, a Republican corruptionist of the first water, and sometime Vanderbilt lawyer, eulogized the Commodore as a hero of material progress, a 'genius of affairs'. Others, with cleaner hands, praised Vanderbilt as a great public benefactor, both as an employer and as a provider of a vital public service: he was an engineering visionary, a manager of operations so complex they required a kind of military genius to master. Much post-mortem opinion in the big city dailies treated his passing with a solemnity that was truly Napoleonic: it found in Vanderbilt's untrammeled individualism a perfect expression of America's national genius and social promise.

One frequently repeated anecdote summed up Vanderbilt's insouciance. When two misguided associates attempted to challenge his position in the Nicaragua Steamboat Company, the Commodore concisely explained: 'Gentleman: you have undertaken to cheat me. I won't sue you, for the law is too slow. I'll ruin you.' This was a true story. Not so the one about how the Commodore, at sea during a fierce storm, the ship floundering, a collision imminent, panic above and below decks, seized the helm and with characteristic daring guided her safely to port. Tales like this were part of the mystique, so enveloping it could lead somebody like Russell Sage, a cold-hearted sociopath, to suggest that Vanderbilt was 'to finance what Shakespeare was to poetry and Michelangelo to art'. His legend crossed the ocean, and even a British observer, who otherwise viewed Wall Street with bottomless contempt, exempted the Commodore who 'assumes the royal dignity and moral tone of a Gaetulian lion among the hyenas and jackals of the desert'. Traveling to London aboard his thousand-ton North Star yacht, his wife, twelve children, caterer, doctor, and chaplain in tow, the Commodore presented a spectacle of surpassing vulgarity, yet gave a British observer pause for social reflection: 'Here is the great difference between the two countries. In England a man is too apt to be ashamed of having made his own fortune . . . It is time that the millionaire should cease to be ashamed . . . It is time that the parvenu should be looked on as a word of honor.' In the end his heroism could be simply explained. Noting that he enjoyed no advantages of birth or education or social position, the *New York Herald* concluded when he died: 'It was one honest, sturdy, fearless man against the world, and in the end the man won.'[32]

Soon enough, fewer than ten years after he died, Vanderbilt's first biographer – or hagiographer – presented the Commodore's story as a model for 'boys and young men', indeed for all who aspired to become 'leaders of their fellows in the sharp and wholesome competition of life'. In the empire of the parvenu, where birth and title counted for nothing, Vanderbilt was the pre-eminent citizen. Before his death and the obligatory piety it produced, even far less enamored commentators like Charles Francis Adams felt compelled to acknowledge the Commodore's monumental grasp, his gargantuan ambition, his 'steady nerve and sturdy gamblers' pride', and the relentless force of will that made him a 'dictator in modern civilization' as he presided over the iron arteries of the nation's economic circulatory system.[33]

The Napoleonic conceit captured what was simultaneously intimidating and grand about these men. Napoleon gripped the romantic imagination of the nineteenth century, as much through the outrageousness of his character as the grandeur of his imperial exploits. Whether idolized or hated, he seemed to epitomize the demiurge of the age, its exaltation of the unfettered individual engaged in perpetual self-creation. By the end of the century, Napoleonic metaphors were deployed widely to signify the imperial, military, and autocratic inclinations of men like J. P. Morgan. However, in this earlier, formative period, the Napoleonic image still conjured up the mountebank, cowboy, and confidence man. It served to transform what might seem at first blush a mere hunger for money into a visionary quest. A 'young Napoleon of finance' was to be admired not for his riches, but for the power with which he moved 'the world's greatest interests'.[34]

A preoccupation with manliness was at the heart of this cultic fascination. E. L. Godkin, a passionate hater of these Wall Street buccaneers, was particularly struck, not entirely negatively, by their roughness and size. Fisk dressed 'like a bartender, huge in nerve as in bulk'. Drew lied and stole his way to wealth with 'tobacco juice drooling from his mouth'. A six-footer, red-cheeked, with a shock of white hair and flowing sideburns, Vanderbilt's feats of physical strength were part of his legend, as was his braving of the British blockade during the War of 1812. The Commodore, moreover, was renowned for the colorful flood of dockside obscenities that embellished his earthy machismo. Even his reputation for heroic bouts of drinking, gambling, and womanizing heightened rather than tarnished his mystique. Similarly, August Belmont, whose confected world of high society would exclude ruffians like the 'four horsemen' for years to come, enjoyed a reputation for sexual allure based as much on his immense financial and political power as on his brooding eyes and dark good looks. With Belmont, sexual prowess, whether real or imagined, became an enduring part of the myth.

Such figures clearly challenged the old-fashioned image of Victorian masculinity, one identified with thrift, perseverance, responsibility, chastity and honesty. Time and again attributes associated with power, will, and force were singled out for special regard, implicitly demeaning the boring utilitarianism and methodical routine of bourgeois masculinity. Such depictions embraced the 'technological sublime', that rapturous faith in the irresistible triumph of technical progress. Metaphors drawn from the new industrial technologies – an iron determination, a will of steel, or a magnetic personality – colored the portraits of Wall Street tycoons and other giants of industry. Beginning with the four horsemen, it crested around the turn of the century, by which time almost anyone who succeeded in high finance and big business, from J. P. Morgan down, was credited with a Napoleonic abundance of the 'Y' chromosome.

Their power was as much about the domination of other men as control over the material world. Wall Street was a man's world; women were considered by nature to be ill-suited to its rigors, lacking the brains, emotional equanimity, and masculine reserve that the life of the speculator demanded. Even the rare exception, like Hettie Green, notorious as the 'Witch of Wall Street', seemed to prove the rule: she was attributed with a man's brain trapped in a woman's body. Green was a fearsome figure. Quaker heiress to a whaling fortune, she dressed from head to foot in black crepe, threatened her rivals with a handgun, and was so miserly that she reportedly washed her own underwear rather than pay the cheap boarding houses she frequented. She made a fortune as a money-lender to speculators and companies in distress, and nurtured a paranoid conviction that her father and aunt were poisoned and that she was herself the target of assassins. Her fellow Wall Streeters considered her a freak of nature, as 'one among a million of her sex', which accounted for her distinctively male ruthlessness.

Aside from Hettie Green, the only other women who dared venture into Wall Street were the notorious sisters, Tennessee Claflin and Victoria Woodhull. Woodhull was a pioneer feminist and suffragist, the first woman to run for President, with Frederick Douglass as her running mate. Her sister was a celebrated faith-healer who exercised a mystic influence over Cornelius Vanderbilt, a man of profligate superstitions (homeopathy, magic spells, séances where Jim Fisk offered business advice). Vanderbilt set the sisters up as Woodhull, Claflin & Company in 1870 at 44 Broad Street. Less fearsome than 'the witch of Wall Street', they were mocked as 'the Lady Brokers' and the 'Bewitching Brokers'. Woodhull in particular was condemned for 'brazen immodesty as a stock speculator'.

A proto-feminist critique was not entirely lacking: Susan B. Anthony and Elizabeth Cady Stanton treated the 1869 conspiracy put together by Gould and Fisk to corner the market in gold as an allegory of sexual politics, proof positive of the 'disqualification of the male man' to be entrusted with money or power. The 'male man' of Wall Street was subject to this sort of ridicule from other quarters as well: the high-wire reveling he enjoyed was sometimes likened to the adolescent machismo of a fraternity party. More often, however, maleness was treated with deadly seriousness, the financiers portrayed as exercising the sort of dominion otherwise associated with western cowboy and military heroes. Nothing more clearly suggested the sexual magnetism of the Wall Street speculator than his icy composure, his capacity to remain under emotional control while others panicked around him.[35]

Earthiness, sexual prowess, folksy simplicity, imperial ambition, nerveless presence, and the gamblers' flash – each in its own way helped crystallize an oddly hybrid image of the great Wall Street speculator as a plebeian aristocrat. This accorded with their ambiguous location in the economy, living off the largesse of state-sponsored enterprise, yet born and bred in the free-for-all atmosphere of the open market. No man possessed every one of the characteristics of the Wall Street hero in equal measure; instead, they assumed distinctive roles within an unfolding allegory. Vanderbilt most clearly assumed the role of the profane and mighty Napoleonic hero. Drew became a self-parodying rustic, a foxily simple soul in the tradition of the Yankee pedlar whose feigned innocence was his cleverest ruse. Fisk came on as pure irreverence, lustily ribald and a moral provocateur. Gould was enlisted as the Devil's lieutenant.

Uncl' Dan'l, the inveterate trickster, was still gulling people half a century after his death. A book purporting to be his diary, 'The Book of Daniel Drew', was published in 1910. It was a fake, but it worked for decades because its 'editor'/ghost writer, Bouck White, had successfully captured Drew's legendary rustic, homespun charm. White, a one-time Socialist, skewered Drew as a greedy rascal and pious hypocrite. (Many years later the Nazis would use a German translation of the book in a propaganda assault on American capitalism.) But White also portrayed an irresistible, wrinkled, twinkly-eyed jokester who fleeced his victims with a certain down-home panache. Thus Drew was alleged to have chortled to himself when spying a gang of his fellow speculators salivating over the prospects of a killing in Erie stock: 'Happy creatures, how merry they be. Wal, I guess I must pinch 'em.' His folksy aphorisms became Wall Street scripture and were widely known and applied beyond its precincts. The most famous, perhaps, was a piece of rhyming folk wisdom: 'He who sells what isn't his'n / Must buy it back or go to pris'n.'

What was perversely fetching about Drew was the ingenuousness of his avarice. 'I had my own fortune to make . . . I didn't feel called upon to keep myself back', is what Bouck had him say – and whether he actually said it or not, it was what people expected a plain-spoken Yankee like Drew to say. He appeared a Jacksonian democrat come to Wall Street without airs, whose self-presentation mocked the aristocratic dress and rhetoric that were so alien to the American sensibility. Drew had two passions – religion and speculation – and they lived happily together inside his untroubled psyche in a way that appalled many, but was probably a secret comfort to those of his fellow citizens negotiating the same American moral conundrum. A Methodist, he founded Drew Theological Seminary, but there was never a hint that he was assuaging some deeper guilt: he felt none. Uncl' Dan'l summed it up best: 'It seems like a dream to me.'[36]

Fisk had his own way with words. 'I was born to be bad', he once said, and who could entirely resist that? He was a comic-opera character, fat, jolly and unabashed. Dressed like a racetrack tout, he paraded around New York with pomaded hair, waxed mustache, and a diamond-studded shirtfront. He often dressed in an admiral's uniform – one paper called him 'the Mushroom Mars' – and flaunted his showgirl friends and lavishly appointed steam yacht. Erie headquarters, widely known as 'Castle Erie', was housed inside Fisk's Grand Opera House at Twenty-Third Street and Eighth Avenue: a sumptuous structure, emblazoned with Erie Railroad royal cartouches, gilded balustrades, and stained glass, where the 'Prince of Erie's' private offices featured a throne cobbled together with golden-studded nails. It was a kind of corporate Xanadu gaped at by passing throngs of Gothamites. Even a Wall Street Brahmin like George Templeton Strong, who considered Fisk 'vulgar', 'unprincipled' and 'profligate', conceded he was 'freehanded with his stolen money, and possessed, moreover, a certain magnetism of geniality'. 'Jubilee Jim' was the P. T. Barnum of Wall Street and never really pretended otherwise. His primitive impiety left one Wall Street insider thunderstruck: 'Boldness! Boldness! twice, thrice and four times. Impudence! Cheek! Brass unparalleled, unapproachable, sublime!' Fisk essentially enjoyed the game: money was scarcely the point, and morality didn't enter into it either. And his sheer cheek was indeed unparalleled: as he breezily quipped when the gold corner collapsed and all its seamy skullduggery was exposed, 'Nothing lost save honor!' Henry Adams was probably right when he guessed that Fisk thought of his Wall Street operations as one 'gigantic side-slitting farce'.

Fisk was a walking scandal. When he visited Long Branch, New Jersey, one of the favorite watering holes of the leisure class, the 'best people' checked out when he checked in. Yet New Yorkers stood transfixed when his lover's playboy lover, Edward S. Stokes, first blackmailed Fisk and then shot him to death in the lobby of the Grand Central Hotel. Talk of lynching Stokes filled the air. Fisk was eulogized for his magnetism and generosity of spirit, and thousands lined the route of his funeral train as it made its solemn way back to his birth-place in Brattleboro, Vermont. Popular singer and song-writer Billy Scanlon memorialized Wall Street's flashiest in a ballad, 'Jim Fisk or He Never Went Back on the Poor', which remained a bar-room favorite for years afterward. Like many a modern celebrity, Fisk was all style and image, admired less for what he actually accomplished than for the raffish glamour and voluptuous irreverence of his pres-ence. His bravado and dash became part of the Wall Street aura.[37]

Even a hundred years later, when the 'robber baron' stigma had long since attached itself to all their names, one can still hear the echoes of a persistent if ambivalent admiration. According to one account from the 1950s, 'These men were as magnificent in their par-ticular ways as they were pathetic in their dude clothes, trying to eat with a fork, wondering how best to approach a chaise longue. They were a motley crew, yet taken together they fashioned a savage and gaudy age as distinctively purple as that of imperial Rome.' The emi-nent historian Richard Hofstadter, certainly no apologist for the Gilded Age, nonetheless considered that these men had 'heroic audac-ity and magnificent exploitative talents – shrewd, energetic, aggres-sive, rapacious, domineering, insatiable. They directed the proliferation of the country's wealth, they seized its opportunities, they managed its corruption.'[38]

Many of the qualities that made romantic figures out of Vanderbilt, Drew and Fisk were also assigned to industrialists who never set foot in Wall Street and even, in some instances, hated the place. Something else in addition allowed Wall Street to be treated as a separate bestiary, set off as if by some translucent curtain from the larger jungle of straightforward industrial mud-wrestling.

The great speculators belonged not so much to a profession or occu-pation as they did to a state of spiritual subversion. Nothing tangible arose from their work. They lived instead in that formless infinity of pure money, a universe with no fixed values where it was unwise to take anything for granted and where the improbable was to be expected. If the great speculator might be likened to Napoleon, he was also compared to the plunger, the wildcatter, the mystic traveler to uncharted and dangerous lands. It was an exhilarating world: those brave or foolhardy enough to expose themselves to its vertiginous atmosphere broke free of the world of work and its inner moral discipline. They recognized no authority, treated all men with egalitarian indifference, responded only to the universal mathematics of the disembodied market. They seemed parodies of Protestantism, sprung free of its repressive commandments. In a culture saturated in Protestant moralizing, they provided an entranced public with a sneaky thrill. They had crossed the border. Waiting on the other side, however, was Jay Gould.

Gould alone was universally loathed. Vanderbilt might be profane, his 'cheaper by the dozen' children a sign of his lechery. But he was an empire builder. Drew was not to be trusted. But his folksy idiom and down-home candor were endearing. Fisk was a born scoundrel. But his native wit and public passions were disarming, and besides he seemed sentimentally attached to 'the people'.

Not so Jay Gould. He wasn't witty and he wasn't sexy. He lacked the common touch. He was taciturn, stealthy, owlish, and humorless, and seemed to be without any of the redeeming virtues of the plebeian aristocrat. To many he appeared demonic: Wall Street gone to hell. He seemed to epitomize what was most reviled about Wall Street by respectable middle-class opinion, by novelists, graphic artists, dramatists, ministers, mugwump reformers, cultural aristocrats, and crusading journalists.

Over the course of a single generation, many Americans had come to admire the country's new class of financial Napoleons. They were awed; they envied them and tried to emulate them. Many others, however, knew in their hearts that these colossuses were first and last confidence men, and they loathed them for it.

4

Wall Street in Coventry

While alive he was the most hated man in America. In the century since his death, and despite history's notorious fickleness, Jay Gould's reputation has remained irredeemably dark. A recent biography of 'the Mephistopheles of Wall Street', the first I know of to attempt his rehabilitation, takes a perverse delight in reviewing this unblemished record of historical denunciation. Alexander Dana Noyes, the dean of turn-of-the-century financial journalism, judged him 'a destroyer'. Gustavus Myers, whose *Great American Fortunes* was a seminal work of Progressive-era muckraking literature, called him a 'pitiless human carnivore, glutting on the blood of his numberless victims . . . an incarnate fiend'. During the Great Depression, Wall Street's ignominious low point, Matthew Josephson's celebrated exposé, *The Robber Barons*, depicted Gould as scarily non-human: 'No human instinct of justice or patriotism or pity caused him to deceive himself or to waver . . . from the steadfast pursuit of strategic power and liquid assets'. As one might expect, things hadn't improved much by the 1960s. One biographer declared his life 'the ultimate perversion of the Alger legend', awestruck by his 'boldness in corruption and subornation'. Another eminent historian writing at the same time concluded that Gould's career 'encompassed almost every known variety of chicanery'. And even though his most recent biographer does yeoman work trying to remove the brimstone from the Gould legend, a *New Yorker* article entitled 'The Confidence Man', appearing just before the turn of our new millennium, echoes Henry Adams' mordant apercu that Gould's plans always demanded that 'someone, somewhere, should be swindled'.[1]

Even when he died, in 1892, no one could think of a kind word to say. *The New York Times,* more than willing to pay its respects to other baronial tycoons, found Gould a purely 'negative quantity in the development of the country where he was not an absolutely retarding and destructive quantity'. *The New York World* captured best the way Gould had become a stench in the nostrils of polite society. For the editors, he was the 'incarnation of cupidity and sordidness'. Lamenting the demoralized state of the nation's spiritual life, its prostration before 'the golden calf', the paper blamed Gould in particular. His success promoted this idolatry, and 'dazzled and deluded multitudes of young men. Jails, insane asylums, and almshouses all over the land are peopled with those who aspired to wealth by similar methods.' Moreover, there were many more, still 'at large, mingling with the community in all the walks of life, excusing, practicing, and disseminating the vices of which he was the most conspicuous model in modern times'.[2]

Silent and secretive, Gould's career nonetheless played itself out inside a luridly lit bubble of public infamy: an editor's favorite foil, a caricaturist's delight. Joseph Pulitzer declared him 'one of the most sinister figures that have ever flitted bat-like across the vision of the American people'. *The New York Times* was scandalized by Gould, noting that the crusade to reform civic affairs could never succeed 'when the insidious poison of an influence like that of Jay Gould can be detected in politics, in finance, in society, and when people claiming to be respectable are not ashamed of being associated with a man such as he'. Even his sometime partner in financial skullduggery, James R. Keene, whose own slyness had earned him a sobriquet as Wall Street's 'Silver Fox', judged Gould 'the worst man on earth since the beginning of the Christian era'. An attorney representing one of Gould's victims went up to the financier while Gould was dining at Delmonicos and beat him up. After a second assault a few years later, he no longer walked the streets alone. Living in garrison-like privacy, at times afraid to travel abroad on his own railroad lines, the target of death and kidnapping threats – including one from a crazed Colorado man who voyaged East vowing to execute Gould on behalf of a mysterious organization known as Christ's Followers – Gould counted on a squad of bodyguards, the iron portcullis mounted at his office, and the protection of his close friend and New York's Chief Inspector of police, Thomas Brynes. He was a marked man.[3]

Many of the people who marveled at the exploits of the four horsemen, who winked at their transgressions and applauded their nerve, were at the same time appalled by what they saw. For those who despised these Wall Street roughnecks while despairing at the credulity of their fellow citizens, Jay Gould had become a metaphor: part of the folklore of a genteel culture wrestling with the paradoxes of raw industrial capitalism. He served this purpose perfectly, in part because he lacked all those features – the bon vivant athleticism, the back-slapping good cheer, the robust, dominating physical presence – that sometimes redeemed his confrères. Diminutive, joyless, shy, unsocial, even bookish, he was easily likened to a spider or a snake, womanish like a treacherous siren. He was a living insult to all those Victorian sentimental illusions which polite society found so necessary to veil its own mercenary ardor. Gould fascinated, however, not because he was unique, but rather because he seemed to distill a set of character traits all too commonly associated with Wall Street and which the world of bourgeois propriety found deeply detestable.[4]

Wealth, even the amassing of great fortunes, did not by itself offend the canons of respectability. Tooth-and-claw, give-no-quarter combat in the competitive marketplace was also acceptable, even a point of manly pride – so long as it was conducted within the implicit ground rules of Protestant morality. But Wall Street, and not just Jay Gould, seemed always to be testing, and often enough transgressing, those ground rules. The problem was the lack of common ground between the Street and the new industrial order. Manufacturing, distributing, and selling the products of American industry and agriculture was carried on, in the main, by small- and medium-sized family firms and partnerships, who had no intercourse with Wall Street. But Wall Street banks, brokerages, and freelance speculators lived off the cyclical crises endemic to this nineteenth-century family capitalism. It was natural enough, then, for the victims of those crises, or those inclined to romanticize a less disorderly past, to treat Wall Street as a special kind of incubus.

When it came to the relationship between wealth and work, genteel culture knew certain truths to be self-evident. Work was good, wealth incidental. Work encouraged self-discipline, probity, and good order, wealth was the tangible outcome. Wealth was the vessel of freedom and security; its accumulation was a perpetual tutorial in self-mastery. Property arising out of work provided the material haven sheltering the patriarchal family. Inside the fortress of land, home, and heritable assets, sentimental affections and the moral education of the young would flourish. Conversely, the loss or dissipation of the ancestral patrimony through recklessness or over-reaching ambition was a specter haunting this family romance. In this world-view, property was more than a mass of congealed, dead labor; it was a vehicle of self-expression, a pathway for creative energies open to all – or rather all men. And indeed the building-up of property through inventive genius or organizational acumen, or by wrestling with a recalcitrant nature, was a chief proving ground of middle-class manhood. Nonetheless, its accumulation, to be legitimate, had to come about through straightforward and transparent dealing, however tough-minded. Should work result in the piling up of excessive quantities of wealth and property, then a self-effacing modesty and civic-mindedness would channel it into worthy undertakings of public benefit.

So it was that respectable society surrounded its preoccupation about work and wealth with a halo of religiosity, worthy intentions, and rules of correct behavior. Everybody recognized that wealth, however beneficent, was also dangerous. It could be flaunted, a sure sign of hubris. Any outward display of great riches, any showiness, was not only a social faux pas but a sign of moral and psychological dissipation. Wealth could feed an insatiable inner greediness, turning self-creation into self-indulgence. Wealth might lure one into dishonesty if not illegality. Wealth might be acquired in what Christian civilization had for centuries stigmatized as the 'Jewish way' – that is, undeservedly, by leeching away the fruits of the honest labor of others. Wealth, like a firearm discharged thoughtlessly or with malice, could wound the innocent. During the last third of the nineteenth century, when middling folk as well as the genteel upper class turned their gaze to Wall Street, they tended to see all that: ostentation, selfishness, dishonesty, parasitism, stealth, and economic death. This was how they could revere businessmen like Andrew Carnegie while reviling speculators like Gould. Wall Street had crossed the line separating honest industry from the dark arts of financial witchcraft.

Negative feelings about Wall Street were shared by a Brahmin upper crust as well as by solidly middle-class citizens, but they were inflected differently. The former cultivated a sense of entitlement based on culture, breeding, and education. Work did not necessarily figure in this, and pursuing it too avidly could be unseemly. But great piles of money mounting up on Wall Street threatened to breach their cherished social exclusivity. The middle classes, however, were existentially committed to the moral rigors of work and hostile to class distinctions. For them Wall Street sowed indiscipline, idleness, pretension, and economic calamity. While the Brahmin was offended aesthetically, for the upright middle classes of town and country, Wall Street was an impiety. The old elite found its social and political pre-eminence challenged. The rising middle classes, meanwhile, feared for their survival and resented the Street's apparent sacrilege.

For both Brahmin elitist and middle-class pietist, however, social position was something that should be earned or deserved, rather than a matter of chance or purchase – or worse. Both groups were proud of their sense of civic responsibility, and together they paid fealty to an origin myth about the Republic: that it had been founded by men who not only exhibited exemplary gentility in their personal behavior – unaffected, independent, diffident, learned, and benevolent – but were also quintessential public servants, virtuous, disinterested, averse to any hint of corruption. Hardly naive, those who subscribed to this myth were ruefully sensitive to the corrosion of the Founders' Spartan political standards. Much of this they blamed on the dirty business of mass politics, but filthy lucre played its own insidious part. Men and women of the genteel persuasion saw themselves as conservators of republican purity, and defenders of the faith against political place-seekers, machine demagogues, and the men with the money. Some of this high-mindedness, of course, was no more than cant; those same people might be caught dabbling in the market or engaged in cut-throat business practices. After all, like everyone else, they lived in a world whose incivility savaged their most precious conceits.

Thanks to its notorious reputation for lavish display, the 'age' we recall as 'gilded' is easily mistaken for one of broad prosperity. However, the Gilded Age in fact encompassed a period of deflation punctuated by frequent panics and depressions. If it was gilded rather than golden, it was nonetheless an age of striking technological innovation and industrial growth. But this occurred in spasms and at a high price. The ruthless efficiency of the market, expressed in the ceaseless outdating of existing forms, methods, and outputs of production, chronically devalued older claims to the means of production. Fourteen of the twenty-five years between 1873 and 1897 were years of recession. It was a 'daimonic' economy, whipsawed by ferocious acts of creation and destruction. Ordinary businessmen saw themselves less as the titanic, Faustian movers and shakers of legend and more like the harassed and anxious strivers they really were, haunted by chaos and insecurity. They lived on treacherous terrain, littered with disabled enterprises and the corpses of once flourishing firms.[5]

Wall Street stationed itself along two vital arteries of this Darwinian organism. It financed the railroads. And it helped determine the flow and availability of credit. Positioned so strategically, it was for that reason wide open to attack.

Railroads were the principal, if not the only form of industrial enterprise whose capital needs were so enormous that they had to resort to sources outside the firm. Half of new private investment went into railroads between 1880 and 1890; every year of that decade another 7,000 miles of track were laid, an unprecedented number. Railroads were themselves subject to the same rigors of market competition: they could come into being and go out of existence with extraordinary rapidity. Speculation was nowhere more feverish: perhaps a third of the new tracks were built to meet current demand, a third might find some useful future, but a final third were of no value to anyone except their promoters and were derided as 'blackmail railroads' by more reputable operators. (In 1884, Moody's estimated that as much as $4 billion in railroad stock represented pure water.)

But as gigantic corporate undertakings with a great deal of capital at risk, they also devised means of survival which propped up the often grossly inflated values attached to the securities issued in their name. Moreover, the railroads themselves enjoyed pre-eminence in an economy increasingly strung together with steel rails and telegraph wire. Farmers, merchants, and manufacturers, not to mention fledgling communities eager to spread their wings, found themselves at the mercy of railroad routes and rates. Wall Street thrived on this largesse and power.[6]

This relationship of dependency was aggravated by the deflated state of the economy. Starved for cash and credit, agrarian as well as urban entrepreneurs faced off against an intractable banking establishment headquartered in Wall Street. The national banking system that coalesced after the Civil War consolidated financial power in the East, New York in particular, leaving regional interests in the West and South on hard rations. Due in part to their holdings in government bonds and to the nation's reliance on British gold reserves to finance its international trade, the great Wall Street banks were unshakably wedded to the gold standard and opposed to all forms of monetary inflation. Add to all this a predilection for gilded opulence amidst chronic privation, and, under duress, this triangulation of the economy by Wall Street's strategic control over credit and transportation was bound to provoke.

Wall Street's power seemed undeserved. It derived as much from the exploitation of the citizenry as it did from the laying of track, the building of drawbridges, and the choreography of freight trains. It seemed tainted, acquired through degrading the integrity of the commonwealth.

The irony was that the ascent of these 'nimrods of the market' depended on their intimate relations with the institutions of political power. For good reason, this moment in the country's history has been ridiculed as 'the Great Barbeque'. Without the active collaboration of state legislators, sitting judges, mayors and city machine bosses, congressmen and cabinet members, the vast wealth amassed by our four horsemen would be inconceivable. This did not devalue their achievement: navigating an uncharted political labyrinth was no mean feat, and another sign of their mastery. However, this intimacy with government, some of it skirting or crossing the borders of legality, did mean that the republic was in danger of being converted into a client state whose legitimacy could naturally be called into question. Thus the elevation of the financial pathfinder was, in a bizarre fashion, assisted by the debauching of republican government.

Erie's story has been told and retold dozens of times – because it's so good, and because it captures this special relationship so perfectly. It stands as a founding legend of the Street, capturing its braggadocio, its cunning, and its outsized ambitiousness. The ingredients are irresistibly delicious: water-logged stock manipulated by maestros; locomotives, passengers' cars, and track left in such sorry condition they killed people; suborned jurors and bought judges; open bribery of the whole New York State legislature and New York City Council; an attempted kidnapping and a harrowing midnight flight across the Hudson in a rickety boat; an armed siege in a converted Jersey City hotel guarded by gangland thugs; a looted corporate treasury and international lawsuits that would continue into the next century.

At first Drew had the Erie all to himself. During the 1850s he used his official positions in the company's management to arrange for the over-capitalization of the railroad and then, making use of his privileged information about the company, made a fortune bearing and bulling its stock on the exchange. The road itself was left in deplorable condition, an accident waiting to happen, as it often enough did. Erie's decrepitude – faulty tracks, broken-down engines, collapsing bridges, exploding locomotives, derailments, and collisions – produced an unending series of mishaps, major and minor, some fatal. Drew was out to milk the road. Precious little of the money raised on the stock and bond markets found its way into upkeep and modernization. But after the Civil War, the road was 'put in play' by others, Cornelius Vanderbilt in particular, who sought to control it in the interests of monopolizing railroad access to the booming New York market.

Vanderbilt clashed with Drew, who was joined by two younger men, each in his own way, as outrageous and shrewd as he was. 'Jubilee Jim' Fisk and Jay Gould attempted to trap the 'Commodore' in his own monopolizing scheme by forcing him to engorge endless quantities of Erie stock at ever escalating prices. The supply of stock was made virtually limitless because it was being manufactured almost at will and on the sly by Drew and the boys. They made clever misuse of a provision in the New York state law allowing the company to issue bonds for the upkeep and operation of the line, bonds which could be subsequently converted into stock. Vanderbilt tried to put a stop to these expensive high-jinks and got a pliant judge to issue an injunction and arrest warrants. But Drew and company purchased their own jurist and had the injunction countermanded. Not to be checkmated, the Commodore's judge ordered the police to enforce his writ. The elderly 'Uncl' Dan'l' fled immediately to New Jersey. Flush with the daredevil confidence of their youth, however, Fisk and Gould hung around partying for almost too long, hailing a small skiff at the Battery just in time to make a fog-enshrouded and nearly catastrophic voyage across the river with the local constabulary hot on their trail. Once in Jersey City they set up Erie headquarters in a hotel, rechristened 'Fort Taylor', guarded by heavily armed 'security' and a small cannon. The artillery discouraged plans to kidnap the threesome and there matters stood . . . until Jay Gould showed up in Albany with a satchel full of cash ready to pay all those state lawmakers willing to vote the Erie a franchise into New York City. Many proved willing indeed. Vanderbilt's agents arrived on the scene with their own bag-loads of money. An auction followed, votes going to the highest bidder.

In the end a compromise was reached. Drew, anxious to return to the comforts of home, betrayed his young protégés and did a deal that saved Vanderbilt from the more extreme consequences of his bullish position in Erie stock. The road resumed its career as 'the scarlet woman of Wall Street'. While its foreign investors, especially the British, tried to call management to account and exercise their 'rights' as shareholders, their lawsuits failed, and for the rest of the century the Erie, growing ever more haggard, looted and re-looted of its dwindling resources, typified Wall Street at its most rapacious.[7]

The Erie was hardly an isolated case. The years after the Civil War were full of similar instances of companies, especially but not only railroads, held for ransom on the Street. Stock-watering, insider manipulations, ruthless wars for control, bribed officialdom, lawsuits, and the piling up of great personal wealth became regular newspaper fare. What is distinctive about this primitive age of Wall Street freebooting is how much of it depended on and inveigled the state.

Two scandals in particular competed with the Erie for public attention, and both involved the government. In the fall of 1869, Gould and Fisk managed for one terrifying moment to corner the market in gold. Their secret weapon was a back-alley channel of influence running directly in to the White House. During the Congressional investigation that followed the 'gold conspiracy', it became clear that President Grant was himself innocent of any connivance in the scheme; although perhaps innocent as well of the financial prudence that might have nipped the plot in the bud, a failing that would years later leave the ex-President the impoverished victim of another Wall Street scam. Grant had long cultivated a taste for high living, avidly encouraged by his wife Julia, and regularly accepted lavish gifts from grateful businessmen (a more or less normal practice at the time).

But if Grant was not their willing creature, Fisk and Gould could depend on the President's brother-in-law, Abel Corbin, a one-time influence pedlar from the St Louis frontier and now a New York lawyer, lobbyist, and speculator. Together with a key Treasury department official, these men, hoping to profit personally, sought to keep the price of gold artificially high by dissuading the government from selling into the market from its own supply of gold. Grant was lavishly entertained by Fisk on his steam yacht and in his private box at

'Jubilee Jim's' opera house, creating the erroneous impression he was a confidante. Gould plied the President with specious arguments about why it would be wise for the government to allow the price of gold to rise, thus supposedly providing American farmers with a windfall when they sold their crops abroad. A gullible newspaper columnist suggested Grant had bought the argument and would keep a tight rein on the government's gold. Only belatedly did Mrs Grant get wind of what Corbin was up to. At last Grant smelled a rat. Just as Fisk and Gould set their cornering scheme in motion, the President ordered the sale of enough gold to collapse the corner. It produced instant pandemonium in the 'gold room', an oddly configured, dingy hall located at the corner of William Street and Exchange Place. The scene there was described by one journalist as a 'rat-pit in full blast'. The sheer heat generated by so many messages flowing back and forth across the 'gold room's' telegraph system melted the wires and produced a telegraphic blackout in much of the Northeast. Crowds gathered hoping to catch a glimpse of the renegade conspirators. Spotted, Gould and Fisk were chased through the streets to 'Jubilee Jim's' Grand Opera House where they lived under siege for days. Grant's action did save the integrity of the government's finances and avoided a more general economic calamity, although plenty of ruined western farmers wouldn't agree. But the stunning memory of financial paralysis and near disaster lingered on; two years later the *London Times* compared the vanquishing of Gould and Fisk to the 'defeat of Hannibal or Napoleon – a victory of Fate over Genius'.[8]

Financial intrigue at the Union Pacific Railroad, exposed not long after the infamous 'gold conspiracy', provided a second spectacular instance of the incestuous carryings on between Wall Street and Washington. The Union Pacific was born out of the wartime effort to traverse the continent by rail and depended heavily on government subsidies and loans. By 1864, it was being run by a group of Wall Street promoters who viewed the treasury as a cash cow. Despite the warning signals, every time management returned to Washington for additional subsidies Congress complied. Indeed, Secretary of the Interior John P. Usher, who was supposed to monitor the undertaking for the government, held stock in one of the road's subsidiaries and knew the promoters personally. Construction was so shoddy that parts of the road could scarcely bear the weight of a locomotive. But nothing was said, as Usher was not alone. Members of Congress and other government officials, including Grant's Vice-President, Schuyler Colfax, accepted campaign money as well as shares of stock in the railroad's construction and land development company spin-offs. Between 1866 and 1872 the railroad handed out $400,000 in graft. Most notoriously, a separate company was established, the Credit Mobilier, which was ostensibly created to build the road but effectively functioned to funnel government subsidies into the hands of its own managers. Not coincidentally, these were the same group of people who were running the railroad. Congressman Oakes Ames also headed up the Credit Mobilier, and to keep the machinery of government subsidy running smoothly he liberally distributed shares in the company to a variety of politicians, including future President James Garfield and Republican Speaker of the House and future presidential candidate James G. Blaine. It is estimated that the Union Pacific was short about $44 million thanks to these machinations. On top of this, the Federal government effectively lent the railroad the use of the army in order to pacify restive Native Americans and discontented workers. When the whole unseemly mess came to light in the early 1870s, the government was naturally embarrassed. But given the density of Wall Street's relations with every level of government, it's doubtful anyone could have been overly surprised.[9]

This was America's first full immersion in the political culture of crony capitalism. It reversed the relationship between business and government Jefferson had once worried about. In those days, government, and in particular the executive, was perceived as the source of corruption, winning over private individuals with favors, emoluments, and cash. During the 'Great Barbeque' it was the public sphere that was seduced and exploited by aggregations of private economic power, by magnates who had long since given up active involvement in governmental affairs. They were more than content to use middling political functionaries to pursue their own self-interest. Gould put it concisely: 'In a Republican district, I was a Republican; in a Democratic district, I was a Democrat; in a doubtful district, I was doubtful; but I was always for Erie.'

One piece of chicanery after another scandalized the post-war public: there was gross corruption at the Indian Bureau, at custom houses in New Orleans and New York, at the ministries to Brazil and England, and in dozens of state and local dealings. An Ohio congressman compared the House of Representatives to 'an auction room where more valuable considerations were disposed of under the Speaker's hammer than any other place on earth.' If Wall Street began its career in Duer's era living off the largesse of the state, by the time of the Civil War it was getting hard to tell who was being kept by whom. Depending on one's point of view, this could be seen as productive ingenuity or gross delinquency.

Thanks to the continuing shortage of private capital willing to take risks on large-scale ventures, state-chartered corporations prevailed well into the 1850s and beyond. This public support encouraged private subscriptions in mixed enterprises in transportation, banking, and various public works. Promoters of these undertakings necessarily looked to the eastern capital markets (as well as to the foreign investment community) for funds; by 1870 a quarter of the financial resources of the country was concentrated in New York. All of these undertakings, particularly railroads, were vital to the accelerating pace of economic growth. All provided unimagined opportunities for speculation and peculation for both businessmen and politicians – sometimes effacing the distinction between them.

Railroad companies depended on the government for lands, loans, and subsidies; between 1862 and 1871, the government donated a hundred million acres to the railroads. Because the government distributed its land and loans only as track was completed, there was an incentive for quick and careless construction; fifteen years after completion nearly all the land-grant railroads had to be rebuilt, all at public expense. By 1880, Federal, state, and local governments had contributed $700 million to the building of the railroads and donated 155 million acres of public land – more than the size of France. Nor does this include the railroads' own sales of land granted to them: in the case of the Northern Pacific alone, this was worth $140 million. Many roads might have collapsed without help from state and local governments, who might agree to underwrite the interest on company bonds, for instance. In the case of the Union Pacific and Central Pacific transcontinental project, the Federal government not only capitalized the roads at $100 million, but made repeated and generous loans for construction costs – as much as $48,000 per mile through the Rockies and Sierras.

In raising capital for his vast new railroad, the Northern Pacific, Jay Cooke relied on political influentials to pump up enthusiasm for the project. He lined up Ohio Governor Rutherford B. Hayes, notable judges, the country's pre-eminent minister, Henry Ward Beecher, respected journalists like Horace Greeley, and such intimates of President Grant as General Horace Porter and Vice-President Schuyler Colfax. After completing a portion of the road up to the Red River so that it wouldn't seem purely chimerical, he went to the government for land grants and bond guarantees – in part to induce European emigrants to settle along the route, in part to convince wealthier continental investors to buy the company's bonds. (The capital of North Dakota was even named Bismarck, because Cooke was trying to peddle bonds in Germany!) The fifty million acres donated to the railroad was larger than the entire territory of New England. To keep the money flowing Cooke hired ex-Senator Benjamin Wade of Ohio to represent the project in Washington. Meanwhile, he underwrote a mass publicity campaign extolling the patriotic virtues of the road. It was to be a great civilizing project that would populate the wilderness, carrying men, goods, and ideas into a rich but unexploited part of the continent. Along with Northern Pacific bonds, his sales agents carried with them maps and posters and pamphlets heralding the cornucopia to come. Celebrities were taken on excursions, traveling exhibits of products from the back country were staged around the country, editors were wined and dined.

Still the aroma of corruption filtered through, as stories of fraud and thievery began to surface. There were derisive allusions to the Northern Pacific as 'Jay Cooke's Banana Belt', mocking a promotional literature that portrayed the region as a lush tropical paradise. Bond sales suffered. Attempts to lure settlers from abroad dead-ended with the outbreak of the Franco-Prussian war. When Massachusetts congressman General N. P. Banks called for an inquiry, Cooke said he 'ought to be expelled from Congress for such outrageous attacks upon the great interests of the country'. His stature was still substantial enough to quiet the accumulating suspicions, and the committee's brief report was favorable. But the relief was only temporary: Cooke was deeply over-extended. The collapse of Northern Pacific securities a year later in 1873 was responsible, more than any other single event, for the next great Wall Street panic and the greatest depression of the nineteenth century.[10]

Like the Erie and the Northern Pacific, railroads became the preferred object of financial gaming. Promoters and financiers were often handsomely rewarded and then sought further ways to reward themselves. If Erie was the most notorious 'scarlet woman of Wall Street', other roads like the Harlem, the Michigan Southern, Prairie du Chien, and the Chicago and Northwestern earned similar reputations through the 1860s and 70s.

The admixture of chicanery and impressive accomplishment involved in the railroads' construction produced storms of public alarm and outrage over the despoiling of republican government, followed by an amazing quiescence. Henry Adams wrote a biting exposé of 'Black Friday', the newspapers' name for the gold panic. It seemed all the more acidic because the Congressional investigation into the scandal, led by James Garfield, exonerated everybody of any real wrong-doing, though rhetorically excoriating Fisk for his 'singular depravity.' (Fisk in turn provided some hilarious testimony that tried, clumsily, to put the finger on Grant.) Battles for control between contending Wall Street financiers became, by necessity, turf wars for political influence. Tammany Hall's Boss Tweed and his 'gang', who controlled New York City's Democratic Party and were a major power in state politics, regularly solicited bribes and participated in speculative pools whose stock prices depended on the actions of the legislature in granting or refusing franchises. Tweed's massive public works project – which endeared him to many working-class New Yorkers – were largely funded with city bonds gobbled up by Wall Street, usually underwritten by fellow Democrat August Belmont, who then resold them in Europe at a handsome premium. The Tweed ring used its control over city funds to manipulate the market on behalf of its favored speculators and to punish their Republican Wall Street enemies. Tweed himself became an Erie director, for which he received a $100,000 annual retainer.

Ultimately Tweed got caught and went to jail (although not for his railroad felonies), but for years he got away with criminal behavior that was more or less public knowledge. During the Erie imbroglio, when the legislators in Albany were being openly solicited, the *New York Herald* sarcastically called the 'Erie bill' a 'Godsend to the hungry legislators and lobbymen, who have had up to this time such a beggarly session that their board bills and whiskey bills are all in arrears and their washerwomen and boot blacks are becoming insubordinate'. The judicial system was similarly compromised. One magazine concluded from the Erie wars that in New York 'there is a custom among litigants . . . of retaining a judge as well as a lawyer . . . it is absolutely essential to each party to have some magistrate in whom it could place confidence.' When the New York State Senate went through the motions of conducting an investigation, it concluded that while large sums of money were on the premises with the clear intention of unlawfully influencing legislation, there was no proof these sums were so used. However, a different sort of proof of Wall Street's impact on the commonwealth was in the offing.[11]

Next to Lincoln and Grant, Jay Cooke was perhaps the most widely admired man in America. What a shock, then, when in the autumn of 1873, Cooke's empire fell apart, precipitated by the collapse of his Northern Pacific Railroad, carrying the economy down with it. The crash ushered in sixty-five consecutive months of deep depression, the longest such downturn in the country's history, and left people in an unforgiving mood. It now turned out that the man famed for his probity was hardly beyond reproach. Reproach was what he got, as darker moments of his past resurfaced. People remembered that Cooke had been a 'moneyed aristocrat' all along. He had led the banking community in insisting that the government redeem its bonds in gold, not the greenbacks demanded by Democrats and credit-hungry debtors. Rumors circulated that he'd tried to bribe highly placed officials in the Grant administration.[12]

Everything, however, paled against the trauma of '73, for which Cooke received sole blame. All the hoopla surrounding the promotion of the Northern Pacific – the celebrity testimonials, the patriotic cant about Progress and the taming of the continent, the lavish fantastical brochures depicting Duluth as the Paris of the prairies, the public forums featuring local celebrities, the traveling exhibits of the unexplored region's flora and fauna, the expeditions to Vienna and other European capitals to drum up bond sales and immigrant settlers for hypothetical towns in a tropical wilderness – all this was not unlike his famous campaign to save the embattled Union's finances. But this time it was largely make-believe, kept aloft by wishful thinking, political corruption, and Federal largesse.

All sorts of middling folks – widows, clerks, schoolteachers, ministers, small businessmen who were normally skeptical about Wall Street – had taken the plunge in Northern Pacific bonds, trusting in Cooke's impeccable reputation. When his great bank failed, the patriot turned into a scoundrel. Angry and bewildered crowds gathered at the shuttered doors of Cooke and Company at Nassau and Wall. A murder trial in Washington adjourned as the judge, jurors, witnesses, and attorneys for both sides rushed out of the courtroom on hearing the news. As dozens of firms, some of ancient lineage, closed up and the New York Stock Exchange was forced to shut for ten days, the panic and depression that followed left an indelible memory for a generation. A broker described 'Black Thursday' as 'the worst disaster since the Black Death'. It would be decades before the small investor returned to the market. A year later half the iron furnaces in the country were closed down. By 1876, half of all railroad bonds were in default. A fifth of the labor force was out of work for most of the decade. Mass gatherings of the unemployed were broken up by police attack. As Alexander Dana Noyes later recalled, 'the financial crash of September, 1873, had been as memorable a landmark as, to the community of half a century later, was the panic of October, 1929.'[13]

Cooke's downfall was shattering enough in its own right. But it happened to coincide with three other events that inflamed public abhorrence for speculative excess and the usurious instincts of the New York banking establishment. The Credit Mobilier revelations hogged the front page throughout the year, with their stunning exposure of the subornation of America's political elite by the directors of the Union Pacific. Then a Republican Party now dominated by its most conservative elements managed to withdraw silver from the nation's circulating currency. This act of legislative miserliness, dubbed by its opponents 'the Crime of '73', infuriated legions of credit-starved businessmen and farmers, who blamed the deed on Wall Street's 'gold bugs'.

Finally in 1873, Mark Twain co-wrote (with his friend Charles Dudley Warner) *The Gilded Age*, the novel whose title has remained in the national vocabulary. The book was an instant bestseller. A year later a version opened on Broadway, where it too became a smash hit that then toured the country. It still seems mordantly funny now. Twain captured the ridiculousness, the cant, and the pretentiousness of a post-Civil War America where 'the air is full of money, nothing but money, money floating through the air'. The following contemplation seems risibly familiar even today:

> Beautiful credit! The foundation of modern society . . . That is a peculiar condition of society which enables a whole nation to

instantly recognize point and meaning in a familiar newspaper anecdote, which puts into the mouth of a distinguished speculator in lands and mines this remark – 'I wasn't worth a cent two years ago, and now I owe two millions of dollars.'

Like all good satire *The Gilded Age* had a moral purpose. Twain and Warner sought to skewer a society which Walt Whitman at just this moment condemned as 'cankered, crude, superstitious, and rotten', overwhelmed by an insatiable greed for money, land, and power. In his considered judgment, 'The depravity of the business classes of our country is not less than has been supposed but infinitely greater. The official services of America, national, state, and municipal, in all their branches and departments, not excepting the judiciary, are saturated in corruption, bribery, falsehood, mal-administration.'

Although we have grown accustomed to associating the phrase 'gilded age' with dissolute materialism and self-indulgence in private life, the novel was much more concerned with the depraved condition of public life, and especially the profound corruption of democratic government. Twain's satirical barbs at Tweed and the bacchanalia of the Gilded Age were informed by a conventional middle-class morality; his iconoclasm was still steeped in the ethos of prudence, thrift, and honest dealing. 'Colonel' Beriah Sellers, the comic foil of *The Gilded Age*, is a man of stupendous bombast. The zaniness of his designs and his good cheer in the face of one fiasco after another inspired a certain sympathy among readers and theater-goers; but it was hardly meant to excuse the debauching of the public purse and the despoiling of the public trust by people like Cooke and his political confederates.[14]

Outrage over the 'Great Barbeque' emanated from two locales which rarely had any intercourse with one another. Elitists from the coastal Northeast and middling folk from the farms and small cities of the heartland shared a foreboding about Wall Street's machinations, but their preferred solutions kept them far apart.

The Adamses, Charles Francis and Henry, co-authored, under the unassuming title, 'Chapters of Erie', what was undoubtedly the most scathing indictment of the whole post-war Wall Street scene. Their elegant and erudite formulations revealed their Brahmin heritage. While they found everything about the 'four horsemen' scandalous, Charles Francis was particularly exercised by the political implications.

Thinking of Vanderbilt especially, he worried about the creation of great financial combines that would overwhelm the state and its citizenry, and he gloomily forecast the advent of a kind of corporate imperialism. He likened the seduction of the judiciary to a 'monstrous parody of the forms of law; some Saturnalia of bench and bar'. At the same time the legislative process was in danger of becoming 'a mart in which the price of votes was haggled over, and laws, made to order, were bought and sold'. The arrangements between Tammany Hall and the Erie were, in Adams' view, 'equivalent to investing Mr Gould and Mr Fisk with the highest attributes of sovereignty'. Charles Francis (a railroad manager of considerable distinction) and Henry were most exercised about railroads – the Erie in particular. But their underlying message, that the integrity of the Republic was in jeopardy thanks to a breed of swindling 'moneycrats', was no less cosmological for that.

Much of the brothers' text concerned the intricate financial chicanery carried out by Gould, Fisk, Drew, and Vanderbilt. In their eyes this spectacle damned a whole culture, one that could no longer tell the difference between piracy and legitimate business, one that could bestow honors and titles on men 'without character' who 'possessed themselves of an artery of commerce more important than even the Appian Way'. Dishonorable men like Drew struck at the very foundations of society and were 'the common enemy of every man, woman, and child who lives under representative government'. Vanderbilt presented an even greater danger. His grasp and gargantuan ambition to control the nation's whole transportation system would overwhelm the state and citizenry. Proof was everywhere. The Credit Mobilier debauch in particular persuaded Henry Adams that 'the moral law had expired – like the Constitution.'

The implications of this corruption were bleak. Graft could no longer be isolated as an abnormality. In a political system ostensibly committed to popular rule, but in which the ambitions of a plutocracy proved irresistible, graft became the essence rather than the excrescence of political life. While the Adams brothers decried this new 'government by moneyed corporations', they had a characteristically Brahmin explanation for its venality: 'the combination of the corporation and the hired proletariat of a great city', by which they meant Boss Tweed's Tammany machine. To the already world-weary Adamses there seemed no remedy.[15]

E. L. Godkin shared their disdain for Wall Street and contempt for the rough and tumble of democratic politics. Godkin was an activist engaged in good government reform, while the Adamses stayed away from the fray. But he, like they, could in the same breath lament the polluting of the Republic by Wall Street money-men, yet condemn efforts by what he considered the unruly to rein in the swindlers.

Godkin felt at home in society and was something of a snob. His magazine was financed in part by James Brown of Brown Brothers, a pre-war pillar of Wall Street rectitude, scandalized by the Street's uncouth arrivistes. Naturally, Godkin too deplored the new buccaneering plutocracy, its subverting of honest government, and the vulgarity of its appetites. But Godkin hated with equal passion the agrarian bitterness and the urban leveling instincts which fueled the Greenback and Labor Party insurgencies then gathering energy in the Midwest. That was the peculiar dilemma of the Brahmin opposition. As in Godkin's commitment to the cleaning-up of the Republican Party and the civil service (dubbed mugwump reform by condescending journalists), it might broadcast its withering scorn of Wall Street and the usurping nouveaux, but its social inhibitions and prejudices left it politically inert.[16]

One famous cartoonist escaped that fate. Thomas Nast was a deeply conservative man. He caricatured immigrants, especially Catholics, as a lesser breed whose fondness for alcohol and the Pope threatened to undermine republican stability. His cartoons in *Harper's Weekly* portrayed striking workers as shirkers and anarchist incendiaries. He was a fervent believer in the free-enterprise system and sustained a Calvinist conviction about the sanctity of the government's gold-backed debt. But he was appalled by the the way corruption undermined faith in the possibility of progress and civic virtue. Credit for the downfall of the Tweed Ring rightly belongs to Nast's gothic-nightmare cartoons that exposed Tammany's ravenous appetite for city treasure. His drawings of a terrifying Tammany tiger unleashed by a cretinous band of Tweed henchmen and slithering city officials led by the obese Boss himself, cartoons which ran week after week in *Harper's*, helped immeasurably in creating an atmosphere of revulsion.

While Nast had no axe to grind against the business community in general, he was unsparing in depicting the complicity of Wall Street and the great railroad speculators in the ravishing of the public. 'The Street', one of his Tweed series, caught the Boss in prison garb with a ball and chain around his neck, walking down Wall Street past a storefront labeled 'Cuthem-Cheatem & Co. Bankers', musing as he strolls: 'Why, a fellow feels quite Honest in this neighborhood.' In another, Tweed is proposed for President, while Fisk, whose buffoonish masquerading as an Admiral was known to all, is to serve as Secretary of the Navy. His 1871 'On to Washington' sketched a White House under ambush by a squad of frontier-garbed characters crawling on their knees and bellies, including a buckskin-clad Jay Gould. They are led by an unsavory figure wearing a plume in his hat labeled 'Erie', sneaking up on an oblivious President Grant, contentedly smoking a cigar on the porch of the White House. 'Dead Men Tell No Tales', which ran following the assassination of Jim Fisk, featured a ghoulish gathering of men around Fisk's tombstone, where Jay Gould comforts Vanderbilt and others with the thought that 'All the sins of Erie lie buried here'. Off to the side, 'Justice' warns that 'I am not quite so blind.'

Politics was Nast's preoccupation, but he would, on occasion, foreground the Street itself. During the gold panic of 1869, 'This Street is Closed for Repairs' left only Trinity Church standing in the background of a ruined Wall Street littered with the corpses of bulls and bears. Given Nast's concern for public morals and the political integrity of the republic, it was hardly incidental that Trinity was left intact, as it was again in his take on the Crash of '73, 'Out of the Ruins'. There the Chief of Police is shown lifting Lady Liberty out of the devastation, assuring this distraught and visibly grateful maiden that 'The Houses in this "Street" have been shaky and on false Bases for a Long Time and you've had a very Narrow Escape.' Trinity's preternatural solidity amidst the wreckage suggested a divine admonition.[17].

Thomas Nast was the most celebrated and popular cartoonist of the Gilded Age. Thanks to the energy, tensile strength, and imaginative richness of his drawings, he was enormously influential in forming middle-class opinion on a range of issues. His drawings contorted images of classical antiquity, as if to convey that western civilization was at stake. They echoed the gothic revulsion felt by a Victorian and Protestant sensibility that regarded a certain species of money-making as unclean and subterranean. He inaugurated a tradition in the graphic arts that would exploit Wall Street, for the next seventy-five years, as a target for mockery and social criticism.

Joseph Keppler's drawings in *Puck*, which ran well into the 1890s and seemed almost carved onto the page, shared a similar aesthetic.

Puck was a cheeky, mildly ironical magazine that attempted to stretch the inelastic boundaries of upper-middle-class propriety. Keppler was a little more distanced from the cynicism and corruption of American politics than the righteous Nast. His work appealed, as a form of high graphic art, to the same genteel audience, revolted equally by money-mad speculators and disorderly proletarians, that devoured Nast. Keppler relished Gould particularly as a subject, and his caricatures sometimes indulged the casual Jew-baiting typical of his class. In 'Shylock's Bad Bargain' a mob of farmers, workers, and businessmen are in hot pursuit of Gould, who is making off with the election of 1884 and flees wearing a banner that says 'Bond for One Pound of Uncle Sam's Flesh'. Keppler's crucifixion of Gould, in this and other cartoons, was a picturesque amalgam, suggesting Wall Street's ancient satanic aroma as well as more high-tech fire and brimstone. 'Monopoly in Hades' displays a devilish Gould arriving in a hell bisected by a railroad track, surrounded by slavish imps working for his various railroads and telegraph companies – 'How the place will be run two years after Jay Gould's arrival,' the reader is informed. Gould is depicted atop a pile of stocks and bonds, skeletal victims in a closet behind him. Fellow Wall Street bad man, Russell Sage, is seated deferentially at his feet in a sketch entitled 'In the Robbers' Den'.[18]

Not only in *Harper's Weekly* and *Puck*, but in most of the leading middle-class magazines and newspapers of the Gilded Age, Nast's and Keppler's demonic cast were over and over again excommunicated from the legitimate world of business and public affairs. In theory any unscrupulous man of business might come under this moral censure. In the main the indicted tended to be habitués of the Street with a special craving for railroads.

The New York Times, even then the paper of record of the haute bourgeoisie, never tired of delineating the boundary of Wall Street's untouchables. It too declared in 1877 that 'The Erie record of Mr Jay Gould should have sufficed to banish him from decent business society. The perpetrators of the frauds . . . should have no place among reputable people. Whatever they touch they defile.' *The Times* couldn't abide even Gould's occasional acts of charity, headlining a report on his contribution of land to a church 'Gould Soothes His Conscience.'[19]

Others, however, saw in cultural philanthropy a means of civilizing the savages among the nouveaux riches. When the new Metropolitan

Museum of Art opened its doors in 1880, its first Director, Joseph Choate – mugwump reformer, corporate trial lawyer, and Brahmin – delivered a fund-raising peroration. Why not convert railroad shares and mining stock, he coaxed his potential donors, 'things which perish without the using, and which in the next financial panic shall surely shrivel like parched scrolls – into the glorified canvases of the world's masters . . . The rage of Wall Street is to hunt the philosopher's stone, to convert all baser things into gold, which is but dross; but ours is the higher ambition to convert your useless gold into things of living beauty that shall be a joy to a whole people for a thousand years.' Some, like members of the Vanderbilt dynasty or railroad financier Henry Gurdon Marquand, were moved by such appeals, supplying a considerable portion of the Museum's early holdings in painting and the decorative arts out of their own private collections. Jay Gould, who counted Marquand among his many vanquished Wall Street foes, was not so easily swayed.[20]

Jim Fisk played in a league of his own. On his death, not long after Tweed's conviction, the *Times* exulted that the mighty had fallen: 'Their wealth is gone . . . some of them are vagabonds on the face of the earth; others perish, in the bitter language of Swift, like poisoned rats in a hole . . . somehow or other . . . the sin of every man finds him out, and the divine laws are just in execution.' Godkin was less sanguine. He lamented that Fisk, the mountebank, had been struck down amidst his 'velvet and diamonds', with his 'gorgeous coach at the door' and a 'dozen physicians round his bed and a hundred reporters outside'; instead, he should have died 'in old clothes, and in penury and neglect', to serve as a warning rather than a model to all.[21]

Public rage was kept at boiling point by some egregious instances of indifference among the wealthy. For example, in the middle of the shenanigans involving the Erie, a train decoupled outside Port Jervis, New Jersey, sending three cars into a ravine where forty passengers were incinerated; the resultant outcry engulfed the railroad's managers. After the '73 panic left the country in deep depression, these overnight tycoons wantonly flaunted not only their ill-gotten gains but their déclassé coarseness. From a great altitude, Henry Adams dismissed Fisk as 'coarse, noisy, boastful, ignorant; the type of a young butcher in appearance and mind', who thought his Wall Street operations a 'gigantic side-splitting farce'. During the boom years following the war, dinner parties where cigars were rolled in $100 bills, where black pearls were stuffed into oysters, diamond bracelets served as party favors, and pet dogs leashed on diamond collars, had been thought amusing, if tasteless. As the tough times lingered, however, when Wall Streeters like Leonard Jerome and August Belmont tried dazzling the populace with teams of thoroughbreds, steam yachts, and private race courses, they were deemed crude and unfeeling. The sheer garishness of such exhibitions unleashed a torrent of sanctimonious judgment that often enough confused bad morals with bad manners.[22]

Fisk represented all that Godkin understood to be morally diseased in a licentious, vain, Mammon-hungry, luxury-loving commercial culture. But the *Nation* editor drew back from schemes to confiscate and nationalize the railroads on behalf of farmers and hard-pressed businessmen. They were crazy notions, in Godkin's eyes, and, by driving capital out of the United States, would prove worse than the problem they purported to solve. After all, he argued, people like Cooke may have been imprudent in their railroad promotions, but they were the same far-seeing, risk-taking people who made the development of the West possible. The only remedy, according to the dour Godkin, was a general raising of the level of public morality – and he wasn't counting on it. 'People are eager for money and as unscrupulous about the means of getting it.'

Godkin's patrician fear of the 'dangerous classes', of the rough and tumble of democratic politics, left him in a dilemma. He would in one breath excoriate scoundrels like Vanderbilt and Fisk; in the next he would defame their enemies as hypocrites consumed with envy; and then, exhaling one final time, conclude that after all Wall Street was just a scapegoat for a universal and unexceptional condition of business civilization, namely the hope for an advance in the value of property – 'Indeed, nothing in the way of moral distinctions is less plainly marked than the line which separates the Wall Street 'operator' from the great bulk of the community.' The moral and political torment of the Brahmin intellectual was painful to watch. It was part of a more general conservative retrenchment that worried more about restricting the franchise than it did about business behavior it once considered scandalous. People like Godkin didn't like the spirit behind popular songs like the following, sung to the tune of 'John Brown's Body':

> For Vanderbilt and Company, 'tis indeed a gilded age,
> But poverty increases, 'tis thus that tramps are made.

Shall it be continued when the people's votes are weighed
As we go marching on?

No. We'll hang Jay Gould on a sour apple tree
And bring grief to the plotters of base monopoly
From the ghouls of booty we shall go free
As we go marching on.[23]

The need to skirt incendiary social anger while maintaining moral censure of Wall Street was peculiar to the upper classes. Organs of public opinion that did not speak for them were less self-righteous and less worried about the social consequences of criticizing Wall Street. Bankers particularly were marked men, violators of republican virtue. Not long after the war ended, calls to continue the issuing of Federal greenbacks and for the coinage of silver swept rural America and reverberated in small towns and struggling industrial cities all across the country. Agitation grew ever more heated: soon silver became the emblem of economic freedom, gold the metal of slavery.

Silver and greenbacks, the currencies of the 'little man' and the indebted entrepreneur, promised liberation from 'the money power', the 'bloated bondholders', 'the moneycrats', and 'the Wall Street sharks' – those 'mere vermin' living off what others produced. Sentimental melodramas like *Esau; or The Banker's Victim*, set in rural Indiana, treated Wall Street bankers like usurious vultures, devoid of human or patriotic sentiment. Hugh McCulloch, Secretary of the Treasury after the War, was labeled a 'tool of Wall Street brokers and capitalists' by radical Republicans from the West. The depression of '73 aggravated this social polarization. Merchant princes, financiers, and wealthy manufacturers were pledged to gold. Farmers, working men, and petty entrepreneurs swore fealty to silver and loathed the Wall Street usurer. An angry Texas congressman and one-time cabinet member of the Confederate government, John Reagan, decried the dire consequences of political corruption, claiming that 'there were no beggars till the Vanderbilts and Stewarts, and Goulds and Scotts and Huntingtons and Fisks shaped the action of Congress and molded the purposes of government.' Ignatius Donnelly, an insurgent Republican congressman from Minnesota, laid open the barbaric logic of the 'goldbugs'. Now that they'd succeeded in demonetizing silver in the 'Crime of 73', these 'Wall Street misers' would next drive gold itself out of circulation, wilfully bringing on the Dark Ages where only the usurer ruled.[24]

A flood of verbal invective supplemented the graphic artillery of Nast and Keppler. From the late 1870s the volume of periodical literature and newspaper column inches devoted to Wall Street increased dramatically. Some of it connected the Street's transgressions to social questions. The great railroad strike of 1877 ignited nationwide urban insurrections, led President Hayes to order Federal troops into the streets, and created in its aftermath a frenzy of armory building in leading cities to prepare for any future such uprisings. Papers like the *Chicago Daily News* were not alarmed only by the danger of anarchism. Those like Vanderbilt and Gould, 'who have been running the railroads and have ruined the finest properties the world has known', were also condemned. These railroad barons having found 'nothing more to get out of stockholders and bondholders, they have commenced raiding not only the general public but their own employees'.

Frank Leslie's Illustrated Weekly appealed to a less prepossessing middle-class reader, especially in small towns and villages, abashed and fascinated by the Street. *Leslie's* worried about how the Street was aggravating 'The Great Labor Question', and suggested sympathy for the downtrodden it normally avoided: 'to make cheap railroad iron for the benefit of Rings and Speculators, while the producers are torn by the pangs of want . . . is not a spectacle likely to cement Labor in the bond which alone can hold the dependent links of the social chain unbroken.' To the editors, Wall Street was a kind of madhouse, mixing pocket-picking with chivalrous honesty, a 'cauldron like to that of the witches in *Macbeth*' where prudential norms were in permanent suspension.[25]

The moral umbrage of the metropolitan media was echoed in the hinterlands. When Fisk's escapade to take over a competing railroad, the Albany-Susquehanna, led to an armed clash between hired thugs on both sides and a head-on collision on a desolate mountain-top, the militia was called in to restore order. The *Albany Evening Times* rejoiced in this victory of rural virtue over the 'money-bags, swagger and braggadocio, and eleven-thousand-dollar diamond pins.' The *Springfield Republican* declared that 'nothing so audacious . . . in the way of swindling has ever been perpetrated in this country' as the interlocking of the Tweed and Erie rings.

Papers throughout the greenback-agrarian Midwest and South

treated Vanderbilt like a blight on the land, as 'profane, a dangerous monopolist, irreligious', and exemplary of an eastern Sodom and Gomorrah. During the gold panic, the machinations of 'the great gorilla of Wall Street, the gold-grabbing Gould', and 'the ring-tailed financial ourangoutang', Jim Fisk, were followed in exquisite detail by papers in dozens of cities.

The earthy language and barbed references to 'monopoly' and 'the labor question' suggested a combativeness and an egalitarianism in the plebeian reactions to Wall Street that Brahmin critics veered away from. From these more homely neighborhoods, Vanderbilt received not only a volley of insults, but occasional threats on his life. Russell Sage, a Wall Street figure whose early fortune in street railways rested on the fathomless corruption of New York City government and whose reputation for mean-spirited selfishness rivaled Gould's, was nearly blown to smithereens by a bomb planted at his office in the Old Arcade building opposite the Trinity Church graveyard.[26]

Moreover, middling Americans caught up in the struggle to survive and rise expressed a fear for their own moral health that elite critics like Godkin never entertained. A cautionary children's literature emerged to draw the appropriate lessons. Story papers, read by strivers from the upwardly mobile working class, advised young men about 'the folly of dabbling in stocks', warning them with tales of forlorn young women left adrift in spinsterhood when their fiancés went under with Cooke. Stressing the 'importance of habits in business', *The New York Ledger* alerted its callow readers to beware heroes like Fisk or else they would trade moments of adolescent excitement for years of 'suffering and anxiety'.

Similar anxieties found voice in a new literature of exposé, tales of the city modeled on the work of Eugène Sue, the French writer who invented the genre. Exposures of glamorous goings on in the big city often contained a chapter or episode about the depravity of the newly rich, and in particular habitués of Wall Street like Gould, Vanderbilt, Leonard Jerome, August Belmont, and Russell Sage. Such stories were as much psychological as moral; despite or even because of their great wealth, these men led less happy lives, anxiety-ridden about their money, slaves to fashion and social ritual, stupefied by excess and tedious gossip, loveless and bored. They floated on a bubble of speculative uncertainty, never knowing from moment to moment where the twists and turns of the market might land them, living in a 'mélange of shocking composition, full of idiosyncrasies, if not monstrosities'. A popular board game of the period, 'The Checkered Game of Life', inscribed this fear of moral backsliding and social dishonor on its playing squares: 'Gambling to Ruin'; 'Idleness to Disgrace'; 'Influence to Fat Office'. The best known painting of Wall Street, *The Bulls and the Bears in the Market* by William Holbrook, showed the Street overrun with rampaging animals, goring and mauling and disemboweling each other in an orgy of violence in front of the New York Stock Exchange, the steeple of Trinity Church visible in the background.[27]

For defenders of the old moral order, the behavior of men such as Fisk and Gould signaled a disease of 'modern skepticism' abroad in the land. It was a skepticism far more dangerous than that represented by modern science, the 'skepticism of the laboratory and the naturalist's closet'. Science at least possessed a pure heart. Denizens of Wall Street, however, had no fear of God. They mocked eternal truths. Speculation described not so much a profession or occupation as it did a state of spiritual jeopardy, a place where the monomania of money subverted all tradition and civilized inhibition. The speculator unleashed an inner frenzy that threatened a general chaos. As the *Herald* unctuously proclaimed, 'Society needs a general purification.' About this the nation's spiritual guardians were in agreement.[28]

For the praetorian guard of American Protestantism, amassing mountains of wealth wasn't at issue. Denominational leaders, especially among the Episcopalians and Presbyterians whose congregations drew heavily from among the gilded rich, were theologically comfortable with the notion that the road to celestial peace could, perhaps even should be paved with gold. Clergymen like Lyman Abbott and William Laurence, among many others, authored tracts on success that effortlessly allied God with Mammon. Russell Conwell was a farm boy from Massachusetts and later a Baptist minister and founder of Temple University, an institution of educational as well as moral uplift for the children of the working classes. Conwell issued the most famous defense of this position. His 'Acres of Diamonds' sermon, first delivered in 1889 – and delivered six thousand times during the next quarter century as well as printed and circulated nationally – made the case not only that the opportunity to make a fortune was open to all, but that striving to do that encouraged, like regular exercise, the muscular development of strong character, and that successful striving –

harvesting those 'acres of diamonds' – would redound to everyone's benefit. In Conwell's circular theology, rich men got rich thanks to their moral superiority, while their wealth counted as incontrovertible evidence of their moral pre-eminence. Official religion in America had no argument with business in general and Conwell was hardly the only man of the cloth prepared to sanctify great wealth. But when it came to Wall Street, a note of ambivalence sometimes disturbed this pious equanimity.[29]

Henry Ward Beecher was the country's most celebrated and highly regarded religious orator and writer for thirty years, from the time he assumed his ministry at Plymouth Congregational Church in Brooklyn in 1847 until 1880. He was a showman whose sermonizing stagecraft even drew an audience of agnostics and atheists like Mark Twain. (Sinclair Lewis once described him as a 'combination of St Augustine, Barnum, and John Barrymore.') His congregants were, by and large, well-to-do businessmen and their families. Beecher's basic message was a pleasing one. Mainstream American Protestantism had for some time given up the older, refractory Calvinism, with its grim sense of congenital sin, in favor of an ameliorative view of man that not only allowed the possibility of self-improvement but made moral room for enjoyment, even luxury. Beecher maintained a sanguine belief in Progress, a reassuring conviction that the spirit of materialism and science was fundamentally benign and did not threaten the moral order of things. In person he was congenial and supremely self-confident, and his fatuous sermons confirmed the social prejudices of his rather complacent parishioners.

Like Nast, Beecher distrusted unions, feared immigrants, and was unrestrained in his denunciation of the 1877 railroad strikers. He was a champion of that new hero, the captain of industry. He could even rationalize the urge for extravagant spending so long as it was devoted to beauty and the edification of the citizenry. Nonetheless, Beecher recognized a certain disquiet among his parishioners. They harbored doubts about the cupidity and corner-cutting behavior they saw around them. Luxury, conspicuous waste, self-indulgent preoccupation with fashion left them vaguely anxious. So even as he defended business and subscribed to the social Darwinism that justified its ruthless competitiveness, Beecher mirrored these underlying misgivings about the businessman's single-minded pursuit of profits and property and his complicity in corrupt practices. Those too intensely eager to pile up possessions, who abandoned their responsibilities as stewards of wealth, were guilty souls and carriers of moral anarchy and social disorder. Wealth accumulated unjustly was 'a canker, a rust, a fire, a curse'.[30]

Some Wall Streeters, most famously J. P. Morgan, were deeply pious, at least outwardly. Morgan would leave his office now and then in mid-afternoon to pray and sing hymns in St George's church. Others on the way to the Exchange would pause at Trinity or stop there or at a nearby Dutch Reformed church after a busy day, to offer thanks for their winnings. Morgan and other financiers were generous with donations for churches or missionary work. Beecher and his fellow clerics were grateful, sometimes fawning, yet remained wary.

'Jubilee Jim' Fisk, who dressed like a racetrack tout and once bragged 'I was born to be bad', was a perfect foil for Beecher's ambivalence, allowing free reign for the preacher's moral high dudgeon without questioning the fundamentals of a civilization resting on business. Indeed, ministers all over the country used Fisk as an exemplar of depravity. On the Sunday following the gold panic, sermonizers drew on Matthew 6 – 'Lay not up for yourselves treasures on earth' – for their text. Fisk's rakish disregard for all propriety infuriated Beecher, who denounced him as 'that supreme mountebank of fortune . . . absolutely devoid of moral sense as the desert of Sahara is of grass'. When Fisk died, Beecher sent him on his way with a eulogy as lush as a Nast cartoon, dismissing him as a 'shameless, vicious criminal, abominable in his lusts'. On Vanderbilt's passing, he found the Com-modore utterly lacking in religious conscience. Foretelling Gould's demise, he described him as 'a great epitomized, circulating hell on earth, and when he dies, hell will groan – one more woe'. These people had gotten their riches through fraud, and as another New York minister, William Van Doren, warned, echoing Hawthorne's *House of Seven Gables*, dishonest fortunes carried with them a curse which 'sooner or later will break forth like leprosy'. Speculators were a breed apart, consigned to a moral gulag, sharply segregated by ministers of the cloth from true heroes of entrepreneurial self reliance and hard work like Andrew Carnegie or Peter Cooper.

Beneath the fiery rhetoric, however, Beecher always maintained his social poise. So he was equally quick to point out that Wall Street was full of people resisting temptations their worst critics sometimes fell prey to. His sermon, 'The Deceitfulness of Riches', cautioned against the lures of excessive wealth, but duly observed that, 'There are men in Wall Street – Brokers and Bankers – who stand near to the heart of God, and who are pouring out their means in a way which gives evidence of a Christian manhood in them.' Moreover, Beecher, whose own fall from grace in the form of an adulterous affair with a parishioner was front-page news for months, was not averse to investing heavily in Gould's transcontinental railroad ventures when 'Mephistopheles' took control of the Union Pacific.[31]

Beecher was hardly the only one caught up in this ambivalence – hypocrisy even. Like many a secular thinker, Rev. C. H. Hamlin, a Congregationalist minister, wrestled with the distinction between speculative investment and gambling. He decided that it depended on the size of the risk: if very big and entailing no work, it was wicked and would lead straight away to physical degeneration and addiction. Most Protestant thinkers agreed that there was something morally dangerous about speculation. Beecher warned young men that 'a Speculator on the exchange, and a Gambler at his table, follow one vocation only with different instruments . . . Both burn with unhealthy excitement . . . they have a common distaste for labor . . . neither would scruple in any hour to set his whole being on the edge of ruin, and going over, to pull down, if possible, a hundred others.' However, critics of speculation, theologians among them, tended to stop short of advising public restraint. They feared violating the laws of the market, trusting to the working out of providential law to punish wrongdoers. Indeed, for some, like Baptist minister, George C. Lorimer, economic and divine law worked hand in hand; panics were a form of celestial wrath meted out to financial sinners.[32]

As the Gilded Age blazed on, the sight of urban squalor, armies of unemployed tramps, and violent uprisings like the 1877 railroad strike and the Haymarket bombing of 1886 pricked the social conscience of some Protestant intellectuals. The Social Gospel movement was the outcome, and Washington Gladdens was among its most distinguished progenitors. In the year of Haymarket, Gladdens published a sermon entitled 'The Three Dangers: Moral Aspects of Social Questions'. He analysed three sources of selfishness – drink, family disintegration, and gambling – and concluded that the last was by far the most dangerous. By gambling, however, he did not chiefly mean traditional forms of card and dice playing. The more insidious villain in his eyes was speculation, though not the mere holding of a piece of property in the hope of a rise in its value, which he thought legitimate and a good thing, even if touched by selfishness. He focused instead on commercial transactions in which there was no real exchange of value, where the hope was of getting something for nothing. 'Speculating in margins', betting on the future value of stocks or commodities, was 'immeasurably worse' than gambling at a casino as it was far more dishonest. The speculator loaded the dice and when the game was done many more people were left injured or ruined. The big-time speculator 'may be a pillar in the church; he may hob-nob with college presidents, and sit on commencement platforms . . . but he is a plunderer'. Gladdens had no patience with people who 'hold up their hands with horror at the rantings of a few crazy communists, sit by and suck their thumbs while operations of this sort are going on'. He for one would challenge the inertia and passivity of the pulpit and work to extirpate this 'evil genius of our civilization'.[33]

Probing this 'evil genius' also became a preoccupation of the literary imagination. As a general rule, narrative art from the genteel tradition had veered away from the world of work and commerce. Its sentimental predispositions kept it at home, where the dramas of family life provided the raw material for novelists and short-story writers wrestling with the moral dilemmas of middle class life. The workshop, the office, and the counting house were studiously avoided. Melville, Whitman, and a tiny handful of others had breached these borders even before the Civil War. Afterwards, the rush to industrialize, the gaudy parade of unparalleled fortunes, and the explosive growth of great metropolitan centers, made business an irresistible subject of fictional representation for a growing number of writers.

The business novel was born in these years, but the concerns of those writing during the first two decades of the Gilded Age remained within the affective universe of the family and the soul of the morally challenged individual. For most of the nineteenth century, after all, the writer functioned as a kind of secular priest, instructing and inspiring. Her or his language, plot design, and character development responded to the powerful undertow of the religious temperament and sensibility. Even when masked as satire, it was, implicitly, a didactic, hortatory literature; an admonishment directed at the Philistine enemy. Only from the 1890s would the worlds of the factory, farm, and office emerge in their own right as central sites of the literary imagination, shorn of their refractory religiosity. Nonetheless, even before then the shadow of business lengthened over the parlor and the drawing room. No place cast a gloomier pall than Wall Street.

Several long-running plays on Broadway, staged consecutively through the 1870s and 80s, catered to theater-goers' fascination with the Street. The dialogue makes clear that playwrights assumed that audiences for these plays were familiar with the argot of the Street – many indeed probably worked there. The first such success, of course, was Twain's *Gilded Age*, renamed *Colonel Sellers* to milk the public's fondness for this incurably good-natured charlatan. The play made the most of the feverish excitement and ridiculous antics aroused by speculative fantasies, each more outsized than the last. A second play, *The Big Bonanza*, opened a year later. Most of its plot was devoted to doings on the New York Stock Exchange. A light comedy intended to poke fun at the smug self-assurance of gentility, it probed the dilemma of a professor who, on a dare, ventures into Wall Street under the mistaken impression that his brains and breeding are more than a match for business talent.

By the mid-1880s, the humor was fading. *Henrietta*, produced in 1887, expressed anxiety about the power of financiers to dominate the business world from their headquarters in Wall Street. The playwright, Branson Howard, applied the strictest Victorian moral code to the Street and found it wanting. This didactic piece of satire was enormously popular; it was even revived in 1913 and later made into a movie starring Douglas Fairbanks.

Howard frankly voiced his contempt: 'I tell you Wall Street represents the fiercest kind of gambling in the world . . . Wall Street is a thousand times deadlier than Monte Carlo.' The play portrayed the Street as a maddening and demoralizing casino, so toxic it poisons the most intimate human affections. A father and son battle each other ferociously for control of the Henrietta Mining Company. The old man is a bull, his offspring a bear who seeks to ruin him. Both epitomize a 'raw civilization and selfish society'. However, the son in particular is a lost soul. While a first generation Wall-Streeter like the father may be unconscionably ruthless, he's still capable of generosity and genuine human emotions like grief; even his larceny is somehow more transparent and so more innocent. But the son is spiritually wasted, the degenerate outcome of idle wealth that 'parades Fifth Avenue in clothes and manners and dialect brought and borrowed from London, and that occupy their minds with clubs, clothes, and chorus girls'. It is, then, a play about decline: even Wall Street, the playwright seems to be telling his audience, was once less morally and psychologically bleak.

Typically for a Victorian melodrama, *Henrietta* was full of sage advice, near catastrophes, and heavy-handed symbolism. A younger son rescues his father from his brother's diabolical financial assault; the evil one is punished with a heart attack and stares death in the face as a stock ticker behind him counts down what may be his last moments, remorselessly recording his downfall after his brief and terrible triumph over his father. Cold-hearted to the end, his dying words mimic the nearby ticker: 'seventy-one . . . seventy-eight'. By the time of *Henrietta*, the high hilarity of *Colonel Sellers* or even *The Big Bonanza* had cooled. Speculation, once a fleeting pastime suggesting native incorrigibility, was now depicted as a professional habit practiced by a dangerous coterie in a diseased locale.[34]

But Broadway playwrights, even at their most didactic, were less lugubrious than novelists and short-story writers. The latter tended to hold the businessman in lower regard, no matter how much he might be respected by economic theorists and admired in the vernacular of popular culture. Fiction writers often attributed the generic businessman with the more specific traits, especially the most loathsome ones, of the financier and stock market manipulator. Much of this literature was really about corrupt practices related to the buying and selling of stocks. Tales of bribery, blackmail, and fraud associated with stock watering, false capitalizations, dishonest promotions, and criminal investment conspiracies betrayed deep if unarticulated hostility to the speculative nature of business more generally.

Such writing deployed the genus of the speculator as a metonym for the broader family of injustices and iniquities that pockmarked the landscape of industrializing America. The indictment was broadly pitched, citing the multiple injuries of the speculator's dark arts: pervasive insecurity, moral dissipation, law-breaking, and preying upon legitimate business. The Wall Street operator inhabited a niche within that larger social ecology: he spread the spirit of risk-taking and infected the wider world of business, leading it into unholy desires for extravagant gains without an equivalent input of honest hard work, diligence, and patient deliberation. He violated a cherished folk ethic inscribed in such hoary Franklinisms as 'lying rides upon debt's back' and 'diligence is the mother of good luck'. In Edward Eggleston's *The Mystery of Metropolisville*, towns are born and killed in a flash of 'speculative madness' spread by railroad promoters full of religious cant and glib promises about the general welfare. Characters like Zedekiah Hampton in H. R. Boyesen's *A Daughter of the Philistines* (1883) or 'Uncle' Jerry Hallowell in Charles Dudley Warner's *A Little Journey in the World* (1889) were caricatured speculators, sometimes bearing a tell-tale Semitic trait: savage, vulgar, and uncultured defilers of the quiet refinement and moral gravity these authors identified with fading New England gentility.

Stories appearing in middle-brow magazines like *Harper's Monthly*, *Peterson's*, and *Scribner's* were often maudlin and preachy. They focused on small-time financial scoundrels who placed their immortal souls in harm's way. Novelists, including William Dean Howells and Mark Twain, as well as some now forgotten but once rather popular writers like Josiah G. Holland and J. W. DeForest, went after bigger game. With real-life Wall Street tycoons like Jay Cooke or Jay Gould hovering in the background of their fictions, these authors tracked not only the moral but the communal and political devastation such characters trailed in their wake.[35]

Josiah Holland was one of the creative editorial minds that made *Scribner's Magazine* the chief competitor of *Harper's Monthly* for the allegiance of the middle-class reader. His *Sevenoaks: A Story of Today*, was a potboiler, except that its social psychology was more complex than usually found in the genre. Thanks to their cupidity and credulity, the people of Sevenoaks, a once sylvan mountain town, are complicit in their own victimization by the novel's anti-hero, Robert Belcher. Belcher is a primordial capitalist whose local schemes and stock manipulations catapult him into the world of Wall Street and the Fifth Avenue nouveaux. He treats actual enterprises, his railroads especially, like playthings, as trophies and as devices designed to achieve ends having nothing to do with their ostensible purposes. They are a means for personal gain and social aggrandizement. In behaving this way he defiles an official morality that honors work and its products. Worse, he adopts the moniker 'General' to celebrate his ascension. This is a kind of sacrilege in a country that still reveres the martial valor of the Civil War. Even more deplorable is the sad fact that the people of Sevenoaks at first take this masquerade seriously, cringing before Belcher's apparent omnipotence.

Masquerade and deceit are at the heart of Belcher's transgression. Not only is he indifferent to the underlying purposes of his industrial enterprises, his nefarious machinations are mainly devoted to concealing an original sin. It turns out that his wealth is founded on an ingenious mechanical invention he stole years earlier from an unsuspecting partner who ended driven insane by Belcher's perfidy – here the tale parallels Jay Gould's, whose fortune was allegedly the result of swindling the senior partner in a tannery business, who then went on to commit suicide. Ever since, Belcher has been busy covering up the deed, gilding his reputation with honorifics like 'General' and armoring himself against possible attack through philanthropic acts. He finally decided (like Daniel Drew, not coincidentally) to endow a theological seminary bearing his name. He was nothing if not cynical about the whole charade, confiding in his factotum from Wall Street:

> Well, all our sort of fellows patronize something or other. They cheat a man out of his eye-teeth one day, and the next you hear of them endowing something or other or making a speech to a band of old women . . . That's the kind of thing I want . . . I behold a vision. Close your eyes now, and let me paint it for you. I see the General – General Robert Belcher, the millionaire – in the aspect of a great public benefactor. He is dressed in black and sits upon a platform . . . There is speech-making going on, and every speech makes an allusion to 'our benefactor' . . . The General bows. High old doctors of divinity press up to be introduced. They are all after more. They flatter the General; they coddle him . . . They pretend to respect him. They defend him from all slanders . . . I look into the Religious newspapers, and in one column I behold a curse on the stock-jobbing of Wall Street, and in the next, the praise of the beneficence of General Robert Belcher . . . I believe I'm pining for a theological seminary . . . It's a theological Seminary or nothing'.[36]

In the end virtue triumphs. The people of Sevenoaks are restored to their senses. Belcher's cheated partner, who has borne his martyrdom without rancor, recovers his sanity as well as his property. A decorous Victorian universe, upstanding and demure, offended by Belcher's flash and ostentation, is put right again. The whole arsenal of the genteel literary tradition – its sentimentality, moral righteousness, stereotypical plot devices, improbable coincidences, Natty Bumpo-like characters of virginal rural simplicity – are mobilized to slay something monstrous that may originate in the deep recesses of the human heart, but has found a nurturing habitat in Wall Street.

If Belcher was a recognizable hybrid of Gould and Drew, *Honest John Vane* recalled for readers all the ugly circumstances surrounding the Credit Mobilier scandal. The novel, published in 1875, was written by J. W. De Forest and was first serialized in the *Atlantic*, just as all the Washington high-jinks surrounding the Union Pacific were being exposed to the light of day. De Forest had been a Captain in the Union Army stationed in Louisiana. *Honest John Vane*, like all of his novels, decried the collapse of public and private behavior that followed the high-mindedness of the War. De Forest hated New York particularly as the epitome of materialist decay, and described its bourgeois patricians as 'half Carthaginian and half Sybarite'.

The novel was an allegorical *Pilgrim's Progress* in reverse, its hero falling from a state of quotidian decency and diligent effort to his destruction, driven there by the temptations of ease and wealth as well as by conspiratorial design. Vane starts out a self-made manufacturer of ice-boxes. His fellow townsfolk, staunch Republicans all, hold him in high esteem and elect him to Congress. But there he falls into the clutches of one Darius Dorman, a creature whose villainy is foretold by his shadowy occupation as a man of general business, a broker of deals. Dorman advises 'Honest John' that once elected, 'Don't go into the war memories and the nigger worshipping; all these sentimental dodges are played out. Go into finance.' That's the way, according to Dorman, 'to make politics worth your while'. Once in Washington the lesson is reiterated by a veteran Congressman, Simon Sharp, who confirms Dorman's insight: 'Capital will become your friend. And capital – ah, Mr Vane, there's the word! My very blood curdles when I think of the power and majesty of capital.' Sharp is a visionary who foresees that the whole land, its people and resources, 'is the servant and I had almost said the creature, of capital . . . Capital is to be, and already is, its ruler. Make capital your friend. Do something for it and secure its gratitude.'

Just before he succumbs, 'Honest John' experiences a last prophetic insight. Watching the common corruption enveloping Congress, he senses that 'this great Republic which brags of its freedom is tyrannized over by a few thousand capitalists and jobbers.' But then the tidal wave of stock deals and fraudulent subsidies washes over him, abetted by the covetousness and social ambition of his wife, Olympia.

Casting his bought-and-paid-for vote for 'the Great Subfluvial Tunnel', 'Honest John Vane' is lost in a sinkhole of public depravity and private greed.[37]

Satire took the place of this rather dreary moralizing in *The Gilded Age*. With Colonel Sellers (like 'General' Belcher's, the Colonel's rank was self-appointed), Twain and Warner invented a character of native charm, a walking-talking catalogue of homespun American foibles. His gargantuan exaggeration was mated to a remarkable faith in his most preposterous schemes. His bombast, softened by the quaint accents of a Southern courtesy already the butt of Northern condescension and ridicule, made him laughable but not repulsive. The pure enthusiasm with which he managed to envision luxury amidst the most miserable discomfort perfectly mirrored the perverse optimism and ingenuous ardor that seemed to mark the national character.

Underneath the belly laughs and intoxicating silliness, however, the novel still pivoted around the moral distinction between the industry and perseverance of Philip Starling, a New England engineer and avatar of science and due diligence, and the scams and speculations of men of power and wealth busy pilfering the public purse. It has little to do with industrialization per se, but rather treats undertakings like railroads as the newest frontier for the devilish talents of the plunger and his confederates. The whole panoply of business-political chicanery is on display: larcenous promotions of railroads and railroad construction, real-estate jobbery, mulcting of Federal agencies, conspiracies to 'corner' the market, and the bribing of legislators with shares. Congress is a caricatured stock market: votes are traded, lobbyists resemble stock promoters, congressmen behave like brokers hiving into factions of bulls and bears battling for Federal booty. The Colonel feels at home here, while Phillip Starling finds Washington 'the maddest Vanity Fair one could conceive'.

Casualties pile up as the novel rolls along. Democracy is disgraced, workmen are left unpaid and abandoned to their fate, intimate feelings among lovers, family, and neighbors end up prostituted or silenced. Twain wanted Sellers to fail in his wacky schemes: 'it would be clearly a crime against society to make him a "success" in life, since this would be to add another Jay Gould to the world's burdens.'

In real life, Twain was his own Colonel Sellers: an incurable speculator with a special knack for failure. At various times he took fliers on timber and mining claims, a steam pulley, a new means of marine telegraphy, an engraving process, some invention vaguely like a television, a self-adjusting vest strap, and the Poise compositor, on which he managed to lose $200,000. His mordant tale about *The Man That Corrupted Hadleyburg* was a metaphor for his own credulity and ruin in the panic of 1893. When he wasn't falling prey to his own credulousness, however, Twain trained a gimlet eye on the 'great game' that preoccupied a society whose motto might well have been *Mundus vult decipi – ergo decipitatur* ('the world wants to be deceived, let it therefore be deceived'). His coruscating wit captured the essence of the era's crony capitalism: 'I think I can say with pride that we have legislatures that bring higher prices than any in the world.' He once described a mine as 'a hole in the ground with a liar standing next to it'. That summed up his attitude to Wall Street.[38]

While Twain in many ways stood outside the 'genteel tradition', William Dean Howells straddled it. For a time he accepted the social Darwinian defense of market society. Those certitudes began to crumble with the panic and depression of 1873, and were effectively destroyed by the sentencing to execution of the Haymarket anarchists, which outraged his sense of fairness. Influenced variously by Leo Tolstoy, the primitive communalism of the Shakers, Henry George's single-tax panacea, and by the liberal theologian W. D. P. Bliss, he became a convert to the Social Gospel, which supplied an ideological fix for his ambivalence. Notwithstanding his fondness for New England gentility, in novels like *The Rise of Silas Lapham* and *A Hazard of New Fortunes* Howells discarded much of its sentimentality and evasive reticence in order to face the social ugliness of the Gilded Age.

In Howells' imagination, the stock market and speculation more generally played the role of the snake in the garden, poisoning the well of the Protestant work ethic, weakening its ethos of self-discipline and modesty. Silas Lapham falls because he can't resist the stock market's temptations. Speculation, for Silas, is a kind of initiation rite into the nether world of modern capitalism, enabling him to shed his identity as farmer, miner, and manufacturer of paint. Only after heavy losses and in desperation does he rediscover the merits of an ancient prohibition and thereby recover himself: 'I always felt the way I said about – that it wasn't any better than gambling and I says so now.' [39]

Such revelations were neither common nor easy to come by, however. As Howells notes in *A Hazard of New Fortunes*, the successful speculator and financier represented 'the ideal and ambition of most Americans'. What went on in Wall Street was like some withering disease. If Silas was unwittingly seduced, Jacob Dryfoos, the tragic patriarch of *Hazard*, is fully attuned to 'the game', subscribes to the harsh orthodoxy that likens business and life itself to an unforgiving game of chance, and epitomizes the Wall Street ethos that honors money, 'especially money that had been won suddenly and in large sums.' Dryfoos, not unlike Silas, started out as an upright, public-spirited, conservative family farmer, a forbidding but devoted husband and father, a practical man of time-tested, rock-solid conviction, 'crude but genuine'. Drawn away, despite his earnest resistance, by the lure of neighborhood land and oil speculations, he changes. He becomes a kind of vampire, sucking the poetry out of life, measuring everything, in his cold-eyed, merciless way, by its rate of return – even the fledgling magazine he invests in to occupy his wayward son and prevent him from becoming a womanish preacher or literary scribbler. Utterly captivated by the Wall Street spirit, he lets his son, Conrad, feel his contempt for the first issue's meager earnings: 'I made that much in half a day . . . I see it made in half a minute in Wall Street sometimes.'

Here was the true hazard of new fortunes, as Jacob 'came where he could watch his money breed more money and bring greater increase of its kind in an hour of luck than the toil of hundreds of men could earn in a year. He called it speculation, stocks, "the Street", and his pride, his faith in himself, mounted with his luck.' Here is where Dryfoos suffers an 'atrophy of the generous instincts'. Traits once heralded as the businessman's virtues are alchemized into their opposite: on the Street 'sagacity' becomes 'suspiciousness', 'caution' turns into 'meanness', 'courage' into 'ferocity'. Dryfoos stares into an abyss devoid of all moral meaning:

> When he broke down and cried for the hard-working, wholesome life he had lost, he was near the end of this season of despair, but he was also near the end of what was best in himself. He devolved upon a meaner ideal than that of conservative good citizenship . . . the money he had already made without effort and without merit bred its unholy self-love in him.

For wealth earned 'painfully, slowly, and in little amounts he had only pity and contempt'. Groveling before those on the Street who'd accumulated even more than he, he harbored a secret resentment and 'respected not them, but their money'.

Howells himself draws back from the edge of this precipice. The novel ends on a note of Christian hope about the future, about the possibility of class reconciliation and moral redemption. But the author's ambivalence has a hollow ring. Jacob's son Conrad, who has enlisted in the Social Gospel movement, is killed in a vain attempt to head off a violent clash between striking streetcar workers and the police. Ravaged by anger, guilt, and remorse, yet out of joint with his son's callow mission of peace, Jacob dimly recognizes the high cost his Wall Street addiction has exacted but is powerless to do anything about it. The reader senses a tug-of-war between Howells' lingering sentimental piety and a foreknowledge of some gathering storm.

Among the novel's gallery of memorable characters, one gives voice to this premonition. Lindau is an embittered, aging German immigrant – probably a refugee from the 1848 revolution – who is convinced to write for the magazine by its new editor, Basil March, himself a refugee from Brahmin Boston. A cantankerous revolutionary, dogmatic in disposition, Lindau is hardly shy about his hatred for the rich. He lost a hand fighting for the Union, and he confides in Basil the bitter significance of that sacrifice, in light of all that's happened since the War:

> Do you think I knowingly gave my hand to save this oligarchy of traders and tricksters, this aristocracy of railroad wreckers and stock gamblers and mine slave drivers and mill serf owners? No, I gave it to the slave; the slave – Ha. Ha. Ha. – whom I helped to unshackle to the common liberty of hunger and cold.

Basil is too insular, too confined by the genteel drawing room, to take this indictment seriously, dismissing it as 'tasteless' at worst, a harmless rhetorical effusion at best. But by the end, when Lindau's leg is amputated in the same savage violence that killed Conrad, Basil is affected by the old man's foreboding that the overbearing power of Wall Street and the trusts will destroy any semblance of a society in which people reap their just rewards. It darkens the mood of pious hope he clings to. Reluctantly, he's driven to the dreariest prognosis:

> And so we go on, pushing and pulling, climbing and crawling, thrusting aside and trampling underfoot; lying, cheating, stealing;

and when we get to the end, covered with blood and dirt and sin and shame and look back over the way we've come . . . I don't think the prospect can be pleasing.[40]

A Hazard of New Fortunes was published in 1890. Wall Street, as Lindau had spied, was poised to embark on a new phase of its career. Once the frontier terrain of financial badmen, it was about to become the organizing center of the nation's industrial economy. Howells' novel grappled with the moral psychology that drove men like Gould and Vanderbilt, Dryfoos figures writ large. *A Hazard of New Fortunes* was genteel America's most nuanced indictment of that species, produced just as their swashbuckling days were drawing to a close.

The new men of Wall Street, the Morgan men, promised to restore order and rationality – to the Street, and to the economy over which they presided in a kind of benevolent dictatorship. The Street would achieve a significance earlier generations of Americans could never have anticipated. It would become the magnetic center of the country's political and social tensions, an abiding cultural preoccupation where once it had been a curiosity. Some would welcome and others abhor the new order. But everybody was forced to wrestle anew with matters of social hierarchy, political power, and even the question of fate and moral action.

PART TWO

The Imperial Age

5

The Engine Room
of Corporate Capitalism

The great fire that ravaged New York's financial district during the arctic winter of 1835 razed seventeen city blocks and could be seen as far away as New Haven. Hordes of suddenly dispossessed businessmen cast about for a savior. Those lucky enough to be policy-holders of the Aetna Fire Insurance Company were especially fortunate. The company made good on every claim. It was owned and operated by Junius Spencer Morgan, patriarch of a colonial-era family of inherited property, European education, and patrician fidelity. Its honorable perseverance in the heat of that horrific conflagration ensured its special reputation on Wall Street. The name of Morgan would be trusted for ever more.[1]

Three quarters of a century later, in 1913, Spencer's son J. P. Morgan died in Rome. It would be hard to exaggerate the reaction to the passing of this investment banker. Poets rhapsodized about his incomparable mastery as he entered the 'heaven of the strong'. His 'giant frame', his 'iron will' were forbidding:

> And yet those eyes so quick to blaze
> And sear, were no less quick to bless . . .
> Keen to acquire, to spend, to give,
> Ardent in all things, small in none.

Like Shakespeare, according to Pulitzer's *New York World*, Morgan had managed to 'bestride the world like a Colossus' – this from a paper not shy about censuring plutocracy. Not to be outdone, the *New York Tribune* depicted him in a front-page drawing by Boardman Robinson as a 'Titan'. Ex-presidents, business rivals, and senators praised his public service and patriotism. King Victor Emmanuel and

Kaiser Wilhelm sent flowers. Pope Pius X pronounced him a 'great and good man'. Secretary of State William Jennings Bryan, who had spent a career reviling Morgan and people like him, conceded the banker's pre-eminence, ordering the American ambassador in Rome to offer the embassy for the funeral service.

Newspapers around the country gave Morgan credit for the spectacular economic development of the nation over the last generation. Superficial observers might have mistaken his preoccupation with the stock market for a money fetish, but that was short-sighted. Rather, editorialists concluded, he was a preternatural banker for whom the ticker tape recorded not dollars won and lost, but a 'panorama of rushing trains and roaring factories'. Financial operations that when performed by lesser men might leave one queasy were cleansed of any impurities in his presence. 'Character First was His Philosophy' declaimed a *New York Times* headline. In a world of imperial rivalries, Morgan had been the nation's champion, 'who first opened the doors for American participation in world financial undertakings'. Meticulously detailed recreations of the deathbed scene (pulse rate, temperature, heroic medical interventions, guards at the deathbed chamber), accompanied by the most solemn descriptions of the New York funeral, lent the moment a sacred air. Cablegrams poured in from all over the world, not just from the rich but also 'pathetic messages from poor persons who have benefited from Mr Morgan's munificence'. Eulogists recollected the stations of his public ascent: reclaiming the country's railroad network from the internecine competition and bankruptcy of the 1880s; bailing out the Cleveland administration during the embarrassing gold crisis of 1895; rescuing the country from economic disaster in the panic of 1907; lifelong philanthropy on behalf of religion, education, and the arts. *Harper's Weekly*'s lapidary encomium declared him a 'matchless upbuilder of properties . . . a faithful trustee of billions . . . full of faith in his country and his fellow man . . . a Christian, staunch, devoted, and untiring in fidelity to Christianity . . . Above all a true patriot . . . a lover of power, but not of money'. In the cool and somber stillness of Trinity Church, Rev. William Wilkinson rendered a final judgment: 'J. P. Morgan will rank in the history of this Republic as one of the greatest men God has yet raised up to serve it.' [2]

Millions at home and abroad dissented violently. They considered Morgan an ogre, a man of unmatched villainy. Why they felt that way is another story, one well worth telling. First, though, his lionization compels attention.

Morgan was utterly lacking in anything resembling the common touch. He was disdainful, secretive, and imperious. The democratic spirit was alien to his being. Unlike the four horsemen of Wall Street's buccaneering youth, who all rose from obscurity, Morgan's ancestry was steeped in the cosmopolitan sophistication of Knickerbocker New York, Brahmin Boston, Rittenhouse Square's Philadelphia: the 'right' clubs and the best schools. He hailed from a place very few of his fellow Americans were ever likely to visit, much less reside in, an exclusive zone apt to arouse plebeian suspicions in a culture saturated in the mythos of its anti-aristocratic birthright. While he could be as implacably ambitious as the Wall Street colossi of the previous generation, the source of his public esteem was very different from theirs. When they weren't being denounced for it, men like Drew, Fisk, and Vanderbilt excited the public with their feats of financial derring-do, their vulgar incivility, their appetite for risk, and their flouting of the law and social convention. Morgan, on the other hand, was all decorum. Prudent, circumspect, risk averse, well-bred, he was a practicing patrician. The Wall Street that preceded him was renowned for its speculative abandon and celebration of the free-for-all. Its heroes were lone desperados stalking the financial badlands of Wall Street. They were in the American grain. Morgan stood outside it. He hated speculation. He hated the free market. And for these very un-American attributes and attitudes he was revered by a sizeable number of his fellow citizens.

It was the fire of 1835 all over again. What his eulogists sought to memorialize was not so much his wealth (he turned out to be considerably less rich than most people assumed, although many times a millionaire) or even the breadth of his financial reach and enterprise. Those were merely tokens of something less tangible, namely that precious sense of trust left behind by a lifetime of service, patriotism, and fidelity.

Morgan presided over a select circle of white-shoe investment bankers and lawyers, a diligent but lugubrious group who exercised enormous power over the whole economy thanks to their financial, professional, and social ties to the corporate leadership of industrial America. Many would double as financiers and corporate executives, combining patrician hauteur with a newer ethos of managerial profes-sionalism. For a long generation, lasting through World War I and arguably even beyond that to the Crash of '29, this Wall Street-cen-tered milieu came as close as anything before or since to constituting America's ruling class.

Instead of plunging into the free-for-all marketplace, the white-shoe brigade earned its spurs by rescuing the economy from the nearly dis-astrous consequences of competitive capitalism gone haywire. This work of reclamation began with the railroads and spread from there into every key industrial sector, where Morgan and his confederates erected a kind of private economic command center. It sternly, if infor-mally, prohibited self-destructive competition, rationed out invest-ment capital, and centralized the management of the economy in ways repugnant to the devotees of laissez-faire. For this work of discipline and deliverance, undertaken in the spirit of the benign autocrat, Morgan was widely admired as the 'Bismarck of the railroads' and the 'Napoleon of American finance'.

Despite these epithets, the world that Morgan made was probably despised by more people than applauded it. Plenty of artists decried its moral transgressions. Even the soberest members of the white-shoe fraternity gave in to bouts of inebriated speculation. The assumption that the governance of the economy and nation might safely take place in bank and corporate boardrooms was challenged by fellow members of the patrician elite – not to mention angry agrarians and the disaf-fected urban middle and working classes – who insisted on the priori-ty of the public realm.

Nonetheless, Wall Street lent the whole political economy a coher-ence and direction it would otherwise have lacked. Its political weight was undeniable. Morgan was an imposing and emblematic figure. The social order he epitomized was extraordinary in the history of Wall Street and the country. Americans have always regarded class distinc-tions as an insult to the national mythos, and the notion of a ruling class has been particularly obnoxious. Yet during the age of Morgan there was what might be called a suspension of disbelief. Without a scintilla of democratic credibility, in open repudiation of the shibbo-leths of the free market, a social caste of highly questionable creden-tials was tacitly granted the right to rule. The Morgans, after all, knew how to deal with fire.

*

In his 'calendar' of mordant observations, that master of the acidic aphorism, Pudd'nhead Wilson, put it like this: 'October. This is one of the peculiarly dangerous months to speculate in stocks in. The others are July, January, September, April, November, May, March, June, December, August, and February.' Pudd'nhead, Mark Twain's misunderstood object of small-minded, local ridicule, had nothing at all in common with the estimable investment banker, Henry Lee Higginson; nothing, that is, except this lowering sense of chronic economic vertigo. Looking back at the thirty years from 1868 to 1898, Higginson remembered the 'constant frights and uncertainties, which gave gamblers a great chance if they could guess right, and which kept decent men in doubt and often in agony'. In his own affairs, Higginson probably experienced few 'doubts'; even less likely that this head of one of the country's venerable and most powerful financial institutions suffered any 'agony'. His was a more disinterested reflection on the anxiety plaguing a business elite, and many others besides, as they lived through the perpetual upheaval and crises of late nineteenth-century competitive capitalism.[3]

Between 1870 and 1900 there were more months of economic contraction than of expansion. More than half those years were times of depression or recession. Beginning with the collapse of Jay Cooke's bank and the panic of 1873, the economy began a long stagnation seasoned by ruinous competition and financial scares. Profits and prices, together with interest rates, commodity prices, and the yield on capital tended to decline. Intense competitive pressures demanded heavy capital expenditures in large-scale fixed investments that were all too quickly outmoded by rivals, leaving everybody on or over the brink of bankruptcy. There was no easy way out. Most industrial capital was illiquid, bound up in solely owned companies or partnerships, not in readily tradable stocks and bonds, so the captain of industry was likely to go down with his ship whether voluntarily or not.

Social violence heated up this already febrile atmosphere. Armies had to protect Vanderbilt's New York Central in 1877 and Jay Gould's western railroads in 1885 as determined strikers stopped the trains. Riots by the unemployed, in New York's Tomkins Square in 1874 and in dozens of smaller cities all through the depressed 70s, were met with mounted police. Young men of the haute bourgeoisie cut short vacations in Saratoga, Long Branch, and Newport and rushed back to New York in fancy carriages to take up arms in the socially select

Seventh regiment, ready to defend property and good order against urban insurgents who William Vanderbilt believed 'belong to the communistic classes'. Then there was the Haymarket explosion in '86, the shoot-out at Carnegie's Homestead works in 1892, and the deployment of Federal troops to break the Pullman strike of 1894. For every national confrontation of this sort there was a score of less visible encounters in small industrial towns and cities all across the country. Proliferating third parties – Greenback-Labor, Workingmen, Populist – portended a political restiveness not seen since the years leading up to the Civil War.[4]

Wall Street lived and died according to the fever chart of this roller-coastering economy. And it did not take a skeptical outsider to notice how prone the whole system was to misdirected undertakings, duplication of facilities, gluts, and panics. Henry Clews, who loved the Street and periodically shared his fascination with the reading public, nonetheless filled his 1888 account, like Scheherezade, with a thousand and one tales of mini-panics, peculations, defaults, defalcations, contractions, foreclosures, frauds, corners, and dozens of ingenious ways to bull, bear, trap, gun, and otherwise manipulate the value of securities so that they lost any connection to the intrinsic value of the companies they represented.

The Street exploded in speculative excitement as soon as the interminable slump of the 1870s came to an end. Gamblers in railroad securities were buying on paper-thin margins, and the deep pockets of returning European investors quickened the game. Henry Villard, the German-born son of a Supreme Court judge who had married the daughter of abolitionist champion William Lloyd Garrison and become a war correspondent, soon turned himself into a warrior of a different sort. He became notorious for organizing 'blind pools' to seize control of roads like the Northern Pacific, with the sole purpose of saturating its stock in water and quickly cashing out. Even Clews acknowledged that the norm in railroad financing was 'intrinsically rotten', resting on 'fictitious capital' which in turn was a 'serious source of social and political disorder'.

This post-depression binge was over again in a flash. A new round of fierce competition, especially among the railroads, signaled yet another collapse. Even while the economy sputtered and stalled, tracks were laid like mad; seven thousand miles a year through the early 1880s, the greatest ever. Much of this consisted of 'blackmail railroads' running parallel to each other, slashing rates to the bone in an insane game of competitive chicken. It wasn't going to take much to burst this bubble, and this time, in 1884, the delusion was punctured by a national embarrassment. Ulysses S. Grant, not at all a rich man since leaving the presidency, had been gulled into a fraudulent investment scheme run by his guileless son, Ulysses 'Buck' Grant, Jr and a wily Wall Street speculator, Ferdinand Ward, a man of 'insinuating and plausible demeanor'. When the firm failed, the rest of the Street followed and the nation's favorite general was left bankrupt. The scandal was saddening and demoralizing since, as *Harper's Weekly* editorialized:

Such painful disclosures . . . have produced a national insecurity which extends beyond the speculators in Wall Street to the great community of staid people who have more or less money to invest. Such events . . . are a public disaster, because they shake faith in the personal honor upon which all business proceeds.[5]

In 1893, all remaining faith was shattered when the economy imploded yet again. As always, the first bad omens traveled cross-country on steel rails. Mighty-looking systems were actually rickety affairs, bloated by debt and grossly over-capitalized, easily toppled by the slightest downturn in production or financial contraction. During the first few months of the new Cleveland administration, the Philadelphia and Reading, the Northern Pacific, the Union Pacific, the Santa Fe, and that perpetual basket-case, the Erie, all failed. Soon firms controlling over a third of the nation's railroads went belly-up. Imagine the impact: a single one of these great rail networks employed more people and invested more capital than the Post Office or the entire US military.

Predictably, the stock exchange panicked. An incipient market in industrial securities went into hibernation, waiting for the economy to warm up again. The selling spree caused the New York banks to call in loans from around the country. That summer alone, 141 national banks closed their doors; the number doubled by the end of the year. Sixteen thousand businesses went under, and even elite universities like Harvard and the University of Chicago laid off faculty as enrollments dropped. More seriously, thousands were left homeless, tramping the roads searching for work while twenty per cent of the labor force could find none. During a single torrid week in July 1893, 607 children under the age of twelve months died in New York tenements. Stories of starvation, death from exposure, and the most dismal despair became commonplace as the Depression dragged on and on. Five years of this anguish were more than enough to make the case against the free market and its cyclical derangements. The system simply didn't work.[6] Even a magazine like *Harper's Weekly* which, by the 1890s, had become a loyal defender of the Street against its host of critics (a Morgan loan had bailed out Harper and Brothers as it teetered near bankruptcy), could acknowledge the damage done. It likened the speculators to lawless gunslingers, train robbers, and drunken cowboys out West, and to an equally unruly assortment of 'negroes, bullies, and tippling colonels' in the South.[7]

There were plenty of efforts to find a way out of the maelstrom the Street had caused, whether driven by economic self-interest or ameliorative visions of social harmony. Informal arrangements to limit or eliminate the epidemic of deadly competition began in the 1870s. Each failure sparked some new piece of ingenuity. There were gentlemen's agreements among all sorts of businessmen – shipbuilders, manufacturers, merchants, railroaders – to limit production, segregate markets, and standardize prices. Under pressure these acts of good faith proved factitious. When they fell apart, sturdier looking fabrications took their place. Trade associations popped up everywhere, bound together by covenants to prevent internecine competition (and also to present a united front against labor organizers). 'Pools' promised to penalize breaches of faith by those too weak to resist the chance to gain a step on their rivals. But the fines were scanty and not easily enforced.

'Trusts' next attacked the underlying problem by proposing to wipe out the existence of independently competing companies altogether. Entrepreneurs traded in their birthright for certificates of ownership in the trust, ceding all prerogatives of control to the creators of the trust. Most trust certificates were not traded publicly, however, and required no brokers or underwriters. They were deeply secretive affairs, open to fraud and manipulation, and were greeted with great wariness. Beginning with Standard Oil, a whole galaxy of raw materials and processing industries, and basic commodity producers – everything from sugar refining to matches to linseed oil, all notoriously and viciously competitive sectors – found themselves trustified during the 1880s and 90s. However, the Interstate Commerce Act and the

Sherman Anti-Trust Act, while not the most robust or lucid pieces of legislation, left these devices for stifling the free market in a kind of legal limbo. Something more all-embracing was required, something that might remove all ambiguity about acting 'in restraint of trade' and so escape the reach of the law and ideological censure.[8]

Anthony Comstock founded the Society for the Suppression of Vice in 1872. Its mission was to wage war on sin, particularly 'pornography' which was, the Society believed, polluting the minds of the young, especially in the cities. How else to preserve the moral fitness of America's future leaders? J. P. Morgan, along with other blue-blood philanthropists, shared Comstock's alarm and sense of trusteeship (although not necessarily his self-righteousness) and signed on as one of the Society's original sponsors. Even at this early point in his long career, the banker displayed a regard for social order and an aversion for unlicensed individualism. For Morgan, the wild gyrations of the free market amounted to a kind of economic pornography. Railroads, the playthings of conscienceless gamblers and sociopathic entrepreneurs, stood at the center of this depravity.[9]

After the dust had cleared and the depression of the 1890s slowly lifted, newspapers and magazines reported widely on the reorganization (or as most of them called it, the 'morganization') of the nation's railroad systems. Many of the bankrupted lines were up and running again, but were now supervised by a handful of great Wall Street banks – Drexel, Morgan and Kuhn Loeb in particular – which in the past had provided only money and advice. In effect, Wall Street went to war against itself. Those elements of the Street that for years had found the roads an endlessly enticing plaything of speculative wilding now confronted the censure of a Wall Street establishment that sought to conserve and guard the nation's main mode of transportation.

'Morganization' had its beginnings twenty years earlier. Jay Cooke's collapse left Drexel, Morgan & Co. and Kuhn Loeb as the chief, although by no means the only sources of railroad capital and credit. At first the roads tried colluding. A New York State investigation in the late 1870s revealed, despite denials by railroad officials, that the big lines had conspired to fix prices and arrange kickbacks and rebates to customers; they'd done so 6,000 times in the first six months of 1879 alone. These were, however, mercurial agreements. To survive crises and defaults, railroads needed capital to reorganize, while in boom times companies increasingly turned to the big investment banks to finance expansion. That was Morgan's opening.

Morgan first demonstrated his extraordinary talent for financial discretion by quietly liquidating a vast sum of William Vanderbilt's holdings in New York Central stock (about $250 million) without unleashing any of the customary hysteria on the Exchange or provoking a bear raid that would have seriously damaged his client's interests. He emerged from the mini-panic of 1884 as the Street's top dog, determined to put an end to the deadly railroad wars which had so destabilized the stock market to begin with. Morgan, and especially his partner, Charles Henry Caster, thought like financial architects, designing reconstructed railroads, grounding them in a sound assessment of their real needs and the real commercial potential of their underlying assets. Like many architects, they met with considerable resistance from those they were supposedly serving.

To begin with, a group of railroad executives, representing the warring Pennsylvania and New York Central systems, gathered on board Morgan's yacht, the *Corsair*, where he extracted an agreement to respect each other's designated spheres of influence. This 'pool' fell apart soon enough; Morgan tried and failed again in 1888. The rail kings were a wilful bunch. George Roberts, president of the Pennsylvania Railroad, who suffered through these bullying peace negotiations, resented Morgan's 'very strong language, which indicates that we, the railroad people, are a set of anarchists'.[10]

Clearly these arm's-length concords weren't worth the paper they weren't written on. To address the linked problems of over-capitalization and competitive overkill, Morgan and other white-shoe bankers sought to reorganize and consolidate the industry. They would thereby dry out the old, watered stock, replace old bonds with new ones at lower rates, merge rival lines, eliminate redundant ones, dismiss old management, and, most important of all, plant their own representatives on the boards of directors to ensure against any renewed outbreak of self-destructive competition. By the end of the 1890s, a sixth of the country's railroads wee under Morgan's control. For these acts of financial re-engineering, Morgan and his confederates were dubbed, in a kind of jokey admiration, 'Pierpontifex Maximus and his Apostles' and 'Jupiter Morgan and his Ganymedes'.[11]

Of course, none of this meant that there would be no further wars between the railroad barons, or between Morgan and his investment-banking colleagues, as the 'Northern Pacific Panic' of 1901 showed. When Edward H. Harriman and James J. Hill began wrestling for control of the Northern Pacific, it was the concluding chapter in a national saga begun well before the Civil War that might with some justice be called 'How the West Was Won'. Winning entailed opening up this terra incognita through extraordinary feats of exploration and engineering as well as exploitation and extermination; opening it up both to settlement and dispossession, development and predation. Hill, a Canadian, built the Great Northern as a rival to the Northern Pacific. When the road was forced into receivership in the crash of '93, Hill allied himself with Morgan. They plotted to seize control of both roads and merge them. Their rival, Harriman, was a rather graceless, sickly, and cold-blooded character who'd spent years as a cautious if shrewd Wall Street broker. Morgan called him a 'two-bit broker' – but he was also an uncommonly intense and combative one. And he nourished imperial dreams, first of a hemispheric rail and water transportation network extending through Mexico and Central America; later of a global one that would run lines through the mainland of Asia. He never tired of talking about 'frontiers to conquer'. But even when he formally departed Wall Street to take up empire-building, he never ceased to be a man of the Street – though at this time, the distinction was blurry at best.

Harriman was a man of considerable financial as well as railroading skill, and he controlled a cluster of major roads to the south of Hill's. Between them lay the Chicago, Burlington, and Quincy, a vital link to Chicago and the markets of the East. Over this the two sides came to blows. Hill and Morgan, thinking they had acquired control of the Burlington, were ambushed by Harriman. He covertly bought up a controlling interest in the Northern Pacific, aided and abetted by Morgan's white-shoe rival, Kuhn Loeb, led by Jacob Schiff and by the long-time underwriter of his grander projects, James Stillman, president of the Rockefeller-controlled National City Bank. Morgan responded in kind. The Exchange reacted in pandemonium as Northern Pacific stock rocketed from $115 per share to $1,000 per share in a matter of days. 'Big men lightly threw little men aside' – there were rumors of suicide and a Troy businessman, faced with ruin, boiled himself alive by jumping into a vat of hot beer. Short-sellers were trapped and forced to liquidate, causing the market to implode until Morgan and Schiff declared a truce.

A plotline like this could have been, indeed was invented long before the age of 'Morganization'; it contained all those familiar elements of 'hoggishness' and piratical public irresponsibility for which it was roundly condemned even in the most conservative business-minded circles. But it was the denouement that was different. Peace was pronounced not by the railroad barons, but their financial overlords. And to ensure it lasted both companies were folded into a new entity, the Northern Securities Company: one so large in capitalization it would discourage any future take-over effort – so large in fact that a few years later the Federal courts would order it dissolved under the Sherman Act, though that's another story. Peace was declared in a form deliberately designed to establish a 'community of interest'. After the panic subsided, Schiff wrote to Morgan offering his firm's services to 'do anything in reason that you may ask or suggest so that permanent conditions shall be created which shall be just to all interests and not bear within them the seeds of future . . . disaster'. This was intended also to reassure a widening investing public that the ruinous railroad raids of the 1870s and 80s were over.[12]

Only the Eastern investment-banking community, Wall Street above all, could mobilize the capital resources it took to carry off these grand consolidations, not only on the railroads, but across broad stretches of American industry afflicted with the same infectious competition. The art of financial dirigisme ultimately orchestrated by Morgan and Schiff in the Northern Pacific case exemplified a new economic order of things, the eclipse of the free market by a private-command economy ministered to by the lugubrious men in the white shoes.

Wall Street's ascendancy had an air of inevitability. As the size and scope of American industry expanded, so did its need for new sources of investment capital. Firms also wanted to escape the legal limitations inherent in the partnership form of company organization. Though some gigantic combines like Standard Oil were financially self-sufficient, and deliberately avoided reliance on outside sources of capital and credit, most could not afford that degree of independence. For the first time in its history Wall Street began to service the capital needs of business in general. This was particularly necessary for high-tech industries like electricity which required vast investments in fixed capital to get started, but it was hardly restricted to such industries: 'going public' also appealed to consumer-products combines like Proctor and

Gamble, for example. New clusters of investment banks and broker-ages emerged to service the capital needs of light industry and mass-consumption-oriented firms. Legal developments helped the process: New Jersey's passage of an incorporation law in 1889, allowing a holding company to control subsidiary firms, was decisive, opening the legal floodgates to an economy-wide merger movement. Integrating once-independent firms into single corporate entities escaped the Interstate Commerce Act strictures against railroad pools and, with some greater ambiguity, the Sherman Act's prohibition against trusts in restraint of trade.

These consolidations at first seemed highly risky and were undertaken by a band of Wall Street promoters who thrived on high-stakes speculations. Men like John 'Bet-a-Million' Gates, the 'Silver Fox' James R. Keene, and Herman Sieleken, the 'Coffee King' were in it for the short term, losing interest once the stock was unloaded at less attractive prices on the broader investing public. Soon enough, however, white-shoe firms became the chief underwriters of these new industrial combines as they proved their sea-worthiness. Firms like Kidder Peabody, Lee, Higginson, the Belmont interests, Seligman Brothers, together with some of the largest commercial banks like Chase National Bank, National City Bank, First National Bank, and others were attracted of course by the considerable profits to be made in servicing these transactions. But they were in it for the long haul as well: they liked the way these corporate restructurings suppressed the destabilizing forces of market competition by ending the existence of free-standing firms. Their very giantism would function as a powerful disincentive to any new entrants contemplating a challenge. For these reasons, the securities issued to finance these corporate reorganizations would not be subject to constant devaluation as price and other forms of commercial warfare chipped away at profit rates. Indeed, in strictly economic terms, what was being consolidated and protected were property-titles to existing means of production rooted in the first phase of the industrial revolution – coal, railroads, iron, steel, raw materials, foodstuffs. What was distinctly discouraged were heavy investments in new and risky technologies, vast plant expansions, or new railroad trackage: anything that might undermine the financial viability and stability of what was already in place.[13]

In industry after industry – coal, steel, shipping, and so on – the great investment-banking houses came to deploy enormous economic power as they rationed out available supplies of scarce capital and undertook to reorganize the core of the nation's productive apparatus. Whatever wider social and political leverage they exercised as a result, the respect and fascination, even reverence which they inspired in others was grounded in this extraordinary economic command. While hardly absolute, it was a privately deployed power more coherent, centralized, and disinterested than anything that preceded or followed it. More than pure financial remorselessness, it operated as a kind of tutelary trusteeship. Sophisticated, highly centralized, and specialized administrative bureaucracies were installed to ensure the durability of these colossal corporate combinations.

In a feudal-like system often described as 'relationship banking', heads of houses would vouch for the moral as well as the financial worthiness of prospective clients. Client corporations in return would be expected to pay fealty to their banking benefactor and welcome its managerial guidance. Law firms staffed by upper-class Protestant Republicans trained in a tiny handful of designated law schools attached themselves to one or another of the Street's pre-eminent 'houses', and made sure frictions between them were dealt with discreetly and in a gentlemanly spirit. A genteel clubbiness thus dampened the impact of competitive rivalries, which lived on but under watchfully suspicious eyes. The grandest undertakings were managed by syndicates of select bankers and brokers, carefully arranged beforehand in a hierarchy of pecuniary participation. In turn, they funneled their corporate offerings to an inner circle of trusted commercial banks, trusts, brokerages, and life-insurance companies, to which they were not infrequently related through the cross-fertilization of their boards of directors.

A small circle of investment banks run by a handful of men, all of whom knew each other socially as well as professionally, comprised a kind of economic central committee. They were trusted implicitly: though their deliberations were conducted in great secrecy, that cloistered confidentiality was a source of trust rather than suspicion. Free of any outside scrutiny, Morgan and his confrères had privileged access to information about the country's leading industrial institutions, leaving everyone else with a psychological stake in their unique trustworthiness.

While Wall Street's pre-eminence was never in doubt, the charmed circle encompassed Philadelphia's Fourth and Chestnut Streets,

LaSalle Street in Chicago, and Boston's venerable State Street. There was a stark arithmetic to their power. Morgan's bank, for example, held substantial interests in Bankers Trust, Guaranty Trust, and the National Bank of Commerce. Morgan and his partners held seventy-two directorships in forty-seven major corporations, including such brand names as GE, USS, and International Harvester. Together Morgan, National City, and First National held 118 directorships in thirty-four banks and trusts with $2.6 billion in assets; not to mention their place-holdings in ten insurance companies with assets of $3 billion, along with 105 directorships in thirty-two rail transportation systems comprising $11 billion in capital investment. This network of institutional as well as personal connections – George Perkins was, for example, a partner in the Morgan bank and chairman of the New York Life Insurance Company's finance committee – formed a community of investors assuring each other's businesses a reliable supply of capital. Whether or not this power was used conspiratorially and malevolently would be an issue for public debate for years. Its existence, however, was undeniable.[14]

A century of economic free-for-all vanished in a decade. Between 1895 and 1904, 1,800 firms, centered especially in the capital-intensive, mass-production sector, were swallowed up in corporate mergers. Here again Morgan pioneered. In 1892, he assembled a number of smaller electrical firms into General Electric. The capitalization of the merged firms quadrupled, and competition in the industry was sharply curtailed. The 1900 Census recorded seventy-three industrial combinations valued at over $10 million; ten years before there had been none. By 1909, a mere one per cent of all industrial firms accounted for forty-four per cent of the value of all manufactured goods. The hundred largest industrial corporations quadrupled in size. In 1909, a mere five per cent of all manufacturing firms employed sixty-two per cent of all wage-earners. Similar trends marked the extractive and distributive sectors. Through the 1880s, with the singular exception of the Pullman Palace Car Company and some large coal-mining operations (all offshoots of the railroad industry and so exceptions that proved the rule), not a single industrial corporation was listed on the New York Stock Exchange. The largest in the world, Carnegie Steel, was privately owned. Already by 1897, even though the Depression had yet to lift, there were eighty-six such companies, each capitalized at over one million dollars. A thousand industrial companies were listed on the Exchange by 1901. Yet there was no Dow Jones industrial average until the mid-1890s; no Moody's manual of industrial securities until 1900. By 1903, the merger movement had revolutionized the economy.[15]

The age of the publicly traded industrial corporation had dawned, mainly in response to price competition and the crisis of capital immobility and illiquidity. It began hesitantly, however: at first, the white-shoe underwriters issued only preferred securities and bonds, not yet trusting to the vagaries and risk-quotient of common stock. Moreover, to assure their control, they reserved a healthy portion of the newly issued corporate stock for themselves. But the scale of these operations was unprecedented; consequently, no matter how tightly controlled, these great consolidations trailed in their wake precisely the sort of uncontrollable speculative booms Morgan and his colleagues sought to rein in.

Soon enough, most such doubts faded away as bankers and a widening investing public came to trust the new corporate order. Between 1898 and 1904, over $4 billion in new securities underwrote this process of industrial amalgamation. Flush with capital resources, these gargantuan businesses were best fit to survive. They had ample funds for research and expanded productive facilities; in turn they became much more attractive and liquid as investments. Morgan left his stamp of approval on the whole transformation, sanctioned the mergers, underwrote the securities, appointed the management, and profited handsomely, taking home about twenty per cent of the value of these new securities. The universe of individual investors nearly doubled between 1900 and 1910, growing from 4.4 million to 7.4 million people. Swelling confidence in the reliable quality of this paper in turn accelerated the merger movement, which of course generated fresh pools of marketable stock. In a favorite conceit of the moment, the market was believed to have safely traversed the seas of 'intoxication', landing safely on the shore of 'sobriety.'[16]

An atmosphere of quiet, understated omnipotence settled over the Street. One contemporary observer remarked:

There is an air of omniscience as if nothing unexpected could ever happen. Doors do not slam, men walk softly upon rugs, voices are never lifted in feverish excitement over profit and loss . . . There is a feeling of space. Ceilings in a banking house are higher than ceilings anywhere else . . . one gets the feeling of space from the manners of the person in uniform who attends to the noiseless opening and closing of the main portal and asks people what business they have to enter.

New York became the unquestioned headquarters of a network of industrial and financial concerns whose scope and perspective were truly national, even international. Indeed, the 'morganization' of the economy was what would enable the US to seize the leadership of the world economy from the still family-based, private capitalism of their British rivals. It was an elite no longer circumscribed by the familial or regional interests of particular industries or the mercenary provincialism and near-sightedness of an earlier Wall Street. Devil-take-the hind-most chaos was to be subjected to a civilizing surveillance, even a kind of planning, albeit one that excluded the faintest hint of public supervision or direction.[17]

Authority without popular mandate or formal responsibility suited the temperament and workaday style of this ascendant elite. Bound together by codes of clubby confidentiality, collective self-interest, gentlemanly mutual regard, and an immense self-confidence, they presumed their own infallibility and civic-mindedness. Most if not all of them stood outside the formal political system. If they held public office at all, it was commonly an appointed not an elected one. But their influence over matters of domestic and international economic policy was nonetheless weighty. Indeed, on certain occasions the Morgan circles came close to running a shadow government, or at least a parallel, private syndicate exercising de facto public power. It was no surprise that they shunned the turbulence and unpredictability of the democratic arena. What is more mysterious is that a sizeable segment of their fellow citizens was prepared to acknowledge their pre-eminence and defer to their prerogatives.

Three primordial motivations help account for this remarkable abdication: disgust, weakness, and fear. Over the course of a generation, rapacious financiers, speculators, and industrial predators had shamelessly connived with political middle-men, machine demagogues, and venal elected officials to loot the public purse. Gilded Age democracy devolved into the politics of the bordello. Disgusted, people reacted in many ways. A genteel milieu of 'good government' reformers sought to purify the process. Their road to integrity was a narrow one, leading away from the economic self-seeking and cultural cacophony of universal suffrage. Wall Street patricians, including J. P. Morgan, Jacob Schiff, and Joseph Seligman, together with venerable members of the old Anglo-Dutch establishment, energetically encouraged this flight from mass politics. In New York they sponsored amendments to the city charter that would restrict the franchise and the powers of popularly elected officials, on the theory that the city, like the corporation, ought to be governed by its propertied stakeholders. Converts among the urban middle and upper classes were not hard to find.[18]

If the stench given off by crony capitalism and outright kleptocracy discredited popular government, that government's own self-evident institutional weakness was a goad to simply ignore it. Once the extraordinary circumstances of the Civil War ended, executive powers in Washington and at every other lower level of political sovereignty declined drastically. Government possessed few administrative mandates and an even frailer apparatus with which to enforce them. The judiciary exerted great influence, but judge-made law was most immune to the popular will. Meanwhile, Congress deferred to the party machines which composed it, and, particularly in the 'millionaires' club' of the Senate, to the incontestable will of big business. Most of all, political authority remained captive to that imperishable ideological legacy of the Revolution: that government governed best which governed least. There was a defect in this formula, however, even for those unmoved by the democratic persuasion. Weakness in the face of economic chaos and social upheaval was a recipe for disaster, a frightening prospect no one could ignore, least of all the new Wall Street regency.

Fear had gripped American society at least since the mass insurrections during the great railroad strikes of 1877. In the immediate aftermath, Morgan's father sent a $500 contribution to help rebuild the Seventh Regiment Armory to help put down any future such rising. Militias like the Seventh regiment, staffed and funded by people like Morgan and Vanderbilt, were in effect armed versions of the rich men's social clubs. They tended to efface the distinction between the disinterested authority of the state and the caste prerogatives of the haute bourgeoisie. Rumors circulated that the railroad financiers had become so disaffected by the democratic experiment that they were hatching plots to make ex-President Grant king, or maybe first consul.

In 1886, during his face-off against the Knights of Labor when labor militants shut down his western roads, Jay Gould boasted that he could hire one half of the working class to kill the other half. This was more than a sadistic case of robber-baron braggadocio; it was a chilling reminder of how antagonistic relations between the social classes had become. People like Rhode Island Senator Nelson Aldrich, Rockefeller's factotum in the upper chamber, made no attempt to conceal his loathing of the mob: a bestial 'horde', a 'swarm' motivated solely by a sense of grievance and animal passion.[19]

Laissez-faire was coming to mean perpetual economic crisis; popular turmoil, in turn, only aggravated economic disarray and social anxiety. All the revulsion, contempt, and fear came to a boil in the 1890s. It was then that the Morgan dispensation first displayed its political sangfroid and sense of trusteeship.

Panic and depression, beginning in 1893, rapidly depleted the Federal government's gold reserves and jeopardized the national credit. This monetary crisis unfolded as populists and plutocrats squared off in the most lethal social and political confrontation since the Civil War. A fifth of the labor force was out of work and Coxey's Army of the unemployed was marching its way to Washington. Meanwhile, the serried ranks of the rich and well-born marched down Fifth Avenue in a 'Sound Money Parade'. In such a context, technical questions of fiscal soundness could not help but turn into matters of state, pitting East against West, the silver of agrarian virtue against the gold of economic sanity.[20]

President Cleveland, despairing of help from a Congress gridlocked by the forces of free silver and gold, turned to J. P. Morgan. As early as the 1870s, the Morgan bank had come forward as an American equivalent of Europe's 'haute banques' or court banks, like the Rothschilds or Baring Brothers. The House of Morgan developed the will and capacity to service Washington's financial needs, freeing it of its customary reliance on Europe. Morgan had not only helped finance Cleveland's recent presidential campaign, but Cleveland had actually worked for a Morgan-affiliated law firm (Bangs, Stetson, Tracy, and MacVeigh) in the interregnum between his two presidencies. Deeply conservative himself on economic matters, the President's inner circle included trusted members of the financial elite – men like corporate financier, William C. Whitney, who candidly shared with Cleveland the prevailing view: 'the impression of you got by the people is that you do not appreciate their suffering and poverty . . . and have your ideas formed by Eastern money powers, etc . . . the usual twaddle.'

'Twaddle' or not, Cleveland knew who his friends were, and as Washington's gold predicament grew acutely embarrassing in 1894, he asked them to come to the rescue. Along with August Belmont, Jr, Morgan formed a syndicate to market US government bonds in Europe (and to New York trust and life-insurance companies as well) thus replenishing the government's perilously depleted stock of gold. The underwriting was carried out expertly, relying on Morgan and the syndicate's foreign connections and impeccable reputation for financial prudence. Everything went so well that the operation would be repeated several times over the next couple of years.

Was this an act of public service or self-service? Opinion varied extravagantly. Some treated it as a capitulation to the 'money kings of Wall Street'; even the respected financial columnist, Alexander Dana Noyes, thought it a harsh and merciless piece of profit-taking. Others, however, celebrated Morgan as the country's 'savior'. Naturally, Cleveland mounted his own post-facto defense, describing the work of the syndicate as an act of patriotism, sarcastically concluding that although Morgan and Belmont might be 'steeped in destructive propensities' and 'sinful schemes', he, for one, was proud to have joined with them at a time of national peril. For millions of middle-class folk driven to distraction by the morbid state of the economy and the specter of political anarchy, restoring the credibility and stability of the nation's credit was essential. Whatever the verdict of public opinion (and warring views continue into the present in the most recent biography of Morgan), the bail-out of 1895 signaled a new demarche. From that moment on, Wall Street presumed a political stature nowhere anticipated in the constitutional scheme of things.[21]

A brief but legendary encounter has come to epitomize this sense of entitlement. Teddy Roosevelt ordered the Justice Department to pursue anti-trust action against the Northern Securities Corporation, the holding company underwritten by Morgan and Schiff which had emerged out of the railroad turf wars between Harriman and Hill in 1901. When Morgan got wind of what was afoot, he went directly to the President in a state of some irritation, to explain that 'If we have done anything wrong . . . send your man to my man and they can fix it up.' An appalled chief executive said nothing, allowed the government's suit to proceed on to its successful dissolution of Northern

Securities, and took due note of this matchless expression of Wall Street imperiousness. Morgan's premise was simplicity itself: the government was no more or no less a sovereign power than the consortia of great investment banks, each ruling in their appropriate sphere, dealing with each other as peers. James Hill once characterized the President as a kind of chairman of the board of 'a great economic corporation known as the United States of America'. In fact, this was probably an overly polite rendition of what the Wall Street elite truly believed: namely, that the government was in fact a second-rate power whom they intended to control.[22]

This overriding self-assurance was born out of the great electoral triumphs of 1896 and 1900, when William McKinley's Republicans banished the silver heresy and crushed its insurgent agrarian constituency. Free coinage of silver, in the dominant view, was code for inflation; inflation in turn fed the craving for credit; unlicensed credit in turn encouraged debt, speculation, and the whole maelstrom of entrepreneurial self-destruction, ruinous competition, panic, and depression. Defeating this madness was the highest priority for the financial consolidators of American industry, and rationing access to capital through a centralized, gold-denominated system of credit and investment was the right prescription to achieve it. So it was that the white-shoe world invested heavily in McKinley's campaigns. They joined with Mark Hanna, Cleveland industrialist, Rockefeller associate, and Republican king-maker, in flooding the country with 'sound money' propaganda of the most sophisticated and persuasive sort. Morgan created something called the New York 'guarantee syndicate' to make sure there was no run on gold during the election season. An assistant Treasury secretary noted 'the curious spectacle of the US finances being controlled by a committee, of which J. P. Morgan is chairman and the majority of whom are Hebrews, while the Secretary of the Treasury sits, practically powerless in his office'. Out on the hustings, pamphlets, cartoons, ads, and editorials competed for the minds of the public. The insidious 'prejudice . . . against everything upon the money question which emanated from the vicinity of Wall Street' had to be extirpated. Through a combination of reasoned argument and unreasoning fear, they convinced multitudes that civilization itself was at stake, that 'massed capital – without which civilization cannot advance, or even exist – is to be dispersed, scattered, redistributed and the sole source of industrial sustenance destroyed.'

Victory meant staffing the McKinley administration with friendly faces, as well as shoring up control of the US Senate, which even by the late 1880s was widely thought of as a 'millionaires' club' each of whose members, in William Allen White's view, 'represented something more than a state, more even than a region. He represents principalities and powers in business. One Senator . . . represents the Union Pacific Railway System; another the New York Central, still another the insurance interests of New York and New Jersey.' Victory also meant the Gold Standard Act of 1900 which would purportedly put an end to the speculative extravagance and recklessness of marginal producers chasing a pipe dream. Victory in 1900 was so exhilarating, confirming as it did the abject capitulation of the enemy, that it ignited an air-borne bull market on the Street, the second highest in the Exchange's history. Above all, victory was an elixir that seemed to provide public validation for Wall Street's soaring self-esteem. [23]

Thus intoxicated, one could easily lose perspective, which is what happened when Morgan's impolitic candor roused Roosevelt's ire. But in practical terms, Morgan was not far off the mark. A series of discreet 'gentleman's agreements', arrived at in confidence between the investment-banking community and appropriate functionaries in the Justice, Commerce, Interior and other interested departments, became the means whereby the desires and deliberations of corporate-financial overseers were translated into public policy. Morgan's wide-ranging interests were watched over and promoted by trusted lieutenants like Elbert Gary representing US Steel and George Perkins acting on behalf of International Harvester. They shared proprietary information on a need-to-know basis with executive branch officials, consulting on possible legislative alternatives, all the while protecting against surprise attacks either through Congress or the courts. Roosevelt's newly created Bureau of Corporations in the Commerce Department would, for example, lay out whatever reservations it might have about the behavior of some particular combine and allow the corporation to clean up these technical transgressions without fear of prosecution.

These agreements amounted to a quasi-private/quasi-public form of regulation, allowing for the private resolution of disputes between the great corporations and the government without exposing them to public debate. The idea, as the *Wall Street Journal* editorialized, was to strike the proper 'balance between the government and the corporations'. The amendments to the Sherman anti-trust law embedded in the Hepburn Act of 1908, which allowed the executive to distinguish between 'good' and 'bad' trusts, were cooked up in just this manner. The initial testiness between the Street and Teddy Roosevelt gradually eased.[24]

'Gentlemen' were assumed to put self-interest to one side in pondering matters of public import. This conceit was less disingenuous than it might seem. The 'morganizers' genuinely sought an end to the economic and social chaos inevitable in a system devoted to the pursuit of the narrowest self-interest. One might say, fairly, that it was in their corporate self-interest to achieve that end; moreover, that some of them at least adopted an even more general view, one that identified the national welfare with their own dispassionate, statesmanlike efforts to guide the country towards economic integration, efficiency, and ordered progress. This was a credible enough fiction to maintain an image of Morgan, for example, as a kind of social umpire and cabinet secretary without portfolio.

The bitter anthracite coal strike of 1902 captured the antimonies. The relations between miners and owners were marked by pure hatred. In perhaps the most infamous utterance of employer arrogance and tyranny, George F. Baer, speaking for the mine-owners, declared that the rights and interests of the laboring man would be best protected 'not by labor agitators, but by the Christian men to whom God in his infinite wisdom has given control of the property interests of the country'. Most of the striking companies were captive mines controlled by Morgan-run railroads like the Erie and the Reading. The mineworkers well knew who pulled the strings and composed this ditty to the tune of a contemporary popular song, 'Just Break the News to Mother':

> Just break the news to Morgan that great official organ,
> And tell him we want ten per cent of increase in our pay.
> Just say we are united and that our wrongs must be righted,
> And with these unjust company stores of course we'll do away.

Yet despite this aggravated class consciousness, Morgan, along with E. H. Harriman, 'paramount symbols of the bloated plutocracy', came forth to mediate the strike, standing alongside the President himself as figures of disinterested sagacity, seeking an equitable resolution of the crisis. In fact Morgan's reputation as a guardian of social harmony preceded the coal strike: a 1901 cartoon entitled 'Hold on Boys' depicted Morgan sturdily separating two embattled figures ready to come to blows, one with his top hat and cane, the other with his lunch box and tool-kit lying on the floor nearby.[25]

Morgan's apotheosis came in 1907. Even now, the financial panic of that year is recalled every time there's a major blow-up on Wall Street, usually with the following interpretation. Those were the days when a single man held the fate of the nation in his hands. He acted with courage, decisiveness, and cool deliberation when all around him dignified bankers and brokers were frozen with fear, paralyzed into fatal inaction, or protecting themselves in a cowardly fashion, no matter the consequences. If Morgan had not intervened to quarantine the rapidly spreading contagion, had he not by the force of his personality and his enormous moral capital as the country's trusted if unofficial central banker, compelled his fellow financiers to pony up the necessary capital to save key tottering institutions, there is little doubt a severe and protracted crash would have befallen the country; indeed the world, since the Tokyo and London markets plummeted on the news from New York and foreign investors relied on Morgan's recommendations and judgments. His heroics were evidence of his extraordinary power and his extraordinarily disinterested deployment of that power. He was a government unto himself acting on behalf of all. Even New York City, in the person of Mayor George B. McClellan (son of the Civil War general) approached the syndicate to save the city from an embarrassing $30 million shortfall in its payroll. The syndicate obliged.

Bernard Berenson, celebrated art critic, writer, and the banker's chief adviser as he went about amassing one of the world's most impressive private art collections, struck a note of exaltation: 'Morgan should be represented as buttressing up the tottering fabric of finance the way Giotto painted St Francis holding up the falling Church with his shoulder.' Dissenting views – that the great banker had personally profited, that he might indeed have provoked the panic as a means to other mercenary ends – were dismissed as calumnies by the President, who was openly grateful. Roosevelt praised 'those influential and splendid businessmen . . . who have acted with such wisdom and public spirit' to accomplish what many were coming to believe ought to be a government responsibility.[26]

In the aftermath of the near catastrophe of 1907, it became customary for Morgan to work with his friendly rivals, George Baker of First

National Bank and James Stillman of National City Bank, to watch over the country's liquidity and money supply and steer its major banking institutions. They came to be known as 'the Trio', carrying out, in effect, the work of a private central bank. Monitoring such a vital artery of national well-being could not remain a strictly private affair for ever, though. The white-shoe ruling elite soon busied itself shaping the legislation everyone anticipated. So it was that in late November 1910, five men traveled to Jekyl Island, a secluded million-aire's retreat off the Georgia coast, disguised as hunters. In fact, Senator Nelson Aldrich (dubbed 'the boss of the United States' by Lincoln Steffens), Henry P. Davison of the Morgan bank, Frank A. Vanderlip of Rockefeller's National City Bank, Paul Warburg of Kuhn Loeb, and Harvard economist A. Piatt Andrew, had no intention of hunting. They were there as draftsmen, determined to put together legislation that would answer the call for public oversight over the nation's monetary system while preserving the prerogatives of Wall Street's trusteeship.

In the end, the Federal Reserve system emerged as a hybrid concoction, reflecting more than the views of the Jekyl Island duck-hunters. It allowed for a greater degree of public control over monetary affairs than they might have wished. Nonetheless, it marked a definitive moment in the evolution of the investment elite's career as a ruling class, translating their economic and social power into formal political authority, albeit imperfectly. Nor was it a provincial and selfish piece of legislation, but one rather conceived with the disinterested intention of keeping the whole social machine in good working order. As James Dill forecast back in 1900, 'industrial combinations are producing a new class of financiers, a new order of corporate men', prepared to assume the burden that went along with functioning as the general staff for the nation's political economy.[27]

Wall Street's 'new order' made itself felt in foreign affairs as well. Henry Adams was among the first to notice that the tidal waves of liquid capital flowing into the Street were the wherewithal of a new American independence from Europe and heralded the dawn of an imperial age. A great creditor nation, in perpetual search of new out-lets for investment and new markets abroad, naturally gravitated towards an imperialist style of diplomacy. Men like Elihu Root – McKinley's Secretary of War, a political *éminence grise* since the 1860s, legal and political adviser to Morgan, Whitney, Thomas

Fortune Ryan and other noteworthies on 'the Street' – pursued a grand vision. Root and his confrères imagined a kind of globalized 'morganization', a trustified, consolidated, centralized world order of enduring stability. The ambassadorships in Paris, Berlin, Tokyo, and London were filled by men long affiliated with one or another of the dominant investment banking groups, men who shared this perspective.

Beginning with the Roosevelt regime and continuing through the 1920s, one initiative of this global strategy extended American power and influence to less developed regions of the world, in Central and South America particularly. Shaky governments in desperate need of capital received private bank loans with the proviso that they also welcome fleets of financial advisers empowered to install modern financial and administrative practices. It was presumed that such hothouse arrangements, incubated by Wall Street experts, would give birth to expanded trade and higher living standards for all, not to mention a more reliable and democratic political environment in which to conduct business. In places like the Dominican Republic, Haiti, Liberia, Nicaragua, and Venezuela, the denouement was not always so neat. Now and again the Marines had to pay a visit to settle things down, and fledgling democracies gave way to military dictatorships. Still, these expeditions were not conceived as naked grabs for power, but rather as statesmanlike efforts by a financial-political elite to replace corrupt and rapacious interests with enlightened ones.

Morgan's bank, along with Kuhn Loeb, National City, and First National Bank led the way in reaching out to the rest of the world; Morgan even arranged a loan as far away as China in 1909. Indeed, he personally involved himself in delicate forms of private diplomacy, so, for example, his energetic efforts to fashion an international shipping trust (International Mercantile Marine) entailed a serious threat to German and British commercial suzerainty and military security. With Roosevelt's blessing Morgan actually met the Kaiser and King Edward VII, together with ministry and State Department officials, to soothe ruffled feathers while relentlessly promoting America's newest manifest destiny. Root, and Adams' old friend, John Hay, lent their support to this Wall Street demarche. The great banker not only lent money to both sides in the Russo-Japanese War, he also lent his services to the mediation efforts of the Great Powers, and then helped bail out the Tsar's bankrupt government when the war ended. London would remain the center of the financial universe until World War I, but the global balance was already tilting West.[28]

Wall Street's forays into both domestic politics and international relations were presumptuous and disinterested at the same time. They were the product of a ruling stratum which saw itself and was seen by others as the bearer of order, reason, and gentlemanly cooperation. An oligopoly of wealth-producing financial über-institutions manned by patricians, if left undisturbed by government meddling, could be trusted to do the right thing. Even their most lavishly appointed social get-togethers had a soberer purpose: 'here too were enjoyed unsung but productive . . . gatherings which helped those in authority to bear the burdens and carry on the tasks of their offices . . . the very walls whisper of the state secrets they have heard, of decisions that have helped mold the political fate of the world.'[29]

As Wall Street occupied the commanding heights of the economy and began to direct matters of state, its more public-spirited members stepped forward as missionaries of high culture and exemplars of a distinct social style. Though this role scarcely appealed to the Street en masse – many were more than content simply to count their money and play with it – a critical number turned their attention to the realm of cultural capital.

High society in New York remained a remarkably provincial, clannish, and cloistered habitat well into the nineteenth century. Edith Wharton's *The Age of Innocence*, for example, is practically an anthropological account of how the old Knickerbocker patriciate armored itself against the gale-force winds of change, blowing in particularly from Wall Street. Social ritual, architectural style, residential geography, interior decoration, marriage arrangements, and dynastic hierarchies all groaned and cracked and finally gave way under the strain: New York society was forced open. Less adaptable elements of 'old New York' fell into social oblivion. Others with a stronger instinct for survival fused, sometimes reluctantly, with the rising plutocracy, as society became infinitely more fluid. In Wharton's novel, Julius Beaufort, a bon vivant and lecherous banker whose enormous wealth wins him a provisional pass into the inner sanctum, is mercilessly cast out once his Wall Street peculations are exposed. But within a generation his daughter marries her way back into the charmed circle. The vector of the future was unmistakable.

The epicentre of these changes was a massively squat building that came to be known all over the world as 'the corner'. 23 Wall Street, catty-corner to the New York Stock Exchange and Federal Hall, was where the House of Morgan presided. Short and dense, towered over by heavily ornamented skyscrapers, it was a widely acknowledged metaphor of the bank's discretion, self-confidence, and quiet power. 'The corner' actually began life as a bank run by George Peabody in London, which the Morgan family acquired in 1838. As well as the bank itself, Peabody's legacy included a serious commitment to cultural uplift: he was probably the first major cultural philanthropist to hail from Wall Street. Praised by both Victor Hugo and William Gladstone for doing God's work, Peabody was responsible for the creation of the Peabody Institute in Baltimore, the natural history museum at Yale, the archaeology/Egyptology museum at Harvard, and an educational fund for emancipated slaves in the South.

For many years Peabody was practically unique. As *The Nation*'s E. L. Godkin remarked, 'Plenty of people know how to get money; but not very many know best what to do with it. To be rich properly is indeed a fine art. It requires culture, imagination, and character.' In a sense, then, 'morganization' as a cultural undertaking entailed the arduous process of converting a plutocracy into a socially conscious aristocracy.[30]

After the Civil War, institutions of high culture were often treated first of all as arenas of invidious distinction and social emulation. This was especially true of the newly wealthy, growing numbers of whom lived lives in and around Wall Street that were consecrated to the purest form of money-making. For their families, wives in particular, money was supposed to purchase an entrée into all the exclusive preserves – clubs, civic groups, social gatherings, honorific posts – of the ancien regime, preserves jealously guarded by the Anglo-Dutch elite. Skirmishes broke out along the lines of social exclusivity: perhaps the most decisive battle was fought at the Academy of Music.

Throughout the mid-nineteenth century the Academy represented the epitome of Knickerbocker clannish elitism and cultural pretension. Its eighteen boxes were reserved for that caste's most lordly families. As the ranks of the nouveaux swelled, as their fortunes dwarfed those of their social superiors, the number eighteen came to seem a cruel mockery of their ambitions. Not only was the old guard determined to hold the line at eighteen, but when the truly astronomical sum of

$30,000 was offered for one of those precious chambers, they closed ranks and refused to sell to someone lacking in pedigree. If such déclassé types – in this particular case the offending parties were William and Maria Vanderbilt – wanted to hear the country's finest singers, they could sit in the orchestra stalls.

Thus was born the movement to found the Metropolitan Opera, whose opening in 1883 signaled a triumph of sorts for this emerging industrial-financial class. A fair number of the notables responsible for this act of social secession hailed from Wall Street or its environs, including Morgan, William Rockefeller, Jay Gould, George F. Baker, and William C. Whitney. The new opera house bore the birthmarks of its money-minded parentage. Its facade included rent-producing stores and apartments. Its fare included Wagner, then much in vogue in America, performed by European artists who could be had on the cheap. The exterior was shockingly ugly, but the interior catered to the patrons' cravings for status and pomp, with terraced hierarchies of boxes arranged in an ascending order of plushness. Opening night was a spectacular social success, at which, according to one discomfited critic, 'The Goulds and Vanderbilts and people of that ilk perfumed the air with the odor of crisp greenbacks.' By 1885, the British impresario of the old Academy of Music, Colonel Mapleson, had abandoned the struggle: 'I cannot fight Wall Street,' he dolefully admitted.[31]

Success in breaching the old guard's redoubts proved both liberating and contagious. The same crew of financiers and industrialists started the New York Symphony Orchestra to challenge the New York Philharmonic (a German musical cooperative) and opened Carnegie Hall in 1891, with Tchaikovsky as the guest of honor. Philanthropic financiers chartered wholly new terrain too: Morgan devoted his greatest energies to the Museum of Natural History, the New York Botanical Gardens, the Cathedral of St John the Divine, the Harvard Medical School, and especially to the Metropolitan Museum of Art.

The museum opened its doors in 1880 and from its inception paid its respects to its Wall Street benefactors. Although ostensibly open to the public, the fact that it closed on Sundays when working people might have used it made clear its snobbish inclinations. Its halls were initially filled with conventional works from private collections and thereby enlarged the public cultural presence of this aspiring financial group of patrons. Moreover, acts of collecting and display were infused with the spirit of Wall Street; works of art were candidly assessed as forms of investment, both speculative and secure. Sanctioned masterpieces were sought in part because their market value was not expected to vary wildly. J. P. Morgan's holdings of art and artifacts from dozens of cultures, living and dead – including porcelains, paintings, tapestries, medieval armor, illuminated manuscripts, rare books, enamels, ivories, and ancient bronzes – was admired all over the world. He bought in bulk. His acquisitions amounted to an attempted cornering of the art market. By the late 1880s, Morgan had become the decisive behind-the-scenes figure at the Met, staffing its board of trustees with his colleagues from the Street, shaping even its acquisition strategy, which showed a decided preference for historical and romantic landmarks in the evolution of world civilization. These were, after all, prudent purchases for a milieu that took seriously the aesthetic aphorism of Wall Street's Henry Clay Frick: 'Railroads are the Rembrandts of investment.' [32]

Inexorably, the social as well as the cultural grip of the old order loosened. Ward McAllister, High Society's most famous gatekeeper ('Butler to the "400"' and 'the world's greatest dude'), helped make room for rising circles of Wall Street grandees without entirely breaching the fortress of the elect. His ingenious plan was to unite the old crustacean dynasties of Knickerbocker New York with the 'swells', those still seeking a secure place but eager, quick-witted, and lavish enough in their entertainments to win acceptance. That way, society would gain a material solidity while excluding the flashiest and most uncouth profiteers. (The 'Social Register' was itself a commercial enterprise which excluded advertisements but was for sale to merchants catering to this clientele.) As McAllister cunningly put the case: 'We wanted the money power, but not in any way to be controlled by it.' Pressure from Wall Street in particular inflated the '400' to something nearer 1,500 by the 1890s, and people derided society's 'watered stock'. But infusions of new blood continued. [33]

To break the Union Club's franchise on social anointment, Morgan began the Metropolitan Club, soon to be known colloquially as 'the Millionaires' Club'. Residential centers of elite life moved further and further uptown, away from the studied and self-effacing brownstone drabness of Irving Place and other traditional Knickerbocker locales. A whole world of arts and crafts grew up to decorate the interiors of the great chateaux along Fifth Avenue ('Millionaires' Mile') which sprouted like mushrooms to house and burnish the cultural reputations of the rising plutocracy. There, according to *Baedeker's*, the pastors from the St Thomas and Fifth Avenue Presbyterian churches 'preached to $250 million each Sunday'. Tiffany glass, fabrics, and wallpaper, La Farge glass, the sculpted detailing of Augustus Saint-Gaudens, imported porcelains, silver tiles, tapestries and furniture filled up the yawning physical space and satisfied the appetite for the insignia of social and cultural pre-eminence.

Like the great fortresses they often resembled, the monumental piles lining Fifth Avenue above Fiftieth Street were the architecture of a psychic and social armoring. They warded off the predictable anxieties of men and women who had rocketed to the top of the social pyramid in a single lifetime, often indeed in a single decade, arriving there without a scintilla of training in the arts of social dominion. History was pillaged indiscriminately in search of some embodied tradition, as each titan tried to simulate the appearance of a princely residence. Echoes of Renaissance France and Italy, of imperial as well as medieval Rome, of Fontainebleau or Azay-le-Rideau rebounded off the stony palaces designed in most cases by the plutocracy's architect of choice, Stanford White. His firm, McKim, Mead, and White, also served the Knickerbocker old guard – which was precisely the point. White made Morgan's Metropolitan Club in the likeness of an Italian Renaissance palace. Cheek by jowl, Romanesque, baroque, and rococo buildings jockeyed for position in a kind of architectural carnival. Ransacked pieces of European artistic history filled their insides. William Whitney (a maestro of stock manipulation on New York City's street-railway system) had Stanford White create a houseleum. It included gates taken from the Palazzo Doria in Rome, while its ballroom once graced a castle in Bordeaux; on the ceilings of its banquet hall and drawing room were Renaissance paintings from a French monastery, while Flemish tapestries lined the walls and medieval stained glass colored its windows.

Hunting after an identity became a full-time pastime. With one eye always trained on Europe, England especially, there erupted an epidemic of international marriages, an aping of French fashions (British ones for men), and a mimicking of the country life of the British gentry, including its immemorial addiction to horses and hounds. The great public halls erected at so much expense to endow the country with the trappings of cultural refinement eschewed American art forms and artists in favor of European paintings, European operas, European orchestras, singers, and conductors. Even the mammoth railroad stations of the nation's principal cities were modeled on the Roman baths. In a simulacrum of family rootedness, Tiffany's actually established a genealogical service, which supplied largely spurious family trees to mask the unpleasant odor of wealth acquired too recently and too suspiciously. Russell Sage and J. P. Morgan, among others, were members of the New York Genealogical Society, which helped to suggest a genetic inevitability to class presumption. Instant oldness, whether in the form of art, furniture, music, fashion, or yellowed manuscript, conveyed a totemic protection against the coruscating effects of the New World's commercially driven iconoclasm.

All this required significant financial support: not only the lavish costume drama of private life, but the whole edifice of museums, libraries, colleges, nature conservancies, concert halls, art galleries, and opera houses which came to comprise the infrastructure of American high culture. For old-stock aristocrats the pace was a killing one. Some managed to join the new order by shifting dynastic assets into railroad bonds, industrial stocks, and investment banks. Many were vanquished, left bitter or nostalgic. What could they do? 'Life here has become so exhausting and so expensive,' reported Frederic J. DePeyster of New Amsterdam vintage, 'that but few of those whose birth or education fit them to adorn any gathering have either the strength or wealth enough to go at the headlong pace of the gilded band of immigrants and natives, the "four hundred".' [34]

Around Wall Street, then, coalesced some rough and ready equivalent of a new American aristocracy. It was less somber than its predecessor, floating gaily on a sea of money, riding the avenues in graceful barouches, soon enough flying about the countryside in racing cars, lunching elegantly at Sherry's, gathering to drink and do deals in the 'Men's Café' of the Waldorf Astoria after the 3 p.m. closing of the Exchange, parading its diamonds in the great horseshoe at the Met, sending its male offspring to Harvard, to the Porcellian and AD clubs particularly, where they were prepped for a lifetime in the upholstered hush of Wall Street's classiest firms. It pleasured itself in walled-off gentlemen's clubs, patronized exclusive resorts, found amusement and challenge in a world of well-bred sportsmanship. But if this overnight patriciate was a sportier one, less weighed down by the insular traditions and claustrophobic rituals of 'old New York', it was also much larger, more heterogeneous and open, less easily fused around a core set of customs, beliefs, and social behaviors.

How cohesive, then, really was this new directing stratum? On the one hand, it is remarkable that this frenetic labor of confecting a tradition on the fly worked at all. Despite the unavoidable frictions, surviving elements of the old mercantile elite were integrated rather well, finding their way into the top echelons of the railroads, investment houses, and New York-headquartered national industrial corporations. All the genealogical fabulism, the clubby mutuality, and cultural philanthropy fashioned a compelling caste consciousness. The President of the New York Central, Morgan intimate and Republican Party power broker Chauncey Depew, thought of himself and his fellows as people of 'superior ability, foresight, and adaptability'. Everything from the inflection of the spoken word to the nuances of table manners reinforced this sense of apartness. The signs of class consciousness were also raw and unsubtle. Chief Police Inspector Thomas Byrnes used the newly perfected telephone to establish an invisible cordon sanitaire around Wall Street, declaring Fulton Street a 'Dead Line' south of which no criminal, or anyone considered unsavory, dared venture as the financial district was saturated with police and underworld informants. (In return, Jay Gould and other grateful denizens of the Street passed a steady stream of market tips to Byrnes.[35])

Yet once the Knickerbocker corps faded away, either cast out of or absorbed into the orbit of the financial-industrial plutocracy, nothing quite as culturally and morally coherent could replace it. Many of the newly enriched were content to retreat into their private sanctuaries, especially as the world outside their barrios became ever more alien and frightening. Moreover, New York was simply too big, too fast-moving, too mercurial for any one group to dictate the character of cultural and social life, as still remained possible for the Brahmins of Boston or the gentry of Philadelphia. Even the efforts of 'the 400', the 'beautiful people', to assume this leadership were taken only half seriously.

Some of Wall Street's most formidable figures – Morgan, Harriman, James Stillman, the Loebs, the Seligmans – were not even members either of Fashionable Society ('the 400') or Polite Society (the Knickerbocker remnant). The money pouring into and out of the Street made the body of the socially elect much too porous.

Sensational rivalries among contending dynasties and their retinues reflected the extraordinary turnover of elites in New York. While the city's largest fortunes at the beginning of the 1890s could be traced to a cluster of tangible trades like shipping, wholesale and retail trade, commission merchant, importing, food processing, and the like, ten years later the richest of the rich were described as 'capitalist', 'corporate director', and 'financier', suggesting the influence of Wall Street in turning concrete forms of wealth production into abstract acts of money-making. The sheer diversity of the city's business classes was daunting. There were old merchants and new manufacturers, new investment trusts and old mercantile banks, importers and exporters, real-estate and entertainment interests, all of them run through with ethnic and religious differences, divergent political and ideological desires. All this worked to undermine a unified outlook except on the greatest matters of national economic and social import: gold and Populism. Moreover, the incorporation of America over which Wall Street presided diffused the concentration of familial wealth, depersonalized it, diluted its ethnic and religious homogeneity, making it that much more difficult to fashion a coherent elite with a single-minded approach to social dominion or cultural patronage.[36]

It was all the more remarkable, then, that Morgan and his circle managed to establish a distinctive style of calming pre-eminence. If August Belmont was the nineteenth century's stereotypical Wall Street banker, Morgan assumed that role in the new century. They couldn't have been more different: Belmont presided over a nouveaux aristocracy that sought every occasion to parade its wealth and insatiable craving for pomp and pleasure; Morgan would have nothing to do with all that sybaritic showiness, the endless hankering after publicity, the gaudy narcissism and frivolous disregard of the public weal. He seemed largely immune to that 'Thermopylae of bad taste' that Edith Wharton mocked.[37]

The 'morganizers' attempted to marry old New York's sense of duty and Tory responsibility to a more worldly immersion in the great economic upheavals of the day. The hybrid that emerged fused a sense of class entitlement with *noblesse oblige*. Ethically it revolved around an ingrained sense of sacred honor, an implicit trust in the word of a gentleman. Culturally it took up the burden of civilizing (which, as Henry James saw it, meant in effect Europeanizing) its fellow Americans. It even took on a palpable physical presence: a look, a body language

marked by a certain hauteur, impeccable self-possession, stoic fortitude, languorous diffidence, and faultless grooming. All of this added
luster to a milieu already deferred to for its economic mastery and
trustworthiness.[38]

The panache, together with the prudence, made up an appealing brew.
Many found their old opinions about the Street transformed. But
'morganization' first of all incited legions of enemies. Some were rustic, poor, and boiling over with rage as they watched Wall Street
undermine their economic wherewithal and run roughshod over their
most cherished democratic sentiments. Others were cosmopolitan,
well-bred, and well-off, and steamed up by their own deep disaffection
from the world that Morgan was making. Listening to the voices of
these great naysayers is a way further to appreciate the Street's penetration into the recesses of the American psyche. Each in its own way
tried to rescue an older view of the good society they were convinced
the Morgan men would blot out for ever.

6

The Great Satan

The two most famous literary expressions of the American utopian imagination appeared practically at the same moment and took the country by storm. Edward Bellamy's *Looking Backward* was published in 1888 and was soon challenging *Uncle Tom's Cabin* and *Ben Hur* as the most popular book of the century. Two years later, readers were devouring *Ceasar's Column* by Ignatius Donnelly. The novels were profoundly similar and profoundly different. Each displayed the moral didacticism that inspired so much nineteenth-century fiction. Each cried out against the gross social inequities, economic chaos, and raw class antagonisms that marked the industrialism of the Gilded Age. Each invoked the ethical certitude and imagined social harmonies of small-town and rural America.

Yet in spirit *Looking Backward* and *Caesar's Column* were utterly at odds. Bellamy's was an upbeat book with a happy ending. His utopia, set in the year 2000, is a place of material abundance, universal enlightenment, and perfect peace. It became that way not by rejecting Gilded Age industrialism, but by extracting and reorganizing its most promising features: its scientific and technological achievements, its rationalism, and above all its aptitude for highly sophisticated and centralized forms of industrial and social organization. Looking backwards, Bellamy told his millions of readers in America and all over the world, it's easy enough to see that the solution to poverty, squalor, and social violence lay ready at hand. It was only necessary for the community as a whole to take over the nation's great productive and distributive enterprises, at present directed by selfishly motivated plutocrats. And then Christian fraternity would soon enough overwhelm individual greed.

Caesar's Column was an infinitely darker book, a dystopia really, whose vision of the future was almost, if not entirely, hopeless and bloody. A degraded and brutish proletariat faced off against an oligarchy of suppurating perversions. One side's horrific sadism was matched by the other's murderous fury in an Armageddon of fire and ash – but one in which it was impossible to distinguish the forces of good and evil. Indeed, that was precisely Donnelly's point. America's industrial and urban civilization, organized by a soulless financial cabal, had turned out to be an anti-civilization, a moral disaster. The New World was like the Old World, only worse, having achieved demonic perfection in the technical means of its own immolation. A saving remnant, escaped to a verdant island off the coast of Africa, represented the novel's frail and solitary hope for a second chance, a rebirth of the human family in the salubrious soil of mother earth.

Both novels inspired political activism. 'Nationalist' clubs formed themselves in towns and cities all around the country soon after *Looking Backward* appeared. Members felt inspired by its utopian vision to work towards an efficient and equitable metropolitan order, taking advantage of the highest technical and organizational discoveries but freed of the fatal distortions introduced by the concentration of financial and productive resources among a tiny handful of men. Bellamy's fundamental premise – that industrialism represented the royal road to social well-being – would be shared by numerous reformers and revolutionaries around the turn of the century. Urban middle-class progressives and labor radicals were scathingly critical of the world wrought by J. P. Morgan. But they remained certain that the great industrial machine over which he presided was a work of human genius which could be used far more democratically and humanely if the stranglehold of the 'morganizers' could be broken.

Seen from the parched prairies of the West and the exhausted cotton fields of the South, however, Morgan's empire seemed infinitely more alien and forbidding. Ignatius Donnelly was a veteran of agrarian politics. Long before he published *Caesar's Column*, he'd served as a Congressman from Minnesota, migrating back and forth between the Republican, Democratic, and various Greenback, Greenback-Labor, and populist parties. He was known far and wide as the 'Prince of Cranks' and the 'Apostle of Discontent'. Soon after his dystopia became a sensation, Donnelly authored the famous preamble to the People's Party (Populist) platform of 1892.

Populism lived in an atmosphere of apocalyptic dread and expectation. It was never the movement of myopic rustics it was sometimes dismissed as. But it imagined its enemy in diabolical colors and conceived of a fiendish financial conspiracy that unless thwarted would overturn the foundations of republican America: an older, better, mythic America. Agrarian rebels who decried subversive plots hatched on Wall Street were no crazier than Jefferson and Madison, who spied monarchist intrigues in Hamilton's wake. Populist economic reforms, once scorned as the schemes of cranks, later became the law of the land. Nonetheless, *Caesar's Column* captured a sense that a world was verging on extinction, that if finance capitalism was allowed to complete its work a whole way of life – small in scale, robustly self-reliant, modest, literate, egalitarian, and pious – would vanish from the face of the earth.[1]

All the highways of global capitalism found their way into rural America during the last third of the nineteenth century. Farmers were in dire straits, though not because they suffered from their own isolation. On the contrary, they lived at ground zero, where the incendiary energies of industrial, financial, and commercial modernity detonated.

The great trunk lines running east and west and into the deep South linked the hinterland to the marketplace on a scale no network of turnpikes and canals could ever approach. But as the iron horse was opening up the American West, it was also forging its way across the steppes of Canada and Russia and into the outbacks of Australia and South America. In no time at all, American homesteaders found themselves competing against family farms and latifundia from all around the world. The railroads which made this possible enjoyed a commanding position. But they were themselves so often submerged by bonded indebtedness and watered stock that they had the strongest incentive to squeeze their agrarian clients and customers.

The explosion in the world market for agricultural products also encouraged well-organized speculation in the prices of their future delivery. Commodity exchanges flooded with real and rumored information about the fate of far-off granaries, and conducted daily auctions of far more agricultural goods than were actually coming off the farm. By the turn of the century, transactions on the commodity exchanges of New York and Chicago's famous 'Pit' exceeded annual harvests by a factor of seven. Prices fluctuated wildly, often without apparent rhyme or reason. Nebraska wheat farmers certainly couldn't figure them out – nor, often enough, could the shrewdest initiates into the mysteries of 'the Pit', however they might delude themselves to the contrary.[2]

To survive this mercantile cyclone, farmers hooked themselves up to long lines of credit that ultimately stretched back to the financial centers of the east. Those lifelines supplied the wherewithal to buy the seeds and fertilizers and machines, to pay the storage and freight charges, to make ends meet while the plants ripened and the hogs fattened. Then came that happy day, perhaps, when all that 'wind wheat', traded and re-traded at fanciful prices, showed up as the real thing and the farmer found out what all his backbreaking toil was really worth. If the news was bad, then those life-support systems of credit were turned off and became the means of his own dispossession.

In a sense, the farmer was the looniest gambler of them all, wagering that he could master this intricate global game, pay off his debts, and come out with enough extra to play another round. On top of that he was betting riskily on the kindness of Mother Nature. But while professional gamblers spun the wheel voluntarily, the farmer had no choice. Instead he was drawn into a kind of social suicide. The family farm and the network of small-town life which it patronized were being washed away into the rivers of capital and credit that flowed toward the railroads and banks and commodity exchanges, toward the granaries, wholesalers, and other intermediaries that stood between the farmer and the world market. In this impersonal world of capital accumulation, the family farm remained a privileged way of life only in sentimental memory.

Malcontented farmers spread the blame for their predicament far and wide. Mortgage holders, grain-elevator operators, absentee landlords, railroad monopolists, farm-machinery manufacturers, local provisioners, commodity speculators and usurious creditors were at various times singled out for censure. However, agrarian anger tended to converge on the strangulating system of currency and credit run out of the great banking centers of the east, and especially Wall Street. Rural hostility to the 'money power' was an entrenched tradition, its roots extending back to Jackson's war against the 'Monster Bank' and beyond. The writings of Edward Kellogg, a one-time Pearl Street merchant turned monetary reformer of the 1840s, who first stigmatized the 'fictitious interest' propagated by Wall Street's money monopoly, were still being studied by the Populists of the 1890s. Greenback insurgents in the 1870s – some would go on to become veteran cadre of the Populist movement – had already fallen in love with the idea of a silver-backed currency, a metal carrying the promise of liberation from 'slavery' to Wall Street's gold standard.[3]

By the mid-1880s, much of rural America was in crisis. The last of the western trunk lines opened up millions of acres on the Great Plains and in the southwest to settlement – and a frenzy of speculation. Inflated farm prices, over-extended loans, overbuilt towns, and mountains of insupportable commercial paper rested on these rickety foundations. It all came crashing to earth amidst biblical afflictions of grasshoppers, blizzards, and the devastating drought of 1889–90. Mass bankruptcies and evictions soon followed.

Many farm organizations had by this time come to believe that their earlier agitation against railroads and various middlemen was something of a diversion. They focused increasingly on the great financial goliath back east, who they believed also controlled the national government. It was, they thought, squeezing the life-blood out of the farm economy by manipulating the currency, forcing up the value of the dollar, leaving behind a mountain of debt no farmer could hope to conquer. Nor were the farmers alone. A range of protest movements concerned with the drying up of entrepreneurial opportunity, including the National Labor Union and the Knights of Labor, fixated on the interest rate and the dearth of credit, uncovering linkages between 'interest, bonds, and the whole speculating power that now owns and runs the government'. So it was that bimetallism and the free coinage of silver, by promising to open up commercial credit, appealed to many beyond the immediate zones of rural misery.

All the torments of commercial agriculture – depressed prices, mortgage foreclosures, crop liens, exorbitant freight rates, commodity, and land speculations – were discovered incubating in the banking networks on the East coast, at the House of Morgan especially. A farmer concluded in 1892 that 'few Reading, thinking men in America, Deny the Slavery of the Masses, to the Money Power of our Country'. The axiom of agrarian unrest became embracingly blunt: the 'agricultural masses' were being 'robbed by an infamous system of finance'. [4]

Wall Street – the Wall Street of venerable and august banking establishments, rather than the plebeian one of gaming rapscallions –

became the *bête noire* of Populist economics. The movement's economic thinking was less wooly-headed than its enemies claimed. Virtually all reform movements of the nineteenth century, whether originating on the land or in the country's towns and cities, reacted similarly to the inequities of power and wealth associated with the commercial and industrial revolutions. They were preoccupied with the financial question, which led them inevitably to the Street. There the 'money power' dictated to the debtor classes by constricting the money supply, rationing credit, and depressing prices. This was a real, not fanciful, predicament.

To address it, the Populists offered the sub-treasury plan as their central economic remedy. It proposed government control of the money supply and credit so as to benefit all the 'producing classes'. The sub-treasury was essentially a kind of purchasing and marketing cooperative run by the government. It would make low-interest loans to farmers in legal-tender treasury notes in return for their crops. Then it would warehouse that agricultural output, releasing or holding back supplies from the market so as to maintain stable prices, prices that would insure loan repayment as well as the farmers' material well-being. Its proponents argued that their scheme would expand the currency without inflation, as the new money was backed by tangible forms of real wealth. The ultimate goal was to wrest control of the monetary system from the Wall Street elite and vest it in the hands of the US Treasury. This was by no means the movement's only economic recommendation. A graduated income tax, strict regulation or even public ownership of the means of communication and transportation, and an end to the protective tariff went after ancillary sources of economic victimization. But the sub-treasury plan, along with the free coinage of silver, were to be the heavy artillery for breaking Wall Street's chokehold on credit.[5]

Populist remedies like the sub-treasury plan were roundly criticized, yet reputable analysts then and since concur that the gold standard was accountable for the secular downward pressure on prices. Killing for all small entrepreneurs, it was especially so for farmers who exported into an overstocked world market. So it was that cotton and wheat prices virtually dropped out of sight: wheat went from $1.37 per bushel in 1870 to fifty cents in 1894; cotton from twenty-three cents per pound to seven.

Most nineteenth-century economic thinking, unlike its contemporary equivalent, was not supposed to be morally or politically neutral. Populist economic language, a lineal descendant of Jeffersonian agrarian republican ideology, was simultaneously a vocabulary and grammar of political and moral criticism. Words like 'robbed', 'enslaved', 'plunder', 'parasite' and 'corruption', which were the lingua franca not only of farm protest but of the whole family of anti-monopoly movements, carried analytic economic meaning even as they thundered out their condemnations. Bankers, financiers, speculators, and money-lenders occupied a distinctive niche in the cosmology of Populist economics: they were, in short, economic deadwood.

James H. Davis, a charismatic orator from Texas, habitually mounted the speaker's platform carrying ten large volumes of the works of Jefferson. He made particularly inventive economic use of the founding father's famous axiom about no generation having the right to bind another, that 'the earth belongs in usufruct to the living; that the dead have neither power nor rights over it'. Davis found the bondholders of railroads, state governments, and corporations to be in open violation. Led by 'private greed alone', they were guilty of taxing 'the unborn generations to pay these bonds'. Another insurgent from North Carolina asked: 'Who are these bankers anyway? What do they produce? What do they distribute? What moral right do they have to cumber the earth?' In Texas an editor of a Greenback paper described bankers as 'leeches on the business body. Bankers prosper when the people mourn. Banking destroys more wealth than any other business.'

Regional economic jealousies thickened the atmosphere as well. Both Southerners and settlers in the West grieved about their colonial status, convinced that 'the effete East wishes to enrich itself at the expense of the rough and rugged West', according to a local Oshkosh, Wisconsin banker, T. R. Frentz. Mr Frentz issued a warning: 'Beware Mr Morgan, Mr Keene and the Standard Oil crowd! You may form steel trusts and other kinds of trusts, but cannot lick the cream out of Mr Frentz' own saucers in his own home.' [6]

The 'money power' was not merely non-productive, it was counterproductive, like an incubus sucking away at the economic vitality of households and businesses. When its critics talked of 'fictitious value' they meant not only to condemn but to explain. Economic practices originating in Wall Street were 'fictitious' in the first instance because they were deceptive and unreal, resting on deliberate falsifications. But they were 'fictitious' in another impersonal, morally neutral sense as well. 'Fictitious value' was the systemic outcome of the mechanisms of trustification, which, without deliberate connivance, produced a parallel universe of paper values increasingly at variance with and greater than the wealth-generating capacity of the tangible economy. At the same time that academic economists and corporate lawyers were justifying the new forms of finance capitalism theoretically, small-town editors, local preachers, and politicians – the whole populist, anti-monopoly intelligentsia – busied themselves showing how this second, phantom economy exacted its heavy tribute. [7]

One acid-tongued observer did a post-mortem on those heavily hyped and extravagantly financed new railroad ventures and found that 'the road was unballasted, the ties are rotting, the station-houses are tumble-down shanties, the trestles and culverts and bridges are dangerous, the quarries and mines and forests have not been discovered.' The only real beneficiaries were Wall Street types foreclosing on railroad mortgages, canceling old securities, organizing new companies, issuing new securities, and floating them out into the world on rafts of fraudulent reports – the cycle primed to repeat itself without end. Critics of commodity speculation, regularly derided as a band of backward-gazing rustic yahoos, were often fully committed to the world of commerce. In their eyes, 'phantom cotton', 'spectral hogs', and 'wind wheat' subverted rather than sustained the market.

William Jennings Bryan's celebrated 'cross of gold' speech nicely captured the contested character of even the most commonplace economic categories. The Republicans claimed to be the party of business, but Bryan pointed out that it was the hardworking farmers, miners, and laborers who carried on the true business of the country, not 'the few financial magnates who, in a back room, corner the money of the world'. In this view, the economic health of the nation was inseparable from its spiritual vigor. James B. Weaver, one-time brigadier general in the Union Army and Greenback congressman from Iowa, issued a 'Call to Action' when he ran as the People's Party candidate for President in 1892. The 'Call' included a long disquisition dissecting the economic rationale of trusts. They might claim to lower prices to consumers, but because 'trusts are speculative in their purpose and formed to make money', they lacked the 'restraints of conscience' and inevitably resorted to 'threats, intimidation, bribes, fraud, wreck and pillage'.

This sense that economic behavior could turn depraved was shared by the Knights of Labor, an organization of urban workers which nonetheless evinced a fundamental sympathy for the producerist ideology arousing the countryside. Terence Powderly, Grand Master Workman of the Knights, traced the perversions of the natural market for wage labor to Wall Street:

The Knights of Labor are struggling . . . for an honest day's pay, for an honest day's work, and because dividends are wanted on watered stock they cannot get it . . . In defense of water – of the thinnest kind – the blood of the Artisan citizen is spilled by alien hirelings who are imported by men who manipulate the Stock Market.

Henry Demarest Lloyd, whose *Wealth Against Commonwealth* became the bible of the anti-monopoly persuasion, penned an 'open letter to millionaires' which used the occasion of a brutal strike of coal miners in Spring Valley, Illinois to draw out the nighmarish implications of Wall Street economics. The poverty and repression in Spring Valley, duplicated in a dozen other mining and industrial towns, were the outward signs of a ghoulish economic metabolism, 'where babies and men and women wither away to be transmigrated into the dividends of a millionaire coal mines of Beacon Street, Boston'. Lloyd tossed a question at those who took refuge in the benign laws of the marketplace: 'Has the bourbonism of the "divine right" of buying cheap and selling dear become so fanatical that you think you have the right to grind up the very bodies of the poor for "6 per cent on the capital" – watered capital at that.'

Today, the arguments seem overheated, the economic thinking lacking in rigor. No modern-day economics department would award a PhD to a Populist dissertation. For example, the critique of the 'money power' made no distinction between the credit and capital markets, cooking them together in a witches' brew of usurious exploitation. And no volume neatly laid out the geometry of populist economics the way orthodox textbooks deployed supply and demand curves. One text, however, came close, and it showed how preoccupied agrarian economics was with Wall Street.[8]

Coin's Financial School was far and away the bestselling piece of free-silver literature of the era. Written by William H. (for Hope) Harvey, it was published in 1894 into a world of twenty per cent unemployment, an avalanche of bankruptcies and bank failures, farm evictions, shuttered mills, panic on Wall Street, and the marching feet of Coxey's Army of the unemployed. People in small-town lyceums, at news-stands, on trains rumbling through the rural South and West read 'Coin', the 'Tom Paine of the free-silver movement', and in no time the book had sold a million copies. Speckled with cartoonish illustrations depicting the principal financial villains, it took the form of a set of mock lectures on the 'money question', interspersed with challenging interrogatories from 'gold bugs' and critically minded economists – people like Marshall Field, Philip Armour, and University of Chicago economics professor, J. Laurence Loughlin – which 'Coin', the precociously wise young lecturer, proceeded to demolish.

Coin's Financial School, true to the eponymous punning of its name, was rather austere, analytic, and impersonal. The book's mock debates were based on a real one at the Art Institute of Chicago between Harvey, 'the little economist', and respected 'experts' from the city's business elite. The book's basic argument was that the free coinage of silver would reverse the gross maldistribution of wealth, thereby relieving debtors, elevating the level of demand, and raising prices to everyone's benefit. Harvey assured those worried about unhitching the United States from the international gold standard that the country could adopt bimetallism without the cooperation of any foreign country – including, most importantly, Great Britain. The *School* extrapolated from a simple market society of small property holders in which money functioned strictly as a medium of exchange. What the 'morganizers' saw as a reckless fueling of further competitive chaos, 'Coin' Harvey insisted was the indispensable means of restoring a stable society of republican freeholders.

Bankers as a class performed an acceptable enough function, according to 'Coin'; only the cabal running things out of New York and London was truly destructive, and Wall Street was particularly to blame for neglecting the obvious explanation for the depression, namely the repeal of the silver purchase act. Although its enemies made fun of the book's errors and amateurism, its core message, that the gold standard was a punishing one, indeed, that some form of inflation was called for to resuscitate a moribund economy even if that meant stepping on the toes of the creditor classes in Wall Street and Lombard Street, was much harder to dismiss.

References to Lombard Street, the British, and the British

Rothschilds cropped up all over *Coin's Financial School*. For Harvey, as for so many others, the 'money question' was never purely economic. It was a political battlefield, the same as that on which the founding fathers, Jefferson especially, had first triumphed over the monarchist counter-revolution. Harvey reminded his readers that 'the conservative moneyed interests furnished the Tory friends of England then, and it furnishes her friends now.' Whatever the merits or demerits of Populist economic attacks on Wall Street, it was in the political realm that the issue would be settled. In an endlessly reiterated refrain, the movement demanded not merely an economy, but a society that raised 'man over money'. As the years passed and 'man' remained on the bottom, many activists looked ahead to a political Armageddon.[9]

The People's Party entered the presidential race for the first time in 1892. The Georgia congressman Tom Watson put together a campaign book in order to educate the public and whip up support. Its incendiary sub-title was 'Not a Revolt; It is a Revolution'. Watson, a rhetorically flamboyant Populist orator, drew a line of descent that connected the People's Party to those struggles of exactly a century ago to preserve the achievements of the American Revolution. 1892 would restage the great confrontation of 1792 between Hamilton and Jefferson. Hamilton, Watson explained, bent all his energies toward erecting a strong national government centered on a national banking system designed to 'interest the rich men in national affairs'. Politically, the idea was to 'create a moneyed aristocracy supported by special privilege'. The Jeffersonians rose up in resistance, and from then on American political life had wrestled with this primordial division between the forces of moneyed privilege and egalitarian democracy.[10]

Even before the formal debut of the People's Party, the agrarian reaction to Wall Street and the 'money power' was grounded in the principles of an earlier era. Not that Populism was anti-modern: many of its proposed reforms foreshadowed Theodore Roosevelt's Square Deal and Franklin Delano Roosevelt's New Deal as well as the legislation of the Wilson administration. When the party assembled in Omaha, Nebraska, to formulate its platform, the delegates cheered a fire-and-brimstone preamble, written by Ignatius Donnelly, which reviewed 'the Thirty Years War' against monopoly and vowed to carry on that ageless struggle against 'the oppression of the usurers'. But the platform itself showed none of that aversion to big government which had once been a Jeffersonian axiom. On the contrary, the sub-treasury plan, as well as a willingness to see the government run the railroads, telegraph, and banking systems were radical departures from the ancestral suspicion of the state. The Party's 1896 demand for a graduated income tax also signaled the movement's eagerness to deploy public power to remedy the private inequities fostered by the 'money power'. Increasingly, these calls for public intervention were heard also in Jefferson's own party, leading to the nomination of Bryan by the Democrats in 1896 and the repudiation of the party's laissez-faire conservatives, including its sitting President, Grover Cleveland.[11]

Yet although populist politics cannot be dismissed as a species of anti-modernism, they certainly owed their fervor and sense of political and moral peril to the republicanism of the Revolution. In the age of Morgan, they conveyed a Jeffersonian conviction that Wall Street and the 'moneyed aristocracy' represented the direst threat to the American experiment in democracy, to its representative institutions and egalitarian spirit. Government itself wasn't bad, but democracy was fragile: it depended on a broadly even distribution of wealth and property, which was in turn the basis for civic independence and vigilance against the usurpations of a self-aggrandizing elite. Those would-be aristocrats amassed their wealth not by honest effort but through the dark arts of financial manipulation; in turn, they used their wealth to seduce and demoralize the institutions of popular government until those instruments were weakened beyond repair – or even worse, themselves became the means of disinheriting and disempowering the People.

Of course, the political chemistry of the country had shifted decisively since the 1790s. A century ago the fledgling financial aristocracy had looked to a state more powerful than itself to bring it to maturity. Since then it had succeeded in subordinating a now much weaker government to its own purposes; and had even exercised its sovereign authority directly over the life of the people, like a private, parallel state, uninhibited by democratic political procedure. Economic expansion had piled up huge fortunes, multiplying the breeding pools of aristocratic sentiment. The great banking houses of the East now gathered in all these tributaries of counter-revolution, concentrating their force. Aware of that shift in the political center of gravity, mindful that the nation was no longer put together as it had been, populists nonetheless grounded their condemnation on an ancient faith. In its attachment to freeholder democracy and its wariness about the 'money power' – and in that sense only – populism might be said to have advocated an older, Jeffersonian order of things.

Stump orators on the prairie were fond of reminding their listeners that in Jefferson's time moneyed corporations and financial types were often 'tories', that 'a man was not considered a sound man to fill a government office if he was a banker or "stockbroker" or corporate man.' An Alabama Populist congressman likened the arrogance and insolence of the Wall Street plutocracy to the French monarchy, Charles I, and of course England in 1776 – all instances of aristocracies 'intoxicated by power', 'surfeited with a redundancy of money', intent on enslaving their subjects. In a speech to a gathering of Populists in Chicago, Henry Demarest Lloyd echoed a widely shared conviction about the two major parties: they were done for, their best work behind them: 'The Republican Party took the black man off the auction block of the Slave Power, but it has put the white man on the auction block of the Money Power.' Two-time People's Party candidate for Governor of Texas, the moderate Thomas Nugent justified breaking away from the two-party system by describing the parties of Jefferson and Lincoln as hollowed-out relics: 'The South can always be trusted for her votes by Wall Street democracy, but never for a place on the national ticket. Contributing the funds, Wall Street has always claimed the right to dictate the candidates and the financial policy of the country . . . Wall Street must, at any cost, be appeased.'[12]

The invocation of 'enslavement' by Lloyd and so many others referred not only to economic exploitation but to the theft of their political birthright as citizens of the republic. The 'money power' cast its chilling shadow over the courts, the legislature, and the state, as well as vital civic and educational institutions. Populist presidential candidate, James Weaver, captured its baleful influence:

> You meet it in every walk of life. It speaks through the press, gives zeal and eloquence to the bar, engrosses the constant attention of the bench, organizes the influences which surround our legislative bodies and courts of justice . . . determines who shall be our Senators, how our legislatures shall be organized, who shall preside over them . . . It is imperial in political caucuses . . . is expert

in political intrigue and pervades every community from the center to the circumference of the Republic.

The People's Party Campaign Book included a biopsy of a sickened party system. The chairman of the National Democratic Party Executive Committee, Calvin Brice, accumulated his fortune as railroad speculator, the Book reported, then bought himself a Senate seat in Ohio and went on to become a 'Wall Street operator; an ally of Jay Gould in corporate combines; a part owner of a convict camp in Tennessee.' Roswell Flower, until recently chairman of the Democratic Campaign Committee, was 'a National Banker of the Wall Street set'. Lamentably, President Cleveland seemed to have 'imbibed the financial views of Wall Street'. The Democrats were hardly alone in this regard. Both parties were predators: 'under the Banking and Bonded Systems all the Roads of Produce lead to the Rome of Imperial Plutocracy.' [13]

Populist insurgents meant to block those roads. Leading up to the final conflict in 1896, their political effectiveness and savvy steadily increased. When General Weaver ran for President on the Greenback Party ticket in 1876 he won only a handful of votes. In 1880 the handful was larger, but still a handful. By 1892, as the People's Party candidate, he attracted 8.5 per cent of the national vote, or over a million ballots, and carried the states of Kansas, Nebraska, and North Dakota. Protest at the whole expanding universe of financial middlemen – financiers, railroad promoters, purveyors of watered stock, bankers and mortgage holders, organizers of trusts and 'combines', a world symbolized by if not synonymous with Wall Street – was raising the temperature of political life. [14]

Agrarian critics and their allies believed that the enormous disparity between the actual output of crops and the sales volume on the commodity exchanges represented a prima facie case of market perversion. They lobbied for bills to ban futures trading, or at least to tax trades heavily when no real goods could be shown to have changed hands. The National Farmers Alliance and Knights of Labor demanded that Congress outlaw 'dealing in futures of all Agricultural and Mechanical Production'. While city papers pooh-poohed these efforts as 'the ignorance of rustics', laws regulating futures trading made it on to the books in the 1880s and 90s in California, Louisiana, and other cotton- and grain-growing states. When the Cleveland administration moved to repeal the Sherman Silver Purchase Act in 1893, tempers grew shorter. Senator William V. Allen of Nebraska defended the act as the 'last feeble barrier between the Patriotic and industrious masses of our people and that hoard of insolent, aggressive, and ravenous money-changers and gamblers of Lombard Street and Wall Street who, for private gain, would . . . turn the world back into the gloom of the Dark Ages with all its attendant evil and misery.' Allen's jeremiad notwithstanding, the act was repealed.[15]

The vitriol tossed at Wall Street grew more sulphuric each passing year. Defenders of the gold standard were prone to dismiss this as the ravings of lunatics and cranks, 'border ruffians', 'cossacks', and 'bandits' out of step with the march of progress. But it is striking how widespread this verbal violence was. Bewhiskered William A. Peffer looked like some Eastern newspaper's caricature of a farmer radical. Actually, he was a rather moderate-minded judge, newspaper editor, and successful Populist candidate for the US Senate from Kansas in 1890. A year after his election, he published *The Farmer's Side: His Troubles and Their Remedy*, which he conceived as a response to Henry Clews' recently issued celebratory *Twenty-Eight Years on Wall Street*. Clews boasted, without warrant according to Peffer, that Wall Street deserved the credit for the country's industrial and commercial development. What Clews got right, however, was that the power of the men assembled in Wall Street 'to catch the driftwood of trade is greater than that of monarchies'. They were despicable hypocrites parading their 'patriotism in lending a few millions of their ill-gotten gains to the government of their imperiled country at 12 per cent interest, when thousands of farmers and wage workers . . . were voluntarily in the army at risk to life and home.' [16]

The question of who were the real patriots dated back to the Revolution. When Cleveland turned to Morgan and Belmont to bail the government out of its gold crisis during the depression, the populists and their sympathisers were sure of the answer. The very same act that in some circles earned Morgan his reputation as a great public benefactor infuriated others who denounced it as a 'wicked Deal'. An *Atlanta Constitution* headline screamed that 'Rothschild, Morgan, and Belmont Skin the Country'. Accusations were rife that the syndicate underwriting the government's bonds came away with an unconscionable profit; even Alexander Dana Noyes, the respected financial columnist for *The Evening Post*, considered it a harsh, even merciless deal.

Armageddon came finally and inevitably in 1896, when the People's Party split apart. Millions flooded back into the Democratic Party, drawn by William Jennings Bryan's eloquent denunciation of the 'cross of gold' and by the alluring panacea of freely coined silver. Legions remained faithful to the populist movement, to its daring and programmatic independence of both major parties. But together they joined battle with the 'Money Kings of Wall Street'. Over and over again, Bryan depicted the campaign as a face-off between 'The People and Wall Street'. In his electrifying peroration at the Democratic convention in Chicago, he quoted Carlyle to challenge the delegates: 'Upon which side will the Democratic party fight; upon the side of the "idle holders of idle capital" or upon the side of the struggling masses?' No one knew the answer, but Wall Street was nervous about the outcome; the just-invented Dow Jones Industrial Average declined that year from 40.94 to 28.48.

Joseph Pulitzer, practically alone among big city newspaper publishers, and in keeping with the spirit of James Gordon Bennett, was willing to grant the silverites a hearing. A month before the election he turned over the Sunday-magazine supplement of his *New York World* to Tom Watson, the vice-presidential candidate of the People's Party. Watson had just visited Wall Street, and his article, 'Wall Street: Conspiracies Against the American Nation', expressed the populist political indictment. An accompanying cartoon featured a giant snake rising out of its nesting place in the Stock Exchange to strangle the businessman, the farmer, and the worker. 'A name more thoroughly detested is not to be found in the vocabulary of American politics' – Wall Street, in Watson's eyes, was a breeding ground for depression, empty houses, and barren fields. It was a hideout for conspirators who controlled those who in turn controlled the President and his cabinet. Cleveland was the merest puppet, his reputation for bull-headed independence a transparent sham: 'since our Republic was founded no President has been so bland and sterile a Wall Street tool as this conceited back number, Grover Cleveland.' Having corrupted legislatures, the bench, the press, the ballot box itself, 'Here is Wall Street: we see the actual rulers of this Republic. They are kings.' For Watson the counter-revolution, feared by Jefferson and all patriots of democracy since then, verged on victory. Resistance was nearly futile. This organized piracy was protected by law, by the armed might of the state, by legislative indifference: 'The Government itself lies prone in the dust with the iron heel of Wall Street upon its neck . . .' Watson was no advocate of violent revolution; he placed what remained of his hope in the vote. Nor did he fear 'revolution rising among the poor. The revolution I fear is coming from Wall Street.' If victorious, it would kill the spirit and achievement of 1776.[17]

Populism took on the world of J. P. Morgan by looking backward and forward at the same time. It anticipated the modern regulatory state far in advance of the urban upper-middle classes, which remained attached to laissez-faire for some time to come. However, the anxieties that Wall Street aroused – about religion and sex, money and race, nature and the city, trust and infidelity – were not, first of all, political, and they long antedated the rise of finance capitalism and its political dominion. Wall Street lit up an antique nightscape in the populist imagination, one populated by the over-sexed and the emasculated, by urban tricksters and sybarites, by moral prostitutes, alien conspirators, and apocalyptic demons. It was a despoiled landscape robbed of natural vigor and hard-earned virtue. This reservoir of cultural discontent proved not only nearly inexhaustible, but charged with Salvationist intensity.

Poetry was a popular medium of social criticism in the late nineteenth century. A folk literature circulated through towns and villages, in newspapers and cheaply bound pamphlets, under such homespun rubrics as 'Grandpa's Rhymes', 'Songs of the People', and 'Forest Runes'. Local poets traded in familiar themes about effete anglophiles, demoralized fops, and arrogant elitists, all of them in thrall to Mammon, all worshippers at the Exchange. Trusts were invariably imagined as tentacled, prehensile creatures, beasts of vaguely Biblical provenance grinding up and devouring their victims. 'Ghouls of booty' made tramps out of able-bodied millions. Vulpine shylocks perched amidst 'Envy and Pride and Lust and Greed' sequestered themselves in 'marble grottos' or 'great mausoleums' of greed. There, these bondholders and speculators demonically chanted:

Money is our dream ideal, money is our highest goal;
Money – money – And for money we crowd out the human soul . . .
Stock and bonds are more than honor. If our brother's blood is shed,
We will overlook the murder; if they pay us for our deed.

This whole 'carnival of wrong', where 'men with itching palms' ignored the pleas of the poor and 'Freedom's right', resembled a black Sabbath where 'stock wizards' gathered like the three witches of *Macbeth* in 'The Genius Loci of Wall Street':

> Down in a wonderful city, near to the foulest slums,
> Where squalor and crime are rife, and the tide flows turgid with greed,
> Where all are greedy and blatant, where peacefulness never comes
> There squats a ravening reptile, Arachne the Spider Queen,
> Her prey is human muscle, with the products of honest toil.[18]

Whatever else one might think about this culture of opposition to Wall Street – expressed in utopian and dystopian fantasies, hell-fire sermons, documentary novels, and cartoon allegories as well as in poetry – it was undeniably luxuriant, allusively dense and dramaturgically alive. It presumed a familiarity with biblical, Shakespearean, and pastoral themes and images. Together they comprised a psychic arsenal with which to defend a sacred honor and fend off the spectre of social oblivion. This repository of metaphor and analogy was also the artillery of a counter-assault through which the strange enemy – Wall Street – would be rendered as gruesomely familiar as the devil.

This was total culture war. No terrain was spared. But there were hot zones of the most concentrated fire. The 'money power' was an impiety and a pollutant that threatened above all the purity of the land, the family, the nation, and the race.

No matter how far into the outback the financial network might extend its reach, it was irreducibly urban, an artifice of big-city life. Populism was ambivalent about the city; sometimes it evinced fellowship with its exploited poor, other times it recoiled from its proletarian squalor and demoralization. In the end, populist culture was pastoral. Proximity to the land was inherently salubrious, the natural soil nourishing manly independence and honest dealing upon which, in turn, a healthy society rested. Wall Street was its antithesis. It ravaged the countryside by converting the land into a medium of commercial exchange and speculation, tearing it away from its pre-ordained role as a giver of life.

Hamlin Garland's grim depictions of a desolated middle border in novels like *Jason Edwards* indicted an eastern seaboard web of financial syndicates, railroads, and overbearing corporations like Standard Oil. The land itself, not to mention those who built their lives upon it, was slowly dying as a result. A 'gigantic system of spoilation' drained away the life-blood of 'the country people and the working forces in the towns', according to Kansas Senator William Peffer. Merciless bondholders reduced once proudly self-reliant farmers to 'hewers of wood and drawers of water'.[19]

In an age filled with looming premonitions of social cataclysm, the virgin land carried sacred meaning: its deflowering at the hands of alien financial interests amounted to a national calamity. Henry George's *Progress and Poverty* was the century's most widely read critique of the new economic order. George's fixation on ground rent reflected a more general cultural preoccupation with parasitism:

> The general intelligence, the general comfort, active intervention, the power of adaptation and assimilation, the free, independent spirit, and energy and hopefulness that have marked our people are not causes, but results – they have sprung from the unfenced land. This public domain has been the transmuting force which has turned the thriftless, unambitious European peasant into the self-reliant farmer; it has given a consciousness of freedom even to the dweller in crowded cities, and has been the well-spring of hope even to those who have never thought of taking refuge upon it.[20]

Agrarian repugnance for city life was, of course, a deeply rooted tradition in Western civilization. It had always been a vital element of the Jeffersonian persuasion – despite the urbanity of its progenitor – which treated the city, European cities in particular, as the site of immoral infection, class inequality, and political corruption. Classics of populist literature like *Caesar's Column* and *Coin's Financial School*, likewise, viewed the city as an amalgam of pretentiousness, avarice, debauchery, and degradation. In the eyes of this adversarial culture, Wall Street was a city institution through and through, marked by all of urban life's most dangerous proclivities, both old and new. Even its geography was suggestive, tucked away at the intestinal end of New York, conducting its business in its serpentine alleyways.

Confidence men were not confined to the city, but they thrived there in its atmosphere of artifice and dissimulation. Henry Demarest Lloyd's wry descriptions of corporate wrecking operations by Wall Street insiders deployed the lingua franca of underworld trickery. Here 'the hidden hand pulled another wire'; here there 'came another can-can in the courts'; here snookered investors 'flung their certificates away for what they could get'. Wall Street traded in fake railroads, impossible canals, and every imaginable sort of con game. Lacking any ethical sense, it treated people as so many 'sheep to be shorn'.[21]

Financial oligarchs wallowed in the immoralities of city life and threatened the moral fiber of the rest of the country. The Street's baleful influence on sexual mores and family integrity was especially alarming. The *Sioux Falls Daily Argus*, which concluded Morgan had done more harm to the world than 'any man who ever lived in it', singled out for special censure his contribution to 'the blighting of womanhood' and 'the premature aging of children'. For Tom Watson, what was acutely galling about the lavish extravagance of the Vanderbilts was the way it was wrung from 'innocent men, helpless women, sweet little children'. His excoriation of the Street in Pulitzer's *World* made sure to mention its callous indifference to the widowed and orphaned, the cold hearths and scattered families. Angry farmers itemizing, often in capital letters, the most repugnant traits and abuses of the 'money power' invariably raised the specter of 'Debased Manhood'.[22]

This fear of emasculation was coupled with an intuition that the unchecked power of these financial overlords bred among them an insatiable and conscienceless lust. Gabriel Weltstein, the ingenuous hero of *Caesar's Column*, learns to his horror that even the 'Brotherhood', that secret proletarian resistance to the 'Oligarchy', shares with its enemy a ruthless masculinity that seeks to ravage every outpost of virtue, female and otherwise. Soon after *Coin's Financial School* appeared, William Harvey published a propagandistic novel typical of a nineteenth-century genre of didactic, social-conscience fiction. The villain of *A Tale of Two Nations*, Baron Rothe, is an international financier of great cunning and ambition. He plots to enrich himself and augment the dominion of the British empire by driving the United States off the silver standard. But his malevolence runs deeper than that: 'We must crush their manhood by making them poor', he confides. As the plot unfolds, the Baron and his nephew, an utterly debauched character, undertake to seduce the virgin daughter of a US senator, driven by the desire both to humiliate other men and to debase women.

An undercurrent of suppressed lasciviousness ran through much populist literature. The denunciation of Wall Street's sexual impropriety and subversion was only part of a broader indictment of its sensual abandon and descent into a kind of over-civilized barbarism. Populists and others still committed to the codes of sensual self-discipline observed with irresistible fascination every behavioral trespass, every sign of dissipation: the more egregious the fall the better.[23]

Wall Street, in the populist imagination, was a boulevard of ravenous appetite. Millions were wasted there on outlandish feasts, while 'gaunt starvation walked the streets'. There men posed as 'missionaries conquering deserts and building republics', feigning piety and wisdom, soaking up the adulation and honorifics of the credulous, while 'living in luxury and ease, renting costly pews in splendid churches and hiring their worshipping done; men petted and feasted by the rich everywhere.' It was the outlandish contrast between their social prestige and sybaritic behavior that supplied endless grist for the populist conscience. Adversarial politicians and jaundiced journalists documented their monumental castles, their yachts 'ready at the wharf', their 'private cars at the depot', their 'private chapels and private priests', and their fancy-dress soirées, all the stigmata of a 'libidinous plutocracy'. While the nation suffered depression, the 'morganizers', who'd looted the Treasury under the guise of rescuing it, spent their ill-gotten gains on 'yacht races, pyrotechnics, and balls'.[24]

Frederick Opper, a brilliant and widely popular 'cartoonist of democracy' at the turn of the century, drew humorous, generic sketches of millionaire tax evaders, venal officials, and Wall Street tycoons that captured their sensuality and insatiable appetite; oily and fat, gleeful, even masterful men, but devoid of 'noble emotions or high ideals'. 'The Common People', on the other hand, were hapless figures in Opper's vision, small in stature and palpably vulnerable. This was one man's rendition of a more universal moral polarity. The opposition between the pleasurized elite and the ingenuous modesty of the 'People' was the axis around which populist melodrama and polemic pivoted.[25]

Prostitution – intellectual, political, and religious – was what happened when this moral cancer metastasized to healthy tissue. It began as an act of consensual hypocrisy. Respectable society genuflected every time a tycoon engaged in an act of public piety or charity. Populists loved to ridicule these philanthropic charades, which so many others admired. About Rockefeller's educational philanthropies, Tom Watson scoffed that just because the oil plunderer scattered 'little doles of booty here and there among Colleges and Schools . . . they all flap their wings and crow; while the press says, "blessed be Rockefeller".' A Populist congressman from Alabama flayed the pious offerings of men like Morgan and Rockefeller as 'blood money' for the

Lord. Charles Schwab, Morgan's right-hand man in the steel trust, was accused of using his church donations as a cover for his scandalous behavior, including his 'gambling exploits at Monte Carlo'.

Hypocrisy tainted everything it touched, and soon enough slid over into a form of intellectual pimping. Orthodox economists and social theorists who defended the new Wall Street order were dismissed as hopeless dogmatists who knew nothing about the empirical reality of the stock market and lived in an Edenic fantasy of primitive hunters and fishermen. They had traded their conscience for a nod of approval from the high and mighty. Delusional and parochial as they might be, the moneycrats had managed to seduce those who ought to know better. In Donnelly's nightmare, the sadistic reign of the 'Oligarchy' rested on terror, but also depended on the support of the press, the church, and institutions of higher education – all of which offered themselves shamelessly. Country editors talked of 'debauched newspapers' and a 'prostituted judiciary'. Wall Street, in an effort to conciliate public opinion and inflate its reputation, had managed to 'seize and subsidize' the press, to buy 'every purchaseable pen, from the pen of the gray philosopher to the pen of the snake editor'.[26]

Populists likened economic inequalities to the impassable scriptural divide between Dives and Lazarus: the rich Dives cast into hell-fire, while the beggar Lazarus reposed in the bosom of Abraham. To stay loyal to republicanism and equality was to defend a Christian way of life, its attachment to hard work and restraint. Wall Street defiled an essential innocence, a core conviction that 'honorable labor in every walk of existence . . . will be counted Monarch among men'. A return to the 'principles and practices of primitive Christianity' was needed: a restoration of that millennial community of sympathy and fellowship. This was a heartfelt Christian romance, a faith in the moral purity of human labor as a form of service free of any attachment to material reward. Unless this etherealized form of the labor theory of value prevailed against the corrosive logic of a leisure-infatuated commercial civilization, there would be hell to pay.[27]

And hell was familiar territory for the populist imagination. The final conflict with the Money Power would inevitably take place on its borders. There the enemy would appear in all its viciousness: a brutal figure of ancient lineage and apocalyptic import. A Populist congressman and the author of *If Christ Came to Congress* called trusts 'institutional vampires'. Wall Street machinations were 'a devil's dance . . .

an orgy of fiduciary harlotry'. Sometimes depicted as a primordial octopus, sometimes a 'great Devil Fish' or vampire, the Money Power engaged not so much in acts of commerce as in 'necromancy'. Strip away Wall Street's veneer of urbane sophistication and what stared you in the face was a demon. The Street's illicit offspring, the trust, was 'soulless'; beneath its avaricious, power-mad exterior beat a heart of pure nihilism, driving the human community backward into some Dark Age. Populist eschatology thought in terms of an 'irrepressible conflict' begun generations earlier. Bred in the bone, it was a war over the very soul of man.[28]

What made the enemy fiendishly difficult to deal with was its conspiratorial nature. Afraid to expose its true purposes, it operated stealthily, spinning invisible webs of intrigue that strung together the power centers of the country and even spanned the ocean. People's Party tracts traced the immediate origins of the crisis to the 'gold conspiracy' which drove the country off the silver standard in the 'Crime of '73': 'For nearly thirty years these conspirators kept the people quarreling over less important matters . . . Every device of treachery, every resource of statecraft and every artifice known to the secret cabals of the international gold ring are being made use of.'

Thinking like this was hardly confined to the countryside. John Clark Ridpath, editor of the *Arena* magazine read by town burghers and middle-class city folk, declared no other conspiracy 'equal in Colossal and Criminal splendor to the profound and universal plot of Wall Street to make perpetual the national debt'. 'Coin' Harvey's Baron Rothe was a creature of the night, carrying forward the insidious work of the international 'gold bugs' while concealing his nefarious intentions. The plotting of the 'Oligarchy' in *Caesar's Column* was as pervasive and cunning as anything one was likely to encounter in a modern spy novel.[29]

What made these conspiracies especially menacing was their alien provenance. Wall Street was foreign in the profoundest sense. It abandoned all sentimental attachments to a people, a faith, or a homeland. It corrupted democracy, undermined Christian fortitude, and felt no national loyalty. The Englishman Baron Rothe's presence is suggestive: his aim was to subvert the American government and install a monarchy that would reign on behalf of the international confederacy of usurers while reducing the country's lower orders to a servant class. Lombard and Wall Street combined to warp the country's foreign policy, too. When passions about the Cuban resistance to Spanish colonial rule began building in the mid-1890s, war sentiment in the Midwest and the silver states of the West was at first rebuffed by the Cleveland and McKinley administrations. Pro-war populists blamed a conspiracy of the international Money Power, centered in England, with links to Wall Street on this side of the ocean and the Rothschilds on the other. British and American financiers stood together in their opposition to the cause of freedom and humanity in Cuba and used every covert means at their disposal to undermine the government's will to act. This ignominious league of 'Wall Street money sharks' and their foreign confederates were to be feared 'a thousand times more . . . than the ironclads of the whole Spanish navy'.

Populist presidential candidate James Weaver told campaign audiences that, 'Wall Street has become the Western extension of Threadneedle and Lombard streets, and the wealthy classes of England and America have been brought into touch . . . We have in late years become an important prop to the British throne.' Talk about 'British gold' exercising behind-the-scenes control of American politics was standard fare on the hustings and in publications sympathetic to the cause of silver. Anglophobia, which stretched back to the nation's beginnings, was still vigorously alive in the nation's heartland. *Coin's Financial School* included a frightening 'map' of the 'Great English Devil Fish', an octopus-like creature native to the British Isles whose monstrous tentacles encircled the whole world.[30]

This talk of conspiracies was lent a certain gravitas by its undercurrent of apocalyptic finality. *Caesar's Column* was grim beyond compare: Donnelly's picture of Armageddon even included the logistical details of hunting down the beast in its lair. 'The Brotherhood of Destruction', as its name signals, had become as violent, brutish, and conspiratorial as its plutocratic tormentors, driven over the edge by oppression and resentment. When the 'Brotherhood' initiates the final battle with the 'Oligarchy', it begins by barricading the area around Wall Street. Once Pine, Cedar, Pearl, William, Nassau, and Water streets are secure the plan is to burst open the great money institutions, loot them of their gold, and use it to buy the services of the most dreaded army of the 'Oligarchy'. This counter-conspiracy succeeds – in a nineteenth-century version of mutual assured destruction – and only then does the horror begin.

The 'Column' turns out to be a truly infernal obelisk named in memory of the Commanding General of the Brotherhood, Caesar Lomellini. It is a giant pyramid erected in Union Square following the insurrection, made out of cement and out of the quarter-million corpses of the vanquished 'Oligarchy' and its minions. It was erected by the forced labor of surviving merchants, politicians, and clergy, to commemorate the 'Death and Burial of Modern Civilization'. To ensure its permanence, Caesar's column is rigged with explosives at its center; should anyone try removing the corpses, the whole monument will blow up. Appropriately, the Column bears an inscription revealing that belief in a final reckoning which inspired so great a loathing for the world of J. P. Morgan. The tablet testifies that the 'Oligarchy' was 'altogether evil'. It had corrupted every public institution along with 'the hearts and souls of the people'. In robbing the poor to give to the rich, the oligarchs had made 'the miserable more miserable' and proved that 'their hearts were harder than the nether mill-stone; they degraded humanity and outraged God.' Their wickedness was now entombed in stone, their execrable vices, festering for generations, punished at last. The epitaph closed with these sear and righteous words:

> Let this monument, O man! stand forever. Should civilization ever revive on earth, let the human race come hither and look upon this towering shaft, and learn to restrain selfishness and live righteously. From this ghastly pile let it derive the great lesson, that no earthly government can endure which is not built on mercy, justice, truth, and love.[31]

'Mercy, justice, truth, and love' – and, Donnelly might have added, anti-Semitism. Drawing from a deep well of folkloric metaphor, the Money Power was stigmatized as satanic, conspiratorial, alien, and Jewish; one might even say, 'and therefore Jewish'. Historians have argued vehemently for generations about whether Populism was anti-Semitic. Programmatically, the answer is no. Its proposals for economic and political reform in no way addressed 'the Jewish question'. They were well- or ill-conceived propositions for dealing with the rise of finance capitalism. They bore no special animus, no legislative provisions or administrative protocols directed at Jews or Jewish financiers. For every populist barb aimed at the Rothshilds there was one fired at the hymn-singing Morgan, as Bryan was quick to point out when rejecting the accusation of anti-Semitism. Moreover, the charge has been unfairly used to discredit the movement's critique of modern capitalism, to dismiss it as a species of political paranoia incubating among the dispossessed in the passed-over regions of rural America.[32]

Nonetheless, populism's morally intense mental universe bound feelings about the city, the East, gold, John Bull, and Wall Street to the sin of usury. And usury, as everyone thought they knew, was a Jewish invention. So among the bestiary of apocalyptic creatures haunting the populist imagination, alongside the vampires, 'Great English Devil Fish', strangulating octopuses, and snakes, Shylock and his hooked nose made regular appearances. Culturally, the populist reaction to Wall Street felt at home with occasional anti-Semitic invective, even though this rarely colored its practical politics. Jew-baiting was a tradition; indeed, it was a particularly lurid instance of a cultural traditionalism which left populism running both with and against the grain of modernizing America.

Wall Street, gold, and the international money power were in any event a preoccupation of the 1890s. Anti-Semitism, whose recrudescence was by no means confined to the populist countryside, tended to settle on the image of the shylock. This shylock, however, was not the petty pedlar or pawnbroker of yesteryear. He was a far more imposing, princely figure who lent the Wall Street plutocracy a distinctly ethnic coloration. This figuration went at least as far back as the baiting of August Belmont during the Civil War as an agent of the Rothschilds. Playing the 'Rothschilds card' never went out of fashion. Thirty years later silverites denounced the Morgan–Belmont syndicate that bailed out the Cleveland government as a Rothschild-inspired scheme for enriching international Jews at American expense. When William Randolph Hearst panted after the presidential nomination of the Democratic Party in 1904, he unleashed anti-Semitic editorial attacks on his enemies in the party's old guard – August Belmont Jr in particular – by asking delegates to repudiate 'the alien pawnbroker who came to our shores just before the Civil War as the representative of the Rothschilds'.

Oddly enough, populist melodrama sometimes mixed heavy-handed Jew-baiting with a genuine philo-Semitism. *Caesar's Column* railed against Israelite avarice while admiring Jewish perseverance. As Gabriel, the novel's hero, is informed about what's what in the modern world, he learns that 'the aristocracy of the world is now almost altogether of Hebrew origin'. The banking coterie running things is 'mostly Israelites' who have accomplished an age-old dream, first acted on by Hannibal; namely, to subject the European races 'to the domination of the Semitic blood'. Yet in the same breath, Donnelly paid his respects to the children of Abraham who, he acknowledged, 'fought and schemed their way, through infinite depths of persecution' to this august perch. 'Tit for Tat', a satirical 'Universal History of How Mr Solomon Moses is Persecuting His Old Persecutors', written by a pseudonymous populist 'professor', felt obliged to point out, amidst its scabrous anti-Semitic vitriol, not only that this was payback time for centuries of persecution, but that in all fairness America had its own share of 'Shylocky Christians', including the Goulds and the Vanderbilts, who were auctioning off 'the last vestiges of American liberty'.

Reservations and equivocations notwithstanding, there is no question that anti-Semitic imagery was part of the verbal and graphic vocabulary of populism. A cartoon captioned 'Shylock's Bank' was not unusual. It portrayed two warriors wielding the swords of the 'people's ballot', assaulting the Money Power that guarded the portals of 'Shylock's Bank', a gateway emblazoned with human skulls. Another sketched a distressed farmer in search of 'Justice'. She's nowhere to be found, according to signs on a nearby church and college, while a big-nosed figure peers around a cornerstone marked 'Wall Street' and asks disingenuously, 'Eish Dodt So?' Gordon Clark, a free-silverite pamphleteer, entitled his crowning work, 'Shylock: as Banker, Bondholder, Corruptionist, Conspirator', and denounced the alliance of home-grown vampires with the 'Bank of England and the Jews of Frankfort'. Defending its breach with the Democrats, the People's Party decried the subjugation of that vessel of Jeffersonianism to the rule of 'red-eyed Jewish millionaires'. Mary Elizabeth Lease, Kansas populist agitator extraordinaire, famous for her exhortation to 'raise less corn and more hell', indicted President Cleveland as 'the agent of Jewish bankers and British gold'.[33]

Rhetoric like Lease's expressed the dyspeptic desperation of an embittered people. 'Morganization' had worked wondrous changes, but its portents were ominous indeed. Often enough Populist insurgents on the western prairies and Southern cotton fields had only recently arrived. Their homesteads might be only a generation old, two at the most. As husbandmen, their fortunes had always been tied to the coming of the railroad and eastern banks – that is, to the infrastructure of modernity. Yet they cherished beliefs far older than that, a sacerdotal commitment to rural and small-town virtues that went back to Jefferson's day. 'Morganization' threatened a way of life as much as a way of making a living. The Populists resisted its coming in ways both perspicacious and retrograde. When they regrettably resorted to forms of sulphurous prejudice, they were hardly alone: Shylockism was abroad in the land and thrived in cooler climes as well.

7

Wall Street and the Decline of
Western Civilization

James Hazen Hyde was practically a caricature of the dissipated financier. His father had founded the Equitable Life Assurance Insurance Company, the largest in the country. Around the turn of the century, James, then only twenty-four, found himself in charge. He was a dandified party animal who brazenly and without conscience put the enormous funds of the company's policy-holders at the disposal of Wall Street operators. James had neither the time nor the talent for business. He could ride, he could sail, and he knew how to indulge the most exotic cravings that marked the hermetic neighborhoods of high society. While he was horsing around, Hyde, together with his cronies in insurance and banking, spent lavishly in order to grease the wheels of political influence in Albany. All the interested companies contributed to a 'Yellow Dog Fund', run by Morgan partner George Perkins. The Fund financed what became colloquially known as a 'House of Mirth', where legislators were pleasured by hostesses from touring musical-comedy productions and other ladies of the night. Scandal erupted in 1905 and led to a highly publicized investigation by Charles Evans Hughes – one that launched the political career of the future Governor, Republican presidential candidate, and Supreme Court Justice. Hyde, meanwhile, high-tailed it for Paris.[1]

In that same year, Edith Wharton published *The House of Mirth*, her first commercially successful novel. 'Successful' understates the case: it sold out its first printing in two weeks and remained a bestseller for four months – a remarkable performance no doubt due in part to the unfolding fiasco in Albany. Critical reactions to the novel were mainly favorable. The *North American Review*, a highbrow journal catering to patrician tastes, zeroed in on Wall Street's pernicious and ubiquitous influence, noting that:

> The presence of Wall Street is felt permeating the whole – the most brilliant fetes champetres, a cruise on the wide expanse of the sea, a ride through country lanes . . . The mere manipulation of other people's capital in finance, the doubtful practices to which it leads, the demoralizing effect upon him who rapidly gains great wealth by those means and upon the community at large . . . [have led to] the gaudy and truly vicious structure of the American House of Mirth.[2]

Wharton's story was not about the business and political misadventure from which it borrowed its title, but the lethal moral and social psychology that lay beneath the frivolity and mercenary preoccupations of the world of James Hazen Hyde. Her withering dissection included a portrait of a merciless shylock: Simon Rosedale is no mere pawnbroker or money-lender, but a man of Morgan-like ambition who nonetheless carries the unmistakable stigma of the oily Jew. Populists weren't the only ones who resorted to ancient prejudice when dealing with the age of Morgan. Wharton's literary inquiry into the manners and mores of newly moneyed Society actually took place over the course of several novels, including *The Age of Innocence* and *Custom of the Country*. These and other writings were part of a more widespread act of cultural distancing undertaken by the 'old money' intelligentsia.

It is hard to imagine anyone more spiritually at odds with populism than Henry Adams. He was contemptuous of its rustic vulgarity, its cultural illiteracy, and its taste for addle-brained political quackery. But Adams was also tormented by foreboding about the advent of a 'Jewish Age', which he gloomily concluded would put an end to everything he held dear. Like many a populist insurgent, this Brahmin intellectual feared the death of a better world at the hands of the 'morganizers'. Unlike those prairie rebels, he was convinced that nothing could be done about it.

A sense of doom, then, was more than a rural hallucination – indeed, it was shared by a slice of America's cosmopolitan cultural elite. The Adams brothers, Henry and Brooks, scarcely shed a tear at the passing of rural America. They did, however, mourn the imminent demise of sanctuaries of civilization such as Washington Square, Beacon Hill, and Rittenhouse Square. There a precious remnant of cultural refinement and ethical high-mindedness was all that forestalled a descent into mercenary barbarism. The Adamses were as pessimistic as Donnelly seemed to be in *Caesar's Column*. Like him, they blamed the situation on the hubris and selfishness of a financial oligarchy whose power had grown irresistible. Like his their language could become lurid, full of nightmarish fantasies of Semitic conspiracies. Others from their spiritual community who felt Wall Street's sting reacted with a mixture of alarm and resignation. Henry James recorded his bafflement. Edith Wharton plotted the psychodynamics of the Street's social corrosiveness. Teddy Roosevelt and Henry Cabot Lodge converted disdain into political resistance. All suspected the Jews. And like their Populist antipodes they feared that the worlds they cherished were being extinguished by the 'morganizers'.

Living in material comfort, urbane and well-connected, this remnant of a faded elite was in some ways more completely estranged from the new age than the populists had the luxury of being. After all, however much the populists decried the ruination of rural arcadia, they were themselves commercially minded and convinced there was a humane and economically rational alternative to Money Power. To believe otherwise would have meant admitting social extinction. The Brahmin disaffection from the world of Morgan, on the other hand, was terminal.

In the immediate aftermath of the 1893 depression, Adams' bitterness came to a head. Though the panic had jeopardised the family's holdings in railroad and other securities, Adams' reaction was too macabre to be explained as a straightforward case of economic nervousness. He confided to his brother Brooks that he was looking forward to the smash-up of his whole world with a kind of ghoulish glee: 'I shall be glad to see the whole thing utterly destroyed and wiped away . . . In a society of Jews and brokers, a world made-up of maniacs wild for gold, I have no place.' The repeal of the Sherman Silver Purchase act, Adams noted, had sealed the victory of finance capitalism. He burned with hatred for the new world it brought:

> I am myself more than ever at odds with my time. I detest it, and everything that belongs to it, and live only in the wish to see the end of it, with its infernal Jews. I want to put every moneylender

to death, and to sink Lombard Street and Wall Street under the ocean. Then, perhaps, men of our kind might have some chance of being honorably killed in battle and eaten by our enemies.

Henry was temperamentally prone to these Götterdämmerung fantasies. Since Lombard Street, Wall Street, and State Street had all been turned into 'Judengossen', he wished the mob would loot this 'financial Ghetto' controlled by 'a Hebrew fraternity' and then end it all by bombarding New York.[3] Judeophobia of such emotional violence was fired by two beliefs: first, that Wall Street was to blame for all the social decay, vulgarity, vice, and avarice that was exterminating whatever remained of the high-minded world Adams had grown up in; and secondly, that history seemed to have decreed it thus. 'We are in the hands of the Jews. They can do what they please with our values . . . Westward the course of Jewry takes its way.'[4]

Brooks Adams, a more eccentric version of Henry, not only agreed with his brother, but transmuted those drear premonitions into a general theory of historical evolution. His magnum opus, *The Law of Civilization and Decay*, assumed a perfect identity between usury, the money power, Wall Street, and Jewry. Rome, Adams argued, fell at the hands of capitalist usurers; the money power had eaten away at the chivalrous imagination of the Middle Ages; parasitic finance capitalism now dominated the industrial revolution. All remnants of patrician noblesse seemed corrupted beyond repair, its disinterested sense of stewardship a pathetic anachronism. He confessed to Henry:

> I suppose there is more concentrated hate of Wall Street in my last chapter than I could have put into a volume of stump speeches . . . I never should have hated Wall Street as I do if I had not first dug the facts out of history . . . I tell you Rome was a blessed garden of paradise beside the rotten, unsexed, swindling, lying Jews, represented by J. P. Morgan and the gang who have been manipulating our country for the last four years.[5]

Anti-Semitism, though not always as heated as this, was as much part of Brahminism as of rural culture in nineteenth-century America. Oliver Wendell Holmes, a patrician intellectual eminence, had early on declared that 'the principal use of the Jews seemed to be to lend money.' Later in the century, the distinguished Wall Street banker, Joseph Seligman, a friend of Lincoln and confidante of Grant, was famously denied admission to an exclusive, old-money establishment in Saratoga Springs on account of his 'race'. Theodore Roosevelt, who in so many ways distanced himself from the fatalism and inertia of this milieu, nevertheless harbored a sympathy for Brooks Adams' 'gloomiest anticipations of our gold-ridden, capitalist bestridden, usurer-mastered future'. The idea that Jewish financiers mysteriously controlled not only America's economy but the world's was also indulged in by people like James Russell Lowell and Henry Cabot Lodge. As they inveighed against the intriguing of Lombard Street and Wall Street, a stateless internationalized money power, their ethnic resentments could even overshadow their innate Anglophilia. Lowell in particular became increasingly dismayed at the eclipse of the cultural universe he cherished, and took seriously the notion that Jewish bankers and brokers ran not only the financial system, but also the army, navy, press, and Society.[6]

Populists and Brahmins shared more than a reflexive anti-Semitism. As Jackson Lears has argued, both have been inaccurately depicted as driven solely by nostalgia when their attitudes to 'modernity' were much more ambivalent. Populists were not trying to dismantle the last hundred years of technical inventiveness, but rather to redirect its energies. And the material and scientific achievements of the industrial revolution were marvelous to Henry Adams, too, even as he shuddered at their spiritual consequences. Theodore Roosevelt made an audacious attempt to accommodate the self-interested motivations of the trustified corporation to the higher purposes of the state, though never relinquishing his inherited disdain for the money-obsessed classes.

Viewed through patrician eyes, the single-minded pursuit of moneymaking, nowhere better exemplified than on the Street, was weakening American life, leaving it dandified, foppish, fat, and slothful. Henry Adams vented a global disdain for this nouveau bacchanal: 'America contains scores of men with five million or upwards whose lives were no more worth living than those of their cooks.' This critique of an over-civilized, flaccid culture, lacking in heroism and self-restraint, had a real affinity with the populist argument against finance capitalism, though it was not identical. How to treat this condition of spiritual enervation was the question.[7]

One way to respond to the bureaucratic emasculation and sybaritic debilitation of modern urban life was to find its antidote where one might least expect to do so. Salvation might lie concealed in the

Napoleonic ambition and derring-do of those captains of industry and finance most responsible for fostering the very institutions and moral indifference which seemed to cause the general malaise. The veneration of financial titans in the popular media around the turn of the century, coinciding with the Morgan-inspired trustification of the economy, showed how appealing this view could be.

The Brahmin remnant wasn't persuaded, however. Some sought their deliverance from the 'Jewish Age' in imperial adventure, in sport, in invocations of medieval martial valor and religious intensity, in a reverence for the aesthetic humanism of pre-industrial craftsmanship . . . or in nothing at all. Whatever the remedy or lack of it, the world of Henry Adams performed an act of cultural excommunication on the world of J. P. Morgan. E. L. Godkin called it a 'Chromo Civilization'. The idea was that there was something irreducibly false, 'gilded', about a society given over to material acquisition and excess. Hypothetically, this accusation might have been leveled even had there been no Wall Street. After all, there was plenty of plundering and shameless extravagance going on all across industrializing America. But as the century drew to a close, Wall Street was increasingly seen as the symbolic location for all the plunder and Mammon-worship.

It wasn't simply that business had established its supremacy; that had arguably been true for some time. In Henry Adams' view, it was the reign of J. P. Morgan, the advent of finance capitalism which was new and ominous. With the Republican victory in 1896, Adams concluded that the great investment bankers had become 'the greatest single power in the country, and infallibly control the drift of events'. This was not merely a political judgment. Adams and his circle, including such lettered patricians as John Hay and Henry Cabot Lodge, conveyed bitterness about a domineering elite which, in their eyes, lacked all traces of moral fiber, any sense of history, honor or public responsibility and whose hubris was limitless. Reacting to Morgan's creation of US Steel in 1901, Arthur T. Hadley, the President of Yale, gloomily forecast that if this sort of thing was allowed to continue unchecked there would be 'an emperor in Washington within twenty-five years'.

Adams' mood fluctuated wildly between outbursts of sour and sulphuric irony, and the resignation of an exhausted 'Puritan aristocrat'. Considering his own education 'magnificently futile', he tried to gain some emotional distance from the expiring world of his ancestors.

Wall Street's supremacy was inevitable, and 'One did not mind the progressive cowardice of one's class . . . the combative spirit of one's Puritan forebears had passed out of one, and one ended, with the rest of the Yankee hegemony, as a pleasing figurine on the intellectual shelf.' When his dander was up, however, Adams' oracular judgments could turn more cutting: he famously observed that American society was the first in history to journey straight from barbarism to decadence without passing through a stage of civilization. [8]

The Age of Morgan, which might be thought to run roughly from 1890 to 1929, gave rise to the country's most enduring imaginative literature about Wall Street. World-class writers, including William Dean Howells, Mark Twain, Henry James, Edith Wharton, Theodore Dreiser, Frank Norris, John Dos Passos, and Jack London, returned to the Street again and again as the ground zero of the era's social and cultural turmoil. Here the aftershocks of the country's stunning economic makeover set off profound reverberations in the way people conducted themselves; not only in the marketplace, but in the bedroom, at the evening party, on the athletics field, before the marriage altar, crossing the Atlantic, dealing with the help. Certain of these artists, like James, Wharton, and Henry Adams (whose novel *Democracy* was preoccupied with the corrosive effect of new money on whatever was left of the country's republican political integrity) were especially absorbed by the relationship between Wall Street wealth and their own world of old money. Because this Brahmin remnant felt ever more marginal to the main currents of American culture, this literature comes down to us as a kind of substitute politics. This was especially so for a milieu that shuddered at the prospect of actual political engagement. Cosmopolitan, familiar with the aesthetic and social upheavals in transatlantic high culture, acutely aware of the fragility and provincialism of their ancestral heritage, their creations still echo with Brahmin contempt. Their work registers the plangent languor of elite disaffection.

Edith Wharton remembered about her friend Henry James that he was thoroughly deaf, dumb, and blind to all the transforming energies of the new America, to its industrial and financial passions. It was all a mystery to him, yet paradoxically one about which he was acutely aware, according to Wharton. James did not suffer so acute a case of sensory deprivation as Wharton implied. He might not feel inclined to penetrate the inner logic of what was happening, but he certainly formed a distinct impression of the moral geography of Wall Street.[9]

In *The American Scene*, James meditates on returning to the country after years abroad: he found himself haunted by the humbling of Trinity Church, now surrounded by ferocious commercial monoliths which crushed and 'dishonored' it. This 'vast money-making structure quite horribly, quite romantically justified itself, looming through the weather with an insolent, cliff-like sublimity'. James felt a 'tenderness' and a 'pity' as the sanctuary seemed a poor, ineffectual thing, overwhelmed by the 'frenzy of Broadway just where Broadway receives from Wall Street the fiercest application of the maddening lash'. At the same time, James was alive to the 'thrill of Wall Street (by which I mean that of the whole wide edge of the whirlpool)'. But he confessed that while he could sense the electricity, he didn't really understand it; he was too old, too much from another age to grasp what was going on. He came away with a presentiment of wild youth on the run, the prize in sight, trampling all the old landmarks in its path. Everything seemed dazzling, crude, and 'over-windowed'. It was all a 'pushing male crowd' of 'monotonous commoness', its dense mass killing any possibility of 'dignity' or 'detachment' or 'meaning'. It was 'appetite at any price'.[10]

Baffled as James may have been, the imprint of Wall Street is nonetheless found on some of his fictional creations. From the earliest stages of his literary career, he was curious about the corrosions of money: it seemed like an acid bath that dissolved relations of love and family and destroyed innocence. Metaphors that draw their energy from commerce and the stock market populated James's work with increasing frequency. 'A Passionate Pilgrim', a short story from 1871, for example, has its protagonist assess the failure of his life as 'a failure as hopeless and helpless, sir, as any that ever swallowed up the slender investments of the widow and the orphan. I don't pay five cents on the dollar.' James himself lived largely off the income from patrimonial securities, which may have pricked this sense of their inherent fragility.

A few years later, *The American* was James's first novel to wrestle with the psychodynamics of money in the life of a representative nouveau-riche American. Though Wall Street is not an active presence in the narrative, it is the material and existential ground on which its eponymous hero, Christopher Newman, stands and confronts the Old

World. Newman amassed his great wealth honestly, but in ways that tethered him to the machinations and machismo of the Street. Finally exhausted by its spiritual pointlessness, uneasy about what it might be doing to his soul, Newman sets forth for the Old World in quest of some nameless replenishment. While all the action takes place abroad, it is the angst engendered by his money fetishism and Wall Street's predations that sets the whole novel in motion.

James is ambivalent about his hero. Newman is naive, profoundly so, and easily tricked by a cynical family of declining French aristocrats. But if he's an innocent, he's a malign one. However much he's victimized by the Bellegardes, he is also a perfect specimen of his peculiar American habitat: boorish, vulgar, self-satisfied, and invincible in his belief there's nothing in the world that can't be bought. This is his fatal and irredeemable flaw, the source of his own social blindness and the irremovable taint in the eyes of his noble French would-be in-laws. The Bellegarde matriarch and eldest son can't abide Newman's driving ambition to marry the family's widowed daughter – the 'magnificent woman' Newman imagines redeeming his life – because they can't get over the fact that he is, after all, 'a commercial person'. To forestall this ultimate insult, they are not only prepared to commit an act of perfidy, but will perversely sacrifice the dynastic future of the family.

James's view is that of a Brahmin outsider. He dissects Newman's more endearing 'americanisms' – his candor, self-confidence, optimism, and extraordinary tolerance for the snobbery of his hosts – as though they are drawn from a catalogue of New World character traits. The younger Bellegarde son, Count Valentin, himself a rakish gambler, is fond of Newman, drawn to his kinetic presence: 'I seem to see you move everywhere like a big stockholder on his favorite railroad. You make me feel awfully my want of shares.'[11]

Late in life, in 1914, still disturbed by the impressions left behind from his last visit to America, James began his final novel. Unfinished and posthumously published, *The Ivory Tower* was his first novel to be set in America since *The Bostonians*, written more than quarter of a century earlier. No hint of native innocence, however crude, remains. Its mordant gaze comes face to face with 'the black and merciless things that are behind the great possessions' of his gilded countrymen. But in the end, James is a stranger to the business world, the Wall Street world of risk and revenge, which shaped men like Christopher Newman. Everything is seen from afar, from the leisured world of the European drawing room, an ocean away from the hurly-burly of the Street.[12]

Edith Wharton worked much closer to home and uncovered Wall Street in the bedroom. Nearing the end of her life, she recalled her colonial ancestors, most of whom had settled in New York. A handful sported aristocratic pedigrees (including a Duer), but most were people of business – merchants, bankers, ship-owners – more interested in 'making money and acquiring property than in Predestination or witch-burning'. Nonetheless they subscribed to a code of comfortable but understated leisure, preoccupied with respectability and with reproducing time-worn tribal rituals. They lived entombed, utterly out of touch with the glittery world of frenzied money-making and party-going swirling around them in Wall Street.[13]

Staid and provincial, Old New York ossified and grew fragile, as is exemplified in *The Age of Innocence*, for which Wharton won the Pulitzer Prize. In that novel, Washington Square's codes of social and sexual correctness are strained to the cracking point. In large measure that's because its airlessness produces fantasies of erotic escape which its hero, one of the chosen, comes perilously close to acting out. But the stress originates from outside as well, from the general direction of Wall Street. The villain of the novel, Julius Beaufort, is, in name and manners, a somewhat malicious caricature of August Belmont. He's a predatory, flamboyant creature, both sexually and financially. He lives amidst Old New York but in flagrante delicto, openly violating its sense of honor, honesty, and noblesse. His mercenary chase after the Countess Olenska, a tainted member of the clan, but nevertheless to be defended, is matched by his legal transgressions on the Street. Beaufort is caught red-handed and banished as Old New York proves itself still able to summon up its reserves of civilized inhibition and decorum. But the novel closes with a premonition. Despite his disgrace, Beaufort's daughter, just a generation later, has risen into the upper reaches of a reconfigured Society, one less duty-bound, less tribal, and less morally constrained. [14]

By the time Beaufort's daughter comes of age, Society is living in a House of Mirth. The atmosphere of Wall Street permeates Wharton's earlier novel of this title. Even the rhythms of sumptuary display are regulated by the pace of the market. When it's down, the narrator tells us, Society sulks in its country houses or puts on a poor face, all the while yearning for the Wall Street magician to bring the good times back. All of its social relations, including the most intimate, have fluctuating conversion rates at which they can be possessed or discarded.

The novel's tragic heroine, Lily Bart, is the coveted sex object of a male world whose animal energies as well as its material wherewithal originate on the Street. Everyone is a speculator, coolly calculating Lily's declining value on the marriage mart, weighing her breathtaking beauty against her shrinking means and diminished social standing. Coolness is the operative word here. Simon Rosedale, the novel's shylock, is no mere plunger, but a man of infinite deliberation in whose hands speculation becomes 'patient industry', very Morgan-like. Early on Rosedale figures that even to be seen walking with Lily in Grand Central Station would be 'money in his pocket'. Nor is this strictly a male game. It is only to be expected, given her patrician upbringing, that Lily finds Rosedale, the oily Jew who crassly quotes her a price for her hand, the most repulsive of her suitors. But Lily herself is a speculator in her own beauty, pursuing its reward with a similar degree of artifice and intention. While still protected by social approbation, Lily develops a creeping anxiety that she's waited too long to strike her bargain with Society, to find her mate and place. At a brilliant soirée she appears in a tableau vivant, gambling on the effect of her stunning presence. She succeeds; the audience is deeply moved; Lily is intoxicated, like any triumphant speculator, with an awareness of her own power. It won't last, however, and from here on Lily's speculations become ever more desperate and less successful.

Lily Bart is simultaneously a creature of the market and its antithesis – at least that is one way of apprehending her tragic flaw. On the one hand, Lily's suicide at the end of the novel is really a kind of social murder. Wall Street systematically devalues her worth, leaving her finally adrift, cast out of Society, descending into the abyss of degrading menial labor. Yet Lily might, at any moment, have chosen differently and made her peace with the commercial calculus of this new world. She not only wants to, she lays careful plans to do just that. Every time something stops her. She draws back not deliberately but in spontaneous, instinctive revulsion. Partly she's inhibited by an inbred, almost subconscious refinement, a deadly ambivalence bequeathed by Old New York. Something more mysterious is also at work, however: a subterranean desire to break free entirely, to defy both the strictures of respectability and the remorseless social arithmetic of the Street. It is that impetuous impulse which scares away Lily's most loyal defender, the patrician Laurence Selden. Aloof and full of disdain for the Wall Street plutocrats, Selden nonetheless lives among them and fears any irrevocable break of the sort Lily proposes. He is in the end a rather hapless, impotent figure, although not so decorative a one as Henry Adams imagined himself to be – so diminished had the Knickerbocker remnant become in the face of Wall Street's dominion.[15]

Undine Spragg suffers from none of Lily's ambivalence and equivocation. The anti-heroine of *The Custom of the Country*, a novel written just before the war at the high noon of the Wall Street regency, Undine is, like Lily, a woman of great beauty, but in every other way unlovely. Where *The House of Mirth* is tragic, *Custom of the Country* is satirical, sometimes given over to farce. Here the culture wars of the fin de siecle are practically over with. Only a faint trace of patrician reticence remains. The Wall Street ethos is the only ethos and Undine is its muse. Love, marriage, and motherhood are Undine's negotiable securities and she puts them in play with dry-eyed calculation.

Dutch Knickerbocker New York hangs on in the presence of Ralph Marvell, the initial target of Undine's machinations to make her way into the inner sanctum of Society. Hailing from provincial western Pennsylvania, Undine has money thanks to her father's mining millions; what she lacks are social credentials, which Ralph's ancestry gives him. Ralph, however, abhors the place Undine pines to go. In his eyes, Society has become 'a muddle of misapplied ornament over a thin steel shell of utility':

> The steel shell was built up in Wall Street, the social trimmings were hastily added in Fifth Avenue, and the union between them was as monstrous and factitious, as unlike the gradual homogenization of growth which flowers into what other countries know as society, as that between the Blois gargoyles on Peter Van Degen's roof and the skeleton walls supporting them.

Ralph is young enough, however, to recognize that the Washington Square world of his parents is aboriginal, doomed to ethnographic extinction. Undine's seduction of Ralph works in part because he wants to believe in a mirage, an artifice of romantic seclusion removed both from the dead hand of Washington Square and the brutish incoherence of Wall Street.[16]

This is fantastical. Real life off the 'Reservation' takes its cue from the Street, and Ralph is no more than its woeful victim. For the Marvells, a stockbroker ranked somewhere between a dentist and shopkeeper, a respectable enough member of the deferring classes. For Undine, however, there are few social stations more alluring, dripping in money and cachet. She's irresistibly drawn towards the Street's gaudy splendor and away from Ralph's intellectuality and moral fastidiousness.

Undine feels an emotional kinship with the Market's unsentimental reckonings. The Marvells are appalled by her casual reference to divorce as a perfectly reasonable strategy for improving one's position on the social stock exchange. She is in this way her father's daughter. Mr Spragg, an otherwise lugubrious type, comes alive when he ventures down to his office on the Street. There his animal passions are ignited, and his face shows the 'glint of half-closed eyes, the forward thrust of black brows, or a tightening of the lax lines of the mouth'. Quickly he figures out that the marriage market is, like the stock exchange, frighteningly unpredictable, that Undine's marriage to Ralph will require a greater capital investment than he anticipated. This leads him to more and more precarious speculations, to losses – and, inevitably, to the souring of the marriage itself as Undine catches on that without a great deal more money than the unambitious Ralph is ever likely to bring them, she will be forever kept outside Society, left to wither on the 'Reservation'.[17]

Practically everything that happens in the story – every character and every emotion – bears the mark of the Street. The undoing of Ralph's literary dreams, his dreams of love, even the abandonment of his honorable but modest legal practice in favour of the more lucrative but demeaning real-estate business, are all casualties of its inexorable workings. Even the lamb-like and self-deluded Ralph wryly observes that marriages of the leisure class ought to be 'transacted on the Stock Exchange'. Whatever his insights into his own predicament, however, it's clear that 'poor Ralph was a survival and destined, as such, to go down in any conflict with the rising new forces.'[18]

Those forces achieve a kind of demonic crystallization in the character of Elmer Moffat. Moffat, once secretly married to Undine when she was still a callow, small-town Baptist teenager, is for much of the book a shadowy figure, appearing and disappearing as he works his way to a surpassing fortune on Wall Street. A borderline felon, always flirting with financial disaster, Moffat's rise can be precisely calibrated with the degree of moral and legal risk to which he opens himself up. He is rootless and amoral, and feasts on the ruination of others.

Elmer and Undine are perfectly matched; together they act out the unholy Zeitgeist of the Street. When Undine rashly runs off with her Wall Street paramour before even securing a divorce from Ralph, it's a daring and irreverent act of speculation during which she shows the same dispassionate sangfroid as Elmer:

> She had done this incredible thing; and she had done it from a motive that seemed at the time, as clear, as logical, as free from the distorting traits of sentimentality as any of her father's financial enterprises. It had been a bold move, but it had been as carefully calculated as the happiest Wall Street 'stroke'.[19]

Elmer and Undine form a sacrilegious partnership. Moffat choreographs a stock scheme, itself put together with political payoffs, whose ulterior purpose is to finance the 'sale' of Ralph and Undine's son, Paul, back to his father. He's been living with his mother, who has no use for him except as a hostage to fortune. Undine finds herself in desperate need of money to finance the Pope's annulment of her marriage, which will in turn free her to marry into the French Catholic aristocracy. Can she trade in her son for the cash necessary to lubricate the machinery of her own social elevation? It is not an overly tormenting decision: after a fleeting twinge of anguish, she licenses Paul's repossession.

Moffat, meanwhile, goes on to triumph after triumph: as he travels to Europe to buy up the heirlooms of a penny-pinched aristocracy, his supreme self-confidence and bravado, his merciless puncturing of all sentimental attachments fills the air. It's the oxygen that keeps Undine's heart pumping as well, but she's become the victim of her own social speculations, as she finds herself a member of that same financially strapped nobility. She is frustrated by and contemptuous of the incomprehensible codes of her new husband's family: they are a maze of commitments and rituals and familial traditions, locked up in the dynastic estate, its land and homes, with no apparent monetary translation or pay-off. Most maddening of all, they are inalienable, stored away in an impermeable cocoon where they can't be traded in for the real stuff of Undine's dreams. When Moffat visits and regales her with tales of his success, conveyed in the argot of the Street which she's never fathomed, she nonetheless 'knew their meaningless syllables stood for success, and what that meant was as clear as day to her':

Every Wall Street term had its equivalent in the language of Fifth Avenue, and while he talked of building up railways she was building up palaces, and picturing all the multiple lives he would lead in them. To have things always seemed to her the first essential of existence, and as she listened to him the vision of the things he could have unrolled before her like the long triumph of an Asiatic conqueror.[20]

This is the canker that eats away at everything. Under its sway, Undine plots to sell the historic tapestries that have been in her new family since they were presented as gifts by Louis XIV, though they are as much part of the family's identity as its name or ancestral lands. But the nouveau aspirations which have coursed through Undine since the days of her family's provincial pre-eminence are deaf to all this senseless tribalism. Moffat, brimming over with the Street's self-assurance, says of Raymond, Undine's French aristocrat husband, 'His ancestors are *his* business: Wall Street is mine.' This could be Undine speaking. She has speculated in husbands as Elmer has speculated in stocks, unloading them like bad investments with no regrets. That she and Elmer should end up where they started, together, is of course only fitting.[21]

Not Edith Wharton perhaps, but other bearers of the same cultural legacy were prepared to draw cosmic conclusions about this spiritual hollowness. In his *Law of Civilization and Decay*, Brooks Adams likened contemporary America to late Rome on the precipice of collapse – a putrefying society stripped bare of its martial valor and imaginative powers. The Rothschilds, in Adams' eyes, were its undertakers: under their reign, usury, once a transgression occurring at the margins of society, became the governing principle of the regime of finance capitalism. Adams' quick sketch of the family's rise singled out Nathan of London, 'despot of the Stock Exchange', for special censure. In his coarseness, his lack of taste or interest in anything but Business, his artfulness at 'bold and unscrupulous speculation', and most of all his squeezing into submission of anything that caught his eye, Nathan gave off the odor of decay that permeated the modern world.

Adams' disgust was truly ecumenical. He rejected all the basic postulates of capitalist life, including the sacrosanct Franklinesque worship of self-interest and the prudential spirit whose bible was the account book. He took up the cultic worship of pre-industrial society, of non-economic man, the chivalrous world of Sir Walter Scott with its obsolescent ethic of courage, enthusiasm, and faith. It all seemed so incomparably superior to the contemporary mercenary age, a world without manners, a sense of adventure, or any instinct for artistic creation; lacking in the honorable disinterestedness of the statesman; a world of plutocrats, bankers, usurers, Jews.[22]

The mood is not far removed from the apocalyptic tone of Populism, and Brooks nearly went so far as to support Bryan in '96, but couldn't get over his elitist contempt for the hayseed. Neither he nor his brother were about to become partisans of a mass movement for democratic reform. By Henry's reckoning, 'nothing could surpass the nonsensity of trying to run a complex and so concentrated a machine by Southern and Western farmers in grotesque alliance with city day laborers.' Nevertheless, Brooks feared the political triumph of the 'Plutocracy'. Their policies were short-sighted, dominated by the narrowest self-interest of the Wall Street banks. They would end up breeding more revolutionaries in droves.

Who could resist the money-men? Even the best people, such as his warrior friend Teddy Roosevelt, were powerless. In the end they would be compelled to sell their swords to the powers that be. Nowadays, one could only fight for 'Wall Street': 'Wall Street is a harder master . . . [It] wants men it can buy and own.' In the heat of the '96 campaign, Adams wrote to advise TR that he might as well strike a deal, as 'Wall Street has desperate need of men like you.' Better to be a barbarian chieftain than a fallen soldier.

One can smell the gunpowder here, and it's hardly surprising that when Adams' mood finally lightened, it did so because he scented a valorous alternative. While the Bryanites sought salvation in The People, Adams found it in Caesar. His brother Henry was already given to acerbic but telling remarks about Wall Street's newly imposing role in global affairs, noting that 'London and Berlin are standing in perfect abject terror, watching Pierpont Morgan's nose floating over the ocean waves, and approaching hourly nearer their bank vaults.' Impressed by America's rise as a world power, financially as well as militarily, Brooks became the staunchest advocate of the nation's imperial turn, especially after Roosevelt assumed the presidency. He shed his former gloom for the exhilaration of the moment, no matter the longer-term prospect. Now he was ready to accept the trust as 'the cornerstone of modern civilization', but only because he could see the emergence of a national administrative elite, a kind of aristocracy of the executive state powerful enough to 'coerce those special interests . . . Call it what you want: empire, dictatorship, republic, or anything else, we have the same problem which Caesar had in Rome when he suppressed the plundering gang of senators led by Brutus.'[23]

Caesarism was only slightly less fanciful than reveries about resurrecting the Middle Age, and a good deal more fantastic than what the Populists were proposing. And even Adams, who really believed in Roosevelt's heroic potential, nurtured an underlying pessimism. Other politically minded Brahmins, equally at odds with the Wall Street dispensation, searched for less melodramatic options.

Henry Cabot Lodge remembered with affection the manners and mores of the social elite that had governed his youth. What a contrast they made to the 'lawless plutocracy' of his mature years, a milieu whose children lacked all conscience or moral restraint, and whose behavior bred a dangerous resentment in the lower classes. Lodge was a United States Senator from Massachusetts and did not dream of some executive *coup de main*. Along with Henry Adams, however, he worried about the vacuum at the center of affairs, the absence of a self-conscious ruling stratum able to rise above the narrow self-interest of the Wall Street crowd. Perhaps some kind of bureaucratic mandarinate might shoulder the burden the patrician old guard had grown too weak and exhausted to bear?[24]

Hopes tended to collect around Roosevelt, whose anti-Wall Street inclinations went way back. As a young, reform-minded New York State legislator in 1882, he'd taken on Jay Gould, calling him a member of 'that most dangerous of all dangerous classes, the wealthy criminal class'. He demanded an investigation into Gould's stock-jobbing schemes on the elevated railroad system; though nothing came of it, the more independent-minded press congratulated Roosevelt for his courage 'in these days of subservience to the robber barons of the Street.' Later on, Roosevelt reviewed Brooks Adams' gloomy tome and while critical in part, sympathized with its melancholic report on modern civilization. He especially concurred with Adams' 'impatient contempt of the deification of the stock market, the trading counter, and the factory'. He chided his friend for the extremity of his political views, most of all his hostility to McKinley and simple-minded defense of the debtor classes. But his antipathy to the Street still simmered. He condemned the Money Power for its pacifism in the run-up to the imperial glory of the Spanish-American war. After the Republican victory over Bryan, he confided that the relationship between 'corrupt wealth . . . the Pierpont Morgan type of men' and 'powerful unscrupulous politicians' was much too incestuous for his liking.[25]

Just how seriously to take these rhetorical fireworks no one would know until Roosevelt unexpectedly assumed the Presidency in the wake of McKinley's assassination. No doubt he dearly disliked the moral flatulence of bloated money-bags, their 'ignoble ease', as any Brahmin gentlemen should. But he harbored no love for democratic politics either, valuing above all the righteous good order and discipline he'd been raised to revere. Like his friend Henry Cabot Lodge, he hated both the 'lawless capitalist' and the 'Debsite type of anticapitalist'. His vision was of public stewardship carried out by an aristocratic administrative cadre. What would happen when those hypothetical guardians of the public interest met up with private trustees of the Morgan regime was not yet puzzled over, as no one expected Roosevelt to rise so far.[26]

Neither the Populist nor the Brahmin reaction to the age of Morgan can be simply dismissed as an old-fashioned attempt to preserve outmoded ways of living. Both groups made trenchant observations about the consolidation of economic and political power. Those observations would be echoed by many other critics of Wall Street – businessmen, middle-class professionals, urban reformers, industrial workers, bohemian radicals, and distinguished jurists – who were entirely enmeshed in modern urban and industrial life. Populists and Brahmins also filled the air with a sense of cultural and moral unease which they shared with many others who didn't live on farms or grow up in pedigreed city enclaves. The vocabulary of opposition invented by the Donnellys and the Adamses, the Watsons and the Roosevelts – 'plutocracy', 'oligarchy', 'the money power', 'parasite' – would remain in vogue, with some modifications, for years to come, deployed by those who accepted the benign logic of industrial progress but who resisted what they saw as Wall Street's pernicious stranglehold on that process.

Yet there was something distinctly old-world about these adversaries of 'morganization'. They viewed its workings as outsiders, from as far away as Monticello and Plymouth Rock. When they looked at Morgan they sometimes saw Jim Fisk instead. When they looked at August Belmont they sometimes saw Julius Beaufort, a lecherous mockery of the Rothschild banker. This was the Wall Street their forebears reviled: the one addicted to speculation and confidence games, the one harboring shylock money-lenders preying on small-time debtors, the Wall Street of the casino, a lawless place of pirates and peculators. This was the Wall Street which had grown up bound to the fortunes of an expanding commercial agriculture and to the prodigious labors of the state to put in place the arterial network of a national marketplace.

No doubt the Wall Street of Morgan's day had a lot in common with the sink of iniquity condemned by Jefferson and Jackson, Melville and Lincoln. But the 'morganized' Street was also something new, situated at the very core of American industrial life, no longer dependent either on the fate of agrarian America or the largesse of the government. It was instinctively cautious, averse to speculative risk-taking, prudent in manner, corporate in style – a sobering place scoured clean of libido. It had adopted as its own the very producerist catechism both Brahmins and Populists so liked to quote in exposing the degeneracy of the Street.

Henry Adams wasn't buying any of this, however. When Morgan created US Steel, the grandest, most expensive corporate amalgamation in the world, Adams spluttered, 'Pierpont Morgan is apparently trying to swallow the sun.' Adams' revulsion wasn't unique. But there were legions of Morgan admirers who felt otherwise. Everybody acknowledged that the creation of this mammoth new business was a landmark event. Legend has it, in fact, that from the moment it germinated as an idea in the head of Charles Schwab, the young man then running Carnegie Steel, this 'deal of the century' – the largest capitalization ever undertaken, at $1.4 billion, dwarfing the Federal budget of $350 million and the national debt of $1 billion – came loaded with portentous visions of world supremacy.

Here's how *Cosmopolitan* magazine greeted the announcement that J. P. Morgan had purchased the vast Carnegie operations (along with others) and merged it with his own (Federal Steel) holdings in the industry. On 3 March 1901, according to John Brisbane Walker, the world ceased 'to be ruled by . . . so-called statesmen':

They were simply in place to carry out the orders of the world's real rulers – those who control the concentrated portion of the money supply. Between the lines of this advertisement headed 'Office of J. P. Morgan & Co.' was to be read a proclamation thus: 'Commercial metropolis of the world'. The old competitive system, with its ruinous methods, its countless duplications, its wasteful-ness of human effort, and its relentless business warfare, is hereby abolished.

In more than a few middle-class neighborhoods, such a portentous proclamation was greeted as very good news indeed.[27]

8

Wall Street is Dead!
Long Live Wall Street!

In 1903, two years after J. P. Morgan called into being the world's greatest corporation and abolished 'the old competitive system', a young writer, with an already established reputation though not long left to live, published the second novel in an intended trilogy. Frank Norris's *The Pit* created a true literary sensation, went through numerous printings, and sold 95,000 copies in its first year. Its fame endured, first as a play staged the next year, and then as a silent film that showed in 1917. Parker Brothers turned it into a board game which was in production as late as 1996 and is still available through specialty stores.[1]

'The Pit: Exciting Fun for Everyone', alternatively advertised as the 'Frenzied Trading Game', was, according to its maker, based on 'the exciting scenes of the American Commodities Exchange', just as Norris's novel was based, with far more verisimilitude, on the hot zone of the Chicago Commercial Exchange, and in particular on action around the 'wheat pit'. Parker Brothers advised players to 'put energy into your trading and trade as quickly as you can'. The object of the game was to secure a 'corner' in one of several commodities – corn, wheat, barley, oats, hay, flax, rye – just as the hero of Norris's story had managed to corner the world's supply of wheat. The game was to be played at a furious pace, signaled by the ringing of an orange bell. Players traded cards amidst a bedlam of yelling and screaming, until someone achieved a 'corner', with the most points awarded to a 'corner' in wheat, and a doubling of their score if the winner happened to be holding a 'Bull' card as well.

Innocent fun! Yet it's hard to imagine that a story about a speculator of practically super-human proportions would have sped so enthusiastically down all the main highways of popular culture – from novel to play to movie to game craze – even a few years earlier. In its own peculiar way, *The Pit* was a cultural seismograph registering a tectonic shift in Wall Street's place in American society during the age of 'morganization'.

Far from fretting about the consolidation of economic power in the hands of a few, a writer in *The Atlantic Monthly* assured his readers that this usefully fixed responsibility where it safely belonged, with trusted men whose accumulated banking resources and cooperative spirit 'are generally recognized to be one of the most potent factors in our recent industrial progress and our present financial security'. US Steel, along with other Morgan inspirations like International Harvester and General Electric, were more than colossal companies: they promised deliverance from a way of doing business which in the eyes of some had come to resemble a form of suicide.

So it was that as the economy underwent its re-creation at the hands of the Wall Street fraternity, what one historian has characterized as the 'anti-competitive consensus' emerged. It articulated the new order's economic logic and historical significance. The consensus never included everybody and was attacked from the moment it was invented. But even today a train of thought treats what might be called 'the Morgan dispensation' as a Darwinian evolutionary adaptation. Formed out of the primordial soup of free-booting capitalism, it perfected systematic organization, rational planning, integration of function, and an aptitude for responsible, risk-averse management.[2]

In 1903 the New York Stock Exchange unveiled its new home on Broad Street. Its grandiose Greek-revival facade was supported by six Corinthian columns and topped by a striking triangular pediment, crafted by John Quincy Adams Ward and bearing the portentous inscription, 'Business Integrity Protecting the Industries of Man'. A mythology was etched on its face. In the center of the stone carving was a figure of a woman, 'Integrity'. Her outstretched arms hovered protectively over sculpted figures frozen in a choreography of productive labor: to her left, Agriculture and Mining; on her right, Science, Industry, and Invention. Beneath Integrity's solicitous gaze a harmonious Commerce reigned. Wall Street, once a scarlet woman, a disreputable habituée of capitalism's badlands, was here miraculously beatified. The 'morganization' of the economy had worked a wondrous change. Wall Street was dead. Long live Wall Street![3]

From the time of William Duer, most middle-class Americans had grown up suspicious about what people did on Wall Street. Was it work or was it gambling; was it moral or not; did it add to or subtract from the value of what the country produced; was it inherently arcane, aristocratic, and conspiratorial or open to all; did it aid the free market or subvert it; was it rational or delusional; in a word, was it legitimate or out of bounds? The verdict had been more often negative than not, but 'morganization' produced a cultural breakthrough. For the first time in its otherwise blighted history Wall Street found itself welcomed into the realm of middle-class respectability.

Nowhere was this more evident than in the way some people – including intellectuals, journalists, and politicians as well as members of the upwardly mobile urban middle class – began to change their minds about speculation. For a culture genetically programmed to venerate thrift and hard labor, this was no mean feat. But by calming a high-strung, erratic economy that seemed perpetually verging on collapse, the white-shoe investment fraternity seemed to prove the once unthinkable: that risk-taking could be rational, that a stable society might rest on acts of speculation.

Moreover, the proliferation of publicly owned corporations at the turn of the century multiplied the opportunities to indulge a taste for speculation on the stock market. Very soon, the traditional sparse menu of railroad and government bonds became a smorgasbord of exotic equities in hundreds of new industrial combinations. At the same time, the increasing numbers of well-paid professionals, mid-level corporate managers, and technical employees – itself an outcome of Wall Street's transformation of the economy – bred a natural constituency supporting the rehabilitation of the Street. The numbers of people investing in the market remained tiny by today's standards – probably about four million in 1900, between seven and eight million by 1910 – but it was many more than participated during the Gilded Age with its far narrower range of securities and reputation for instability. And that strange phenomenon of 'public opinion', which grew weightier yet also more elusive as mass-circulation magazines for the urban middle class proliferated, increasingly articulated the desires and anxieties of the new corporate white-collar world. It was from just those precincts that the stock market was drawing its newest recruits.

The major exchanges – both in New York and at the Chicago Board of Trade, the great center of agricultural commodity speculation – helped promote this new attitude. They waged war on the 'bucket shops'. These were one-room walk-in affairs in towns all across the country, housed in dingy, dilapidated buildings with a ticker and chalkboard. Gathered there was a picturesque brotherhood of greed – men, always men, with a 'tip' from a 'Trolley insider'; or an unassuming barber who happened to trim the beard of some 'Napoleon of finance'; or perhaps an old eccentric loaded down with elaborate charts of some infallible mathematical system; characters of infinite hope and desperation, hanging on until one day they vanished.

These 'bucket shops', also known colloquially as 'funeral parlors', conducted a shady business wagering on the ups and downs of stock prices, often without any stock changing hands, sometimes without even the benefit of a real 'wire' reporting the real prices. They were run by pretend brokers unconnected to any stock or commodity exchange, rigging the local market until suspicions heated up and they fled into the night. By attacking these larcenous operations, the 'securities industry' redefined the moral status of speculation. The activity itself wasn't evil; but there were evil forms. 'Bucket shops' demonstrated that the real historic conflict was not so much a cosmological one between virtuous producers and speculative parasites, but a more everyday one between producers and consumers. In this new way of looking at things, the reputable exchanges were themselves producers, committed to high standards of efficiency, service, and professionalism. Indeed, speculation, properly conducted, could be considered a profession in its own right, whose expertise consisted in the making and interpretation of markets and the taking of risks. [4]

Risk itself went through a metaphysical transformation. If it could inspire such prodigious economic enterprise, perhaps it could and should be rescued from its Puritan excommunication. And some credited it with still greater virtues. Around the turn of the century, men like Teddy Roosevelt and William James, seeking a way of revitalizing a society apparently overcome with industrial routine, Victorian convention, and debilitating femininity, pondered the idea that the gambling instinct was a therapeutic elixir. For Roosevelt particularly, risk-taking – whether in combat, or on expeditions into 'darkest Africa' or the polar wilderness, or in pioneering scientific and technical investigations – came to seem like the essence of red-blooded masculinity.

The very notion of chance was undergoing a philosophical re-evaluation. Modernist thinkers like James and Charles Pierce abandoned an older mechanistic world-view resting on the laws of cause and effect. They came to terms with an inherently uncertain universe governed by probabilities, and devised notions of the 'standard deviation' and 'risk assessment' to lend it coherence. Chance was thereby made both inescapable and controllable. The gambler's mad conceit, that he depended not on luck but on a kind of magical inner divination, was smuggled into the 'science' of speculation. For characters like Simon Rosedale, Lily Bart's predatory suiter in Edith Wharton's *House of Mirth*, playing the market was not gambling but 'patient industry'. As Walter Benn Michaels notes, the world seemed not so much rule-bound as controllable by artifice and intention. The stock market and its oscillations were merely phenomenal instances of this deeper orderly disorder.[5]

Drawing Jesuitical distinctions between speculation and investment had been a cultural preoccupation for generations. But now the former began to merge into the latter. At the turn of the century, commodity trading in agricultural goods still affected many more people than the stock market. Seven times the annual crop was traded each year on the various exchanges, particularly in Chicago. Prices fluctuated wildly. Distant speculators were roundly denounced for profiting from 'wind wheat'. For the first time, however, a counter-argument gained credence. Defenders of the exchanges maintained that the speculator was a specialist, facilitating a wider and more stable distribution of commodities; without him the farmer's exposure to risk would be even greater. Metropolitan newspapers decried 'the ignorance of rustics' who persisted in hunting down bogey-men.[6]

Industrial America's rapprochement with speculation went further. Even the nineteenth century's favorite self-made producer-hero, Andrew Carnegie, who kept Wall Street at arm's length, could acknowledge the service it provided to investors while condemning its speculative side: 'All pure coins have their counterfeit; the counterfeit of business is speculation.' Moreover, before he got religion and determined to keep his steel holdings private, free of the 'mercurial changes of the Stock Exchange', Carnegie speculated like a champion. The steel master's faint approval was light years away, however, from the new spirit of the times articulated by financial journalist and storyteller, Edwin Lefevre. The peculiarly 'American type', according to

Lefevre, was 'the speculator – the gambler if you will'. It was he, not the conservative investor, who really made the market work. Without him it 'would be difficult, perhaps impossible . . . to build railroads, to erect factories, to consolidate industries, to become a world power'. This hyperbolic sense that all that separated civilization from savagery was the capitalist visionary had been around at least since the first hagiography of Cornelius Vanderbilt: without the Commodore, 'no railroads or steamships or telegraphs; no cities, no leisure class, no schools, colleges, literature, art – in short no civilization.' Now Wall Street inherited this exalted reputation.[7]

Popular middle-class magazines like *The Atlantic Monthly* spread the word. The stock market was a vital piece of economic machinery, lubricating the wheels of capital mobility. The country's progress depended on making sure that investment capital didn't lie idle, stagnating in useless hoards. The judicious stock-market promoter was an economic matchmaker, introducing the desiring investor to a bevy of attractive investment options. The magazine congratulated the Street for facilitating that process by devising a host of new securities, artfully designed to meet a host of particular investment needs. It was a mark of the national genius; the Old World had much to learn from the way in which the American stock market attracted whole new classes of the population, widening its orbit of financial as well as cultural support.

For the editors of *The Atlantic Monthly* or *The Century*, the rise of the great combinations was a revelation. They seemed for the most part models of efficiency and economies of scale. They put an end to destructive competition and the irrational duplication of facilities. True, they were sometimes mimicked by less well-grounded undertakings. The editors cautioned against an 'unfettered stock market' whose seductive glitter might permit 'rich buccaneers to upset values and threaten the tranquil ownership of property'. But the remedy was not to consign Wall Street to some moral and financial quarantine: it would be better to rely on the wisdom of a select group of trusted financiers. Their sense of responsibility, the concentration of banking resources at their disposal, their collegial spirit of cooperation made them 'generally recognized to be one of the most potent factors in our recent industrial progress and our present financial security'. And after all, 'the financial powers which control these institutions seek the best brains.'[8]

Among those 'best brains', academic economists and social scientists likewise theorized and justified the new order. 'The formation of trusts is a process of natural selection of the highest order,' one which put 'undertaking genius' at the head of these new 'progressive' industrial organizations, weeding out the 'weak entrepreneur'. The voices of 'Progress' and 'History' could be heard speaking the language of corporate consolidation, according to gatherings of the American Economic Association and the American Academy of Political and Social Science, where the old competitive marketplace was denounced as outmoded and socially dangerous. Yale professor Henry C. Emery published a talmudic commentary exploring the subtlest distinctions between gambling and speculation. Distinguished economist Charles Conant thought of the stock market as a kind of economic gyroscope, signaling capital shortages and surpluses and allowing for the quick transfer of capital from sector to sector to restore balance. He also stressed its social significance. Like a magnet, it attracted a pool of savings spread among a diffuse mass of smallholders, giving them all a common stake in the new corporate order, while leaving control of large and complex properties in the hands of a centralized and expert management. [9]

For as long as anybody could remember, 'watered stock' epitomized what was fraudulent about Wall Street. The merger movement managed to undermine even that article of faith. In 1899, the Civic Federation of Chicago convened a 'Conference on Trusts'. There, J. W. Jenks, the statistician of the US Industrial Commission, raised the question of just what constituted 'over-capitalization'. It was not at all clear to him whether the capital value of a corporation should be arrived at conservatively – that is, measured by paid-in capital, cash on hand, and a prudent estimate of plant and equipment – or more liberally, taking into account the company's earnings potential, a far less tangible entity. While Jenks was agnostic, others, like George Gunton, publisher of *Gunton's Magazine*, were not. Gunton was inclined to minimize the problem of over-capitalization, confident that the stock market would set a fair rate. He and others denied the claim that high capitalization resulted in abnormally high prices to sustain investors' dividends. Naturally, they conceded that speculative swindles did and would occur, and should be punished. But the regular operations of the stock market were benign. Wall Street 'manufactured' stock and bonds like any other commodity producer. The Market received these 'goods', presented them to the public where they were 'quality tested'; some found permanent resting places with investors, others, like the infamous Erie, remained perpetually in play. Speculation was a vital part of the market's metabolism. To be without it would be like a human body 'without lungs, heart, stomach, and other organs as well as without flesh and blood'. Wall Street was the ultimate legitimating agency, a 'toll-gate in the Highway of American Progress'.

The 'Final Report' of the US Industrial Commission, issued in 1902, echoed these deliberations. The great industrial consolidations were accepted as inevitable and beneficial. Alternative approaches to capitalization were duly noted. While observing that there were considerable profits to be made by promoters in the first months after a new merger, noting that the secrecy surrounding these dealings might advantage the wicked and seduce the innocent, the Report nonetheless concluded optimistically. These evils, in particular the temptation to over-capitalization, were already diminishing, thanks to popular skepticism and in particular, the intervention of the great prudential investment houses that were superseding the more unruly and less scrupulous freelance promoters.[10]

No doubt the commissioners first of all had in mind that 'Bismarck of the Railroads' himself. Frequently accused of being a deft stockwaterer in his own right, Morgan's reputation nonetheless remained in some circles unimpeachable. Indeed, his most recent biographer offers a defense in keeping with the fresh approach to stock-market valuations that first surfaced a century ago. Morgan's re-financings of the railroads wrung most of the 'water' out of the new systems. Moreover, in keeping with this elite's broader sense of fiscal and social responsibility, Morgan's syndicates received payment for their services in high-risk common stock, not in bonds or other preferred securities. In this view, the proof was in the pudding, as Morgan and his associates imposed a chastening regimen on the 'gigantic waste and fraud and duplication' of the railroads.

A *New York Times* reporter, trying to account for Morgan's extraordinary stature, concluded that it had little to do with his money. Rather the House of Morgan functioned, in the popular mind, as a synecdoche for Wall Street, which many now perceived as a quasi-benevolent organization whose benign ministrations caused banks and corporations to flourish, gave employment to millions of workers, and allowed the stocks of 'widows and orphans to rise in value and give off dividends'. *Harper's* observed, during the terrifying panic of 1907 when Morgan raced to the rescue of the economy, that there were in effect two Wall Streets. One was the old den of speculators and swindlers, perhaps never to be entirely expunged. But the newly risen Wall Street was an 'essential partner of industry and intelligence in material production', and it could be trusted implicitly.[11]

Wall Street's rising legitimacy, its pivotal role in forming huge, publicly traded corporations, and its attractiveness as a money-making outlet for widening segments of the middle class had significant consequences for the nation's legal culture. Lawyers and legal theorists homed in on this newly popular form of shareholder ownership, wrestling with concepts of limited liability. They crafted new definitions of property that could take account of the right of return on intangible assets like 'good will', and helped to open up the portals through which industrial stocks might travel out into the general population. James Dill, the Wall Street lawyer mainly responsible for drafting the 1889 law making all this corporate merging and acquiring legally defensible, argued that if these new industrial securities could be made safe for 'small capital', it would help to win the loyalty of the middle classes for this new incorporated system of private property. This was itself a significant cultural revolution, as until then most people assumed that the connection between ownership and control of property was absolute and indissoluble. Now these same middle-class folk, prospective shareholders in America Incorporated, would be weaned away from any vestigial belief that ownership included actual control over the use and allocation of property.[12]

Certain brokers and banking houses began to covet the small investor. Kidder, Peabody and Lee, Higginson in particular looked to sell securities to those seeking income rather than capital gains, and the latter created a sales force and marketing strategy specifically aimed at this niche. Because this clientele was predictably naive about financial matters, the first independent investment-counseling concerns surfaced, and investment banks too began to provide such advice.[13]

On his visit to America in the late 1880s, James Bryce, a British peer, had already noticed this simmering American middle-class appetite to play the market. In Europe, this remained the province of professionals. But in the New World, 'there are times when the whole community, not merely city people but also storekeepers in country towns, even farmers, even domestic servants, interest themselves actively in share speculations.' He saw lists of share prices hung up on posts in the streets and outside newspaper offices, where they were changed every hour or two. The center of this all-American activity was New York, 'and as the centre of America is New York so the centre of New York is Wall Street', which Bryce considered the 'nerve centre of all American business'. He found it 'the most remarkable sight in the country after Niagara Falls and the Yellowstone Geysers', so struck was he by the violent passions that swirled through its serpentine corridors. Bryce concluded that middle-class enthusiasm for speculation had implanted itself deeply in the American character, that it had 'already passed into the national fiber'.[14]

By the turn of the century, a diverse literature catered to this swelling audience of amateurs, friendly to the market but arguing that it should become a more transparent place, and to that end publicizing relevant facts about the new securities and the corporations they financed. Edward Jones, partner in a brokerage, along with Charles Henry Dow, a financial journalist, were weary of the secretive manipulations that distorted the operations of the market and damaged its reputation. Dow in particular was a rather dour New Englander, conservative and ascetic, with a somewhat anal faith in the predictability of things. Together they sought to codify the causes of stock fluctuations. By locating long-term influences in general 'sentiments' that were themselves based on broader economic conditions, the tides of unreason might be tamed, breaking people's hypnotic fixation on the random daily fluctuations of the Exchange. Dow and Jones issued their first 'average' of stock prices in an 1884 issue of their 'Customers Afternoon Letter', a sheet read by market professionals. There were no industrial stocks on that list. In 1896, the Dow Jones 'industrial average' made its debut, a pool of information drawn from twelve major stocks, that best expressed the prevailing 'general sentiment'.[15]

The *New York Times* began running 'Wall Street Talk' and 'Financial Affairs' columns. *Harper's Weekly* started one called 'The World of Finance', which followed doings on the Street, lifted the stigma attached to stock speculation by treating it as part of everyday life, and reassured its financially unsophisticated readers about the safety of the new stock. By force of habit, the magazine continued to extol the virtues of the free market. Now, however, it pointed out that 'competition brings also evils', including shoddy and adulterated goods, discriminatory railroad rates, child labor, unsafe and unsanitary working conditions, and sheer waste. Trusts and combinations, while liable to their own acts of selfishness, were enemies of waste. One way or another they represented the future, and that future would be bright as long as these mammoth undertakings were brought 'within the law of the stock market' and subjected to skeptical assessment by the investing public.

Magazines like *Harper's* flattered the small investor as the key ingredient in the country's economic growth, while reassuring the reticent that the stock market encapsulated the audacious spirit 'that sent Peary to the Pole and got Wilbur Wright off the ground'. An act of speculation could even provide a metaphysical release from the anonymity and deadening conformity of industrial society. The clerk, the 'filing girl', the lonely could 'enlarge their destiny' and 'ally oneself with mystery' and 'romance'. The stock market, once rid of its less savory denizens, might just provide that 'spiritual adventure' missing from the lives of the 'common folk'.

For some, the rise of the publicly traded corporation even promised to improve the country's class relations. John Bates Clark, Richard Ely, and other reform-minded economists were hardly Pollyanna-ish. They worried about the inherent conflict of interest between investors and the promoters of these giant consolidations, and between corporate managers and the anonymous mass of common shareholders. But Clark, for one, also prophesied that the widening of the class of stock owners to include workers would dampen class conflict: 'The socialist is not the only one who can have beatific visions.'

Confidence men, unscrupulous promoters, shifty brokers had not vanished, but were less feared in the new and more professional Wall Street. F. B. Thurber, President of the United States Export Association, cited a New York brokerage firm circular to explain why he felt safe. Acknowledging the lightning-like 'manufacture' of securities on the Street, the pamphlet noted that previously Wall Street only needed to know about railroading. Now 'we must inform ourselves . . . as to steel billets, barbed wire, freight cars, paper bags, baking powder, electric and air power cabs, passenger and freight elevators, hard-rubber goods, typewriting machines, smelters, cigars, cigarettes, beet-root sugar, pumps, potteries, etc.' Bankers and brokers examined these candidates for investment with great caution and were not 'so enthusiastic as the promoters of these various consolidations, and therein lies the safety of the situation.' While Thurber predicted a 'checkered career' for these proliferating industrial stocks, he remained sure that 'the test of time will separate the sheep from the goats.'[16]

Henry Clews, always an irrepressible champion of Wall Street, sensed the shift in the wind. His *Twenty-Eight Years in Wall Street* censured the clergy in particular for spreading the canard that the Street was a den of parasitic gamblers. On the contrary, for Clews and many others, risk, speculation, and even the periodic panics that regrettably followed in their wake were an essential part of 'our vast pioneering enterprise', in a country bursting at the seams with gigantic (and inevitably uncertain) new undertakings.[17] Middle-class magazines like *Munsey's* and *The North American Review* articulated a swelling pride in the nation's remarkable prosperity and especially its emergence as a player in world affairs. While journalists might still depict the market habitué as a 'nervous dandy with watery eyes and muddy complexion', a certain glamour crept into these descriptions, especially those of the 'bulls', admired for their all-American boldness and gregarious good cheer. The regular use in national celebrations of blizzards of tickertape, once a piece of Christmas revelry confined to the Exchange, was symptomatic of the changed mood.[18]

More than glamour and glitter were at work here, however; after all, sensationalism had attached itself for years even to the most reprobate 'robber barons' and Wall Street buccaneers. Journalists had long tracked their familial intrigues, their parties, their lavish voyages abroad, their dalliances, the fate of their offspring. But now genuine social esteem, even a sense of awe grew up alongside the Street's new legitimacy. Lord Bryce observed about people like James Hill and E. H. Harriman that 'When the master of one of the great Western lines travels toward the Pacific in his palace car his journey is like a royal progress. Governors of States and Territories bow before him; legislatures receive him in solemn session; cities seek to propitiate him.' The doings of the Morgan fraternity became a daily spectacle: when J. P. Morgan launched his 241-foot ocean-going yacht, *Corsair II*, people found it the perfect symbol of America's global financial might. When the patriarch's son, Jack, married Jane Grew of the Boston banking family, the *New York Times* ran the illustrated story on its front page as if it were a state affair. And it was believed that crowds parted when the world's most famous banker walked down the street.[19]

Of course, such reverence for the Wall Street caste was hardly spiritual – in the end, it was based on money. As the nineteenth century drew to a close, the Social Register and similar indices increasingly measured pure wealth, whether or not it was weighed down with blood lines and social pedigree. This was a world, in Henry James's telling aperçu, of 'bottomless superficiality'; it was a society of the Spectacle. Great weddings paraded down Broadway, where masses of people gridlocked as they gazed at the jewel-encrusted barouches and the oceans of exotic flowers. Despite ingrained republican distrust of pomp and circumstance, city people were powerfully attracted to artifice of all kinds: food displays erected into dramatic tableaux, richly decorated interiors, insignia of royalty and nobility carved into bedsteads, suits of armor, medieval spears doing double duty as drapery stanchions. When the Duke of Marlborough married a Vanderbilt in 1895, *The Times* reported that 'women and children almost threw themselves under the feet of the horses in their desire to get a look at the occupants of the vehicles.'

The velocity at which millionaires were produced was nowhere greater than on Wall Street. Many of the Fifth Avenue palaces ogled by New Yorkers were inhabited by families enriched by the Street. Papers never tired of relating Society's prodigality, providing detailed accounts of James Hazen Hyde's $200,000 ball at Sherry's in 1905, and Henry Lehr's 'dog dinner' where his friends' pets supped on pâté and chicken. When the creation of US Steel led to an explosion of new Pittsburgh millionaires (Carnegie's top management were invited to the feast), the orgy of splendor that followed was hypnotic for many. Mansions with Ivanhoe-like drawbridges, gold-plated pianos, heraldic decorations on cigar bands, gifts of gold-plated bicycles to chorus girls were catnip for the tabloids.

By the turn of the century, New York was developing a global reputation as an Oz of wealth and power. Wall Street was the dynamo that called into being the monumental public buildings and houses of high culture. *The Times* went so far as to sing the praises of 'the public service trust', by which it meant all the great beneficences funded by Wall Street nabobs: 'It is impossible to consider what New York's public activities would do without these men'; they ran 'a trust of the public spirit'. 'Society' pages helped cook up a strange new social consciousness that mixed emulation with envy, ersatz familiarity with an intimidating remoteness. A new publication, *Town Topics*, devoted itself entirely to gossip about the more risqué Wall Street figures, some of whom were blackmailed to keep their names out of circulation.

But such publications did not diminish Wall Street's mystique: there was a peculiar kind of alchemy at work, one that changed gold into a rarer element. Though newspapers like *The World* and *The Tribune* ran competitions to see who could sniff out the most millionaires – *Tribune* 4,047; *World* 3,045 – they and similar publications also helped transmute the homelier qualities of mercantile shrewdness into sacerdotal acts: financial acumen became 'vision', avarice was reborn as business 'foresight', rapaciousness morphed into 'military strategy'.[20]

It was in this context that the creation of a uniquely large corporation like United States Steel could be viewed as earth-shattering, an almost divine re-making of the world as it had once been known. The deal was indeed stupendous, involving 300 underwriters, including bank and insurance company presidents. Carnegie was paid $480 million at a time when the Federal budget was $350 million. The new company absorbed eight already gigantic amalgamations and seven more individual companies. Capitalized at $1.4 billion (the world's first billion-dollar corporation), it accounted for a sixth of the total value of American manufacturing.

Alexander Dana Noyes, dean of American financial writers at the turn of the century, commented at the time of the US Steel announcement that:

> Men and women and even children all over the country drank thirstily every scrap of news that was printed in the press about these so-called 'captains of industry', their successful 'deals', the off-hand way in which they converted slips of worthless paper into guarantees of more than princely wealth, and all the details concerning their daily lives, their personal peculiarities, their virtues, and their vices.

Some of this hullabaloo was deliberately whipped up by PR flaks and Morgan allies, like market manipulator, James R. Keene, to prepare the ground for the unloading of the new securities. Much of it, though, was unadulterated enthusiasm. For instance, *World's Work*, a soberly middle-class magazine, mesmerized its readers with a double-paged map, in color, outlining the great railroad empires of Vanderbilt, Gould, Rockefeller, Morgan, Hill, and Harriman, as if they were armed legions massed for battle.[21]

Peter Finely Dunne, the great fin-de-siecle satirist of all forms of American hypocrisy and self-inflation, loved to parody this sense of grandeur and omnipotence. But his Mr Dooley riffs on J. P. Morgan were so hilarious only because they drew on a reservoir of popular adulation. Take the following:

Pierpont Morgan calls in wan iv his office boys, th' prisident iv a national bank, an says he, 'James', he says, 'take some change out iv th' damper an' run out an' buy Europe f'r me, he says. I intend to reorganize it an' put it on a payin' basis . . . Call up the Tsar and the Pope an' th' Sultan an' the Impror Willum, an tell thim we won't need their services after nex' week, he says. Give thim a year's salary in advance. [22]

If the reader thinks Mr Dooley had lost all contact with reality, then try sampling popular opinion about the esteemed banker's testimony before the Pujo committee early in 1913, just months before his death. The Pujo committee (chaired by Louisiana Congressman Arsenia Pujo) was conducting a Congressional investigation into the 'money trust'; that is, it was seeking to determine whether or not in fact the country's financial and economic resources were closely controlled by a small investment-banking clique. A sizeable part of the population believed the accusation was true. Everyone eagerly awaited Morgan's testimony before the committee. Would this most reserved and taciturn man, zealously protective of his privacy and prerogatives – the man who when asked if he owed the public an explanation for the Northern Pacific panic of 1901 replied, 'I owe the public nothing' – be compelled to reveal his most secret undertakings? Would he prevail or might he even be publicly humiliated?

Morgan prevailed – then, and since then in the historical record. Samuel Untermeyer, the committee's chief counsel, interrogated him politely but relentlessly. Nonetheless, Morgan flatly denied that he possessed the kind of overwhelming power that everyone knew he did. In a frequently quoted colloquy, when Untermeyer suggested that Morgan and his confederates exercised financial favoritism that rewarded those already endowed with resources and connections, the banker emphatically demurred: 'The first thing is character, before money or anything else. Money cannot buy it.'

Morgan's modesty was preposterous, but sounding the ancient cry of 'character' was just right, exactly what many people wanted to believe about this newly risen elite in whom so much trust was vested. So while many scoffed at his testimony, papers like the *Chicago Tribune* reacted in ways Mr Dooley would appreciate. The editors called Morgan 'a master of the mighty processes that move in the modern world, shaping the material destinies of nations and their millions of souls.' Another, a 'Bull Moose' paper, congratulated the banker for the dignity of his presentation: 'He talked like a statesman. There was in his testimony no touch of the stock gambler, no suggestion of the rat-like cunning that has marred similar interviews with men who probably have greater fortunes than he.' These were editorial leaps of faith, rather than reportage or considered opinion.[23]

The cultural raw material of Dooleyism had been accumulating for years. Hanging in the Metropolitan Museum of Art is a legendary photo of Morgan by Edward Steichen, posed in 1903. Steichen was particularly taken with Morgan's eyes. (What might be called 'tycoon eyes' amounted to a minor visual fetish in those days: a *New York World* reporter once said of Harriman's eyes that they 'could look through the steel side of a battleship'.) Steichen compared Morgan's gaze to the experience of confronting the on-rushing headlights of a locomotive. The photographer found Morgan's physical bulk (he was six foot, big-chested and portly) intimidating as well, and was struck by his deep booming voice, his abrupt speech, and his aggressive presence. The picture does indeed rivet the viewer on those enormous, glowering eyes and, inescapably, on Morgan's famously bulbous, inflamed and diseased nose (which Steichen retouched to remove some of its more unsightly spots). The Morgan nose had become a kind of public monument, so much so that the financier rejected the surgery suggested by the Russian diplomat Count Witte because, Morgan explained, 'Everybody knows my nose. It would be impossible for me to appear in the streets of New York without it.' In its forceful self-assertion and imposing dignity, the photo captured the wonder and respectful distance that Morgan elicited from many of his contemporaries.[24]

In Henry Adams, this economic vainglory set off a range of reactions, mainly negative ones, and it also contributed to his gathering fatalism: the reign of finance capital was inexorable. After the Republican victory over William Jennings Bryan and the Populist insurgency in 1896, Adams concluded that the investment bankers had become 'the greatest single power in the country, and infallibly control the drift of events'.[25]

Lincoln Steffens was younger and less gloomy than Adams. However, they shared a sense of Wall Street's looming omnipotence. Although Steffens would go on to become a famous muckraking writer, early in his career as a reporter, in 1892, he was assigned to cover Wall Street for Laurence Godkin's studiously proper and conservative *Evening Post*. Naive and impressionable, he approached those he admiringly described as 'the constructive engineering financiers' as if they were the most formidable figures of the day:

> My approach to high finance was that of most of the world . . . It was the awed approach of a boy brought up in the belief that there were heroes, really giants and great persons, whether good or evil, in life . . . My Wall Street assignment was an opportunity to see giants.

Morgan, of course, was first among them. Looking back, Steffens remembered the financier's aloofness, how unapproachable he seemed, how he was feared even by his own partners, who considered it risky to even open up a conversation; when called for 'they looked alarmed and darted in like office boys'. The cub reporter admitted that he too felt 'a vague awe of the man'. There, brooding in the solitude of his office, Morgan seemed to him a great mathematician, 'alone with himself and his mind'. There was no question in Steffens' view that Wall Street's operations were perfectly legitimate: the Street, he explained, was for most people not only a central economic reality, but a 'moral and wise' place. Although he would later in life come 'to despise and pity' these men who lived and thrived at the expense of others, at the time he was so taken with their affairs that he empathized as they took their daring plunges. The world of business at the turn of the century seemed to him 'all good', the world of politics 'all bad'. For a time, he treated Morgan's Wall Street like the economy's Vatican, a holy of holies. Even when he was brought face to face with its uglier aspects – its chicanery, its use of the law to evade the law – at first he could scarcely believe what he saw.

The same sort of 'vague awe' was felt by other less likely observers. Scott Joplin, of all people, caught the mood musically. He composed *Wall Street Rag* in 1909, an unusually programmatic piece in four named parts: 'Panic in Wall Street, Brokers Feeling Melancholy', followed by 'Good Times Coming', 'Good Times Have Come', and a finale called 'Listening to the Strains of Genuine Negro Ragtime,

Brokers Forget Their Cares'. Legend has it Joplin wrote and first performed the *Rag* in Fraunces Tavern close by the financial district. Whatever Joplin's actual thoughts about the Street, *Wall Street Rag* struck a note of mirthful good cheer and easy optimism.[26]

A whole literature grew up in response to this mass fascination. There were stories and diatribes, novels and exposés, jeremiads and briefs for the defense. Some of it mixed fact and fiction, like the stories of Edwin Lefevre. People loved these tales that seemed to provide a real feel for life in the financial district and its personalities. For anyone in the know, Lefevre's characters clearly mirrored figures like Keene and Harriman, set in motion on the romantic 'battlefield' of the Street. Stories like 'The Break in Turpentine', 'The Tipster', and 'The Last Opportunist' struck an amused and bemused tone, an air of ironic detachment about Wall Street's adventures and misadventures.[27]

Munsey's was the most popular general magazine of the 1890s, read by 700,000 people. Frank Munsey, who himself did a fair amount of speculating on the Street, ensured that his magazine conveyed the glory and enchantment of financial success. Articles about Wall Street's mysteries thrilled rural storekeepers and city clerks alike. Pieces on 'Ball Giving in New York', 'The Equipage of the Millionaire', and 'Two Miles of Millionaires' betrayed no hint of envy or resentment.

The change was subtle, a matter of inflection. Textual and visual portraits of Wall Street titans in magazines like *Munsey's* still gave off dangerous vibrations, but they were also more flattering, more respectful, more humane. The *Munsey's* profile of Jay Gould's son, Edwin, for example, noted his athleticism, his vigorous participation in Troop A of the First Dragoons, his fondness for horses, his crewing for Columbia. The monikers and eccentricities of other Wall Street notables were recorded with a sense of endearment. Even depictions of the shady world of the promoter were lightened with amusing tales about schemes to run a milk pipeline from Orange County to New York City; or a deal offered to Collis P. Huntington to purchase the Great Salt Lake, evaporate it, and sell it as salt back East; or a proposition made to Vanderbilt to buy up all the Civil War battlefields and convert them into what today we would call 'theme parks'.[28]

Munsey's, along with *Century*, *Cosmopolitan*, and similar magazines, hailed 'The Reign of the Business Man' and defended the trusts as, oddly, the newest terrain on which heroic individuals might prove their mettle. Wall Street hagiographies became a minor literary industry, some of them even appealing to children.

E. H. Harriman's prodigal career on the Street – he started out as a fourteen-year-old 'pad shaver' carrying buy and sell messages from office to office – served as one of the more popular models for dime novels about Wall Street wizards aimed at an audience of young males. Credited with transforming the decrepit Union Pacific – sometimes likened to 'two streaks of rust' – into a model of modern railroad efficiency, Harriman enjoyed a reputation as a kind of financial magician. Though he has been much criticised since then, Harriman's most recent biographer resurrects that image in describing the railroad baron's turn of the century struggle for supremacy in the West: 'Here truly was Harriman in the role of a railroad Napoleon, risen from obscurity to a position of power in which the destiny of his world rested in the choices he made between war and peace.' Like Napoleon, and like the rest of the imperial financial elite to which he belonged, Harriman, according to this historian, saw himself as 'wielding power to serve not himself but larger, nobler causes'.[29]

Always popular, the Napoleonic comparison became practically universal in attempts to capture the sense of grandeur inspired by the age of Morgan. But it was no longer Napoleon the upstart, the obscurely risen, the scourge of the old regime, that thrilled and inspired. One didn't read much any more about industry and thrift, honesty and piety. Heroes now were men of will and force: Titans, figures of enormous strength, wielders of earth-shaking power like their Greek predecessors. Their traits mimicked the technologies they lorded over; they were men of iron, with wills and jaws of steel; they radiated magnetic personalities; in a word, they were a Darwinian super-race, the tycoons. It was Emperor Napoleon that writers invoked when they introduced 'The Young Napoleon of Finance', or described Morgan, as Munsey did, as 'the plumed knight of finance'.

Men like Morgan were revered for 'moving the world's greatest interests'. B. C. Forbes, the founder of *Forbes* magazine, saw in him 'the financial Moses of the New World'; others thought they spied Lorenzo de Medici, St Francis, or General Sheridan, the Indian fighter and Civil War hero. While biographers and feature writers would serve up the obligatory fare about their habits, amusements, philanthropies, and peccadilloes, what really drove this literature of industrial and financial heroism was a sense of these men as masterful engineers of human and material affairs. The *New York Sun* eulogized Morgan as 'the embodiment of a heroic age in American industrial history'. The Morgan men seemed to have absorbed into themselves all those traits that once distinguished earlier military, political, and artistic elites: valor, sagacity, creative perseverance. For Frank Munsey, the financier had become a kind of modern genius: 'In this country of ours . . . genius asserts itself in the financier and becomes most forceful and most dramatic. The most dramatic spot on earth today is Wall Street.'[30]

There was a deep irony to these Napoleonic comparisons. The men that were idolized stood at the head of vast, impersonal corporate organizations. Naturally enough these complex institutions, run by layered bureaucracies, were ecologically unfriendly to the survival of the heroic individual marching to his own tune. Neutered, faceless administrative machines aroused anxiety among many who also worried about the corrosion of manly independence at the hands of organizational routine and corporate conformity. As that most Napoleonic of tycoons, John D. Rockefeller put it, 'The day of combination is here to stay. Individualism has gone, never to return.' By endowing the leaders of a highly centralized finance capitalism with almost superhuman powers of free will and masculine self-assertion, this Napoleonic mythos offered psychological compensation for a sense of irretrievable loss: somewhere character and individual action still mattered. That was especially reassuring to a swelling salaritariat of anonymous functionaries who nonetheless felt themselves drawn to the new Wall Street order of things, eager to identify with its achievements and élan. It was morale-boosting to find frontier valor alive and well on Wall Street, just at the time when the frontier West, that once inexhaustible reservoir of male fantasy, had been declared permanently closed.[31]

New York, and Wall Street in particular, emerged around the turn of the century as a new frontier in the literary imagination, full of colorful characters, tall tales, and urban legends. It was a rowdy arena where Bunyanesque figures stood toe to toe, and raids and ambushes lent an air of perpetual suspense. Bluster and aggression, bluff and deception of the sort associated with tricksters and badmen in the lawless frontier towns made the world of finance and business seem suddenly rather picturesque. While some of this literature was decidedly

hostile to Wall Street, other writers rediscovered it as a site of sentiment, romance, and high adventure. Though the Street itself was
becoming dominated by the facelessness of the corporation and the
investment bank, a hunger for something bloodier demanded satisfaction.

Titans in white shoes! Writers wrestled with the contradiction: what
becomes of romantic heroism and moral action in a world seemingly
overrun by impersonal corporate behemoths and the tidal flows of
capital? A shift in literary culture was under way. It entailed first of all
abandoning the genteel critique of business and finance. Uneasily,
some novelists worked their way towards a naturalistic acceptance of
this new economic universe, finding a kind of physics of finance congruent with the lawful structure and benign indifference of the natural
world – this, in the end, was the way things were and were meant to
be. Yet those individuals who were in touch with this cosmological
constant had about them the aura of supermen, romantic beyond
imagining, wilful, controlling, and free. They were primitives of
exquisite sophistication.

This literary cocktail of determinism, fatalism, and amoral liberation was served up by a number of minor novelists at the turn of the
century, including Will Payne in *The Money Captain* and Henry Blake
Fuller in *The Cliff-Dweller*. Books like *The Short Line War* and
Calumet 'K' by Samuel Merwin and H. K. Webster were great publishing successes, running into multiple editions. Webster's *The Banker
and the Bear* and Harold Bell Wright's bestseller, *The Winning of
Barbara Worth*, concerned confrontations between speculative titans,
great gamesmen in quest of mastery over the forces of fate and chance.
Some engaged Wall Street directly; all exploited the Exchange's aura
and explored the intercourse between normal business and financial
empire building. Many were first serialized in up-scale middle-class
magazines like the *Saturday Evening Post*, *Cosmopolitan*, and
Everybody's. They were often formulaic books about men written for
men. However, in the work of Frank Norris and Theodore Dreiser in
particular, all the moral, philosophical, and psychological counter-
pulls set in motion by Wall Street's reconstruction of the economy
reached a new level of imaginative salience.[32]

Frank Norris's novel, *The Pit*, was not about Wall Street. Its plot
was loosely based on a real-life attempt by a Chicago commodities
speculator, one Joseph Leiter, known fleetingly as the 'king of the

wheat pit', to corner the market in wheat in 1897. But its hero, Curtis Jadwin, was the quintessential and universal speculator. Norris's invention was a landmark cultural event, because Jadwin seemed to call into question all those certitudes which for generations had confined his particular sub-species to its own cultural exile.

Jadwin's audacious, even outrageous attempt to control the world's wheat supply came amidst the greatest agrarian political unrest in American history. From the wheat fields of Kansas to the cotton plantations of Georgia, commodities speculators and financiers were the favored targets for vituperation: the parasitic scum of the earth. Yet Jadwin's spectacular coup, whose aftermath is a series of social and personal disasters, evokes no unambiguous moral censure from his creator. Indeed, for Norris, traditional codes of conduct seem, at times, no more than desiccated forms of hypocrisy. Instead, what's at work here is the cosmic non-human: forces of nature and economic law that operate above the heads, as it were, of a benighted humanity that is swept away to a destiny not of its own choosing. Norris evokes that organicism in this tableau of the commodity exchanges: 'Within them a great whirlpool, a pit of roaring waters, spun and thundered, sucking in the life and tides of the city and then vomiting them forth again, spewing them up and out . . . sending the swirl of its mighty central eddy far out through the city's channels.'[33]

The retribution for Jadwin's hubris, his vaunting conviction that he can direct this flood, is somewhat uncanny and perverse. As a 'bull', his strategems on the Chicago Board of Trade actually drive up the price of wheat, momentarily benefiting producers everywhere. But they unleash a tidal wave of production which in the end overwhelms his Napoleonic scheme. In a kind of inversion of the American ethos, the forces of production, those vessels of righteousness and good order, turn nightmarishly into demonic carriers of destruction, burying the hopes of producers and speculators alike.

Standing at the center of this maelstrom, Jadwin retains a certain grandeur. He's a kind of primitive genius. On the one hand, his knowledge of the market is intricate and exhaustive, the pre-requisite of its mastery. The book is full of detailed accounts of the way the Pit operates, itself a departure from earlier 'business' novels which stayed close to the drawing room and men's club, out of earshot of the factory floor or mercantile exchange. But full mastery of the speculative art depends as well on a form of creative intuition, and Jadwin possesses a feel for the psychological state of his fellow speculators. His intuition extends farther than that, however. Here the novel leaves the realm of social realism, venturing into the shadowy world of post-Victorian romanticism in search of some saving remnant of the lone individual.

In Norris's eyes, Jadwin's drive to control the world's wheat is a kind of demiurge, an insatiable compulsion, an utterly male lusting after control and conquest which, in the existential confusion of the novel, both erases any last traces of free will and provides the inner spring of heroic action. Jadwin is on a quest, like King Arthur and his knights; Norris wants the reader to believe that an aura of medieval heroism can be rediscovered in the 'romance and adventure in Wall Street or Bond Street'. Norris, fascinated by the blood-lust and heroism of the medieval warrior, viewed the winning of the West as a modern form of the Viking conquest saga. Struck by the contrast it presented between pulsating vitality and the debilitating over-intellectuality of modern life, he sought to rediscover the healthy aggressiveness of that primitive questing urge in the high drama of imperial war and big business.

That quest is both psychological and sexual. Norris had familiarized himself with the latest clinical studies of hypnosis, hysteria, and the subconscious in order to grasp the emotional metabolism of market panics, but something profoundly erotic is at work as well. Laura Dearborn, the love of Jadwin's life, born and bred in New England gentility, is at first repelled, or at least perplexed by the distinctly male odor of commerce. As the novel progresses, however, she finds herself drawn to Jadwin's Promethean defiance of the implacable power of the Pit, coming to see him as 'a fighter, unknown and unknowable to women . . . hard, rigorous, panoplied in the harness of the warrior, who strove among the trumpets, and who, in the brunt of conflict, conspicuous, formidable, set the battle . . . in a rage around him and exulted like a champion in the shoutings of the captains.'[34]

Jadwin's openness to the primitive world of instinct is an invigorating release from the deadening, de-sexualizing inhibitions of over-civilization. Speculation for him is a monomania so all-consuming that for a while, and with nearly fatal consequences, it causes Jadwin to neglect his beloved Laura; but it also serves as the vessel of an *élan vital*, a newly revealed metaphysical life force. What an extraordinary trans-valuation! Speculation, once a shadowy realm of psychological

chaos and moral death, now a passway to erotic and existential fulfill-
ment, even an aphrodisiac. And Jadwin's impossible quest – in effect,
to corner the earth itself – calls upon such deep-rooted passions that it
is made to seem not at all venal, but tragic.

However, the constant oscillations between high heroism and stark
objectivity leave the novel in a kind of aesthetic limbo. Some have read
it as a bitter, moralizing tract, reflecting an ongoing cultural ambivalence about the new economy. Jadwin may be on a quest, but it is
never clear just what that quest is about. The language used to invoke
it becomes murky, miasmic, and overblown; capitalized nouns dominate the typography. Whether the speculator is a hero, a villain, or an
automaton is shrouded in ambiguity. Jadwin champions the tillers of
the soil, but only inadvertently, and shears the hapless 'lambs' mewing
about the Pit with pitiless contempt. Part social criticism, part fantasy,
the bifurcated portrait of the financier as *Übermensch* and soulless
atomic particle of the natural universe seems incoherent. The novel's
supposedly unblushing realism is undermined by the author's eliding
of certain dissonant facts about the real Joseph Leiter: that he was not
self-made, but the son of a millionaire; and that the real 'corner' was
not quite an intuitive act of genius, but abetted by bad weather
through widely dispersed wheat-producing regions in India, Australia,
the winter wheat belt of the US and North Africa, and by the locusts
and late rains that plagued the Argentinian yield. Despite Norris's
regard for the 'facts', he was even more profoundly committed to the
mythopoetic.[35]

But Norris is hardly unaware of the silliness and cynicism that often
accompanied Napoleonic myth-making in the real world. Jadwin
becomes a public spectacle pumped up by a publicity machine, just as
the actual 'King of the Wheat Pit' had been. The media can't get
enough of this 'Napoleon of La Salle Street': reporters scurry after
every anecdote and recycle old ones if they run dry. Every cliché is let
loose: Jadwin is a 'cool, calm, man of steel with a cool and calculating
grey eye', 'piercing as an eagle'; a 'desperate gambler, bold as a bucca-
neer, his eye black and fiery', he is like a 'veritable pirate'. This is all
part of the persiflage that went along with the newly established cultural stature of the businessman financier. Norris knows it for what it
is, yet he shares its unspoken assumption: that it's time to discard the
moral stigma that for generations has surrounded the speculator. But
in the end something holds him back: he can't quite go all the way.[36]

Theodore Dreiser does. Different in many other ways, Dreiser, like Frank Norris, was an economic Darwinian, although of an aberrant sort. Orthodox social Darwinism, as espoused by William Graham Sumner (the Yale professor who was Herbert Spencer's chief exponent in America) held that: 'The millionaires are a product of natural selection . . . It is because they are thus selected that wealth . . . aggregates under their hands . . . They may be fairly regarded as the naturally selected agents of society for certain work. They get high wages and live in luxury, but the bargain is a good one for society.' Dreiser, however, would have nothing to do with Sumner's social meliorism or moral teleology. He was rather a Darwinian fundamentalist. Fitness implied nothing one way or the other about social progress or moral order. It was a fact of nature, barren of any higher meaning or human solicitude. With his willingness to live in his imagination with this appalling natural indifference, Dreiser escaped the aesthetic and intellectual compromises and confusions that marred Norris's work, and thus came closer to the emotional heart of the Morgan dispensation.[37]

The first volume of Dreiser's trilogy, *The Financier* (the others were *The Titan* and *The Stoic*) appeared a decade after *The Pit* and in the year of Morgan's death. It opens with a Darwinian epiphany. As a young boy, Frank Algernon Cowperwood, the trilogy's protagonist, makes a life-defining observation. Watching a heavily armored lobster devour a vulnerable squid, young Frank discovers the answer to the question, 'How is life organized?' 'Things live on each other – that was it', is his spare and unblinking conclusion. Anything else was so much weightless vapor: that ethos was the red thread running through Cowperwood's whole career as a financier. This occupation was neither benign nor demonic, in Dreiser's view. It was predatory to be sure, but so was all of nature. It could bring on calamity, but the universe was not an orderly place: it was inherently unstable, out of anyone's control.[38]

As a young man Dreiser was influenced by Herbert Spencer's ideas about the social implications of Darwinian theory. Spencer, however, sought to reconcile individual and social evolution, to find some way of defusing conflict as society inevitably became more complexly integrated. But Dreiser not only rejected social Darwinism's optimistic veneer, he sustained a simultaneous belief in the sheer contingency of existence, a kind of evolutionary open-endedness more in vogue today. And indeed, *The Financier* is a tale informed as much by chance as by predetermination: for Cowperwood, 'life was war', filled with a kind of 'jungle-like complexity . . . a dark, rank growth of horrific but avid life – life at the full, life knife in hand, life blazing with courage and dripping at the jaws with hunger.'[39]

Like Curtis Jadwin's, Frank Cowperwood's story is loosely based on the real life of a notorious financial tycoon. Charles T. Yerkes started out as a daring young broker in Philadelphia, handling state bonds for the impeccably reputable Drexel and Company. Yerkes, however, was impatient, and lacked the scruples of his employer. He connived with the City Treasurer, one Joseph Marcer, to invest city funds secretly to their own account in Chicago. The lucrative plot went up in flames along with the city itself in the Great Fire. Exposed and convicted as an accessory to embezzlement, Yerkes was sentenced to two years and four months and actually served seven months in the state penitentiary before he was pardoned. (Marcer, who lacked Yerkes' political adroitness, not to mention his money, was sent away for twice that length of time.) Out of that ignominy he rose again to resume his financial career, this time in Chicago, where he became a street-railway magnate whose empire rested on his conviction that 'in normal times somebody can be found to buy a bond on anything, and that with the power to issue bonds the gathering of great fortunes is simpler than the gathering of ripe apples.' He might be called the original junk-bond artist, and his Chicago traction monopoly was once characterized as 'the most picturesque lot of junk ever seen in the world'.

Yerkes fascinated Dreiser as did other great tycoons of the day, some of whom, like Armour, Carnegie, and Cyrus Field, he interviewed for *Success* magazine. In preparing the trilogy, Dreiser researched the lives of Morgan, Gould, Russell Sage, and other notable and notorious financiers and businessmen. Frank Cowperwood's curriculum vitae mirrored that of Yerkes, but his character was an imaginative composite of what Dreiser sensed to be fundamentally true about them all. In *The Financier*, Frank put it with a kind of brute pithiness: 'I satisfy myself.' [40]

Cowperwood's epic rise and fall and rise roughly tracked the tectonic upheavals in the nation's economic understructure. He was born in 1837, the year when manic land speculation swamped the agrarian-mercantile order and brought the country's rickety financial system, including Wall Street, to its knees. By 1857, Frank had ventured forth as a stockbroker, only to learn at first hand how precarious a trade it was. That year's economic implosion, again ignited by insupportable real-estate fantasies, closed that phase of the Street's formative history, in which its fate was still tied to the fortunes of American agriculture. Cowperwood becomes frightened. He backs out of 'stock gambling', getting into 'bill brokering' instead, a business of fixed and relatively tangible values, promising the same orderliness and security as the homespun farming life it purportedly represents. But that stability runs against the grain of Frank's character. He is drawn back into the world of speculation, investing in city securities and crossing the borders of criminal manipulation. Here he feels at home, in love with an alluring abstraction: 'Money was the thing – plain money, discounted, loaned, cornered, represented by stocks and bonds – that interested him.' Disaster strikes, however: he's jailed, but not chastened. On the contrary, he surfaces again like some ageless shark in the great panic and depression of 1873, another significant year which marks Wall Street's inveiglement in the new industrial economy. Cowperwood thrives as a bear, feasting on the financial desperation spreading all around him. With his new fortune he sets out for Chicago where his sangfroid and political shrewdness sweeps away even his most ruthless enemies. Total victory comes amidst the maelstrom of the mid-1890s which delivered the last rites to the old agrarian and competitive order and installed the Morgan system. Carried aloft by financial and political storms, over which Cowperwood can exercise no control, he watches as his rivals succumb to fear and selfishness. Having vanquished his competitors, he is now the unchallenged traction king of the windy city, long since in control of its supply of natural gas. Frank finally leaves its provincialism behind to complete his destiny: life in the land of the fittest – New York and Wall Street.

What a ride! In the course of it, Cowperwood abandons every vestige of convention. He becomes a living impiety, offensive to polite society, a defiler of Christian ethics and bourgeois decorum. He gives up his belief in the priority and enduring worth of material production. He becomes not only a speculator, but a bear, that particularly obnoxious breed that lives off the misery of others. He jettisons any deference to the ossified maxims of competitive free-market capitalism, frankly embracing monopolism. He mocks the culture's pious faith in democracy, cooly suborning numerous public officials. And his faithlessness is not only in the public sphere. He cheats shamelessly on his wife, Lillian, a priggish, dispassionate creature of great social rectitude; and unlike his peers, Frank doesn't bother to conceal his transgressions. Nor is his adultery a petty fling, but rather a grand sexual passion for an indecently young girl, Aileen Butler, herself a creature of fecund beauty – impulsive, sexually ravenous, and highly dangerous to Frank's fragile social reputation. Indeed, Cowperwood's eroticism is not only as potent as his magnetic attraction to financial empire-building; it is fundamentally the same craving. It brooks no interference in its urge for conquest and control. It inevitably leads Frank to overcome lingering scruples and betray Aileen as well, despite her fierce loyalty during his trial and imprisonment. [41]

Dreiser is not squeamish about any of this. The trilogy is free of moralizing and harbors no second thoughts. There's no trace of Norris's romantic heroism, no attempt at metaphysical rationalization. One of Cowperwood's rivals admits he has the heart of 'a numidian lion'. But if he is pitiless, if he worships accumulation – money, women, works of art – for accumulation's sake, it is because that is the way the world has irresistibly come to be. It is no more to be made sense of than Jay Cooke's collapse, which came like a 'financial thunderclap in a clear sky'. But Cowperwood is a more interesting figure than someone merely given over to the belief that life is all gamble.

Even as he defies social convention, Frank can barely contain an inner rage at his exclusion from society. He craves its respect while mocking its pieties, and even cuts himself loose of Aileen once convinced her crudities bar his acceptance. His imperishable wish is to rank among the great Titans of the East, 'the serried Sequoias of Wall Street'. It's a quest of awful incomprehensibility, a blind flight from death and meaninglessness. Dreiser's account of it does not lapse into the kind of facile stigmatizing then so much in the air: though the final scenes of *The Titan* display an armed populace, lusting for revenge, Dreiser portrays this as so much manipulated mass frenzy, set in motion by the cynical elected representatives of 'the people' – a piece of political stagecraft which Cowperwood was just as capable of managing for himself when he needed to.

Dreiser's distanced view, free of irony, is at the core of his understanding of a world reconstructed by the great forces gathering around Wall Street. Cowperwood is a mighty player of the game: powerful and ruthless, an exploiter to be sure, but one who is also a creator of wealth and builder of cities. And he always conceives of his own power as rooted in his control over great enterprises, not in the buying and selling of securities like some mere broker or merchant. He is, in keeping with the new Wall Street scheme of things, the financier qua industrialist, the industrialist qua financier, a merger giving birth to an exhilarating sense of Olympian dirigisme. A figure such as Cowperwood is not easily reducible to the moral polarities of an earlier age: he stands at the heart of the awesome, amoral, brutal world that Dreiser perceives and portrays. [42]

Dreiser's trilogy did not enjoy the critical acclaim or popular success that greeted *The Pit*. Critics were put off by its amorality and what might be called its anti-lyricism. Nonetheless, Dreiser bored deeper than any other contemporary writer into why so many people felt drawn to the remorseless Darwinian mystique of the Wall Street financier in the age of 'morganization'. A strange alchemy transformed the sober and methodical businessman into a great gamesman, the roguish and disreputable speculator-gambler into a director of the material world. Yet Dreiser left behind a displeasing aftertaste as well; showing that there was something about what people liked that was dislikable, frightening even. [43]

During the first decade of the new century broad stretches of the urban middle classes began to perceive Wall Street as a threat to their very existence. The populist and Brahmin oppositions to 'morganization' could be and were dismissed as atavisms, representing past ways of life and therefore bound to die away. Now, however, Wall Street would face the mobilized ire of millions whose fate was bound up with the life cycle of modern industry and finance.

9

Other People's Money

An American President lay mortally wounded for the third time in thirty-seven years. William McKinley was shot twice, once in the breastbone, once in the abdomen, on 6 September 1901. He was attending a reception in the Temple of Music at the Pan American Exposition in Buffalo. The shooter, Leon Czolgosz, an ex-metal worker and anarchist from Cleveland, was arrested on the spot, confessed to the assassination, and claimed to be a follower of Emma Goldman, the country's most notorious champion of the black flag.

McKinley lingered on for a week, rallying briefly before dying on 14 September. It was more than enough time for the emotions of the moment to cool into sober reflection. At first people wanted Czolgosz lynched or burned at the stake; in the event, he was electrocuted little more than a month later, unrepentant to the end. Emma Goldman was arrested but soon released, as there was not the faintest trace of her involvement. Never easily intimidated, Goldman eulogized the immigrant assassin as an idealist. Police authorities cracked down on socialist and anarchist clubs around the country. At his own request, J. P. Morgan was placed under police guard. Carrie Nation kept the pot boiling by celebrating the deed in a speech at Coney Island, praying the shot would prove fatal since the President supported the rum sellers and beer brewers. Memories of dismembered police corpses in Haymarket, of a river running red with blood in Homestead, of Federal cavalry riding down Pullman workers, of inflammatory declamations against mankind's crucifixion on a 'cross of gold', were so fresh they weren't even memories; they were haunting premonitions in a society living with a precarious sense of its solidity.

Though McKinley's victory over Bryan in 1896 and again even

more resoundingly at the turn of the century had proved to be the last rites for populism, nobody believed America's class relations had miraculously improved. The President, a man of studied caution and Midwestern modesty, was nonetheless the standard-bearer of a party that had become the wholly owned subsidiary of a national corporate and financial elite. Led by Cleveland industrialist and Rockefeller ally, Mark Hanna, it made no secret of its commitment to the supremacy of the business classes. McKinley's cabinet was a *Who's Who?* of financiers, corporate Poo-Bahs, and Wall Street lawyers. Not since the Jacksonian era had the electoral arena opened itself up to such raw expressions of class fear and hatred. Under these circumstances, witch-hunts and vigilante justice were predictable.

Despite the initial hysteria, however, fears of social insurrection soon subsided. A different set of anxieties disturbed the Republican regency. Administration insiders like ex-Treasury Secretary John G. Carlisle worried that this third presidential assassination in a single generation might bring prolonged depression. Most stockbrokers disagreed, convinced the country's prosperity was so deeply rooted that it was impervious to this sort of exogenous shock. J. P. Morgan was typically taciturn. Incredulous at the news, he offered no public comment except to declare it 'sad', and to assure everybody that his banking fraternity would not permit the tragedy to 'derange' the economy. It is likely, however, that his stoic reserve concealed real misgivings, not so much about the prospect of a depression but about the depressing prospect of who was waiting in the wings.

At a time like this one expects government to mount a united front to convey a sense of unbroken political resolve and coherence, so it is noteworthy that hints to the contrary began to seep out almost right away. The chairman of the New York Republican State Committee said he was sure Vice-President Roosevelt would make no mistakes, 'no matter what people say'. After all, 'Colonel Roosevelt' had consulted with Senator Platt, the party's New York State boss, and they found themselves, according to the chairman, in perfect accord. But it was common knowledge that Platt despised Roosevelt as a reckless adventurer. He had connived to undermine the presidential ambitions of the 'Colonel' by removing him from the platform of the New York governorship into the Siberian gloom of the vice-presidency. Platt must have been incensed at the undoing of his schemes by an obscure anarchist fanatic, and if he wasn't about to admit this in public, others were less circumspect. The chief counsel of Standard Oil lauded McKinley's political integrity and prayed for his recovery; 'Colonel Roosevelt', he confided, would not be as safe a President and the market would suffer accordingly.

The 'Colonel' tried to do his own reassuring. At the swearing-in ceremony he promised to continue the policy of the fallen President 'absolutely unbroken'. Mark Hanna, the Republican Party's kingmaker and now Ohio Senator, welcomed the new President with a great display of cordiality. But this was all for show. Hanna had even opposed TR's interment in the vice-presidency, warning his fellow chieftains, 'Don't any of you realize there's only one life between this madman and the Presidency?' Like Platt, Hanna didn't trust Roosevelt or consider him a member of the club, and privately voiced his dismay that fate had catapulted 'that damn cowboy' into the White House.[1]

Leon Czolgosz's bullet, some speculated, was poisoned. If so, the contagion it carried was not anarchy but a more insidious and slow-working virus that would disrupt the metabolism of 'morganization', shattering its immunity to public surveillance. The 'damn cowboy' turned out to be less of an uncontrollable ruffian than Hanna feared. But just when Wall Street seemed to have vanquished its oldest foes, Roosevelt's accidental elevation opened up a decade of challenge from an altogether different cast of characters. These men and women were comfortable with the cosmopolitan city and corporate bureaucracy, but doubted that it was best administered by an elite cloistered at 23 Wall Street.

'Progressives', whether acolytes of the 'Colonel' or the 'professor', Woodrow Wilson, or muckraking independents or socialist intransigents, could all revert to a Christian vocabulary when denouncing the 'morganizers'. They could sketch the lineaments of financial conspiracy as vividly as any prairie-fire populist or dyspeptic Brahmin. They could be just as ardent in defense of Jeffersonian democracy as any critic of the Wall Street aristocrats. But the people who would disrupt the Morgan–Hanna entente were also in tune with the intellectual and cultural currents of modern times.

Facts were their favorite ammunition. They devoured exposés; they were empiricists before they were moralists, pragmatic not apocalyptic. Their scripture resided in the natural and social sciences. They were confirmed secularists. If Wall Street under Morgan's suzerainty was indictable it was not from a biblical point of view, but because it failed the test of rational social organization, standing in the way of economic progress. These progressives were the nation's first converts to planning and the ethos of non-partisan expertise. They were pre-occupied with trusts, and above all else the 'money trust', but not because they worshiped at the altar of 'small is beautiful'; quite to the contrary, they admired recent industrial innovations and were convinced they were in danger of suffocating in white-shoe Wall Street.

If the Street's overweening power caused a serious political problem, these middle-class rebels didn't expect to solve it by reverting to the town meeting and village democracy. They were among the first architects of the modern regulatory state, an administrative apparatus national in scope and with executive powers robust enough to match the encompassing grasp of the 'money trust'. While they were dubious about the class struggle, they nonetheless believed in national solidarity, an imagined communal coming together around opportunity and abundance. This was New Testament democracy, the democracy of strong government that would turn the language of classical liberalism inside out. Thanks to its confrontation with Wall Street's 'money trust', democracy in America would never be quite the same again.

These new democrats were debunkers by instinct, the writers and readers of realist and naturalist fiction, people who wanted to see things as they were. Deflating the grandiose illusions that had grown up around the heroes of finance and industry was an act of cultural revolution in which they delighted. When they mocked Napoleonic romancing they did so not because they thought these men were devils, but because they enjoyed dismantling their spurious heroism, uncovering their naked pettiness. Iconoclastic and meritocratic, they detested and ridiculed the caste-like exclusivity and presumptuous secrecy of Wall Street's inner sanctum.

Two assassinations punctuated a long decade of withering criticism: McKinley's at the beginning and the Archduke Franz Ferdinand's in 1914, which brought the process to an abrupt end, well short of its objectives. One reason the movement petered out – aside from the chilling effect of the war itself on all serious forms of dissent – is that from the outset it spoke in many tongues. Roosevelt and his circle were certainly suspicious of Wall Street, but the ambitions of the 'Colonel' were imperial rather than democratic and he was prepared to find common ground with the country's financial oligarchs that would leave their economic dominion intact. His declamations against 'malefactors of great wealth' were more inadvertently inspirational than the President anticipated or could tolerate. When the air filled with bellicose propositions to uproot the power of the 'morganizers', the 'damn cowboy' holstered his weapons.

Others pushed harder and further. People like Louis Brandeis and Senator Robert LaFollette, in league with a diverse array of middle-class reformers, hound-dog journalists, and injured businessmen, wanted to use democratic government to prise open the financial oligarchy's stranglehold over commercial life and curb its political influence. Their motivations and intentions were various, and sometimes at odds: their ranks included both substantial Wall Street interests who felt excluded from the Great Game, and socialists who wanted the rules rewritten from scratch. All of them, however, wrestled with the dilemma of the age: namely, bigness and complexity in modern economic affairs and what to do about it. And all agreed that the mother of all combines, the one whose looming presence became a national obsession as the decade wore on, was the 'Money Trust'. They believed that it rested on a stupendous act of usurpation: it traded, in Louis Brandeis's famous phrase, in 'other people's money'.

This was a damning apercu. It lent an air of illegitimacy to the deliberations of the directors and trustees of the country's most formidable financial institutions. It implied an offense more than strictly economic, like the theft of a birthright. Yet it also suggested something else: that these people wanted their money back. They were stakeholders – or sought to be – in a market economy that the 'Money Trust' was ruining for everyone but itself. To bring Wall Street before the bar of public opinion was not to attack the capitalist system but to restore it to good health, to open it up to vigorous participation by enterprising businessmen and middle-class investors, to assure consumers and citizens that the system could indeed work to maximize efficiency and satisfaction.

John Hay was a young man of twenty when he served as President Lincoln's personal secretary during the Civil War. By the turn of the century he was still on the scene, a diplomat and *éminence grise*. Like Roosevelt he came from a background of genteel wealth, which fastidiously believed that money ought to know its place and stay there. But just like Roosevelt, he operated under no illusions and was prepared to deal with the devil, especially if it served a higher national purpose. As early as the 1880s, Hay delivered his own cold-eyed view of the state of the union: 'This is a government of the people, by the people, and for the people no longer. It is a government of corporations, by corporations, and for corporations.'[2]

The new President would have subscribed to that view without demur. That was precisely why people like Mark Hanna and 'Boss Platt' were worried. Roosevelt was determined to assert the prerogatives of the government over matters that the overlords of American finance capitalism had come to presume were theirs to decide. He was jealous of his own executive powers, sought to widen them, and would tolerate no challenge from private citizens, no matter how mighty. This was as much a matter of asserting his imperial will as it was a crusade to make government more responsive to the will of the governed.

Roosevelt was a democrat of the Napoleonic variety, speaking in the name of the people but trusting to his own genius to intuit its will. But he also realised that the Morgan elite was afflicted with a dangerous myopia. They imagined themselves as a disinterested ruling class, one with the wisdom to transcend their own narrow self-interest, or rather to find that happy meeting ground where what was best for incorporated Wall Street was indistinguishable from what was best for the country. This was the constitutive delusion of the 'morganizers', and TR saw right through it.

Naturally enough, therefore, not long after McKinley's body grew cold, Roosevelt shelved his pledge to continue in the footsteps of his fallen predecessor and began acting like a 'damn cowboy'. In his very first message to Congress, mainly given over to sentiments of consolation and reassurance, he slipped in a more ominous word or two about the 'baleful consequences' of over-capitalized trusts. Early on in his administration he encouraged the Justice Department to prosecute the Northern Securities Company under the Sherman anti-trust act. Northern Securities was the corporate confection crafted by Morgan and Kuhn Loeb to resolve the wild speculation and panic that followed in the wake of the railroad wars between Harriman and James Hill. The spectacle had nauseated everybody; even the redoubtable *New York Times* deplored this vulgar display of commercial megalomania, truculence, and indifference to the public interest. It was an inviting and vulnerable target.[3]

Roosevelt's decision to press forward with the suit shocked the

Street, but there was little it could do except bluster. The President's action was 'beyond comprehension'. It led to Morgan's ill-considered expression of wounded hauteur: why hadn't the President, a fellow chief executive and a gentleman after all, assigned a second to settle the matter privately with some factotum of Morgan's. 'The community of interests', the banker had long ago cynically concluded, was merely 'the principle that certain numbers of men who own property can do what they like with it'. Morgan's exquisitely hubristic utterance turned out to be a colossal faux pas and only stiffened Roosevelt's resolve. His Attorney General, Philander C. Knox, let it be known that in his judgment thirty per cent of the company's capital stock was pure water, an insult to investors and a burden to the railroad company's customers. One paper gleefully applauded the government's demarche: 'Even Morgan no longer rules the earth and other men may still do business without asking his permission.' Henry Adams gloated that 'Our stormy petrel of a President . . . hit Pierpont Morgan, the whole railway interest, and the whole Wall Street connection a tremendous shot square on the nose.'[4]

As the Northern Securities case made its way through the judicial system, the President fired off round after round of rhetorical artillery, some of it pretty high-caliber. He denounced 'malefactors of great wealth' who shirked their public responsibilities and made it clear that he did not regard the money-besotted financial titan highly. He confided in his closest political friend, Massachusetts Senator Henry Cabot Lodge, who shared Roosevelt's disdain, that he loved his recently published remembrance of *A Frontier Town* especially for its implied indictment of people like Harriman and Rockefeller, for their callous and perilous indifference to the public welfare.[5]

According to Henry Adams, Roosevelt was 'pure act', and there were indeed actions that went along with all the censorious language. Every presidential intervention into what had once been a protected private marketplace alarmed Wall Street. Whether it was Roosevelt's efforts to compel the coal barons to negotiate with their workers, to make the railroads show some restraint in their chronic demands for rate hikes from the ICC, or to punish the meat packers and others for their egregious disregard for the public health, Wall Street was offended. This was after all the age of Morgan, when the line between the world of big business and its financial overseers was virtually invisible, a distinction without a difference.

Tensions between the Street and the President eased a little, but never really went away. When Roosevelt was attacked by segments of the financial community in the aftermath of the panic of 1907, particularly in a nasty pamphlet entitled 'The Roosevelt Panic' he believed emanated from the 'Standard Oil and Harriman combinations', Roosevelt plotted a counter-assault on 'predatory wealth'. He singled out 'manipulating securities' and 'stockjobbing' for punishment. Convinced that Harriman and William Rockefeller were conspiring to undermine the Republican Party and put Hearst (the publisher TR most loved to hate) in the White House, the President let it be known there was 'no form of mendacity or bribery or corruption they will not resort to in an effort to take vengeance'. His arguments verged on paranoia: the panic itself, he suggested, had been deliberately fomented to intimidate the government, to scare Roosevelt away from investigating the railroads and other corporate redoubts. The President wasn't about to let them get away with it. He railed against the conscienceless press that fronted for these tycoons, allowing them to hide behind the mask of journalistic objectivity. He likened their behavior to gamblers, saloon keepers, and brothel owners. They had managed to make 'the very name of "high finance" a term of scandal'.[6]

In a way Roosevelt couldn't help himself. His conviction that financial plutocrats were the 'most sordid of all aristocracies' was bred in the bone, part of an upbringing that dismissed materialistic strivings as unworthy, debilitating, and effeminate, encouraging behavior that ranged 'from rotten frivolity to rotten vice'. He worked at showing respect but confessed:

> I am simply unable to make myself take the attitude of respect toward the very wealthy men which such an enormous multitude of people evidently feel. I am delighted to show any courtesy to Pierpont Morgan or Andrew Carnegie or James J. Hill, but as for regarding any of them as, for instance, I regard . . . Peary, the Arctic explorer, or Rhodes, the historian – why, I could not force myself to do it even if I wanted to, which I don't.

(Morgan's feelings towards the President were no warmer: he was alleged to have said, once TR left office and was about to set sail for a safari in Africa, that 'I hope the first lion he meets does his duty.')[7]

Roosevelt's verbal pyrotechnics were a force in their own right and their impact should not be underestimated. No President since Lincoln had uttered a truly unkind word about doings on the Street. No President since Jackson had thought to single out the financial establishment as a political danger. So Roosevelt's pronouncements changed the social landscape: they were the equivalent of a royal invitation to peer behind the facade of Wall Street's intimidating omnipotence. Many a crusading journalist and publisher took up the invitation, and for a while Roosevelt valued what they managed to uncover about the seamier inner workings of business and finance.

Hanna's worst premonitions seemed prophetic. By 1903, the Republican Party high command was frantically searching for ways to deny the 'cowboy' the Party's presidential nomination, and Roosevelt knew it. The 'whole Wall Street crowd' was against him, he told Lodge, but he was ready for a knock-down, drag-out fight against both 'the criminal rich' and 'the fool rich'. Wisely, Lodge sought to rein in his friend's temper. He agreed there were capitalists out to get the President, but they were mainly confined to 'a group of Wall Street and Chicago people'. Moreover, even in Wall Street he had allies, and in Boston's State Street too: firms like Lee Higginson, for example, which actually approved of the President's approach to the trust question. Lodge had his ear to the ground. Whatever Hanna might have hoped, by 1904 fantasies about getting rid of Roosevelt were defunct. Not only was he enormously popular, it was also becoming clear to many that his bark was worse than his bite. And as Lodge intimated, the 'morganizers', some of them at least, were in a mood to compromise.[8]

To claim that Roosevelt talked loudly and carried a small stick is not to accuse him of being disingenuous, or no more so than most Presidents. There is no question that his low moral opinion of the Wall Street crowd was heartfelt; he acknowledged his membership of a fraternity of disdain that included the Adams brothers and others. But on economic matters the approach of the President and his inner circle, including Lodge, Senator Albert Beveridge, Hay, Elihu Root, George Perkins of the House of Morgan, and others was something else again. It amounted to a kind of twentieth-century Hamiltonianism. The point was to enlist the country's dominant economic classes, especially its financiers, in collaboration with the state in a quest for national glory. Hamilton of course was an eighteenth-century gentleman, less comfortable with democratic behavior, more at ease with the notion of a natural aristocracy; not so concerned, even after the William Duer scandal, with curbing the appetites and ambitions of liquid wealth.

However guilty of stock-watering and stock-manipulating shenanigans the trusts might be, they were in the eyes of the Roosevelt group institutions of proven economic viability. Their massiveness matched the power of an industrial order of daunting technical and organizational complexity that spanned the nation and even beyond. Trusts of the sort put together by the 'morganizers' were the imperfect vessels of that high-velocity, high-volume system of production and distribution which carried the promise of abundance at home and mastery abroad. Correcting their imperfections made sense; shattering them did not. If their judgment was clouded by self-interest, Roosevelt was prepared to call them to account. When, for example, following the panic of 1907, the Wall Street-dominated rail systems groaned under a burden of watered stock and gutted assets, Morgan's people pressured the ICC to license a huge rate increase. This not only infuriated shippers everywhere, but jeopardized economic recovery more generally. Roosevelt told Morgan's emissary, George Perkins to back off.[9]

The President was ultimately searching for common ground with Wall Street, however. Despite his reputation as a 'trust-buster', the Northern Securities case (the company was ordered to dissolve by the Supreme Court in 1904) was actually the last significant anti-trust case of the Roosevelt years. Instead administration functionaries arranged 'gentlemen's agreements' (though Roosevelt was less than convinced of the Wall Street crowd's gentlemanliness) with their counterparts from the corporate-financial establishment to avoid issues that might cause the government and the great corporations to collide. And near the end of his second term the President supported Senator Hepburn's proposals to amend the Sherman Act in ways that would permit the law to distinguish between 'good' and 'bad' trusts.[10]

Trusts were steeply hierarchical command institutions whose role was to preside over orderly business. Morgan, not unlike Roosevelt, practiced his own code of Spartan discipline; his trusts after all were designed to rein in the riotous free-for-all of the free market. Roosevelt insisted only that they apply this same uplifting spirit of martial restraint to themselves. So long as the trusts kept within the sphere of their own legitimate authority and respected the government's prerogatives to protect the commonweal, they actually shared a basic kinship with the way Roosevelt conceived the political universe.

The 'Colonel' was not a democrat in any grassroots sense of the word. To the end of his days, he nurtured an abiding distrust of the 'mob': almost anything was better than rule by the 'popocrats' as he once sarcastically described Bryan and his allies. But he maintained a highly developed sense of social obligation and recognized that the cynicism and callousness of people like Jay Gould and George Baer were an invitation to social chaos. Roosevelt's conception of a new order incorporated a genuine concern for the social welfare of the many. He sought to protect the demos, but shivered at the thought of becoming its creature. Roosevelt considered himself the architect of a cadre of men trained to exercise power, not to chase after meaner forms of success or popular favor. Such a class of leaders was more likely to be recruited from the world of old money, with its custodial traditions and sense of noblesse, but it might also be assembled in the mahogany-walled conference rooms of the patrician investment banking houses – that is, if these institutions could be persuaded to give up living in impromptu fashion, in day-to-day pursuit of their 'interests'.

Roosevelt, then, was an elitist in the public interest. Social stability depended on a broadly shared sense of fairness as well as material well-being. One of the reasons he was so alarmed at the selfish behavior of the plutocracy was that it caused people to doubt the fundamental equity of the social order, and inspired dangerous schemes that might elude the control of the 'Colonel'. Such rashness could up-end the arrangements of private property and wealth upon which Wall Street and the corporate order depended. Wall Street, in the President's eyes, threatened to damage its own interests. If at first the Pooh-Bahs of the Street failed to catch on, studiously cautious magazines like the *Saturday Evening Post* understood right away and lambasted the financiers for stupidly abusing Roosevelt, who was seeking to save, not dismantle the business system.

It was a delicate game: chastising the 'morganizers' in public while pursuing detente in private; inciting popular animosities but not allowing them to detonate. The 'community of interests' crafted by Roosevelt was capacious and disinterested in a way that Morgan's more cynical formulation was not. It offered relief from the worst abuses of the old crony capitalism without removing the white-shoe regency from its commanding position over the economy. This equilibrium between Wall Street and the White House was subject to chronic oscillations and adjustments. Whenever it saw the chance (and the coming of the Great War brought plenty), the Street worked to restore the old fin-de-siecle order of things. But until the Crash of

1929 this fragile equilibrium defined the chemistry of elite rule in America.[11]

Muckraking was a pejorative phrase, coined by the President to return the genie released by his own incantations back in its bottle. Whether he saw it that way or not, his theatrical use of the 'bully pulpit' of the presidency had helped ignite a wild-fire of social criticism. No institution or center of power was spared – certainly not those whose shadow had grown more menacing during the preceding generation. Had Roosevelt never uttered an unkind word about Wall Street and the trusts, their day of inquisition was bound to come. But the President provided both inspiration and license. At first he seemed to welcome help in exposing the back-room machinations of corporate financiers. He read Upton Sinclair's nauseating revelations about the country's meat-packing plants and it heightened his resolve to pursue a pure food and drug law. Ray Stannard Baker, one of the earliest 'muckrakers', whose work had illuminated the dark side of the railroads' financial affairs, was invited by Roosevelt to discuss stiffening the regulatory reach of the Interstate Commerce Commission. Soon enough, however, the President grew visibly wary of these associations.[12]

Were the muckrakers and the spirit of middle-class rebellion they invoked more radical than Roosevelt? Yes and no. Their language was often more temperate than the President's. He loved to indulge a vocabulary so full of violent anathemas it might have been banned had it not also first been published in the Bible. The prose style of the investigative journalist, on the other hand, was usually drier, bearing freightcar-loads of facts and numbers – the arithmetic not the pornography of financial debauch. Progressive-minded critics also offered detailed, precise, and heavily footnoted proposals for legislative reform, the product of much archival research. For the most part, these people were not driven by a sentimental anti-capitalism. On the contrary, they were less interested in soaking the rich than in getting in on the deal. Progressives maintained a bedrock faith in the promise of economic opportunity for all, under a closely monitored system of free enterprise. That scarcely qualifies as red- or black-flag radicalism.

Yet Roosevelt treated them as if they were Jacobin rabble-rousers, a radical menace to civilized order. He invented the 'muckraker' metaphor as a term of opprobrium when David Graham Phillips published *The Treason of the Senate*, an indecorous undressing of the naked huckstering that usurped the public interest in the nation's loftiest legislative chamber. After that, the President took to the low road with regularity, stigmatizing those who dared take their criticisms too far as a 'lunatic fringe'. In a certain sense he was right: the progressive agitators, the muckrakers, and their millions of readers were not content to reach some accord with the 'morganizers', to place their trust in a 'gentleman's agreement'. They didn't want to learn to live with the Money Trust, they wanted to level it. They were driven, in short, to democratize the economic order, to open it up to the scrutiny and participation of outsiders. Democracy, even with these limited objectives, is always risky; one can't with any confidence predict where things will end up once the invitation to participate is extended, and it was this that made Roosevelt bristle. For a man of his breeding and disposition, it was hard to tell the difference between democracy and anti-capitalism. In his overwrought imagination, one might bleed naturally into the other once the appetites and resentments of the mob were unleashed. It would be reckless to tamper with the species of leaders and commanding institutions the social organism had evolved.[13]

Other People's Money was the quintessential muckraking assault on the world according to J. P. Morgan. First published in 1913 as a series of nine articles in *Harper's Weekly* (gathered together and expanded a year later in book form), it was an instant journalistic sensation in an era that sometimes seemed defined by them. Roundly praised for its temerity and intelligence, its enemies treated it with caustic contempt; Frank A. Vanderlip, president of National City Bank, dismissed the whole notion of a 'money trust' as pure 'moonshine'. But *Other People's Money* would color public policy and popular opinion about Wall Street for the next half century. [14]

Louis Brandeis, the book's author, was an eminent jurist and trusted adviser of the newly elected President, Woodrow Wilson. He amassed much empirical research to prove the exposé's principal argument: that a 'money trust' did indeed exist; that it was headquartered in a handful of Wall Street investment banks; that it exercised a virtually unchallengeable control over the flow of credit and capital; that it deployed that power on behalf of a charmed circle of favored corporate clients in industry, transportation, and public utilities; that these gargantuan businesses were themselves directly under the influence of emissaries from the 'money trust' who sat on their boards of directors;

that conversely, the 'trust' denied new firms access to vital capital resources; that by virtue of its control over both the institutions in need of capital and those in a position to meet that need, this clique of investment bankers controlled the basic functions of the economy; that through deft manipulation of this web of interests the 'money trust' feathered its own nest with unconscionable fees and insider stock transactions; that its access to 'other people's money' innocently deposited in the 'money trusts' network of banks, insurance and trust companies and brokerages allowed it to carry out this financial legerdemain; and worst of all, that the 'money trust' had a debilitating effect on the rest of the economy, clogging up its circulatory system with inefficiencies, artificially high prices, watered stock, and technological blockages. [15]

Brandeis's journalistic tour de force distilled the work of a fact-finding mission carried out under the auspices of the Pujo Committee, actually a sub-committee of the House Banking and Currency Committee, chaired by Louisiana congressman Arsene Pujo and charged with determining, first of all, whether there was a 'money trust'. The notion in some ways belonged to the realm of myth, akin to the serpents and devil fish to which the 'money trust' was frequently compared. But what Brandeis and the Pujo Committee engaged in was an act of demystification. They wanted to detach the real-life 'money trust' from the myth, find out just where on earth it lived, and describe how it went about its business. Their hopes for legislative remedy would live or die by the persuasive power of the facts they assembled. Such was the confidence that typified so many progressive-era reformers. They were indefatigable researchers, dispassionate analysts; pragmatists, free, so they believed, of ideological predispositions. They were determined to drag the bogey-men of their nineteenth-century predecessors into the light of day, and to subject Wall Street to probing social-scientific scrutiny.

Under its remorseless chief counsel, Samuel Untermeyer, the Pujo Committee accomplished a Herculean task of research. In an age when business records were largely immune from public inspection, the Pujo staff probed and dissected whatever material they could obtain about what today we might call the financial services sector. Untermeyer supplemented this mass of statistics with a relentless public interrogation of the captains of finance. Appearances by the principal financial luminaries naturally drew the media: Morgan arrived accompanied by a platoon of lawyers and partners while a standing-room-only crowd looked on entranced.[16]

What Pujo unraveled and Brandeis displayed in bite-sized pieces turned out to be a metaphor in its own right. Instead of a creature from some fantastical nightscape, they discovered a web, constructed with architectural precision, each of its arms fluidly articulated with all the others, lending the whole structure impressive resilience and elasticity. Included in the Committee's exhibits and in the pages of Brandeis's book were illustrations resembling electrical grids, constructed to show all the interlocking connections: between overlapping boards of directors; between the four or five top investment houses and their allied commercial banks and a whole network of underlying financial and industrial corporations; between the country's leading insurance companies, trust companies, savings banks, brokerages, railroads, and top-rank industrial concerns like United States Steel, International Harvester, and AT&T. Together these connections formed a force field whose central generating station was located very near Morgan headquarters at 23 Wall Street. Nor was there only a single web; subsidiary webs deployed power in local domains – 'provincial allies', 'auxiliaries', and 'satellites' like the Boston nexus and the Chicago group – all in the end wired back into the master grid.

Case studies documented how Morgan or Kuhn Loeb functionaries, in their dual roles as investment banker and corporate director, determined strategic decisions about when, how, and at what price securities were marketed. Brandeis cited Morgan partner George Perkins as a prime example: as a vice-president of New York Life, the country's largest insurance company, he steered it into major purchases of securities underwritten by the House of Morgan, even though, as a mutual insurance firm, such decisions fell in theory within the province of the policy-holders – a proviso Pujo called a 'farce'. This same power was also used in reverse to close off sources of capital and deflate the value of rival securities. Brandeis chose the Harriman railroad empire and its Kuhn Loeb banking partners to illustrate how high finance in the transportation business was not directed at needed capital improvements. Those, he argued, might have been easily financed out of earnings. Instead, the Union Pacific and other lines went to market with large blocks of securities to finance paper transactions in the stocks and bonds of other roads and to acquire a slew of non-railroad related speculative assets.[17]

The Pujo report and the Brandeis exposé delighted in showing the arithmetic of power. According to the jurist, Morgan partners held seventy-two directorships in forty-seven of the country's largest corporations. Pujo performed a grander summing up: all in all the House of Morgan and its allies (First National and National City banks) occupied 341 directorships in 112 corporations with an aggregate capitalization of more than $22 billion. When Morgan created that godfather of all industrial trusts, United States Steel, the whole country tilted to the East, according to Brandeis. The combination absorbed 228 separate companies in 127 cities in eighteen states, all once locally owned and financed. Wall Street trustifications of this magnitude warped the country's financial geography, wiping out the financial independence of communities and regional banking centers.[18]

As it was prised apart and then re-sutured, the web emerged as a matchless metaphor particularly appealing to middle-class urbanites infatuated with science. Although steered by human hands, it resembled nothing so much as a highly reticulated machine: nothing but intersecting vertical, horizontal, and diagonal lines of motion primly labeled with an alphabet of institutional acronyms. Stark and abstract, the web, as a visual experience, was also a masterpiece of modernist social science.

Confessions before Congress's committee were more equivocal than these reports suggested. Morgan was the only witness openly to condemn stock manipulations by the web. Others denied it existed, or, conversely, rescued the practice by rechristening it as a way of 'making a market'. George F. Baker of First National Bank pleaded ignorance and memory loss, unable even to recall the companies he directed or just where the New York, Susquehanna and Western Railroad (one of his) began and ended. Frank Sturgis, President of the New York Stock Exchange, zigged and zagged as Untermeyer quizzed him about the web's organized short-selling, maintaining that it was a morally distasteful yet justifiable form of self-defense, even during panics – although he conceded that such behavior actually aggravated the panics. Others coyly insisted their stock-market deportment was a private matter, while some – like the 'Silver Fox', James Keene – boldly supplied chapter and verse on how the bloodless business was carried out. William Rockefeller, John's remote and far less pietistic brother, avoided the problem altogether, developing an acute case of laryngitis when Committee investigators came down to Georgia to ask him some questions at his Jekyl Island retreat.[19]

Silences like that echoed loudly, of course, as did the implausible terseness with which Morgan responded to the following line of questioning by the Committee's chief counsel:

UNTERMEYER: You do not have any power in any department of industry in this country, do you?

MORGAN: I do not.

UNTERMEYER : Not the slightest?

MORGAN: Not the slightest.

UNTERMEYER : And you are not looking for any?

MORGAN: I am not seeking it, either.

UNTERMEYER : This consolidation and amalgamation of systems and industries and banks does not look to any concentration, does it?

MORGAN: No, sir.

UNTERMEYER : It looks, I suppose, to a dispersal of interests rather than to a concentration?

MORGAN: Oh, no; it deals with things as they exist . . . [20]

But if Morgan's self-possession and sangfroid could produce this sort of preposterous obtuseness, others came forward with refreshing candor. Jacob Schiff admitted there existed a certain concentration of power, but found this no cause for concern; after all, the power was in 'good hands', which for the 'morganizers' was the ne plus ultra of their right to rule. Schiff helped as well to clarify the true nature of competition within the web. While its two great branches – the Morgan/First National Bank/US Steel cluster and the Rockefeller/National City Bank/Standard Oil cluster – might find themselves at odds, generally speaking it was not considered 'good form to create unreasonable interference or competition'. George M. Reynolds of the Continental and Commercial National Bank of Chicago candidly acknowledged even before the Pujo hearings convened that 'I believe the money power now lies in the hands of a dozen men. I plead guilty to being one of the dozen.'[21]

By turns frank and duplicitous, forthcoming and evasive, the testimony did nothing to disprove what many already believed: that the web was real. One could admire its structural elegance while sensing the danger of its capacity for perpetual self-reproduction. Thus even as he pursued his relentless interrogations, Untermeyer insisted he did not necessarily consider these men dishonest or venal; on the contrary, he accepted that they often acted with self-restraint and with a regard for their own nice sense of justice. What bothered the interlocutor was not the men but the system, the web that organized and set in motion this choreography of domination. So intricate in composition, it was hard to see how anyone could completely control its workings.

Untermeyer feared that if left intact this system would end in 'a moneyed oligarchy more despotic and more dangerous to industrial freedom than anything civilization has ever known'. Why more dangerous? Because, as Brandeis explained, it was unlike the great wealth of the Astors, for example. However socially objectionable and unjustly acquired, that was 'static wealth' and strictly personal, unlike the 'dynamic wealth' of the 'morganizers'. Theirs depended on control over the capital assets of others, which in turn allowed them sway over great industrial combines and vital financial institutions, with only a fractional investment of their own money.

This pernicious system of interlocking directorates was an all-round disaster. It stifled the entrepreneurial spirit, intimidated business and professional people, discouraged efficient management, destroyed sound business judgment, injured innocent stockholders, bank depositors, policy-holders, and consumers, blocked new inventions and production processes in order to protect investments in antiquated technologies, kept prices artificially inflated, and was patently unfair. In Brandeis's view, the whole web of interlocking relationships needed to be outlawed as offensive to laws both 'human and divine'. That was the royal road to the 'New Freedom'.

Other People's Money concluded on an adamantine note: 'We must break the Money Trust or the Money Trust will break us.' Armageddon-like language was hardly new to the anti-trust persuasion. What was new, however, was the scientific esprit with which the challenge was offered. Brandeis's book was full of references to despotism and industrial democracy; 'money kings', 'banker barons', and their crushing of the American spirit of free enterprise. Brandeis's locutions were more than mere rhetorical varnish: he meant them all, as did Woodrow Wilson, Robert LaFollette, and the magazine writers and the armies of anonymous middle-class insurgents ready to face off against the 'money trust'. But it was a case of old wine in new bottles. The final chapter of *Other People's Money* was entitled 'The Inefficiencies of the Oligarchs': Brandeis and his muckraking colleagues finally rested the case against the 'morganizers' on their unfitness to rule.[22]

Arsene Pujo was a Democrat. But his hearings were first called to life by Charles A. Lindbergh, Republican congressman from Minnesota and father of the future aviation hero. Suspicion about the 'money trust' was a bipartisan phenomenon, shared by broad swathes of the middle classes. True, some conservative media, including the trade press of the finance industry, congratulated Morgan for his coolness under fire, although eye-witness accounts described the banker's rising uneasiness as he chewed his lips, banged on the table, and looked for approval from his lawyers and family members. Other publications pooh-poohed the Pujo investigation as a witch-hunt. John Moody, a deeply conservative business publicist, praised the advent of economic giantism and took the existence of the web for granted. In his view, its peak institutions collaborated in a wise administration of the economy: 'It is felt and recognized on every hand in Wall Street to-day, that they are harmonious in nearly all particulars.'[23]

However, even journals of impeccable respectability and restraint like *The Nation* had to admit that Pujo had unearthed some unseemly truths about Wall Street, while turning up its nose at what it considered ridiculous notions of a 'giant conspiracy'. *The Baltimore American*, known for its Republican sympathies, went as far as to declare the Committee's findings a 'menace' and a 'disgrace'. On the other side, liberal publications were still more outspoken. In *Collier's* the 'Trust' was likened to Peer Gynt's Boyg – shapeless, slippery, cold, and all over the place. Cartoons laughed off Morgan's testimony: one pictured the banker sitting atop a pile of $25 billion, his pudgy hands holding lucrative properties – ships, railroads, banks, buildings – and running underneath a verbatim rendering of his testimony denying any special power over the economy.[24]

Pujo's hearings and Brandeis's book were signals that popular skepticism about the web and the world according to J. P. Morgan had reached critical mass. The explosive ingredients had been accumulating for years, at least since that fatal shot in Buffalo. Magazines and newspapers throughout the decade had filled their pages with evidence – piecemeal and usually focused on some particular industry but always rich in detail – about the way the web conducted its affairs. Between 1903 and 1912, periodicals whose readership once numbered in the hundreds of thousands were now read by twenty-five million people. Financial coverage became a regular feature of this literature, including hot exposés and inside dope on the way the pros played the markets, and especially about how promoters gulled the public selling sham securities that were 'three-quarters wind'.[25]

Ray Stannard Baker's careful reconstructions in *McClure's* ('The Generals Up in Wall Street') exposed the way financial titans exercised authority over the great rail systems, revelations Teddy Roosevelt found so persuasive. Striking a chord with the increasingly consumer-conscious middle class, Baker homed in on the way Wall Street used its captive rail systems like a tax farmer, levying usurious rates to drain away the income of its customers (both commercial and passenger), enabling it to recycle the revenue into the acquisition of other far-flung outposts of American industry. Baker told Roosevelt that the real solution was government ownership, but the 'damn cowboy' found this too hot to handle. [26]

A similar excavation was performed on the underground operations of New York's mass transit financiers by Burton Jesse Hendrick in *Great American Fortunes and Their Making*. Raking up the muck left behind by the likes of Thomas Fortune Ryan and William Whitney (often in collaboration with the Morgan interests), Hendrick's was a sordid but precisely itemized tale of stock watering, construction kick-backs, shoddy, unsafe work, bribed judges and legislators, and circumvented city regulations – neatly arranged by Morgan attorney and sometime Secretary of State, Elihu Root. It was typical of a whole subgenre of progressive periodical writing designed to explore the impact of the web on public services. Whether it was gas, water, electric, or even the ice trust, consumers of municipal services were the ultimate losers, according to the damning evidence unearthed by muckrakers like Hendricks and Charles Edward Russell.[27]

Given that much of this literature was brimming over with the driest sort of data, it is remarkable that it nevertheless had an avid readership. Not so laden with the ideological baggage of the last century, it appealed to cosmopolitans who participated in modern urban life and resented being taken advantage of. The reputation and commercial success of whole magazines rested on this taste for the methodical demystification – 'just the facts, mam' – of big business in general and high finance in particular.

Frenzied Finance was arguably the most spectacular instance of this sort of journalistic wonder drug. Its serialized publication by *Everyman's* magazine in 1904 transformed an under-read monthly into the country's bestselling progressive magazine. Circulation quadrupled to one million while the series ran. Its special sizzle came from the fact that its author, Thomas Lawson, hailed from the belly of the beast. Lawson was a well-known Wall Street speculator on a first-name basis with all the masters of the web, a high-flyer who'd seemingly gotten religion: he was prepared to tell all and take no prisoners.

Lawson's defection was hardly unique. Rumblings of discontent were audible from opposite sides of the Street. There were distinguished investment firms, some of more recent vintage like Goldman Sachs and Lehman Brothers, less than enamored with the Morgan regime. They made their way by bringing to market the initial offerings of companies in mass-consumption and new-technology sectors – retailers like F. W. Woolworth, mail-order firms like Sears Roebuck, auto companies like Studebaker, office-machinery manufacturers like Underwood typewriters, and so on. Though prosperous enough, they nonetheless felt like outsiders looking in, and wanted to break the Morgan chokehold. After all, even the *Wall Street Journal* worried now and then about how the 'money trust' might imperil the capital stock of the country, by shifting too much of it into speculation and by encouraging an unnatural piling up of resources in New York.

Critics often imagined the 'community of interest' within the Wall Street confraternity to be more seamless than it really was. Fissures were inevitable, however, especially in an economy just then straining to make the transition from heavy to mass-consumption industry. While Wall Street grew in size and power, the economy grew even more expansively. The Street was never able to exercise the degree of control it wished to. New regional centers of economic influence emerged, independent of the Street's dominant institutions. New competitors appeared who relied on internal financing or on local or regional banking resources in the Midwest and West. The great merger movement was essentially confined to eight basic industries, and even in those new competitors arose. Down below, the economy was far less concentrated and stable than either the 'morganizers' or their enemies believed.

Newer Wall Street firms, as well as investment houses with venerable pedigrees, were naturally enough drawn to these emerging sectors. Still, such houses, particularly those originating in the German-Jewish financial old guard, cultivated, like the 'morganizers', a sense of dynastic exclusivity and devotion to duty. Cloistered with their unimaginable wealth, they nonetheless prided themselves on their modesty, prudence, sensitivity to the arts – music especially – and civic-mindedness. [28]

As if from another planet were the Street's hoi polloi. They were Wall Street's men on the make: flashy, full of wild financial enthusiasms and misguided speculations, carriers of the Street's democratic promise that anybody could play the game and come out on top. And they too harbored a grudge against the 'morganizers', whose grip over the market was so vice-like no one else could get a finger-hold. *Where the Money Grows* was one such *cri de coeur*. Garet Garrett was no innocent. A friend of Bernard Baruch's, the Street's most eminent speculator, he warned his readers about the innumerable mysteries and treacheries of a street he called 'The Hall of Delusions'. But what he found irresistibly attractive was its egalitarianism. Everybody – everybody, that is, except the 'Great Ones': the Morgans, the Rockefellers, the Harrimans – dealt with each other in a spirit of good fellowship. They shared their petty dreams and grand illusions, their stories of faded glory, their infallible schemes; altogether an odd community of hangers-on, wannabes, and once-wases, ready to trust to fate and perhaps on occasion to a 'hoodoo man'. What spoiled this democracy of luck were 'the invisibles', the malevolent 'theys' who used their hidden powers to bull and bear the market behind the backs of the Street's common folk. [29]

Thomas Lawson's withering exposé seemed to emerge from both these worlds. He was a rather dandified, glib, and remarkably charismatic one-time stockbroker from Boston. The son of a carpenter, he'd risen fast by trading on his amiability, good looks, and rakish irreverence. A teenage speculator, he was a millionaire at thirty, decked out in black pearls and enjoying his castle-like estate on the Massachusetts coast. While some of the more pious from State and Wall Street resented his Barnum-like jocosity and gambler's insouciance, over the years he'd become a financial confidant and deal facilitator, especially in that domain of the web where the Rockefeller interests predominated. Standard Oil executive Henry Rogers, James Stillman, and William Rockefeller himself were the men he dealt with. However, while Lawson was trustworthy enough, by Wall Street standards, he was no mere functionary, but a man with his own outsized ambitions to master the market. The tale he told in *Frenzied Finance* was like a revenge fantasy come true for a speculator who felt he'd been used and abused by the web.

'The Story of the Amalgamated', the first of Lawson's grenades, was lobbed directly at the Rockefeller-directed machinations to set up a copper trust. Lawson had helped to make the market for the Trust's stock offerings among Yankee blue-bloods and New England bankers. Making a market understated what happened. Lawson called it 'dollar hydrophobia' as he sauntered through the Waldorf, whipping up the avidity of the well-heeled. But then he was betrayed. Lawson's was a blow-by-blow account of the way the 'top dogs' arranged it so that only they skimmed the cream from the initial underwriting. Everybody else, including not only speculators like himself but a mass of middle-class amateur investors, was victimized by plummeting share values, especially after McKinley's assassination, and rocketing copper prices; all in all, he claimed, the Trust fleeced the public of $100 million. Lawson sketched an empire of money run out of Standard Oil headquarters, its reach extending to mines in the West, factories in the East, colleges in the South, churches in the North. He named names and reported sick-bed confessions, flights from prosecution, and midnight intrigues. Full-page illustrations of Rogers and Rockefeller ran alongside the text. The foreword to the series was reprinted in daily papers across the United States as well as Canada. A completely silly play – a cross between 'Colonel Sellers' and the Keystone Cops, starring Douglas Fairbanks and entitled *A Case of Frenzied Finance* – lasted through eight performances on Broadway. Through all the hullabaloo, Standard Oil stayed mum. Lawson was lionized; but also branded a traitor, a fraud, and a hypester by his erstwhile colleagues on the Street. [30]

As if he still needed to scratch a festering sore, Lawson then announced in the December installment of *Frenzied Finance* that 'I am now going to cause a life insurance blaze . . . so bright that every scoundrel with a mask, dark-lantern, and suspicious-looking bag will stand out so clear that he cannot escape the consequences of his past deeds, nor commit future ones.' With the assistance of confederates in other muckraking journals and the Pulitzer media machine, he succeeded beyond his wildest imagining. Soon enough the New York State Department of Insurance ordered an investigation to determine whether the management of the Equitable Life Assurance Society was guilty of the misuse of funds. Had the company and others like it become violators of the people's trust, mere 'playthings of the Morgans, the Harrimans, the Ryans, and other speculative exploiters and gamblers of their ilk'?[31]

The Armstrong Commission, led by its Chief Counsel, Charles Evans Hughes, a man of unimpeachable reputation, conducted a dispassionate dissection of the life-insurance business, which nonetheless provoked a passionate response. It zeroed in on the industry's three giants – Mutual of New York, Equitable, and New York Life – all watched over by the Morgan and Rockefeller interests. Like Baker's railroad revelations, the Commission's discoveries proved particularly alarming to an urban middle class increasingly self-conscious about protecting its rights as consumers and investors in the new economy. Hughes posed the bedrock question: how could the investment bankers who directed both the banks that sold and the insurance companies that bought these multi-million dollar securities not find themselves in a conflict of interest? The traditional response of people like Schiff and Perkins was to point with reassuring pride to their professional probity. That answer was wearing thin.

Armstrong's probe uncovered the way the web used the deposits of policyholders to support its own underwritings while premiums ballooned and dividends shriveled. Investigators tracked those hard-to-come-by premium dollars as they filtered into newsrooms, editorial offices, and legislative chambers (including the infamous 'house of mirth'), where they bought silence about or loud endorsement of the big three's stratagems on behalf of the web. Ryan was cited, for example, for dipping into these idling pools of insurance-company capital to float his far-flung promotions in traction, tobacco, mining, and even an escapade in the Congo. James Hazen Hyde, the notorious young sybarite running the Equitable, always a target for magazine satirists and cartoonists, sold his holdings and decamped for Paris.

All of a sudden a normally sleep-inducing subject became the raw material of one of the era's most celebrated pieces of muckraking journalism. 'The Story of Life Insurance' by Burton Jesse Hendrick ran in *McClure's*, where it not only laid bare the extravagant salaries awarded to top executives, but traced the evolution of a staid industry into a racy sub-region of the Wall Street web. The 'sharpies' had in effect colonized these insurance companies, freely funneling their vast pools of capital into railroads and utilities verging on bankruptcy. Cartoonists had a field day making fun of insurance-company executives for their self-indulgence in food, dress, mansions, and lavish party-giving. The urge to reform the industry, to bar it at least from participating in Wall Street underwritings, spread from New York to states all across the nation.[32]

Lawson, however, was incorrigible. He presented himself as a repentant sinner, a reformer who knew all too well what needed changing and had a basket full of remedies at hand – stock-exchange regulations to control margin sales, interlocking directorates, undistributed profits, suspiciously large dividends, and so on. But even while he penned *Frenzied Finance* Lawson continued his career as a speculator – he couldn't resist. His editor at *Everybody's*, E. J. Ridgway, wrote him a public letter: 'I shall never cease to believe that if you had kept out of Wall Street after you began the series with us you would be the biggest man in the country today.' Maybe so, but the love affair between Lawson and his loyal readers ended badly. His credibility damaged, the progressive community abandoned him and he it, contemptuous of 'the people' and their petty dreams of stock-market riches.[33]

Lawson went through several more fortunes, ending as a bankrupt. But *Frenzied Finance*, together with all the other anatomies of the web – including Gustavus Myers' 1907 tome, *History of Great American Fortunes*, whose encyclopedic inventory showed 'inert masses' of dynastic wealth originating in stupendous acts of larceny – changed the cultural atmosphere. Wall Street's grandees, worshipped so recently, now seemed to wilt away under a remorseless scrutiny, some of it carried out by their former admirers.

Lincoln Steffens went to work at *Everybody's* magazine just after it placed its bombshell under the insurance business. Having taken a break from Wall Street to write, among other things, his muckraking classic, *Shame of the Cities*, Steffens returned to find everything changed, including himself. He'd once been openly awe-struck in the presence of Morgan and his ilk. But now he was put off by what he dubbed the 'boss system' – that is, the web. For Steffens the drift toward dictatorship was unmistakable. Wall Street under Morgan had become 'an organization of the privileged for the control of the sources of privilege, and of the thoughts and acts of the unprivileged'.[34]

Steffens' epiphany was a not uncommon experience, though many continued for the moment to treat the captains of finance and industry as giants. To others, however, they began to seem more dwarf-like. As periodicals, novels, and short stories picked away at their Napoleonic armor, their cultural authority began to slip. Magazines which at the turn of the century had been filled with the Herculean exploits of the paladins of business, now shifted their attention to statesmen, scientists, explorers, and others whose lives now seemed more exemplary. *American Magazine* announced that 'the old gods are dying in the world of greedy finance', and with them their Napoleonic mystique. Serialized biographies of Morgan, Gould, Rockefeller and others now took the view that these were rather duplicitous men, callous and given to cheating. The aim of the debunking was to turn heroes not into ogres, but rather into ordinary men whose claims to deference turned out, on close inspection, to be groundless.[35]

Were the 'money-trusters' responsible for the nation's industrial growth? Not at all. That was due to the initiative, endurance, and ingenuity of thousands of anonymous entrepreneurs. Did the web-meisters deserve credit for the country's extraordinary technological progress, which had transformed the lives of so many? Far more deserving were the scientists and engineers admired round the world. Could the 'morganizers' in good conscience congratulate themselves for the miracle of American mass-production? Better to reward the production managers and highly skilled labor force who day by day grappled with the intractability of the inanimate world.

But there was always the Hamiltonian defense. Wasn't it right and fair to assign the 'money trust' the chief responsibility for mobilizing the capital resources of the country, a daunting burden which it had assumed with spectacular results? Did not the investment houses assume the risk in 'making the markets' in liquid capital which irrigated industrial growth? Did not their guaranteed underwritings of new corporate issues, even on occasion their willingness to buy up whole issues outright, justify the financiers' power to dictate their price, and where, how, and to whom they would be sold? Alas, even here, the masters of high finance were found wanting. They performed their singular role with marked ineffectiveness. Their gentleman's understandings discouraged real competition and opened the way to indefensible underwriting fees, grossly distorted security prices, illogical dividend payouts, and insider profit-taking. They institutionalised the separation between the Wall Street cognoscenti and the unwashed investing public. In a word, the system they presided over was defunct.[36]

Those who championed the Wall Street elite saw it as a vanguard leading the rest of the country to the summit of a new manifest destiny; others took a long look at this vanguard and found it barbaric. When Morgan died, Walt Whitman's close friend, Horace Traubel, called him a 'brute'. He meant that less as a personal insult than as a means of characterizing 'a certain civilization', with which the Morgan name was synonymous: 'What the power of wealth stood for: he was that. He was stocks, bonds, banks, railroads, trusts, financiering; chicanery, profit . . . He was the shadow of his time . . . We put his age away in the hole in the ground with him.'

Traubel registered a sudden change in the cultural temperature. As one observer noted, 'When the nineteenth century closed, America worshipped great wealth . . . In five years' time, America has learned to hate great wealth.' Already one can sense an early intimation of the crisis that would eventually undo the ruling elite, whose self-sufficiency and confidence depended on the indivisible linkages between its dynastic property and managerial authority. The house that Morgan built stood midway between an old world where wealth and power were invariably vested in great magnates and their families, and the modern universe of the impersonal bureaucratic corporation, where the impress of even the mightiest individual was growing fainter. The confrontation between 'morganization' and progressivism was a first reckoning with that historic crisis.[37]

All of that was still a Great Depression away. But no one could deny the growing skepticism that picked away at the vaunted rationality of the 'morganizers'. What defenders of the web saw as its greatest virtue – that it stood above the fray, overseeing and integrating whole industrial sectors, imposing a healthy equilibrium – its opponents treated as its fatal flaw. Invested, like the Church or some feudal potentate, with sovereignty over the economy, the banker-barons had turned it into a system of tribute levied on everyone – railroad and shipper, investor and consumer, citizen and worker. To ward off threats to its existing investments, it discouraged new inventions and processes, using its control of patents to freeze whole industries. Nay-sayers surfaced even from the innards of industry. *The Engineering News* observed that American manufacturing, iron and steel metallurgy particularly, trailed German technical development because 'those who control our trusts do not want to bother developing anything new'. Instead of fast-forwarding economic progress, the web aborted it. [38]

Around the turn of the century, a chorus of academic criticism reinforced the conviction that 'morganization', far from representing the acme of economic modernism, was retrograde and dysfunctional. Distinguished economists like John Bates Clark, Richard Ely, and James Mead subjected the publicly traded corporation to close inspection. At a time when the academy was not quite so segregated from public debate, such voices further disturbed the equanimity of the 'morganizers'. On the one hand, these men welcomed the emergence of large-scale industry for its efficiencies and economies of scale. Moreover, the dispersion of shares of these giant combines into the hands of a broad middle class, and even into the hands of their blue-collar workers, struck these reform-minded scholars as a positive social development. If carried far enough it could ameliorate class antagonisms and extend democracy into the authoritarian heart of American industry. However, the superceding power of the web placed all of this in jeopardy, dividing the average shareholder seeking regular and reasonable returns from the web-meisters who manipulated securities for short-term gain. Clark, the most daring member of a commission set up by New York Governor Hughes to investigate the stock exchange, declared the investor the trust's 'most conspicuous victim'. Moreover, banker control opened up another fissure between the management of these corporations who served at the sufferance of web-dominated boards of directors, and the shareholders whose 'ownership' had been so diluted as to preclude any say over the deployment of the corporation's assets.

The fraying connection between ownership and management was a newly observed dilemma at the turn of the century. Its ramifications were not only legal, organizational, and economic, but also cultural, and would ripple on for decades. What was to become of the sense of personal and familial identity and social esteem once associated with control over productive property? As shareholding began to diffuse more widely, a dawning realization of this loss no doubt fed some of the middle-class disquietude about the web's wrenching disruptions.

Still, in these early days everything seemed reversible. The academics spied the tantalizing prospect of a shareholder democracy that could turn industrial giantism into a blessing for all. As Clark rhapsodized, 'the old line of demarcation between the capitalist class and the laboring class will be blurred and at many points obliterated . . . The socialist is not the only one who can have beatific visions.' Only the distortions introduced by a regressive Wall Street plutocracy stood in the way of the progressive economists' urban middle-class utopia.[39]

Progressivism lent its name to a school of history which registered the decisive impact of economic forces on the course of the nation's development. Wall Street in particular cast its shadow backward to the nation's founding. Charles Beard's *Economic Interpretation of the Constitution*, published at the time of the Pujo hearings, was perhaps the most provocative work of 'progressive' historiography. His controversial discovery that the founding fathers had been motivated to junk the Articles of Confederation and substitute the Constitution's federalism by their desire to protect their investments in government securities was shocking. Yet it also seemed to make sense. After all, titans of finance, the contemporary incarnations of those eighteenth-century bondholders, seemed to be calling the shots from behind the scenes, dictating the direction of economic as well as political life: this was 'morganization' read backwards, history as orchestrated from the Street. Beard despised Morgan and was appalled at the vulgarity of this gilded civilization. He never tired of recording its more freakish excesses: a private carriage and valet for a pet monkey, a pair of opera glasses costing $75,000, beribboned dogs driven for afternoon rides in the back seats of luxury Victorias, a symphony orchestra hired to serenade a newborn baby.

Charles Edward Russell argued in his scathing series in *Everybody's* (provocatively entitled 'Where Did You Get It Gentlemen?') that these men's wealth and power did not come from work connected to the nation's productive enterprises, but from their control and manipulation of property-titles. How unworthy of adulation this was Russell proceeded to document, in a case-by-case demolition of the romance of Napoleonic success. He took particular delight in rewriting the mythography of Thomas Fortune Ryan, who was virtually the apotheosis of that romance. The nation's Secretary of State, Elihu Root, was his attorney; he maintained a brigade of loyal senators and congressmen in Washington; from Kentucky to the Congo, from London to San Francisco, 'men are employed by him and are subject to his will; he says to them, Do this, and they do it.' How had he managed it? Was it a fairy tale of desperate beginnings, unsquashable pluck, unimpeachable trustworthiness, and dedication to business? Not exactly. It was, Russell tried to show, the product of a marriage made in hell, a 'union of rotten business with rotten politics'. Ryan and his confederate William Whitney were paragons of venality, over-bearing bullies who held other men in contempt. Scrape away the glamorous veneer and what you uncovered was something much cheaper: a tawdry spectacle of 'debauched public officials' in league with the web to loot the public treasury, leaving the consumers of municipal services to pick up the bill.

Muckrakers like Russell clearly enjoyed moods of righteous indignation. Even as he discussed the practical costs of this Wall Street syndrome – he noted that New York was one of the last great cities to electrify its transit system because so much capital had been swallowed up in stock manipulations – Russell couldn't resist levying a moral indictment as well. It was directed not only at the captains of finance, but at his fellow citizens, who had become hypnotized by the ethos of success. By worshipping men who caused them harm, the citizenry was complicit in its own fleecing. Of course, this was the cultural dilemma with which Wall Street had confronted the country for generations.[40]

Finley Peter Dunne's send-ups of the Street aimed to puncture this very misapprehension. When Dooley's bartender friend, Mr Hennessy, asked him what a 'Titan of Finance' was, Dooley left him in no doubt: 'A Ti-tan iv Fi-nance . . . is a man that is got more money thin he can carry without bein' disorderly.' Dooley described what happened when two such titans went at it hammer and tongs:

'And im th'gr-eatest consolidator in th' wurruld,' says Scaldy Harriman, 'I've consolidate th' U.P., th' K.R. and L., th' R.O. and T., th' B.U. and M., an th' N. and G.,' says he. 'I've a line iv smoke reachin' fr'm wan ocean to th'other,' he says. 'I'm no ordin'ry person,' he says . . . 'I'm a Titan an' I'm lookin' f'r throuble,' he says, 'an here it comes,' he says. 'You a consolidator?' says Scrappy Morgan. 'Why,' he says, 'ye cuddenit mix dhrinks f'r me,' he says. 'I'm th' on'y ruffyan consolidator in th'gleamin' West,' he says. 'I've joined th' mountains iv th' moon railway with th'canals iv Mars, an I'll be haulin' wind fr'm the caves of Saturn befure th' first iv th'year,' he says . . .

Dunne could be just as unsparing when it came to sizing up the popular infatuation with the Street. Dooley recounted the binge accompanying the Northern Pacific bubble of 1901:

> Niver befure in th' history iv th' world has so manny barbers an waiters been on th' verge iv a private yacht . . . Th' barber on th' third chair cut off part iv the nose iv th' prisident iv Con and Foundher whin A.P. wint up fourteen pints. He compromised with his vicitim be takin' a place on th' board iv the comp'ny. But it's all past now. Th'waiter has returned to his mutton an th'barber to his plowshare . . . Th' jag is over. Manny a man that looked like a powdher piegeon a month ago looks like a hinchback to-day.[41]

Novelists too took a second look at the warrior cult. Robert Herrick's ingenuous hero in *A Life for a Life* at first buys into the notion that this seemingly gray world of credits, reorganizations, and receiverships is the modern analog of a battlefield, full of 'powder, shot, and shell'. He's saved from this illusion by an older, wiser man, who shows the callow country boy that all this talk of crusaders, warriors, and heroes is just so much after-dinner cant and hypocrisy, meant mainly to titillate the archaic imaginations of the women folk.[42]

David Graham Phillips did something different in *The Deluge*, by fictionalizing the life of Thomas Lawson – ripe raw material indeed. The novel was a story of Wall Street heroism in reverse. Instead of standing in awe of the financial titan, the Wall Street insider, *The Deluge* made the Wall Street outsider its redeeming protagonist. Phillips was already well known for his exposés of the medical and law professions, the church, press, and higher education. A year after publishing the novel, he would write *The Treason of the Senate*, which made Roosevelt apoplectic and inspired his charge of 'muckraking' for its assertion that the government was run by a claque of financiers, 'the Seven'. In a sensational story in *Cosmopolitan*, he fingered 'the chief exploiter of the American people' (by whom he meant Rockefeller) and his 'chief schemer' (by whom he meant Rhode Island Senator Nelson Aldrich, linked to Rockefeller by marriage and to Morgan by handsomely rewarded political services). Phillips would pay the heaviest price for his audacity. He was assassinated a few years later, shot six times as he walked through Gramercy Park in New York by Fitzhugh Coyle Goldsborough, the scion of a prominent Maryland family. While the motives for the killing remain obscure – Goldsborough took his own life immediately after the murder – the

Phillips family speculated that Goldsborough sought to avenge Phillips' scathing portrait of the lifestyle of the idle rich in one of his recent novels.

The Deluge was published into the afterglow of the Lawson revelations, which no doubt contributed to its considerable popularity. Matt Blacklock, the novel's stand-in for Lawson, is a folk hero of Wall Street's new frontier. He's self-made, democratic in spirit, and rather picturesque; like Lawson he's a bon vivant, a free-lance and not afraid of a fight. He's a genuine enthusiast, a promoter who works with but is never allowed inside the inner spirals of the web. He revels in his insouciance and bumptious egoism. Blacklock gives voice to the civilian investor facing down the old guard: it's not that he doesn't want in, but he can't stifle his caustic assessment of their flimsy pretensions and supercilious rectitude. Blacklock doesn't fear the great titans; on the contrary, he's realized they are really weak and passive characters with no claim to join him in the aristocracy of doers.

One, however, is a more fearsome opponent. Roebuck is a villainous caricature of Morgan, full of pious delusions of grandeur, who believes his reorganization of the economy is God's work, and that he's saving the poor, the unemployed, widows, and orphans from the chaos of deadly competition. Roebuck exercises his dominion over both political parties, the press, and the courts, his power nearly beyond challenge. He is a consummate hypocrite and delights in the humiliation of his rivals, but is at the same time a figure of practically irresistible hypnotic force.

Blacklock's truest insight is that 'Financiers do not gamble. Their only vice is grand larceny.' With this bon mot, speculation wins a reprieve from the moral gulag to which it had been consigned for more than a century. Blacklock/Lawson trusts to luck, fate, and his wits to see him through. His is the esprit of the sportsman: honorable, courageous even. The web-meisters, on the other hand, leave nothing to chance. The fix is in before they ever sit down to play the game.[43]

Nowhere was the ethic of good sportsmanship, of playing by the rules, more hallowed than in the weekly escapades of Frank Merriwell, a series of enormously popular adventures aimed at teenage boys. Just after the panic of 1907, Frank finds himself up against 'the wolves of Wall Street'. Frank himself is heavily invested, but he's a straight arrow, a man's man of the sort TR would have loved. While there are others on the Street just as honest as he, and some hopelessly crooked, the far darker force Frank must deal with is the mysterious 'System'. Its rigging of the market fouls the nest it grew up in; it threatens to make the Street, once a place where legitimate companies could turn, into a sinkhole of trickery and very bad sportsmanship. 'Putting the Wolves to Rout' becomes a kind of middle-class revenge fantasy. To tame the great magnates, you need someone with Frank's mental agility, dogged determination, unflappable rectitude, and manly courage – someone suspiciously like Teddy Roosevelt, in fact.[44]

Frank Merriwell slew his Wall Street dragon in the aftermath of the truly terrifying panic of 1907. The irony of that event is noteworthy. This was the time when the tides of cultural opinion seemed to shift decisively against the 'morganizers' – yet it was also Morgan's supreme moment. When everyone else seemed frozen in place, while the government looked on helplessly, he'd rescued the economy and the nation from what seemed certain disaster. For just that reason, however, some began to wonder aloud whether any one man, however 'safe and sane', ought to be entrusted with such fateful authority. Others went much further and suggested that Morgan had deliberately fostered the panic in order to feather his own nest.

Upton Sinclair's *roman à clef*, *The Moneychangers*, published in 1908, suggested as much. It's a clumsy novel full of cliché and caricature: oversized furniture inside over-sized buildings, all bronzed and marbled; tapped phones; snoops reading other people's mail in a climate of conspiracy lorded over by a Morgan figure (Don Waterman) so brutalized and despotic he can risk committing rape without fear of punishment. But the real point of the story is an accusation that the Senate Judiciary Committee later investigated, and that even sober-minded insiders like John Moody took seriously. Morgan, so the story went, wanted to acquire the Tennessee Coal and Iron Company to extend his US Steel empire into the South and to block the emergence of a dangerous competitive rival. The panic allowed him to do so (with TR's acquiescence) at a rock-bottom price. Although the Senate investigation concluded that Morgan had indeed forced the 'surrender' of TC&I and might be in violation of the Sherman Act, George Perkins called the charge an 'infamous lie'. Morgan's most recent biographer agrees with Perkins, and Teddy Roosevelt denounced the charges as calumnies. Sinclair, despite his notoriety, could find no magazine willing to serialize the tale, and only an obscure publisher willing to put it between hard covers. Nonetheless, the fact that such accusations could attain the status of urban myth indicates how damaged the prestige of the Wall Street elite had become.[45]

Everything went downhill from there. Arguably, business did not fully recover from the trauma of 1907 until the outbreak of war. It sputtered along, and wide segments of the business community blamed the Street for the general sluggishness. Inertia seemed to take the place of that heady sense of forward march which inspired enthusiasm at the turn of the century. There were no new railroads being built, no new cities rising from nothing, no vast manufacturing facilities undergoing expansion. The panic seemed to confirm that the 'morganizers' were superintendents, or worse, undertakers of the old, not the engineers of an exciting new explosion of industrial energy. James Hill himself granted that most trusts were created 'not for the purpose of manufacturing any particular commodity . . . but for the purpose of selling sheaves of printed securities which represent nothing more than good will and prospective profits to promoters.'[46]

Immediately after the panic, Roosevelt called for legislation to regulate speculating and trading on margin. He lashed out at financiers who he believed were trying to use the hysteria to embarrass the government. Anxiety that the nation's system of credit was antiquated and incoherent infected even the soberest banking circles. A cartoon in the *Denver Daily News* showed a smarmy fortune-teller reading a Republican elephant's palm: the forked tongue of a serpent, a 'finance capitalism' snake whose sinewy form could be seen coiling in the background, indicated the elephant's impending demise. 'The Bear Dance . . . or Wall Street Jubilee' made its debut as song and musical theater, featuring a ghoulish group of ravenous grizzlies whooping it up in the forest at a midnight witches' coven. In another Broadway musical, a chorus of demons fanned the flames of a glowing griddle in Hades, chanting delightedly, 'This seat's reserved for Morgan / That great financial Gorgon.' Movies, the infant medium of mass entertainment, discovered the inherent melodrama of high finance. An attempt to film Sinclair's *The Moneychangers* came to nothing when his screenplay was rejected. But in 1909 D. W. Griffith's first featurelength film, *A Corner in Wheat*, shocked audiences with its scenes of manic speculation in the pit. In a terrifying denouement, the 'Wheat King' stumbles into one of his own gigantic wheat bins and is literally buried alive by his ill-gotten gains. A card game called 'Commerce' became the enormously popular still-life equivalent of Griffith's early masterpiece. Its brilliantly lit chromolithographs depicted a whirlpool of concentric circles sucking the 'farmer', 'merchant', 'scientist', and 'mechanic' into its vortex of 'bankruptcy', 'dishonor', 'failure' and 'ruin'.[47]

This cultural subversion of white-shoe Wall Street's honorific status naturally spilled over into the political arena. After 1907, the movement for reform of the web steadily built. Paradoxically, Morgan's midnight rescue served to increase this pressure: lingering doubt about the existence of a 'money trust' was hard to sustain in the teeth of such salvationist heroics.[48]

Questions about what its presence meant for the future of middle-class democracy and middle-class capitalism became irrepressible. They surfaced in both parties and spilled over into presidential campaign rhetoric; they forced their way into Congressional investigations and demanded legislative resolution. Anti-trust sentiment is sometimes too loosely thought of as a plaint of the resentful, as an assault on property by the dispossessed. But what lent the movement so much political heft and cultural salience was its anchorage in diverse niches of the commercial and professional middle classes. It was an unlikely and yet characteristically American liberationist rising.

Historians have argued for generations about the difference between Teddy Roosevelt's 'new nationalism' and Woodrow Wilson's 'new freedom', or about whether there was any real difference at all. Roosevelt suggested a kind of national trusteeship administered by a disinterested political elite, prepared to collaborate with or police the country's economic overlords. However much Roosevelt concerned himself with matters of social justice – he vigorously endorsed legislation to restrict child labor, institute a minimum wage, and compensate injured workmen – the 'new nationalism' was flavoured by a kind of American-style Tory socialism. Woodrow Wilson's 'new freedom' relied more on the democratic energies of the middle classes. Roosevelt's barbs to the contrary, it indulged no nostalgia for some earlier species of small-scale capitalism: 'We shall never return to the older order of individual competition,' Wilson proclaimed, observing that the 'organization of business upon a great scale of cooperation is, up to a certain point, normal and inevitable'. What excited urban as well as small-town progressives was Wilson's conviction that 'The men who understand the life of the country are the men who are on the make and not the men who are already made.' And nowhere was one more likely to run into made men than at the 'money trust'.[49]

Woodrow Wilson already nurtured serious presidential ambitions in 1908 when, still president of Princeton University, he delivered speeches to the Commercial Club of Chicago and to the American Bankers Association. His speeches warned that citizens had good reason to fear that their God-given and democratic right to achieve economic self-sufficiency and to help determine their nation's fate was in danger of being usurped. This was no 'old world' plot by conspiring aristocrats, however. Nor need Americans fear, as their ancestors had, the baleful influence of the sinful city, the rape of a virgin land by an alien industry, or even that most formidable of ancient enemies, the Government. Now it was the life-and-death grip over capital exercised by a remote group of imperial bankers that frustrated all attempts at restraint. There were men, Wilson insisted, who 'stood outside the formal organizations of the greater enterprises and manipulated their securities', and caused everyone else to suffer. 'The truth is,' Wilson confided, empathizing with a widely felt middle-class unease, 'we are all caught in a great economic system which is heartless.'[50]

Once his presidential campaign got under way, the New Jersey Governor made the 'money trust' a live issue and consulted regularly with Brandeis about how best to tackle it. His acceptance speech at the Democratic Party convention placed the 'money trust' first among equals in the rogues' gallery of the nation's enemies. Walter Lippman might consider this as indulging paranoia – 'men like Morgan and Rockefeller take on attributes of omnipotence that ten minutes of cold sanity would reduce to barbarous myth,' he remarked with disdain. Upton Sinclair might be blacklisted for inventing bogeymen. But the man who would soon become President spoke plainly about something he considered all too real:

> There are not merely great trusts and combinations . . . there is something bigger still . . . more subtle, more evasive, more difficult to deal with. There are vast confederacies of banks, railways, express companies, insurance companies, manufacturing corporations, mining corporations, power and development companies . . . bound together by the fact that the ownership of their stock and

members of their boards of directors are controlled and determined by comparatively small and closely interrelated groups of persons who . . . may control, if they please and when they will, both credit and enterprise.

This 'combination of combinations' must be firmly, if delicately prised apart by a vigilant government. [51]

Unquestionably, the censorious moralizing of genteel Protestantism continued to fire up progressive politics. This was emphatically true of Roosevelt, as it was of Wilson. The 'Bull Moose' candidate evangelized: 'we stand at Armageddon, and we battle for the Lord.' The Democratic President-elect, a minister's son, devout and didactic, had this to say about anyone foolhardy enough to deliberately sow the seeds of financial panic: 'I will build the gibbet for him as high as Haman's.'[52] Progressivism was, in part, a revival meeting of superannuated elites. Second- and third-generation New England federalists, their New York Knickerbocker cousins, urban mugwumps of the Gilded Age, expatriate Southern reformers like Walter Hines Page, William Gibbs McAdoo, and Wilson himself, rejoined the battle for supremacy. Still fluent in the oratory of Jeffersonian and Protestant righteousness, they applied it to modern finance capitalism. In one way or another they were determined to rein in the plutocracy, realizing that it had become a chronic incitement to political and social turmoil.

For years editorial opinion warned that if a tiny group of financiers were allowed to dictate the 'capitalistic end of industry, the perils of socialism . . . may be looked upon by even intelligent people as possibly the lesser of two evils.' Partisans of Wilson's New Freedom feared that the reign of the 'money trust' might end up proletarianizing American society, recalling the old Jeffersonian phobia about a 'moneyed aristocracy' breeding European-style sinkholes of urban dependency in the New World. Brandeis went so far as to call the conflict 'irreconcilable', cautioning that 'our democracy cannot endure half free and half slave'. He worried about the crushing not merely of economic liberty but of 'manhood itself which the overweening financial power entails'. Progressivism, inside and outside the Democratic Party, was in some sense a cultural purgative. It meant to revivify a spirit of egalitarianism and self-restraint that the rule of the plutocracy, and especially the 'money trust' which epitomized its hubris, seemed bound to destroy.[53]

Wilson's nomination itself came only after a fierce fight within the Democratic Party, the denouement of a nasty internal feud with Wall Street running all the way back to Bryan's capture of the Party in 1896. At the 1912 Baltimore convention, the old Belmont faction lobbied for New York's Alton B. Parker, whom William Jennings Bryan openly accused of being Wall Street's creature. Numerous telegrams from the hinterlands echoed that belief. Bryan felt emboldened and introduced a resolution declaring the Party unalterably opposed to any nominee 'who is the representative of or under obligation to J. Pierpont Morgan, Thomas Fortune Ryan, August Belmont, or any other member of the privilege-hunting, favor-seeking class'. There were cheers, along with cries to 'lynch him' and 'beat him up'. Bedlam ensued. The resolution passed – only after Bryan agreed to remove a clause calling for the expulsion of delegates representing those nefarious circles; Ryan and Belmont were both delegates – and Parker's candidacy was dead.[54]

Wilson's nomination thus marked the convergence of two oppositional cultures inflamed by hostility to Wall Street. Bryan championed a venerable rural and ethnic suspicion of the eastern big-city 'devil fish'; Wilson the self-confident iconoclasm of the economically more secure and respectable urban middle class. It was a marriage of convenience which would end in mutual recrimination in the 1920s. For the moment, however, it was a striking measure of Wall Street's demonic stature in the nation's political iconography.

Across the aisle, chastened by the panic of 1907, the Republican old guard grew ever more wary. Nonetheless, sentiments similar to Wilson's were alive and well in the Grand Old Party, especially among those faithful to that father of progressive reform, Wisconsin Senator Robert La Follette. He was a crusader of the old school: indeed, his rhetoric was less temperate, his demands for legislative remedies more strident than Wilson's. Like Upton Sinclair, La Follette was willing to ask the unaskable: had the panic been deliberately provoked to suit Morgan's darker purposes? On the Senate floor he produced documents that proved the control of American industry and transportation by a clique of fewer than a hundred men. When the ICC revealed what a mess Morgan had made of his New Haven Railroad system, the Senator wasn't shy about fingering the country's Napoleonic banker: 'these men . . . are but hired megaphones through which a beefy, red-faced, thick-necked financial bully, drunk with wealth and power, bawls his orders to stock markets, Directors, courts, Governments, and Nations. We have been listening to Mr Morgan.'

La Follette led the insurgency within the Republican Party and gave serious thought to instigating a third-party rebellion. He talked ceaselessly about democracy. He did not mean social democracy: no collectivization of the means of production and distribution was contemplated. But the Senator warned that economic and industrial as well as political democracy of a distinctly middle-class sort was being strangled by the web. In a speech delivered in Philadelphia in 1912 and then circulated nationally as a pamphlet, La Follette described the trustification of the economy as an attempt to 'Mexicanize it'. Standing at its headwaters was the 'money trust' roped together by directorships from the command centers of the Morgan and Standard Oil dynasties. Worse even than its baleful influence on the economy was the way it crushed the democratic impulse, reducing the country to a condition of 'complete industrial and commercial servitude'. A captive media, muzzled by the cross-fertilization of publishers, bankers, advertisers, and special interests, insulated the web from public criticism. The 'end of democracy' was in sight.[55]

When the bolt from the Republican Party actually happened in 1912, it was Teddy Roosevelt who became the standard-bearer of the new Progressive or 'Bull Moose' party. La Follette was bitter, noting that George Perkins along with other leading Wall Street bankers financed the ex-President's candidacy. The Progressive Party did indeed acknowledge that economic concentration was inevitable, and not necessarily a bad thing. At Roosevelt's insistence, it scrapped a call to strengthen the anti-trust law that the ex-President considered pandered to reactionary sentiment. But the new Party also raised the specter of an 'invisible government'. Albert Beveridge – an ex-Senator from Indiana, Roosevelt ally, and temporary chairman of the Party convention – declaimed against over-capitalization and manipulated prices. While he judged the Sherman Act antiquated, he called for the criminal prosecution of 'the robber interest'. Only put these men behind bars, and Beveridge would be confident of the Republic's grand future: a time when round the world it would be said of the American businessman, 'as it is said of the hand that shaped Peter's Dome, "he builded better than he knew".'[56]

Beveridge's sunniness typified the fervor of the Progressive Party's cadre. College-educated, self-employed professionals, public intellectuals, journalists, and social workers, they fancied themselves the embryo of a public-service mandarinate. Indeed, some would go on to play just that role. Dean Acheson, Walter Lippman, Felix Frankfurter, and Henry Wallace, among others, served their apprenticeship as Bull Moose partisans.

This political sound and fury simultaneously yielded a great deal and not very much. On the one hand, in the election of 1912, the country's center of political gravity shifted. The issue of the trusts lent the campaign its dramatic tension. Whether people voted for Teddy Roosevelt, Woodrow Wilson, or Socialist Party candidate Eugene Victor Debs (as they did in sizable numbers), a large majority of the electorate registered a desire to break the power of Wall Street's 'money trust'. Wilson's New Freedom promised an end to 'Hannaism', a system in which the country was given over to Wall Street to be 'exploited like a conquered province'. The nation now entertained a once heterodox sentiment, nurtured over the course of a decade: that a reconstruction of the economic order of things might be called for and that the government had some leading role to play in that reconfiguration. Would the state compel the country's leading financial and corporate institutions to behave in the public interest? Would it instead work as a kind of anti-coagulant, opening up the arteries of financial and industrial life to regulated competition and innovation? These were undecided matters, but they were, for the first time, on the agenda.[57]

Yet Wilson himself, just like Roosevelt, maintained close ties to the financial elite, including people like Paul Warburg of Kuhn Loeb, who helped draft the Federal Reserve legislation (and whom Wilson immediately appointed to serve on the new Federal Reserve Board). Bernard Baruch was a Wilson intimate, and members of the German-Jewish 'our crowd', including Jacob Schiff, Henry Morganthau, Sr, Nathan Straus, and Hy Goldman became Wilson loyalists. Consequently, circles of left-leaning Democrats as well as La Follette denounced the 1913 Federal Reserve Act as a banker's bill. Wilson had always kept his distance from the more ideologically driven wing of the anti-trust movement, considering himself a 'practical idealist', not a leveler: 'I am for big business and I am against the trusts,' he explained. Like Roosevelt, Wilson worried about the forces of 'envy' that battened on Wall Street, making it the target of choice for class animosities that progressivism of whatever persuasion tried to stay clear of.

Legislative and executive action was indeed muted. The Federal Reserve Act, while establishing a measure of government oversight and at least a theoretical power to rein in speculative trading, hardly did away with the 'money trust'. The bank bill made no attempt to break apart the system of interlocking directorates that had revved up 'money trust' accusations for years. The disproportionate power of the New York banking establishment was left nearly intact. Indeed, Carter Glass, a Virginia Democrat and chief architect of the bill in the Senate, subsequently boasted that it was always intended, notwithstanding its decentralizing language, to confirm New York's pre-eminence; indeed, Glass 'even hoped to assist powerfully in wresting the sceptre from London' and eventually to make 'New York the financial center of the world'.

None of this stopped elements of the business community from labeling the bill 'socialistic' and the 'preposterous off-spring of ignorance and unreason'. But it was a long way from the system of nationalized control over the country's system of credit, which the 'progressive' critics of the web had for years envisioned. William Gibbs McAdoo, Wilson's son-in law and Secretary of the Treasury, irritated the business establishment as he jealously gathered in as much power over the monetary system as he could. But he was an experienced railroad executive with many ties to the Street. No ideologue, McAdoo was perfectly prepared to work out informal arrangements with the leading commercial and investment banks that left most of their prerogatives undamaged.[58]

The new system first of all devoted itself to ensuring stability in the capital markets, a cause in which even the web-meisters believed, having gotten religion in 1907. Various mechanisms at the disposal of the Board facilitated this general purpose, while insulating the Board itself and its regional banks from the storms of partisan politics and the public discipline of executive fiat. Credits were made available to a wider range of newer, smaller enterprises. In this way the system responded to the middle-class complaint that the web had restricted opportunity. This was tacit recognition of an underlying dilemma: that the modern economy somehow had to accommodate the need for centralized direction and good order while not killing off the goose that laid the golden egg – that ever-renewable desire for private capital accumulation.

Wilson's special message to Congress early in 1914, in part intended to compensate for the deficiencies of the Federal Reserve Act, featured tough talk about outlawing interlocking directorates, beefing up the powers of the ICC to regulate railroad financing, and stiff penalties for other business malpractices. Noises were heard around the Capitol about forcing railroads to sell securities at competitive auctions, prohibiting corporations from designating a bank as its sole fiscal agent, and special taxes to penalize short sales. The Clayton Act, however, was a disappointment. It did make it illegal to hold directorships in two or more corporations if these corporations were direct competitors. But even though Pujo had called for government regulation of the stock exchanges, Federal supervision of new securities issues, and measures to outlaw stock manipulation and control trading on margin, none of that made it onto the statute books.

Gathering signs of depression may have scared the President into mending fences with the financial elite: Morgan was invited to the White House. Soon enough the outbreak of war in Europe would simultaneously dampen the enthusiasm for reform and go a long way to rehabilitate the Morgan elite. The war would change many things. Ironically, by compelling Wilson to make peace with Wall Street, it would prepare the way for the Street's own Armageddon.[59]

War and Peace on Wall Street

Horse flesh flew through the air. Windows half a mile away were shattered by the blast. Flames soared into the sky, twelve storeys high, and a cloud of green smoke obscured the sun. Thirty people were killed instantly; ten more died from their wounds soon thereafter. Another hundred and thirty would nurse their injuries for weeks and months to come. One eye-witness reported hearing a bang 'like the explosion of a volcano . . . followed by the most awesome shrieks and howls'. A man ran down the street with one hand holding his other arm just barely attached to his shoulder.

The target of the explosion – the House of Morgan at 23 Wall Street – was pockmarked with flying shrapnel on its facade, all the windows on its north face blown inwards. Inside a bank clerk lay dead and Junius Morgan, the son of J. P. (Jack) Morgan Jr, was painfully if not seriously hurt, a shard of metal penetrating his buttock. Morgan himself was out of the country. Trinity Church shook to its foundations. On the floor of the New York Stock Exchange, brokers scurried for cover, terrified that the building's great glass dome would cave in on top of them. Fortuitously, the bomb had gone off that sunny September morning in 1920 just before the Street's customary late-break for lunch; otherwise scores more would have perished or been mangled in the crush of lunch-time crowds in the narrow roadways of the financial district.

The perpetrators were never found. To this day no conclusive evidence exists showing who did it, or even exactly what happened. Everyone presumed it was an anarchist plot: a sub-species of anarchism had always countenanced terrorism as a legitimate political tactic, so it was hardly far-fetched for the media and government to leap to that conclusion. Bomb scares and real bombs had been surfacing throughout the previous year amidst a nationwide 'Red Scare' fostered by the country's Attorney General, A. Mitchell Palmer. Fear of Bolshevism and anarchism in the wake of the Russian Revolution, compounded by war-time xenophobia, encouraged government raids on left-wing political parties and newspapers and mass deportation of alien radicals. In response bombs had been planted here and there, including one that severely damaged Palmer's house in Washington. Thirty-six more were discovered at the New York Post Office waiting to be delivered to Palmer, Morgan, Rockefeller, and Chief Justice Holmes, among others. Like these, the one that went off outside the Morgan bank – across the street from the New York Stock Exchange, cattycorner to the Sub-Treasury building – could not have been more plainly addressed to the cynosures of finance capitalism.

At the crime scene, however, confusion reigned. All anyone remembered seeing, shortly before the blast, was an old, single-top wagon drawn by an old dark bay horse, driven by a man of indeterminate description. No one agreed on what was in the wagon, but afterwards investigators found pieces of window sash, the wagon's axles, and parts of a dismembered horse, including two hooves. Some speculated it might have been an accident caused by a Du Pont or some other explosive company's wagon on its way to a demolition site in the area. A scrutiny of company records turned up nothing definite, however. Some deliberate act of anarcho-Bolshevik terrorism remained the favored explanation, especially as bombs continued detonating in Philadelphia, Pittsburgh, Cleveland and elsewhere in the days immediately following the disaster at Broad and Wall.

Hysteria, already at boiling point thanks to Palmer's raids, boiled over. Fifty policemen were assigned to guard Morgan's home. The financial districts of Boston, Chicago, and Philadelphia were cordoned off. Some papers published crudely composed threats promising revenge for Palmer's actions, signed 'American Anarchist Fighters' and allegedly found in a nearby mailbox. There were retaliatory calls for the death of all radicals, blaming everyone from the Wilson administration to the 'blood-crazed proletariat'. The ideal composite villain, according to the papers, was a German still suffering the agony of defeat, who also happened to have lost money on the stock exchange while somehow trafficking with Communists. The rector of Trinity Church denounced disloyal intellectuals. Law enforcers trawling for suspects came up with a netful of foreigners. All across the country public officials, Rotary Club presidents, Chamber of Commerce publicists, and newspaper editorialists clamored for the government to rid the country of its alien red menace.

Panic was everywhere . . . except at 23 Wall Street. The event transmogrified bankers, brokers, and speculators into patriotic heroes, bloodied but steadfast as they stared into the face of barbarism. If you walk up the shallow steps of 23 Wall Street today and peer eye-level at the building's facade you will, with little trouble, see the pitted scars, some as much as an inch deep, left there by the high-velocity air-borne shrapnel nearly a century ago. Those scars were left there on purpose on the orders of Morgan and the banks' senior partners. Like saintly stigmata, they were to be the visible signs of martyrdom. More than that, however, they were intended as a symbol of the bank's resolve not to be intimidated. Together with New York City officials, Morgan and stock exchange authorities mobilized an around-the-clock brigade to clean and repair the area at lightning speed. The bank itself was open the next day. Nor did the Morgan men vent the same alarmist rhetoric about the country verging on revolutionary chaos that so many businessmen and other middle-class folk voiced. Thomas Lamont went so far as to call the event an accident, suggesting the circumstances did not point to a premeditated bombing. Morgan himself remained on holiday at his English country house, barely commenting on the event except to reassure everybody the damage was minimal.

All of this – the carefully preserved artillery, the business-as-usual sang froid, the studied reserve of the public utterances – was a bravura piece of political theater by a circle of immensely powerful investment bankers. But it was more than mere show. Wall Street's elite had emerged from that dark thunderhead of moral and political opprobrium that hovered over the Street right up to the outbreak of war. And while the war midwived upheaval and social revolution across broad stretches of eastern and central Europe, in America it was the undertaker of such aspirations. It was this underlying shift in the temper of the times and in the global balance of power that accounted for the remarkable composure displayed by Wall Street's white-shoe fraternity. They sensed that the bomb that went off in their front yard was not a reveille for radicalism, not an overture but rather a finale: the last desperate act of an exhausted anti-capitalist opposition.[1]

*

Since the turn of the century Wall Street's critics had been divided into two schools of thought. Bull Moose progressives, Wilsonian idealists, and gimlet-eyed muckrakers could be unsparing in their undressing of Wall Street. It served as a whipping post for all the assorted ills of an obnoxious form of trustified capitalism. But as for capitalism itself – well, that was a different matter. For most middle-class progressives the old dog had plenty of life left in it; and a life of plenty for all, if only it were reorganized and regulated.

An articulate minority remained unconvinced, however. 'Morganization' bred legions of intransigents, who were determined to move on, to junk the system, and start over. The labor and socialist movements, the radical bohemias of Greenwich Village and other cities, the 'hobohemias' of self-educated rebel proletarians, the scattered redoubts of maverick intellectuals and artists all lived in a state of profound and permanent disaffection. On the one hand, people like Thorstein Veblen, Eugene Debs, and Jack London shared a lot with progressive reformers; indeed, without them their own presence in public life would have loomed less large. Like their more conciliatory allies, they too recognized something inexorable and forward-looking in the evolution of economic enterprise. They too treated Wall Street's dominion over that process as a fatal irrationality. They too charged that a clique of finance capitalists had hijacked the political system.

Unlike many an ambitious reformer however, these intransigents relished their position as outsiders – cut off from the centers of power, cut out of the system of material reward and social prestige. They didn't consider themselves stakeholders or want their money back; their attitude was more Olympian than that. They were convinced, for one reason or another, that Wall Street's days were numbered. For them the 'Money Trust' was not some excrescence, a cancerous growth to be surgically removed from an otherwise healthy body; on the contrary, it was the essence of a way of life so diseased it was bound to die.

No social theorist of this period worked up a more original and global argument about the imminent demise of American pecuniary civilization than Thorstein Veblen. He was hardly an ideologue, even less an apparatchik of the left – his political activism was episodic and infrequent. But his intellectual vantage point from outside 'the system' was characteristic of left-wing intellectuals in general, when they turned their attention to Wall Street. Veblen's *Theory of the Leisure*

Class (1899) and *Absentee Ownership* (1923) bookended the cultural rise, decline, and rehabilitation of the Wall Street elite. Veblen was the era's most acerbic and quirkily original social critic, a man of daunting erudition who approached the contemporary American scene like an anthropologist observing the strange rites of an alien and primitive culture. At the turn of the century he was particularly struck by the acts of 'conspicuous waste' and 'ostentatious consumption' that typified the behavior of the country's 'upper tendom'. Memorably, he pronounced this milieu a permanent 'leisure class', and scathingly picked apart its slavish mimicking of warrior and aristocratic cultures: it panted after all the insignia of prestige, finding in them sources of psychological self-esteem and social overlordship.

Like Brooks Adams, Veblen adopted a stance of galactic distance from the sordidness below. His tone, however, was one of dryly amused irony and detachment – nothing like Adams' coruscating rage. Moreover, the professor was a meticulous scholar, while Adams mixed insight and research with snobbish demagoguery and raw prejudice. But both men took the long view, and thought they spied in Wall Street the signs of a civilization in deep decline. For Adams it was the sacrifice of the warrior virtues for commercial and utilitarian egoism. For Veblen it was nearly the opposite. The 'leisure class' was decadent and atavistic, lost in a pantomime of mock heraldry, its preoccupation with 'pecuniary emulation' and 'invidious distinctions' cutting it off from the principles of efficiency and utility which were the foundations of any healthy civilization. In a tart apercu about habits of dress, he noted that the glistening top hat, shiny patent-leather shoes, and walking stick, that de rigueur uniform of the Wall Street nabob, not only enhanced the impression of great wealth, but situated the wearer in a privileged caste exempt from any demeaning obligation to work.

According to Veblen, 'financeering operations' particularly characterized a predatory class, standing in ironic contradiction to the very values of work and technical ingenuity American business supposedly embodied. Wall Street was history's little joke, a place that boasted of its warrior-like exploits even while shadowed by a reputation for the dishonorable and unworthy. 'Captains of industry' was a misnomer; members of the 'leisure class' were masters of the pecuniary realm who lived off, but remained ignorant of the science and technology that underpinned modern industry. To the degree that Wall Street in particular embodied this pecuniary urge, it stood outside the industrial

order. However undeniably powerful it was, in Veblen's historical cosmology it was functionless: not a history-maker but a relic of 'barbarian culture', sharing its primal disdain for work. Indeed, all those
qualities associated with the Napoleonic financial titan – fear, force,
ferocity – were, in Veblen's eyes precisely what condemned that figure
before the bar of history. His combative machismo marked him for
cultural obsolescence in a world whose survival depended on peaceable acts of collective endeavor.

Veblen admired the engineering mentality of the 'tool-makers': it
was the industrial age's simulacrum of the old craft ethos in its devotion to the rational, to the peaceful pursuit of practical knowledge and
functional efficiency. But so long as the economy remained in thrall to
the 'absentee owners' of the leisure class, it would fail again and again
to realize the social abundance latent in the sophisticated technical
means at the disposal of modern industry. To escape that cul de sac
would require, if not the 'Soviet of engineers' some would later advocate during the Great Depression, then at least a rupture with private
property – which, in Veblen's view, emerged simultaneously and not
coincidentally with the leisure class.

This was where Veblen parted company with other critics of the
'money trust' like Brandeis, who arraigned its irrationality but were
not prepared to jettison the whole system of private accumulation. But
as Veblen saw it, the inherent technical and social interdependence of
modern economic life made such a step inescapable. In his *Engineers
and the Price System* (1921) and even more mordantly in *Absentee
Ownership and Business Enterprise in Recent Times*, he lamented the
capture of the whole of American society, even that secular sainthood
of engineers, by 'pecuniary culture'. The 'new order' had originated at
the turn of the century through the coalescence of the 'masters of tangible assets' with the 'masters of credit and solvency', reached its cul-
mination after the war, and was run in the interests of the 'funded
power'. Wall Street's absentee overlords had taken effective control of
key industries 'out of the hands of corporate managers working in sev-
erality and at cross-purposes', and lodged it instead in 'the hands of
that group of investment bankers who constitute in effect a General
Staff of financial strategy and who between them command the general body of the country's resources'. Veblen called it, with mocking
irony, 'One Big Union of the Interests'.

For most people, business and industry were practically interchangeable terms in the vocabulary of everyday life. For Veblen, however, they were profoundly incompatible. Business implied pelf, patriarchy, and pecuniary emulation. Under the sway of the 'morganizers' it had lost all earlier connections to creative work and the husbandry of means. Its purely paper transactions 'constitute no part of the country's material possessions and have no creative part in the tangible performance of the country's industrial forces. They are wholly in the nature of an absentee claim to a share in the country's income . . . to which they have contributed nothing.' The principle of business, Veblen pronounced, was 'ownership'. Industry, on the other hand, was the outgrowth of the impersonal scientific outlook; it was agnostic and dealt in matters of fact. Its principle was 'workmanship'. From the latter he expected the socialization of property and the egalitarian family to flow naturally, like water running downhill. All of this was a matter of anthropological not moral judgment: the insight of a social scientist, not a theologian.[2]

Veblen was hardly the first to declare that finance capitalism had reached an evolutionary dead end. Edward Bellamy's *Looking Backward* had voiced, a generation earlier, what might be called left-wing social Darwinism, a dispassionate judgment about the inexorable logic of economic development. Julian, Bellamy's time-traveler, discovers that a hundred years hence it has become simply inconceivable that the industry and commerce of the nation should be left in the hands of capricious individuals and irresponsible corporations pursuing private profit. Instead, the whole of the economy was entrusted to a single syndicate, 'representing the people to be conducted in the common interest for the common profit'. All previous and lesser monopolies were to be swallowed up in a 'final monopoly . . . in which all citizens shared. The epoch of the trusts had ended in the Great Trust.' In the estimation of people like John Dewey and Charles Beard, no book since 1885, with the exception of *Das Kapital* itself, was more significant in persuading people that finance capitalism was doomed.[3]

Doomsday atmospherics sometimes backlit the era's more acidic magazine literature, too. Various muckraking journalists, including Upton Sinclair and Charles Edward Russell, flirted with socialism, migrating into the orbit of the Socialist Party when Wall Street's most egregious behavior convinced them that it was becoming extinct. Russell, who ran as the Socialist candidate for Governor of New York in 1910 and for various other local and state offices in the years that followed, treated the trust as an evolutionary phase that would inevitably give way to some form of public ownership. Sinclair's book-length and self-published exposé of the kept press, *The Brass Check*, struck a harsher note, suggesting that Wall Street's grip on all the means of mass communication was so suffocating that only the over-throw of the whole system could re-oxygenate the air of public life. 'System' was the operative word here, as the once serviceable 'plutoc-racy' did not convey a more global apprehension of systemic break-down. Of course, the fact that Sinclair could find no commercial publisher for *The Brass Check* in 1920 seemed to confirm his argu-ment, while at the same time signaling that Wall Street had acquired immunity to its sting.[4]

A pre-war bohemian disdain for capitalist culture left its imprint on Wall Street. Oscar Wilde's bon mot – 'With an evening coat and a white tie, even a stock broker can gain a reputation for being civilized' – was typical of a cultural radicalism that sometimes found common cause with socialism and other varieties of proletarian rebellion. When H. G. Wells paid a visit to America, he was particularly struck by the country's fascination with the financial *Übermensch*. These men were not voluptuaries, Wells noted, nor were they 'artists nor any sort of creators'; they betrayed no high political aspirations, but were instead 'inspired by the brute will . . . to have more wealth and more, to a sys-tematic ardor'. While other lusts were constrained by the country's puritan heritage, this one alone flourished and was 'glorified'. The men themselves were hardly criminal; taken as individuals they were rather commonplace and pious enough. It was the game itself that was criminal, part of an 'ignoble tradition', a miscarriage of money and honor. David Graham Phillips detected an odor of cultural putrefac-tion that threatened to spread from Wall Street to the rest of the coun-try: 'This New York that dabbles its slime of sordidness and snobbishness on every flower in the garden of human nature. New York that destroys pride and substitutes vanity for it. New York with its petty, mischievous class-makers, the pattern for the rich and the "smarties" throughout the country.'[5]

But it was in the heart of New York itself, in the intellectual salons and cheap coffee houses of Greenwich Village, that the most biting depictions of Wall Street's death throes were fomented. Village radicalism before the war was a buoyant brew of Marxism and modernism, mixing aspirations towards artistic experimentation and sexual liberation with ecstatic visions of social revolution and proletarian emancipation. Novelists and cartoonists, painters and pamphleteers, journalists and poets formed a fraternity of the estranged. They communed with more hard-boiled partisans from the socialist movement; in particular those exotic renegades of the anarcho-syndicalist Industrial Workers of the World, who seemed like a virile blue-collar incarnation of their own pagan defiance of bourgeois propriety. Left-wing bohemians expressed an all-consuming contempt for bourgeois life: its psychological repressiveness as well as its political chicanery; its sexual hypocrisy as well as its economic injustice. They not only wrote, sketched, and rhymed, they were engaged – as publishers of incendiary magazines, activists at demonstrations and picket lines, and organizers of such stirring events as the 1913 'Patterson Pageant', staged to aid the embattled silk workers of Patterson, New Jersey.

Looking back, there seems something indelibly naive about this political and existential exuberance. Not long after the war this union of artistic and political radicalism would fall apart acrimoniously. Many a bohemian revolutionary would later reappear in conventional bourgeois costume. What had once seemed genuine fraternal sentiment later soured into elitist condescension. Before the war, however, they were borne aloft by an end-of-days optimism. Like their putative comrades in the socialist and syndicalist movements, they believed not only that the capitalist order was nearing its day of reckoning, but also that some vaguely described but infinitely more egalitarian, erotic, and pacific future would take its place.

No institution better encapsulated bohemia's sense of bourgeois inhumanity and exhaustion than Wall Street. No magazine better represented that sensibility than *The Masses*, whose publication was subsidized by a socialist-minded vice president of the New York Life Insurance Company – talk about social estrangement! In the pages of *The Masses* cartoonists like Art Young, Boardman Robinson, and Robert Minor, painters like John Sloan and George Bellows, and writer-editors like Max Eastman distilled a kind of furious humor and poured it liberally over bloated, balloon-like figures representing 'The Master Class'. Invariably decked out in standard-issue top hat and tails, these capitalists-cum-financiers conveyed both fear and mania, bestiality mixed with weakness. Young in particular was unrelenting. His send-ups of smiling, smug plutocrats mocked not only Wall Street but its puppet-mastery of judges, senators, subsidized writers, college presidents, and the clergy. John Dos Passos, then an apprentice writer and an admirer of revolutionary journalist, John Reed, spurned his patrician roots, threw himself into the struggle against class privilege, and fantasized about guillotines on Wall Street. When the war did come, it was self-evident to bohemia that America's involvement was prompted and plotted for by its financiers, 'to make the world safe for the French and British securities in the hands of the Morgan group of international bankers'. 'Having Their Fling', a Young cartoon with a hint of the grotesque, showed the master classes having an uproariously good time, fiendishly filling the coffers of war to chants of 'all for Honor', 'all for Jesus', 'all for Democracy'.[6]

Jack London, although by no means a charter member of the Village left, expressed his own idiosyncratic version of this bohemian zeitgeist. *The Iron Heel*, his futuristic Armageddon in which 'the Oligarchy' crushes its proletarian opposition with sadistic brutality, inaugurating a three-hundred-year reign of terror, was a kind of *Looking Backward* in reverse, staring into the abyss of capitalist depravity. As a novel it suffers from a nearly unbearable allegorical simple-mindedness. Its characters are utterly conventional, either impossibly pious or impossibly insensate. Its hero, Ernest Everhard, is a 'natural aristocrat', austere, chivalrous, fearless, and aflame with muscular idealism. But the book is also a perfect representation of that sentimental rationalism which so inspired the intransigents. Remorseless in his philosophical materialism, Ernest deflates every Christian and metaphysical attempt to cauterize the open wound of class exploitation. The novel conveys the conviction that finance capitalism, for all the ferocity of its death agony, is not only inhumane but irrational, and so must pass away. Ernest mocks the anti-trusters as Luddites, their vain efforts to save small business powerless against the irresistible drift of 'morganization'. The proletariat, instead of resisting, welcomes the onrushing tide, recognizing the wave of the socialist future. Society 'was a lie', but the master class believed in it, convinced of its own ethical and social superiority. Only the proletarian vanguard – austere, free of the gluttonous cravings of their overlords – sees the plain truth. In the mean time, however, the 'Oligarchy' rules by turning the 'people of the abyss' into a maniacal, brutalized mass, seduced to the work of the Iron Heel, feeding the ravenous lust of the 'Oligarchy' to revenge the misery of its own life.[7]

Burning Daylight, published in 1910, was the sort of Nietzchean fable London specialized in. Set in Alaska and on Wall Street, it combined frontier socialism with an etherealized meta-eroticism. Its hero, the Bunyanesque 'Burning Daylight' (his real name is Elam Harnish), is a man of immense animal charm, good fellowship, and physical endurance. He carries on a love affair with life, which he treats with unaffected impiety as a great game, an endlessly exciting gamble. When he strikes it rich in the Klondike he outwits a band of Eastern money men seeking to plunder the northern wilderness. He finds the experience so exhilarating he seeks greater adventure of the same sort on the 'Outside' – first in San Francisco where he becomes a multimillionaire financial operator, and then, inevitably, in New York. There the rough-hewn but innately honest Burning Daylight tests his powers against 'gentleman bankers/financiers', and comes up short. Unprepared for their skullduggery, their bald-faced prevarications and smooth talk, he's gulled and fleeced, though still enough of a frontiersman to take back his losings at gunpoint.

A rickety tale in many respects, *Burning Daylight* nonetheless incorporates much of the irreligiousness and sensuality characteristic of the bohemian socialist critique of Wall Street. There is for instance, its Nietzschean reversal of the familiar genteel condemnation of Wall Street as a haven for gamblers. Instead it's the gambling instinct itself that's celebrated as salubrious, a sign of life at its most vigorous and daring. What drew Burning Daylight to the Street was his embrace of the primitive (therefore natural, therefore good) urge to play, to chance. His Wall Street disillusionment makes him savage, 'a veritable pirate of the financial main', always on the move. He is convinced his fellows are capable of any deceit, players in 'a vast bunco game' siphoning off the real wealth produced by the world's workers. Touted as modern supermen, his rival financiers stand naked, a gang of 'sordid banditti'. The taste for life itself curdles in his mouth; it seems purposeless, random, and futile. Burning Daylight grows hard-hearted, more brutal, cruder – but he is made that way not by the Yukon wilderness but by civilization, and in particular the Street.

Feminism of a peculiar type saves our hero in the end. Physically as well as psychically debilitated by the nastiness of his new life, he's nearly lost his native love of horses, of nature, of the simple majesty of life. Awakened by a slowly ripening love for a chaste, athletic, and independent-minded woman working as his stenographer, Burning Daylight seemingly comes to his senses. He recognizes that he's become a parasite, and even more perilously that he's robbed himself of that old Klondike joy of fashioning something useful and enduring out of the primal chaos of nature. Sexuality, the generative urge, trumps the purely masculine drive for dominion. Renewed, he becomes a master builder and turns down-at-heels Oakland, California into a booming entrepot of shipping and industry, street railways and hotels, people's parks and ritzy clubs.

Without quite realizing it, however, Burning Daylight has made himself into a benevolent version of the Wall Street Napoleon, indulging a secret pleasure in crushing his more venomous financial rivals. Even this compromise, then, won't work. A life of urban dissipation and sedentary money-making is going to kill him in the end. Just before that happens, he makes his final break with the whole capitalist dream, and even with the 'good works' his fabulous wealth has subsidized. He returns with his heart's love to Nature, to the life of boyish energy and simplicity that is the true secret of his remarkable power and endurance. No matter how it's played, *Burning Daylight* tells us, the modern game of high finance and capitalist striving is a mortal disease.[8]

Village radicalism's faith in the imminent demise of finance capitalism was shared by a broader proletarian insurgency. Lenin's *Imperialism: The Highest Stage of Capitalism* was only one version of a Marxist literature that purported to demonstrate empirically that the progressive concentration of capital under the world's great investment banks had sharpened the system's fatal contradiction – that between social production and private appropriation. That system had reached the point where it was ripe for expropriation by its socialized producers. Wall Street (and its equivalents in London, Paris, and Berlin) was to be the reluctant midwife of a new socialist order – either that, or global carnage lay ahead as the finance capitals of rival nations warred for supremacy.

Since the turn of the century, socialists had distinguished themselves from the broader anti-trust movement by welcoming the centralization of capitalist production and finance, even as they denounced trusts for their profiteering. Around the turn of the century, the socialist faction within the American Federation of Labor managed to win a mild endorsement for the notion of nationalizing the trusts, seeing in their size, interdependencies, and latent efficiency a natural evolutionary progression towards collective production and distribution. The Socialist Party actually called for the repeal of the Sherman Anti-trust Act: the idea was that Wall Street's creations ought not to be broken up, but rather taken over – either purchased, according to the party's conciliatory right wing, or confiscated, as the left wing insisted. When Morgan died, left-wing publications duly noted his crimes, but they also emphasized his singular triumph in consolidating the nation's capital resources. It had paved the way for his own undoing, by fostering great combinations of rebellious workers and making transparent that society's welfare rested on collective labor. Big Bill Haywood, charismatic leader of the syndicalist IWW and, until purged, a member of the Socialist Party's executive, viewed the trusts as almost ready-made industrial governments, now headquartered in Wall Street but easily transferable to the councils of workers, which could make them work for the benefit of the international working class.[9]

Bought and paid for or simply seized, the point was the same: the quintessentially selfish world as put together by J. P. Morgan was history's antechamber to a glorious future of fraternal fellowship and general material well-being. That delicious irony was savored by more and more citizens in the years leading up to the war. The vote for Socialist Party presidential candidate, Eugene Debs, doubled between 1908 and 1912 to almost a million. When Morgan died, the socialist left greeted the news enthusiastically. The official publication of the Socialist Labor Party noted that the engine of capitalist finance purred smoothly on, despite the great man's passing. This proved that he, just like the 'Capitalist Class', was superfluous: 'Its mission is performed . . . To deliver this object lesson was J. P. Morgan's main mission. It took his death to perform that task . . . The Socialist Movement gratefully acknowledges its obligation to J. P. Morgan for having died.' The IWW concurred: 'Let us praise Morgan then for having helped to create a society in which labor is united . . . not only for the profit of capital, but also for its own emancipation.' Socialist sentiment was sometimes hard to distinguish from more mainstream progressive assaults on Wall Street. Their objectives were different, but in the bill of particulars they directed at the Street, socialists and progressives had a lot in common.[10]

THE IMPERIAL AGE

It did make a difference however whether one was a warrior for the Lord or for Karl Marx. The latter discarded the vocabulary of moral judgment – words like greed, deceit, and theft – and treated such behavior as the inevitable outcome of finance capitalism's deeper systemic logic. Proletarian socialists could be more bloody-minded, implacable, and serene all at the same time. In the cafes of the Lower East Side, revolutionary workers and street intellectuals had for many years nurtured dreams of revenge that no one from the reform-minded middle classes could stomach. As early as the 1880s, the idea had circulated that 'the best thing one can do with such fellows as Jay Gould and Vanderbilt is to hang them on the nearest lamppost.'[11]

Nor did feelings of class resentment always assume overt political form. Urban working people comprised the principal audience for silent movies in their formative years, and the content of the films reflected that fact. Many silent melodramas were directed by political radicals, and they often featured a banker dressed in stereotypical Wall Street garb as the principal villain. Pictures like *The Bank Defaulter* (1906) emphasised the social message by allowing the class prejudices of the criminal justice system to acquit a bank president transparently guilty of making off with his depositors' money. Many movies trafficked in predictable tales of thwarted evil and romance fulfilled that might have appealed to any audience, but often enough, they included not only a picturesque account of a financier's personal moral failings, but also allusions to his victimization of the working classes. In the remarkable *Spirit of the Conqueror, or, The Napoleon of Labor* news reaches the River Styx of a great war on earth between Labor and Capital. The shade of Napoleon is dispatched, disguised as the son of financier, Peter Morgan. Repulsed by his father's mistreatment of the workers, he ends up leading a worldwide general strike, which triumphs when the army refuses to fire on the peaceable proletariat.[12]

Such films reflected the uncompromising attitude of the left towards Wall Street. The *Appeal to Reason*, a socialist publication with half a million readers during the new century's first decade, editorialized in favor of seizing the gang of Eastern financiers – 'transient trash' the magazine labeled them – and putting them to 'honest work'. When Big Bill Haywood, along with two other Wobbly and Western Federation of Miners leaders, were effectively ambushed and kidnapped by police officials in Colorado and spirited across state lines to stand trial for

304

the assassination of the ex-Governor of Idaho, the *Appeal* published Deb's call to arms: 'Arouse, Ye Slaves.' The head of the Socialist Party accused the powers that be, including their 'pals in Wall Street, New York', of plotting murder. If Haywood and his compatriots didn't make it out of Idaho alive, Debs vowed, then the governors of Idaho and Colorado 'and their masters from Wall Street, New York to the Rocky Mountains had better prepare to follow them'.

Right up to and through the outbreak of war, the Socialist Party of America could still muster this defiant air, despite severe internal divisions over many issues. Alone among the socialist parties of the West, it stood by its orthodox Marxist opposition to imperialist war. The Party met in emergency session to denounce America's decision to enter the conflict, proclaiming that it had been instigated by those 'predatory capitalists' concerned to protect their huge investments in wartime loans to the Allied powers. This was 1917, however – much too late to make a difference. Popular as well as official attitudes had begun shifting sharply in favor of Wall Street three years earlier. Not long after the Socialist declaration, the Justice Department shut down *The Masses* for its purported violation of the Espionage Act. Art Young's cartoons were under indictment. The specter of the 'Money Trust' was speedily receding from view. Wall Street was winning the war, at home and abroad. [13]

Rapprochement between Washington and Wall Street began soon after the conclusion of Pujo's hearings. While legislation like the Federal Reserve Act and the Clayton Anti-Trust Act was far from toothless, it hardly met the more stringent requirements of people like Brandeis, La Follette, and even President Wilson himself. Even before war began to darken the horizon, the economy slipped into worrying recession and Wilson, like most Presidents before and since, sought to allay the anxieties of the business classes. Not only was Morgan invited to the White House, but Wilson issued public reassurances that the President was no enemy of the financial elite and opposed big business only when it used 'methods which unrighteously crushed those who were smaller'. The regulation of business was 'virtually complete'.[14]

War turned a fledgling friendship into a passionate patriotic union. Once America joined the fray, national solidarity required that any thought of domestic reform be shelved for the duration. But even before that, with the first outbreak of hostilities in Europe in 1914, the

Street sensed the turning of the tide. There was shock, of course, when the armies started marching. The New York Stock Exchange closed for the first time since 1873 (along with the principal exchanges throughout Europe) and essentially remained closed for four months, fearing, with good reason, that the liquidation of European investments in America would crush the market and foment panic and depression.

Soon enough, however, the Exchange revived, and by mid-1915 it was booming. Bethlehem Steel stock rocketed from $33 a share in 1914 to $600 in 1916. General Motors went from $78 to $750. Nine ordnance stocks averaged an increase of 311 per cent in their share price over eighteen months. Regional stock and commodity markets mimicked their big brother in New York. Investors, according to one observer, rushed to get their hands on 'war-stocks, semi war-stocks, possible war-stocks, stocks that beyond the range of human imagination could not by any possible metamorphosis be converted into war-stocks'. 'Peace scares' that the war might be mediated to an early end passed quickly in 1916, producing only momentary deflations in war orders and stock prices. Every sector of the economy – foodstuff, war materials, basic steel, clothing, machinery, cotton – produced in unprecedented volumes.[15]

All this reflected a tectonic shift in the foundations of international economic life. The United States had become the Allied powers' bread basket, its arms supplier, and above all, its financier. This was bound to improve the self-confidence of the country's great financiers and industrialists after a decade living under the gun. More tangibly, it confirmed the United States' emergence as the world's premier economy, as a leader in international trade and creditor to the West. America's centuries-long dependency on European sources of capital was over. The war signaled the historic transfer of capitalism's financial center of gravity from Lombard Street to Wall Street.

The global economy was pulled westward, like some great locomotive, by the war loans to the Allies floated by the Street's principal investment houses. It was these loans that made possible European purchases of American foodstuffs, raw materials, industrial necessities, and the hardware of war. It was the need to pay off these loans that caused the liquidation of foreign-owned US assets and their repatriation into American hands. It was these loans that hung over a ravaged post-war Europe like the sword of Damocles and assured Wall

Street's financial dominion. And it was these loans which lubricated the relationship between Washington and Wall Street throughout the war and which left the Street so remarkably composed when a bomb exploded on its doorstep in 1920.

The House of Morgan, with its extensive British and European connections, took the lead in arranging the first foreign loans. For his pains, Jack Morgan was subjected to threats of assassination by German sympathizers and assorted lunatics. Strong expressions of neutrality kept public interest in these initial offerings tepid at first. Even the President implied that staying neutral meant financial abstinence as well. His Secretary of State, William Jennings Bryan, announced even before the guns of August had a chance to reload that 'loans by American bankers to any foreign nation which is at war are inconsistent with the true spirit of neutrality.'

When the *Lusitania* (the ship that had rushed a critical supply of gold across the Atlantic to staunch the panic of 1907) was torpedoed, it took with it Wilson's financial circumspection. Bryan resigned, Robert Lansing took his place, and by October 1915 the administration had given its blessing to the first Morgan flotation of a $500 million loan to Britain and France. Soon other leading investment banks joined to underwrite these issues, which carried substantial fees and other incentives. Banks like National City, with long-standing commercial ties to the Central Powers, conducted business as usual, so long as the United States remained a non-belligerent. Only the German-Jewish houses at first abstained entirely. Henry Goldman of Goldman Sachs retained a filial loyalty to his homeland until American engagement made that impossible; a not uncommon attitude among the German-Jewish bourgeoisie in America. Jacob Schiff of Kuhn Loeb couldn't stomach loaning money to the notoriously anti-Semitic Tsar, tried to get the Russians excluded from the Allied loan, and when that inevitably failed, stood aside.

War finance underpinned a strengthening collaboration between the Wilson administration and Wall Street. Foreign loans were only one element of that intimacy: Wall Street functioned as purchasing agent for the Allies, facilitated trade in key commodities, and helped stabilize exchange rates. The Morgan bank in particular took responsibility for the centralized purchase of food stuffs, munitions, and other supplies vital to the war effort. Nothing more strikingly signaled the entente between progressivism and the 'Money Trust', however, than the appointment of Bernard Baruch to run the war economy as chairman of the War Industries Board.[16]

An odder coupling than Wilson and Baruch is hard to imagine, although the financier and notorious speculator had contributed heavily to Wilson's 1912 presidential campaign. His reputation, however, shadowed him everywhere. During the Pujo hearings he'd candidly identified himself as a speculator. What else could he do? His career as a wheeler and dealer, a master of arbitrage, someone who Morgan scorned to do business with, stamped him indelibly in the public mind, despite his efforts to present himself as a financial statesman. He was a soft-spoken debonair Southerner, a lover of horses and roulette, the 'lone wolf of Wall Street' known far and wide for his merciless bear raids on the market.

Baruch seemed to reaffirm that reputation when he, along with an even less savory bear, Jesse Livermore, were found selling the market short during the 'peace scare' of 1916, as President Wilson seemed on the verge of brokering a peace with the belligerents and the British Prime Minister hinted at talks with the Germans. But the rather mild public reaction to that ephemeral scandal was itself an indication of a shift in the wind, and hardly arrested Baruch's ascent. Indeed, when he appeared before a House investigating committee, Baruch boldly defended his chosen occupation. Wall Street was no 'upper-class race track', he declared, but 'the total barometer of our civilization', and speculation was a specialized science of human behavior.

Wilson had already appointed Baruch to the Advisory Committee of the Council of National Defense, despite some predictable public skepticism. With the decision to enter the war, the President formed a 'war cabinet' dominated by businessmen with Wall Street connections. Though the drift of events was unmistakable, it was nonetheless a singular rite of passage for Wall Street when a nationally notorious stock-market speculator, and a Jewish one at that, was given command over the country's industrial economy in a time of national emergency. And as it turned out, Baruch exercised his power (not as great as advertised, not nearly as absolute as his unofficial title as the 'czar' of industry suggested) as head of the War Industries Board to rein in the more selfish impulses of war profiteers. Sometimes he succeeded. Sometimes he largely failed, as when he was faced with the recalcitrant steel, auto, and Dupont interests, who resisted all government priorities, insisted on getting paid top dollar, and wouldn't cut back on their civilian production. Nonetheless, his tenure in Washington enhanced Wall Street's newly earned credit for social responsibility. Alvin S. Johnson, a war planning colleague of Baruch's, put the case hyperbolically, but with some insight into the Street's vaulting prestige: 'The old capitalism of Morgan had no adequate answer to Lenin. The new capitalism of Bernard M. Baruch has a wholly adequate answer. Democracy under Morgan's capitalism was a dream. Under Bernard M. Baruch's capitalism democracy became a reality.' Actually, Baruch's version of state capitalism was an emergency expedient, which evaporated along with the poison gas on the fields of Flanders. Its halo of victory, however, lingered on, hovering benignly over the citadel of finance capitalism.[17]

Baruch's statesmanship aside, it was the Street's broader participation in what amounted to a mass campaign of financial patriotism that counted most heavily in its cultural rehabilitation. Once the United States entered the war, the government had enormous financial needs, and it turned to the same investment houses to help underwrite and market successive issues of what became known as 'Liberty Bonds'. Treasury Secretary McAdoo went to the investment-banking community for advice about the size of the issues, payment terms, and methods of distribution. Each of the twelve regional Federal Reserve banks created 'Liberty Loan Committees', which in turn enlisted bankers, brokers, bond houses, businessmen, newspapers, press associations, fraternal organizations, and even the Boy and Girl Scouts in a vast nationwide solicitation. Railroad trains toured the country, carrying veterans and exhibits of captured war material. All-day 'liberty loan' rallies gathered in town squares, addressed by celebrity speakers. Actors pitched to their theater audiences between acts. Caruso sang for the cause at Carnegie Hall; movie stars like Mary Pickford and Douglas Fairbanks endorsed 'Liberty Loan' ads; Charlie Chaplin stood on Fairbanks' shoulders exhorting the thousands gathered at 'the Corner' for a Liberty Loan rally. One hundred thousand clergymen delivered Liberty Loan sermons.

It was all an outstanding success. Public debt, mainly in the form of four Liberty Loan issues, rose from $1.3 billion in April 1917 to $26.6 billion in August 1919. Two thirds of the cost of the war was paid for this way (one third by taxes). For twenty-three million Americans, it was their initiation into the elementary rites of investment, a kind of toe-in-the-water experience that would embolden many to plunge deeper in the decade ahead.

Swarms of underworld con artists buzzed around this enormously enlarged pool of potential investors. These 'pirates of promotion' – who 'Are After Your Liberty Bonds With Their Get-Rich-Quick Schemes', as one publication warned – hawked dozens of fraudulent stock promotions: 'Kent Holme's anti-aircraft gun' with its twenty-four barrels capable of downing enemy planes 'without the necessity of accurate aiming', fictional arms manufacturers with fantasy foreign or domestic contracts, tapped-out gold mines and oil wells. Their obvious criminal provenance, however, was precisely the point. By demonstrating the wrong side of the Street, they defined the border of legality and respectability. Just before the outbreak of war, the New York Stock Exchange, conscious of its own need to do something about its public image, had established a public relations committee. The committee thought about launching an 'anti-stock swindling campaign' and briefly considered hiring Ivy Lee, the public relations guru famous for salvaging the poisonous reputation of John D. Rockefeller after the massacre of silver miners in Ludlow, Colorado. Basking in the warm glow of its service to the nation, however, the Exchange decided it could do without Lee's special talents.[18]

Magazines which a few short years before had filled up their pages with a rogues' gallery of 'malefactors of great wealth' now resumed their deference towards the businessman as hero; not so much the Napoleonic loner but rather the managerial genius heading a dauntingly complex organization. *The Saturday Evening Post* issued a wartime valedictory for Wall Street: 'The first vigorous effectual response to the call to arms came precisely from Wall Street . . . War, with its demand for a common purpose and a common sacrifice, makes this a good time to discard popular prejudices against Wall Street as merely stupid and demagogic.' Evidence of the Street's patriotism indeed showed up very early on. The National Security League, a Wall Street group, formed late in 1914 to engage in war preparedness and patriotic education. Its creation so long before the nation had committed itself to either side strongly suggested that Wall Street had already made that choice.[19]

For the white-shoe fraternity, the Great War was more than an enticing economic opportunity, although it certainly was that. Nelson Aldrich has argued that for the world of 'Old Money', it was also a life and death struggle to defend European civilization, particularly its British incarnation, with which Morgan had always been eager to affiliate. American financial and industrial elites had spent decades borrowing, buying, and imitating European artifacts, customs, and rituals, hoping to smooth out their own social rawness. The war became a testing ground for acts of selfless sacrifice, feats of heroic athleticism, loyalty, and magnanimity that carried with them the promise of a kind of secular grace. It was the Ordeal that would prove their worthiness to rule, through pure acts of voluntary service that mirrored the honorific codes of conduct that supposedly guided their European exemplars. Wilson's war 'to make the world safe for democracy' was, in its high idealism, sufficiently congruent with this 'Old Money' sense of calling that its aura added to the luster of Wall Street's wartime public esteem.[20]

Young men of Old Money were bred for this moment. For example, Nelson Aldrich's relative, Winthrop Aldrich (himself the son of the famous Senator from Rhode Island and Rockefeller factotum) was a devoted yachtsman who joined the Naval Reserve. Called to active duty, he was assigned command of a training regiment which left him frustrated. Finally, his repeated requests for sea duty were honored and he served on the USS *New Orleans*, convoying merchant ships across the treacherous North Atlantic. When the war was over, he returned to his career as a Wall Street lawyer and banker.

This was an archetypal story of breeding, money, and service, one that was repeated by numerous other Wall Street aristocrats. A young college student at Princeton, James Forrestal, who would later go on to become president of Dillon Read and then Secretary of the Navy under FDR and the nation's first Secretary of Defense, cultivated his social and business ties to the WASP establishment early on. He interrupted his fledgling career at the Wall Street investment firm of William A. Read and Company to serve as a lieutenant, junior grade, in the conspicuously upper-class Aviation Division in the Office of Naval Operations.

Robert Lovett was similarly well connected: his father had looked after Harriman's railroad interests in Texas and served on the War Industries Board. Robert, who would go on to become Secretary of Defense under Truman, graduated from Yale before serving as a navy pilot during the war. In fact, he joined a flying unit of the Naval Reserve made up of fellow 'Yalies' and financed by Henry Davison, senior partner at J. P. Morgan. Known as the 'millionaires' unit', these rakish aviators trained at Davison's Long Island estate. Lovett was the squadron's most heroic pilot, and led night-time dive-bombing raids on German submarines. After the war, he resumed his Wall Street career at Brown Brothers.

Investment banker, diplomat, and future Senator Dwight Morrow, a graduate of Columbia Law School, served as director of New Jersey's National War Savings Committee and was a key figure in the Allied Transport Council charged with resolving inter-Allied conflicts over the allocation of scarce shipping resources. After the war he went on to became a senior partner in the House of Morgan. Henry Louis Stimpson, a partner in Elihu Root's Wall Street law firm, was forty-nine when war broke out. Nonetheless, this son of a New York mug-wump, graduate of Phillips Academy, Teddy Roosevelt Republican, and future Secretary of State and Secretary of War volunteered. He became an artillery officer and saw active duty in France. James Paul Warburg, offspring of the famous German-Jewish banking family, graduated Phi Beta Kappa from Harvard where, to the chagrin of his Germanophile father, he editorialized in the *Harvard Crimson* on behalf of the Allies. Enlisting before America's entry, he hoped to become a pilot. His poor eyesight prevented that, but he invented a new kind of aviator's compass that was put to immediate use in combat planes. Finally, Robert Patterson, who would later serve as Truman's Secretary of War, joined Elihu Root's law firm just in time to leave – first to join New York's Seventh Regiment chasing Pancho Villa along the Mexican border, and then to become a captain of infantry in France, where he received the Silver Star (twice) for 'gallant and meritorious' behavior, the Distinguished Service Cross for leading a charge against German machine-gun nests, and a Purple Heart for wounds suffered in the encounter.[21]

This collective biography of Wall Street wartime service and bravery was epitomized in the fabled career of New York's 'Silk-Stocking' Regiment. The 107th Infantry Regiment, made up mainly of Society boys from Manhattan, but with a sprinkling of upstate country 'apple-knockers', took on the impregnable Siegfried Line in the fall of 1918. The 'Line' consisted of a formidable zigzagging series of stony fortresses (each named after a Teutonic folk hero) interlaced with underground tunnels so vast they could house and conceal town-sized armies with all necessary provisions and munitions, buried so deep they were impervious to bombardment. The Regiment suffered the highest single-day casualty rate in US history, but managed to punch a hole in the 'Line' – the first regiment, along with an Australian troop, to do so – and earned a sacred spot in its nation's conscience.

This was a remarkable turnabout. For seventy-five years the 'Silk-Stocking' Regiment had served as the praetorian guard of New York's high bourgeoisie. Its Armory on Park Avenue was privately funded and included a reception parlor, library, mess hall, and gym decorated and furnished in Gilded Age splendor. New York's luminaries could watch from a grand gallery as scions of the Vanderbilts, Belmonts, Van Rennsselaers, Roosevelts, Harrimans, and Schermerhorns paraded in their military regalia in the drill hall below. The 107th's upper-class membership and its deployment putting down risings of the lower orders, from the draft riots of 1863 to the Croton Dam strike at the turn of the century, earned it a large measure of suspicion and even scorn. Maligned as a cowardly collection of snobs, the regiment was hardly taken seriously as a fighting unit. Indeed, Robert Patterson volunteered for another assignment, fearing he'd otherwise miss the war, and he wasn't the only honor-bound blueblood in the regiment to do so.

Then came its moment of redemption in Germany. Six months later an immense crowd, drawn both from the city and from as far away as Pennsylvania and Connecticut, gathered along Fifth Avenue to welcome home the 27th Division of which the 107th was a part. At its Park Avenue armory, deafening cheers of 'Welcome Home Seventh' greeted the veterans. Bloodied and bemedalled, the 'Silk-Stocking' Regiment stood before the country like some knighthood of the Street.[22]

Together with the honor and glory, underpinning them in fact, was a breathtaking new power that Wall Street had long dreamed about and plotted to achieve. To be present at the creation of a new American empire was an exhilarating experience. It helps further explain the remarkable equanimity of the Morgan men when a bomb blew up on their doorstep. Lenin might view imperialism as finance capitalism's terminal disease, but others took a more salubrious view. The outcome of the war seemed to confirm Wall Street's sense of America's coming of age. The idea that America might supplant Britain as the globe's imperial hegemon had excited the imaginations of people like Brooks Adams and Teddy Roosevelt for a generation. Ever since Elihu Root's turn-of-the-century proclamation of the 'open door' in China,

American businessmen and financiers had lusted after a position in the world's markets more in keeping with the nation's prodigious economic weight.

Once upon a time, however, such grandiosity had aroused accusations of political venality and conspiracy. The tale that best captured the air of popular suspicion surrounding Wall Street's earliest foreign intrigues, the one that left behind the sourest aftertaste, was that of the Panama Canal. In the heat of the presidential election of 1908, Joseph Pulitzer's *World* published an extraordinary exposé that threatened to de-rail the candidacy of William Howard Taft. It was a story of nepotism, political intrigue at the highest levels, financial skullduggery among the doyens of American banking and law, and conspiracy by the executive officers of the government to foment revolution and secession. The story was set in Panama and its characters included J. P. Morgan and Theodore Roosevelt.

Nothing made TR prouder than his acquisition of the Panama Canal. It was the capstone of his strategic ambition to project American power globally, a muscular assertion that the nation intended to be a major player in world affairs. Certainly the Canal's construction would carry enormous geopolitical as well as economic significance, providing the country with a two-ocean presence, ending once and for all the lingering challenge to United States hegemony in the hemisphere. So it's easy to imagine his rage when, just five years after he'd acquired this jewel, tabloid headlines screamed that the Canal was the sordid outcome of presidential collusion in bribery, financial scamming, and bloody insurrection against a sovereign state. Roosevelt exploded. He pledged to 'bring to justice this villifier of the American people'.

Pulitzer hated TR and the feeling was mutual. Nonetheless, *The World*, and the other papers that soon picked up the story, were not dealing entirely in fantasy. A Congressional investigation followed: though it proved nothing, it contributed to a pervasive anxiety about Wall Street's unseemly ambitions and influence.

Panama, according to Pulitzer and others, happened like this. William Cromwell, the head of Wall Street's most prestigious law firm, Sullivan and Cromwell, formed a syndicate of investment bankers, beginning with the House of Morgan, whose most intimate business affairs his firm handled. In addition to a roster of Wall Street heavyweights, the syndicate allegedly invited in Taft's brother and

Roosevelt's brother-in-law. Cromwell, an embodiment of white-shoe panache, sporting a wave of white hair, striped trousers, a silk hat, and a morning coat, was on a first-name basis with every important investment banker and Washington power broker.

The syndicate's purpose was to buy up the now defunct French canal company that still held the original franchise to build the transoceanic water route across the Isthmus of Panama. The securities of the canal company were spread far and wide among the citizens of France. Agents of the syndicate scoured the French countryside buying up these securities cheaply, their value at a steep discount thanks to the moribund state of the old company. The plan then was for the syndicate to sell the rights to the US government for $40 million, a sum around three or four times what the syndicate had paid to acquire them. The problem was that the House of Representatives had earlier voted to sanction the construction of a canal at an alternative site in Nicaragua. The syndicate's plan then became to undo that decision through the judicious exercise of political influence and high-octane hype. It worked, and the Senate re-voted, this time for Panama. But the problem then was that Panama was not itself a nation, but part of another nation, Columbia, and so lacked the authority to auction off a piece of its real estate to the American government. The syndicate's plan then evolved to engage in what today might be called 'nation building'. Cromwell and his confederates, so Pulitzer claimed, financed and armed an insurrection among restive Panamanians, some with purely mercenary motives, others more genuinely driven by a desire for national independence. Roosevelt, who was probably unaware of the syndicate's financial hanky-panky, was more likely apprised of its political machinations. US warships appeared off the coast just as the army of Cromwell made its move, discouraging any serious thought of resistance by the Columbian government.

As a military action it was a transparent charade. The 'rebel' army was in part officered by Cromwellian business agents. 'Troops' were paid at bargain-basement rates. Even the circumspect *New York Times* called the Canal 'stolen property' and identified the 'thieves' as a gang of promoters, speculators, and lobbyists who 'came into their money through the rebellion we encouraged, made safe, and effectuated'. Roosevelt himself later bragged in his inimitable way that he'd taken the Isthmus – 'I took the Canal Zone and let Congress debate' – but omitted any reference to the Wall Street syndicate or the choreographed uprising. Finally, all problems were solved. The syndicate got its $40 million. Panamanian nationalism, such as it was, was gratified. And Roosevelt had his waterway to world dominion.

If all or much of this was true, then it was scandalous and perhaps illegal. Given his temperament, Roosevelt could afford to do nothing less than react in outrage when the headlines appeared. He ordered the Justice Department to pursue a libel suit against Pulitzer: he fumed that there was no Panamanian syndicate, and the 'abominable false-hood that any American had profited from the sale of the Panama Canal is a slander'. Pulitzer had 'wantonly and wickedly' sought to 'blacken the reputation of reputable private citizens'.[23]

Roosevelt lost his libel case, but Pulitzer could never come up with the hard evidence to back up his most serious charges. Inconclusive as a political and legal event, the Panama brouhaha nonetheless provid-ed sustenance for the pre-war suspicions that shadowed Wall Street's forays abroad, and which only world war would finally vaporize.

'Dollar diplomacy' was an epithet coined in the Taft era to condemn the slavish subservience of the nation's foreign policy to American business interests, especially in the Caribbean. Wall Street banks, in collaboration with agencies of the State Department, effectively took over the financial affairs and even the rickety and corrupt political sys-tems of one Central American country after another. Such open finan-cial imperialism was sometimes conducted with the greatest probity and foresight. They were often not so much rapacious raids as acts of rational reform, albeit in the interests of capitalist stability. But at first they offended the democratic and anti-colonial sensibilities of a sizable slice of public opinion.

Before the war, Wall Street's insatiable appetite for foreign booty had been widely lampooned and excoriated. A cartoon in the maga-zine *Puck* showed Morgan holding a giant magnet, sucking the insignia of European civilization across the ocean – statutes, furniture, medieval armor, jewels, Egyptian antiquities, manuscripts, paintings – all headed for New York, its already famous skyline dimly lit in the background. Another appearing in the *Minneapolis Journal* displayed a manic Morgan gleefully embracing a huge snowball-like globe imprinted with the logos of mines and mills worth $25 billion, entitled 'And Growing'. When Taft sent off two thousand marines to Nicaragua in 1912, Bryan declaimed against the capture of foreign policy by 'gold standard financiers'. Midwestern progressives like senators Borah and Norris described the ensuing treaty with the Central American nation as a transparent arrangement to turn its government into a Wall Street puppet. The Nation would later call Nicaragua 'the Republic of Brown Brothers'. A few years after the fact, Lieutenant General Smedley Butler recalled:

> I spent thirty-three years and four months in active military service
> . . . And during that period I spent most of my time as a high-class
> muscle-man for big business, for Wall Street, and the bankers . . .
> Thus, I helped make Mexico and especially Tampico safe for
> American oil interests in 1914. I helped make Haiti and Cuba a
> decent place for the National City Bank boys to collect revenues
> in. I helped in the raping of a half dozen Central American
> republics for the benefit of Wall Street.

Even theological imperialists like the reverend Josiah Strong found 'dollar diplomacy' embarrassing, its naked profit-seeking an insult to the loftier cultural and religious mission of Anglo-Saxon civilization.[24]

As in the case of the 'Silk Stocking' Regiment, however, what a difference a war could make. For it was war that reversed a historic relationship between Europe and America, which Wall Streeters had not been the only ones to resent. After all, not only the Street, but through it a great deal of American industry, in particular its railroads, were in debt to and/or owned by British capital. Powerful as he was, Morgan's extraordinary cachet derived in part from his access to British and European money (and this was true of other Wall Street grandees like Belmont and Schiff). This dependency was widely and painfully felt, even in the populist outcry against the 'English devilfish', the latest incarnation of the Tory counter-revolution.

Every new war loan was a nail in the coffin of that 'enslavement'. Assuming the imperial mantle once born by the British would soon enough bring its own special conundrums for the American political and financial elite. The dawn of American global supremacy would produce a flurry of awkward fits and starts. The money seemed appealing but no one in power was quite prepared to assume the social responsibility of Empire. This in turn would contribute significantly to the traumatic crash and worldwide depression at the end of the 'roaring twenties'. At first blush, however, the view from the top of the mountain was exhilarating, producing a triumphalist self-assurance.

In four years the United States went from being the world's leading debtor nation to its leading creditor. Its allies were now not only its financial subordinates, but had to reconstruct their war ravaged economies. Germany, which along with the US had surpassed the British at the turn of the century as an industrial superpower, now lay prostrate in defeat. All the while the American economy boomed. Overnight, the country liquidated its age-old debt to Europe. Meanwhile, rivers of capital from all over the world flowed into New York, the only place they could safely settle without fear of depreciation. America found itself in possession of nearly half the world's gold supply.

Moreover, the timing of the war was arguably fortuitous from Wall Street's point of view. Pools of idle capital building up over the previous decade, flooding the markets and causing panics in 1901, 1903, and most famously 1907, had made the whole system fragile. This seemed the historic price of 'morganization', a massive thundercloud of fictitious values that grew and grew, finding no release in the 'normal' cyclic crises of the free market, hanging there ready to inundate everybody. War loans and government-subsidized war production cleared the atmosphere, providing outlets for all that inert capital. [25]

In this atmosphere, opposition to the war and to Wall Street's role in its conduct did not so much vanish as drown in a tidal wave of martial enthusiasm. The left was raided, its publications closed up, its resolutions against finance capitalism and imperialist war ignored; or worse, used as evidence in the post-war 'red scare' hysteria to jail Socialist Party presidential candidate Eugene Debs. Old-time fire and brimstone Populists like Tom Watson, who told people that 'where Morgan's money went, your boys' blood must go', were treated as political freaks. They may as well have been bona fide kooks and German propagandists like the pseudonymous pamphleteer, Charles A. Collman, whose 'War Plotters of Wall Street' talked of 'Wall Street's British Gold Plot', designed to 'ruin a country and its people in the interests of a foreign race'.

It was not only the opposition on the always vulnerable left who were confined to a gulag, real or metaphorical, however. William Randolph Hearst – bad boy of the upper classes – came out early against the war loans to Britain, editorializing that war talk would benefit only Wall Street banks seeking to protect their investments. Cartoons in Hearst papers depicted top-hatted financiers glowering over scenes of horrific devastation. It didn't even matter that once

America joined the combat Hearst became a jingoist. He was widely vilified as a traitor anyway, and accused of employing German spies on his staff. 'Peace progressives', including Senators Borah, Nye, Norris, La Follette, and Shipstead carried on an increasingly lonely and isolating vigil against a war whose purposes they openly identified with Wall Street. Norris in particular was lambasted for his vote against a declaration of war (only five other senators joined him), because he was so bold as to argue that vast war loans to the Allies were producing irresistible pressures to ensure the value of those bonds: 'The enormous profits of munitions manufacturers, stock brokers, and bond dealers must be still further increased by our entrance into the war . . . We are going into war upon the command of gold.' It was an old populist refrain sung now by a rapidly shrinking minority of Americans. A rhetoric that had once electrified millions was receding to the fringes of public life, on its way to becoming a marginal subculture.[26]

When the war ended Bernard Baruch, Thomas Lamont, and Norman Davis, another Morgan partner, accompanied Wilson to Versailles, there as special advisers to the President on how to reconstruct the West's economy. No one doubted that Wall Street would play a decisive role in designing the new architecture. Alexander Dana Noyes, the conservative financial journalist of the *New York Times*, concluded a book he wrote a few years later with a gentle admonition directed at this new mandarinate. America was in a unique position, Noyes claimed. The whole world had changed and 'the course both of political and economic history will be largely shaped by the capacity of our bankers, merchants, investors, and statesmen to meet the resultant new responsibilities.' If that was indeed the case, it's no wonder the explosion of 1920 left the white-shoe fraternity so remarkably unfazed.[27]

11

A Season in Utopia

Montauk is a small town – half year-round fishing village, half summertime resort – perched at the easternmost tip of Long Island, a hundred miles from Wall Street. To its west, just a handful of miles away, lie the Hamptons, playground of the rich and famous. While Montauk harbors its own population of the transient rich (and a small enclave of celebrities seeking seclusion in cliff-side mansions overlooking the ocean), it is really an unprepossessing place. It lacks the glamour and fashionableness of its western neighbors. Nor does it compensate for that deficiency with anything resembling rustic charm, any buildings one might sentimentally take for a seventeenth century seamen's hideout, preserved for the edification of the modern vacationer. Surrounded and traversed by water everywhere, hilly and green, the locale is undeniably fetching, beautiful even. The town itself, however, is much like dozens of other modestly middle-class beach resorts. As you drive down the few blocks of its one main street what you see is the predictable line-up of pizza joints, chochka shops, ice-cream parlors, gas stations, a miniature golf course, the 'Memory Motel' (memorialized by Mick Jagger and Keith Richards), and delis stocking nothing more exotic than standard cheddar cheese and no-name cold cuts. Naturally, these are all simple wood and brick structures, hovering close to the ground, as if in deference to the Atlantic Ocean just a few hundred yards south of the main drag. But then you come to The Fossil.

There is nothing natural about The Fossil. Located just off the village green, it is a stout, seven-storey stone 'skyscraper', done up in mock-Tudor style, topped by an airy penthouse and a graceful triangular pediment. It not only dwarfs everything in the vicinity, it is utterly unlike anything for fifty miles around, an imposing case of mistaken identity. It simply doesn't belong. And as it turns out, it is indeed a monument to a bygone age, a remnant of a dream world that flashed in and out of existence during the 1920s, Wall Street's first season in utopia.

Carl Fisher built the Fossil to be his headquarters, the centre of a vast undertaking designed to transform a sleepy fishing village into the 'Miami Beach of the North'. An Indiana boy from a family of modest means, Fisher was, by the 1920s, fabulously wealthy and already famous. Having made his first fortune in the car-parts business, he carried on a lifelong love affair with the automobile and built the Indianapolis Speedway and the first transcontinental highway. What ensured his fame, however, was the truly breathtaking entrepreneurial vision that turned a Florida mangrove swamp into the world-renowned vacationland most people assume Miami Beach always was. Will Rogers called Fisher the 'Barnum of real estate'. And sure enough the spectacular success of 'the Beach' was the engine driving the legendary Florida land boom for which the 'Jazz Age' would become notorious. In turn, some say, the Florida fantasy of the decade's early years was infectious, and soon spread to Wall Street, causing the hyperventilation and collapse of the decade's end. Be that as it may, by 1926 Fisher had grown a bit bored with his Miami extravaganza; now that it was up and running his inner eye turned North.

Most fascinating and emblematic about Fisher's plan for Montauk was the way it combined recherché elegance and exclusivity with a play-land for the middle classes. Fisher's wealth and renown had made him the familiar of Wall Street financiers and corporate tycoons. He was friends with people like Walter Chrysler, William K. Vanderbilt II, and Bernard Gimbel. He also socialized with media celebrities including strong-man Johnny Weismuller, the auto-racing champion Barney Oldfield, and a bevy of movie stars, an intermingling of the heroes of popular culture with old wealth that first became common in the 1920s. Their tastes, their sense of themselves as a kind of social aristocracy but one open to the modern currents of café society and celebrity culture, led Fisher to conceive a very special kind of Potemkin village. Spread over ten thousand acres, this Montauk Shangri-La for the plutocracy would come fully equipped with polo fields, stables for thoroughbred polo ponies, a professional-quality race course for sports cars, a golf course, and glass-enclosed grass tennis courts. Hunting to hounds was penciled in as a regular pastime. Plots were reserved for fellow nabobs, including Goodyear, Chrysler, Champion, and Woolworth (another racing-car enthusiast). And for those who chose not to erect their own rococo getaways (Fisher had already built one for himself), a luxury hotel sprang up practically overnight.

Fisher thought of a perfect name for the hotel. 'The Manor' sat atop a steep hill commanding an aerial view of the ocean, Lake Montauk, Long Island Sound, and all the rolling countryside. It came equipped with a broker's office, beauty salon, personal valets, and house doctor. Designed to look like a cross between a French renaissance castle and an English Tudor manor house, it was a striking piece of architectural stagecraft in a grandly entertaining feudal fantasy. Scattered here and there across the fiefdom were facsimile thatch-roofed Tudor 'cottages', some spacious and opulent enough to house visiting dignitaries. Others, clustered together like a micro-village, were much simpler and designed as homes for the workmen and their families, there to build and maintain this amusement park for the super-rich. Basque shepherds and shepherdesses, outfitted in traditional costume, were imported, along with veteran sheepdogs, to tend flocks of pure-blooded sheep. No wool-raising was expected of them, of course; the sheep and their keepers were there purely to heighten the atmosphere, as were the windmills that sprouted randomly here and there like the weird remains of a world that never was.

Getting to this seaside arcadia was not easy, so Fisher invested heavily in dredging an entrance to Lake Montauk from Long Island Sound that would be deep enough to accommodate the ocean-going yachts favored by the 'upper tendom'. Once there, these seafarers could bed down at the richly appointed Star Island Yacht Club (which conveniently did double duty as a bootlegging entrepot). Fisher also entered into a collaboration with the financiers running the Long Island Railroad to modernize the trackage, equipment, and station servicing this under-utilized outpost. Now bankers and industrialists could arrive at Montauk in their private parlor cars, where chauffeured limousines would whisk them up the hill to 'The Manor'.

But there was an ulterior motive behind all this digging and upgrading. Fisher's fantasy was ecumenical: it catered not only to the sophisticated pleasures of America's faux aristocracy, but also, like Miami Beach, to the more plebeian tastes of the country's burgeoning culture

of fun. Fisher was a great sport and utterly without pretension. If robber barons could now de-train at Montauk, so could unassuming middle-class families out for the week or the month, perhaps in the market
for a small bungalow of their own. If steam-powered yachts could
now moor in Lake Montauk, Fisher's dredging operations envisioned
a time when ocean-going cruise liners, even trans-Atlantic vessels,
would dock there as well discharging hordes of passengers who
couldn't afford their own boats. And when they got there they would
find not only pristine beaches, but a huge public saltwater pool, casinos, a boardwalk, a skating pond, a theater, a radio station, apartment
houses, a school, a Protestant church, a small hospital, even a college
– and land lots for sale, where they might indulge their own homelier
version of Carl Fisher's dreamscape.

This phantasmagoric Montauk opened officially for business in the
summer of 1927. Present at the founding ceremonies held at the
Manor were the president of the *Wall Street Journal*, C. W. Barron,
Vice-President of the United States, Charles Dawes, and the polar
explorer Robert E. Byrd. An auspicious beginning! But most of this
phantasm never came to be. There was indeed a casino from which it
was rumored that New York bon vivant Mayor Jimmy Walker had to
flee one night, disguised as a waiter, when the premises were raided by
the district attorney. There was a saltwater pool, but it would take a
minor archaeological dig to excavate its location now. There was and
still is the Manor, today a condominium complex for well-off middle-
class folk which might have pleased Fisher. And of course there is The
Fossil. But almost everything else, like some eccentric utopian fantasy,
never materialized, or if it did it was blown away one late October day
in 1929.[1]

Fisher's folly was a utopian misadventure of a peculiar sort. It tried to
bottle that aura of carefree high-living, surreal optimism, and guiltless
sensuality which together make up the legend of America's Jazz Age.
In Montauk as in Miami Beach, the pleasure principle was to be uni-
versalized. To be sure, great wealth would still enjoy its privileges,
indulge its rarefied desires, shelter its inflated self-esteem in comic
masquerades of social superiority. And like Fisher's dream for
Montauk, the era had a background radiation of recklessness, of the
faintly illicit: there was something ineffably frangible and Gatsby-like
haunting the glamor and excitement. But it was the promiscuous

opening up of the dream world to the unpedigreed middle classes that makes Fisher's fantasy a simulacrum for a decade's distinctive delusions.

Wall Street, together with bootleg booze, jazz, and the flapper, came to symbolize an era. Moreover, the Street's association with these insignia of sensual abandon was hardly adventitious. For a brief but unforgettable moment, the stock market became that horizonless terrain on which millions of people spied a future of limitless good times for all. This 'democratization' of the Street was unprecedented. Never before had Wall Street enjoyed such universal acclaim. Never before had Wall Street been so intimately identified with the mainstream of American cultural life. Never before had the Street managed to escape from the dark cloud of Old Testament judgment which seemed always to follow it around like a bad conscience. Never before had the missionary futurism so much part of the American grain been grafted onto the goings-on in lower Manhattan. And just like Fisher's Montauk reverie, the Street's exaltation would vaporize in an instant in the Great Crash and Depression. Not until the late lamented 1990s would Wall Street again presume to limn the meaning of the national quest.

All the stars aligned to make this remarkable happening possible. First of all there was the Street's wartime patriotic rapprochement with the government and the internment of the pre-war reform impulse. Then Wall Street's post-war global hegemony made it the arbiter of European reconstruction and lent it new luster. After an initial episode of demobilization and deflation, the domestic economy boomed, ushering in a period of real prosperity – albeit less universal and far shakier than its publicists pronounced – for which the Street took credit. In Washington, the Republican ascendancy enshrined Wall Street's political triumph in the person of financier/industrialist and Treasury Secretary Andrew Mellon, who served as the country's true chief executive officer until the debacle of 1929. Meanwhile, a rush of Wall Street outlanders crashed through the gates of the white-shoe fraternity, encouraging the chronic misapprehension that the Street was once again open to the lowly. Whether old wealth or new, Wall Street heavily invested in the era's frontier technologies – radio, aircraft, the movies, automobiles – deriving from that association a reputation for being in the vanguard of progress. All of this fed a widely shared premonition that a new era was beginning, one entranced by

America's triumph, one that promised to banish old social antagonisms, one that would make mainstream an underground ethos of immediate gratification which Wall Street had long enjoyed but had been too embarrassed to admit to in public. A new era indeed: high-tech, futuristic, democratic, triumphant – satisfaction guaranteed. A Wall Street utopia!

Henry Ford sensed this future earlier than most, divined its source in Wall Street, and declared the whole business unutterably foul. Beginning in 1920 and continuing without interruption for nearly two years, he published a series of articles in the *Dearborn Independent* (a paper he controlled) under the inflammatory title of 'The International Jew'. Talked about everywhere, the articles were later collected together to become a bestselling book.

In many respects Ford's was garden variety anti-Semitism. The articles frequently referred to and sometimes excerpted the 'Protocols of the Elders of Zion', that infamous forgery concocted back in the 1890s by the Ohkrana, the Tsar's secret police, to help foment pogroms against the Jews. Ford bought into the Protocols' notion that an international Jewish conspiracy, one dominated by leading Jewish financiers in Europe and America, was poised to take control of the world, to exercise an 'economic pogrom against a rather helpless humanity'. The world war had been perpetrated for this purpose. The great Jewish investment houses had profited, vampire-like, from the blood of all the belligerents. A stateless tribe after all, the Jews were devoid of patriotic sentiment and cynically exploited that feeling in others to accomplish their own nefarious purposes. This cabal of international financiers was the only real victor in the war which had otherwise laid waste to much of Europe and exhausted its resources. Such devastation meant nothing to these Jewish bankers who cold-heartedly calculated its costs in profit and loss and in a power over mankind long plotted for and now nearing consummation. What else could one expect from a race of parasites and shylocks that over generations had fine-tuned the art of living off the labor of others?

Fiendishly clever, these conspirators enlisted the aid of their apparently inveterate enemies, those Jewish Bolsheviks whose tyranny in Russia was a foretaste of a world to come. Back home in America, circles of Jewish finance secretly plotted with the IWW and the Socialist Party to make war on the world of Gentile capitalism. Bernard Baruch was America's Trotsky, exercising an autocratic control of the nation's capital resources, honeycombing the agencies of war mobilization with his co-religionists. While finance and speculation were inherently dubious activities, their Jewish practitioners, whose craving for world domination was insatiable, were in a class by themselves. Their Judaism notwithstanding, they would not scruple even at allying themselves with the avowed enemies of all religion.

Ford's belief that a sinister league of bankers and Bolsheviks really existed would remain an undercurrent of popular superstition rising to the surface of public life again in the McCarthy era. What it suggested to the faithful, first of all, was the triumph not so much of the devil but of a godless atheism. Wall Street had long been depicted as a hothouse of sin where tormented souls wrestled with Satan and generally lost. There was plenty of this, to be sure, in the *Dearborn Independent* series. But Ford intimated something new in his panoramic survey of the 'international Jew'. Wall Street, or at least its Jewish segment, the car manufacturer labored to show, was the fount of a pervasive hedonism that threatened to destroy the moral fiber of the nation.

The *Dearborn Independent* articles ranged widely across the terrain of modern life in a perversely painstaking effort to unearth the hidden pathways linking these Jewish financial conspirators to every Sodom and Gomorrah of post-war America. Here they were peddling pornography through their control of the movie business. There they were befouling the national pastime in the 'Black Sox' scandal of the 1919 World Series. Their tentacles extended into the criminal underworld, as they ran vast stock frauds to loot the innocent. Determined to undermine what was left of the nation's self-discipline, they saturated the country in bootleg gin. Because they were the masterminds behind the publishing industry, they arranged an endless flow of sex and sensationalism in newspapers, magazines, and pulp novels. They fed the nation the same titillating diet of cheap thrills and sexual innuendo in one scandalous Broadway production after another thanks to their backstage domination of the Great White Way. 'Jewish jazz', bankrolled by the same circles, was on its way to becoming the national music, its mood and rhythms an open invitation to the lewd and lascivious. Encouraging every form of vanity and self-indulgence, Jewish Wall Street was the incubator of a modernist debauch. Controlling vital capital resources, Jewish financiers subjected American industry to a demeaning vassalage, eating away in the process at the country's historic obedience to the discipline of productive labor, that lodestone of national well-being. This was a nightmarish rendering of a web whose reach was far vaster and more insidious than anything ever imagined by Brandeis and Pujo.

Henry Ford had always hated Wall Street, and not just its Jewish faction: he resented the power of finance capital to dictate to industry. For years he'd resisted turning to the investment houses for credit and to meet his longer-term capital needs, preferring instead to draw on his company's earnings. He reacted angrily when Wall Street interests tried to buy up shares in his newly opened British manufacturing operations. In these respects, Ford's animus against the Street was shared by sizeable segments of the business community, especially in middle-American mid-sized cities and towns where the independent family-owned manufacturing enterprise was a *point d'honneur* as much as it was the source of patrilineal continuity. Moreover, Ford's anti-war sentiment was genuine, as was his conviction that the war was little more than a financial boondoggle. But his wartime efforts to broker a peace – he commissioned a 'peace ship'(the *Oscar II*) carrying delegates across the Atlantic and around Europe to a conference of neutrals in Norway – ended in pathetic futility, further persuading the eccentric manufacturer that the financiers ran things as they chose.

A poll conducted in 1923 rated Ford among the two or three most popular men in America. People semi-seriously talked of Ford as a presidential possibility; the numbers showed him beating President Harding easily. Ford was more than popular, he was legendary, a folk-hero of American business. In the minds of millions, he exemplified an older, earlier America, one with rural roots, committed to the godly verities of abstemiousness and hard work, endowed with that peculiar national genius for practical inventiveness. He neither drank nor smoked; he dressed modestly and showed up for work at dawn. Like all legends, Ford's was partly true, partly concocted, but it helped account for the warmth with which his exposé of 'the international Jew' was received in the American hinterland. The acceptance of Ford's fabrication was also helped by the after-taste of xenophobia, and particularly of anti-Semitism, that was left behind by the war.

Despite that initial welcome, however, *The International Jew* turned out to be a colossal false step. The currents of American society were running in a different direction from the ones that Ford invoked. The articles were almost immediately denounced by Woodrow Wilson, William Howard Taft, William Cardinal O'Connell, and other luminaries of official society. The American Jewish Committee led by Louis Marshall joined with the Federal Council of Churches to organize a boycott of Ford cars, demanding an apology and retraction. Ford dealers, normally a subservient lot who for years helped finance the company by accepting consignments of cars on onerous terms, felt the pinch and added their pressure on the auto tycoon to give in. Finally, he did, forced to retreat by the very forces of consumer capitalism he'd helped unleash. The book was withdrawn from circulation and Ford issued a rather mealy-mouthed *mea culpa*.

For Adolf Hitler, Ford's financial anti-Semitism and denunciation of the Versailles peace treaty rang a bell, and he made reference to it in *Mein Kampf*. He kept a life-size portrait of Ford in his Munich office and later, as Führer, he would award Ford the Grand Cross of the Supreme Order of the German Eagle, the first American to receive that honor. But in America, so long as the Jazz Age lasted, Ford's notion that Wall Street, Jewish or not, might deserve credit for movies, booze, sexual excitement, and easy money did not seem a bad thing at all. After all, America was admired and deferred to all over the world.[2]

It was at Versailles that Wall Street first registered its newly exalted stature in the world. The peace conference soon enough dissolved into bitter quarrels among the Allies over the spoils of victory. One thing was clear, however. Victors and vanquished alike would depend on American financial largesse to get out of the hole they'd dug for themselves. Britain and France were of course deeply in debt to the United States. Both countries, but especially the latter, because the war had mainly been fought on its territory, faced an immense task of physical and economic reconstruction. They might look longingly at Germany, at German industry in particular, as a source of material and financial sustenance. But pursuing war reparations from a defeated nation that could barely hold itself together was a short-sighted strategy at best. They might use the leverage of their indebtedness to the Americans (and the threat of default) to prise loose additional credits and to justify their recalcitrance when it came to dismantling their own closed trading blocs, in defiance of Wilson's call for unencumbered international trade. Whatever maneuvers they adopted, however, there was no denying the commanding position of Wall Street, not only in

Western Europe, but in the capital markets of the world, including of course its traditional sphere of influence in Latin America, as well as in the newly emerging nations of Central Europe and the Far East.

The Street was amply represented at the peace conference, not only in the person of Bernard Baruch, but by Thomas Lamont and Norman Davis, senior partners from the House of Morgan. Bolshevism was the spectral presence at the table. Just as would be the case after World War II, all the conferees agreed on the urgent need to jump-start the Western economy to meet the real threat of social revolution. But the Europeans wanted the capital to come from America and from the indemnities and reparations exacted from the defeated powers. The United States, on the contrary, viewed a revived Germany as the linch-pin of general economic recovery, a recovery that would never get off the ground if they were forced to bear an insupportable load of finan-cial retribution. The American delegation was determined to deal firmly with the British. Baruch confided that 'I intend to carry as many weapons to the peace table as I can conceal upon my person.' What Wall Street sought, aware of its enhanced leverage, was a militant ver-sion of the Open Door policy designed to break open the system of trade preferences, price controls, and cartel arrangements that had frustrated American finance and business for years. But ultimately Versailles satisfied nobody and left behind much unfinished business, in part because the United States proved unwilling to assume the full burden of global suzerainty.[3]

Nonetheless, no one doubted that the Americans, and Wall Street in particular, carried the biggest stick. After Versailles, each time the fragile financial relations between the Allies and the Germans threat-ened to collapse, it was American emissaries like Charles Dawes in 1923 and Owen Young of General Electric in 1929, together with American bankers, the House of Morgan especially, who rushed in to reorganize Europe's finances. These efforts at financial stabilization and statecraft also included close consultation between the Federal Reserve and Europe's central bankers. Throughout the ensuing decade, the Morgan bank in particular would extend its influence abroad, financing governments from Japan to France, from Austria to Cuba, even including Mussolini's Italy. Wall Street arguably conduct-ed a foreign policy of its own, in lieu of Washington, where post-war isolationist sentiment inhibited consistent involvement overseas. Dwight Morrow, a Morgan partner and later ambassador to Mexico, conjured with the bank's peculiar role, in which its strictly commercial dealings were promiscuously intermingled with highly delicate political negotiations. He reflected that 'the Morgan firm is an anachronism. It is accountable to nobody but its own sense of responsibility.'[4]

Even before the war, Wall Street had viewed the State Department as at best a junior partner in the pursuit of its global objectives. Since the 1890s, the ambassadorship to the British Court of St James had been the private property of Wall Street's mandarins: John Hay succeeded Joseph Choate of Standard Oil; Whitelaw Reid, owner of the *New York Tribune* and long-time Morgan associate followed Hay; next came Walter Hines Page of National City Bank; then John W. Davis from the House of Morgan, followed by George Harvey, whose professional blood lines ran to both the Morgan and Rockefeller dynasties. Willard Straight, who had shuttled between the foreign service and work for Edward Harriman and J. P. Morgan, helping them open up Asia, China especially, to American capital and trade, believed, like Morrow, that politics and business should be joined at the hip. When the war came, Straight sensed the historic opportunity. He left Morgan and together with Frank Vanderlip of National City Bank formed the American International Corporation. Its express purpose was aggressively to promote American investment and commerce in Asia and Latin America, filling the vacuum left by European financiers. The idea was to seize those markets while the time was ripe, rather than waiting for the government to act.

Morrow and Straight belonged to Wall Street's old guard. American power in the post-war world was for them an open invitation to pursue the private interests they'd always served. They trained their financial wisdom and legal talents on ways for American investors to take advantage of Europe's weakness. They weren't imperialists, at least not in the traditional European sense: colonial conquest and exploitation of pre-capitalist societies did not accord with their objectives. What the new dispensation of global power invited was the financial and industrial penetration of the most advanced capitalist economies in Europe. This would be accomplished less through the deployment of cumbersome statecraft or the projection of military might than by using the sheer economic throw-weight now in Wall Street's exclusive possession. And that was just the point. While the United States emerged from the Great War as cock-of-the-walk, neither the political system, nor popular sentiment, nor the conjunction of external events had ripened enough for an aging political elite to assume an imperial trusteeship. It was neither prepared nor called upon to accept the disinterested political responsibilities that inevitably accompanied American economic supremacy.[5]

Whether exercised responsibly or not, Wall Street deployed its unilateral power most freely in its own backyard. Wall Street lawyer Henry Stimson, who served as secretary of state or war under Taft, Hoover, FDR, and Truman, led a mission to Nicaragua in 1927 to settle the civil war that erupted there after the withdrawal of American marines two years earlier. As in all these cases of 'dollar diplomacy', the objective was to create a peaceable and orderly framework for investment and trade. A brash self-assurance accompanied these ventures, encouraged by the triumphalist atmosphere, and undisturbed by any second thoughts that these might be societies with their own histories and cultural preferences. Managing these countries as if they were delinquent children encouraged a post-war delusion of American racial superiority, a natural enough outgrowth of the nation's financial and geopolitical pre-eminence. A film starring Victor McLaglen, *Cock-eyed World*, inscribed this celebratory myth on celluloid, depicting battle scenes of heroic marines looking like the cavalry in Indian country subduing the local bandits. President Coolidge congratulated Stimson on a job well done. It should be noted, however, that soon thereafter a rebel general, one Augusto Sandino, launched an insurrection against the American's client regime, and once the last marines were shipped home another man, Anastasio Somoza Garcia, someone Stimson thought a 'likeable young liberal', installed a brutal family dictatorship that would last nearly half a century. [6]

Nicaragua at least carried with it the illusion of social responsibility. However, no such pretense was plausible when Wall Street, with utter recklessness, elsewhere exploited its newly won role as, in Paul Warburg's phrase, 'the world's banker'. Governments with the shakiest hold on power, presiding over economies verging on collapse, queued up for American loans, and the Street's investment houses fell over themselves to oblige. Just as they were growing accustomed to hawking the most dubious of domestic securities to the American investing public, so too agents of Wall Street banks practically camped out in South American and Central European nations, sometimes cajoling and bribing these rickety regimes to issue even more debt that the bankers might then unload back in the States. Fees on these loans were so lucrative that they dampened any residual instinct to warn their potential purchasers of their inherent riskiness. Competition among American banks to get these loans was intense, further inflating the prices of already very suspect securities. 'Peruvian bonds', practically worthless even before they were officially issued, soon became the most infamous instance of Wall Street's foreign malfeasance. State Department functionaries helped Kuhn Loeb float a $90 million loan to bail out the Chilean military dictatorship and collaborated with Wall Street financiers to keep the brutal Machado regime on its financial feet in Cuba. By 1934, a third of these international loans were in default. This was a terminal case of power without responsibility, and its effect on domestic affairs was equally damaging.[7]

Wall Street's commanding position in foreign affairs was more than matched by its political cachet at home. There have been three periods in the country's history during which its political system might aptly have been characterized as a version of crony capitalism. The Gilded Age was the first and the 1990s the last, to date. The 1920s was that third era during which the government bent its efforts to serve the narrowest interests of the business classes, and especially its peak institutions. Crony capitalism implied more than mere corruption; or rather it raised corruption to the level of state policy, to a form of extra-legal mercantilism in which one could no longer easily tell the difference between the representation of a political constituency and the servicing of a corporate client. Businessmen, according to economist and social critic Stuart Chase, were 'the dictators of our destinies', supplanting the 'statesman, the priest, the philosopher, as the creator of standards of ethics and behavior'. This was true in the loftiest realms of tax, monetary policy, and trade policy, and also in the shadier areas of influence peddling and outright graft. All sorts of big businesses had their needs met, as did the rich more generally. But it would be imprecise to leave it at that. Crony capitalism in the 1920s (and again in the 1990s) had a distinctly fiduciary character, reflecting the overbearing presence of Wall Street in particular.[8]

Republicans were the party in power throughout the decade, although the Democratic Party harbored its own powerful Wall Street faction and was nearly as sensitive to the Street's desires. The Republicans' attitude might be likened to that of their party forbears at the turn of the century – people like Mark Hanna, Henry Cabot Lodge, and Nelson Aldrich – except that this older generation could arguably on occasion muster enough independence to master the plutocracy, while the party's top operatives in the 1920s were faceless retainers who served on the sufferance of their financial overlords. William Allen White, a Midwestern, middle-of-the-road Republican journalist and the Party's wise man, described the whole class-conscious structure, in a biography of Calvin Coolidge, as a 'fiduciary invention'. It was 'possessive rather than creative' and floated on a 'lake of capital, placid on the surface, sustained in its waterline by constant springs in the hills while it was being drained slowly into Wall Street'. President Coolidge, according to White, was ill prepared to staunch the drainage, not so much because he lacked the political fortitude (which he did), not so much because he knew of no ideological and moral alternative (in fact he grew up with one), rather because property, properly decked out in imposing corporate regalia and 'guarded by a silk hat, was sacrosanct to him'. The 'wizards of Wall Street' found an open sesame at the Coolidge White House so long as their wizardry didn't descend into black magic.[9]

All three of the decade's Republican presidents were alike in this fundamental regard, although starkly different in style. Warren Harding let the good times roll and loved to drink and play with his cronies, most of whom were well connected to the fat-cat world of business and finance. He conceived his role as President as being to report 'on the state of affairs of the stockholders of the Republic'. In an eerie foreshadowing of his own administration's disgrace, he entitled one of his rare literary forays 'Less Government in Business and More Business in Government'. Predictably enough, then, his regime came close to ruin in the Teapot Dome scandal, a sordid tale of political bribery of administration functionaries, aimed at securing leases on valuable Federal oil deposits for exploitation by favored petroleum companies. Harding died before the whole mess resolved itself in the courts with the jailing of the nation's Interior Secretary, Albert Fall (although not until 1931 and only for nine months); some thought the President's death may even have been caused by the scandal. One lubricant notably used to grease the wheels of this rather spectacular act of cronyism was bonds delivered to Fall in return for opening up the Navy's oil deposits.[10]

Herbert Hoover was Harding's antithesis: dour, overflowing with rectitude and high purpose. As Commerce Secretary, his private worries about excess speculation were dismissed as alarmist by Coolidge and Mellon. But while he harbored reservations about White's 'fiduciary invention', he was afraid to buck the tide publicly – afraid, that is, until it was too late and that 'lake of capital' had been all but drained dry.[11]

It was during the regime of Calvin Coolidge, however, that the era's crony capitalism achieved a kind of perfection. Just five months after Harding's death, his Vice-President famously declared that 'the business of America is business'. While the new President might abhor the shenanigans of the Teapot Dome felons, he felt no qualms about the piling up of the securities of the nation's key industries and public utilities by Wall Street's banking elite. He confided in his friends from the financial district that to make sure nothing like the post-war deflation marred his administration, the lid was off the sources of speculative credit. He would make such reassurances at every hint of a downturn. William Allen White described a crowd of 'little tin Croeseuses, wise and foolish, honest and rapacious' that were 'beating a path to the White House door'.

It was virtually impossible to tell the mountebanks from the mandarins. Investment trusts of more or less dubious pedigree were sprouting like mushrooms. One, the United Corporation, was a blue-blooded Morgan confection that managed to seize control of a vast network of public utilities stretching across twelve states from Michigan through New Jersey, generating twenty per cent of the electrical power of the whole country. To guarantee its political safety, stock in the United Corporation (along with other Morgan enterprises) was offered privately at insider prices to a select circle of luminaries that included: ex-President Calvin Coolidge, World War I hero General Pershing, recent Secretary of War Newton Baker, Wilson's Secretary of the Treasury, William Gibbs McAdoo, Democratic Party chairman and GM executive John Jacob Raskob, Wall Street lawyer and 1924 Democratic Party candidate for president John Davis, Coolidge's Vice-President, Charles Dawes, not to mention the CEOs of the nation's largest industrial corporations. William Allen White confessed that this brazen variety of crony capitalism left him with 'a twinge of mean distaste' for a system which had abandoned any lingering instinct for social justice.[12]

Crony capitalism achieved its apotheosis in the person of Andrew

Mellon. The Pittsburgh industrialist and financier served as Secretary of the Treasury under Harding, Coolidge, and Hoover – or, in Senator George Norris's apt inversion, 'Three presidents served under Mellon.' It was during his reign that the quotidian practices of grab and gain took on the aura of disinterested high policy.

Mellon was the plutocrat's plutocrat. A gnomish man, barely a hundred pounds in weight, almost mousy-looking, studiously reserved, bashful, and cold, he lived a life of luxury on his Pittsburgh demesne. His daughter's wedding at the Mellon castle was an extravagant multicultural pastiche staged to show off the rarities of half a dozen civilizations. There were Chinese cockatoos swinging in gilded cages, a sculpture garden of Greek gods, and 'rugs from Irak formed cushions underfoot'. There were tapestries from Iran and the mountains of the Caspian, and a simulated Hindu temple 'surmounted by mystic light'. Meanwhile, striking workers at the Pittsburgh Coal Company were being evicted from their homes and others were blown to bits in an explosion at the Mellons' Riter-Cowley Coal Company.

When he assumed public office, Mellon was certainly one of the richest men in America, and although deeply involved in weighty financial undertakings, his geographical distance from the Street was probably a political asset. But his singular dedication to the art of money-making was the equal of any Wall Street banker. In the divorce proceedings that ended his first marriage, his long-suffering wife (an Irish landed aristocrat named Nora McMullen) testified to his monetary monomania and to her husband's profound insensitivity to the lives of those legions of minions and dependents who made his world possible. While the Irish ingenue had 'dreamed of another Hertfordshire, with Hertfordshire lads and lassies', the owlish financier treated the 'Huns and Slavs' toiling away on the great estate with a chilling indifference. The spirit of the community 'was as cold and hard as the steel it made', and while Nora sequestered herself in her baby boy's bedroom, 'my husband locked in his study, nursed his dollars, millions of dollars, maddening dollars, nursed larger and bigger' at the expense of domestic peace and happiness. Biased evidence to be sure, but in spirit, if not in detail, entirely in keeping with the great man's self-assurance that what was good for the very, very rich was best for the country.

And great man indeed he was. Harding once said of his Delphic presence, 'It's no use. He's the ubiquitous financier of the universe'. He was the only one to receive a standing ovation at the 1924 Republican Party convention. As a bona fide titan of finance of the first rank, he was effectively precluded from a run for the presidency (although some in the Party allowed themselves this fantasy). But soon enough he was lionized as the 'greatest secretary of the treasury since Alexander Hamilton'. With every up-tick in the Dow Jones average, his popularity soared towards the rarefied realm of sainthood. If any one person enjoyed the credit for the decade's prosperity, however flawed, it was Mellon who over and over again was lauded as a kind of Olympian seer of the dismal science. And in a sense he deserved all the praise.[13]

The Secretary's tax and monetary policies were a study in the care and feeding of White's 'fiduciary invention'. With unflagging enthusiasm he encouraged the Federal Reserve, which sometimes entertained doubts about the matter, to keep the spigot of bank credit wide open, even as the stock-market boom reached unprecedented proportions in 1927 and 1928. Mellon interests were heavily invested in power, electric light, and railroads, so there might have been a tincture of self-interest at work. But this was neither a necessary nor sufficient condition for a conviction that transcended private gain. Nothing quite like Mellon's unalloyed confidence in the free market and in the flawless wisdom of those elite circles who dominated its operation would be seen again until the age of Reagan and Bush. During his nine-year watch, thanks to his relaxed attitude about credit and a package of tax cuts that openly rewarded his class, income from dividends rose sixty-five per cent. Four Mellon tax cuts between 1921 and 1928 reduced the rate on top incomes from seventy-seven to twenty-five per cent, lowered corporate taxes, and repealed the excess profits and gift taxes. The Supreme Court proved a willing accomplice, ruling that corporate dividends paid in stock could not be counted as taxable income, furthering the quest for speculative gains. At the same time, the FTC and the Justice Department stood aside as a mania of corporate mergers excited the market. During the Mellon era, of the 1,268 mergers of 7,000 corporations, only sixty caused even a raised eyebrow and only one was actually blocked by the government. By the decade's end, sixty thousand families at the top of the income pyramid were worth as much as the twenty-five million at the bottom.[14]

Diffident and wraith-like, the baronial financier presided over the nation's political economy in the same distant manner that characterized his human dealings in his private life. He, not the Presidents he served, best captured the era's infatuation with money-making and the stock market. Yet while his presence practically blotted out the grayer figure of Calvin Coolidge, from a cultural standpoint it is 'silent Cal' who is much the more interesting character, the one who can tell us something about how modernizing America reconciled with its past.

Coolidge was intriguing precisely because he was so silent. By 'silent', people meant that he was dour, taciturn, parsimonious in body and spirit, emotionally zipped up – in short, a perfect exemplar of New England country reticence and simple living. His Vermont upbringing was written all over him and he had no desire to wash it away. Every aspect of his public image was the antithesis of all the pleasure-seeking and funny money-making so many millions were drawn to. In his plainness of manner and dress he stood there like a mute monument to a time when hard work, delayed gratification, frugality, and modesty of means were the unchallengeable verities of everyday life. He signified all that even as he presided over and tacitly encouraged an orgy of national self-indulgence – that was the Coolidge genius. If 'silent Cal', a veritable apparition from nineteenth-century small-town America, could tolerate these goings-on, could indeed smile benignly at their metastasis, then maybe they weren't after all the fall from grace they seemed to be at first glance.

Homespun, old-fashioned, limited but shrewd, Coolidge was a kind of sentimental anachronism; in William Allen White's apercu, 'a Puritan in Babylon'. Had he been a more militant Puritan, he might have spoiled the party by excoriating the mood of riotous speculation. But he was too politic to make that mistake, even while his provincial temperament was scandalized by his predecessor's seamy corruption and malfeasance in office. When Harvard economist William Ripley published an alarming, widely discussed series of articles on the dangers of holding companies and trusts, and the absence of public oversight over their vast over-capitalization, the President invited him to the White House for lunch, listened to his warnings, but kept his own counsel. Privately he was probably offended by all the loose living, but he was, after all, 'silent Cal', the national icon of painless repentance.[15]

This peculiar dialectic between President and people supplemented the more heavy-handed domination of Party and government by the friends of Wall Street and helps further account for the Street's stunning elevation. Moreover, the culture of narcissism that lent the Jazz Age its unique éclat dissolved most lingering vestiges of public consciousness, making political life itself seem beside the point. To stand in opposition was to live in exile. Those pre-war Village radicals who kept the faith found themselves writing for magazines like the *Liberator*, where they penned and drew caustic undressings of Morgan's global machinations and outed 'the giants of Wall Street' as the stage managers of Teapot Dome. But their exposés were only read by a tiny and dwindling sub-culture of immigrant revolutionaries, who were in any case already won to the cause.[16]

As the 1920s wore on, the remnants of populism and progressivism in Congress maintained a lonely vigil against the 'money trust'. Meanly christened 'Sons of the Wild Jackass' by their political enemies, a handful of senators mainly from the Midwest and Great Plains – Borah, Norris, La Follette, Shipstead, Brockhart, and others – constituted a parochial, largely agrarian-based holdout. They inveighed against speculation on the commodities markets, kept aloft the banner of productive labor, and made futile attempts to give the Federal Reserve powers to prevent the use of its credits by stock-market gamblers. 'Peace progressives' in Congress, who were more anti-imperialist than isolationist, lambasted post-war dollar-diplomacy sorties into Latin America. *The Nation* might call Nicaragua 'The Republic of Brown Brothers', but the Marines scarcely noticed.

La Follette went so far as to bolt the Republican Party and run an independent presidential campaign in 1924, during which he accused the Federal Reserve Board of being a captive of 'the great banking interests of the country'. But the Wisconsin Senator's Progressive Party did miserably at the polls. Senator Brockhart of Iowa, an old Bull Moose Progressive, was practically excommunicated from the Grand Old Party for daring to endorse La Follette. Hearings were held and the air filled with a bygone rhetoric of political moralizing about Wall Street's looting of the hinterland, about starving farmers and 'a wild orgy of speculation'. But it all seemed as old-fashioned as Alabama Senator Thomas Heflin decked out in his Prince Albert coat, mixing his sympathies for the Klan with denunciations of an ungodly Wall Street as the 'most notorious gambling center in the universe'.[17]

In short, the political opposition was disarmed and Wall Street couldn't help but gloat. Just on the eve of the great crash of 1929,

Joseph Stagg Lawrence, a well-known Princeton economist, published an enormously popular book that epitomized the arrogance and smug self-assurance of the ruling order. *Washington and Wall Street* exuded all the snobbish disdain of a modern Tory aristocrat for those political dinosaurs in the capital who pathetically resisted the new age. People like Borah, La Follette and Brockhart were 'gentlemen of high moral voltage and abysmal prejudice'. They were, in Lawrence's view, a provincial, bigoted, puerile bunch whose hatred for Wall Street was a part of that same 'saturnine crusade' for purity which bred prohibition and hysterical isolationism. Lawrence took the long view and considered the present clash of cultures the denouement of an historic confrontation that went all the way back to the country's beginnings. Since then the 'wealthy, cultured and conservative settlements on the seacoast' had been pitted against 'the poverty-stricken, illiterate and radical pioneer communities of the interior'. Lawrence left no doubt as to where his sympathies lay, nor about his confidence in the outcome. Steeped in prejudice and resentment, these benighted regions had waged war for generations on a demonized Wall Street, a war they were about to lose.

Lawrence's confidence rested on evidence of the Street's miraculous success in piloting the economy to undreamt-of altitudes. Wall Street had proved itself over and over again, rendering great service to 'banking, finance, trade, commerce, agriculture, and to government itself. It has served intelligently and unostentatiously. It has maintained no lobbies. Its books have been open. It has enforced upon its members a code of ethics which it is well for the supreme legislative body of the land to emulate.' For just those reasons, because the Street had performed so ably in facilitating the movement of capital, deploying its wonderfully self-correcting mechanisms to ensure stability and progress, legislative proposals like Senator Carter Glass's proposal to levy a five per cent tax on sales of stock held less than sixty days was really an act of 'vandalism'. If passed it would usher in an era of 'bootleg finance'.

True enough, in the dim past a 'fringe of fraud' had given a bad name to speculation. Now that stigma had faded away along with high-button shoes and the ancient religious tendency to conflate gambling and speculation. The modern world recognized not only that uncertainty and risk were inherent to life, but also that they were responsible for most of mankind's heroic achievements. And here

Lawrence showed how infectious the mood of the Jazz Age had become, its improvisational rhythms penetrating the mental reserve and hauteur of an Ivy League academic. It turned out that the whole long-lived Jesuitical disputation about the difference between gambling and speculation was a big waste of time, a mere artificial ethical distinction. It was, judged Lawrence, like condemning dancing, the Broadway theater, or smoking, deeming them bad or less worthwhile or anti-social just because they didn't contribute to the general fund of material value. What the past decade had proved, however, was that whatever people derived pleasure from was legitimate, so long as it didn't entail harm to others. The ultimate discovery of the new era was the supreme value of psychic income, a swiftly running stream of pleasurable sensations.[18]

Had it been published just a few months later, *Wall Street and Washington* might have seemed grotesquely mendacious and absurd. But Joseph Stagg Lawrence was neither a liar nor an idiot. He was simply very, very sure of himself. And what accounted for that was the material muscularity of the underlying economy, its connection to frontier technologies, and a stock market that behaved as if the laws of Newtonian physics had been indefinitely suspended. Hovering over it all, like a benediction, was a faith that the future had arrived – not, as Lincoln Steffens imagined, in the Soviet Union, but right here in America. And indeed, as Steffens had concluded, the future worked.

If the Coolidge years marked the apogee of Wall Street's influence and reputation, it was because they were the noonday of economic good times. When Coolidge was inaugurated in 1925, employment, prices, and stock values were all riding the up escalator. The air crackled with revelations about new technologies and new products: radio, sound movies, air-conditioning, electrical appliances (electric irons, vacuum cleaners, washing machines, refrigerators), synthetic fabrics, and other breakthroughs in chemistry (Pyrex, Bakelite, rayon, cellophane, neon signs). Radio, the hottest of the new mass-market technologies, sold in astounding numbers, vaulting from sixty million sets in 1922 to 842 million in 1929. Industrial production rose fifty per cent between 1920 and 1929. United States national income exceeded that of the United Kingdom, France, Spain, Italy, Germany, Japan, and a dozen others combined. The number of companies listed on the New York exchange quintupled between World War I and the end of the decade. Dozens of the nation's largest corporations installed more or less elaborate 'welfare capitalism' schemes that rewarded their employees with pensions, stock ownership, and profit-sharing plans.[19]

An undertow of impending disaster went unnoticed and unattended: western farmers and lumbermen in deep distress; erosion in the inundated Mississippi valley swelling the population of the uprooted and itinerant; a fifth of the nation's citizens in the South, in urban ghettos, industrial hovels, and coal-mining hollows, living in shameful conditions. Three quarters of American families lived on less than $3,000 a year; forty per cent survived on less than $1,500. But even this damning evidence of failure was, perversely, yet another marker of Wall Street's triumph – precisely because none of it succeeded in disturbing the national mood of equanimity and optimism.[20]

One obscure instance of technological inventiveness suggests the on-rushing momentum. A running contest took place behind the scenes at the New York Stock Exchange among mechanics and engineers, who were trying to improvise a makeshift solution for speeding up the ticker-tape so that it might keep pace with the soaring volume of transactions. The wheels driving the tape could only revolve at a fixed speed. The technicians tried shortening the symbolic abbreviations for stocks, but people complained. They tried changing the paper. They tried switching the ink. Nothing really worked, although the basement of the Exchange building contained more mechanical equipment than most factories, including duplicates of all the key machinery and spare parts, and standby tickers all interconnected, ready and waiting.[21]

Ticker-tape technicians faced a nearly insuperable task. For decades, Wall Street had grown at roughly the same pace as the rest of the economy. Now it was the Street that ran on ahead like a team of wild horses. While GNP in the 1920s rose less than fifty per cent, the Dow Jones quadrupled. Urban construction boomed in response to the stock market as luxury apartment houses and office skyscrapers changed the cityscapes of New York and a dozen other business centers.[22]

During the week of 3 December 1927, more stock changed hands than in any previous week in the Exchange's history. And that was just the beginning of a raging bull market that stampeded prices for the next two years. New levels of zanyism, a 'victory boom', followed Hoover's election. Seven-million-share days, once considered inconceivable, became common. The annual total of new domestic industrial securities tripled from 1920 to 1929. 'Financial department stores', integrated financial-service enterprises, pioneered by National City Company (the brokerage/investment offshoot of the National City Bank), opened up branches with securities subsidiaries all over the country to cater to the new retail-investment market. In 1922 only sixty-two commercial banks were in the investment-banking business as well. By the end of the decade that number was 285. Radio Corporation of America stock, the dot.com of its day, rocketed from $85.25 in 1928 to $549 in September 1929, although the company had yet to pay a dividend. Other hot, high-tech glamour securities, like Wright Aeronautical, Pan American, Boeing, United Aviation and Transcontinental did likewise. Lindbergh's transatlantic triumph sent aeronautical stocks into orbit.

With the advent of the 'talkies' and the need to finance expensive sound studios, Wall Street invaded Hollywood. Adolph Zukor at Paramount teamed up with Kuhn Loeb to do battle with the other sound pioneer, William Fox, who heavily leveraged his studio to Halsey Stuart. Upstart Warner Brothers mounted its challenge to the established movie moguls with saddlebags of cash from Goldman Sachs. By mid-decade the Street was well represented on the boards of most major studios. The industry appealed to the bankers not as an art form, but on the basis of its neat mechanical inventiveness, its vertically-integrated, assembly-line-like production system, its global distribution capacity, air-conditioned theaters, and prudential book-keeping. Investment analysts did cash-flow deconstructions of 'star value', assessing stardom as an 'economic necessity', because the star delivered not only a 'production value', but also 'trademark value' and an 'insurance value', which 'are very real and very potent in guaranteeing the sale of the product to the cash customer at a profit'. Old-line production chiefs like Darryl Zanuck, Jack Warner, and Cecil B. DeMille resented these East Coast number crunchers – DeMille lamented that there had been 'joy in the industry' when the studios relied on their own money, 'grief' thereafter – but they were there to stay.

Mid- and low-tech companies like Montgomery Ward also surged on the rising tide. Above all the horseless carriage drove everything before it and the stock of the four major public companies – GM, Fisher Body, DuPont (because of its hefty holdings of GM stock), and Yellow Cab – were regarded as the four horsemen of the boom. By

1928, the value of corporate securities issued as common stock was two and a half times what it had been just four years earlier. Nor was the excitement confined to issues of common stock: the volume of bond issues doubled during the 1920s. Even the most outlandish numbers lost their shock value. By the summer of 1929, the paper value of Samuel Insull's great utility empire – a Mount Everest of holding company piled on top of holding company – was appreciating at $7000 per minute.[23]

Commercial and investment banks, brokerages, and securities dealers created investment trusts to satiate the appetite of amateur investors. Middle-class neophytes bought shares in these new trusts, which in turn invested in whatever they felt like. Some were fly-by-night operations, others carried the brand of a Morgan or some other white-shoe institution. Goldman Sachs ran the era's most spectacular trusts – the Blue Ridge Corporation and the Shenandoah Corporation – which heavily leveraged the issuing of vast quantities of new securities. This was common practice. Investment trusts, unlike modern-day mutual funds, regularly had recourse to borrowed money beyond what they took in from the sale of their own shares. It enhanced their power in the market, but of course left them as vulnerable as any speculator operating on margin. All worked in the greatest secrecy, rewarding their directors with lucrative fees and insider prices on premium securities. By 1929 a new investment trust was born each day, even though most of their clients hadn't a clue about what they were doing with their money. [24]

The 'roaring twenties' left an audible echo in the national consciousness, in part because of their reputation for speculative flamboyance and excess. The reputation is well deserved: 'pools', essentially legal conspiracies of market professionals and their privileged clients, manipulated the market through carefully planted rumor and quick, concentrated infusions of cash, pulling out with overnight gains while a wider, unsuspecting public was just getting its feet wet. The thrice-bankrupted founder of General Motors, William Crapo Durant, was the era's most notorious pool-meister, who magically levitated the stock of a faltering International Nickel by sixty points and the profitless Baldwin Locomotive by 135 points. Little more than con games, like the one that pumped up enthusiasm for RCA in the late 1920s, these 'pools' were nonetheless put together by the most distinguished circles – in RCA's case by Durant along with Charles Schwab,

John Jacob Raskob, Walter Chrysler, and Woodrow Wilson's one-time aide and confidante, Joseph Tumulty. Often enough pool organizers were themselves directors of the corporations whose stock they put in play, dumping it on the public when the time was ripe. For these privileged insiders pools were sporting as well as money-making affairs, bringing something of the thrill of hunting to hounds. One who tracked their peregrinations talked of 'the lure of action, of quick profit, the thrill of battle, the call of the chase, the glamour of admission into a charmed circle, the attraction of mysterious enterprise'. Such pools operated in 105 of the 550 stocks listed on the NYSE.

'Pools' and other mechanisms of speculative investment fed the demand for call loans; in the early years they'd averaged about a billion dollars, but by 1929 they approached six billion. Call money was so coveted that interest rates soared from five to twelve per cent, money poured in from abroad to meet the 'need', and even industrial corporations lent excess cash to the call market, a painless road to high returns without the headaches associated with actually producing something. 'Reloaders' and 'dynamiters', high-pressure stock promoters, roamed the land, pumping up and deflating expectations, often on the flimsiest, or even fabricated pretexts. On rare occasions – as in the case of 'the Wall Street Iconoclast', one Graham Rice – they ended up in Sing Sing.[25]

This whole three-ring circus of frenzied finance – investment trusts, pools, financial department stores, boiler-rooms and bucket-shops, inside traders and felonious stock tipsters – was ballasted by the weight of the underlying economy, empowered by the subservience of the political order, and infused with the élan of Wall Street's global supremacy. Above all, however, it depended on the enthusiasm that was supplied by faith.

Soon after the war ended, an Italian ex-vegetable dealer and one-time forger and smuggler made his sensational debut in America. Charles Ponzi was forty-two, handsome, and glib. The scam he invented was stunningly simple. You lend him $10, without collateral, and he promises to pay back $15 in ninety days. To the legions who lined up to join his scheme, he explained that he would invest their money buying up International Postal Union reply coupons overseas, redeeming them in various markets around the world to take advantage of fluctuations in the value of foreign currencies. He set up the

Old Colony Foreign Exchange Company and the money rolled in at the rate of $1 million a week. He bought a controlling interest in the Hanover Trust Company to enhance his liquidity as well as his legitimacy, moved into a fancy house, and drove around in a flashy 'Locomobile'. By the early summer of 1920, he was famous. By the end of the summer, he was in jail for fraud, where he stayed until 1934, when he departed for Italy and the life of a minor Fascist government official. He died a pauper in Rio de Janeiro in 1949. What's remarkable is not that Ponzi's scheme collapsed, but that so many were credulous enough and so swayed by their own cupidity that they actually believed they'd realize a fifty per cent return on their money in the space of ninety days.[26]

Only a small part of what went on in Wall Street during the 'roaring twenties' can be fairly likened to a 'Ponzi scheme'. But the atmosphere of fantastical expectations that gave the Street its incandescent glow was fired by the same misplaced faith, a widely shared cultural conviction that Wall Street, that old 'street of torment', had become the passway to an El Dorado of prosperity and pleasure. How widespread was this delusion, how large the congregation of the Wall Street faithful? No one seems to know for sure. It was not nearly so large a percentage of the population as became participants in the market in the 1990s – perhaps only a tiny fraction of that fifty per cent. But big enough, compared to anything before that time, to convince every contemporary observer and many since then that the Street had penetrated the country's psychic and cultural mainstream.

William Z. Ripley, a harsh critic of the Street and the way a handful of trustees, directors, and corporate officers had seized control, disenfranchising the mass of stockholders, estimated that of the 14.4 million shareholders, 3.4 million had been brought on board by the Liberty Loan campaigns and stayed on after the war. He considered the 'passing of ownership from Wall Street to Main Street' an optical illusion, since these new 'owners' had virtually no say over what they owned. Nonetheless, he assumed that these disenfranchised proprietors were on the scene in great and growing numbers. [27]

A lot of them, it seems, were women. The Pennsylvania Railroad became known derisively as the 'Petticoat Line', because half its stockholders were female; so too were fifty-five per cent of AT&T's investors. Tabloids talked of 'lady bulls' while more genteel publications referred to 'ladies of the ticker'. Some were businesswomen, others 'ladies of leisure' – altogether a mixed crew caricatured by one observer as 'aggressive, guttural dowagers, gum-chewing blonds, shrinking spinsters who look as if they belonged in a missionary society meeting watch, pencil in hand, from the opening of the market till the belated ticker drones its last in the middle of the afternoon.' What lent this new social fact a certain electric shock was the prevailing prejudice that women were not up to the challenge. Their incompetence was presumed: they lacked the right toughness of temperament, the sangfroid as well as the business experience, and were in every regard out of tune with the macho music of the Street (this in a decade notorious for its 'liberated' view of women). When one tried to secure a seat on the NYSE in 1927 she was turned down. Yet there the women were, 'mudhens', loitering about the ticker tape. And Wall Street responded, establishing 'specialty shops', opulently appointed lounges, women's rooms in beauty parlors; it even hired women brokers to recruit this new population of market mavens.[28]

Indeterminate but substantial numbers of middle-class men – salesmen, car dealers, doctors, small businessmen, retirees, engineers, mid-level clerks – although described with greater respect than this female congeries of banshees and celibates, were observed to be similarly mesmerized. Anecdotal estimates of the market's reach extended downward into the working classes as well. There were stories of newsboys and chauffeurs, elevator operators and valets, plumbers and speak-easy waiters taking a plunge. *Harper's* concluded the stock market was no longer reserved for a handful of 'hard-boiled knights', but had become a place 'for the butcher and the barber and the candlestick maker'. The same social mix was witnessed among the women: journalists reported sightings of working girls – typists, scrub-women, farmers' wives, cooks, switchboard operators – communing around the ticker with their social betters. Volume on regional exchanges in places like St Louis, Los Angeles, and Chicago expanded exponentially as the number of players soared. Branch offices of Wall Street brokerages opened in every major city, spilled over into the suburbs, and even showed up in out-of-the-way towns like Steubenville, Ohio; Gastonia, North Carolina; and Chickasha, Oklahoma. Charles Mitchell, the enteprising president of National City Bank and a salesman at heart, set up the National City Company with a big high-pressure sales force to peddle securities at railroad stations, nightclubs, and wherever else crowds of people might gather long enough to indulge their financial whimsy. Edmund Wilson dubbed Mitchell the 'banker of bankers, the salesman of salesmen, the genius of the new economic era'.[29]

Hard estimates about the actual number of investors are hard to come by and even harder to evaluate. Despite all the hoopla and lingering legend of mass infatuation, it may be that as little as two million people were actively involved. Other educated guesses go as high as fourteen million, if one includes the passive holders of securities in pension funds, corporate stock-ownership plans and so on. Certainly the New York Stock Exchange responded to its widening public. Its publicity committee commissioned hortatory pamphlets and fatuous magazine articles ('The Stock Exchange: Its Relation to the Building of Proper Manhood', 'The Stock Exchange as a Moral Force'), and even a movie, *Smith's First Investment*, designed to educate and reassure novice investors.

On the other hand, probably seventy-five per cent of the dollar value of all outstanding securities were held by not many more than half a million people. And it does seem certain that most traders were still drawn from among wealthy insiders, upper middle-class amateurs, and peversely from the servant caste – butlers, doormen, chauffeurs, bellhops – in a kind of upstairs/downstairs democratization of what remained an Edwardian marketplace. But no matter the actual number, it seems undeniable that blood was stirring where it hadn't before. As one clearly astonished journalist perceived, what was most remarkable about the boom was not its unprecedented longevity (discounting some momentary slides, it ran on for five years), nor its record-setting trading volumes, nor its upper atmosphere prices, but rather that it was fed by 'great new hordes of small investors who were never in this game before and have come out of it with six passenger coupes or whitened hair'. A Wall Street persuasion seeped deep down into the cultural bedrock. [30]

Signs were everywhere that Wall Street was on people's minds. Ticker tapes appeared not only in beauty parlors and railroad depots, but on ocean liners like the *Ile de France*, the *Bremen*, and the *Leviathan*, short-waving their trades across the Atlantic to Wall Street. Cartoonists poked endless fun at the mass obsession. Frederick Opper, still scenting out the credulity of the Volk, depicted a line-up of rakishly clad tipsters promising some hapless country yokel the inside dope from 'J. P. Morgan's barber' or the elevator man at the stock exchange or 'the window cleaner in a big broker's office'. 'The Golden Stairs' captured the buoyant mood following Hoover's election as a ticker-tape machine tap-danced its way up a stairway called 'GOP victory'. One classic *New Yorker* sketch showed a cadaverous-looking character stretched out on an operating table being prepared for surgery, telling the doctors huddled over him to please 'keep your eye on Consolidated Can Common', and should it go down while he was still under the knife to kindly call his broker with a message to sell 'four thousand shares of P&Q Preferred on the usual margin'.

Just in case people like our *New Yorker* patient didn't make it, burial societies, especially in the New York metropolitan area, promoted custom-designed mausoleums to house the remains of Wall Street tycoons, roomy enough to store private papers recording their more memorable deals. This sacerdotal air filtered into the sanctuary of the church as well. The Swedish Immanuel Congregational Church in New York offered all who contributed $100 to its building fund an 'engraved certificate of investment in preferred capital stock in the Kingdom of God'. Church magazines carried articles advising the faithful on how best to invest; recommendations included mortgage bonds, public-utility bonds, and even 'Bible Annuity Bonds'. While Protestant churchmen paid rhetorical tribute to Christianity's traditional wariness of materialism, the churches fawned over businessmen as the era's spiritual heroes. After all, this was the decade when advertising executive Bruce Barton's *The Man Nobody Knows* extolled Jesus Christ as a business genius ne plus ultra, a figure of surpassing salesmanship worth emulating in an age devoted to hedonism and the hard sell. It was a piece of outlandish literary stock-jobbery which kept Barton's book on the bestseller list for two years. [31]

Europeans as well as Americans were swept away by the craze for American stocks. An Italian paper marked the changing of the guard: 'with more authority than the League of Nations, and with more subtlety than Bolshevism, another world power is making a direct appeal to the strongest instincts of human nature. The new power is Wall Street.' Daily quotations from the Street were printed in all major European cities. Malcolm Cowley, in his memoir about expatriate writers trying to escape the baleful influence of American materialism, noted that 'having come in search of values, they found valuta' as

Europe too was swept away by the Exchange! Wall Street became a tourist destination as travelers from abroad as well as from all over the United States came to gawk at the 'Canyon of Gold'.[32]

Systems for prophesying the market assumed a dozen faddish forms. One 'system' predicted no bearish downturns in any month containing the letter 'r'. Another tracked sunspots. Yet another derived its picks from a code assembled from comic-book dialogue. Evangeline Adams, a famous fortune-teller whose clients included European royalty, Charles Schwab, and movie idol Mary Pickford, held court in her studio above Carnegie Hall, where of course she consulted her own ticker-tape. She issued a monthly newsletter that explained how shifts in planetary positions were bound to affect the market, 'a guaranteed system to beat Wall Street'.

New radio shows and newspaper columns, presumably more down to earth, sprouted up everywhere to appease the hunger for investment advice. One couldn't assume their reliability, however. PR firms prowled newsrooms seeding stories about hot stocks, and sometimes handing out stock options, even cash, to pliant reporters. Temptation was great for radio and print journalists to take kick-backs for producing favorable news about dubious companies. Ex-*Daily News* columnist William J. McMahon, known in print as 'The Trader', supplemented his salary as a radio commentator by secretly pocketing $250 a week from PR flak and stock promoter David M. Lion. Lion himself was rewarded with stock options by front-rank firms like Hayden Stone & Co., Eastman Dillon & Co., and E. F. Hutton, when it was running a pool in Kalster Radio securities. It was the age of the confidence man all over again, as 'the wire', 'the rag', and other con-game permutations flourished. The 'boiler room', a pre-war invention of the financial underground, came into its own. Their telephone salesmen kept up such a deafening volume of high-pressure calls that the noise sounded like the inside of a boiler, as they hawked 'specialty' penny stocks, options, and commodities to 'sucker lists' of 'marks' anxious to get in on the action. All the channels of mass communication were saturated with news of big killings by insiders which only incited seething ambitions among the vast population of outsiders. The floor of the stock exchange itself, one observer noted, had become an iconic image of modern American life in all its furious perpetual motion. [33]

There was something irrepressibly whimsical, binge-like and fun-loving about all of this. There may arguably be an invariant connection between cycles of speculative excess and bouts of extravagant consumption accompanied by a seductive sense of moral/erotic abandon. In any event, Wall Street, which in the past always seemed to wear a lugubrious mien, now seemed sportier, a recreational arena where one could not only spectate but join in the game. A whole new vocabulary associated with the culture of abundance – pleasure, plenty, play, leisure, self-fulfillment, instant gratification, celebrity – supplanted the harsher poetry of the work ethic and attached itself to the goings-on on the Street. As even Max Weber once remarked, while in its formative stages capitalism seemed to draw its moral energy from Protestantism's worldly asceticism; later on, and especially in America, its religious and ethical moorings fell into disuse and the pursuit of wealth aroused 'purely mundane passions, which often actually give it the character of a sport'.[34]

Take those iniquitous 'pools' for example. Pools, which were in fact conspiracies of the few to bilk the many, were nonetheless reported on like great sporting events, even while they were under way, and without the taint of disapprobation. After-dinner gossip dwelt on sagas of market exploits and disasters and slaked the sporting man's thirst for statistical measures of athletic achievement and failure. One keen observer of national mores recognized that 'The market has fitted perfectly into the interests of a highly mathematical nation which can really give its heart to no sport which cannot be tallied in batting averages . . . strokes per hole, or stolen bases'. The phrase, 'playing the market' as if it were some sporting contest, first entered popular parlance in the 1920s. What a turnabout from the days when similar conspiracies to manipulate the market had been resented and censured. Loaded images of diamond-studded waistcoats and silk top hats yellowed with disuse. [35]

Shakespeare in Wall Street, published at the height of the spree, was a parody that caught the light-heartedness of the moment. Hamlet was cast as a bond salesman, Macbeth as a 'timid bull' and his wife as 'always bullish', chastising her husband's cowardice:

> Give me a stock
> with a rocket's rush
> A shooter for the stars.

Hamlet vacillates:

The future trend of ups and downs, why, then
we'd know
whether to go long or short, the eternal question
never answered yet
And never will but by the hand of chance.

The three witches (the 'three traders') prophesy a crash, but Shakespeare, who himself plays the role of a kind of average Joe dreaming of hitting it big and escaping life as an impoverished writer, confesses:

The market is the nation of fever
deep-seated in its blood
Now who am I to be so strong I can escape the germ?
Lead on, you
bulls, And strong be he who first shall scent a bear.[36]

This miscible brew of the carefree and the careless (a carelessness whose toxicity F. Scott Fitzgerald would memorialize in *The Great Gatsby* and elsewhere) was intoxicating and sexy. Noted behavioral psychologist John Watson mapped the cultural synapses linking the speculative craze to the permissiveness of the Jazz Age: 'Sex has become so free and abundant that it no longer provides the thrill it once did . . . gambling on Wall Street is about the only thrill we have left.' An English visitor remarked that some male Americans viewed 'financial success, particularly success on the stock market . . . as evidence of virility' and boasted about their exploits there the way a 'primitive' might about real sexual triumphs.

Tin Pan Alley and Hollywood caught the bug. Louis Armstrong growled 'I'm in the Market for You'. The tabloids kept everyone apprised of the market escapades of stars like the Marx Brothers, Irving Berlin, Charlie Chaplin, and Eddie Cantor. Groucho, the most stock-addicted of the brothers, got his tips from theatrical producer Max Gordon, but when he was out of touch in Boston performing in *Animal Crackers* he relied on the elevator operator at the Copley Plaza. At the height of the boom, women's magazines observed that their readers found stockbrokers sexier than movie stars. Once the lingua franca of male shop-talk, doings on the market reportedly competed with sex and romance as the favored topic of female conversation at fashionable social gatherings. Faddish stocks like airline securities got to be known as 'high steppers', a piece of Wall Street slang itself borrowed from the voguish term for the socially glamorous and well turned out. Popular magazines of the time were visual catalogs of moneyed sophistication: slim, leggy women with stylishly bobbed hair were escorted by equally lean and perfectly coiffed money men, sharing witticisms laced with sexual innuendo. The Street had become home base for a vanguard of trendsetters. [37]

The atmosphere of glamour and play carried with it an undercurrent of irreverence and irony that infused the culture and the air of reckless abandon that hovered over the market. A stock exchange in the high heat of a bull-market fling instinctively disrespected the past, recognized no cautionary voice, and paraded its iconoclasm like a rebuke to all the maxims of Victorian caution and propriety. In this way too, the spirit of Wall Street evinced a surprising sympathy with the era's plangent intellectual and artistic mockeries of Puritan hypocrisy and banality – everything from the novels of Sinclair Lewis to the journalism of H. L. Mencken. These coruscating critics of babbitry might have appreciated the irony. The Street, that synecdoche for power and seriousness of purpose, had become a folk carnival, an inversion of that once indissoluble bond between capitalism and the ethic of self-renunciation. As the old taboos lost their sting, Wall Street's instinct for the Dionysian and demonic, which had always lurked in its shadows, now surfaced as a kind of salubrious consumerist hedonism and creativity. The revolution, however temporary, that so distinguished the decade – in manners and morals, in fashion and sexual relations, and in codes of conduct – shared an esprit, an aggressive irreligiousness with the Great Bull.

Out of this goulash of fast money and erotic agitation, there arose, like a distilled vapor, a peculiar kind of utopian projection about a new world; Wall Street was its midwife. It transcended the era's heavy irony and cynicism and spoke the language of democracy and techno-futurism that went down particularly well in America. It lent the Street a kind of Salvationist, even messianic aura, which would evaporate without a trace in the great crash of 1929, not to be seen again until the turn of the millennium.

William Allen White intuited these popular implications of the Coolidge boom. It was, he claimed, 'ordained by the American democracy. It came out of the people. It was woven inextricably into the lives of the people. It was their conscious purpose, their highest vision . . .

And in so far as Coolidge was the embodiment of the big bull market . . . he was democracy's perfect flower.' The British social critic, James Truslow Adams, wondering why Americans seemed hypnotized by the ticker-tape, also decided it was an instance of pure Americana. In a civilization first, last, and always dedicated to doing business, one lacking a court aristocracy, a country gentry, or an established church, where no great prestige attached to diplomacy, government service, or even the armed forces, the stock market towered over the landscape, Adams observed, redolent and unchallengeable, emblematic of national purpose.[38]

Wall Street's reincarnation as the voice of the people could take on metaphysical or homelier guises. A generation before Charles Merrill's firm adopted 'bullish on America' as its signature slogan, the great investing public was enjoined to 'Be a Bull on America' and to 'Never sell the US short'. Patriotic puffery showed up as advertising copy, as in an advertisement by a group called Incorporated Investors, which in the *Wall Street Journal* appealed to 'The American Birthright'. That 'most precious' right turned out to be the chance to share in the cornucopia which was the country's 'greatest discovery'; any citizen might participate and Incorporated Investors would provide 'an ideal method' for doing so. Mayor Jimmy Walker of New York called the bull market 'the eighth wonder of the world'. [39]

Moreover, this seepage of 'market consciousness' into the lower social orders was thought to help ballast the market itself. Mass participation would, it was forecast, provide the Exchange the backbone it always seemed to lack in volatile times, rendering it less treacherous and blessing it with a stabilizing homogeneity and democratic unity: 'When the country follows the same tips, finds comfort in the same reassuring signs that normalcy is here to stay . . . we know . . . that this is a united people.' Corporate-sponsored stock-ownership plans for employees, although they enrolled tiny numbers, were celebrated as an ingenious way for the United States to avoid 'a caste system like England's' with its nasty outbreaks of class acrimony, as in the General Strike of 1926. Paul Warburg of Kuhn Loeb encouraged the idea of tailoring particular securities for sale among immigrants and 'the working classes'.[40]

All these reassurances made middle Americans feel at home in a place once so foreign to their experience. The Street basked in the glow of an economy of mass production and consumption, of Fordism and installment credit, proud of its efficiency, technical innovations, and mass purchasing power. Pundits fell over one another to echo Coolidge in proclaiming a 'new era' which would change everything, even that most mysterious 'street of torment'.

Economists and journalists discovered approaches to investment that miraculously eliminated the element of risk that always plagued the market. The 'science of investment' was soberly compared to that of insurance, where one 'appraised the character of unavoidable risks' and then neutralized them through a combination of diversified holdings. Authorities like Clarence Barron, publisher of *Barron's Financial Weekly*, dismissed market manipulations as ephemeral aberrations. He was confident that in the long term the market was buoyed by the strength of the underlying economy, so that the wise investor need only diversify his holdings; he could safely assess his investments not on their current book value but on the rosy prospects of future earnings.

Insight into the workings of the market and the economy had so improved as to eliminate the dangers of the past – that at least was the prevailing conceit. With better statistics and research, a new 'management science' could now reliably forecast the future. New formulas designed to establish the present value of common stocks based on the discounting of their future earnings lent an illusory precison to what were after all highly speculative exercises. As investment sage Benjamin Graham later wryly remarked, 'Calculus . . . [gives] speculation the deceptive guise of investment.' Allied to this reassuringly 'scientific' knowledge was the Federal Reserve which, if things somehow got out of hand, could abort incipient panics with timely open-market interventions to regulate interest rates.[41] However, the skeptics who actually dared suggest that the Federal Reserve ought to exercise some restraint over the tidal wave of easy credit were treated like benighted ignoramuses who'd failed to understand the enlightened view of speculation. Congressman James O'Connor of Louisiana let loose this hosanna: 'The world could not afford . . . to stem that wonderful tide which has made for a development of natural resources and opulent growth of a stupendous civilization, paling into insignificance the glory that was Greece, the grandeur that was Rome.'

Science of this sort really functioned more like religion; it instilled confidence in what most people still believed was an uncertain future; it conveyed a consoling if misleading sense of control; it told people that what seemed to be too good to be true was, after all, true. The most legendary expression of this misplaced confidence was the remark on the eve of the crash – later richly ridiculed – by the renowned Yale economist, Irving Fisher, that 'Stock prices have reached what looks like a permanently high plateau.' Fisher was no fool, and his certitude was widely shared. At just the moment Fisher uttered his regrettable prophecy, Thomas Lamont of the House of Morgan, a confidante of the new President, assured Hoover that 'the wide distribution of ownership of our greater industries among tens or hundreds of thousands of stockholders, should go a long way to solve the problem of social unrest', and that if 'the future appears brilliant . . . it is the future which the stock market has been discounting.' John Jacob Raskob, raised in a slum tenement, but more lately of DuPont, GM and the Democratic National Committee, displayed a similarly exquisite sense of timing. His widely noted article in *The Ladies' Home Journal*, 'Everybody Ought to Be Rich' (really an interview conducted by Samuel Crowther) echoed Lamont's sunniness and came with its own plan for financial deliverance. An Equities Securities Company, run by a trusted board of directors, would buy common stocks and turn over the profits to working people. There would be 'nothing secret about its transactions', it would not 'deal in speculative stocks'. One might invest as little as $15 a month and if the dividends were left to accumulate, $80,000 would be waiting there in twenty years. What might be called Raskob's 'twenty-year plan' would not only abolish the need for charity and end poverty among the elderly; it would, he sententiously declared, cultivate 'ambitious, contented children'.[42]

All this rhetoric, together with the gravity-defying performance of the market, produced a kind of mesmeric optimism. Claud Cockburn, a scion of English gentry with leftist inclinations, visited America in 1929 (the first Cockburn to make the journey since Admiral Sir George Cockburn helped burn down Washington DC in 1814). Cockburn frequented 'Gatsby country', either on Long Island or in 'steel boxes on Sutton Place' where, he reported, 'you could talk about Prohibition, or Hemingway, or air conditioning, or music or horses, but in the end you had to talk about the stock market . . . There was a "mystique" about the market.' Although people might differ violently about politics, about the merits of various investments, about every other conceivable subject,

What you could not with impunity do was to suggest, not by words only but by so much as an intonation, that there was any doubt about the fact that the market as a whole was going up and up and up, that every 'recession' there might be in the near future would be 'temporary', 'technical', 'an adjustment', after which the new era of American life would resume its swift, inevitable progress toward a hardly imaginable stratosphere of prosperity.

To do otherwise was considered sacrilegious, like insulting the Pope. Cockburn perceived an 'element of sympathetic magic' at work, as if to speak ill of the market was unlucky. Behind the elaborate statistical analyses and sober market reports, he observed, there was a primitive belief that 'the whole thing was a kind of marvelous subjective trick; a séance where the table moved and the spirits spoke.' Europeans were under a misapprehension about Americans whom they regarded as overly and inherently 'materialistic'. What the worship of the market revealed, however, was quite the opposite: that Americans 'believed in miracles'.[43]

Everything about Wall Street, even its architecture, seemed beguiling evidence of its mastery over the future. William Lamb, the Street's architect of choice during the 1920s – the man charged by John Jacob Raskob with the task of razing the old Waldorf Astoria and erecting the Empire State Building in its place – presided over the transformation of the financial district into the towering apparition now recognized all over the world. Although the Empire State and the Chrysler Building got most of the attention, the real heart of the process was in the Street. There, at nos. 1 and 60 (the site of the old buttonwood tree), sleek thousand-foot edifices visible from the sea lorded it over the turn-of-the-century buildings, more massive but less soaring. The art-deco ornamentation of the new skyscrapers was a declaration of independence from their predecessors' slavish echoing of classical columns and European decorative allusions. The Standard Oil building at 26 Broadway was topped off in the 1920s with a great tower and enormous cauldron filled with kerosene, a symbol of inexhaustible economic combustion. In its very physicality, the Street invoked gravity-defying force, kinetic energy, and voluptuousness. For millions around the world, its skyline became the best symbol of Wall Street's modernist dreamscape.[44]

*

Not everyone was taken in, either by the blue-skies economic crystal-ball gazing or by the Edenic musings about a 'new era' civilization. A handful of renegade economists, skeptical bankers, doctrinal leftists, and repatriated artists and intellectuals swamed against the tide, but few paid much attention to these Cassandras.

William Z. Ripley, writing from inside the academy, decried the 'financialization' of the economy. He had no quarrel with the corporation as the economy's fundamental institution, but he worried about the concentration of control among a very few individuals. Free of public restraint, they abrogated the rights of most shareholders, and could if they chose ignore the needs of their employees and the communities in which they did business. This was not news. What was strikingly new in Ripley's eyes was the stock market's penetration of the back country, which made an old predicament intolerable. Ripley called 1925 'the year of the vanishing stockholder': closed clubs of elite managers and directors could no longer make key decisions about the terms and timing of new issues, whether to buy or sell corporate assets, whether to enter into or break off relations with other industrial combines, and so on, without making a mockery of the promise of shareholder democracy. Main Street deserved a voice within the great corporations, and Ripley called for permanent minority-shareholder representation alongside boards of directors, to monitor their doings and represent the views of the voiceless. Unless this was done, unless the rupture between ownership and responsibility was repaired, abuses of power would eventually bring down the whole system. *Main Street and Wall Street* was a catalog of such abuses, focusing particularly on the stock manipulations, insider dealing, and pyramiding of grossly inflated stock values by public-utility holding companies. [45]

Warnings like Ripley's would, after the deluge, become the orthodoxy of financial reform during the New Deal. Now, however, they hardly disturbed the equanimity of those in charge. The skepticism of more conventional economists could sometimes cause a stir, but it passed quickly. Doubts voiced by popular if eccentric market gurus like Roger Babson were a different matter. When, in early September 1929, his 'Babsonchart' (based, he claimed, on Newtonian physics) predicted a market crash, radio programs interrupted schedules to announce the forecast, a fleeting hysteria ensued, the market took a severe dip, and Babson was anointed the 'Prophet of Loss'. Sources more circumspect than Babson chimed in as well. *Moody's* warned that stock prices were insupportably high. Editorials in the *New York Times*, in the *Commercial and Financial Chronicle*, *Forbes* and elsewhere, though never using the frightening word 'crash', delivered cautionary sermons that had a sobering effect for a day or so.

The Ripleys and Thorstein Veblens had little in common with pinstriped investment bankers, but there were some from that guild who also knew something was awry. John Foster Dulles, later Dwight Eisenhower's Secretary of State but then a lawyer with Sullivan and Cromwell, worried about the over-enthusiasm of the small investor. The problem, as he saw it, was not that stock prices were too high or that the Fed was asleep on its watch, but rather 'one of psychology'. Dulles was convinced that the country's credit base 'cannot, under present conditions, meet potential speculative demands as well as the economic needs of the nation as a whole'. Paul Warburg, too, let it be known that he saw the signs of calamity, that the 'colossal volume' of margin loans might bring on 'general depression involving the entire country' – for which he was indignantly charged with 'sandbagging American prosperity'. Before the fact, B. C. Forbes blamed any eventual collapse not on establishment Wall Street, whose conservative financial practices he quite mistakenly considered impeccable, but on those nouveau riche 'pool' operators, men of reckless temperament like Durant, Jesse Livermore, Arthur Cutten, and others who in Forbes' view were really interlopers on the Street.

Federal Reserve Board officials believed the market was overextended, but powerful forces within and outside the central bank whittled away at its will to act. Big corporations with idle cash were so lucratively rewarded for loaning into the call market that they resisted any effort to rein in credit. Charles Mitchell, the head of National City Bank, whose instincts for the salesman's hype had gotten the bank knee-deep in the hawking of 'Peruvian bonds' and other second-rate securities, denounced warnings by the Fed about speculation and defied the government by letting it be known that he would make bank funds available to the call market. And after all, Mitchell was himself a director of the New York Federal Reserve bank.[46]

Charlie Mitchell's insouciance epitomized the zeitgeist. Malcontents might carp, Jeremiahs might bemoan the new era's cultural debauch, but the congregation wasn't listening. *Civilization in the United States*, an anthology edited by cultural critic Harold Stearns, attempted to take the measure of this 'new era'. The book's essay on 'Business' argued that in a country given over to the pursuit of fast money the notion of business morality had lost all meaning. Soulless corporations, rather than individual men, now ran things without the faintest trace of ethical responsibility or moral liability. The purest expression of this impersonality, according to Thorstein Veblen, was Wall Street's fiscal relationship to the vast aggregations of property it controlled. All material and sentimental attachments to the workaday world of wresting a living from nature were effaced, 'whereby the livelihood of the underlying population becomes, in the language of mathematics, a function of the state of mind of the investment bankers.' Democracy, Veblen demonstrated, sickened under the strain.[47]

The literary and political avant-garde was similarly appalled. Cartoonists on the left sought to capture the grotesque consequences of this subversion of democracy. Art Young's 'Rake's Progress' in the *Liberator* (one of half a dozen left-wing political-literary publications that barely clung to life during the decade) was a 'sabre-toothed' depiction of a diabolical John D. Rockefeller dancing lasciviously with 'Miss Liberal Ideas' while the 'whole Babbit family' looked on in shock and dismay. Maurice Becker, an artist steeped in the styles of European modernism, drew a cubist depiction of 'Morgan über Alles', which evoked the banker's fearsome overlordship in Europe and Latin America, but marked his face with bestial craziness, making him appear terrifying yet weak and self-destructive. Bohemian literary magazines like *The Broom* ran spoofs of Wall Street roués who couldn't tell the difference between their chorus-girl mistresses and hot stock-buys. The era's cynicism left its mark even on these committed literary leftists who hated consumer culture and despaired of mass politics. In *Manhattan Transfer*, John Dos Passos's modernist rendering of hedonistic New York, Wall Street generates an atmosphere of infidelity, evanescence, and ennui. It's populated by ruined stock wizards and effete snobs huddled away from the teeming life around them. Wall Street, its reputation for command notwithstanding, seems at a loss, in control of nothing, and thus perfectly at home in a world full of random events and deflected hopes, pointless and living on the edge of a nervous breakdown.[48]

Malcolm Cowley, who helped edit *The Broom*, lamented the experience of his fellow expatriate artists in his *Exile's Return*: 'We had come three thousand miles in search of Europe and had found

America,' a disturbing discovery for many artists seeking refuge from the mercenary ethos of the Street. But the Street, along with the rest of the country's business civilization, had other plans in mind for these young rebels, eager to exploit their talents as copywriters, public-relations flaks, graphic designers, romance writers and illustrators, and servants of the new era's play economy. Even while many went on to take precisely these jobs, they sustained a 'professional hostility' to the 'middle-aged bankers and corporation executives' running their lives, hating their 'high collars and white-piped waistcoats, beautifully tailored over their little round paunches'. Cowley concluded that too many of his comrades 'accepted too much from publishers and Wall Street plungers', so that 'we became part of the system we were trying to evade, and it defeated us from within.' Citing Zelda Fitzgerald's cultural epitaph, Cowley pleaded guilty for his generation of writers of 'being lost and driven like the rest'.[49]

Zelda's husband was the poet laureate of this disorientation. In *The Great Gatsby* and elsewhere, F. Scott Fitzgerald captured the peculiar blend of eroticism and money-making that epitomized the 'new era'. Despite the free-floating libido and free-flowing cash it was not a happy picture; yet it was not the same picture of moral depravity that for generations was associated with Wall Street. In Gatsby's world the rich were no longer vicious, but careless; no longer lascivious but oversated; less devilish than they were cynical; bored, eaten away and enervated by the enveloping envy of consumer culture.

So Gatsby loves and envies Daisy's weightless self-possession. Her voice, 'full of money', vibrates with every dream of romance and social elevation that Gatsby cherishes. He hates and envies Tom Buchanan's 'effeminate swagger' and supercilious arrogance. The world they toy with, the world Jay Gatsby pants after, is kept aloft by Wall Street. That's where Yale graduate Nick Carraway, Gatsby's chronicler, works as a bond salesman, when he can tear himself away from the narcotic fascinations of West Egg night life. Nick's ambivalent mix of awe, sympathy, and censure for Gatsby mirrors his own lingering pietistic attachment to his native Midwest. Nick works for 'Probity Trust', a bastion of Wall Street respectability, yet like so many in that white-shoe world, he's irresistibly drawn to Gatsby's underworld, a seductive world of money laundering and trafficking in illegal bonds. There old boundaries are erased, ancient taboos weakened, and a kind of American genius for audacious rule-breaking is given its head. Nick feels the romance of this illicit capitalism, the alluring wonder a whole culture has vested in the Market. We know, without being told, that it's Wall Street supplying the juice, that intoxicating elixir of money and style which is distilled in its purest form in the barrios of the Street, or on its shadier back roads where Gatsby has accumulated his stash. Moreover, beneath all the glitter, the waterside mansions and glamorous sports cars, there is for Gatsby something fundamentally immaterial about it all, a kind of sacramental reaching out beyond the world of commodities.

For Fitzgerald, the Market punctuates the era's tragic trajectory. It is the magnetic north of its spiritual inertia, pervasive dissipation, compulsive gaiety, and looming air of loss. The Street records the arithmetic of the new era's destructive self-regard and adolescent bravado, yet there is also an elemental innocence at work. Gatsby's downfall is a kind of premonition of the Crash: the wreckage of the era's money-dream, the run-down of its speculative mania, the echoing sound of waste and disillusion. But Gatsby's romantic speculation on Daisy is both naive and profound. His longing for the promise of the past – his and Daisy's past, the American mythological past – sheds the cynicism of the era's Wall Street operators. It is a spiritual speculation, akin to that yearning Nick imagines gripped the first Dutch sailors on spying the 'fresh green breast of the New World'.[50]

Thorstein Veblen assumed the position of the disinterested social scientist. The writers for *Civilization in the United States* were confirmed secularists. Mencken and the *Liberator* cartoonists were avowed atheists. Dos Passos flirted with nihilism. Cowley, Fitzgerald, and the expatriates were modernist romantics, who found Wall Street's hubris more retrograde than sinful. Other Jazz Age dissidents, however, felt the hand of God.

Until this moment, the religious conscience had always formed the core of cultural opposition to the Street. In the Jazz Age, for the first time, that ceased to be the case. The desacralization of the country, the withering away of its Protestant spiritual fervor, and the decline in the church's moral and psychological authority meant that Wall Street, like so much else in the secular world, was no longer so vulnerable to the sting of the righteous. Religious voices could still be heard, however, as the furore over Darwinism in Tennessee, the rebirth of the Klan, the meteoric popularity of Ford's anti-Semitism, and the venomous anti-Catholic, prohibitionist attacks on Al Smith's candidacy for the presidency in 1928 made evident.[51]

For the pious, the country's reverence for the Street remained a sacrilege. Rural politicians talked of brokers as apostles of evil, flouting the laws of God as well as the law of the land. The perfidy of these 'moonshine promoters' was limitless, as they deployed 'moving picture shows, flamboyant and deceptive talk, and bombastic figures and advertisements' to inveigle the innocent. According to the *Christian Century*, society was headed for hell, helped along by a compliant church: 'The gap between the New Testament and the mind of the man who sits in the pew worshipping what Amalgamated Wireless is going to do tomorrow is too wide to be bridged by most sermons.' 'What kind of society will it be that is composed of get-rich-quick, something-for-nothing citizens,' the editors asked, alarmed that 'speculation in stocks has become a national affair'.[52]

You didn't have to be a regular reader of religious newspapers to hear this message. In fact, you were probably more likely to see it in the dozens of silent movies that depicted Wall Street as the modern pathway to hell. Films like *The Plunger*, *Extravagance*, *The Blasphemer*, and *The Silent Partner*, age-old tales about the moral pitfalls of easy money, the way it ate away at homespun ethics, marital fidelity, and honest effort, still commanded an audience. But it was a dwindling one, as most movies catered to the popular appetite for the good times.[53]

In 1919, Vachel Lindsay composed *Bryan, Bryan, Bryan*, a poetic elegy to the great crusade of 1896 'as Viewed at the Time By A Sixteen-Year Old'. Lindsay was no religious zealot, nor a Victorian throwback, yet there is something irreducibly old-fashioned about his verse recollections. The poet remembers how he had marched and chanted and bragged of Bryan, the candidate 'who sketched a silver Zion'. He had 'scourged the elephant plutocrats / with barbed wire from the Platte', and his faithful had leapt the Mississippi to confront 'the towns of Tubal Cain', the eastern lair of Hanna and his men. As the hosts of Bryan assembled, 'the demons in the bank-vaults peered out to see us pass' and in 'July, August, suspense / Wall Street lost to sense.' But Hanna rallied, 'threatening drouth and death / Rallying the trusts against the bawling flannelmouth.' Election night and defeat:

> Defeat of western silver
> Defeat of the wheat
> Victory of letterfiles
> And plutocrats in miles . . .
> Defeat of my boyhood, defeat of my dream.

The language has an antique ring, a jarring echo from a bygone time. Its vocabulary, rich in religious allegory, must have seemed entirely out of sync with the morally neutered apostrophes of the roaring twenties.[54]

Like Fisher's folly in Montauk, the poem lies there like a fossil, buried under tons of new-era wit and faddish wisdom. Unlike Fisher's monument to a make-believe past, however, the moral specter of *Bryan, Bryan, Bryan*, nostalgic yet prophetic, would once again come to haunt the Street – and much sooner than most people imagined possible.

PART THREE

The Age of Ignominy

Who's Afraid of the Big Bad Wolf?

The Three Little Pigs, an eight-minute Walt Disney cartoon, was a sensation from the moment it appeared in 1933. Ministers sermonized about it, the new President quoted from it, radio stations played its theme song, 'Who's Afraid of the Big Bad Wolf?', over and over again. Indeed, 'Who's Afraid of the Big Bad Wolf?' became an alternative national anthem – sung, hummed, and whistled, on trains and buses, in taxis and hotels. There was a near riot in Dallas where a local theater forgot to run the cartoon as scheduled; management quickly interrupted the feature film to get the three little pigs on the screen before things got really out of hand.

Commentators then and since have recognized in this universal craze a deep emotional reaction to the trauma the country was living through. The song itself echoed the President's first, reassuring fireside chat about people having 'nothing to fear but fear itself'. And of course, long before the Great Depression, the wolf served as a haunting figure of material want and starvation. Political cartoonists were quick to borrow the movie's imagery, dressing up the New Deal's political opposition to resemble the 'big bad wolf'. Critics treated the short as a populist parable affirming hope and celebrating the bravery and solidarity of the community against its enemies. The wise little pig in particular reaffirmed a venerable faith in hard work and planning ahead that repudiated the devil-may-care recklessness of pre-Crash America.

Though it had no explicit political message, the cartoon served to resurrect a distinctively American romance with the 'producing classes'. A recent biographer of Disney calls this cultural subtext the folksy, denim-shirted cartoonist's 'sentimental populism'. Many of the great

Disney classic full-length animations and shorts of the 1930s – *Snow White and the Seven Dwarfs*, *Pinocchio*, *Dumbo* – are infused with veneration for honest toil and contempt for those outside its charmed circle: tricksters, con men, landlords, bankers and their minions. Dozens of other works of art, including the movies of Frank Capra, the music of Aaron Copland, the plays and poems of Archibald McLeish, and the novels of John Steinbeck, similarly aestheticized 'the people' and their perseverance. What lent Walt Disney's brief comic fantasy such extraordinary resonance was the way it recapitulated the emotions raised by the Great Depression: terror slowly gave way to anger and then to a sense of impending triumph over and finally ridicule of a once fearsome enemy.

There were plenty of candidates for the role of 'the big bad wolf', but the biggest and baddest was Wall Street. Rightly or wrongly, the Street was blamed for an unprecedented calamity. It aroused every animosity that Americans had ever felt for those 'lords of creation' who controlled what others produced while adding nothing themselves to the commonweal. Wall Street, it seemed, would take the blame for everyone who had transgressed, from the confidence man to the money trust. Only then would the temple, cleansed of its money-changers, be restored. And Wall Street would be sent ignominiously packing: no one need be afraid of the big bad wolf any more.[1]

The Civil War and then the Great Depression were the two profound trials of modern America: they live on indelibly in the national memory bank, unusually for a culture that prefers to live in the present and future. The Great Depression not only altered the national mentality for good: it also carved out a great generational divide, coloring people's attitudes to work and security, wealth and justice, democracy and the role of the government, for decades to follow. Even in the United States of Amnesia, there are a few moments nobody forgets.

Just as the Civil War had called into question the legitimacy of the nation state, the Crash and Depression posed a similar challenge to capitalism. Not that revolutionaries were roaming the streets, though their apparitions disturbed the equanimity of some – but this was certainly the severest crisis the system had ever suffered. This is not so much a matter of the numbers of victims, for there were plenty in 1837, 1873, 1893, and other years too. The thing that no previous panic or slump had managed to do, however, was produce a foreboding that the whole system of production and distribution had reached a state of terminal breakdown. Moreover, the nation's political institutions also seemed implicated, either by virtue of a decade's worth of crony capitalism, or due to their inaction and ineptitude in the early years of the slump. It was by no means certain that democratic protocols could be maintained in such an emergency. Fascist military upheavals in Central Europe, Latin America, and the Far East, reactions to what was, after all, a global economic collapse, were hardly reassuring. Inevitably, the cultural authority of those figures in the media, politics, the academy, the church, and above all business who had spent the previous decade celebrating the 'new era', was now severely compromised. All this formed the makings of a true crisis of confidence.

The confidence in which Wall Street traded is the psychic understructure of any market economy. To say that people lost confidence in the stock market during the 1930s is to commit a gross understatement. Since that time, and especially during the last twenty-five years, some economists and other writers have labored to separate the Crash from the Depression, arguing that whatever accounts for the stock market meltdown in late October 1929, it did not push the economy at large into its own free-fall descent. They note that the market soon revived, later that year. Some argue that even in the late 1920s, stock prices were hardly as over-valued as legend has it, at least assessed by modern methods. Some more timely tinkering by the Federal Reserve might have prevented the whole debacle. In this view, the Depression was brought on by events and less visible underlying economic processes, especially in Europe, for which Wall Street can't be held accountable.[2]

Maybe not, but for most people living then and long after, the Crash and the Depression were joined at the hip. Wall Street was not merely accountable for the country's dilemma; it was its perpetrator, the principal villain in a saga of guilt, revenge, and redemption. The Crash did more than discredit the immediate circle of financial oligarchs and nouveau riche speculators who'd helped make the twenties roar. It invoked the whole historic iconography of shame that had shadowed the Street since the days of Jefferson. It was like the return of the repressed after a decade of laughter and forgetting. The popular imagination transformed Wall Street into a menagerie of parasites, shylocks, web-meisters, defrocked aristocrats, gold worshippers, psychopathic anti-heroes, noxious confidence men – and fools. Fools, because mixed with the predictable anger at the Street's pernicious omnipotence was an even more chilling sense of its utter incompetence.

Laughter and mockery as much as righteous wrath and political reform virtually erased the Street from the forefront of public consciousness. How extraordinary, when one considers that throughout the country's history, the magnetism of Wall Street had attracted the most febrile emotions and the most strenuous intellectual labors, all grappling with the Street's relationship to the American experiment with democracy, opportunity, and equality. Yet from the outbreak of World War II until the presidency of Ronald Reagan, that lightening rod lost its charge. The Street retreated into cultural anonymity, still exercising immense economic weight and political influence, but no longer a source of public desire and anxiety. Forty years of silence are perhaps the most telling evidence of how indissolubly the Crash and the Depression were connected in the popular mind. From 1929, the sedimentary deposit of generations of cultural animosity descended on the Street, and it was buried alive.

Winston Churchill happened to be visiting the United States at the time of the Crash. He found himself on the floor of the New York Stock Exchange on one of its very worst days. Expecting pandemonium, he was taken aback by the slow-motion decorum that prevailed instead. Soon afterwards, however, the future British Prime Minister would witness a man leap to his death from a building near his own hotel.[3]

Reactions to the Crash ranged just this widely, from dazed somnambulism to terminal depression. Though suicides connected to the market's implosion were far fewer than people assumed, the fact that such an urban legend gained instant currency shows how distraught everybody was. F. Scott Fitzgerald converted the legend into a metaphor, noting that the Jazz Age had 'leapt to a spectacular death'.[4]

At first, fear mixed with a vertiginous disorientation. Shock was quickly cauterized with denial, both official and mass-delusional. It didn't take long for that to wear off. A Dow Jones average that had registered 381 in September 1929 plummeted to 41 by the beginning of 1932. An unemployment rate of 3.2 per cent swelled to 23.6 per cent. The share values incinerated on the exchange were twenty times the value of all cars manufactured and sold in 1929, five times the value of all farm and agricultural products. As weeks turned into months and years of the bitterest disappointment, fear, guilt, and denial gave way to more muscular emotions. Anger, thirst for revenge, camaraderie of the disinherited, and even on occasion a perverse sense of liberation formed a psychic united front that vastly overmatched Wall Street's dwindling reserves of cultural capital.[5]

A madness swept the Exchange on Thursday 24 October, and especially on that blackest of all Black Tuesdays, 29 October. The tidal wave of sell orders inundated the market. Neither men nor machines could keep up. Millions were lost simply because orders disappeared in the chaos, or were later found and registered far past the time when they could be executed at their original price. When United States Steel stock, the bluest of the blue chips, collapsed on Tuesday, brokers and speculators 'hollered and screamed, they clawed at one another's collars. It was like a bunch of crazy men.' Frantic rushing about soon enough gave way to bewilderment and exhaustion as $10 billion in share value was lost in a day. One reporter compared the swarms of shell-shocked ticker-tape watchers to 'fiends about the bedside of a stricken friend . . . There were no smiles. There were no tears either. Just the camaraderie of fellow-sufferers.'

As news spread, curious crowds pooled outside the Exchange, alarming enough to the powers that be that four hundred mounted police cordoned off the Exchange building. Ten thousand people formed an impenetrable mass from Broadway to the East River. Similar crowds collected throughout the city and at brokerages around the country. Newspapers voyeuristically reported a 'world series of finance' and relayed ghoulish rumors of window-jumpers, ambulances rushing to the floor of the Exchange, men weeping helplessly, praying, or kicking over ticker-tape machines in uncontrollable rage. Trinity Church was packed all day.

Bedlam even disturbed the Washington Square home of Edgar Speyer, a patrician German-Jewish banker with impeccable social credentials. There, amidst the rare Chinese paintings and porcelains, a red-faced butler burst into the dining room, to the astonishment of the assembled guests. There was uproar among the servants downstairs, the man explained, as they sat around their own ticker-tape in the kitchen watching their savings go up in smoke while their employer was 'calmly sitting upstairs eating pompano and saddle of lamb'. The master's attention was urgently required, and Speyer left his guests.

Everybody reacted characteristically. On 'Black Tuesday' Mayor Walker, chronically upbeat, proposed an antidote: instead of showing newsreels of the panic, 'I appeal to movie exhibitors to show pictures that will reinstate courage and hope in the hearts of the people.'[6] There was little chance of that, but right from the outset the mandarins of the Street put their moral authority on the line. Richard Whitney, Vice President of the New York Stock Exchange, was an old-money thoroughbred. From the top of his silver mane to the burnish of his Wetzel suit, he exuded self-assurance. He was the Harvard-educated son of a bank president and brother of a senior Morgan partner, George. His wife socialized with the Vanderbilts and Morgans. His father-in law was an ex-president of the Union League Club. Richard relaxed at the most recherché country clubs and spent weekends hunting foxes and raising champion Ayrshire cattle on his five-hundred-acre New Jersey estate. Immaculately coiffed, lean and graceful, Whitney personified the physical ideal of the WASP elite – and like most men of his ilk, he was at ease with his own power and accustomed to its efficacy.

It was this Richard Whitney, symbol of Wall Street's old guard, who walked onto the floor of the Exchange to quiet its clamor. In an act of studied theatricality, he made his way to the floor where US Steel was traded and boomed out a bid for 25,000 shares at $205, well above the last quoted price. His promenade then moved on to the posts for AT&T and other bell-wether stocks, where Whitney repeated the ritual, although at less inflated prices. This was designed to staunch the bleeding, and for a moment it did.

Whitney's excursion was made on behalf of the Street's Brahmin inner circle. Partners in the most prestigious houses like Morgan and Kuhn Loeb never ventured onto the floor themselves or held seats there; its atmosphere of hurly-burly huckstering was considered déclassé. But on 'Black Thursday' Thomas Lamont, the most senior Morgan partner, the house's ambassador to the peace conference at Versailles, convened a meeting at 'the Corner'. In a reprise of the elder Morgan's celebrated heroics during the 1907 panic, the Street's blue-ribbon banks and investment houses met in the second-floor board-room, appointed to resemble an English clubroom with its wood-burning fireplaces and tastefully worn easy chairs. Though they usually gathered in privacy, now these 'saviors' made their arrivals quite conspicuous, to enhance a mesmerized public's anticipation of relief and restoration. The bankers agreed to pony up a sizeable sum, about $25 million; a blood transfusion for the market, aimed at getting it off the critical list. Most of the money, though, was spent buoying up stock of companies like USS, Bethlehem Steel, and GM in which their institutions were already heavily invested. The temporary lift in market confidence allowed them quickly to sell out of dangerous positions, before it was too late.

The stagecraft of Whitney, who was treated like a matinee idol by the media, was reassuring, and his money was welcome. But like an opiate, its effect was short-lived. The very next day, the market resumed its downward plunge. Though it would rally again briefly, when the relentless decline resumed the bankers stayed silent.[7]

As time went on other titans of business and finance made similar rescue efforts, counting on their personal aura and once unimpeachable social prestige to turn things around. John D. Rockefeller himself let it be known that 'the fundamental conditions of the country are sound', and he and his son then proved their conviction with an ostentatious purchase of common stock. Eddie Cantor, everybody's favorite cynic, was quick to retort: 'Sure – who else has any money left?' There was something pathetic about these gestures: Thomas Lamont was observed making his softly modulated, chin-up reassurances as 'the pince-nez gently waved away ill-informed rumors of the disaster, moving to and fro in the dim light from the high windows heavily covered with anti-bomb steel netting.'

These were the fleeting days of false optimism – the song 'Happy Days Are Here Again' was copyrighted on 7 November 1929. A cartoon cheered everybody up with a picture of a car-full of 'high-powered' speculators crashing into a telephone pole, while the rest of the country, 'the people who are really going somewhere', drove safely away in a car full of 'salaries and wages'. Secretary Mellon pronounced the economy 'sound and prosperous'. And of course President Hoover, although trying to further the distance between himself and the Street's more notorious speculators, had little choice but to issue those prognostications about imminent prosperity which now seem so ridiculous and damning.[8]

None of this made any difference. Two months after the October debacle, restive crowds continued their disturbing vigil outside the Exchange. One eyewitness later recalled the sound they made: 'It wasn't an angry or hysterical sound. That was the most ominous thing about it. It was a kind of hopeless drone, a Greek dirge kind of thing. It was damned distracting, I must say.' Gloomy reports of business closings, insurance policies cashed in to cover margin loans, college plans foregone, and other signs of disaster filled the air. 'The stock market crash was to count for us', Edmund Wilson reported, referring to his fellow intellectuals, 'almost like a rending of the earth in preparation for the Day of Judgment'. Will Rogers delivered a comedic version of the same perception: 'The situation has been reached in New York hotels', the folk-hero humorist quipped, 'where the clerks ask incoming guests, "You wanna room for sleeping or for jumping?"' There were numerous smaller premonitions of disaster, too. Newspapers disconnected their electric clocks to save power; paper mills asked their employees to use wood shavings instead of paper when they visited the bathroom; Conrad Hilton decided to remove guest telephones and ordered his clerks to dole out hotel stationery by the sheet.

Idols of a profligate age crumbled. Wall Street's wise men no longer seemed so sagacious. New-era prophets morphed into failed rainmakers. All this could be frightening but also exhilarating, as Edmund Wilson recorded:

Yet to the writers and artists of my generation who had grown up in the Big Business era and had always resented its barbarism . . . these years were not depressing but stimulating. One couldn't help being exhilarated at the sudden and unexpected collapse of that stupid gigantic fraud. It gave us a new sense of freedom and it gave us a new sense of power to find ourselves still carrying on while the bankers, for a change, were taking a beating.

Though not everyone shared Wilson's high spirits, watching the bankers take a beating became a popular spectator sport.[9]

There were two distinct species of bankers who went to the wall. One was a new breed, risen to riches and public notoriety on the bubble. Brash and nervy, they were the latest incarnation of the Napoleonic confidence man. Then there were the aristocrats like Whitney, Lamont, and Morgan who scorned the market's latest crop of arrivistes. But as both breeds were brought low, it was discovered that they had intermarried; it had become nearly impossible to tell the cowboys from the cavaliers. Suddenly all those solemn 'morganisms' about 'trusteeship' and 'social responsibility' seemed like so much self-serving cant.

Ben Smith was born poor and grew up rowdy. He made pots of money as a lone speculator and pool operator in the 1920s, never hiding his contempt for Wall Street's patricians. When the Crash happened he made additional millions selling the market short. Such market savvy might have been applauded and emulated just months earlier. Now 'Sell-em Ben Smith' was pilloried for making like a vampire and went everywhere with two bodyguards in tow.[10]

Like Ben Smith, characters like Samuel Insull, Jesse Livermore, Ivar Kreuger, Michael Meehan, and others had come from nowhere and hogged the limelight in the 1920s. Livermore, like Smith, was a notorious bear – 'the man with the evil eye' – a practicing Calvinist and lecher who had been around since the War. Supremely vulgar – he called Wall Street a 'giant whore house', brokers 'pimps', and stocks 'whores' – he flaunted his yellow Rolls Royce, steel yacht, and huge pinky sapphire ring. When the Crash happened, he was tough-skinned enough to ignore his own public shaming – but not for ever. Reduced to penury by 1940, a two-time bankrupt, Livermore shot himself in the cloakroom of the Sherry-Netherlands Hotel. A rambling eight-page suicide note reiterated a stark judgment: 'My life was a failure.'

Other Wall Street *Wunderkinder* were perhaps not as ruthlessly bearish as Ben and Jesse, but their rise was as meteoric and their fall just as bottomless. Meehan, for example, was an Irish upstart, part of a gang that included Ben Smith and Joseph Kennedy, although the latter was already a generation removed from his grandfather's lowly beginnings. Meehan was a one-time theater-ticket broker who first made an impression securing aisle seats at Broadway hits for a white-shoe Wall Street clientele. Later he struck it rich running a pool in RCA, but remained excluded by the old-boy network. After the creation of the Securities and Exchange Commission, he faked insanity to avoid prosecution, but still ended up expelled from all the exchanges. After the Crash, he was shunned by everyone.[11]

Big Money, the third volume of John Dos Passos's modernist undressing of America's toxic financial world, was published in 1936 and contains a scathing portrait of Samuel Insull. The public-utility, traction and coal-company magnate spent the 1920s evangelizing his stock to his employees and the wider public, deploying the proceeds to create a network of holding companies and voting trusts that controlled about ten per cent of the nation's power output. Insull, a poor

British stenographer who worked his way into the inner sanctum of
Edison Electric as Thomas Edison's secretary, was king for a day. But
the vast pyramid of over-capitalized companies he'd put together
couldn't survive the Crash. One hundred thousand investors lost a billion dollars, at that time the grossest fleecing in American financial history. Charged with cooking the books, Insull fled in disgrace to
Canada to avoid prosecution. From there it was on to Europe, one
step ahead of the extradition proceedings. Finally he was hauled back
to the United States, where his trial became a public spectacle, his
career a cautionary tale for Dos Passos as well as the new President.
FDR cited the 'Insull Empire' as the most egregious example of bilking
the public through fraudulent finance, and Insull himself as a man
'whose hand is against every man's'. High-priced lawyers and publicity agents saved Insull from imprisonment, but a man accustomed to
wearing spats and a homburg hat died a few years later in a Paris sub-
way with eight francs in his pocket.[12]

Ivar Kreuger, 'the Match King' and a titan whose industrial empire
stretched across the globe, was the idol of Sweden and the financial
savior of a brace of Central European nations in the 1920s. One country after another granted him a match monopoly in return for life-
preserving loans. Kreuger and Toll securities traded everywhere. After
the deluge however, it emerged that the Kreuger kingdom had rested
on fraud and deceit not detected by his negligent investment bankers.
Ivar Kreuger committed suicide in Paris in 1932: his rise and fall
stunned those who thought they'd seen everything when Charles Ponzi
absconded to Italy.[13]

The fate of such men – who, starting with next to nothing, were
borne aloft on a cloud of paper wealth and public adulation – became
more than an object lesson in greed and hubris: they were the living
refutation of 'new era' hype, of Raskob's 'Everybody Ought to be
Rich' fairy-tale, of Wall Street as the yellow brick road to fortune. It
had been heartening, inspirational even, that unvarnished people like
these could rise so far in the face of old-guard hostility. The fact that a
good many turned out to be confidence men or worse was a disillusionment from which the notion of a people's Wall Street would take
a long time to recover.

It was as if the whole country awoke from a delirium, a decade-long
infatuation with Herman Melville's confidence man. Writers from the

left, right, and center took note. An editor at the *Baltimore Sun* confirmed that the middle class's idolization of the great men of business was finished; Pare Lorentz, whose documentary film-making became a vital part of the Depression era's populist aesthetic, declared that 'the great American game of starting over from scratch is definitely over.' John Dewey, philosopher and political activist, wrote about 'The Collapse of the Romance', charting the demise of the faith that gambling unleashed human energies and led to economic good times. It had all rested on an act of 'confidence', and the confidence was gone. Conservative economist Virgil Jordan pronounced that 'the sacred bull is dead'. That 'potent symbol of the economic millennium', which, according to Jordan, had replaced the eagle as the nation's favorite emblem, had now betrayed a once worshipful citizenry. While 'the high priests of the speculative synagogue' might not admit the bull's de-horning, everyone else knew it to be an imposter. No country and economy so anchored in scientific methods and sustained effort could give itself over to 'vast speculative adventures' without reaping the whirlwind.[14]

Now the era of such mass psychic maladjustment was over with – at least for the time being. Confessionals by one-time 'trusted agents' of the Street, chastened and seeking redemption, spiced their memoirs with talk of 'ballyhoo brokers', 'oily promoters', 'financial follies', 'reaping the whirlwind', 'a new race of speculators', and 'bandit bankers'. All of American society had been turned into a 'madhouse' – a favorite metaphor – where confidence men preyed on that native American instinct to risk everything in a rush of optimism. The Crash and Depression were a kind of shock therapy.[15]

The victims had always been partly blamed, or at least made accomplices before the fact, alongside the indictment of the Wall Street confidence man. Jacksonian America, for example, was preoccupied with its own fathomless credulousness and failure to resist speculative phantasms. The urban middle classes were particularly vulnerable to this sort of mea culpa, as they felt embarrassed by their own naive frivolity during the Jazz Age. Herbert Hoover, of course, had his own reasons for scapegoating Everyman. In hindsight, he claimed to have done all that was humanly possible to discourage speculative excess, but 'when the public becomes mad with greed and is rubbing the Aladdin's lamp of sudden fortune, no little matter of interest rates is effective.'

There was also a kind of we-told-you-so scolding by those who'd been revolted by the babbitry and stock-market idolatry of the 1920s. Social activist writers like Gilbert Seldes, Anna Louise Strong, and Sherwood Anderson had their way with avaricious businessmen, but also believed the economy had foundered on an all-American greediness – 'America is being caught up,' declaimed a self-righteous Anderson. Seldes wrote about the depression as a chastening for collective sins in *The Years of the Locust*. Left-wing political philosopher James Rorty looked back at the roaring twenties as if they were a social hallucination, a 'flight from reality' by an infatuated society. Even the Communist left in the early 1930s threw brick-bats at 'the people', the very same anonymous mass it would soon revere. *The New Masses* dripped scorn on 'cockroach capitalists' who'd fancied themselves big money men: 'Every barber was dabbling in Wall Street. Every street cleaner expanded his chest proudly as he maneuvered his horse droppings into a can. Wasn't he a partner with Morgan and Rockefeller in American prosperity?'

In *The Crisis of the Middle Class*, Lewis Corey argued that because the middle class had grown drunk on the 'heady wine of speculative profits' and indulged a reverie about a new social order of universal middle-class affluence, it was woefully unprepared for what befell it. A dangerous mood of 'enraged bewilderment and despair' gripped it instead. Ideologically disarmed, having become loyal subordinates in the corporations' bureaucratic hierarchy, the new salaritariat especially found itself adrift. Sensitive to the way the depression had stirred up primitive political emotions among the ravaged middle classes in Europe, Corey worried about something similar happening in the United States. Wall Street's unconsummated flirtation with people's capitalism not only discredited the Street and its clairvoyant confidence men; it left a residue of disappointment and rage.[16]

Ridicule and shame, however, were the more common reactions to the death of Wall Street's democratic mystique. Black humor and a spirit of iconoclasm – only occasionally carrying a political charge – served to flush out all the indigestible toxins of an over-indulged Jazz Age. There were no end of jokes: like the one about the oil promoter who can't get through the pearly gates because the quota on oil promoters is all filled up, so he announces the discovery of oil on Jupiter; all the speculators rush out of heaven to cash in, and even the original rumor-monger gives up his chance for eternal salvation, exclaiming 'There may be some truth in that report.' Will Rogers and Eddie

Cantor let loose a stream of quips inspired by the Crash: 'There's a proverb on Wall Street,' Rogers advised, 'What goes up must have been sent up by somebody.' Cantor told audiences, 'My uncle died in September. Poor fellow. He had diabetes at 45. That's nothing. I had Chrysler at 110.' Suicide jokes made for painfully funny cartoons, like one showing two Wall Streeters leaping hand in hand, captioned 'The speculators who had a joint account'; or the one called 'Club Life in America', in which a butler races about with a serving tray carrying guns, ropes, poison, and other implements of self-destruction, while top-hatted bankrupts prepare to commit various forms of hara-kiri next to an open window with a sign instructing the members 'to close the window after them'. In *The People vs. Wall Street*, a mock trial composed by a left-wing satirist, the Street is charged with criminal lunacy. Duke Ellington, who'd lost almost everything in the market, kept his spirits and those of his fans up with a rather rousing and light-hearted *Wall Street Wail*.

Little Orphan Annie, Harold Gray's otherwise quite conservative and capitalist-minded comic strip, mixed mockery with revenge. Daddy Warbucks spent a good part of 1931 as a financial lone ranger plotting successfully to do in 'Shark and his crowd', a miserable bunch of speculators, and later on his old nemesis, the aptly named 'Bullion' – himself a mere flunky, as Daddy tells Annie, for the 'big boy, J. J. Shark'. In Annie's grim and menacing world, full of lowering skies, even the tuxedoed Warbucks, not shy about his own outsized financial appetite and with no liking for the New Deal, could nevertheless be pressed into service against market tricksters and short-sellers. After all, the Crash had had its way with Daddy too: 'over-production' and 'poor collections' had driven him into bankruptcy, leaving him house-less, carless, and yachtless.'[17]

Movie melodramas in the early years of the Depression sentenced financial mountebanks either to an early grave or heartfelt repentance. Forgettable films like *Clancy in Wall Street* and *Big Executive* featured the Crash as the just deserts of avaricious upstarts. The truly absurd *Toast of New York* starred Carey Grant as 'Jubilee Jim Fisk' in a biopic so filled with historical silliness it even had Jim assassinated by an outraged stockholder rather than the lover of his ex-mistress. However, the film amply illustrated Hollywood's near universal skep-ticism of anyone associated with the stock market.[18]

Dos Passos's *The Big Money* included a scathing portrayal of a hotshot aviation-stock promoter, bubbling over with inside information but otherwise utterly ignorant of anything about the manufacture or flying of airplanes. But Nat Benton's sedulously applied hype does its insidious work, causing Charlie Anderson – one of the novel's little anti-heroes – to lose his unsophisticated love of machines and inventions, becoming instead an addict of the 'big money' dream. Charlie is left dead by the side of the road, a drunken fatality of a car crash in Miami – lying there like a deadly premonition of the road ahead, he represents a whole universe of little people, clerks and shop girls, whose lives are destroyed by the stock market.[19]

Ever since nineteenth-century newspapers started running sentimental sketches of ruined speculators expiring next to empty liquor bottles, weeping widows at their bedside, Wall Street had been linked to inebriation. For many writers, addiction to the speak-easy and to the stock market was essentially the same thing. Addiction is at the core of *Babylon Revisited*, F. Scott Fitzgerald's post-mortem of the Crash. For the protagonist, the whole decade was one long drunken spree. Stocks functioned like booze, lubricating childish daydreams about eternal good times, anaesthetizing any sense of responsibility, fostering careless and criminal negligence. The end seems preordained: after the Crash the story's sad and ruined hero crashes himself. Wallowing in narcissistic despair and an alcoholic daze, he is just like Charlie Anderson – except that this time it's his wife who lies dead by the side of the road, leaving behind a terminally guilt-ridden husband and an estranged daughter, victim of an era's fatal recklessness.[20]

While the Crash and the Depression killed off the confidence man and his numerous accomplices, the death toll was far greater than that. As one disaster followed another, it was revealed that for every free-booting Jesse Livermore or Ivar Kreuger there was a pillar of financial rectitude up to his eyebrows in the same sort of immoral or felonious behavior. And this presented a far more lethal threat.

In 1933, Edmund Wilson wrote an acidly humorous portrait of a one-time Wall Street legend called 'Sunshine Charlie'. The butt of its joke was Charles Mitchell. Charlie appeared out of nowhere, much like Mike Meehan or Ben Smith. Like Meehan or Charles Ponzi, he was a born pitchman: Wilson compared him to a high-pressure Fuller Brush salesman. But there was one big difference. Charles Mitchell was no freelancing financial privateer, but the president of National City

Bank, the nation's largest. He was the mastermind of the bank's head-first plunge into the mass marketing of Wall Street during the 1920s. It was Charlie, 'that genius of the new economic era', who set up the bank's sixty-nine district sales offices and thousands of local branches, toggled together by 11,386 miles of wire stretching from coast to coast. It was Charlie who established National City's investment banking affiliate, National City Company, to underwrite and market securities. It was Charlie who, according to Wilson, bullied, bribed, and inspired his four-hundred-odd clerks and brokers to pitch securities, especially National City Bank stock, 'like groceries' of dubious quality.

In the aftermath of the Crash, word leaked out that it was also Charlie, that 'banker of bankers', who had played fast and loose with the commercial bank's depositors' funds, investing them in the wobbly stocks and bonds the investment affiliate was busy hawking. It was Charlie who skirted the law prohibiting a commercial bank from trading in its own stock by having its investment affiliate dispose of two million shares. It was Charlie (among others) who employed his salesman's guile to hawk the insupportable loans of the Brazilian state of Minas Gereasi and the 'Peruvian bonds' of a government his own bank privately considered 'an adverse moral and political risk'. It was 'Sunshine Charlie' who'd speculated in the stock of his own bank. And finally, it was Charlie who'd concocted an elaborate transfer of stock to his wife at a fire-sale price to escape the taxman. In court, the man who had once inspired awe looked 'cheap' and his sangfroid evaporated on the witness stand: his ruddy face, his high stiff collar, blue serge suit, and white breast-pocket handkerchief were all that was left of 'those millennial boasts of the bankers, the round-eyed hopes of the public.' Charged with income-tax evasion, Mitchell eluded the law, but his reputation was forever muddied. [21]

After the financial and corporate frauds at the start of the twenty-first century, we are no longer quite as shocked to learn that the officers of major banks and investment houses are inclined towards larceny. The aura of rectitude which surrounded such men in this earlier era, however, made the transgressions of 'Sunshine Charlie' more profoundly disillusioning. Mitchell seemed like a grotesque inversion of those conventional bankerly attributes of propriety, prudence, and restraint. Yet Charlie couldn't be dismissed as a freak of nature, since as it turned out he was hardly alone.

Albert Wiggins, the head of Chase National Bank, had been as eager as Mitchell to have his bank chase after alluring speculations. Like National City, Chase formed its own investment adjunct, the Chase Securities Corporation, with scant regard for the 'Chinese wall' that many assumed separated the commercial bank's inherent prudence from the far riskier undertakings of its investment twin. By birth and breeding, Wiggins came not much closer than Charlie to that white-shoe image of disinterested trusteeship. But he served on the board of directors of fifty-nine corporations and on the executive committee of the Federal Reserve Bank of New York. These credentials were a masquerade, however. Wiggins, everybody now learned, had actually sold his own bank's stock short, using money loaned to him by that same bank, profiting from his insider's knowledge of its calamitous position, while issuing public assurances to the contrary. Bank officers who had to approve these transactions were themselves heavily in debt to Wiggins in pursuit of their own speculations. The resemblance to our very recent past is of course striking. Then, however, the legal ambiguity surrounding insider trading meant that Wiggins had to deal only with his public humiliation, not the district attorney. And the humiliation he handled well, insisting that 'I think the market was a "God-given" market,' unruffled by his interlocutor's rejoinder: 'Are you sure of the source?'[22]

Again and again, Wall Street's old guard, which had a well-developed disdain for the likes of Joseph Kennedy and Ben Smith, found itself linked with such unsavory types, and singled out for censure in congressional hearings and in the tabloid accounts of the more sensational findings. Partners of the Goldman Sachs Trading Corporation allegedly accepted huge fees for touting securities that left their customers pockets' emptied. Halsey Stuart fed their clients a steady diet of Insull stock without telling them the firm was deeply invested in the utility king's properties and that several Halsey Stuart principals sat on the boards of directors of Insull companies. The redoubtable firm of Dillon, Read engaged in similar misalliances. The lines separating the two Wall Streets had grown hopelessly fuzzy.

Jack Morgan and his partners had paid no income tax in 1931 and 1932, the public learned. Lists of dignitaries who'd received preferential invitations from the Morgan bank to buy new offerings at way below market price were published in the daily press, along with confidential thank-you notes from the likes of John Jacob Raskob,

Democratic Party chieftain, conveying his hope that 'the future holds opportunities for me to reciprocate.' The most notorious of these insider deals involved the Allegheny Corporation, a giant railroad-holding company put together by the Van Sweringen brothers from Cleveland, the sort of shady pool operators white-shoe Wall Street was supposed to spurn.

Otto Kahn, scion of the great banking dynasty of Kuhn Loeb – a patron of the arts, sponsor of the Provincetown Players, the Metropolitan Opera, the Ballets Russes, and Arturo Toscanini ('I must atone for my wealth,' he explained) – was no more public-spirited when it came to squirreling away cash. Although now full of regrets, he'd been blind to the dangers of mixing everyday commerce with speculative adventuring. Dapper and cosmopolitan-looking with his handlebar mustache, the elderly Kahn confessed that 'a great deal must be changed', but failed to mention he'd paid no income tax since the Crash. Nor was he forthcoming with information about how the partners pocketed millions, dealing privately in the stock of a railroad-holding company while the investing public suffered losses of over $100 million. 'We were all sinners,' Kahn admitted.

Even if they weren't sinners they'd become untouchables. In 1933, FDR confided to his old friend and Morgan partner, Russell Leffingwell, that as President-elect, he couldn't consider him for the post of Assistant Secretary of the Treasury because 'We simply can't tie up with No. 23' – an address familiar as the House of Morgan.[23]

Richard Whitney's story took a bit longer to unravel, because it was shrouded in criminal secrecy. Whitney spent the first half of the Depression decade denouncing every effort of the New Deal administration to reform the New York Stock Exchange. As its President, he pronounced the purity of the ancien regime, dismissing every accusation about its malfeasance with an aristocratic éclat. Inside the Exchange, more and more people knew something different. Whitney had for years been on a long downward slide, greased by failed speculations. He was overextended, his condition ever more desperate as his debts mounted, to his brother George among others. As he wore out his welcome and his last available lines of credit dried up, Whitney resorted to embezzlement and fraud to keep himself afloat. He even used his position as treasurer to misappropriate funds from the New York Yacht Club, a favorite Brahmin hang-out, and from the Stock Exchange's own gratuity fund. That he managed to keep it hidden for

as long as he did is evidence of his own ingenuity and the aura of invi-
olability that still clung to old money. He was eventually discovered,
tried, and convicted of embezzlement. FDR embodied the nation's
sense of shock, repeating over and over again, 'Not Dick Whitney.'
Richard Whitney went off to Sing Sing dressed in his somber black
coat and bowler hat. There his former Groton headmaster, the
redoubtable Endicott Peabody, visited him and asked if there was anything he needed. 'A left-handed first baseman's mitt,' Whitney replied,
the grace and bonhomie he'd imbibed at school still intact.[24]

White-shoe Wall Street suddenly seemed no better than a gang of common criminals, skimmers, double-dealers, and confidence men,
stripped of every last vestige of moral authority and heroism to which
they had once laid claim. A veritable cottage industry grew up, devoted to the unmasking of those who had been glorified during the war
and the Jazz Age. Gustavus Myers' *History of Great American
Fortunes* – a doggedly detailed accounting of ill-begotten wealth in the
Age of Morgan, first published in 1907 and long since out of print –
was reissued as a Modern Library classic, to greater acclaim than the
original edition. Matthew Josephson, who worked for a brokerage
after returning from Paris, published his classic dissection of *The
Robber Barons*. Although these were the industrialists and financiers
who lorded it over the Gilded Age, their peculations, arrogance, and
callous abuse of democracy brought their present-day equivalents into
everyone's minds, and the book went on to become a bestseller and a
Book-of-the-Month Club selection. A series of debunking biographies,
including Lewis Corey's *The House of Morgan* and Harvey O'Connor's
Mellon's Millions, delighted in dressing down their subjects.

Ferdinand Lundberg's *America's Sixty Families* was less personal in
approach, as it attempted to penetrate the force-field of power emanating from the country's great dynastic groupings. The author called
the Morgans 'American Bourbons', and compared the Rockefellers to
the Hapsburgs, the Mellons to the Hohenzollerns, and the DuPonts to
the Romanovs. The book did nothing to enhance the heroic reputation
of the financiers it depicted as utterly self-serving and corrupt. They
were worse than the robber-baron generation that preceded them:
those men had at least accomplished great feats of construction, but
their heirs were 'common burglars' who left behind only a 'complicat-
ed tangle of worthless hierarchically graded stocks and bonds.'

According to Lundberg's widely quoted account, they'd become 'a psychopathic class' whose gross self-indulgence made the plutocracy of the Gilded Age seem ascetic by comparison. Lundberg relished the absurd details: private islands and fleets of automobiles and airplanes, jade-encrusted toilets, a wedding where five thousand chrysanthemums were dyed bluish-pink at a cost of $2000 to match the icing on the three-hundred-pound wedding cake, a dinner where the ballroom was transformed into a replica of Belmont Race Track with prize horses performing for the guests – all this during the misery of the Depression.[25]

If such exposés emphasised the extravagance of Wall Street, popular culture brought out its hapless, comic air of incompetence. A movie called *Bottoms Up* spoofed the topsy-turvy world left behind by the Crash; houses, lampposts, streets, and people listed at a forty-five-degree angle as if suffering a hangover from a tornado, while stocks were peddled in open-air fruit stands for fifty cents a piece. Bankers themselves, however, hardly showed up as dramatis personae in the performing arts of the thirties. This may suggest not just that they were held in low regard (which of course they were), but that they ceased to be regarded at all. Their absence from the movies probably also owed something to the industry's self-censorship through the Hays office, whose business it was to keep dangerous sexual, political, and social issues off the screen, where they might cause damage to the industry. Wall Street's heavy hand was also a presence in Hollywood: the major studios relied on the big banks for money, and the bankers in turn took an interest in which films got made and which didn't. Nonetheless, on the rare occasions when bankers did appear on stage or screen, they tended to be overweight anti-heroes.

The mogul in Frank Capra's *Meet John Doe* is a sinister Machiavellian with fascist inclinations. Played by Edward Arnold, whom Capra felt had 'the power and the presence of a J. P. Morgan', the character is exquisitely unctuous, yet cruel and frigid. Capra, perhaps the era's best known 'sentimental populist', never forgot his boyhood resentment for 'big fat businessmen, wearing big fat coats, big fat necks overflowing tight white collars, entering big fat limousines'. Obesity had at one time served as the fleshy incarnation of bankers' power. Now, the Depression era's populist aesthetic entombed these moguls in rolls of baby fat, which rendered them less menacing and rather toothless.

The era's socially conscious art – the drawings and cartoons of William Gropper, the classic documentaries of Frontier Films (*Native Land*, *The Plough That Broke The Plains*), the Hollywood melodramas of Capra and Welles, King Vidor's agrarian fable, *Our Daily Bread*, the rousing folk music of the labor movement – relied on a symbolic vocabulary that elicited a predictable hiss at the sight of a Morgan or Mellon-like visage. This was an aesthetic that presumed the guilty presence of a financier: the black magician of national disaster, the despoiler of 'the people'.

Panic: A Play in Verse by the poet Archibald MacLeish was a piece of experimental, agit-prop expressionist theater that had a brief run at the Phoenix Theater and starred Orson Welles. McGafferty, the play's central figure, is a ferocious young banker, the biggest in the land, seemingly fearless, a kind of Brechtian ogre. But while he fancies himself a gothic *Übermensch*, a capitalist hero accustomed to cowing the masses, he reacts to the Crash first with sententious bluster and then with psychopathic hysteria. Convinced the shadows of doom he once dismissed as phantoms are real, he cracks up:

> Yes, You think they're shadows!
> You think this creeping ruin is a shadow!
> You think it's chance the banks go one by one
> Closing the veins as cold does – killing secretly
> Freezing the heart – ruin follows ruin . . .
> Chance that does it? You think! So did I
> I do not think so now. I think they wish it.
> We cannot see them, but they're there: they loom
> Behind the seen side like the wind in curtains

Lost in the bleakest paranoia, McGafferty kills himself.[26]

Back in the real world, the man once heralded as the greatest Secretary of the Treasury since Alexander Hamilton, a modern wizard, was now treated like an aging nincompoop. Mellon had earned this derision with remarks like 'I see nothing in the present situation that is either menacing or warrants pessimism,' delivered as New Year's balm in 1930. For a while he was a prime scapegoat, investigated for conflicts of interest and threatened with impeachment until mercifully farmed off by Hoover to a British ambassadorship. Meanwhile, on his radio show, Will Rogers observed that it was not 'the working classes that brought on the economic crisis, it was the big boys that thought the financial drunk was going to last forever . . . Why is it alright for these Wall Street boys to bet millions and make that bet affect the fellow plowing a field in Clakemore, Oklahoma . . .' In his sketch of 'Sunshine Charlie', Edmund Wilson drew an unflattering caricature of the whole species of defrocked bankers then being publicly undressed: 'Enormous, with no necks, they give the impression of hooked helpless frogs, or of fat bass or loggy groupers hauled suddenly out the water and landed on the witness stand gasping.' No one was more deliberately ridiculed than Jack Morgan himself.

Morgan arrived in Washington one June day in 1933 to testify before the Senate Banking and Currency Committee. Just as he was settling in, two publicists plopped onto his lap Miss Lya Graf, a twenty-seven-inch German midget, a plumpish, pretty young woman in a doll-like peasant costume from the Ringling Brothers, Barnum and Bailey Circus. Photographs of the avuncular, bushy-eyebrowed, white-mustached banker with Miss Graf perched beatifically on his knees circled the globe. It was a minor moment of transformation in popular culture: the archetypal villainous banker suddenly appeared as a doddering old fogey. People would never entirely lose their belief in the old guard's wickedness. But the Crash – because it was identified as the old guard's Crash – left them looking silly and pathetic. (Miss Graf, incidentally was half Jewish: she was killed at Auschwitz, bearing the double curse of Jewishness and a status as a 'useless person', thanks to her size.)[27]

The House of Morgan had been the emblem of Wall Street's sobriety, wisdom, and statesmanship for two generations. When Lya Graf cozied up on Jack's lap, the aura evaporated in a flash of laughter: the solemnity and reclusiveness of the Morgan bank, and the half-dozen or so others like it, were gone for ever. Clarence Dillon, for example, a man of studious aloofness who had turned the drowsy house of William Read and Company into a major player in the Latin American 'junk bond' market, found himself lampooned, *Alice in Wonderland* style:

> How cheerfully he seems to grin,
> How neatly spreads his claws,
> And welcomes little fishes in
> With gently smiling jaws.

Dinner at Eight, a popular movie featuring Lionel and John

Barrymore, captured the despair, self-destruction, and hapless scheming which infected the post-Crash aristocracy. The film's financier is
simultaneously brutish and fawning, merciless and deceptive. He
swoops down, vampire-like, into a dinner party that includes a failing
shipping tycoon, his bird-brain social-butterfly wife, an alcoholic has-
been silent-film star, and an aging grand dame of the intercontinental
celebrity set. All of them have fallen on hard times, and the financier
seeks to profit from their plight and win an entree into society for his
foul-mouthed trophy wife. An air of doom hangs over the party's nervous gaiety – this is a world nearing its end.

Sometimes that world, lost in self-regard, made unintentional fun of
itself. Morgan lectured reporters, after yet another congressional
investigation, that 'If you destroy the leisure class, you destroy civilization. By the leisure class I mean families who employ one servant,
twenty-five million or thirty million families.' Commentators raced to
their typewriters and microphones to report Morgan's bizarre view of
the nation's domestic life, pointing out that the 1930 census counted
fewer than thirty million families in the whole country, and sadly,
fewer than two million cooks and servants to tend to them.

A satirical painting by Jack Levine, called the *Feast of Pure Reason*,
reduced the stubby-fingered banker, the oily politician, and the cop on
the take to diminutive figures conniving furtively in the shadows, their
capacity for inflicting serious harm severely constricted by the claustrophobic space the painting allots them. *The Daily Worker*, not
renowned for its sense of humor, began running a comic strip, 'Little
Lefty' (a riposte to *Little Orphan Annie* and Daddy's anti-New Deal
jibes) which made fun of the tattered remains of the old guard's laissez-faire faith. Nathaniel West's novella, *A Cool Million: On the
Dismantling of Lemuel Pitkin*, was a parody of America's cherished
Horatio Alger myth. Poor Lemuel, out to make his fortune and save
his widowed mother from the clutches of a carnivorous banker, is
gulled, imprisoned, and physically brutalized by the guardians of the
moral and social order as well as their con-artist soulmates. Set in
Vermont, the central villain is an ex-President, Shagpoke Whipple (an
unmistakable portrait of Calvin Coolidge) who has become a banker.
When his bank fails, he rants like a madman about an international
conspiracy of Jewish financiers and Reds. Whipple overflows with
homilies about self-reliance and hard work, but sweats cupidity from
every pore, and becomes the prisoner of his own paranoia when he

forms a ragtag citizens' militia – 'the leather shirts' – to take on the cabal of Jewish bankers and Bolsheviks.[28]

A global meltdown of finance capitalism naturally enough bred this image of ruling-class decrepitude and demoralization. Wall Street was perceived as the centerpiece of an international ancien regime gone to rack and ruin, its leading lights hanging on to what they could, dispossessed of self-confidence and social pre-eminence. Christina Stead's *House of All Nations* borrowed its title from a famous whorehouse in Paris. In her novel, it's a brokerage house, run by a circle of Parisian speculators and cynical servitors in the years right after the Crash. Their clientele consists of rootless European aristocrats and American plutocrats in search of safe havens for their liquid wealth, 'the same crowd you'll see at Biarritz and at Deauville and at Le Touquet . . . the International Upper Ten Thousand'. There are coupon clippers and tax evaders, a 'few old Spanish hogs', Hollywood 'sky-rockets', 'Eton playboys', and a 'few Theosophist bankers' – a thoroughly contemptible and pitiable lot. The house managers know that it takes boot-licking and flattery to lure this crowd: one needs to 'serve their vices'. Once considered seers and lions, these financiers are now only 'great mythomaniacs . . . their explanations and superstitions are those of primitive men.' The atmosphere at the *House of All Nations* becomes one of precariousness and sophisticated fatalism. Here all the national branches of the ancien regime have gathered as their world nears exhaustion, bound together for one last feed before the lights go out. After all, as one of the House's nihilist operators coolly muses, 'Life went on under Attila, went on in the Dark Ages. These will be the ages of night looking back from the days to come, but we're alive; we can't go dead dog . . . this is the time to move in.'[29]

There was a dawning realization that the ruling class was unfit to rule. Archibald MacLeish published an open letter to 'The Young Men of Wall Street', informing them that 'only the credulous hope for anything further from the generation now in control . . . of American capitalism.' That generation had accepted power 'but refused to govern'. The journalist Heywood Broun remarked that 'the only thing our great financial institutions overlooked during the years of boom was the installation of a roulette wheel for the convenience of depositors.' Even before the debacle Walter Lippman had decried the woeful state of the American leadership class, a class educated for success but not 'to exercise power', living from day to day, governing in impromptu fashion if at all. They were obeyed, but had no true authority.[30]

This is what made the Great Depression one of the two great turning points in American history: not the misery alone, but the conviction that the nation's bankruptcy was also the bankruptcy of an elite – of its beliefs, traditions, and sense of entitlement. Every nightclub punchline and lampooning cartoon, each literary satire and iconoclastic biography, every cinematic exposé and editorial jeremiad whittled away the puissance of the old ruling class. Wall Street's chances of holding its own against the onslaught of the New Deal were fatally compromised by these works of cultural subversion. A ruling elite might survive a reputation for imperial aloofness; indeed, under the right circumstances disinterested cruelty might even enhance a sense of its impregnability and social superiority. What was harder to weather was the popular conviction that the ancien regime was foolish, frail, and inept – like a big bad wolf of whom no one is any longer afraid.

13

Evicted from the Temple

Adolph Berle, Columbia University professor and original member of FDR's 'brains trust', received an odd communiqué from Richard Whitney early in 1934. Ever since the Crash, Whitney had served as the Exchange's principal public defender, fending off threatened legislative intrusions from the outside while resisting attempts from within the Exchange to reform the way Wall Street conducted its business. Whitney relied mainly on his ancestral sangfroid to see him through, but he was not entirely deficient in the new arts of public relations. So he invited Berle to serve on an advisory board whose ostensible purpose was to help the New York Stock Exchange get its house in order. Berle seemed a savvy choice. He was a charter member of the New Deal, so his presence would prove the Street's openness to serious reform. He also had considerable experience as a Wall Street lawyer, and so, Whitney anticipated, was apt to sympathize with the practical realities of money-making on the Street.

Berle accepted Whitney's invitation, as FDR encouraged him to do. But the President also cautioned his adviser that

> The fundamental trouble with this whole stock exchange crowd is their complete lack of elementary education. I do not mean lack of college diplomas, etc., but just inability to understand the country or public or their obligations to their fellow men. Perhaps you can help them acquire a kindergarten knowledge of these subjects. More power to you.[1]

Power was indeed the issue. FDR was prepared to wield it against the upper-crust milieu from which he sprang. His patrician relative Teddy had done this before him, as had Woodrow Wilson, a Southern gentleman of impeccable breeding if not great wealth; all Presidents whose 'elementary education' did indeed ready them to 'understand . . . their obligations to their fellow men.' In Britain, this form of upper-class political defection had already acquired a name: 'Tory Socialism'. In the United States it never assumed the same programmatic or institutional coherence: it was far more personalized. Nonetheless, this willingness to bump heads with the rich and powerful signaled fateful divisions within the country's most powerful elites. And it was an astonishing spectacle. After all, Richard Whitney and FDR both went to Groton, where Endicott Peabody raised them to honor a code of public service, to recognize that their privilege carried with it a call to duty. FDR was less imperious in his disdain for the selfishly wealthy than TR, less righteous than Wilson. Despite his native geniality, however, and when circumstances forced the issue, he knew his classmates to be woefully untutored about their public obligations. In the eyes of his peers, he committed an act of unforgivable betrayal: 'that man in the White House' was insane, a closet Jew, a drunk, a syphilitic, a 'foul' communist, and so on. The extreme nature of the insults was an index of Wall Street's exile.

It is arguable that the New Deal order, which would determine the shape of American political life for the next half century, filled the power vacuum created by the default of Wall Street. It wasn't Wall Street's demise alone, of course. The upper reaches of corporate America more generally came to feel the heavy hand of the New Deal regulatory state. But the Street was singled out for special attention, especially in the formative years of reform.

Venturing into the unknown during a breakdown as devastating as the Great Depression was bound to produce great anxiety. It is hardly uncommon for reforming or even revolutionary movements to borrow from the past, in order to shore up the courage to move ahead. Writers and artists like Disney, Dos Passos, and Capra drew on reassuring images of an older America, a society of republican virtues, as ballast for their iconoclasm, and a similar restorationist atmosphere inspired the work of political reform. Phantoms of populist financial octopi, progressive money trusts, and Jewish financial conspiracies hovered over the rallies and congressional hearings, the legislative deliberations and extra-legal mass actions that supplied the decade's political energy. Some of this spent itself picking apart the ethical failings of individuals. Mostly, however, it arraigned 'the system' for crimes and misdemeanors of long standing. Every denunciation of the Street resonated with the voices of Jefferson and Jackson, Bryan and Brandeis, TR and Debs, a chorus that overwhelmed every effort of the old regime to defend itself.

Farmers, who by and large had remained fairly quiescent since the Populist conflagration burned itself out, took to the fields and roads in shocking displays of lawlessness. Even in the halcyon days of the 'New Era', rural America had remained an outpost of opposition, its congressmen still invoking the specter of the old populist 'devilfish'. Now, in the brutal winter of 1933, agrarian rebels across the corn belt banded together to forcibly prevent evictions of fellow farmers. While the immediate objects of their wrath were local bankers foreclosing on unpaid mortgages, the Farm Holiday Association kept a larger prey in sight. Its leaders used language that would have been entirely familiar to populist champions like Tom Watson and General Weaver. According to Milo Reno, president of the association, the real culprit for agrarian misery was the system of usury run out of Wall Street. It would take a wholesale house-cleaning in Washington, Reno concluded, to 'break the grip of Wall Street and international bankers on our government'. Perhaps so, but in the immediate aftermath of the anti-foreclosure uprising, four major New York insurance companies holding hundreds of millions of dollars in mortgages in Iowa alone were compelled to suspend foreclosures, and the states of Iowa, Nebraska, Minnesota, among others, declared moratoria or extensions on overdue mortgage payments.[2]

For generations, ever since the Jeffersonians had tried to rid the country of a usurping 'moneyed aristocracy', Wall Street's alleged control over the sources of credit had inflamed farmers and other small producers who found themselves overrun by debt. Wall Street's usury was a sin against hard work and honest effort, against America's egalitarian promise, and against nature, in so far as farmers fancied themselves the earth's midwives. Trapped in appalling poverty, living under the daily threat of dispossession, vast stretches of the agricultural Midwest and Great Plains, which had been reliable Republican territory for years, went over to the Democrats during the New Deal heyday.

Of course, that was in part thanks to vital acts of legislative relief and reform like the Agricultural Adjustment Act and the Tennessee Valley

Authority. But it was also caused by the wholesale discrediting of the Republican Party by association with Wall Street. A farmers' manifesto renounced force except as a last resort, but warned that 'We are free men and refuse to become the serfs and slaves of the usurer and the money king.' Lester Barlow, a tempestuous and erratic stump orator from the farmers' movement – he'd fought for Pancho Villa in 1914, then invented depth bombs for the Navy in World War I, and later voted for FDR in 1932 – wrote a book called *What Would Lincoln Do?* In it Barlow recommended compulsory labor for financial parasites and the founding of something he called the 'Modern 76'ers'. That organization would function as a parallel government, issue its own temporary currency, '76'er script', and organize a national citizens' militia to run the country. Here one recognizes not only an ancient Jeffersonian suspicion of 'high finance', but also a hint of fascistic alienation from democratic politics. While the farmers' movement had plenty of orthodox left-wingers, including a Communist Party contingent that sought to ally the unemployed with the rural poor 'against finance capital in actual struggle', it also had its share of Barlow types who felt instead an affinity for leaders like Huey Long.[3]

Demagogues like Huey Long and Father Coughlin, the 'radio priest', mobilized impassioned followers with images of fat-cat parasites, gold-obsessed Eastern bankers, and usurious Wall Street Jews. Long's 'Share-the-Wealth' movement had rubbery economic foundations – its proposal to tax and redistribute great personal fortunes would hardly have had a measurable impact on the stalled economy. But the Louisiana Governor roused millions when he talked about how 'Rockefeller, Morgan and their crowd' stepped up and took the riches God had created for all, leaving behind but a pittance for the rest of the country. Ruled by his megalomania, Long overreached himself when he attacked FDR for temporizing with the plutocracy. While the inner circle of the Roosevelt administration worried, even after the Governor was assassinated, that the Long movement might undermine support for the President's re-election in 1936, it is far more probable that his invective further diminished the rapidly shrinking constituency of the Grand Old Party. Certainly it further reinforced the stigma attached to Wall Street.[4]

Like Long, Father Charles E. Coughlin, whose modest parish at the Church of the Little Flower outside Detroit was the platform from which he reached millions, started out in Roosevelt's corner and then moved into the opposition. His charismatic radio sermons and gymnastic live performances were spellbinding recitations of an old refrain. His mellifluous voice and trim, athletic body (Coughlin was an ex-football player and coach) charmed multitudes into believing the Depression was first and last the fault of the Eastern banking establishment. These 'high priests of finance' cared only about gold, Coughlin argued, and having built an altar to gold they invented 'both a liturgy and a worship which they have imposed upon the peoples of the earth'. Wall Street was prepared to beggar the rest of the country; indeed, 'international bankers' had subjected people from every civilized nation to a 'torture more refined than was ever excogitated by the trickery of the Romans or the heartlessness of slave owners'. Not only that, Wall Street was prepared to compromise the nation's independence. Coughlin repeated charges first leveled by the Populists and reiterated by Henry Ford and others during and after the Great War, that the Morgan bank colluded with British financiers to drag America into the war and inveigle it in financial alliances that had helped precipitate the Depression.

Coughlin's sermons in the early years of the Depression were typical of mainstream populism. To escape Wall Street's grip, the nation would have to return to the fundamental Christian principle of economic life: 'By the sweat of thy brow thou shalt earn thy bread.' Labor must always take precedence over capital. To sustain the speculative profits and dividends of big-time stock operators, 'the laborers are paid the lowest possible wages'. The Detroit cleric enjoyed considerable support among the motor city's auto-workers. Deliberately echoing the newly elected President, the radio priest claimed that thanks to the war, 'the money-changers came back into the temples of government'. So long as the President seemed to see things that way, the priest praised him as a hero, leading the nation in 'the Wall Street battle . . . as great a battle as Runnymede or Gettysburg.' But when FDR seemed to depart from the faith, Coughlin grew increasingly sour.

By 1936, the priest had endorsed William Lemke's quixotic Union Party campaign for the presidency and raised the caliber of his verbal artillery. Lemke, a Republican Congressman from North Dakota, described both major parties as 'run by the ventriloquists of Wall Street', and launched a crusade against 'financial slavery'. Now, in the eyes of the radical right, the New Deal had become too intrusive, its regulatory reforms really a disguised version of 'financial socialism'.

The Gold Act of 1934 and the Banking Act of the following year were, in Coughlin's view, Roosevelt's version of 'Leninism', contributing to the centralization of the money power in the hands of the international banking fraternity. In the charged atmosphere of the campaign, his rhetoric grew more and more bombastic: he likened the New Deal to 'a broken down Colossus straddling the harbor of Rhodes, its left leg standing on ancient Capitalism and its right mired in the red mud of communism.'[5]

Anti-Semitism, always latent in Coughlin's assault on Wall Street, became explicit, especially after the Union Party's miserable showing in the 1936 election – less than five per cent of the vote and ten times less than Coughlin had anticipated. He published the *Protocols of the Elders of Zion* in 1938, and his sermons were speckled with references to 'thirty pieces of silver', to shylocks and 'pagan usury', 'gentile silver' and 'bad international Jews'. Coughlin's earlier populism gave way to a variety of Catholic fascism: it openly abandoned democracy, called for the abolition of political parties, and proposed instead a Corporate State organized to represent society's main functional groups – farmers, capitalists, industrial workers, and so on. The priest's National Union for Social Justice, which had always respected the 'sanctity of private property', now devolved into the Christian Front Against Communism. The Front reiterated its denunciations of speculative wealth, but more and more directed its animus at Jewish financiers, whom it depicted as leagued with atheistic Bolshevism.

Others in the Union Party camp, including Huey Long's political executor, Gerald L. K. Smith, veered away from outright Jew-baiting, but steeped their hatred for Wall Street in patriotic Christianity. Clutching the Bible, coatless, sweating profusely, Smith exhorted the Union Party convention delegates to end the rule of Wall Street, confident that 'there are enough good people who believe in the flag and the Bible to seize and control the government of America.' Even further from the political middle ground were men like William Dudley Pelley, an ex-Hollywood screenwriter and founder of the paramilitary Silver Shirts. Pelley adopted Ford's 'International Jew' as his political Bible and railed against a Jewish banking conspiracy out to destroy gentile civilization. He found blue-blood financial angels to support his Foundation for Christian Ethics, and composed vicious little Christmas-card ditties like this:

> Dear Shylock, in the season
> When we're all bereft of reason,
> As upon my rent you gloat,
> I would like to cut your throat.

It was an ignoble tradition stretching back to the regular slandering of August Belmont as a traitor, thanks to his association with the House of Rothschild. The usurious Jew had always been part of the satanic Wall Street of the popular imagination.[6]

Ironically, even as Coughlinites zeroed in on Wall Street shylocks, elements of that very same conservative business community took after the left-wing Jews who were allegedly running the New Deal's assault on laissez-faire capitalism. Grassroots insurgencies like the Union Party and elite anti-New Deal organizations like the American Liberty League had precious little in common. But the notion that Jews might be blamed for everything had potential. Henry Ford had been the first to concoct a conspiracy of Jewish financiers and Jewish Bolsheviks. Coughlin pioneered a new archetype: an Eastern elite which was part Anglo-Saxon, Ivy League financiers, and part Jewish left-wing government bureaucrats. FDR was the demiurge of this new aristocracy of money and power, serving to inspire communism and finance capitalism all at once. This ideological phantasm took root among hard-pressed small-businessmen, precariously positioned white-collar employees, and better-off elements of the Irish Catholic working class, whose Anglophobia and religiosity found a perfect foil in this bizarre amalgam of banker and Bolshevik. After World War II, the McCarthyite right wing would play this card with some effectiveness. During the New Deal years, however, the animus against Wall Street was so overwhelming that the attempt to cross-breed Jewish communists with Jewish bankers remained politically still-born. As the radio priest descended further into this swamp of Jew-hunting, his national political influence declined as well. He was still a radio celebrity, able to incite an act of street thuggery here and there. But repudiated and silenced by the Catholic hierarchy in the interests of wartime unity, he was no longer an important political figure. It was a reckoning with Wall Street most people were after, and the New Deal seemed to deliver that, whatever its religious and political associations.[7]

*

A populist rhetoric once considered the property of outsiders was now entirely mainstream. It was one thing to hear this talk coming from the likes of Long, Coughlin, and rebel farmers. It was another matter entirely to hear it coming from the *New York Times* and the White House. While most of the metropolitan press kept its skeptical distance from the new administration, when it came to Wall Street they joined in the general hostility. As for the President, his relationship to the business community blew hot and cold. During the early years – sometimes labelled the 'first New Deal' – FDR went to great lengths to mollify the corporate industrial elite. Even then, however, Wall Street functioned as a convenient whipping boy.

It was the President, after all, whose inaugural address announced that 'the money changers have fled from their high seats in the temple of our civilization.' Those 'unscrupulous money-changers', he confidently averred, 'stand indicted in the court of public opinion, rejected by the hearts and minds of men'. Recalling Louis Brandeis's still much-used phrase, the President vowed to end 'speculation with other people's money'.

Roosevelt's first fireside chat during the height of the banking crisis singled out those bankers who had 'used the money entrusted to them in speculations and unwise loans'. The President invoked the language of the Pujo 'money trust' investigations to excoriate his enemies. Roosevelt concluded that the first generation of robber barons, though unscrupulous, had at least left behind a mighty industrial infrastructure. But their successors, the money-trusters Wilson had fought, led the country down a dead end of economic oligarchy, choking off new avenues of property-holding and mobility. Now the President could proclaim that 'the day of the great promoter or the financial titan, to whom we granted everything if only he would build or develop, is over.'

It was FDR who referred to the new era's stock-market seers and fantasists as object lessons in how the country had departed from the basics of Ben Franklin republicanism. It was FDR who decried Samuel Insull's pyramid of watered stock, its arbitrary write-up of assets, its milking of subsidiaries, and vast over-charging of customers. It was the President who confirmed a long-held populist suspicion that 'fewer than three dozen private banking houses and stock-selling adjuncts in the commercial banks, have directed the flow of capital within the country and outside it,' pledging that the government would become the effective counterweight to this financial oligarchy. And it was FDR who encouraged those Congressional investigations of Wall Street that so embarrassed the old regime, where Morgan, Lamont, Mitchell, and Wiggins had their dirty linen held up for public view.[8]

The Pecora Committee was the natural heir of the Pujo Committee. Organized under the auspices of the Senate Banking and Currency Committee, it began its investigations into the stock-market crash under Hoover, but really picked up steam once Roosevelt was inaugurated. Its chief counsel, Ferdinand Pecora, was a Sicilian immigrant, an old 'Bull Moose' progressive who'd converted to the Democrats and conducted his own investigation of bucket shops in New York when he served as District Attorney in the 1920s. His confrontation with the Morgan faction was political theater at its most hypnotic: an immigrant's righteous inquisition pitted against the monarchical self-assurance of the nation's most distinguished banker.

Deliberations continued for more than two years. When it wasn't pillorying particular Wall Street malefactors the Committee tried to examine the systemic origins of the Crash. It used Brandeis's *Other People's Money* as a canonical text, attempting to reproduce its meticulously detailed picture of the 'web' at work. For example, it revealed that Morgan partners held 126 directorships in eighty-nine different corporations worth $19 billion. But here it largely failed to uncover the empirical evidence necessary to prove what it presumed: namely, the existence of a 'money trust' which acted with deliberation to control the economic fate of the country. It did, however, reveal numerous Wall Street deals that left insiders heavily rewarded and the investing public cheated. It showed how pools brought Wall Street's elite together with lower-level operators in acts of mutual enrichment. It exposed the incestuous relations between the commercial and investment-banking arms of the same financial institutions. It documented the way pool-meisters employed publicity agents to tout targeted stocks and paid journalists and radio announcers to recommend them. And of course it left an indelible impression of the Street's great figures as men of little character and less scruple.

If the Pecora Committee allowed its pursuit of individual financial outlaws to overwhelm its critique of the system, if its analysis was less sharp than that of the Pujo inquiry, politically it was considerably more potent. This reveals how much the times had changed. Pujo had to work against the grain of a generally prosperous economy, and its findings were unwelcome in a White House initially occupied by William Howard Taft. Pecora rode the tidal wave of hostility towards a financial elite already blamed for the country's dire predicament. The political weight of the report was only reinforced by the number of ways in which it found Wall Street violating the public trust. Both the press and the President loved the Committee and its fiery chief counsel. FDR urged it to produce legislative remedies, and incorporated its findings into the administration's securities acts of 1933 and 1934 and the Public Utility Holding Company Act of 1935.

The Committee and other related public investigations painted a nineteenth-century picture of financial parasitism. Senators talked about how 'the lambs have been sheared', of how the 'rascals on Wall Street' had 'soaked millions of dollars out of the South'. Some revived accusations that a cabal of financiers, munitions makers, and shipbuilders had conspired to drag the country into World War I. Others compared the Street's inner circles to the gangland world of Al Capone, an analogy favored by newspapers around the country. Sometimes the rhetoric recalled the progressive-era depiction of Wall Street as an industrial superpower whose influence dominated the boardrooms of corporate America. Although Pecora exposed Morgan's tax-dodging, what most exercised him was the power his bank wielded over vast resources, a power subject only to the will of one man, free of public obligation or scrutiny.[9]

Intellectuals and others removed from the public arena attempted more coherent dissections of the Street than were possible in the highly charged atmosphere of a hearing room. These comprised the first serious analytical reckonings with modern capitalism since the Progressive Era; though dispassionate, they were intended to make a political difference. This was, after all, the decade of the socially conscious intellectual.

In *Who Owns America: A New Declaration of Independence*, a group of prominent writers known as the 'Southern Agrarians' combined a down-home populism with a modern critique of late-stage finance capitalism. Added to its sacrilegious violation of the work ethic, Allen Tate argued in 'Notes on Liberty and Property', there had emerged a dangerous rupture between the legal ownership and effective control of corporate property. These writers sought to avoid a

socialist response to the situation: they warned that a highly centralized system of production and finance logically tended in the direction
of corporate collectivism, 'a corporate structure that strives toward
the condition of Moscow'. This economic tropism would extinguish
what was most precious about the American love affair with property: its rootedness in families and communities, which endowed the
individual with moral significance and lent society a solidity that the
market undermined. Under the regime of the stock market, the wide
dispersion of stock ownership conferred neither control nor a sense of
responsibility. It emasculated its possessor, robbing property of its
capacity to draw the individual into active transformation of the physical world. Finance capitalism as mediated by the stock market de-
materialized wealth, liquefied social relations, and eroded any
lingering sense of communal obligation. Tate envisioned a final conflict first joined by Jefferson and Hamilton: it would end either in a
'tyrant state', or a return to 'real politics' and the 'reassertion of the
rights of effective ownership'.[10]

Who Owns America caused a stir, if only because it originated in a
region not known for pioneering social theory. New York was a more
likely incubator of such thinking, and it produced the decade's most
influential piece of public-policy research. Adolph Berle and Columbia
University economist Gardiner Means produced a sober, scholarly
work, The Modern Corporation and Private Property, which soon
became canonical among many New Dealers. Berle gave up his Wall
Street legal practice to move to Columbia, where Means was a graduate student. Their book laid out a rigorous case for dispossession that
the 'southern agrarians', among others, would later echo. It converted
a generation's worth of muckraking polemic into authentic scholar-
ship. Although dry in tone and laden with statistics, its publication in
1932 was greeted with great excitement. Charles Beard pronounced it
a 'masterly achievement', perhaps the most important book on statecraft since the Federalist Papers. And Time magazine rightly described
it as 'the economic Bible of the Roosevelt Administration'.

The book resurrected and updated the notion of absentee ownership which had surfaced during the first wave of publicly traded industrial corporations at the turn of the century. William Z. Ripley (a
mentor of Berle's) and Thorstein Veblen had already lent the idea
empirical and theoretical richness. A 'silent revolution' had stripped
the great body of security holders of any meaningful control over the

corporate resources they theoretically owned. By default that power had settled in the hands of a caste of managers often in league with a bloc of minority shareholders. Yet by virtue of their widely dispersed ownership, these corporations were quasi-public institutions. Moreover, Berle and Means' statistics demonstrated how dominant these corporations had become over the whole economy. By their reckoning about two thousand people ran half the country's industry; this endangered the interests not only of the investing public, but also of the workers, consumers, and communities whose lives depended on the corporations.

'Nearly social institutions', the new corporations were burdened with obligations which its executive functionaries showed no inclination to honor. And there was nothing their stock-holding 'constituents' could do about it. The power to control property – now vested in a clique owning insignificant fractions of the company's stock – had been abruptly separated from the benefits of owning property. The authors detailed the stratagems deployed by management/stockholder elites to implement control and to disenfranchise everyone else: holding-company pyramids, the proliferation of non-voting preferred stock, stock-purchase warrants, super-shares bearing extra voting privileges, legal feints allowing for the issue of non-voting common stock. They concluded that effective control was regularly possible while holding as little as one per cent of the company's stock. And these were only the formal means: most control was exercised informally through a combination of share ownership, strategic position, and social connections, which entrenched the position of a caste virtually immune to challenge.

Without robust government intervention, Berle and Means averred, a tiny clique of managers with minimal proprietary stake in the corporation would remain able to control its operations without regard for the common shareholder, much less the commonweal. Like the 'southern agrarians', Berle and Means compared this corporate dispensation to communism in the way it diminished the historic rights of private property. They likened boards of directors to committees of commissars, Wall Street to the Kremlin. Like the 'southern agrarians' and many others pondering a way out of the Depression, they sought a middle ground between the plutocracy and the proletariat.

Unlike the defenders of the agrarian order, however, these economists accepted the fateful logic of the modern corporation. It was a devil's pact: the separation of ownership from management had produced the liquidity and mobility of the securities markets and thus the wonders of modern industry; but that liquidity came in exchange for trading away the old proprietary control. The evolution of the modern corporation represented a historic transformation. Without the smooth functioning of the securities markets, the modern economy had become inconceivable. Yet that very evolution raised the urgent question: in whose interests should these quasi-public institutions be operated, 'who should receive the profits of industry?' Berle and Means might have argued that 'shareholder value' was the only answer, and so arrived at that justification for asset-stripping, mergers, and acquisitions which made the 1980s notorious. Instead, for these two New Dealers the question was a political, not a financial one. And the answer for these public intellectuals was obvious: the corporate-financial order, which Wall Street had organized and which now lay in ruins, had to be democratized.[11]

Everybody, not just reconstructed southern populists and academic theorists, steered clear of socialism – even though there was a broad consensus that capitalism at home and abroad was experiencing a breakdown. Moreover, the Soviet Union was accomplishing prodigious feats of industrialization that left some marveling and others anxious and puzzled. Despite all this, socialism never made it onto the public agenda.

The left, communist and non-communist, had long since concluded that the Crash and Depression signaled the long-scripted terminal phase of finance capitalism. Before Roosevelt's ascendancy, left-leaning writers such as Edmund Wilson and Theodore Dreiser entertained radical solutions, authoring a 1932 manifesto, *Culture and Crisis*, which declared the hopeless bankruptcy of the capitalist system, affirmed their willingness to meet force with force, and endorsed the Communist Party presidential candidate, William Z. Foster. An insurgent labor movement, upon which the left rested most of its hopes, came closest to propounding a democratic system for planning production and investment. Papal indictments of finance capitalism's usuriousness – *Rerum Novarum*, 'The Condition of the Working Classes' (1891), and *Quadragesimo Anna*, 'On Reconstructing Social Order' (1931) – further inspired the working-class movements. But both socialism and Catholic radicalism, however personally uplifting, remained politically inert. Most of the movement's energies were devoted to breaching the walls of industrial tyranny at the workplace and to defending the more limited objectives of the Roosevelt administration against its enemies in Wall Street and the American Liberty League. Journalists like the *New Republic*'s John T. Flynn – who would later serve on the Pecora Committee and help draft securities legislation – argued that New Deal attempts to regulate 'the speculators' were doomed. It was either socialized investment and planned production, or back to the bad old days, because any vigorous attempt to regulate would quickly dry up the well of private investment capital. But the practical politics of the left-wing parties never crystallized around this Marxist analysis; instead they took up positions in more or less critical support of New Deal reform.[12]

Liberal thinkers also adopted a glum view of 'mature capitalism'. They were pessimistic about its prospects for further unaided expansion, applying Frederick Jackson Turner's meditation on the closing of the western frontier to the exhaustion of new opportunities for innovation on the industrial frontier. Thanks to the technical efficiencies of capital, the chronic tendency to generate over-capacity, the decelerating rate of population growth, and the decline of confidence, the private economy would remain stationary without a jumpstart from public investment. But these reform-minded intellectuals never took seriously the idea of jettisoning the system. For economists like Alvin Hansen and Stuart Chase, the burning public question was how to administer the economy so as to avoid recurrent collapse. Managed capitalism, in one form or another, was the response to Wall Street's debacle throughout the political spectrum.[13]

Eventually 'Keynesianism' became shorthand for the whole system of state-regulated capitalism that supplanted the free-market orthodoxy of the last generation. John Maynard Keynes was hardly a household name in 1930s America, but his thinking was well-known by influential circles in and around the New Deal. During the 1930s, Keynesian remedies fitfully informed the administration's policy-making. Sometimes they were joined to incompatible approaches to getting out of the Depression; sometimes they were abandoned entirely. However, the British economist's views about speculation and the economy of mass consumption reflected more widely shared if less methodically argued opinion about the relationship of Wall Street to the Depression and to any hoped-for permanent recovery. Speculation and under-consumption were the twin evils of the old order – New Dealers went after them both.

Since the turn of the century, financial speculation had emerged from the cloud of moral and economic censure that had dogged it from the days of the Revolution. Though severe critics remained, many had come to think of speculation as a positive contributor to technological innovation and economic growth, that impulse to risk-taking that powered the American economic dynamo. Moreover, economists and others had offered systematic proof that what seemed like gambling and guess-work was actually a rational process, amenable to sophisticated mathematical calculation. But after 1929, academic theorists and market analysts like Benjamin Graham began to backtrack. The Crash and its aftermath had dashed the romance and removed the scientific certitude – temporarily.

Keynes's *General Theory of Employment, Interest, and Money*, published in 1936, included a dissection of speculation's impact on economic well-being. He noted that a rise in the proportion of capital invested by people who neither knew anything about nor took any managerial responsibility for actually existing businesses resulted in a decline in 'the real knowledge in the valuation of investments'. Furthermore, conventional stock valuations, which were, in his view, purely the product of the mass psychology of innumerable more or less ignorant individuals, could change suddenly due to a mass response to developments irrelevant to the likely yield on an investment. Investment prospects were utterly mercurial, shifting precariously along with 'the nerves and hysteria and even the digestions and reactions to the weather' of market amateurs. Mathematical certainty in this environment was a pipe-dream. Moreover, because the outlook of professional speculators was inherently short-term – a year at most – their behavior, even if savvier, could not act as a counterweight to the irrationality of the herd; indeed, the aim of the professionals was to stay just ahead of the short-term fluctuations instigated by the fickleness of public moods. This structure certainly did not permit accurate long-term forecasts about the economy in general or companies in particular. While Keynes acknowledged there were still those who invested for the long term, he considered the likelihood of their prevailing negligible.

All of this was the inevitable outcome of the stock market's underlying 'fetish of liquidity'. Champions of the market had long identified liquidity as its great achievement, allowing it speedily to mobilize otherwise scattered and inert capital resources for the building-up of the country. But now it seemed that the same mechanism that inspired capital investment could also impede it. In Keynes's eyes, the fixation on liquidity was profoundly anti-social, as it conveniently forgot that 'there is no such thing as liquidity of investments for the community as a whole.' One might hope that skilled investors would apply their craft 'to defeat the dark forces of time and ignorance which envelop our future', but day to day they were preoccupied instead with outwitting the crowd. Even in the eyes of the most august bank and investment-trust directors, the long-term view had come to seem rash and eccentric. It was all 'a game of snap, of Old Maid, of Musical Chairs'. After all, the most socially advantageous investment policy might not be – under current conditions was almost bound not to be – the most profitable.

American economic culture aggravated the tendencies of the stock market. In New York, Keynes observed, the influence of speculation was 'enormous'. He cited those who claimed that when the Street was going through a typical bout of hyperactivity, at least half of each day's transactions were undertaken with the intention of reversing them on the same day. Americans rarely invested for 'income', as people still tended to do in England. In the Old World, the stock market remained inaccessible and expensive, a socially exclusive arena, not an amusement park for the middle classes. There, speculators might in theory remain harmless, no more than 'bubbles on a steady stream of enterprise'. But in the New World, the relationship was reversed: 'enterprise becomes the bubble on a whirlpool of speculation'. Under such circumstances, where the whole country's development had become 'a by-product of the activities of a casino, the job is likely to be ill-done. The measure of success attained by Wall Street . . . cannot be claimed as one of the outstanding triumphs of laissez-faire capitalism.'

Here the specific indictment of speculation merged with a more global judgment about capitalism as currently practiced. Others before Keynes, including some of the best-known Wall Street economists of the 1920s, had focused on the system's worrying tendency to depress the level of demand below what a mass-consumption-oriented economy could tolerate. Although this could show up on the shop floor in concerted managerial efforts to keep wages low, it could also arise from the peculiar configuration of capital represented by the Wall Street old guard. According to these critics, the lion's share of liquid capital had been locked up in various forms of short-term speculations, which grossly inflated the paper value of existing property-titles to the means of production. Investments in new industries, and in new productive capacity in older industries, were thereby blocked or inhibited, for fear of depressing the fictitious values associated with this mass of speculative paper. So long as that was the case, the chances of expanding employment and rising wages would be fatally compromised. The sources of insufficient demand could thus be traced back to Wall Street and its short-term, speculative preoccupations. A cluster of the Street's peak institutions had kept the economy in that precarious state until the Crash and Depression broke the log-jam by sweeping away all the logs. The underlying productive organism now lay inert, waiting for a transfusion of capital to resuscitate it.[14]

New Deal economic reform addressed this toxic mixture of coagulated capital and sickly mass consumption. Deficit spending and public-works projects were designed, however imperfectly, to shore up mass purchasing power. And together with the legislation aimed directly at the Wall Street old guard – such as the Glass–Steagall Banking Act, the creation of the Securities and Exchange Commission, and the Public Utilities Holding Company Act – it was aimed, however inadequately, at breaking the choke-hold on capital flows once exercised by the 'morganizers'. While the government would monitor the flows of private capital, it also became the largest mortgage and investment bank in the country, thanks to the Reconstruction Finance Corporation (set up initially under Hoover to bail out the nation's bankrupted railroads), the Federal Home Loan Act, the Farm Credit Association, and other public agencies. The New Deal was as close to a show-down with Wall Street as is reasonable to expect in a political environment that effectively excluded more radical alternatives.

None of the legislation formulated to deal specifically with Wall Street, either in theory or practice, fully realized the objectives of the Street's harshest critics. It focused on felonious behavior and the secretiveness of the Street, rather than the system of 'speculative greed' which had doomed it. Senator Carter Glass, chief architect of the banking act of 1933, was certainly no populist, and planned no purge of the banking establishment. However, Congressman Henry Steagall of Tennessee didn't like Wall Street's domination of the nation's banking system and wanted to decentralize the balance of power. And so the Glass–Steagall Act did sever the connection between commercial and investment banking, an incestuous relationship that had nurtured some of the most flagrant conflicts of interest and had undermined the public trust in both the stock market and banking. That relationship epitomized the way capital had congealed in a tiny handful of institutions. The Act's passage meant that commercial banks could no longer invest their depositors' money in high-risk stocks, securities for which they were often also functioning as the original underwriter. No longer would those same banks be permitted to make highly dubious loans to boost the share prices of securities that their investment affiliates owned or were charged with selling. Moreover, the Federal Reserve was granted the power to regulate bank loans secured by stocks or bonds. Glass-Steagall lasted nearly seventy years, and its nullification in 1999 was regretted by at least some during the financial scandals of the turn of the millennium.

The two securities acts of 1933 and 1934, similarly, were not perfect reforms or revolutionary in intent. Those designing the legislation – Ben Cohen, Tom Corcoran, and James Landis, all intimately acquainted with Wall Street – would have preferred stiffer margin requirements. William O. Douglas, who'd worked earlier for the prestigious Wall Street firm of Cravath, de Gersdorff, Swaine, and Wood, and became SEC chairman in the late 1930s, always considered the commission a conservative institution designed to reassure the middle-class investing public that the marketplace was safe and did not need overthrowing. These men and others argued for strict prohibitions on 'wash sales' (purely paper transactions between conniving speculators which fostered the illusion of real activity in a stock when in fact there was none), pools, and short-selling. But the final act omitted these prohibitions. Left-wing critics were unhappy, but FDR settled for what he felt he could get, disappointing Pecora, for one, who ruefully concluded that 'Wall Street may prove to be not unlike that land, of which it has been said that no country is easier to overrun or harder to subdue.' Nonetheless, the acts considerably widened the access of the public to vital, uniform, and accurate information about old and new stocks and the companies issuing them, made insider trading a crime, and tightened the Federal Reserve's control over margin requirements for stock transactions. More fundamentally, it ended the stock exchange's long reign of self-regulation, placing all stock markets, at least in theory, directly under government supervision.[15]

FDR's appointment of the notorious bear and pool operator Joseph Kennedy as the new Securities and Exchange Commission's first chairman seemed at first a shocking capitulation, as a number of newspapers observed. (Indeed, Kennedy's bear pool during the brief bull market of 1933 had been one of the inspirations for the second securities act, which he was now charged with enforcing.) Roosevelt was repaying a political debt, as Kennedy was one of very few men from the Street who'd actively supported his run for the presidency. But Kennedy also hated the Morgan crowd, who'd shunned him for years, and his brief tenure made it clear that the government and not the Exchange would set the rules. 'The days of stock manipulation are over,' he informed his one-time colleagues. 'Things that seemed all right a few years ago find no place in our present-day philosophy.'

When William Douglas, a man of Brandeisian convictions, succeeded to the SEC chairmanship in 1937, he considered it his mission to democratize the financial system, to prevent 'the exploitation and dissipation of capital at the hands of what is known as "high finance"'. The problem with the world of 'high finance', in Douglas's view, was that sitting atop their Mount Everest of stocks, bonds, notes, and debentures, the financiers had lost sight of the life-giving economic activities down below. And with that blindness came a loss of any social responsibility. Shortly before becoming commission chairman, Douglas addressed the Bond Club of New York, whose membership included every major investment banker in the city. His audience was 'shocked into a state of profound grumpiness', according to *Time* magazine. With extraordinary frankness, he talked about the danger of investment-banker control and collusion, exercised not only openly, through interlocking directorships, but also more covertly, through trusteeships, informal associations, and favors rendered through 'zones of influence'. All this took place behind the backs of the average investor, fortified the monopoly position of the investment-banking elite, and facilitated its extortion of tribute from dependent corporations.

For Douglas, there was even more at stake than fair dealing with investors and corporations. He wanted the Commission to help force a redirection of capital flows to ensure economic growth and stability, a system that consciously worked to steer capital to where it was most economically and socially useful, if not most immediately bankable. He imagined a reformed investment-banking community functioning as a kind, disinterested middle-man, relinquishing its 'remote control by an inside few'. The old system of 'financial royalism' might have made some sense during an earlier era, when the universe of investors was a tiny one. Now it was a dangerous anachronism, a usurpation of the democratic rights of share-owners, employees, and consumers. Douglas vowed that in the end, democracy would prevail.

Looking back from the vantage point of late-twentieth-century free-market triumphalism, all this talk of a public-service-oriented Wall Street, of a nationally monitored system of capital allocation, may seem at best hopelessly naive, at worst a form of economic serfdom to the state. It is striking, then to realize these were not the idle ramblings of a discontented intellectual, but the strategic perspectives of a powerful government official. His views were widely shared throughout the administration, so much so that by 1938, in an atmosphere made extremely tense by the precipitous re-collapse of the economy, the old guard of the New York Stock Exchange was finally ousted.

Richard Whitney's disgrace and conviction naturally accelerated this process. An editorial in *The Nation* observed that 'Wall Street could hardly have been more embarrassed if J. P. Morgan had been caught helping himself to the collection plate at the Cathedral of St John the Divine.' But even without Whitney's demise, the reformers inside the Exchange knew it was long past the time when the Street had to take serious measures to recover its reputation. The new regime proceeded to adopt rules allowing for greater public oversight of its activities, including the appointment of three governors to represent the public, a concession once considered unthinkable. Meanwhile, the SEC adopted a rule requiring any director or officer of a corporation who bought and sold stock in that company within a six-month period to turn over any profits realized on such transactions to the company. The old-boy network hated this regulation, but it had grown far too weak to do anything about it. No one could argue that the fundamental role of the investment-banking community in the national economy had changed, but the way it conducted its business certainly had.[16]

In the same way, the Public Utilities Holding Company Act of 1935, originally crafted by Tom Corcoran to break up utilities monopolies, was ferociously fought over by the utilities industry and their financial allies. It suffered a thousand cuts, but the wholesale pyramiding, obfuscation, and book-cooking that had become industry trademarks wouldn't be seen again until the era of deregulation and 'Enronization' at the end of the century. Moreover, the Federal Power Commission was given jurisdiction over the interstate transmission of electrical power, and bank officers and investment brokers could no longer serve as officers of public-utility companies.

The plutocrats, both old and new, rose up over FDR's wealth-tax act. It threatened inheritances and to disable the generational transfer of wealth through gifts. The President tried explaining that 'I am fighting communism, Huey Longism, Coughlinism . . . I want to save our system, the capitalistic system,' but the bill had several of its teeth extracted before it became law. Still, the New Deal inaugurated a tax regime under which corporations would be taxed more heavily than ever before on their undistributed surplus, until they were relieved of that burden by Ronald Reagan and the return of the free market. Top inheritance-tax rates reached ninety-one per cent (where they stayed until the 1950s), while the rebates and loopholes of the Mellon years were repealed and closed. Ferdinand Lundberg, always skeptical about the New Deal's seriousness when it came to attacking 'capital', nonetheless assessed its tax policy as an attempt to 'smash the synthesis of finance capital completed under Harding, Coolidge, and Hoover'.[17]

Franklin Delano Roosevelt, a man of genteel upbringing who was familiar with Wall Street – he'd invested in blue chips and gambled and lost on an oil speculation, although he'd kept away from buying on margin – would never have vowed to 'smash the synthesis of finance capital', but his rhetoric nonetheless contributed mightily to the Street's political downfall. Only Wilson and Teddy Roosevelt before him, and no President since, spoke about the country's financial elite the way FDR did, for the better part of a decade. Spoken at the right moment, words can carry a power as telling as a legislative enactment or executive fiat. This was such a moment.

Even in the first year of his administration, when the President was still trying to reassure an anxious business community, he nevertheless warned that responsibility for directing the nation's economic affairs had resided in special-interest groups not moved by the general welfare: despite such men's useful expertise, 'we cannot allow our economic life to be controlled by that small group of men whose chief outlook upon the social welfare is tinctured by the fact that they can make huge profits from the lending of money and the marketing of securities.' He was engaged in an historic struggle, Roosevelt confided to Colonel House, Woodrow Wilson's factotum:

> The real truth . . . is, as you and I know, that a financial element in the larger centers has owned the Government ever since the days of Andrew Jackson – and I am not wholly excepting the Administration of Woodrow Wilson. The country is going through a repetition of Jackson's fight with the Bank of the United States – only on a far bigger and broader basis.

Echoing Berle and Means, FDR observed that a handful of men ran most of the country's industry, and that everyone now suffered the result: 'Unrestrained financial exploitations which created fictitious values never justified by earnings have been one of the great causes of our present tragic condition.'[18]

By the time of his re-election campaign in 1936, Wall Street's enmity for the President was raw and unconcealed. FDR taunted his enemies with memories of how these same speculators had pleaded with him back in 1933 for help, pledging their cooperation and swearing they had learned their lesson – with the first up-tick in the market, however, they returned to their old selfishness. Addicted to trading 'other people's money', deeply distrusting of popular government, they were convinced that power 'should be vested in the hands of one hundred or two hundred all-wise individuals controlling the purse strings of the Nation'. Presidential campaign rhetoric recalled the old 'money trust' investigations, full of references to interlocking directorates, private governments, and infernal stock and bond machines that killed off independent business, stifled innovation, and undermined efficiency. Making use of the public's fixation on the Lindbergh kidnapping and John Dillinger's own banking escapades, Roosevelt likened his Wall Street villains to 'kidnappers and bank robbers' eluding capture in 'high powered cars', racing across state lines with the Feds hot on their trail. The campaign reached its climax at a rally in Madison Square Garden at the end of October, where the President invoked 'Nine mocking years with the golden calf and three long years of the scourge! Nine crazy years at the ticker and three long years in the breadlines!' Powerful forces were arrayed against him, full of venom. FDR voiced his defiance: 'They are unanimous in their hatred of me – and I welcome their hatred!'

A year after the election, the country was sinking again into severe recession. As new capital investment withered away, the President confided to his Cabinet that he blamed the predicament on a 'capital strike' against the New Deal: 'Organized wealth, which has controlled the Government so far, seizes this opportunity to decide whether it is to continue to control the Government or not.' Interior Secretary Harold Ickes compared the President's plight to Jackson's war against the monster bank, with 'big capital' in 'the role of the bank'. FDR agreed: he may not have believed in an actual conspiracy (Ickes probably did and made radio addresses about the plots of Lundberg's 'Sixty Families'), but a mood of 'irreconcilable conflict' hovered over the most committed New Dealers. Robert Jackson, who headed the anti-trust division of the Justice Department, wasn't shy about fingering the 'Sixty Families', describing their purported maneuvering as a 'strike of capital . . . a general strike – the first general strike in America', aimed at coercing the government.[19]

From the beginning, Wall Street treated this rhetoric as a declaration of war and reacted accordingly. The administration was overrun with communists, madmen, and Jews, its opponents cried. Its reforms would worsen, not cure the economy's malaise. The stock market was the proven instrument of the country's gigantic industrial achievements and global financial pre-eminence. Under the guise of protecting the weak and the innocent, the New Deal would smother freedom, crushing the initiative and self-reliance that made America what it was. And all of this to punish a set of institutions – the Street – which was guilty of nothing more than obeying the inexorable laws of the free market. As Henry O. Havemeyer, the head of the American Sugar Refining Company, candidly put it: 'Let the buyer beware; that covers the whole business. You cannot wet-nurse people from the time they are born until the day they die. They have to wade in and get stuck and that is the way men are educated and cultivated.'[20]

Until he was dispatched to Sing Sing, Richard Whitney maintained his aplomb, denying any wrongdoing on the part of the Exchange, dismissing his congressional interlocutors with icy disdain. He testified that he'd never come across pools, wash sales, or any other stratagems for rigging the market. Speculation was as all-American as baseball, and a part of human nature that ought to be cherished, not condemned. Senators marveled at the grandeur of his disingenuousness.

But the atmosphere grew testy: when Iowa Senator Brookhart told Whitney he'd visited the 'greatest panic in history' on the country, the Exchange's president haughtily responded that 'We have brought this country, sir, to its standing in the world through speculation.'

At the same time, the Exchange itself waged a bitter lobbying campaign against the securities legislation emerging unstoppably from these government investigations. Republican defenders of the Street lashed out at Cohen and Corcoran, 'the scarlet fever boys from the little red house in Georgetown'. The bill they were cooking up would 'Russianize everything worthwhile'. Roosevelt himself, it was intimated, was a bit pinkish. Rumor had it that the Morgan partners kept photographs of FDR out of Jack Morgan's sight, fearing they might upset his weak heart. Once the Securities Act became law, the Street at first reacted by refusing to float new issues, hoping to accomplish its practical nullification. When the new recession hit in the fall of 1937 and the market crashed again, the Street, led by Winthrop W. Aldrich of Chase National Bank, blamed the new Federal regulations and became so bellicose that SEC chairman Douglas came close to seizing the Exchange.[21]

The American Liberty League was an organization of elite businessmen and financiers opposed to the New Deal. It was assembled by John Jacob Raskob of DuPont (the biggest corporate-financial dynasty of them all) and figureheaded by the ex-Governor of New York, Al Smith. Among its anonymous donors were those who'd made their fortunes on Wall Street. While the Morgan bank kept clear of formal affiliation, J. P. Morgan made personal contributions. When the Public Utility Holding Company Act was up for debate, the League warned it would be even worse than the Securities Act of 1933, which 'was so severe as to hold back the flow of capital necessary to the revival of industry'. At a dinner early in 1936, held to launch the League's campaign against FDR's re-election, Smith declared that the New Deal smelled of 'the foul breath of communistic Russia'. Nasty League propaganda circulated fake genealogies to prove FDR's Jewish heritage, and called his wife a Communist. The head of a big Wall Street bank told the *New York Times* he considered the President a 'pathological case'. Ex-President Hoover became increasingly defensive and shrill, claiming the economy had been well on its way to recovery in 1932 when fear of the New Deal returned it to panic and depression. Wendell Wilkie, a charming, tousle-haired country lawyer from

Indiana, later president of Commonwealth and Southern Corporation, a public-utility holding company, railed against the Holding Company Act (it would 'destroy' the industry's ability to supply cheap and reliable electricity) and big government in general; when he ran for president against FDR in 1940, he would be damningly labelled a 'simple barefoot lawyer from Wall Street'.

John W. Davis, the Wall Street lawyer and 1924 Democratic presidential candidate, issued a grim warning that administration legislation 'constitutes the gravest threat to the liberties of American citizens that has emanated from the halls of Congress in my lifetime'. Wall Street frequently resorted to this sort of scaremongering: when Upton Sinclair ran for Governor of California in 1934 on the End Poverty in California (EPIC) ticket, investment houses in New York circulated groundless rumors that capital was fleeing the state, causing state, municipal, and corporate bonds to tumble. In the depths of the late 1930s recession, David Laurence, a staunchly conservative newspaper columnist, accused FDR of arousing 'fear amounting to almost terror and distrust', which had in Laurence's opinion 'broken . . . the spirit and faith of the business and financial world in the actual safety of the citizen's property and his savings'.[22]

Not all of Wall Street was of one mind. Thomas Lamont, Morgan's most senior partner, thought of Roosevelt as a bulwark against social chaos, even though he opposed most New Deal economic policy. Men like Paul Warburg and the guilt-ridden Otto Kahn recognized the need for outside supervision of the exchange. Averill Harriman, along with Vincent Astor, started a weekly magazine, *Today* (later reinvented as *Newsweek*) to support the New Deal. Nelson Rockefeller and Winthrop Aldrich of Chase backed FDR's re-election in 1936, as did James Forrestal of Dillon Read – more because they feared the isolationism of the Republican candidate Alf Landon than out of sympathy for the New Deal's domestic objectives. Certain investment houses more closely allied with mass consumer industries – Goldman Sachs, Lehman Brothers, and the firm led by E. A. Pierce which would form the kernel of Merrill Lynch – had for some time identified the roadblock erected by their financial rivals to new investment, expanded purchasing power, and the mass marketing of stocks. They recognized the real value in having the government sanction the honesty of the Street.[23]

Warburg was a fiscal conservative. He'd warned for years that 'unrestrained speculation' would end in depression. He was a Roosevelt family friend who defended the new regime until Roosevelt abandoned the gold standard and Warburg abandoned him. Paul Mazur was another Wall Street analyst who had looked askance at the 'sterile' capital funds accumulating in corporate coffers and offloaded into suspect foreign bonds or into the highly speculative call-loan market. Throughout the 1920s, Mazur pointed to the system's gathering crisis of under-consumption, but few on the Street were paying any attention. After the collapse, he lobbied vigorously for public works and corporate taxation to release dammed-up idle capital. Otto Kahn's associations with the modernist art world signaled his rebel temperament. He shared with the Pecora Committee his cyclical theory about the relationship of the market and the commonweal, concluding that every thirty years or so the economy required a good shaking out. Teddy Roosevelt had challenged the first generation of financial jungle-fighters. Now, thirty years later, Kahn knew 'a good deal must be changed. And I know the time is ripe to have it changed. Overripe in some ways.' By 1936, both the economy and the market were enjoying a lift, and segments of the Street were ready to accept the legislation they'd once denounced.[24]

The economic collapse a year later soured the atmosphere again, but the real political battles were essentially over. What lingered on were the rancid musings of people like Russell Leffingwell, a Morgan partner and Roosevelt family friend: 'The Jews do not forget. They are relentless . . . I believe we are confronted with a profound political-economic philosophy, matured in the wood for twenty years, of the finest brain and most powerful personality in the Democratic party, which happens to be a Justice of the Supreme Court.' Here the ingrained anti-Semitism of the upper class functioned as a warped expression of WASP dispossession, bitterly resentful of the ethnically diverse and newly empowered New Deal elite. From Wall Street to Park Avenue, the country's 'natural aristocracy' whispered that 'that man in the White House' was 'morally weak', a 'cripple', a 'liar', a tool of 'niggers and Jews', a megalomaniac dreaming of dictatorship.

Slander, denial, bigotry, paranoia, and outrageous bluff: these were the symptoms of an unhorsed elite, losing its grip and thrashing about on slippery political terrain. Before he was defrocked, Richard Whitney revved up a final publicity campaign and toured the country delivering inspirational speeches. But no one was listening, except

Eddie Cantor who found them rich material for his comedy routines. It was the end of an era.[25]

An odd little spot on Vesey Street in the financial district was known by 1934 as the 'securities graveyard'. There the auction firm of Adrian H. Muller and Sons conducted surreal auctions of worthless stock from bankrupt companies. The bidders were pathetic souls ready to invest a dollar for a bushel basket full of waste paper, in the vain hope that one of these dead businesses might somehow come back to life.[26]

The end of an era indeed . . . yet there was always hope. Two striking developments suggest how deep in the American grain that ran. Henry Luce founded *Fortune* magazine in the depth of the Depression in 1930. While *Fortune* would sometimes whine about the New Deal in the same way as the rest of the dispossessed business elite, in the main it took a very different tack. It was upbeat, stylish, and witty; its production values mirrored the sumptuous tastes of its readership. Hand-sewn bindings, elegant typefaces, expensive paper, and art nouveau covers were aesthetic arguments against a mood of gloom. Its voice was deliberately insouciant, gay, and lyrical, whistling amidst the ruins. Heavily illustrated, it depicted a world of country clubs, debutante balls, and prep schools, as if nothing had happened to interrupt the party. The magazine awarded Walter Chrysler and Nelson Doubleday prizes for being the best-dressed Wall Streeters. Luce was determined to maintain the Street's esprit. The magazine would on occasion note the dark side – Archibald MacLeish's sobering look at poverty in America, for example. But mainly it wore a brave and smiling face. It opened with a profile of the Rothschilds, dubbed Ivar Kreuger 'brilliant' and 'noble', and mounted a retrospective on Morgan family heroism from J. P. senior's gold bailout of 1895 to Jack's wartime financial patriotism. The 'great businessmen', Luce unblushingly announced, 'were the new supermen of civilization'. In the summer of 1937, *Fortune* published a sunny, rather arch account of a newly booming Wall Street; office space filled up, brokers wearing buttonaires as they enjoyed three-hour lunches in fashionable restaurants, the whole neighborhood enveloped in a balmy atmosphere of peaceful co-existence with Washington. *Fortune* was dedicated to the proposition that in the end nothing would disturb the rectitude and social authority of the country's natural establishment.[27]

In 1933, a salesman, Charles B. Darrow, invented a game on a piece of oil-cloth and played it on his kitchen table. He played with his family and even sold a few models to his friends. Then he thought he'd try to get Parker Brothers to distribute the game. The company found it to be filled with fatal design flaws – fifty-two, it reckoned. So Darrow kept at it on his own. His success convinced Parker Brothers that the error was theirs, and in 1935 the company began selling Monopoly. It quickly became the best-selling game in Depression-era America. In other words, while real capitalism was tanking, make-believe capitalism became an unprecedented triumph. And Monopoly was a fantasy with only one merciless objective: not to get rich at any cost, but to drive everyone else into bankruptcy. If that could delight the multitudes, there was life in the old dog yet.[28]

14

The Long Goodbye

For two generations – from 1870, when a waspish Henry James observed the 'grotesque' elephantine mansions disfiguring its minia-ture coastline, until 1930 – Newport, Rhode Island served as the social capital of the country's East Coast elite. Financiers gathered there, together with diplomats, politicians, eminent jurists, fashionable artists, and industrial tycoons. They partied in 'cottages' so grand that Mrs Ogden Mills once matter-of-factly noted that she could host a dinner for a hundred without adding to her full-time staff of house-hold servants.

By World War II, the ravages of history and the sea had dealt this gilded getaway a mortal blow. The ocean ate away at the coastline and the Crash devoured great fortunes. Many a monolith that had once lorded it over the sea – 'with the air of a brandished proboscis', according to James – now fell into decay. Estates were suddenly worth a fraction of their pre-Depression value, and they were sold or aban-doned as new taxes became too onerous to bear. Servants were harder to find or else too expensive to maintain. Moreover, 'fashionable soci-ety', which had once managed to patrol the perimeters of its exclusive enclaves with a reasonable degree of rigor, after the war found itself dissolving into the more promiscuous world of celebrity culture. Pedigree counted for less, and the Newport palaces that had embodied it consequently fell into disrepair. Soon enough Newport became an historical curiosity. Tourists came to view these monuments to a dead way of life, as they still do: the great homes were the fossilized record of an extinct social species, mementos of the world of dynastic capi-talism.[1]

Soon enough, the same air of abandonment, if not the same

piquant curiosity, hovered over Wall Street, the location from which this fading aristocracy had drawn its power. Just a month before Pearl Harbor, *Fortune* magazine published a 'Letter from a Blighted Area: Wall Street', written by a blue-blooded habitué of the Street, one Washington Dodge II. Despite all rumors to the contrary, Dodge insisted, signs of life could still be detected in the financial district. But he couldn't point to many, except to note that, again contrary to popular belief, most Wall Streeters welcomed the new SEC as a protection against felons and a way to restore their damaged reputations.

Dodge's letter provided a sorry inventory of Wall Street's woes. It was arguably the only business not significantly helped either by the general improvement in the economy or by the defense build-up. Dodge also admitted that the place was tainted: good families didn't send their sons to work there or marry off their daughters to men who did. Back in 1928, seventeen per cent of the graduates of the Harvard Business School started careers on the Street; in 1941, only 1.3 per cent did. A near universal conviction held that 'nobody in Wall Street knows what hard work means'. And indeed, Dodge ruefully observed, the Street seemed overpopulated with Hamptons playboys, everyone else having evacuated. The disgraced mountebanks and financial daredevils who had once made the Street sizzle were all gone: 'Sunshine Charlie' ran the staid firm of Blythe and Company, Dick Whitney was out of Sing Sing, farming on Cape Cod. In 1929, ten thousand ticker-tape machines had provided the jazzy accompaniment to Wall Street's fandango. By 1941, only two thousand were left, their rhythms slowed as the Street grew quiet.[2]

Post-war Wall Street seemed a becalmed and ghostly place. Yet just at that moment, men who'd grown to maturity in its shadow were crafting the institutions and strategic outlook that led *Fortune*'s creator and the nation's most illustrious publicist, Henry Luce, to proclaim the advent of the 'American Century'. Throughout World War II and its immediate aftermath, men like John McCloy and Dean Acheson, born or bred into the Street's white-shoe traditions, occupied key positions in the defense and diplomatic establishments. There they devised those critical international interventions that defined the post-war world: the International Monetary Fund, the World Bank, the Marshall Plan, NATO. By the mid-1950s, people had begun referring to them as 'the Establishment', a loose collective exercising an authority not provided for in the constitution. Some found them exceedingly wise; others accused them of belonging to 'a conspiracy so immense' it threatened the very existence of the republic.

For forty years then, from roughly 1940 to 1980, Wall Street led a double life. After three generations in the limelight, it receded into the shadows. Yet its most prestigious institutions and formidable figures were believed to exercise a vast imperial power. This was a strange interlude for a nation accustomed to the Street's cultural omnipresence.

Wall Street had long exerted huge influence over the nation's politics: counting backwards from FDR, six of the last eight Presidents had found their administrations bedevilled by its overpowering presence. Several generations of Americans had experienced the disquieting sense that the country was becoming 'two nations', and that Wall Street had become a universal metaphor for that fatal division.

How strange it was, then, to see it vanish from the stage and fall silent. No longer did it preoccupy newspaper reporters, magazine editors, congressional investigators, Presidents, cartoonists, ministers of the cloth, and all those other makers of our common cultural experience. Every now and then, of course, there was news about Wall Street – 'white sharks' raiding corporations in the 1950s, high-flying stock-pickers in the 'go-go years' of the mid-1960s, an SEC investigation or two. But this was news about Wall Street as a private place whose doings no longer seemed to implicate the rest of the country.

Vacancy and silence can signify emptiness and death – or, like dark matter, it can conceal an alternative universe. Wall Street's cultural disappearance in the post-war era was of the second variety: that is to say, if listened to closely its silence could be deafening.

Everything begins with the New Deal, that exorcist of the old Wall Street. However one characterizes the New Deal order – the 'welfare state', 'corporate liberalism', the 'mixed economy', social democracy in the American grain – once empowered, it clearly reduced class animosities. Frictions between a gilded elite and the urban hoi polloi, between capitalist financiers and the rural dispossessed, between robber barons and proletarians, had dominated the cultural landscape since before the days of the Populists, and Wall Street always figured prominently in these divisions. By shaming Wall Street and subjecting it, along with the rest of the corporate world, to public regulation, however rickety and ad hoc, the New Deal made a convincing case that the ogre had effectively been defanged. 'Two nations' might again become one.

Thanks to a more muscular government, the big bad wolf of Wall Street no longer set off that general fear and trembling it once had. A mixed economy subject to public supervision and social regulation promised to excise the class struggle. No one needed to worry over-much about wealthy malefactors and the machinations of the 'money trust'. The corporation became the locus of normative but not economic dilemmas: it might leave people with an identity crisis in the race up the slippery slope, but at least their security was assured. Wall Street, singularly blamed for the insecurity that had traumatized everyone, was now monitored by government watchdogs who allowed the rest of the country to relax.

Social consensus (race relations conspicuously excluded) was the watchword of the post-war world. Wall Street, for so long identified in the popular mind with hierarchy and privilege, with elitism and inequity, thus lost its grip on the collective imagination. This yearning for consensus was reinforced by the victory over fascism, by the pre-eminence of America in the international arena, and by the new national crusade against communism. While a down-home Harry Truman could still now and again inveigh against moneycrats and the plutocracy, his was a dying vocabulary. Collaboration between big business, big labor, and big government promised to massage away social conflict. Furthermore, post-war prosperity, which lasted with only occasional interruptions into the early 1970s, provided the sturdy material foundations of this social harmony.

Shunning any reckless talk about fast money and the great game, Wall Street instead emphasized its anti-communist patriotism and talked a blue streak about safety and security, which after all was what the New Deal promised a ravaged generation. At the same time, the contours of the Anglo-Saxon elite, within which Wall Streeters had always occupied front rank, grew hazier. Its ethnic and religious borders became more porous so outlanders could get in. But even more portentously, insiders increasingly wanted out, especially of their genetic affiliation to the Republican Party. Key public servants who hailed from the Street were notably non-partisan or even Democrats, and in any event had made their peace with the New Deal order. While they helped design the lineaments of the 'American Century' abroad, they did so with discretion and probity, eschewing publicity. All this further lowered the profile of Wall Street as the haven of a ruling caste.

Talk of cooperation and consensus led some intellectuals to formulate a distinctively American question: did the country have an identifiable ruling class, or was the whole notion irrelevant to the American experience? The faith had always been cherished that in America class didn't exist, or if it did, that it was always going out of existence. Yet in practical terms precisely the opposite conviction had run through much of the country's history. It is virtually impossible to make sense of the great epochs of American history or of the grander narrative of American democracy without encountering 'Tories', 'moneycrats', 'the slavocracy', 'robber barons', 'plutocrats', 'the money trust', 'economic royalists', and other variations on a single theme: namely, that despite the fluidity of the American experience, elites have arisen at key junctures which have succeeded for a time in dominating the country's political economy and even on occasion its cultural and social life. Popular wisdom had more often than not identified Wall Street as a principal headquarters of the ruling stratum.

Suddenly, before the previous decade's social turmoil had died down, a new literature appeared arguing that all this rhetoric about ruling and subordinate classes was empirically empty; or worse, an intellectual anachronism, alien to the American ethos; or even worse than that, an expression of paranoia by people looking for someone to blame for their social displacement. A new ideology of political pluralism leveled the landscape, shrink-wrapping all the contending parties into interest groups, none of which was thought to have the grandeur of vision necessary to preside over the whole of American society. Such a persuasion further downsized Wall Street, minimizing its metaphorical resonance in the cultural life of post-war America.

Not quite everyone agreed with this neutering of the Street. Those right-wing populist circles which in the 1930s denounced the unholy alliance between international bankers and New Deal Bolsheviks remained alive and well after the war. Senator Joseph McCarthy exploited these festering suspicions when taking on the 'striped pants' traitors in control of the country's foreign-policy establishment, stigmatizing their Wall Street affiliations. From the left, C. Wright Mills theorized about a new 'power elite', many of whom came of age as white-shoe lawyers and investment bankers. Running against the grain of the country's new consensual persuasion there persisted a vague but nagging intuition that something like an 'Establishment' was actually in charge of the big questions. Though Wall Street naturally figured in these musings, it no longer occupied pride of place, as it had during the age of Morgan. The effective silencing of Wall Street arguably marked a sea change in American political culture. Moreover, its forty years in the wilderness would clear the ground for its return to the limelight during the Reagan era.

A visitor to Wall Street some time around 1960 might have done a double-take at what he saw there. Most of the people filling the streets, congregating on the floor of the exchange, working away in high rise-offices were either past sixty or under thirty. Middle-aged men, ubiquitous in every other American business, were scarce as could be on the Street. One thing that kept them away was the protracted sluggishness of the market itself. As late as 1940, the number of shares traded on the NYSE was less than it had been in 1905. Unlike World War I, World War II witnessed only modest growth in the investment-banking business, as these institutions played at most a supporting role to the government in financing war production. Fear of a post-war depression kept the Dow depressed; in fact, it dropped twenty-five per cent between 1939 and 1942 while volume shrank beneath what it had been in 1900. The picture improved a bit in the closing years of the war, so that in 1945 the three million shares traded matched the level last seen in 1937. This was progress, but of the sort that might give heart to those tracking the recovery of a patient still on life support. The Dow was still at half of its September 1929 level.

Nothing in this situation would encourage large numbers of people once again to consider a career on the Street; after all, there wasn't much to keep people busy or make them rich. Commissions were few. Even exclusive Wall Street luncheon clubs, desperate for business, opened their doors to outsiders. *The Journal of Commerce* gloomily predicted Wall Street would become a residential backwater as banks and corporations moved their headquarters to the more fashionable uptown. The shift of power was evident in the buildings constructed: after the war, as mid-town Manhattan established more extensive direct rail links to the suburbs, the newest skyscrapers there dwarfed those of lower Manhattan. The scent of decline filled the air, at least for a while.

It is a stunning testament to the profound after-shock of the Crash that it took twenty-five years for the Dow Jones average once again to reach the heights of 1929. More telling still, volume on the exchange didn't surpass its 1929 highs until 1961. A place once synonymous with risk now fled it. Memories of the Crash were seared into the public mind. When the market acted bullish in 1946, it set off negative vibrations and *The New Yorker*, for one, rushed to reassure its readers that although a speculator or two might still be on the premises, 'there are no Morgans, Goulds, or Fisks. There are no titans to twist the finances of the nation to their personal will. Nor are there ever likely to be again.' Those who ventured near Wall Street now did so with extreme caution. A sedated ticker-tape registered that timidity.[3]

Early in the 1940s, when Charles Merrill, founder of what became Merrill Lynch Pierce Fenner, and Smith, first set out to evangelize the stock market to the 'thundering herd', he took a survey of public opinion. It showed what he already suspected: namely, that despite the existence of the SEC there was broad distrust of Wall Street and its brokers. Merrill told his new staff that most Americans were 'suspicious of the motives and operations of the securities business', and it was their job to dispel those doubts. Aware of these same inhibitions, the NYSE undertook a modest public-relations campaign to reassure potential investors. It flopped. The director of the New York chapter of the Public Relations Society of America told a group of investment bankers that Wall Street was a public-relations disaster area, that most of their countrymen viewed them as 'paunchy, silk-hatted tycoons', a discreditable bunch of 'selfish, conniving schemers'. He advocated a publicity counter-attack through the press, radio, and that newest mass medium, TV. But the task was daunting: how to get people to shed the image of the market as a casino, to reimagine it as a seaworthy vessel, manned not by drunken sailors posing as brokers, but by careful 'professionals', sagacious investment counselors.

It would take a generation and more for this to sink in among any sizeable number of people. Only one in sixteen adults bothered with the market at all through most of the post-war era. Nearly half of all dividend income was collected by 0.1 per cent of the adult population. The number of shareholders in 1959 – 12.5 million – was a smaller percentage of the total population than the roughly ten million people who owned securities in 1930. Even finance departments in schools of business pretty much ignored what went on in Wall Street. When the

fear of a post-war collapse had passed away, when the economy surpassed the most sanguine expectations in the 1950s, the market still
stayed cool, poking along at what Merrill derided as a horse-and-
buggy rate. *Barron's* identified Wall Street as a 'depressed industry'.
Fortune magazine declared the market a 'voice in the wilderness of
lower Manhattan, unheeded and often off key'. Seats on the Exchange
were selling at 1899 prices.[4]

It was as if a cultural boundary had been crossed: as if the country had
reached a point of no return and could only look back with a sigh of
good riddance, wiser at least for having lived through the worst Wall
Street could do. Indeed, *Point of No Return* was the title of a novel by
J. P. Marquand, published in 1947. Together with similar novels by
Louis Auchincloss and others, *Point of No Return* captured that atmosphere of revulsion, angst, and insecurity which enveloped the post-
war Street.

Fear was a primordial emotion driving the New Deal. Roosevelt's
clarion call to wage war for the four freedoms – including the freedom
from fear, want, and insecurity – made the purging of fear a global
crusade. Bedrock pieces of New Deal legislation – unemployment
insurance and social security especially, which even seventy-five years
later and in a very different political atmosphere, retain an aura of the
untouchable – were attempts to reckon with fear and insecurity.
Together with Keynesian counter-cyclical manipulations of fiscal policy, alongside the great massing of statistical information about the
economy, population trends, occupational reconfigurations, and so
on, these were all attempts to moderate but not eliminate the fearful
unpredictability of capitalism. Modern life had become permanently
unsafe. To make provision to insure the unemployed or the aged was
to assume that there would forever be unemployed and elderly in
need. Actuarial foresight and collective action might function as useful
prophylactics or antidotes – George Bernard Shaw's Fabian confidence
that 'when dealt with in sufficient numbers, matters of chance become
matters of certainty' – but no one expected a perfect inoculation
against the burdens of the modern economy. Nor, therefore, could
anyone escape that nagging fear of their reappearance.
Psychologically, as well as on more tangible economic terrain, the
post-war era was marked by a quixotic quest for security.

Marquand's protagonist, Charles Gray, burrows inside the cloistered confines of an ancient firm, monkishly devoted to husbanding the blue-chip investments of its blue-blooded clientele. A sacerdotal atmosphere pervades this old-line family bank, where the very notion of risk is verboten, where rumors and hot tips are considered unseemly, where ambition must conform to the measured pace and the prehistoric protocols of ascension. After hours Charles hides out in the utterly predictable routines of an upscale Westchester suburb and pays meticulous attention to the subtle but reassuring nuances of social prestige. Whatever tensions surface in his life – competition for favor and preferment at the firm, frustrated ambitions to rise within the country-club pecking order back home – they remain manageable, slowly corrosive but not explosive.

Charles is fleeing the past. His whole life and character were irreparably disfigured by his father's unconscionable Wall Street speculations at the height of the Jazz Age. Patriarch of a financially strapped but socially distinguished Boston family, hapless and ineffectual but yearning to recapture its fading distinction, John Gray loathes the sanctimonious, antiseptic, self-assured world of the Boston investment house. He's determined to break loose of those constraints and hypocrisies and recover the family patrimony. Instead he loses everything. A series of inebriated and reckless plunges ends in his suicide, and Charles is left to pick up the pieces. Romance, social elevation, career are all sacrificed on the altar of his father's malignant Wall Street fantasies. This, then, is Charles's point of no return. His life will forever be marked by his father's shame, and by revulsion for everything he attempted, even the daring urge to break loose that a more callow Charles once admired. It's as if Charles has taken a vow of never again: he lives instead in perpetual self-denial, losing his free will in a life of suffocating resignation.

For Marquand, Charles's point of no return is also the country's: there is no going back to those childish dreams of erotic thrill and perpetual ease. Those Jazz Age fantasies of love and adventure that turned out so cheap and shabby and ruinous would be the last American flirtation with its indigenous optimism. Taking the place of Wall Street's flash and dash is the gray flannel suit and the suburban cocoon. Life ever after is filled with regret and stultifying caution, with a poignant sense of loss – and of the unforgiven.[5]

Louis Auchincloss's *The Embezzler*, published in 1960, is a reckoning with Wall Street's unforgiven. His embezzler, like Richard

Whitney, is a Wall Street insider of the 1920s. Guy Prime is handsome, charming, and supremely self-assured, a charter member of every club and association worth belonging to. Money rolls toward Guy on waves of promotional patter. Self-absorbed, shallow, a sexual athlete, he is too smug to be cynical: he never doubts that his social cachet and the financial wherewithal that undergirds it will continue indefinitely. But when the Crash descends, Guy is caught up in desperate, felonious efforts to save himself. Now he must pay for his fecklessness and moral myopia. His embezzlements will be discovered, and for that he will be punished by a community now outraged by the profligacy and selfishness of the old order. And he will be punished a second time by his own Wall Street fraternity. Hoping to win some mercy, Guy testifies against fellow members of the old-boy network before a Federal tribunal, run by a hectoring Jewish prosecutor he despises – Ben Cohen, we are led to assume. He betrays a venerable code of honor – never to tattle on a fraternity brother, no matter how dishonorable his public behavior – and exposes their secrecy and insider trading. His testimony marks the 'Götterdämmerung of an era'. Guy's inquisitor enunciates a new code of ethics, one that insists on loyalty to the public interest and not to a circle of privileged friends. Guy joins the ranks of the unforgiven: he lives out his life estranged from his country, family, and friends, passing away his remaining years in the bars of Panama, brooding over his fatal errors and indulging a bitterness about which we learn from the post-mortem pages of his memoir. Guy, like the Street that made him, is an exile – never forgotten, never forgiven. [6]

Both Marquand and Auchincloss wrote of a world they knew intimately. Marquand made a noisily triumphant marriage to the niece of Henry Dwight Sedgwick, whose lineage went back to the Hookers of colonial Connecticut. Auchincloss's father was a broker in the 1920s. His son became a partner in a smart Wall Street law firm, where he grew familiar with that world's rituals of hierarchical snobbishness, its exceedingly fine stratifications of old and new wealth. But one didn't need to be to the manner born to express that universal post-war rejection of the Street and the attitudes that had presumably died with it.[7]

American success literature had been a staple of popular culture since at least the days of Horatio Alger, and the aggressive, masculine character traits that literature celebrated were widely associated with the lions of Wall Street lore. After the war, however, the Street largely vanished from the pages of those inspirational guidebooks. It gave off the wrong vibrations in a world grown more cautious, where the power of positive thinking had come to mean the crafting of an amiable personality that would function cooperatively, if anonymously, as part of the corporate team. Success depended on adopting a more modest mien, a kind of bureaucratic self-restraint utterly at odds with the assertive, risk-prone temperament for which Wall Street had become notorious. If Wall Street did show up here and there in this advice literature, it was practically indistinguishable from the rest of the white-collar universe, a place of stable salaries and security in which Charles Gray would have felt entirely safe.[8]

Napoleonic financiers from yesteryear no longer supplied the folklore of popular emulation. When they did make a rare appearance, they came across as anachronistic, out of touch with the new corporate order of things. Cameron Hawley, popular novelist of the 1950s, who was a businessman before becoming a writer, found these tensions plot-worthy. In *Cash McCall* (published in 1955 and filmed in 1959), the hero is a distant relative of those turn-of-the-century financial *Übermensch* that writers like Norris, Dreiser, and London found fascinating. The story is riddled with stereotypes, sentimentality, and moral simpletons. Yet Cash is interesting. He's easily confused with those earlier raiders of corporate properties who buy and sell with scant regard for the workers and communities whose fate they determine. Jackals of just that sort populate the background consciousness of the novel's characters. But Cash is not quite that; rather he intrigues to get hold of an old family manufacturing firm and keep it out of the hands of rival predators – not to strip it but to save it (and marry the owner's withdrawn daughter). Cash's mysterious, hermetic life expresses his existential alienation from the bureaucratic conformity of post-war corporate life. He exercises his heroic individualism on behalf of a family capitalism that seems otherwise doomed to extinction.[9]

Cartoonists and moviemakers registered a similar depletion of raw material when it came to Wall Street. That more imposing, muscular, 'morganized' Wall Street, which graphic artists had skewered for generations, had withered in size. Cartoonists no longer selected Wall Street as a target for spoofing with anything like the frequency they once had. And when they did, their visual vocabulary seemed downsized, stripped of the lush symbolism and the allusions to titans, gorgons, snakes and Mephistophelean evil-doers. Now their sketches were more quotidian, haunted by the recent debacle. A cartoon appearing in 1946 pokes fun at a ditsy dowager instructing her suitably befuddled investment adviser to make sure he switches her holdings from stocks to bonds 'just before the next depression'. And a deeply distraught character from a mid-1950s cartoon, dressed in a pinstriped suit, lying on an analyst's couch, complains that 'I could have bought GM in 1949 for $26 a share' and continues a long litany of lost opportunities that fades eventually into an angst-ridden 'I could have . . .'[10]

During the silent era, film-makers relished the moral frisson hovering over every appearance of the villainous banker and kindred Wall Street types. But after that, they rarely found the Street cinematic enough for their liking. This would remain the case until the Reagan era. *Force of Evil*, a 1948 film noir, was exceptional in this regard, perhaps in part because of the left-wing sympathies of its director, Abraham Polonsky. The story of two brothers, one a big-time lawyer with Wall Street connections, the other a petty-ante operator of a numbers racket, draws the starkest equation between these two worlds; indeed the moral advantage, if any, is with the latter. Here, exceptionally, one still feels the presence of capitalism's dark side.

The sunnier environs of the corporate office, instead, became a frequent site for commercial fiction, as well as movie melodrama and comedy, after the war: *The Man in the Gray Flannel Suit*, *The Apartment*, and *How to Succeed in Business Without Really Trying* are three of the most memorable instances. Here the dramatic space was filled with the unheroic intriguing and the guarded social climbing of management apparatchiks. Here excessive ambition and greed could threaten hearth and home and were sharply censured. Wall Street's reputation was still too risqué and lawless to make it a likely site for such bloodless confrontations. True enough, corporate executives and Wall Street bankers both came to work dressed in white collars. But the collar symbolized a cautious conformity that did not seem to fit comfortably around the bulbous neck of the Wall Street financier. Like American business in general, popular culture sought to distance itself from the country's favorite bogeyman.[11]

Wall Street's intimate relations with the nation's core industrial corporations had been in place ever since the merger movement at the turn of the century. But in the great silence that followed the war, both parties did all they could to erase that tainted association. Corporate America engaged in what might be called ethos-building, crafting an ideology of cooperative-minded business, concerned about its social responsibilities. This work was meant to neutralize its reputation for selfish and belligerent behavior. Gigantic post-war strikes (or threatened strikes) by rubber, steel, electrical, railroad, coal, auto and other workers against many of the country's industrial behemoths quickly followed demobilization. The militant Congress of Industrial Organizations launched a serious organizing drive among the brokerage, banking, and insurance industries; in fact in 1947 it led a walkout at the Brooklyn Trust Company, the city's largest non-Wall Street bank. A more spectacular uprising happened a year later. No spot on earth seemed less likely to hear the chorus of 'Solidarity Forever' echoing through its corridors than the New York Stock Exchange. But in March 1948, its clerical employees, this time organized by an AFL union (along with their fellow workers at the Curb Exchange, the predecessor of the American Stock Exchange) tried to shut down the stock market. New York City police charged the picket lines in a bloody confrontation newspapers dubbed the 'Battle of Wall Street'. All this, however, turned out to harbinger nothing at all – the storm before the calm. [12]

After this season of aggravated class antagonism, most, although not all corporations were in full flight from anything that might conjure up unhappy memories. Business did all it could to widen the gap with the Street, beginning on the beleaguered terrain of the family firm. In 1947, practically on his deathbed, Henry Ford had sourly vowed to 'take my factory down brick by brick before I'll let those Jew-speculators get stock in the company'. Anti-Semitic assaults on the Street like Ford's were becoming increasingly rare, especially in the aftermath of the war against Naziism. But defenders of family capitalism still had it in for Wall Street, and with good reason. [13]

By the late 1950s, a roguish collection of Wall Street takeover artists waged proxy fights to acquire undefended corporations. They roamed the land, picking off troubled companies in industries like railroads, shipbuilding, and metal manufacturing to fold into their polymorphous empires. One such shark boasted his strategy was to look for 'a family company run by a third-generation Yale man who spends his afternoons drinking martinis at the club'. Because of the sedated state of the stock market, shares in such concerns could be had on the cheap from exhausted patriarchs ready to cash out. In the 1980s the same maneuverings – leveraging the purchase of allegedly mismanaged companies with debt to be paid down by re-engineering those businesses into a state of lean and mean efficiency – would be hailed as a lifesaving, a kind of tough love. Not so in post-war America. Back then these men were known as the 'white sharks of Wall Street', 'boardroom pirates', the 'Proxyteers', 'the liquidators'. They were censured by government investigators, and Senator Estes Kefauver and Congressman Thomas Dodd warned of legislative sanctions. They got nothing but bad press in the nation's opinion-shaping weeklies like *Life* and *Look*, and were treated as uncouth ruffians at odds with the new corporate ethos of 'people skills'. Their nouveau flash seemed offensive and embarrassing, especially to a decorous elite that had sold off its great mansions, dismissed the servants, and accepted a more seemly level of compensation from the corporations it ran. These nasty proxy fights and the consolidated businesses that emerged out of them threatened to exterminate a whole species of family-based industry, and along with it the mythos of entrepreneurial manliness which still inspires many today.

It is telling, though, that no one any longer remembers the names of these 'white sharks' – Louis Wolfson, Robert Young, Art Landa – or even that men like them existed. They failed to leave a permanent imprint on the country's cultural conscience, unlike their forebears during the Gilded Age or the Age of Morgan; unlike, for that matter, their successors during the 1980s, the age of Gordon Gekko. No novels or films, no refractory sermons or legislative investigations commemorate their passing. No one wanted to mimic the style of a 'white shark', to dress or show off like one. Yet in the essentials, their behavior and modest social origins were identical to those of Michael Milken or Ivan Boesky; indeed they were the first generation to be nicknamed 'corporate raiders' by a scandalized media. That their cultural resonance turned out to be so faint is the sound of silence.[14]

If the remnants of family-based industry felt threatened by Wall Street, the giant, publicly traded corporations maintained a wary distance. This aloofness was facilitated by the financial independence of post-war corporate America, especially at its upper reaches. Flush times meant plenty of internal capital resources to finance expansion and innovation. Between 1950 and 1973, non-financial corporations funded ninety-three per cent of their capital expenditures out of internal resources. During the post-war era, seventy per cent of corporate profits were on average reinvested in the company, as compared to thirty per cent in 1929. First National City moved its headquarters uptown to be nearer its biggest clients, signaling an historic reversal: the great corporation had supplanted Wall Street as the defining institution of power, property, and prestige.[15]

But although Wall Street might not be running the show, its footsteps could still be heard in the background. *Executive Suite*, a 1953 movie starring William Holden, was based on another Cameron Hawley novel: its plot revolves around a struggle for control of a corporation, a not unromantic tussle for the hearts and souls of the board of directors. A top-level financial functionary intrigues to become the new CEO, his covert purpose to subject its operations to the ruthless calculus of short-term financial return. His ally on the board of directors is a venal Wall Street speculator who cold-bloodedly sells the company's stock short when he happens to witness the firm's old CEO drop dead on the street outside the offices of his Wall Street creditors. Holden, an engineer by training – the modern, high-tech carrier of that ancestral ethos of productive labor – opposes his scheming. He's committed instead to the notion that the corporation is there to produce something tangible (in this case high-quality furniture) and to share the rewards with the community within which it is embedded. All this takes place sotto voce as everybody, especially the rather uncharismatic Holden, is well groomed in the mores of corporate teamwork. But Holden rises to the occasion, summoning up an inspirational faith in technical progress and company fidelity. On that hallowed ground, Wall Street's presence seems suspicious; yet the real menace is that the Street has bored its way into the heart of the business. It must be expelled, and in Hollywood, it is.[16]

In real life, of course, saving the corporation from the siren song of shareholder value did not proceed quite so idealistically. If it happened, it did so through the leveraging of economic and political influence within the organization, through factioneering and alliance building. Nonetheless, *Executive Suite* captured the business community's instinct to detach itself from past intimacies with 'the street of torment'.

Ivy Lee, the public-relations wizard who'd salvaged John D. Rockefeller's reputation from the ignominious savagery of his attack on striking miners in Ludlow, Colorado before World War I, had long prescribed a simple remedy to those businessmen who cared about how they were viewed by the rest of society. Because Americans felt at home with democratic and populist points of reference, Lee advised his corporate clients to claim those values as their own. A corollary of that axiom naturally implied an arm's length relationship to places like Wall Street that were still viewed as elitist.

Whatever the precise degree of corporate independence of Wall Street's financial resources, the men occupying the boardroom and the executive suite disassociated themselves from the outlook of the pre-Depression financier. The business community certainly hoped to roll back or at least halt government regulation of the economy. And as the years wore on, they were modestly successful in this effort. But this political retrenchment proceeded in the shadow of the Great Depression, so organizations like the Committee on Economic Development, which brought together many of the country's dominant corporations, stayed faithful to a moderate Keynesianism. It recognized that the government needed to suppress the wilder market fluctuations of the old days, or else face unacceptable levels of social upheaval.

Keynesianism was more than an economic theory or set of policy prescriptions. Just as today millions of Americans take the virtues of the self-correcting free market as axiomatic, so back then it was equally self-evident that such faith was a cruel joke. During the golden age of post-war prosperity it was the unifying conviction of the West that there was indeed a way to preserve the framework of a capitalist economy while banishing those sickening cycles of boom and bust, those yawning inequalities of wealth and income which had called the system's very existence into question. Averill Harriman, whose father was a legendary railroad titan and cold-blooded speculator, voiced the new persuasion in 1946: 'People in this country are no longer scared of such words as "planning" . . . people have accepted the fact that the government has got to plan as well as individuals in this country.' In the new age of deft fiscal management, there would be no panics, like the one E. H. Harriman helped precipitate in 1901. And panic, of course, was Wall Street's middle name.[17]

Compared to today, there was only muted talk about shareholder value; on the contrary, that anonymous and passive mass of stakeholders took a back seat to the corporation's livelier, more demanding constituencies: employees (often unionized), customers, civic groups, the government. And the approach to managing those relationships was a study in industrial diplomacy, far removed from that of the robber barons. Management, CEOs especially, were depicted as powerful but benign, their pre-Depression reputation for cruelty and greed leeched away. Instead they presented themselves as trustees, public servants, peace-loving men ready to do business with old foes from the labor movement and the government. They were a new species of management which had in effect expropriated the old-time expropriators.

Managers of this corporate commonwealth to be sure abhorred the class struggle and fretted over the statist tendencies of the New Deal. A few no doubt read the British academic Friedrich Hayek's wartime bestseller (excerpted in the *Readers' Digest*) *The Road to Serfdom,* and grew genuinely alarmed by the specter of the 'leviathan state'. But in general, this milieu made its peace with the 'limited welfare state' and believed in the possibilities of social cooperation administered by a disinterested business elite. Society itself seemed to dissolve into the embracing arms of the corporation. Indeed, all the great social enemies of the recent past – Wall Street, the plutocracy, the bosses, the fascists – receded into the background, blotted out by the radiance of military victory, post-war prosperity, the real egalitarian drift in the division of national wealth, and the singular preoccupation with the red menace abroad. There was much mild-mannered talk of teamwork, as was dramatized in Sloan Wilson's signature novel of the new managerial class, *The Man in the Gray Flannel Suit.* It was the ethos that William Whyte identified with *The Organization Man,* his sociological classic of 1956, in which one learned to 'get ahead by going along'.[18]

Even when the Street seemed to reassert some of its old swagger during the 'Go-Go Years' of the 1960s, its enthusiasm and scandals remained largely confined to the business section of the daily newspaper. New technology – computers and electronic consumables particularly – accounted for much of the market's spectacular oomph. But there was much less of that prophetic hyperbole about 'new eras' and 'Dow 36,000' which inflated the biotech and dot.com market euphoria of the 1980s and 90s.

The great conglomerate movement of the early 1960s – the mashing together into obese unions of utterly disparate corporations like Ling Temco Vought, Litton Industries, Texetron, and most famously Gulf and Western (made notorious as 'Engulf and Devour' in the movie, *Network*) – was not, to begin with, a Wall Street invention. Although it was undoubtedly an abuse of managerial prerogative, the movement was driven by internally generated surpluses accumulating in corporate treasuries. Like those geological formations containing bits and pieces of random stones, after which the conglomerates were named, these firms made no sense except as financial devices often with no higher purpose than to circumvent anti-trust law. They deployed the assets of their own pension funds as speculative profit centers, cooked their books, relied on press touts to boost their reputations, and eventually lured in the more reputable investment houses, mutual funds, and brokerages to peddle their securities. The mighty 'conglomerateurs' of that go-go era – men like Harold Geneen of IT&T, Royal Little of Texetron, and Charles 'Tex' Thornton and Roy Ash of Litton Industries – audaciously flirted with the unethical and even the illegal, and they were trailed after by excited managers of mutual funds and flocks of freelance speculators. When the go-go market crashed in 1970, David Babson, a respected investment analyst, chastised the Street for falling prey to 'confidence men'.

However, unlike the investment trusts of the 1920s, or the junk-bond confections of the 1980s, these were not original works of art crafted by the Street. Moreover, the ruthlessness of the conglomerateur was tame by modern measures. While they could strip assets like champions, their corporations followed the rules of welfare capitalism, adhering to the prevailing principles concerning vacations, health benefits, pensions, holidays, and sick leave – all things considered unimaginable in the 1930s, all scarcely imaginable again at the turn of the millennium under the reign of 'shareholder value'. Even the big institutional investors who were caught up in the go-go market's sudden raciness were nonetheless Keynesian loyalists. They believed that deft steering of the economy by government functionaries, together with the underlying profitability of the companies they were invested in, kept the market buoyant – and above all, on an even keel.

John Brooks, one of the most astute chroniclers of Wall Street, concluded his book on *The Go-Go Years* with the prophecy that 'this may be, conceivably, one of the last books to be written about "Wall Street" in its own time'. Brooks believed that the Street's days as a vital national social institution were numbered and that, the go-go years notwithstanding, it had lost its fascination for the public.[19]

Though Brooks turned out to be wrong in the long term – but who isn't? – his observation that the Street had ceased, if only temporarily, to rivet the nation's attention was not only apt, it was one that Wall Street itself had labored to produce. Too much of what used to fascinate people about the Street, especially after the Crash, was not helpful to a business flat on its back and wondering how it might one day expunge all those bad memories.

The post-Depression craving for social security together with the cold war anxieties about national security presented themselves as ideal purgatives, if only they could be digested by the Street. Charles Merrill instantly recognized the allure of the former. His new firm's 'Declaration of Policy', issued in 1940, told its employees, managers, and partners that everything rested on overcoming popular suspicion of the market. Right after the war, the firm began marketing stocks as if they were a safe and sober alternative to insurance policies – slightly more risky, but much better able to provide for long-term well-being, even into retirement. Merrill Lynch Pierce Fenner and Bean, in their pioneering effort to bring Main Street to Wall Street, knew that before one could dream of that happening, people would have to overcome their fear of the stock market. Abolishing commissions for their brokers was one way of reassuring potential investors that salesmen had no ulterior motives when they traded a customer's stock (although actually the firm's top producers were rewarded with bonuses). Strict separation of the company's brokerage and underwriting businesses was a gesture pointedly aimed at the old Wall Street's most dangerous practice. Running off reams of free, fact-based, studiously neutral literature about particular companies was yet another way to undermine nagging insecurities about the Street: no advice was offered, just the bare facts. Ad campaigns were pitched to the neophyte, and their very simplicity in laying out the basics of investing was comforting. The essential message was always the same: blue-chip investments as the royal road to security.[20]

It had been long ago, back in the days of Abraham Dayton and his self-effacing Knickerbocker world, that the Street last presented itself as the prudential conservator of the trust funds of widows and orphans. Now, cautious promotions picked up on the domestic preoccupations so characteristic of the 1950s. Some were aimed at women, on the hunch that the Street's makeover could appeal to their presumed maternal protectiveness. Sylvia Porter told the readers of *Good Housekeeping* that Merrill Lynch offered a four-week 'investment course for women' which had been quickly over-subscribed.

Colleges and other brokerages were sponsoring similar 'ladies only lectures', all of which walked through the ABCs of investing and emphasized only the most conservative approaches to handling any excess cash – beginning with savings accounts, insurance policies, and government bonds, and only then the stock market, and only the most rock-solid of securities. Men, of course, were hardly neglected. The New York Stock Exchange launched a public-relations campaign that mimicked Merrill Lynch's information-only format, aimed especially at the higher reaches of the expanding corporate salaritariat and wealthier professionals. The Exchange's literature carried tellingly soporific titles: 'Understanding the Exchange', 'Investors' Primer', and 'The Public Be Served'. It was full of cautionary words about speculation: 'Don't invest if you can't afford it,' 'Don't put the rent money or the insurance money in the stock market.' An article in *Esquire* appealed to upscale suburbanites as the 'Gentleman's Adviser' and talked about mutual funds as if they were savings plans, professionally managed and designed to meet long-term family needs like college tuition and retirement. Image management cleaned up the Street's most basic vocabulary. 'Broker' gave off too many intimations of 'bawd' and 'pimp', from which it long ago derived – better to describe the Street's emissaries as 'total financial planners' and 'account executives'.[21]

Nonetheless, the public remained acutely suspicious. The Dow Jones Industrial Average climbed steadily all through the 1950s; indeed, its rise of 239.5 per cent during the decade was its best ever ten-year performance. However, it didn't take much to make everyone jittery. Harvard economist John Kenneth Galbraith testified before Senator William Fulbright's Banking Committee in 1955. He carried with him the galleys of his soon-to-be bestseller, *The Great Crash*. When he compared the current market and its reliance on speculative margin loans to what had happened during the year of the Panic, the senators weren't the only ones alarmed. The market nosedived and the professor's mailbox filled up with hate messages from frustrated investors.[22]

This quest to reconcile the desire for security with a place identified with the opposite was an improbable one, but it nonetheless captured the imagination even of academic economists and mathematicians. In 1952 Harry Markowitz, a University of Chicago economist, published an eye-opening article on risk. How much risk was necessary and inherent? Was there a method to minimize it, to maximize not only the size of return on investment, but to ensure there was a return?

Markowitz would help usher in a mini-revolution in the way people would manage their investments. His approach was geared not to individual stocks, but to managing a portfolio of securities. This was the first rule of the new method: diversify in order to reduce the possibility of loss. That way, even if a whole category of investments plummeted, all responding to the same set of underlying economic conditions, the widely diversified holder would be protected against catastrophe because his holdings extended beyond that sector. Linear programming models were soon developed to establish rules or guidelines for this new kind of security-conscious stock playing. The market as a whole would remain risky, always subject to fluctuations, but if one honored the key prohibition – to avoid any 'co-variance' in the portfolio's holdings – Wall Street could be domesticated.

Eventually this rethinking of the marketplace would bolster the confidence of pension funds, mutual funds, and insurance companies, releasing them from the 'prudent man rule' that demanded that every stock purchased be free of any speculative taint. The fund manager emerged as a new Wall Street type: soberly turned-out, reassuringly unflashy, carrier of the Street's featureless 'institutionalization'. Institutional investors' holdings ballooned from $11 billion in 1949 to $219 billion in 1971. Almost all of that was parked in blue-chip, high-capitalization Dow industrials, safe and sound companies like GE, GM, and Proctor and Gamble. These were dubbed 'one-decision stocks' – you bought them once and held onto them forever. Prices for the 'nifty fifty' only went up, as their institutional purchasers rarely sold. The Street even underwent an organizational make-over. At the height of the 1960s boom, new Wall Street firms, along with a sizeable number of old-line houses, shed the partnership form and became corporations instead, further distancing the Street from an era when decisions had depended on connections not algorithms.

Notwithstanding the rise of the institutional investor in the 1960s, for a long time, well into the 1970s, much of the new mathematical theorizing remained inside the ivory tower. But it was indicative of a national mood: the Street would only win back its legitimacy if it could first prove it knew how to behave itself . . . or at least that 'mathematical science' and computer technology had helped it guard against the inherent randomness of the market's behavior. [23]

Security of a quite different sort – the search for security on a planet threatened by nuclear Armageddon – was now everyone's obsessive concern. And even the stock market could be enlisted in the country's twenty-four-hour-a-day vigilance against the omnipresent threat of the Soviet Union. Merrill again explained how: 'I can think of nothing that would build a stronger democratic capitalism, nothing which would provide a stronger defense against the threat of Communism, than the wide ownership of stocks in the country.' Not only the New York Stock Exchange, but also non-partisan commentators like New Deal brains-truster Adolph Berle and business economist Peter Drucker advocated a 'people's capitalism' in which annual stockholder gatherings functioned like the 'town meeting', that evergreen image of American democracy. There was a certain immateriality to this 'people's capitalism', given that a smaller percentage of people directly owned shares in 1960 than had done so in 1929. Nonetheless, in his Annual Report of 1952 Keith Funston, President of the New York Stock Exchange, claimed that, 'we have learned in short how to put capitalism to work for all the people. The NYSE is the symbol of our democratic capitalism. The hate poured on us by the Soviet press is good proof that we are regarded as a solid barrier against the spread of Soviet theories.' The Exchange's 'Own Your Own Share of America' campaign, Funston explained, was a special form of public ownership of industry, clearly distinct from socialism or nationalization. Funston, along with Merrill and GM's Alfred Sloan, answered President Eisenhower's call to fight communism by linking the crusade for national security with the quest for domestic tranquility. *Newsweek* heralded the widespread enthusiasm for the 'new capitalism', whose practical rebuttal of communist propaganda was found in the steadily widening base of the stock market.

Lyndon Johnson's remarks, when he signed a bill amending the Securities and Exchange Act in 1964, echoed Merrill's. He poked fun at Soviet denunciations of American capitalism as pitifully out of date, 'for under our system the worker is also the investor. The people are also the owners of our productive system.' As a statement of fact this was utterly preposterous. But its sheltering of Wall Street under the blanket of national security provided welcome camouflage. It was a position from which the Street's defenders launched pre-emptive strikes against their old enemies. By now, the pre-war talk about the imperial ambitions of American finance capitalism was virtually inaudible – dismissed either as right-wing isolationism, or worse, as communist-inspired. At the height of the McCarthyite panic in 1951, the chairman of United States Steel, Irving S. Olds, declared it a malicious and dangerous lie that a tiny elite controlled the American economy: 'In short, stock ownership is one of the most completely democratic institutions to be found anywhere.'[24]

Harry Truman, who after all presided at the creation of the cold war, would not have agreed. He was the last American President to adopt an adversarial position towards Wall Street. With memories of the Depression still fresh, Truman would now and again deploy the vocabulary of class warfare, vowing that the days of the 'divine right of business' were over with for good. When shortages first appeared in 1946, the President called those speculating in grain 'merchants of human misery'. During his miraculous comeback in the presidential election of 1948, he revved up populist sentiments by pointing to those Wall Street 'gluttons of privilege' who he alleged dominated the Republican Party. Truman of course was old school, and had come of age at a time when it made good political sense to compare the financiers of the Missouri and Pacific Railroad to Jesse James, and to recall that the Rockefeller Foundation was 'founded on the dead miners of the Colorado Fuel and Iron Company'. After Truman, however, Wall Street was barely mentioned in Presidential public papers. Here and there one can find a reference to an up-tick or down-tick in the market and what it might signify for the economic future. There was LBJ's paean to investor democracy in 1964. Otherwise, political silence. And this was less because presidents had rediscovered some basic sympathy for the Street, than because the Street no longer served as an effective lightning rod for the gathering in of political energy. [25]

The fate of Henry Wallace, Truman's predecessor as Vice President during FDR's third term, was indicative of the political drift. During the war Wallace invoked a vision of 'the Century of the Common Man' – a global version of the New Deal. It was offered up in answer to Henry Luce's forecast of an 'American Century' of imperial grandeur once the Axis was defeated. Wallace warned that if the century was to belong to the 'common man', the old plutocracy must not be allowed to make a comeback. The great American and German cartels must be controlled by institutions of the popular will; there could be no 'military nor economic imperialism'. A global New Deal would direct the flow of capital investment in order first of all to raise the general standard of living, as the foundation of an economy of mass consumption.

TVAs across the Mekong River Delta, straddling the Tigris, Euphrates and elsewhere, would irrigate and electrify the ex-colonial world. An international regulatory regime would guard against speculative excesses in the commodities, currency, and capital markets.

For some, the 'Century of the Common Man' was an inspiring prospect: the triumph over fascism seemed to mark the end of the most rapacious version of finance capitalism. But for others the 'global New Deal' was a more dubious proposition. Within a few years, Wallace was an outcast: expelled from the Truman government, a presidential candidate in 1948 of a Progressive Party that not only did poorly at the polls, but which carried the fatal stigma of Communist Party association.[26]

Luce's 'American Century' won the day, helping to spawn a culture of political consensus as the cold war grew icier. That consensual zeitgeist squeezed out all that hot-tempered talk about class and power, economic inequality and democracy, which had inflamed American politics for the previous seventy-five years. Wall Street, once everybody's preferred symbol of social abrasiveness and ill-will, now subsided beneath the waves of national solidarity.

Scholars and intellectuals – writers like Daniel Bell, David Riesman, J. K. Galbraith, David Potter, Reinhold Neibhur, Robert Dahl – declared the 'proletarian metaphysic', the notion that class struggle somehow explained the course of history, a dead letter. Consensus historians labored to show that America had always enjoyed a robust immunity from these sorts of social divisions; they might have arisen now and again, but the pursuit of abundance, in Potter's felicitous phrase, weighed in more heavily and bound the country together. Revisionist historians like Allan Nevins re-imagined Matthew Josephson's 'robber barons' as industrial statesmen, valued for their functional fitness; baiting big business and Wall Street financiers was passé, to be treated as a 'cheap bohemian flourish'.[27]

And even if political conflict had in the past been driven by contending economic interests, that was all over now. The idea of 'class conflict' was tainted red rhetoric, kept alive by a Stalinist tyranny that used it in cynical pursuit of its own self-aggrandizement. Language familiar to Americans for generations seemed suddenly suspect, liable to weaken the national resolve to confront a totalitarian menace – all the more reason, given the global contest between freedom and communism, to expel it from the national vocabulary.

Moreover, New Deal provisions for social security and Keynesian financial stabilizers, together with the booming post-war economy, would ensure that old antagonisms would remain precisely that: old. No chilling panics and demoralizing depressions would reignite memories of the 'money trust' and 'malefactors of great wealth'. Instead, economic growth would bury earlier divisions over the distribution of wealth. Median income rose from $19,500 in 1947 to $26,800 in 1959; home ownership from forty to sixty-six per cent of American families between 1939 and 1955. The proletariat – even assuming it ever existed in a nation so single-mindedly dedicated to individual opportunity and social mobility – was well on its way to obsolescence. Buoyed by the compression in income distribution that began with the New Deal, it was not too far-fetched to envision a purely middle-class nation in which pre-war social fractures would heal and disappear.[28]

Of course, nobody maintained that politics in the United States was suddenly conflict-free. But the point was that whatever differences existed did not threaten bedrock institutions like private property, a capitalist economy, and parliamentary democracy. Groups, not classes, pursued their interests in a pluralist political universe set up to achieve compromise among countervailing centers of power. David Riesman characterized the new equilibrium as an historic shift from 'the power hierarchy of a ruling class to the power dispersal of "veto groups"'. This was the American political genius at work, damping down the ideological zealotry and implacable absolutism that had so despoiled the Old World, producing the disasters of the last quarter century. It was the end of an era of conflicts in which Wall Street had figured so darkly, of malignant utopias – the 'end of ideology', as ex-leftist intellectual Daniel Bell proclaimed. The promised land turned out to be a realm of pragmatic realism, though intellectual approaches to it varied. A sense of tragic pessimism about the possibilities of human improvement permeated the historical meditations of Louis Hartz and Richard Hofstadter. Popular historian Daniel Boorstin expressed a sunnier confidence about the prospect of endless technological progress. Either way, the culture of consensus concluded that fundamental questions of social and political transformation had been banished from serious public debate. Everyone sought to position themselves within the 'vital center'.[29]

Wall Street, so long a magnetic pole for class animosities, was thus ushered into a kind of political and intellectual oblivion, erased from presidential rhetoric, party platforms, and campaign oratory. *The Affluent Society* (the title of J. K. Galbraith's 1958 bestseller) had its problems, to be sure, but they were largely cultural, psychological, and sociological. Although Galbraith noted the silent exclusion of poor people from this middle-class idyll, most writers emphasized the existential travails of the 'lonely crowd' and its search for meaning, identity, and status in a world of gray flannel and homogenized suburbia. Anxieties about social status diffused across the fluid terrain of middle-class life, rather than fastening onto old-fashioned enclaves of elitist pretension like Wall Street.

Journalists and intellectuals were not the only ones who sensed that the Street's days as a gathering place for the American ruling class were over with. The Street itself seemed to have made its peace with the New Deal order. The new guard running the Exchange had welcomed the basic reforms promulgated by the SEC, though other economic and social reforms of that era, and in particular the inquisitorial atmosphere to which investment bankers found themselves subject back then, still rankled. On matters of civil rights and foreign policy, however, little separated liberal intellectuals from Wall Street's most distinguished leaders (even if the latter's public commitment to racial equality remained strictly rhetorical).[30]

At one time, twentieth-century American liberalism – whether under the guise of the 'Square Deal', the 'New Freedom', or the 'New Deal' – sought to rescue the country from the grasp of concentrated economic power. But now mainstream analysts wondered if it any longer made sense to talk of a ruling class. Had it vanished? The search began.

Social scientist David Riesman was among those who believed that the whole notion of a ruling class was an anachronism. Power in an American society defined by the anonymous corporation, he maintained in *The Lonely Crowd*, was much too 'mercurial', 'situational', and 'amorphous' to support something as fixed and durable as a ruling class. It made no sense any longer to talk of a 'we' and a 'they'. Reinhold Neibhur in *The Irony of American History* agreed, suggesting that the fluidity of American society tended to dissolve every incipient hierarchy of power. The business economist Peter Drucker argued that it was impossible to define a distinctly upper-class (or for that matter lower-class) way of life.

The incorporation of distinguished Wall Street figures within the upper echelons of the Roosevelt administration seemed a stunning refutation of older, more polarized depictions of the class fissures in American politics. A real rapprochement between Washington and the Street was there for all to see; a concord of the enlightened from finance and politics presided over the essential regulatory innovations of the New Deal and promised to heal wounds from the past. This sort of thinking was naturally encouraged by the pressing anxieties of the cold war, and by a political environment increasingly preoccupied with communist subversion – at home, in the State Department, in the labor movement, and elsewhere. A ruling class might crop up in Europe, might even perversely characterize the Stalinist tyranny that ran Russia, but for just that reason it could find no traction in the 'Free World'.[31]

Yet nagging doubts remained. Something tangible, if hard to define, seemed to be in charge. Henry Fairlie was a conservative British journalist who first invented the phrase 'the Establishment' in 1955 to illuminate the mechanisms of power and prestige in England. Fairlie's formulation soon crossed the Atlantic, picked up by journalists like Richard Rovere and public intellectuals like Galbraith. 'Establishment' sounded less harsh than 'ruling class' or even ruling elite: it evoked images of a semi-official and venerable institution rather than a cabal of men meeting in a mahogany-paneled room to conspire against democracy. Rovere in particular seemed to accept and dismiss the notion all at the same time. His ironical take on 'the Establishment' conceded that men like John McCloy, whose ties to Wall Street law firms and banks were widely known, did indeed exercise considerable power; yet he was at pains to make fun of those on the left, like sociologist C. Wright Mills, who still insisted that an organized, self-conscious group, a 'power elite', made the country's key decisions.[32]

Whether treated half seriously by Rovere or with the acerbic gravity of Mills, these intellectual expeditions in search of a ruling class didn't home in on Broad and Wall Street as they would previously have done. For liberals especially, the cold war reconfigured ideological and social assumptions. Men like McCloy, Dean Acheson, the Dulles brothers, and Robert Lovett (and a younger generation that included the Bundy brothers, Dean Rusk, Paul Nitze, Douglas Dillon, and Charles Bohlen) seemed to be less plenipotentiaries from Wall Street than 'wise men' who made disinterested decisions on behalf of

the whole nation. If their Wall Street background counted for anything, it was as training in the complex political economy of international affairs. If the Street still incubated men of power, their
dominance no longer seemed worrying, but rather benignly exercised:
such men were like an American equivalent of the upper ranks of the
British civil service.

For a man of the dwindling left like Mills, the demotion of Wall
Street from its position as the central committee of the ruling class was
more ambiguous. On the one hand, Mills noted that in the post-war
world it was 'not "Wall Street financiers" or bankers, but large owners and executives in their self-financing corporations [who] hold the
keys of economic power'. It was this more anonymous world of managers and directors of great national corporations that comprised the
understructure of the new ruling elite. Together with peer groups of
military proconsuls and political leaders, with whom they shared a set
of social practices, educational affiliations, and cultural beliefs, they
formed a cadre of decision makers. Their overriding priority was the
well-being of corporate capitalism at home and abroad.

Anyone during the cold war who defended the notion that there
might be identifiable elites endowed with disproportionate power was
laying himself open to cold war accusations that he was suffering from
paranoid delusions and expressing resentment rather than reasoned
analysis. Mills, whose *Power Elite* was published in 1956, labored to
fend off such charges. He noted that the era of great dynastic alliances,
of America's 'Sixty Families', was over. He deliberately stayed away
from Marxist nomenclature, especially the loaded phrase 'ruling
class', as it implied too deterministic a relationship between economic
and political power. He cautioned that the 'power elite' did not constitute a conspiracy, nor were these men always of the same mind, nor
were they immune to mistakes, nor omnipotent in their reach. They
did not make all decisions, only the most fateful ones. Wall Street still
showed up on this map of the nation's new power structure. But it was
no longer its lodestone.

Yet at the same time, Mills maintained that Wall Street remained a
critical nodal point, that its financiers and lawyers were inherently
perfect go-betweens, moving gracefully from economic to political to
military realms, acting to unify the country's 'power elite'. Their function was to transcend the narrower interests and points of view
endemic to a capitalist economy. Mills pointed particularly to the firm

of Dillon Read as the transit point between Democratic administrations and the corporate world, singling out such figures as James Forrestal and Ferdinand Eberstadt who'd gone from Dillon Read to the War Production Board. He took due note of other key Wall Street firms like Sullivan and Cromwell, and of McCloy and Winthrop Aldrich from the Chase Manhattan/Rockefeller group, who felt at home in both Democratic and Republican regimes. The Eisenhower administration, Mills observed, filled its three key policy-making departments – State, Defense, and the Treasury – with men like the Dulles brothers (John Foster at State and Allen at the CIA) who regularly moved between Wall Street law firms, corporate boards, bank directorships, and non-elective posts in the executive branch. These circles no longer viewed the government as a happy hunting ground for pelf and favor, as their ancestors once did. Rather they sought to transfer their portable talents as managers and directors, equipped to take their long view into the realm of national policy-making.[33]

Most observers, however, found Mills' portrait of a cohesive, commanding, and self-conscious power elite far-fetched. After all, one could no longer assume the filial political loyalties of the ancien regime; for example, they were no longer all Republicans. Clearly there were strategic differences within 'the Establishment'. Men like John Foster Dulles, who wanted to confront the Soviet Union with the threat of nuclear annihilation, distrusted people like Dean Acheson, who by comparison seemed almost pacific. Moreover, assuming the burden of global overlordship inevitably diminished Wall Street cosmopolitans' attachment to local and regional political hierarchies. While their presence spread horizontally from Western Europe, across the Middle East and into the Far East, their reach downward into the topsoil of urban America grew shallower. While they worried about goings-on in Paris, Berlin, and Cairo, they were less concerned about what was stirring in New York, Boston, and Chicago. It was partly for this reason that twenty years later, 'masters of the universe' like Tom Wolfe's Sherman McCoy I in *Bonfire of the Vanities* found themselves under siege and out of touch with a hostile city.

Internal divisions compounded this sense of alienation. Among the upper classes generally, some were more prepared than others to accept the new post-war dispensation – that is, the New Deal order of things. Sociologist E. Digby Baltzell, in his 1964 anatomy of *The Protestant Establishment*, noted the schizophrenia infecting the outlook of 'old money'. The 'wise men' and their ilk were ready to allow the meritorious into their ranks, whatever their origins. Many of their peers, however, preferred to huddle in their bunkers of caste exclusivity, offering stiff-necked resistance to or ignoring the social changes around them. Meanwhile, 'the 'Establishment' became conspicuously bi-partisan: Sullivan and Cromwell sent its emissaries to work in the upper echelons of the executive branch, regardless of which party happened to be in control. By the 1960s, there were as many notable Wall Street Democrats as Republicans.[34]

Ambiguity about Wall Street's political identity and intentions was compounded by a post-war fascination with the insidious workings of 'mass society' and 'mass culture'. That phenomenon left the Street's social profile if anything even less distinct than its political presence. The blurring of the boundaries of social status had always been an American characteristic, but after the war, the energies driving this remarkable social fissioning and recombination multiplied exponentially, even penetrating the most intimate recesses of upper-class exclusivity. It was becoming harder to spot a plutocrat by the cut of his swallow-tail morning coat, or by his artistic preferences and moral code. Even more perplexing, the capacity of people to make such judgments, to discern the very existence of a ruling elite, had withered. Cultural antennae once sensitive to vibrations of social and political inequality were overwhelmed by the deafening noise of 'mass culture'.

Mills was both fascinated and troubled, like many other commentators in the 1950s, by the emergence of this phenomenon. They feared first of all those specific features of crowd hysteria upon which the fascists and Nazis rode to power. But the anomic individual so typical of modern bureaucratic-industrial society in general was susceptible to similar emotions. In this truly new world, they hypothesized, the everyday life of ordinary people was so dominated by the mass media that they had lost the internal fortitude to resist its machinations, to form independent judgments. 'Informed publics' were undermined by the standardized delivery of vacuous information and mindless entertainment, creating a passive, deluded, and politically sedated population incapable of identifying its own manipulation. This allowed the 'power elite' to rule without admitting it ruled, to earn a kind of artificial legitimacy for its decisions that no democratic public either understood nor had any role in formulating. Soon enough the popular upheavals of the 1960s would highlight the short-sightedness of this view. In the meantime, however, 'mass culture' seemed another black hole into which Wall Street had vanished.[35]

One principal medium of that mass pacification was the culture of celebrity, whose emphasis on fleeting fame and 'personality' monopolized the attention of the media. Movie stars especially, but also politicians, businessmen, and athletes gathered together in a socially promiscuous nocturnal world of glamour and souped-up sexuality, which fixed attention on the fast-moving and the evanescent. It was a café society of the fashionable where lineage mattered less than media charisma or off-color notoriety. In the process more durable landmarks of personal and social privilege assumed a lower profile. Dynastic marriages, heraldic and genealogical displays, feudal masquerades, and trans-Atlantic alliances of wealth and pedigree no longer commanded the front-page priorities of metropolitan newspapers. Indeed, such spectacles began to seem just a little quaint.

Some dignitaries from the Street had already made themselves at home in the more mercurial and heterogeneous environs of the celebrity bazaar. As far back as the 1920s, for example, Averill Harriman, after his second marriage to Marie Norton Whitney, had become a regular partygoer at the Algonquin, where Alexander Wolcott, Helen Hayes, Harpo Marx, Ernest Hemingway, George S. Kaufman, and Dorothy Parker – literati and glitterati – intermingled. Nelson Rockefeller inherited a fondness for modern art from his extraordinarily open-minded mother, Abby Aldrich Rockefeller, the godmother of the Museum of Modern Art. Her son was devoted to collecting and championing abstract expressionist art, which defied the conventional aesthetic habits of the larger social world he was born into. While David assumed the paternal inheritance as the head of Chase Manhattan Bank, other Rockefeller offspring followed Abby's highbrow deviance – especially the eldest son, John, who developed a reputation as a 'parlor pink' for his social philanthropies and anti-war sentiments. Robert Lovett, likewise, cultivated a taste for modernism and became a fan of jazz, movies, and popular mystery novels.

A process of ecological decay set in, burying those imposing political and cultural signposts that once helped everyone identify a titan of finance when they saw one. It was not just that some doyens of the Street were abandoning their mansions and the furniture of their feudal pretensions. Consumer culture accelerated the erasure of age-old

hierarchies of taste. Clear marks of class distinction and social preferment in dress, residences, recreation, and everyday manners were
eroded by post-war prosperity. Once quarantined behind impassable
barriers of style and language – by golf, polo, and grass-court tennis –
the upper classes opened themselves up to the onrushing tide of
demotic youth culture, with its rock 'n' roll and blue jeans. A corporate middle-class invasion of recherché country clubs, exclusive
restaurants, and Ivy League universities showed how porous the
boundaries of privilege had become. Of course, new and more subtle
and invidious distinctions would arise; after all, that was inherent in
the nature of consumer culture. But property, breeding, and power, the
cardinal signposts of the old social hierarchy, undoubtedly no longer
carried the weight they once did.

'Grace . . . the greatest artistic effect of the Old Money class', which
once defined its ineffable psychological authority, made a fainter
impression in a world that preferred a utilitarian pragmatism in its
leaders. Those reiterated social rituals which had lent permanence to
that world now seemed oddly frozen, out of joint with the times: the
debutante ball, the prep-school apprenticeship, the eating-club initiation. This loss of *amour-propre* fostered a detectable demoralization. The hapless hero of Louis Auchincloss's *I Come as a Thief*, a
Wall Street lawyer of impeccable lineage, is not only morally indifferent, but plagued by a sense of aimlessness, as he watches the lines of
dynastic privilege and exclusivity disintegrate in front of his eyes. An
air of rueful resignation hovers over this world, a consciousness that
its social entitlement could be assumed no more.[36]

During the go-go years of the 1960s, the Street was overrun with
young men, salesmen and analysts, infected with the decade's cultural
irreverence, sporting sideburns, necklaces, and flowery leisure shirts –
men who hailed from nowhere special. It was then that the Street's
language first became known for its locker-room crudity, while the
upper-class accents of yesteryear became more rare. Wall Street had
always left space for the 'rough trade'; that was part of its popular
allure. But not since the days of Drew and Fisk had such insouciant
rebel financiers commanded center-stage, giving the Street a democratic facelift. The fact that many of these men were lower middle-
class Jews from the outer boroughs and no-name colleges was
noteworthy precisely because their origins no longer proscribed their
ascent. Among the most aggressive 'gunslingers' of that mid-60s fling

were people like Gerald Tsai and Fred Alger, who ran high-risk mutual funds and considered themselves maverick rebels against the old order on Wall Street. When the then youthful upstart, Saul Steinberg, failed in his brash attempt to take over Chemical Bank due to the concerted resistance of the old guard, including Governor Nelson Rockefeller, he reacted with bemused shock: 'I always knew there was an Establishment – I just used to think I was part of it.' Meanwhile, the Street retired the last of its ornate financial temples: the modish utilitarian starkness that characterized corporate architecture further uptown began to displace the monumentality and the patina of antiquity that had once lent the Street its distinctive grandeur.[37]

Political bipartisanship and cultural assimilation could cut both ways, however. Wall Street's vanishing act ran up against the incontrovertible evidence of its looming presence at the creation of the post-war order. If the Street was a ghost, it was the ghost in the machine, still a power to be reckoned with. Indeed, that very 'American Century' that had installed a Pax Americana across the 'free world' and consigned the class struggle to history's proverbial dustbin was the handiwork of men who'd spent their lives shuffling between Wall Street and the country's foreign-policy establishment. The International Monetary Fund, the Bank for Reconstruction and Development (the 'World Bank'), and the Marshall Plan – together with NATO the key institutions of America's economic and political hegemony – were designed by men like Henry Stimson, John McCloy, Dean Acheson, James Forrestal, Robert Lovett, and Averill Harriman. Furthermore, these and other post-war channels of trade and investment denoted the commanding material presence of the Street in post-war economic affairs, however obscure its cultural presence might be.

It is virtually impossible to exaggerate the dominance of the United States economy at the end of the war, and the strategic positioning of Wall Street figures within the post-war international apparatus. When the war ended, the United States accounted for two thirds of the world's industrial output. In 1950, sixty per cent of the capital stock of the advanced capitalist world was American. That same year, US corporations accounted for a third of the world's total GNP. Two out of every three tons of steel were made in America. As late as 1970, the United States still accounted for half the world's capital stock and half its industrial output. Right after the war, the country's economic weight was almost too much for the rest of an impoverished western European economy to bear as huge export surpluses piled up on American shores. No one had anticipated the paralysis that gripped the Continent, or the extent of its physical devastation, technological retrogression, monetary chaos, and workforce demoralization. The British Empire, or its sickly remains, hung on like a mortally stricken patient on life-support. Measured against such bleakness, the economic and financial power of the United States government and Wall Street's imposing international banks was daunting indeed. [38]

From the outset of war, the institutions of domestic economic mobilization as well as the military were honeycombed with Wall Street lawyers from peak firms like Cravath, de Gersdorff, Swaine, and Wood. Henry Stimson was Roosevelt's Secretary of War, ably assisted by two younger Wall Street protégés, John McCloy and Robert Lovett (a one-time Wall Street partner of Averill Harriman). Stimson, who felt equally at home in Washington and on the Street, acted as elder statesman and *éminence grise*. McCloy and Lovett, together with Averill Harriman and James Forrestal, who became Under-Secretary of the Navy after a tour of duty at Dillon Read, were representative of a younger generation from the Street that first came of age during the Great War. Their careers during the interwar years made them familiar with international finance and the political negotiations that invariably shadowed that business. They soberly considered the prospects, once the war against fascism was won, of the United States assuming the position of dominance that had once belonged to Great Britain – in other words, they were prepared to shoulder the responsibilities that Walter Lippman had once accused their fathers' generation of abdicating at Versailles. Wall Street had flirted with visions of empire since the days of J. P. Morgan, and the prospects were heightened by the Street's special triumph in World War I. But at ground level this had devolved into sordid episodes of 'dollar diplomacy', parochial defenses of particular financial interests in out-of-the-way places like Nicaragua and the Dominican Republic. Something far grander now surfaced among policy-making elites in Washington: an 'empire of the free world' that no longer gave off the aroma of old-fashioned imperialism.

These men comprised what would soon enough be characterized as 'the American Establishment', a world described by Arthur Schlesinger, Jr as headquartered in the New York financial and legal community, whose 'household deities were Henry L. Stimson and Elihu Root, its present leaders Robert A. Lovett and John McCloy, its front organizations, the Rockefeller, Ford, and Carnegie foundations, and the Council on Foreign Relations.' As Schlesinger's sketch suggests, this world spilled well beyond the confines of Broad and Wall streets. It intermingled Wall Street statesmen like Harriman with captains of industry like Charles Wilson of General Motors and Robert McNamara of Ford, and brought them all together in collaboration with policy intellectuals at strategic policy salons like the Council on Foreign Relations, which for years was chaired by McCloy.

Many in this charmed circle had grown up together, been schooled together, dined together, done business together, fought together. They might even be related. Kennedy administration strategist William P. Bundy, graduate of Groton, Yale and 'Skull and Bones', a 'connected' corporate lawyer, was also Dean Acheson's son-in-law. Cosmopolitan, steeped in trans-Atlantic high culture, they were on the whole deeply private men who shied away from elective office and the hurly-burly of democratic politics. Nelson Rockefeller and Averill Harriman turned out to be conspicuous exceptions, but their electoral confrontation for the governorship of New York in 1958 scarcely registered their Wall Street provenance. Although mainly Republicans by birth – some like Acheson and Harriman would go over to the Democrats – they adopted an ecumenical bipartisanship when it came to holding public office. So, for example, C. Douglas Dillon, member of the NYSE, international banker, an Episcopalian Republican who'd served Eisenhower as under-secretary of State, whose father had founded Dillon Read, became John Kennedy's Secretary of the Treasury. Dillon's career was typical of this world's patrician calling to public service, performed out of a sense of stoical duty and honor; such men were infused from boyhood with a belief in their Christian obligation to use their riches wisely on behalf of God and the nation. They were presumably free of any tincture of self-seeking, either after wealth or personal political power. They bore also a sense of entitlement: that it was precisely their social training and their careers in finance that prepared them to deal with international politics, and with affairs too dangerous to be left to a less knowledgeable, more mercurial public to decide.[39]

A 'committee of three' – Stimson, McCloy, and Forrestal – helped fashion many of the key policies regarding the occupation of

Germany, the creation of the United Nations, revamping America's national security complex (this was Forrestal's black bag specialty as Secretary of Defense after the war), and the international financial arrangements conceived at the Dumbarton Oaks conference in 1944 to establish the IMF and the World Bank. The formative plans for the Bank and the Fund were sketched by a sub-group of the Committee for Economic Development. These were the two key institutions for ensuring long-term capital investment and short-term exchange-rate stability, and once the cold war began, they functioned as organs of United States foreign economic and political policy. The system of international currency exchange conceived at Bretton Woods and which reigned for a generation was designed, in part, to purge the moneylenders from the temple of international finance. How better to capture the chastening experience of the Crash?

McCloy epitomized this prepossessing Wall Street elite, and his resumé maps the social geography of power in post-war America. At one time or another, McCloy was a partner in various top-rank Wall Street law firms (Cadwalader, Wickersham, and Taft, as well as Cravath, de Gerdsdorf, Swaine and Wood and then Milbank, Tweed, Hope, Hadley, and McCloy), President of the World Bank, US High Commissioner to Germany, chairman of the board of Chase Manhattan Bank, Chairman of the Ford Foundation, Chairman of the Council on Foreign Relations, legal counsel to the 'seven sisters' oil companies, director of a dozen or so *Fortune* 500 corporations, and perennial adviser to American presidents. J. K. Galbraith once called him 'chairman of the board of the American Establishment'.

Like the public-spirited Wall Street fraternity he associated with, McCloy was ever mindful of its social responsibilities, alert to the choreography of multilateral diplomacy, yet determined to mould the post-war world in accordance with America's pre-eminence. This in turn implied the pre-eminence of international capitalism. By 1946, McCloy was running the World Bank. He steered it away from 'global New Deal' relief policies, and buried any lingering notions that the bank might be used as an engine of welfare economics, much less social reconstruction. Instead, the Bank would adhere to conservative, low-risk business principles reassuring to the Wall Street world McCloy hailed from and which the Bank would depend on to invest in its bonds. One foreign director of the World Bank sardonically referred to meetings of the Bank's board as 'a meeting of the Chase

Bank'; McCloy ran the Bank as if it were a United States creation, which effectively it was, since its foreign members were virtually powerless.

But the Bank did more than carry out its fiduciary responsibilities to Wall Street; it became an engine of the Cold War, funneling desperately needed loans to the French government in 1947 on condition that the Communist Party be removed from its minority position in the Cabinet. When it came to the 'third world', McCloy intended its loans to 'blaze the trail for private investment', although as a matter of fact no significant investment from that quarter materialized for at least two decades. Nonetheless, the point was well taken. When McCloy left the Bank to become German High Commissioner in 1948, his mission was to guide the new West German government in the direction of free-market parliamentary democracy, to restore the German industrial machine to its axial place in the European economy, and thereby to help save Europe for the West.[40]

More than any other single piece of post-war foreign policy, the Marshall Plan was a perfect marriage of political and economic objectives. Dean Acheson presided over its creation. He was Truman's Secretary of State and perhaps the most publicly recognizable member of that newer generation of Wall Street lawyers-cum-statesmen; he'd rowed with Harriman at Groton, and they were classmates at Yale, where many of these 'wise men' were educated and formed their first associations, often in the secretive conclaves of the legendary Skull and Bones club. Acheson recognized that containing the Soviet Union and saving capitalism in the West depended first of all on bailing out Europe. In 1947, wheat production on the Continent was half what it was in 1938; British coal output was twenty per cent less than in 1938; in Germany there was forty per cent less coal mined than in 1938; industrial production in the three occupied Western zones was a third of pre-war levels. And France harvested its smallest wheat crop in 132 years. There was no way of financing vital imports, including a huge surplus from the United States. Europe's once robust invisible earnings from overseas investments, shipping, insurance, and so on were gone. Paralyzing strikes gripped France and Italy. Wild inflation stirred up unhappy memories of Weimar. Starvation reappeared in the heart of Europe.[41]

Russell Leffingwell, a Morgan bank partner who was included in the deliberations leading up to the Marshall Plan, wrote of 'the gravity of food, fuel, finance, and communism impending in France. It is a matter of great practical business importance to this bank. We cannot afford to have the Paris officers and directors living in an unreal Pollyana dream.' Acheson translated those ground-level concerns of a distressed banker into the strategic demarche of a foreign-policy elite. For that milieu, the near-term interests of Wall Street were completely integrated into the disinterested crusade to save Western civilization. The Marshall Plan emerged as a massive, multipurpose undertaking to save capitalism and democracy in Western Europe through the infusion of American capital, a system of economic containment presumed to be in the general interest. Paul Nitze, a younger member of this elite and former partner of Forrestal's at Dillon Read, authored the detailed reports evaluating the economic needs of each country. The Plan was an act of international Realpolitik and a striking departure from the traditional isolationism of the Republican Party to which most of these men had been at least loosely affiliated. It committed the United States to preserving and leading an open system of global trade and investment. It was a neat mixture of restraint and imperial prerogative, of multilateral pragmatism and crusading zeal, of ambition and moral purpose.[42]

'The Establishment' presided for a generation, undergirded by a mutual balance of nuclear terror and an extraordinary era of economic prosperity and multilateral diplomacy. Vietnam blew it apart, both from the outside and internally. Indeed, when Senator Eugene McCarthy challenged Lyndon Johnson for the presidential nomination in 1968, his chief fundraiser was the head of the Dreyfus Corporation. A solemn anti-Vietnam war demonstration at Trinity Church in 1969, at which leaders read the names of dead American soldiers, was attended by executives from Brown Brothers, Lehman Brothers, Kidder Peabody, and other distinguished houses. But of course most of 'the Establishment', including its prominent Wall Street statesmen, closed ranks in support of LBJ's disastrous misadventure in Vietnam. By the time of the Nixon administration, however, its fissuring was a matter of public knowledge, headlined in *New York Magazine* in 1971 as 'The Death Rattle of the Eastern Establishment'.[43]

Senator Joseph McCarthy, had he been alive to read it, would have derived a visceral thrill from that obituary notice. While others spent the post-war years wondering whether or not a ruling elite existed, and if so who belonged to it, and just where if anywhere Wall Street fitted in, the Wisconsin Senator and those ignited by his demagoguery were not plagued by such doubts. Years after the passions aroused by the New Deal had cooled, during a time when the country's impressive capacity for social amnesia had buried unhappy memories of the Street, the one place it continued to haunt was the dyspeptic imagination of right-wing populists like McCarthy. What an irony! That site, which more than any other had inflamed anti-capitalist sentiment, now stuck in the craw of people who were feverish over the threat of communism: communism abroad and communist subversion at home, but mostly the latter.

Henry Ford and Father Coughlin might be counted the progenitors of this deeply conspiratorial view of how the country was being undermined by a bizarre alliance of Bolsheviks and bankers. Both men were infected with virulent anti-Semitism. For them and many of their followers, it was the Jewish gene, first of all, that accounted for the mercenary inhumanity of Wall Street's financiers. While a distinct ethnic parochialism lay beneath their global paranoia, McCarthy instead went right for the heart of the WASP Establishment. No doubt the horrors of the Nazi extermination camps eliminated anti-Semitism as a viable political ploy for all but the lunatic fringes of American politics. But McCarthyism was after bigger fish, in any event. It gave voice to a politics of resentment directed against the mainstream institutions of post-war America and the people who ran them.

Reds could be found everywhere, according to this persuasion: in colleges and universities, among writers and performing artists, in advertising agencies and the mass media, leading trade unions and civil-rights movements. Far more worrisome, so the Senator averred, was their covert presence in the highest councils of the government, especially its foreign-policy apparatus. There, charged with defending the country against an enemy bent on world domination, they instead engaged in 'a conspiracy so immense' to betray the nation. This was especially galling because these traitors came from the most privileged precincts of American society, from places like Groton, Harvard and Wall Street. The country had bestowed them with great wealth, the best educations, the highest social honors, the most eminent public offices. Nonetheless, they'd worked to turn wartime triumph into post-war retreat and debacle. Just like their spiritual godfather, FDR, they were traitors to their class. They'd lost half of Europe and most of Asia, China most gallingly. Nor could this be written off as well-intentioned but misconceived policy. It was treachery.

Men like Secretary of State Dean Acheson and German High Commissioner John McCloy woke up one day to find their motives impugned and their social origins mocked. McCarthy mesmerized a sizeable audience that cheered his baiting of these people for their cosmopolitan associations, their anglophilia, their aloofness, their silver-spoon upbringings, their gilded careers as international bankers. McCloy was a pro forma Republican, but more ardent members of his party's right wing considered him a knowing dupe of the communists. In particular, they railed against his multilateralism, his friendliness to the United Nations, and his early advocacy of international control over atomic energy. Republicans denounced the Marshall Plan as a 'bold socialist blueprint', an 'international Works Project Administration'. Senator Robert Taft, the political and ideological standard-bearer of the Republican right, vetoed McCloy's rumored appointment as Eisenhower's Secretary of State because he distrusted his intimacy with 'international bankers' and 'Roosevelt New Dealers'. Earlier on, when Taft lost the Republican presidential nomination to Eisenhower in 1952, he vented his general resentment against these Wall Street internationalists, claiming that 'every Republican candidate for president since 1936 has been nominated by Chase Bank.'

J. Edgar Hoover quietly encouraged these sentiments, both about McCloy and Acheson, and circulated scurrilous reports about their alleged links to communist spy rings. When Alger Hiss was first accused of belonging to such a ring back in the 1930s, his old friend Dean Acheson came to his defense. Hiss and Acheson were perfect foils: patrician in manner, Harvard Law School-educated, devoted New Dealers, and yoked together by Alger's brother, Donald, who'd been Acheson's Wall Street law partner. Revanchist Republican congressmen, offended by Acheson's hauteur, jumped on his defense of Hiss and ridiculed the Secretary of State as a pretentious 'Yalie', an 'overdressed, overeducated wise guy'. And when in 1950 McCarthy first unveiled his purported list of underground reds in the government at a memorable public performance in Wheeling, West Virginia, he referred to Acheson as 'this pompous diplomat in striped pants' with his 'phony British accent', parading about with his 'cane, spats, and tea-sipping little finger', running a State Department infested with spies and their dupes who secretly yearned for the Soviets to win the Cold War. Acheson would later characterize this 'attack of the primitives' as a 'shameful and nihilistic orgy', a 'sadistic pogrom'. But in the humid atmosphere of the early 1950s, the 'red Dean of the State Department' and his co-architects of the post-war order couldn't escape the political heat.

Nor were they, according to their tormentors, a random gathering of closet communists, but rather the soured cream of a spoiled elite enjoying 'the finest homes, the finest college educations, and the finest jobs in Government we can give'. Paul Nitze was a younger member of 'the Establishment' working in the Defense Department when he was fired by Defense Secretary Charles Wilson of General Motors, who succumbed to McCarthyite pressure. Nitze was amazed that McCarthy went after him not for his foreign-policy ideas, nor even with accusations that he was a red, but because he was 'a Wall Street operator'. The Senator even charged McCloy with sheltering Communists in the army during the war, and warned that men 'with a top hat and silk handkerchief' were, at best, ill-equipped to deal with a worldwide communist conspiracy. This accusation of cowardice came at a time when McCloy functioned as a central node connecting practically every public and covert agency charged with waging the Cold War; it was directed against men who together had taken the decision to drop the atomic bomb, which was certainly not what the Senator had in mind when he questioned their virility and patriotism.[44]

Why, one might ask, would such a favored few find common cause with those inveterate foes of upper-class privilege, with communists who meant to destroy the foundations of their capitalist good fortune? Partly because, McCarthyites explained, their pampered existence had sapped their will and cut them off from the grassrooted patriotism of more common folk. Their cosmopolitan style of life had exposed them to cultural viruses that ate away at their Americanism, at that bedrock pietistic individualism which made the country what it was. Here a tincture of traditional anti-Semitism could be plausibly surmised to lie just beneath the surface rancor about this elite's excessive fondness for urban life. If they weren't themselves Jews, they consorted with New Dealers who were. And if not exactly Semitic, their urbanity implied a kind of impiety, a social and psychological dissipation and a loss of frontier vigor. More specifically and insidiously, they'd been captured by the ideology of the New Deal state. This leviathan threatened, like its Soviet counterpart, to overawe the individual all in the name of social welfare. So long as they exercised their mastery over that vast bureaucratic machine – and in the realm of foreign policy, they most assuredly did – these nabobs were prepared to dance with the devil, to choreograph relations of mutual self-interest with their counterparts on the other side of the Iron Curtain.

Like a raging fever, McCarthyism severely weakened the body politic and then subsided. However, it was also symptomatic of an underlying unease with the way the New Deal order behaved at home and abroad. Its hallucinatory co-mingling of commissars and capitalists was a striking indicator of this condition. For a minority, whose numbers and political influence would grow and grow over the next few decades, Wall Street remained an ominous force – just as powerful as it had always been, just as capable of stifling the initiative and freedom of action of others. Now, however, it lay concealed within the corporate-bureaucratic welfare state, where it incubated a primal urge to make the free individual conform to the organizational discipline it shared with the Kremlin.

McCarthy appealed to all sorts: anglophobic Irish and Germans; Slavs with family and sentimental ties to the 'captive nations' under Soviet domination in Eastern Europe; Midwestern isolationists suspicious of the 'one worldism' inside their own Republican Party; and all those for whom the state's intrusion into social life, whether initiated by the Bolsheviks or the New Deal, represented a new species of slavery. Businessmen also harbored such feelings.

Robert Young was one of those audacious 'white sharks' of the 1950s who'd managed to take away the venerable New York Central Railroad from its long-time Wall Street handlers after a ferocious proxy fight. Young made the case for his proxy wars for corporate control in terms that would become increasingly common in the run-up to the Reagan era. He explained at a Congressional hearing that the old Wall Street crowd, Morgan's men, were a deeply anti-democratic cabal. They didn't give a damn about shareholders, manipulated the media, and lorded it not only over major industrial corporations but also over the government agencies charged with regulating them; in a word, they were, Young argued, just like Soviet bosses. He, on the contrary, portrayed himself as the champion of a beleaguered people, in this case, innocent shareholders denied their rightful share. Young was an ardent McCarthyite. Indeed, from the first fall of the Iron Curtain, business patriots issued warnings to the Street to root out its communists, claiming there were more there even than in Hollywood, including partners at some of the industry's top brokerages.[45]

In the recombinant New World, old money never gets to be very old. While the war economy doled out public treasure to many of the country's blue-chip corporations, it also incubated industries and companies in newly industrializing regions of the country like Texas, California, and the Southwest. New entrepreneurial fortunes piled up but did not necessarily carry with them political access or social prestige. This could and did cause resentment, as it had many times in the past, among a milieu of nouveaux riches who in style, language, and emotional tone were much closer to their plebeian roots than to the trans-Atlantic mores of 'the Establishment'. They hailed from German and Irish-Catholic neighborhoods in East Coast cities, from middle-sized towns in the Protestant heartland or upstart suburbs further west, from secondary state colleges or unknown denominational schools. In their eyes, patrician institutions of the Eastern elite like Harvard transmogrified into bizarre hothouses of egg-headed, homosexual, left-leaning financiers. They were an effete lot, disarmed by their own aristocratic pretensions, unfit to function in the tough post-war world. These new men of the free market hated the snobbish exclusivity they associated with the Street, its air of Eastern sophistication, its sympathies for the lower orders, native and foreign. Old money's social graces offended the egalitarian nerve-endings of men on the make by seeming presumptuous and silly. Fancying themselves the 'underprivileged rich', they disregarded, as had many before them, the origins of their own great fortunes in the government's wartime largesse, on the contrary nurturing a zealous distaste for government and its demoralizing welfarism.

Out of this soil flowered an anti-establishmentarianism of the right, which trained its sights on the New Deal state. Because Wall Street's old guard filled the upper echelons of that hated apparatus, it too bore the stigmata of the leviathan. Post-war multilateral codicils governing international trade and investment, when added to the heavy burden of New Deal domestic economic regulations, would only stifle the most dynamic sectors of American business, crushing initiative beneath a mountain of bureaucratic constraints. That rule-bound orderliness might appeal to a risk-averse and imperialistic financial establishment, but not to audacious new entrepreneurs. Their future anyway had precious little to do with a reconstructed Europe run by Wall Street and its blue-chip corporate partners, and everything to do with an unfettered expansion of the free market in the USA. Their distinctive anti-communism expressed itself as an isolationist aversion to the pink-tinted internationalism – or what they derided as the 'one worldism' – of the Wall Street elite. And so, even as the Wall Street establishment warred against communism abroad, right-wing populism warred against a communist Wall Street at home. It would be a generation before the Street itself became a liberated zone, where rebel financiers dethroned the old guard and proclaimed the rule of Everyman. Until then, for this world of middle-class business-minded malcontents, Wall Street remained a target of opportunity and resentment. For the most part, however, the rest of the country took no notice.[46]

PART FOUR

The World Turned Upside Down

15

The Return of the Repressed

It was a 'happening' that almost didn't happen at all. On that hot August day in 1967 when Jerry Rubin, Stew Albert, and Abby Hoffman approached the security guard at the entrance to the New York Stock Exchange, they looked suspiciously scruffy. The guard, sensing they were up to something, was about to turn them away when the three 'yippies' began accusing him of being an anti-Semite. They were loud enough for the assembled press to hear, loud enough to embarrass the guard into relaxing his vigilance. The three then made their way up to the visitors' gallery overlooking the trading floor of the Exchange. And there they provoked a signature New Left spectacle. A shower of dollar bills (fives and ones) came raining down on the heads of the brokers, clerks, and runners, setting off a hilarious pandemonium. Trading stopped as everybody gathered up the loot, cheering or jeering their long-haired benefactors from above. When the cash began to run out, the yippies had to resort to change, eliciting some catcalls from below. All in all, however, spirits stayed high. Albert exulted because, for a moment at least, all that 'high speed greed' had ground to a halt. 'It's the death of money,' another yippie ecstaticlly exclaimed. Outside the Exchange, fellow yippies burned dollar bills, danced in the streets, and announced to the press that they were emissaries from a 'new generation that laughed at money and lived free'. Three weeks later the visitors' gallery was enclosed by bullet-proof glass.[1]

A far grimmer scene unfolded three years later, in May 1970, at Broad and Wall on the steps of Federal Hall. There an anti-Vietnam war demonstration, called to protest about the recent killings at Kent State University, turned into a bloody rout. An organized body of construction workers, many of whom were then building the World Trade Center, descended on the plaza from four different directions. Chanting 'All the way USA', the two hundred enraged men used their tools and work boots to bludgeon any demonstrator they could lay their hands on. Terrified, the anti-war protestors fled as best they could, many to the sanctuary of Trinity Church. The neighborhood's real habitués – the brokers, bankers, and lawyers of the Street – looked on, horrified, from their skyscraper sanctuaries. The sympathies of many ran to the kids. For some time, the Street had grown bearish on the war. Defense contractors were no longer considered blue-chip investments, and the market turned bullish on rumors of peace initiatives following the Tet offensive. Perhaps that plus the sheer ugliness of the attack accounts for the fact that one Lehman Brothers partner was himself assaulted while trying to protect a young activist. A few others courageously tried to help, but most looked on, pained but aloof.[2]

'This is the end': The Doors intoned their malediction. If not exactly signaling the Götterdämmerung of western civilization, these two moments nonetheless helped shatter the equanimity of post-war America. Wall Street would be reborn from the wreckage and help inter the New Deal order which had been responsible for its eclipse. 'Morning in America' would dawn in its place, as the Reagan 'revolution' directed its fire at its own version of 'the Establishment'. It would tap into the energies driving the choreographed street violence of the New York's hard hats, who also loathed those 'limousine liberals', and give it political heft. But it was a curious upheaval. Its triumph would open the door to America's second great 'Gilded Age', a return of the repressed that would transform Wall Street tycoons into liberators. No dancing yippie or bloodied anti-warrior could have imagined such an outcome.

A striking fact about both events is that although they happened on Wall Street, they weren't about Wall Street – at least not in the old sense. In fact, they confirmed the Street's provincialism: it was no longer the metaphorical center of some vast and malevolent power. The New Left, of which the yippies were an absurdist sub-division, mostly laughed off slogans like 'lackeys of Wall Street' as cartoonish leftovers from the 1930s, stale even to the captive congregations forced to imbibe them in Moscow and Peking. For Abby Hoffman and company, the aim of their political theater was to mock the material-ism of mainstream America. The Stock Exchange served that specific symbolic purpose, but it was no longer the headquarters of an American ruling class.

Instead, power originated in the government, in those leviathan-like bureaucracies of the Defense Department, the Pentagon, the CIA, and the whole apparatus of the welfare state which together comprised the sinews of the post-war liberal regime. It was an animus against the cruelty and hypocrisy of the government – and of those kindred bureaucracies running the country's universities and corporations – which led those unlucky demonstrators to congregate at Federal Hall and not at the Stock Exchange diagonally across the street. Economic interests still mattered, especially the great banks, the munitions mak-ers, and the household names atop the *Fortune* 500. But in the eyes of the 1960s insurgencies, they were less important than the leviathan state.

Wall Street mirrored its own political and cultural demotion. It seemed cut adrift. Somehow it boomed through the second half of the decade, unfazed by urban riots and insurrections, the Tet offensive, the thundering herds of anti-war demonstrators, the assassinations of Robert Kennedy and Martin Luther King, the debacle in Chicago at the Democratic Party convention; it shrugged off the ominous por-tents that the dollar's pre-eminence in international trade and invest-ment could no longer be taken for granted. A 'young Wall Street' aped the hip informality (if not the back-to-nature romanticism) of its puta-tive counter-culture critics and otherwise seemed oblivious to the social chaos around it. Meanwhile, the remnants of the old guard suf-fered their own crisis of confidence. The Lehman Brothers executive who risked his safety at Federal Hall was acting out doubts about the durability and worthiness of the prevailing Establishment order.

For quarter of a century, the liberal state had presided over a domes-tic and international order grounded on material abundance and the amelioration of social conflict. Wall Street had disappeared into the capacious embrace of that consensual order. Its most distinguished fig-ures were architects of the country's global dominion. The system they helped design called upon the Street and the corporate community to acknowledge the right of public institutions to oversee the market-place and ensure equity and stability. Now that system was breaking apart. Racial iniquity dashed illusions of social harmony. A violent acting out of imperial hubris abroad undermined the political author-ity and democratic sincerity of the 'wise men' responsible for it. Cultural disaffection ran deep, calling into question the prohibitions, the sobriety, and the earnest work ethic of Wall Street's Protestant elite. And then, just as the tumult of the 1960s was subsiding, the economy entered a long decline. The golden years were over and with them Wall Street's interlude of invisibility.

One sign that the Establishment was becoming unmoored was the loss of its cultural gravitas, its susceptibility to irony. Voices as disparate as Adam Smith's and William Gaddis's echoed the irreverence of the yip-pies in their puncturing of Wall Street's self-importance. Smith (a.k.a. George Goodman) was a confirmed snob with an utter disdain for the gullibility of the amateur investor. But his bestselling book of 1967, *The Money Game*, was no brief on behalf of the prevailing Wall Street order. He was just as contemptuous of the boring ideology of long-term growth, the persiflage about 'owning a share of America', the pseudo-science of professional money-managers, the emphasis on security that had stultified the markets since the War. Smith was a kind of effete romantic; he longed to restore the sense of speculative adven-ture that had once defined the market as a frontier zone. He spoke to all those who yearned to be players again, who knew instinctively that in the end the game wasn't about money, but about the sheer libidinal excitement of playing. His book was full of the decade's psychobab-ble, with facile profundities about the Zen mysteries of the market and a faith in the intuitive rather than the scientific. Smith quoted Freud and Norman O. Brown and turned the market into an arena of upper middle-class psychotherapy, aimed at curing suburban ennui. The book was more a form of entertainment than an investment guide; for the latter purpose, it was essentially useless. Playing the market was an art form, the speculator a hipster of financial cool locked in to the zeit-geist's fundamental commandment to know thyself. His portfolio was not some computer-derived artifact of mathematical reasoning, but a self-portrait of the inner man. Smith particularly admired the Street's newest version of the aggressive gunslinger, the hot-to-trade portfolio managers with ice in their veins, men like Gerald Tsai and Fred Alger, who ran with their hunches and scorned the prudential orthodoxies that had been frozen in place since the Depression. James Ling, the era's king of conglomerateurs, captured this mood. He rhapsodized about his surreal corporate potpourri (Ling-Temco-Vought), combining everything from tennis rackets to airplanes; it was an 'adventure' he likened to some weird work of art. Ling's corporation was a vision of himself, a form of financial narcissism; this was a world of pure testosterone.[3]

Down with prudence, long live the playful! The partisans of the counter-culture defined by this cry had virtually no interest in the stock market, or even in more prosaic forms of money-making. The fact that this sensibility had crept inside the fortress of post-war financial correctness was a sign the walls had already started to crumble. There was a dangerously anarchic spirit at work here; in his own way, Smith, like Abby Hoffman, wanted to shoot the moon. And after all, for all his waspish debunking of the conventional wisdom, the fabricated conglomerates, the phony accounting schemes, and insider manipulations, Smith still loved the Street. Others, who didn't, further diminished the cultural gravity of the Wall Street establishment.

William Gaddis's *JR*, winner of the National Book Award in 1975, was, in part, a send-up of this surreal Wall Street with which Smith was so infatuated. In the fabulist world of an inscrutable schoolboy, financial gamesmanship achieves a kind of sublime ridiculousness. JR, a sixth-grader, erects a huge business empire out of nothing even as substantial as paper; the line between real empire and pure gaming vanishes, and along with it that between fiction and reality. *JR* takes an absurdist view of the legendary imperial financier, who leaves behind nothing but a paper trail. The stock market functions as a metaphor for the impermanent, counterfeit character of American culture more broadly. JR's school is preoccupied with real estate and stock deals; the school principal is also a banker. It's natural for JR to conclude that school, like everything else, is essentially a money-making enterprise. He talks a confabulatory language about stock and bonds and sleights of hand: abbreviated, encoded, mirroring the lingua franca of the market, the verbal equivalent of the ticker-tape. Yet despite all the fakery, there is a zany energy emanating from this world of make-believe, and a fascination with the arcana of financial coups and virtual money.[4]

Even in the more earthbound *Ragtime*, published a year later by E. L. Doctorow, the image of J. P. Morgan has an element of risible insanity about it. In the rear-view mirror of 1960s iconoclasm, the prodigious banker, that soul of caution and rectitude, turns out to be a pathetic captive of his own mythos, prone to psychotic raptures. He's laughably self-inflated, as are his confrères in the novel, men like Carnegie, Harriman, and Rockefeller; asses all, empty of real intelligence, although capable of serious harm and so not funny at all. *Ragtime*'s deathbed scenes of Morgan as a crazed mystic before whom all of Europe prostrates itself finds echoes in the real-life collapse of the imposing post-war Establishment.[5]

About the same time, a British rock group, 10cc, recorded the *Wall Street Shuffle*, a pedestrian tune which nonetheless rose to no. 2 in the British charts and played widely in America. It too conveyed a sense of the endgame as a kind of manic sport, with lyrics like:

> Do the Wall Street shuffle
> Hear the money rustle
> Watch the greenbacks tumble
> Feel the sterling crumble

As in many cultural manifestations of the time, doom-laden premonition was freely mixed with comic irony. [6]

Long before Daniel Bell wrote about *The Cultural Contradictions of Capitalism*, Wall Street embodied them. The craving for immediate gratification contended against the faculty to calculate, the instinct to accumulate, to delay gratification in favour of a longer-term purpose. What Bell observed in his 1976 book was the contagious spread of this play culture. A preoccupation with self-realization activated through compulsive consumption had become so ubiquitous as to undermine the prudential logic that still guided economic activity.

Whether or not this instinct found release in the stock market, it was a reproach to the values long preached, if not always practiced, by 'the Establishment'. Living still within 'the compulsions of theology' – seeking divine sanction for the pursuit of wealth – that aging world was losing ground to one more invested in the amoral anarchy of the game. The faculties of this new culture for recognizing and addressing the social consequences of its own behavior were already beginning to shut down. If the sport's spectators, ordinary people without the wherewithal to play, turned out to be the game's main losers, they were what today might be dismissed as 'collateral damage'. Smith's *Money Game* was the first, but far from the last screed to articulate the new ethos. Michael Maccoby's *The Gamesman* (a bestseller published in the same year as Bell's book) turned gamesmanship into a metaphysics. And once the Reagan revolution took hold, vast stretches of the business world would be beguiled by this flattering delusion.[7]

There might never have been 'morning in America', however, without the midnight of Vietnam. Cultural disaffection took on the weight that it did because the political and economic order established at the end of World War II entered a terminal phase that coincided with and was exacerbated by America's Vietnam debacle. This was a fatal blow to Establishment Wall Street.

Recovery in Western Europe and Japan was a central purpose of the Bretton Woods agreement and the Marshall Plan. By the mid-1960s, they'd worked wonders, so much so that American industry, based largely on the older and more costly technologies of the war years, for the first time felt competitive pressure from its more up-to-date and cost-efficient rivals. West Germany's exports rose 109 per cent and Japan's 333 per cent during the decade, while US export growth trailed behind at 67 per cent. The United States began running trade deficits not seen since the 1890s. The huge burden of funding both the war and the War on Poverty, as well as new middle-class entitlements like Medicare, aggravated the financial predicament. Pressures accumulated through the second half of the decade, threatening the system of fixed exchange rates which had been critical to regularizing trade and investment relations in the industrial world. As early as 1956, Harold Wilson, the future British Prime Minister, had blamed the 'gnomes in Zurich' for wreaking havoc in the money exchanges. By 1967, speculators had forced a devaluation of the pound. As deficits mounted, even the dollar, the apparently impregnable international reserve currency, proved vulnerable: in 1971 President Nixon announced the death of the gold-backed dollar and the beginning of the end of the Bretton Woods system. The President too condemned the 'gnomes of Zurich', who 'thrive on crisis, they help to create them'. In extremis, struggling to control runaway inflation with proposals for wage and price controls, Nixon admitted that 'we are all Keynesians now'. But in fact the devaluation of the dollar, the threat of protective tariffs, and the unmooring of the world's key currencies from their fixed positions amounted to a repudiation of the Keynesian system which was the pride of Establishment Wall Street.[8]

Doubts about the foresight and disinterestedness of the country's 'wise men', once confined to the marginalia of political life, now entered the mainstream. The Establishment itself began to break up. A civil war inside the Council on Foreign Relations over Vietnam policy led to a rancorous struggle. Dean Acheson's son-in-law, William Bundy, was the choice of John McCloy and the older Wall Street generation to become the new editor of *Foreign Affairs*, the Council's prestigious house-organ. He was challenged by a dissident faction led by public intellectuals like Ronald Steele, Richard Falk, Richard Barnett, Arthur Schlesinger Jr, and Walter Lippman, who considered Vietnam a strategic and political disaster. Council deliberations were normally conducted with great discretion: a nasty public fight like this not only breached decorum, but also ended that think tank's once unchallengeable position as the repository of national strategic intelligence.

David Rockefeller would try to re-establish the transcontinental influence of the corporate-financial elites through the creation of the Trilateral Commission in the 1970s. The Commission sought to restore the bipartisan post-war order of international free trade and investment, to abort the dangerous trend toward trade wars and currency devaluations and promote transnational corporate expansion. Trilateralists – 'the Traders' – were less exercised by the old bugaboo of communist military aggression than with the prospect of international economic disorder. But the Commission often found itself on the outside looking in (except during the Carter administration). It became subject to bad-tempered sniping from widening circles of the Republican Party, who accused the Commission (and sometimes even Presidents Nixon and Ford) of being overly friendly to the Soviet Union and having insufficient regard for the sovereign independence of the United States.

All this had the familiar ring of paranoid red-baiting. Indeed, Wall Street liberal Republicans had begun losing face inside their own party with the repudiation of Nelson Rockefeller's presidential aspirations by the Goldwater forces in 1964. Their anger in turn echoed some of the same resentments first given voice by the 'isolationist' or Taft wing of the Republican Party, and by Joseph McCarthy in the aftermath of World War II. The economic crisis and military defeat at the end of the 1960s left the Establishment wide open to the anti-elitist onslaught. It came both from businessmen and financiers outside the old charmed circle, and from more plebeian, middle-class and blue-collar precincts anxious about the cultural and racial cosmopolitanism of 'limousine liberals'. Moreover, from the Johnson administration onwards, even presidents chafed at the hauteur, the in-born sense of rulership that their patrician advisers so effortlessly assumed. LBJ relished embarrassing the very 'wise men' he relied on with displays of studied vulgarity. And Nixon, his Keynesian conversion notwithstanding, was overrun by bitterness and suspicion about his East Coast enemies. To ward them off, he surrounded himself with a younger group of political thugs sympathetic to his view – which ultimately led, of course, to Watergate. While Establishment types would continue to populate the executive branch in the 1970s – men like George Herbert Walker Bush out of Yale, James Baker out of Princeton and a white-shoe law firm, Nicholas Brady out of Dillon Read – the Establishment itself had lost its cohesive and bipartisan presence in public life.[9]

What compounded this loss of legitimacy, turning an undercurrent of resentment into a flood, was the gradual and disturbing recognition of a country in decline. Military defeat, however dressed up with talk of the 'Vietnamization' of the war, was a shock. Devaluation was another. But their convergence signaled an even more fatal fall from grace. The United States entered two decades of secular economic stagnation and decline. Henry Luce's 'American Century' seemed to have been granted only a quarter of its appointed time. The Establishment could not recover from this blow, so wounding was it not only to its *amour-propre*, but to the optimism crucial to the country's sense of itself.

Wall Street crashed in 1970. It began when an unknown Texas hillbilly, Ross Perot, lost $450 million, a sum greater than J. P. Morgan's entire fortune (which still left Perot a billion dollars with which to carry on). The 'go-go years' were over. The reign of those 'sideburned gunslingers', the brash young men familiar from Adam Smith's writing, flamed out, sometimes ignominiously. The likes of Charles Bluhdorn, the brash Czech immigrant who'd erected the era's most notorious conglomerate, Gulf and Western, wouldn't be seen again for a decade and more. Bernie Cornfeld was particularly notorious. A Brooklyn College graduate and ex-socialist, he skirted the law by putting together the era's best known offshore fund, where the international rich could park their money and avoid currency restrictions and taxes. While living it up in a castle complete with moat and drawbridge, he lubricated the transactions of his Investors Overseas Services with lavish payments to influentials like the ex-vice-chairman of the Federal Republic of Germany. He ended the decade fleeing half a dozen US and international investigatory agencies.[10]

Although the repercussions of the crash were mild by past standards, it nonetheless caused great anxiety, since the post-war order had promised to inoculate the economy against such events. Words such as 'panic' and 'crash' were supposed to have been eliminated from the lexicon of economic discourse, consigned to the status of historical curiosities by a set of national and international regulatory institutions. By and large that promise had been kept, but from the 1970 panic onward, the old specter of bubble and bust returned from the dead. It punctured the post-cold war dream in which communism would crumble beneath the onslaught of a 'People's Capitalism' where everyone would 'own a share of America'. Indeed, Wall Street would play dead for another decade and more, until rescued by the financial euphoria of the mid-1980s, the golden years of 'morning in America'.

Signs of decline appeared everywhere: in OPEC's ransoming of the West to the price of oil in 1973; in the jettisoning of fixed exchange rates that same year; in the desperate rooftop evacuation of the American embassy in Saigon; in the resignation of a President to save himself from impeachment; in the combination of runaway inflation and high unemployment soon dubbed 'stagflation'; in President Ford's callous indifference to New York City's fiscal emergency (captured by the immortal headline in the *Daily News*: 'Ford to City – "Drop Dead!"'); in President Carter's hapless jeremiad about the country's descent into a quagmire of cultural narcissism; in the damping down of the heartland's smokestack industries, soon dubbed 'the de-industrialization of America'; in the wounding realization that the Japanese had overtaken the United States in technological development and economic growth; in the depressing statistic that American steel, once accounting for over sixty-five per cent of the world's output, now chipped in fifteen per cent, less than Spain or South Korea; in the feelings of national impotence aroused by the sight of American hostages in Iran and the pathetic failure of the effort to rescue them.[11]

After the hyper-activity of the 'go-go years', Wall Street sank back into a kind of prolonged torpor. The percentage of households with any assets in the stock market shrank from 24.3 per cent in 1968 to 8.5 per cent in 1978. The Dow lost three quarters of its value between 1968 and 1982, a noiseless crash, but a sickening one nonetheless. The market simply mirrored a more fundamental decline: the period of worldwide economic growth that followed World War II had come to an end. Some industrial countries, Japan and Germany for example, might prosper, but now only at the expense of others. In America the industrial core was burdened with antiquated technologies, huge administrative overheads, high labor costs, and a looming crisis of over-capacity. Innovation, productivity, wages – every vital sign of economic growth slowed, stopped, or regressed.

De-industrialization – an antiseptic term for social devastation – overturned a whole way of life, transforming the country's economic geography and political demographics, bringing enormous social and cultural ramifications. Whole towns, regions, unions, churches, schools, local businesses and community hang-outs, political alliances, venerable traditions, and historic identities went down with the smokestacks. But the Street would soon enough figure out how to profit from this great dilemma. Barry Bluestone and Bennett Harrison, in their landmark book of 1982, *The De-Industrialization of America*, targeted this fateful interconnection. De-industrialization, as they saw it, entailed the diversion of capital 'from productive investment in our basic national industries into unproductive speculation, mergers and acquisitions, and foreign investment.' At first, however, the depressed state of American industry depressed Wall Street. The rate of profit in industry began a long-term decline which naturally registered on the Street. Only the world economy's willingness to support the swelling US trade and current-account deficits – the alternative was too grim to ponder seriously – put off the day of reckoning.[12]

Two remedies promised short-term relief. One was to shift the burden of economic stagnation to the country's competitive rivals, Germany and Japan in particular, by letting the dollar decline on world markets, thus improving the position of American exporters relative to other industrial producers. The second was to artificially sustain corporate profitability. This could be done by cutting taxes, loosening the constraints of government regulation, floating ever larger budget deficits (in part to finance expansion of the arms industry), and forcing down costs – labor costs, the social costs of the welfare state, and the costs associated with the bloated corporate bureaucracies.

None of this would address the underlying problem of over-capacity and depressed profit rates, in manufacturing especially. Only a depression performed that kind of radical surgery – and with great thoroughness and brutality. Draconian credit tightening of the sort attempted by Federal Reserve Board chairman Paul Volcker at the end of the 1970s came scarily close to that kind of ruthlessness. Business failures soared to rates not seen since the Depression. Manufacturing output fell ten per cent, and unemployment climbed to eleven per cent, a post-war high. Some of the dying branches of American industry were pruned away in the process, but the cure threatened to be worse than the disease. The Volcker recession was the severest since the 1930s, and was soon enough abandoned by the new regime, although not until suffering through two more years (1981–82) of punishing economic contractions.

Short of these heroic yet terrifying purges, however, devaluation, deficits, deregulation, tax cuts, and an armored assault on the ossified structures of corporate America would have to do. These measures would certainly serve to reinflate Wall Street, in a way that would return it to its Hamiltonian days as chief speculator in the public debt. They would also prepare the terrain on which an unheralded generation of Wall Street raiders would stand before the country, posing as champions of disenfranchised shareholders against the complacent old guard running the stodgiest banks and corporations. They would usher in an age of unapologetic hedonism such as the country hadn't seen for a century.[13]

It was called a 'bacchanalia of the haves' when the New Rich and the New Right gathered in Washington in their sumptuous threads for Ronald Reagan's inaugural ball in January 1981. He was emphatically their President. When he moved into the White House, one of his first acts was to remove portraits of Jefferson and Truman from the Cabinet Room and replace them with a canvas of Calvin Coolidge. This seemed to say it all: a decade of devil-may-care greed had begun. Forty years in the wilderness were over; the Great Fear of the Depression had finally been laid to rest. Diana Vreeland, style guru and confidante of the Reagans, put things in perspective: 'Everything is power and money and how to use them both . . . We mustn't be afraid of snobbism and luxury.'[14]

Yet what made this trumpeting of appetite and guileless social pretension possible was something far less materialistic. It was the exhilarating sense of victory over an entrenched elite, a conviction that America's revival was as much about unleashing entrepreneurial adventure and creativity as about unlocking the cap on the Federal treasury and the storehouse of liquid wealth locked up in corporate America. Conviction and self-interest, idealism and resentment fused together to form the Reagan political explosion. Wall Street felt its heat almost immediately, and soon exemplified the era's faith as well as its fatuousness.

A decade of economic decline that seemed impervious to the normal Keynesian remedies emboldened the already convinced, and won many new converts to the belief that the government constituted the chief obstacle to recovery. This amounted to a 180-degree reversal of the reigning political persuasion of the last half-century. Looking back at the whole history of Wall Street, it is clear how unusual an interlude the New Deal order represents. Under virtually all circumstances except for the trauma of the 1930s and its aftermath, the Street's inclination was to take advantage of whatever lucrative opportunities the state might offer, but otherwise fend off any intrusion into financial affairs and the marketplace more generally.

Outside the most committed Establishment circles, the Street's political opinions were as fickle and ephemeral as the market they chased after. But it could hardly help but respond favorably to the promise of tax cuts aimed at corporations and investment communities; or fail to warm to a regime eager to pare down regulatory agencies like the SEC; or not applaud 'supply-side' economic theorizing which advocated lightening the tax burden and channeling subsidies to the already well-off (a notion of 'trickle-down' familiar to Andrew Mellon sixty years earlier). Nor could it be anything but flattered by the shift in the zeitgeist, which made the flaunting of stupendous personal wealth a badge of honor as well as prestige. After half a century in the shadows of skepticism and disrepute, it was this turnabout in its public reputation that above all proved that, for Wall Street at least, it was indeed 'morning in America'.

A capitalist version of liberationist theology, at one time the eccentric faith of revanchist businessmen and marginalized conservative intellectuals, gathered momentum throughout the dolorous 1970s. An ideological alloy that had been around for years, it combined reverence for the free market with resentment of state interference and the servile demoralization it allegedly encouraged. At first this was the propaganda of far-right foundations set up by people like Richard Mellon Scaife and John Olin. Soon enough it migrated to the center of public debate through the American Enterprise Institute and the

Heritage Foundation. Front-rank economists like Milton Friedman provided the latest and most sophisticated formulation of that capitalist alchemy which transmuted private vices into public virtues. In a world where self-interest became the basis of social order, that old bogeyman, the speculator, could again play a productive role. Friedman argued that under optimal conditions, even infamous frenzies like the South Sea Bubble or the Tulip mania could be considered 'rational bubbles'. As the 1980s drew to a close, two economists pronounced that 'speculation has come of age; it can sit quite comfortably side by side with investment; and it is as legitimate and necessary as the securities markets themselves.'[15]

Segments of the liberal Wall Street establishment, including Citicorp's chairman Walter Wriston, were eventually won over to more pragmatic versions of the free-market counterculture. These latter-day Wall Street conversions were helped along by the evident failure of Keynesian principles to arrest the process of decline. They were hardly in the vanguard of this revolution, but trailed along contentedly in its wake, miming its laissez-faire incantations on behalf of more down-to-earth propositions for relaxing the regime of government financial regulation. Who could object, after all, to government bailouts of troubled financial institutions or even the whole savings and loan industry? The formation of the Business Roundtable in the 1970s, with its galactic cast of *Fortune* 500 CEOs, already signaled that the financial and business elite was mastering the art of self-interested lobbying. It was fast shedding what remained of its taste for disinterested public service and for the social-gospel vocabulary of liberal Protestantism.[16]

Of course, ideas about the superior virtue and efficacy of the free market were pretty old, even if newly defended by the latest applications of differential calculus and probability theory. But what gave this old-time religion added force among a rising generation on the Street was the unprepossessing social origins of these young men. Because many of them, like Ivan Boesky and Carl Icahn, were not to the manner born, but were instead strivers from the middling classes, they genuinely believed (and could convince others) that they had come to storm the fortresses of the ancien regime. Carl Icahn, for example, was a lower-middle-class Jewish kid from Queens whose intelligence got him to Princeton and then Wall Street. Once there, he exercised a raging temper and a petulant contempt for the Street's old-boy network, from whom he regularly exacted tribute in the form of 'greenmail'. Self-proclaimed champions of the disenfranchised shareholder, saviors of a business underclass denied access to life-sustaining bank credit, men like Ichan turned Wall Street into a zone of combat between fading overlords and the forces of market freedom. Such men were capable of the most cynical and self-interested deceptions, while remaining true believers in the moral allegory and economic axioms underlying their actions.[17]

It was this sense of mission that transformed 'corporate raiders', merciless practitioners of the 'lean and mean' approach to corporate reorganization, at least temporarily into cultural heroes. Wall Street's deal-makers during the Reagan era promised to open up the marketplace for capital to that mass of American businessmen who lacked the size and connections to command the attention of the big banks. They fearlessly attacked the managements of the very largest corporations, whose timidity, addiction to routine, and limited vision kept stock prices artificially depressed, depriving their shareholders of their rightful gains. In this brave new world the legality of property rights trumped all other social claims. This principle had been momentarily obscured by the New Deal, but now 'shareholder value' would be restored to precedence over the interests of other stakeholders, no matter how transitory that shareholder might be. This was old-time, nineteenth-century liberalism with a vengeance.

Every act of this Wall Street insurgency had a disinterested or even non-material justification. If outsized mergers and acquisitions made speculators stunningly rich, they also produced handsome returns for the millions of stakeholders in mutual funds, college endowments, savings and loan institutions, and pension funds, who bought the 'junk bonds' that financed these transactions. If men like Saul Steinberg, Carl Ichan, Ron Perelman, and the immaculately coiffed circle of anonymous suits serving them seemed almost indecently awash in money, at least they worked like demons, often from four in the morning till midnight. For them hard work was an aphrodisiac, a living reproach to the stereotypical Wall Street banker whose day began at ten and ended at three with an intermission for a three-martini, two hour liquid lunch. Taking on the stuffed shirts like the urbane, French-accented Michel Bergeac, head of Revlon – as Ron Perelman, an uncouth upstart from Philadelphia did in his hostile takeover of Revlon in 1985 – was depicted as class warfare, American-style. The have-not-enoughs were confronting the have-too-muches, and the fate of the American dream itself seemed at stake, not just mere lucre.

And if in the immediate aftermath of root-and-branch corporate reconfigurations, landmark industrial plants shut their doors, if whole communities became ghost towns, if middle management lived in terror of its own extinction, in the long term this was a kind of tough-love patriotism: it would strengthen America against its rivals in a global economic jungle where only the fittest survived. When they lobbied ferociously for a defanging of the government's regulatory apparatus, or for the repeal of New Deal legislation like the Glass–Steagall Act, Wall Street's young lions did so to extend the realm of freedom. Remove the dead hand of the government bureaucrat and unleash the creative energies of the individual – this was no mere public policy scrap, but a crusade.[18]

Freedom morphed into a synonym for free enterprise. An anti-elitist revolution from above, it exuded a messianic aura. Corporate America was to be saved from its fat-cat complacency: stripped of poorly earning assets, malingering workers and their feather-bedding unions, doddering and absentee managers, American business would rise again. Only men who had themselves risen from social obscurity could meet the challenge. They came armed with the necessary irreverence, fearlessness, and appetite. Only they had the foresight to spot, and the confidence to resurrect. companies that were languishing in commercial oblivion but latent with untapped potential.

Michael Milken's Aladdin-like junk-bond corporate buy-outs, mega-mergers, and acquisitions made him the chief knight of this new order. Raised in California, nerdy, supremely arrogant, and notably modest in what he drove, dressed, and lived in, he was perhaps an unlikely candidate for the role. He nonetheless exerted a mesmerizing influence, a charisma that had limos lining up on Rodeo Drive in Beverly Hills at four in the morning to do deals, convinced, as one of his more fervent admirers gushed, that 'Michael is the most important individual who has lived in this century.' Why not? Contemporary observers thought they spied a 'social revolution' in the making, and Milken was its Lenin. In just half a dozen years, 225 industrial and financial companies issued nearly $20 billion in junk-bond debt, (roughly thirteen per cent of the total corporate-bond market). Household names in American industry – TWA, United States Steel, Gulf Oil, Walt Disney – were suddenly in play and threatened with absorption into some alien acronym of financial abstraction. Every major and minor Wall Street house had to have a merger and acquisitions department and staffed it with its top-gun lawyers and traders. Three thousand mergers worth $200 billion took place in 1985 alone.

Michael's 'social revolution' overturned the Street's historic hierarchy. The firm he worked for, Drexel Burnham Lambert, had been distinctly minor league; now it and a handful of other new arrivals were cocks of the walk. 'Relationship banking', that genteel world lined with mahogany walls hung with old masters, resting on traditional dealings between banks and their corporate friends, gave way to 'transactional banking'. Here every new deal was open to negotiation; each was a new test of the commercial bona fides of some Wall Street financial house, and all deals were subject to the single criterion of producing the highest profit in the shortest time. Milken believed in and exploited his reputation as a warrior against the 'corpocracy'. Nasty struggles for control took place inside venerable firms like Lehman Brothers, between languorous Ivy League patricians in rimless glasses and shirt-sleeved, uncouth, cigar-chomping geeks from the trading floor. Such battles gave off a sense of freedom, of fresh blood being pumped through the arteries of an aging financial organism. [19]

It was an undeniably odd revolution, sanctioned from above, pursued by a vanguard of the already well-heeled. Donald Regan, onetime chairman of Merrill Lynch, came aboard as the President's chief of staff and Treasury Secretary. Right away he let the country know where things were headed: 'We're not going back to high-button shoes and celluloid collars. But the President does want to go back to many of the financial methods and economic incentives that brought about the prosperity of the Coolidge period.' It had been half a century since anyone in high office had even mentioned the name of 'Silent Cal' in public, much less invoked it with such high praise. But President Reagan's closest advisers and house ideologues were weaned on this reborn faith in the free market, issuing clarion calls from the *Wall Street Journal* against bloated corporations and an obese government bureaucracy. Administration policy bent over backwards to minister to the needs of this rather bizarre anti-establishment uprising. Government deficits far larger than any in peacetime history generated a bond market that Wall Street soaked up: for the first time since the mid-nineteenth century, the Street suckled at the public breast.

Corporate income taxes fell, the defense budget soared, but more important than that the ethos of public service changed. Now a hands-off approach sanctioned all sorts of risk-taking in the way savings and loan institutions conducted their affairs, removing the ceilings on the interest rates thrifts were allowed to pay their depositors. The change was truly revolutionary: as if by magic, once homely home mortgages were transmuted into glamorous bonds that became the hottest item available at investment banks like Salomon Brothers. Now S&Ls could make loans not just to home builders, but to just about anybody, and could invest in whatever they felt like, including junk bonds and other maximum-risk securities. The government greased the wheels of this new machinery by guaranteeing mortgage loans and amending the tax codes so that thrifts could unload low-interest, underperforming mortgages and amortize their losses over the life of the debt.

John Shad, a free-market fundamentalist, was Reagan's choice to run the SEC. Shad's idea was to turn the Commission into a public detective agency, ferreting out cases of individual cheating. Meanwhile, he provided official benediction for a tidal wave of new securities – the offloaded fragments of public and private debt, stock options, and assorted other financial instruments dubbed 'derivatives', a term that neatly captured the aura of pseudo-science enveloping the Street. Designed as prophylactics against risk, in the end they proved riskier than traditional forms of financial intercourse. Indeed, the Street's new lingo was positively Orwellian: 'risk arbitrage' was supposed to lower risk but turned out to be a very high-risk business; 'portfolio insurance' was designed to ward off disaster but actually helped trigger it; 'hedge funds' didn't so much hedge bets as inflate them. The administration made clear to the Federal Reserve its preference that margin requirements need not be scrupulously observed when it came to financing the leveraged buy-outs then shaking up the established corporate pecking order. At the Justice Department's anti-trust division, at the Federal Home Loan Bank, at the Federal Trade Commission, the same laissez-faire spirit prevailed.

Public opinion which by the early 1980s harbored greater distrust of the government than of big business made it entirely unnecessary to conceal this relaxation of public vigilance. While popular skepticism persisted about the relationship between wealth and virtue, only a rapidly declining percentage of the population was willing to countenance any legal limits on the right to accumulate. Indeed, for a while at least, the relationship between the newly rich and famous and the hoi polloi was a case of love at first sight.[20]

After a long generation of obloquy and public indifference, no one anticipated this new era of mass infatuation with the Street. Looking back, it's less hard to understand. There was to begin with a hunger for tangible signs that the country was finally emerging from defeat and decline. All the 'big swinging dick' posturing of Wall Street deal-makers in the 1980s helped gratify a wilted national masculinity. And a willing suspension of disbelief in the utopianism of free-market ser-monizing seems less credulous when measured against the backdrop of Keynesian dead-ends that discredited big government in the 1970s. Moreover, the compulsive narcissism inspired by consumer culture, which had first surfaced in the 1920s and catalyzed some of the cul-tural upheavals of the 1960s, was alive and well. And this was the per-fect psychological antidote for any lingering feelings of Protestant (or Jewish) guilt about living it up. Together, these and other cultural undercurrents immunized the Street's new breed of raiders, greenmail-ers, junk-bond salesmen, downsizers, buy-out artists, and derivatives dealers from public censure – at least until the crash of 1987. Before that, it is hard to exaggerate the extent to which Wall Street once again hogged the limelight.

No arena of cultural endeavor remained untouched. Preachers and newspaper editors, magazine entrepreneurs and board-game creators, novelists, playwrights, movie-makers and television soap-opera pro-ducers, historians, publishers, gossip columnists, and even choreogra-phers were all infected with a kind of bug-eyed fascination. They couldn't take their eyes off what Michael Thomas, a columnist for *Manhattan Inc.*, waspishly dubbed 'The New Tycoonery'.

Coverage of this phenomenon could be gushing, bemused, or a bit of both. Reagan's lavish inaugural balls were reported by *The New York Times* like a deliverance from purgatory. Nancy Reagan's bejew-eled appearance announced a new gilded aesthetic, 'an upwardly sub-urban sensibility . . . founded on buying power and unabashed appreciation for luxury'. One *grande dame* candidly confessed that it had been 'getting a little tiresome to always have to apologize for our-selves'. On the first Labor Day of the new regime, the *New York Times Magazine*'s annual 'Fashions of the Times' sighed with relief that 'at long last' luxury was back.[21]

Catholic theologians like Michael Novak joined televangelists in scouring the Bible for injunctive commandments to multiply and accumulate. Jerry Falwell found 'the free enterprise system . . . clearly outlined in the Book of Proverbs'. Great wealth, Falwell professed, was 'God's way of blessing people who put him first'. He and his fellow celebrity evangelicals certainly practiced what they preached, transforming their ministries into multipurpose businesses that included theme parks, cable TV stations, colleges, and hotels. Nor were they shy about flaunting their personal opulence: Jim and Tammy Faye Bakker had six homes, one of which came equipped with an air-conditioned dog house.[22]

New magazines like *Success, Manhattan Inc., Venture, Millionaire*, and *Vanity Fair* sprang to life as awestruck documentarians of the era's power dressing, its manly horseplay, its philanthropic social climbing, its OK Corral financial stare-em-downs and shoot-em-ups. A 'letter from the editor' in *Manhattan Inc.*'s maiden issue proclaimed 'the business of New York is, in a word, power – economic, political, social, and cultural.' She envisioned that the audience for the magazine would consist of 'Manhattan based men and women who operate on a grand scale'. On the magazine's third anniversary, its newly appointed editor congratulated his publication for capturing an 'impressive share of the minds of the decision and opinion makers of the city', a city he anointed the 'headquarters of the American century'. Its ad pages filled up with solicitations from high-end real-estate brokerages offering 'historic mansions' all around the metropolitan gold coast, in Old Lyme, Connecticut, Westchester, or Bucks County, where 'sophisticated living' and 'blue chip investments' might be had. Reports of art and antique auctions (especially the one that disposed of Jay Gould's daughter-in-law's Impressionist paintings) read like junk-bond offerings or IPOs, with the heaviest emphasis on the prices bid and asked. The art market was systematically deconstructed so as to better gauge the values on offer according to 'difficulty', 'materials', 'supply', 'size', and 'collector cachet'.[23]

The after-hours social life of Wall Street's newest moguls had a narcotic effect on journalists. They filled page upon page with who wore what, who sat next to whom, and what edible art-work was served at the latest fete for the Metropolitan Museum of Art. Tidbits like one about Susan Gutfreund, the spouse of Salomon Brothers' CEO, booking two seats on Concorde to fly a bottle of Coke to Paris to celebrate her husband's sixtieth birthday were too delicious to resist. Philanthropy as a form of social climbing became an indoor sport with an avid following. Saul Steinberg, the period's most notorious greenmailer and an original corporate raider from the late 1950s, was ushered into Society at a gala affair reported like a coronation. The Brooklyn-born son of a mid-sized plastics manufacturer, Saul was welcomed aboard thanks to a newly mastered social poise and a generous disbursement of funds to the favorite cultural institutions of the city's elect. The Street's nouveau robber barons competed with rock stars for off-the-business-page coverage in style-conscious publications like *New York*, which meticulously traced their footsteps across the art market, the city's night-life, and the white sands of the Hamptons. Journalists mapped the social geography of their residential splendor, often enough 'tear downs' in newly fashionable faubourgs replaced by kitsch palaces equipped with tanning parlors, motorized chandeliers, petting zoos, and heliports. Chroniclers showed almost as much interest in the parallel career paths of their wives, who displayed feminine sangfroid and managerial toughness as designers, magazine publishers, and philanthropic impresarios.

Male sartorial splendor became an item for editorial comment as well as commercial advertisement. Wall Street modeled a return to a kind of rococo extravagance: red braces, assertive midriffs encased in vests that simulated the look of nineteenth-century clubmen, custom-tailored suits from the Old World. Saks Fifth Avenue offered a pair of penny loafers for $610. *Manhattan Inc.* invented a column called 'Power Tools' offering advice on power fashions for Wall Street movers and shakers, including a pair of 'Aggressive' wing-tipped patent leather shoes for $335, a $135 silk scarf embellished with a Napoleonic bee design, and a late-nineteenth-century ebony, ivory, and gold walking stick available at $485. Aston Martin slyly promised prospective customers that the car would 'demoralize thy neighbor'.

Power portraits of the biggest deal-makers on the Street marveled at their all-round fitness, their regimen of physical workouts that prepared them for 'all-nighters'. A high-class athletic club offered 'The Fitness Program Fast Enough for Wall Street'. These were financial athletes at the peak of their game, in it not for the money but for the je ne sais quoi which always seems present in true sportsmen; men like 'The Liquidator', Asher Edelman, who confided his 'Nietzschean desire for control', echoing Frank Cowperwood's Nietzschean candor,

'I satisfy myself.' Bond traders made out like professional hit men and boasted of 'ripping the faces off' their clients, while the more cerebral samurai of the financial wars carried around copies of *The Art of War* by Sun Tsu, the Chinese Clausewitz. *Forbes* rhapsodized about Michael Milken's 'one man revolution'; *Business Week's* cover story compared the junk-bond maestro to Morgan; *Institutional Investor* anointed him 'Milken the Magnificent'.

A whole sub-genre relived familiar tales of transfiguration: like the story of Bruce Wasserstein (playwright Wendy's brother), who grew up in the middle-class neighborhood of Midwood in Brooklyn, spent time as a poverty worker and Nader raider, only then, like some character out of *The Big Chill*, to go on to negotiate the four largest corporate mergers in American history. He was compared to a bloodied general, perpetually embattled. However, Wasserstein's incongruous beginnings turned out to be not so odd after all, as a small cohort of young men living on the fringes of the counter-culture and the New Left brought its feistiness and audacity, if not its politics, to this bizarre version of the class struggle on Wall Street.

There was no denying the fact that for the new journalism of the 1980s, Wall Street had shed its cocoon and was once again a 'sexy' place, full of 'real cliff hanger stuff'. There was, to be sure, an element of self-promotion and self-delusion in all of this, satisfying a craving for glorious deeds at a time when there were slim pickings. So it was that a face-off at an unsexy institution like Lehman Brothers between two otherwise colorless figures – Lewis Glucksman, a jowly merchant; Pete Peterson, a faceless one-time political functionary – could serve as a facsimile of knightly combat, a tale of 'greed and glory'.[24]

Supplementing these real-life dynastic confrontations, millions of Americans tuned in with unwavering dedication to each new installment of *Dynasty*, *Dallas*, or *Falcon Crest*, caught up in the soap-opera melodramas of the nouveau riche. Indeed, peeking at the 'real lives' of the rich and famous became an international video pastime far exceeding in intimacy anything achieved by the 'Society' pages in the age of Morgan. As Robin Leech's *The Lives of the Rich and Famous* proved, tittle-tattle whisperings and envious gazing at the gilded super-rich was once again, in Leech's words, 'out of the closet'.[25]

Book publishers discovered an insatiable demand for titles purporting to illuminate the mysteries of business gamesmanship. *Winning the Money Game*, *The Takeover Game*, *The Game-Players*, and dozens of others featured the stories of financial 'geniuses' and takeover Michelangelos. Like Adam Smith's prescient *Money Game*, these books expressed a cultural ethos light years removed from the Protestant catechism about hard work and frugal living once the staple fare of tycoon wisdom. Now it was the element of risk and play that got top billing, in an economy increasingly dominated by financial high-wire acts. It was a more precarious world, but a fairer one for it, according to scholars like Milton Friedman or Peter Berger, whose *The Capitalist Revolution* likened the system to a great wheel of fortune that spun in such a way as to best assure material progress and social mobility.[26]

Biographies and autobiographies of men like Lee Iacocca and Donald Trump exemplified the idolization of a business braggadocio that Jubilee Jim Fisk might have envied. Indeed, for the first time in nearly a century, scholars began revising the sordid history of Fisk's own founding generation of robber barons. New studies of Jay Gould, Morgan, and E. H. Harriman reconceived them as master builders and economic statesmen. This historical revisionism did more than simply mimic the Gilded Age hagiographies of Vanderbilt or Jay Cooke or the fawning Napoleonic magazine literature of the turn of the century. Instead, the well-publicized faults of the old tycoonery were duly noted – but reconceived as the natural, inevitable, and even admirable traits of a bumptious country preparing to burst onto the world stage.[27]

Their present-day likenesses matched them in grandiosity. *Trump: The Art of the Deal* stayed a bestseller for nearly a year, as its in-your-face ethos of 'make it and show it' became not only tolerable but even desirable social behavior. Arbitrageur Ivan Boesky's *Merger Mania* modestly attributed his triumphs to hard work and common sense. But this was a mere rhetorical gesture, since everyone knew his real allure was that of the riverboat gambler. The book was enough of a success to earn Boesky an invitation to enlighten the students at Berkeley's business school in 1985. In fact, the book was loosely based on earlier lectures of Boesky's at the business schools of Columbia and NYU, and was first suggested to him by Marty Peretz, the owner-editor of the one-time bastion of New Deal liberalism, *The New Republic*. Like his book, Boesky was such a hit at Berkeley, he was asked back. A year later he delivered the commencement address, in which he proudly recalled his working-class, Jewish-immigrant origins, and famously assured the graduates that 'greed is healthy', a revelation they greeted with a healthy round of applause. It was an axiom of the age soon immortalized by Gordon Gekko in the film *Wall Street*, although Gekko managed to lend it added moral wallop through his critical emendation of the original: 'Greed is good.'

Berkeley students weren't the only ones won over to the notion that life on the Street could be healthy and good. The most hallowed precincts of American higher education promised to become vocational schools for the Street. In 1976, thirty per cent of Harvard Business School graduates opted for careers in manufacturing corporations, three times the number headed into investment banking. Ten years later those numbers reversed. By then the starting salary of MBAs joining the Street was $80,000, with a fair prospect that a true hotshot would clear a million dollars three years down the road. Suddenly investment banking – and allied occupations as money managers, venture capitalists, and Wall Street lawyers – defined the curricular choices of students at the top schools. Ivy Leaguers who used to hold their noses at the more 'hondling' features of the Street, now lined up for interviews to become bond salesmen duking it out on the trading floor. Their mathematical skills and financial professionalism minted in new, portentous-sounding departments of 'financial engineering' lent a meritocratic air to old-fashioned wheeling and dealing.[28]

Toy manufacturers echoed Wall Street's penchant for intrigue and cut-throat competition with board and video games like 'Greed', 'The Bottom Line', and 'Arbitrage'. Slang from the Street insinuated itself into the language of everyday life. And whole thesauruses migrated in the opposite direction – from civilian life back to the front lines – to capture the atmosphere of bloodthirsty romance. Metaphors for corporate mergers leaned heavily on the language of sex: there was talk of 'white knights', of 'shot-gun' corporate matings, of financial 'angels' and 'sweethearts', not to mention those 'sleeping beauties' targeted by a rogue's gallery of 'black knights', 'killer bees', and 'hired guns'.

There was even a small corpus of graphic and performing art that took the Street as its subject. *Homage to Wall Street*, a serigraph print by Edwin Salomon, depicted a single-file parade of bulls, growing ever leaner as they receded from the foreground of the picture; it showed not just in galleries but in public spaces as well. *Wall Street Boogie*, an enamel on steel kinetic sculpture, lent a physicality to the Street's renowned freneticism of cascading people, careening cars, and drunken buildings, and was discussed in leading art magazines. Karole Armitage, avant-garde choreographer, staged a multimedia ballet at the Brooklyn Academy of Music loosely based on the life of Michael Milken, and in particular on the bestselling account of Milken's empire, *Predators' Ball* by Connie Bruck. While it appeared years after Milken went to jail, its very presence testified to the durability of the legend. Hiphop performers shared the stage with dancers dressed like Wall Street traders, who combined classical ballet with martial arts and breakdancing. Set pieces included a 'stock market dance' and a 'robber barons' prance'. Armitage conveyed a certain ambiguity as to whether 'Michael the Magnificent' more resembled Paul Bunyan or Al Capone. But the ballet's most striking comparisons were to Martin Luther and Copernicus. Milken came across as a 'cold but brilliant visionary', an evangelist for the excluded, driven like some Greek hero to act beyond the bounds of worldly prudence.[29]

Flattery was not the only note sounded by these cultural effusions. An undertone of can-you-top-this for chutzpah, vainglory, and sheer greed was sometime audible beneath the applause. The hero of *Dallas*, after all, was one cruel Texas megalomaniac in a world full of Midas wanabees. 'Grumpies' – grim, ruthless, upwardly mobile young professionals – were the Wall Street sub-species of the 'yuppie', itself a neologism that revealed popular resentment at the trendy princelings bidding up the price of urban real estate.

Michael Thomas's 'new tycoonery' column tirelessly mocked the pretensions of Wall Street's insurgents. He contrasted their avid hunt for publicity with the sense of decorum characteristic of 'old money'. Captives of celebrity culture, the new tycoons loved to posture and pose as philosophes, gurus, style-setters. The media ate this up, 'the *luxe*, *calme*, and *volupté* that business success or inherited wealth can bring' – and Thomas's own outlet, *Manhattan Inc*, was exhibit A. But the magazine also ran feature after feature in which the reader got to learn about the uglier personal as well as professional attributes of the Street's financial big shots, including their peculations, frauds, and gargantuan over-reachings. Wall Street workaholics could only pull all-nighters, reporters noticed, because they employed a bevy of servants to clean up after them: personal shoppers, hairdressers, gift-buyers, manicurists, and half a dozen other 'experts' to keep the rest of their mundane existence on track. One writer called their penchant for gathering up and displaying helter-skelter the dishes, toiletries, paintings, furniture, and other leavings of half a dozen cultures and as many centuries, the return of the 'robber baron aesthetic'. Newspapers occasionally found some spare ink to measure the gulf opening up between Wall Street and the nation's have-nots.

All but the most zealous and unabashed registered a certain queasiness about the sudden appearance of a new plutocracy. But through the middle of the decade, this unease failed to rise to the surface. Michael Thomas and Lewis Lapham might perform exquisitely comical dissections on the mores of Wall Street's new moneyed elite in the pages of *Manhattan Inc.*, but the magazine sustained an air of ironic knowingness: arch, yet still fascinated and awe-struck. Only with the panic of 1987 did novels like *Bonfire of the Vanities* and exposés like *Liar's Poker* attempt to puncture the infatuation – and even then they fall far short of reversing the Street's cultural momentum.[30]

Soon enough all these goings on became commonly referred to as America's new Gilded Age. The label would last well beyond the Reagan era, into the dot.com mania of the next decade. Although its meaning would shift as 1990s Wall Street became an arena of mass (some would say democratic) participation, the gildedness stuck. Certainly everything about 1980s Wall Street justified the adjective. The arithmetic of yawning inequality, for example, was as impressive as anything recorded a century earlier. The Reagan years did more than slow the 'great compression' of income and wealth that distinguished the post-war Keynesian commonwealth – that deceleration was already under way in the 1970s – it moved the scissors in the opposite direction, thanks to draconian cuts in social welfare and the corrosive spread of the rust-belt. And on the other side of the ledger, a permissive government rewarded corporations and the wealthiest individuals with tax cuts, subsidies, deregulatory freedoms, and a financial safety net installed to save failing businesses.

The numbers are stark: between 1979 and 1989 the percentage of national wealth owned by the richest one per cent of the population almost doubled, from twenty-two to thirty-nine per cent. What was astonishing about this was not only the extent of the change but the incredible speed with which it happened, the fastest rise in wealth inequality ever recorded in the country's history. Of the total growth in American family income between 1977 and 1989, the top one per cent of households took seventy per cent and the next nine per cent took the rest. Meanwhile, the social consequences of maximizing shareholder value were calculated with explicit mathematical precision; a single lay-off at a debt-leveraged corporate acquisition was found to return $60,000 to the bottom line. Alongside the Reagan recovery, ten million lost their jobs to plant closures and layoffs, in an epidemic of downsizing. At the same time, compensation packages for the ten leading corporate CEOs ballooned 500 to 700 per cent over the course of the decade; average CEO pay, once twenty-five times that of the average hourly production worker in 1968, was nearly a hundred times that amount by the early 1990s . . . and that proved just the start. Distribution of the tax burden in the United States became the least progressive in the industrialized world. Amidst industrial ghost towns, soaring rates of child poverty, central city rot, shuttered mines and factories, and small-town atrophy, *Business Week* observed that 'the great divide between rich and poor in America had widened in perhaps the most troubling legacy of the 1980s.' Kevin Phillips, by this time a Republican apostate, likened the drama of flagrant excess and invisible want to a 'tale of two cities'.[31]

Alongside this metabolism of gilded affluence and downward mobility other telltale memories of fin-de-siecle America showed up as well. There was the same self-conscious extravagance that betrayed a similar desperate quest to erect a faux social hierarchy on the fly. Naturally enough, the insignia of social pre-eminence had changed; nobody now chased after titles of nobility, which seemed quaint or comic at best. But excess was in with a vengeance. Society hostesses threw gilded shindigs at 'Club Met' (the Metropolitan Museum of Art). 'Social Susie', an ex-stewardess and now wife of Salomon Brothers CEO, John Gutfreund, redecorated their Fifth Avenue apartment for $20 million. 'Fast Eddie' McBinney who ran Sun Belt Savings and Loan in Dallas threw a party to celebrate the bank's speculative killings, where he dressed as Henry VIII and fed his guests lion meat.[32]

Muscle flexing was also de rigueur, but here one could measure a real decline in machismo. Back in the glory days of the last century, a man exercising his virility on and around the Street was attributed with a standard repertoire of Victorian character traits originating in organs other than his genitals. Indeed, the exemplary notion of male character assigned to people like Morgan or Harriman emphasized fortitude, discipline, foresight, and steely determination, as well as the requisite ambition and audacity. In the Reagan era much of this was

de-sublimated into dick size. It's not so much that our forebears simply didn't talk publicly about dick size; it's more that a generation living too long on a starvation diet of defeat and decline (one
commentator referred to the 1970s as Wall Street's 'death march')
congealed all its frustrated hungers into a compulsive locker-room
pissing contest. The young lions in the bond-trading department at
Salomon Brothers – depicted in Michael Lewis's *Liar's Poker* – lorded
it over the wimps in corporate finance, not to mention their fellow 'big
swinging dicks' at competitive firms, in the same way a dominant
baboon might exert his brood prerogatives. It was brash with a tincture of cruelty. Liar's poker, a game played not only at Michael Lewis's
firm but at all the big investment houses, was not much more than a
juvenile contest to see who would blink first, played for big-money
stakes.

Whatever the differences, however, the strident machismo of the
two gilded ages is undeniable. One young trader caught up in the
throes of some superheated deal was overheard to exclaim: 'I love it.
It's just like combat. It's the real thing.' Like those weekend warriors
who went off into the bush to engage in mock paramilitary warfare –
another of the decade's chest-thumping pastimes – this 'real thing' was
pure male fantasy. Even as a tiny handful of women found jobs on the
Street – most in clerical posts, a few in unglamorous positions as stock
analysts – Wall Street remained, as it had always been, male turf.[33]

And on the distaff side of this relationship, a familiar Gilded Age
form of feminine social climbing reasserted itself. People whom Tom
Wolfe would memorably christen the 'social X-ray' wives of the new
Wall Street power elite competed like Amazons for social preferment.
At the great masquerade balls of the 1880s and 90s, arrivistes mingled
with financially strapped old money in Marie Antoinette-like flaunting
of unimaginable riches amidst urban poverty. Not much separates
these astonishing elite circuses from the displays organized by the
uninhibited, if drastically slimmed-down *grandes dames* of New
York's latest belle époque. However lost in self-indulgence and social
amnesia our Victorian forebears might have been, they would have felt
right at home in the gala narcissism of morning in America's *Wall
Street Boogie*.

Then there is the striking similarity in the way these gilded
moments justified their amazing good fortune. Victorian tycoons borrowed copiously, if indiscriminately, from the natural sciences. Social

Darwinism supplied the intellectual gloss that aligned the era's social and economic inequality with the impersonal forces governing the evolution of life on earth. How much separates that exercise in pseudo-science from the trickle-down supply-side economics and the 'thousand points of light' mouth-wash that passed for serious social policy during the Reagan era? And just in case this didn't go down well, there was the harder stuff on tap as well. A tough-love defense of unrestrained accumulation and ruthless economizing converted slash-and-burn executives like the notorious 'Chainsaw' Al Dunlap of Scott Paper into practitioners of life-saving, heroic corporate surgery. He was prepared, unlike the faint-hearted, superannuated managerial relics he replaced, to face up to the triage-like choices a sick economy demanded: shades of J. P. Morgan's fabled Darwinian implacability.

All of this, moreover, fueled a triumphalism on Wall Street and its satellite financial circles reminiscent of the days when Morgan first introduced the Street as a major player in world affairs. The second time around, in the 1980s, it smelled all the sweeter as the Japanese and Germans, one-time pretenders to the throne, were compelled to swallow enormous mouthfuls of US debt, to suffer the loss of their trade advantages with the up-valuations of the yen and deutschmark, and to bring their 'economic miracles' to a screeching halt, from which the Japanese struggled to recover throughout the succeeding decade. America was back on top, led by its financial supremacy. In his 1985 State of the Union address, President Reagan boasted that the US would become 'the investment capital of the world'.[34]

Both gilded ages also left behind the indelible mark of crony capitalism. This did not necessarily entail corruption. First of all, it meant the dropping away of a set of protocols keeping normal – as opposed to downright illicit – business–government relations at arm's length. Society, or the society that counted, was made up of insiders, whether they were actually engaged in insider trading and other sub-rosa transactions or not. Being on the inside bred a certain cynicism regarding the law, whether in the Iran and contra scandals in Central America or more down-home rip-offs of the poverty program in central Harlem. A kind of guilt-free acquisitiveness by any means necessary, fueled by the high-octane wheeling and dealing on the Street, permeated the ranks of government and business just as it had a century before.

During the 'great barbeque' following the Civil War and in the years of merger and acquisition mania in the 1980s, a free-for-all atmosphere, one the government either pretended not to notice or actively sanctioned, invited a back-and-forth crossing of the lines, a mutuality of interest that could lapse into illegality. Incestuous relations between financiers and kept politicians scandalized the Reagan era just as the Credit Mobilier/Union Pacific disgrace and the rape of the Erie Railroad had tainted the Grant administration. Shady dealings at HUD, at the EPA, and in the procurement practices of the Pentagon implicated Reagan's inner circle, including Ed Meese, Michael Deaver, and Lyn Nofziger. The collapse of the savings and loan industry at the end of the decade damaged the reputations of half a dozen powerful senators and what was left of the regulatory apparatus of the executive branch, just as the Credit Mobilier revelations had exposed the corruption of the Vice-President, cabinet officials, and leading members of Congress.[35]

There is, then, something about gilded ages – the nakedness of their mercenary monomania, perhaps – which breeds cronyism as its natural offspring. This need not entail actual venality, only a casual and pervasive insiderism. At the height of Michael Milken's fame, his Beverly Hills 'predators' ball' (a name, by the way, chosen not by some judgmental journalist, but by the Milken crowd itself, in a characteristic gesture of chutzpah) attracted a clutch of United States senators: Alfonse D'Amato, Senator from New York, both senators from New Jersey, Bradley and Lautenberg, Howard Metzenbaum of Ohio, Alan Cranston from California, and Edward Kennedy from Massachusetts. D'Amato, who chaired the Senate banking sub-committee on securities legislation, which was considering bills to curb junk-bond-initiated takeovers as well as restraints on what savings and loan banks could buy, received sizeable campaign monies from Milken associates and, for whatever reason, stalled any progress on the sub-committee's deliberations. Cranston would eventually leave the Senate under a cloud created by the savings and loan debacle. But the point is not so much the possible malfeasance of these two senators, and more the presence of those other unimpeachable dignitaries at an affair where the era's most notorious corporate raider held forth like some imperial potentate. It is this kind of consanguinity that was the essence of cronyism in the 1880s: the Senate was a 'millionaires' club' then, and it functioned that way again in the age of Milken.[36]

*

Under Reagan, however, something new also transpired: the paradox that a government sworn to laissez-faire rushed in to bail out financial institutions, whose recklessness had been encouraged by its own very lack of supervision. Financial commentator James Grant called this the 'socialization of credit risk'. The rescue of the savings and loan industry, which also included many banks, by the Federal Resolution Trust Corporation was the era's biggest example of this new financial welfare state. By 1990, the RTC's assets, performing or otherwise, were larger, at $210 billion, than those of any corporation in America; it was a fiduciary smorgasbord that included shopping malls, junk bonds, two thirds of the thrift assets of the state of Arizona, and a piece of the Dallas Cowboys.[37]

However much they may have resembled one another, the two gilded ages were essentially different. When the captains of industry and finance lorded it over the country in the late nineteenth century, no one would have dreamed of calling them rebels, either against overweening government bureaucracy or some entrenched set of 'interests'. There was no government bureaucracy to speak of, and these men were themselves 'the interests': people like Morgan, Harriman, and Schiff worried about being overthrown, not about overthrowing someone else. How different this is from the faux-radical rhetoric of 'morning in America' with its pointed barbs at obstructive regulators, sclerotic managements, and timorous financiers. A gilded age peopled by irreverent, leonine youngsters out to shake up the old order is distinctly different from one run by lugubrious patriarchs.

Yet as the rescue of the savings and loan industry suggests, the anti-authoritarianism of the new Wall Street had its limits, and these point in turn to an even more fundamental distinction between the two gilded ages. During the last third of the nineteenth century, Wall Street was bound up with America'a transcontinental industrial explosion. It had its hand in all the nation's great undertakings – coast-to-coast railroads, gigantic steel, oil, and raw materials industries, pioneering technologies in electricity and chemicals – and it was those stupendous feats of production and innovation that drove the economy. Wall Street capital lubricated the great machine and came away with a fat share of the proceeds, but it did not itself generate the energy that drove it. A hundred years later, however, Wall Street sat at the center of a decaying productive apparatus. The billions of dollars that changed hands during the Reagan era signaled what one commentator has aptly called the 'financialization' of the economy. In one sense, of course, 'financialization' is an omnipresent feature of any developed capitalist economy: as Joseph Schumpeter observed, the money market is 'always, as it were, the headquarters of the capitalist system, from which orders go out to its individual divisions'. But the second great gilded age concealed an underlying stagnation.[38]

The 1980s were marked by a relative lack of investment in new plant and machinery, research and development, a smattering of scientific breakthroughs with limited immediate technological impact, and the contraction of precisely those core industries that were the bedrock of the first gilded age. The Reagan administration was staffed by people interested neither in entrepreneurial new technology nor in saving the rust-belt. Instead, the economy relied on the ballooning financial services sector, which became a revolving door for the exchanging and re-exchanging of nominal assets: corporations buying other corporations, public companies taking on freight loads of debt to go private – a kind of 'paper entrepreneurialism', as Kevin Phillips described it. Between 1980 and 1988 the cumulative value of mergers and acquisitions, corporate takeovers, and leveraged buy-outs amounted to two-thirds of a trillion dollars. Between 1979 and 1990 the proportion of total private investment in plant and equipment that went into the finance, insurance and real estate sector (FIRE) doubled, and between 1984 and 1990 a quarter of all private investment ended up there. By the mid-1980s FIRE led the pack in campaign donations and lobbying budgets. That's why a regime that came to power as rebels against government bureaucracy felt compelled to rush to the aid of any major financial institution in danger of toppling. Under this new version of financial mercantilism, even companies who had relocated their major productive facilities abroad could count on the government's help. The S&L bailout alone cost the taxpayers the equivalent of three years' private investment in plant and equipment. By the end of the decade, the Federal Reserve had reduced short-term interest rates to near zero in order to ward off the collapse of overly leveraged financial institutions, ending a wave of bank failures not seen since the Depression.[39]

A British observer tried to sound the alarm in a 1986 book, *Casino Capitalism*, whose opening line was: 'The Western financial system is rapidly coming to resemble nothing so much as a vast casino.' No one was listening. But then in the fall of 1987, it seemed for a moment as if the whole system might crash. On 19 October, the Dow fell twenty-three per cent or 508 points – a record for a single day, doubling the infamous descent of 1929's 'Black Tuesday'. The situation worsened the next day, as trading in stocks, options, futures, and other instruments virtually ceased. Values on the futures market fell by nearly a third. Even blue-chip corporations found no buyers for their stocks, and banks began calling in loans. Nicholas Brady, then the CEO of Dillon Read and later the Treasury Secretary for the first President Bush, blamed the collapse on computer-driven, automatic sell-offs by a handful of the largest institutional investors. There was a telling irony here. The computer-generated sales were part of an elaborate system of portfolio management and 'insurance' designed by the Street to win back public favor, to overcome the lingering nervousness of the middle classes about risk in a highly volatile global economy, to put to rest the last memories of 1929.

Whatever the reasons for the market's implosion (and Brady's explanation hardly won universal assent), its impact was paradoxical: terrifying like a bad dream, yet virtually gone overnight. Felix Rohatyn of Lazard Freres thought the stock market was an hour away from complete disintegration. Reacting to the immediate panic, the Federal Reserve rushed in with a quick infusion of credit shoring up the liquidity of the key banks and investment houses. Within forty-eight hours, the market had rallied, thanks to the alacrity of the government, which was rhetorically at least the bete noire of orthodox Reagonomics. It was then that Alan Greenspan first donned the mantle of economic seer and savior last worn by J. P. Morgan during the great fright of 1907.[40]

This flirtation with disaster might have led to a serious reckoning with the Street, with its vanguard of purported revolutionaries and their visions of economic transformation, and with the culture of shareholder value that had come to permeate social relationships far removed from the trading floor. But as the market's quick comeback hinted, this was not quite what happened.

At first glance, that may seem inaccurate. After all, there were those, like the redoubtable J. K. Galbraith, who'd been issuing Cassandra-like warnings for some time. Just a year earlier the liberal Harvard gadfly had made dour comparisons with the Coolidge era: there was the same speculative fever, insupportable debt, unfounded technological euphoria, heavily leveraged LBOs that looked suspiciously like Jazz Age investment trusts and holding companies, and tax cuts for the well-off that financed further speculation in the markets, not the new savings and investments advertised by Reagan's supply-siders. James Grant, another prophet of economic doom but far more conservative than Galbraith, predicted as early as 1984 that the whole junk-bond world would get buried in an avalanche of illiquidity. Felix Rohatyn, a Wall Street insider, was hardly shy in decrying all this paper-empire building which he likened to a magic show done 'with mirrors'. Ross Perot compared the ballyhoo entrepreneurial heroics of the Wall Street insurgents to the work of Jesse James.[41]

Soon enough some of the era's most celebrated financial Jacobins found themselves in the dock, facing fines and even serious jail time. Drexel Burnham Lambert pled guilty to six felony charges of mail, wire, and securities fraud, paid a $650 million fine and was bankrupt by 1990. Michael Milken was indicted on ninety-eight counts of racketeering, fraud, and insider trading. His comrade Ivan Boesky cut his own plea bargain with the government. Milken was sentenced to ten years, of which he served twenty-two months, and other Wall Street felons preceded and followed after him. By this time, whatever distinction may once have separated the upstarts from their putative foes in 'the establishment' had evaporated, as all the big investment houses were neck-deep in the 'financialization' of the economy, in its highly speculative and highly leveraged corporate takeovers and reorganizations.[42]

Indeed, in the aftermath of the crash every rationale for the new economic order seemed dubious at best. Studies showed that most of the companies targeted by the merger-meisters were not actually failing, but on the contrary were quite well-managed concerns with underpriced assets. Takeovers were often captained by firms with no usable experience and tended to impair, not improve efficiency. Financial objectives in these deals were remorselessly short-term – milk the cash cow as rapidly as possible – so research, development, and technological modernization were starved of funds. Since the choreographers of these mergers and acquisitions were invariably specialists in finance, they knew little about production. Often they watched helplessly as productivity fell, until the day for dismantling the whole misbegotten undertaking inevitably arrived. Supply-side theorizing notwithstanding, net new investment in plant and machinery during the 1980s dipped below the average for each of the previous three decades. Junk bonds whose performance initially seemed to live up to their hype were defaulting at a rate of thirty-four per cent by 1988. The rate of return on those still solvent fell to 9.4 per cent, less than what money-market funds were paying, and the latter were of course risk-free. Those companies financed with 'junk' often avoided defaulting by massive layoffs or by selling off pieces of still viable companies at panic prices. What had begun as an exaltation of entrepreneurial liberation ended in the fabrication of even more cumbersome, giant-sized corporations. Once again, the risk-takers were rolling the dice with other people's money. [43]

No wonder, then, that many had second thoughts about this new gilded age and the Street that made it all hum. Surveys recorded a shift in popular attitudes: the Street was now viewed by many as a haven for gamblers who relied more on insider connections than luck. Criminal lawyer Edward Bennett Williams, who defended the likes of Jimmy Hoffa and Mafioso dons, declared the investment bankers of the 1980s the worst of the lot: 'The worst charlatans I've found in my old age . . . They go out there and sell glass insurance to glass houses while they break windows . . . They don't give a shit for the shareholders.' When the Museum of Financial History first opened its doors in the old Standard Oil building (once the site of Hamilton's law offices), the *Economist* noted that it would be a 'Wall Street hall of fame, not its hall of shame – but then the latter would need far larger premises than the lobby of 24 Broadway.' In the wake of Milken's indictment, a *Time* magazine cover story bore the wide-eyed headline: 'What Ever Happened to Ethics?' Louis Auchincloss's 1986 novel, *Diary of a Yuppie*, suggested the answer. It told the story of a bottomlessly unscrupulous Wall Street lawyer, a study in self-absorption and crude ambition which had wiped out whatever remained of those withered codes of honor once respected on the Street. The habitat of the 'yuppie', the era's favorite social pejorative first coined by *Newsweek* in 1984, was not confined to Wall Street, but nowhere else did it feel quite so at home. A widely circulated joke caught the sentiment: 'What happens when you cross a Wall Streeter with a pig?' Answer: 'There are some things even a pig won't do.'[44]

Scan the titles of some of the bestselling books we now associate with the Reagan era: *Liar's Poker, Predators' Ball, Den of Thieves, Greed and Glory on Wall Street, The Fall of the House of Hutton,*

Serpent on the Rock, Barbarians at the Gate, Bonfire of the Vanities, American Psycho. Not to mention movie 'heroes' like Gordon Gekko, or the movie version of *American Psycho* and plays like the off-Broadway hit *Other People's Money.* Most of these symptoms of psychological dyspepsia only came on the scene after the crash of '87. Their titles suggest that the iconography of evil discoloring our ancestors' perceptions of Wall Street lived on – but perhaps more as an afterlife. The white-hot class abrasiveness of the first Gilded Age had, it turned out, cooled considerably.

An atmosphere of comic irony or knowing fatalism, or sometimes both, suffuses most of this literature and theater. The 'liars' morph into a bunch of wild and crazy Salomon fraternity brothers. The Predators living it up at the Beverly Hilton reveal voracious appetites as gargantuan as the old robber barons. But except in extremis, their chronicler, Connie Bruck, regards them as necessary, even inevitable facilitators of economic circulation. Those barbarians storming the gates of RJR Nabisco are not a threat to western civilization, as the *Nation*'s Victorian founding editor, E. L. Godkin, perceived Vanderbilt and Russell Sage to be. They merely menace Wall Street's old guard, a battle between titans with little moral significance. 'Thieves' like Milken, Boesky, and Martin Siegel of Kidder Peabody hunker down in their den, but it's a claustrophobic tunnel cut off from the rest of the world. 'Houses' like Hutton full of sexy women and villainous men may fall, but no one feels the aftershock. Indeed, 'houses' were falling left and right, but the 'greed and glory' associated with *The Fall of the House of Lehman* (a bestseller by Ken Auletta) were noticeably less grand and tragic than the demise of the great European dynastic families. The Wall Street 'psycho' in *American Psycho* is so unimposing and anxious he even harbors serious doubts about his own existence. And the Vanities Tom Wolfe so brilliantly skewered belonged to 'masters of the universe' like Sherman McCoy so fragile and unprepossessing as to call into question their mastery of anything. Hard to imagine them with Morgan's preternatural eyes, those terrifying headlights of an oncoming locomotive.[45]

This is not to suggest that *Bonfire of the Vanities*, the movie *Wall Street*, and the play (subsequently made into a motion picture) *Other People's Money* are lightweight indictments of Wall Street's most recent adventures in exploitation and megalomania. Hollywood, perhaps because of its traditional resentment of money-men interfering in the creative process, always seems to frown on the Street, even when the rest of the country is enamored. In the 1980s, cinematic representations of the business world became less benign, less suburban in feel, more naked in portraying raw ambition than they had been during the golden years of the post-war era. Still, these novels, plays, and films lack the high moral seriousness of William Dean Howells' *Hazard of New Fortunes* and shy away from the appalling amorality of Theodore Dreiser's *Titan*; and they are too knowing to indulge the moral simplicities of those one-reel silent-era films featuring venal bankers.

On the one hand, Tom Wolfe's novel in fact restores Wall Street as a central player in the country's social drama, after a generation in which such tensions had largely vanished from the American imagination. Moreover, *Bonfire of the Vanities*, which was initially serialized in *Rolling Stone* magazine, is the first attempt to register the Street's racial coloration, to update the social context within which it fended off public criticism. Until then its whiteness had always been utterly taken for granted, so colorless in fact it seemed to have nothing at all to do with the country's racial dilemma. Wolfe's story, however, revolves around the racial animosities that the Street arouses. *The New Republic* called it a tale of 'white greed', describing the hilarious scenes of 'young white men baying for money' on the trading floor of the protagonist's Wall Street firm.

Yet the novel's overriding tone is one of cynical satire. How seriously are we meant to take a protagonist whose self-designation as a 'master of the universe' is borrowed from one of his six-year-old daughter's favorite overmuscled superhero toys? This constricted emotional range infects nearly every character, no matter their social and racial origins. Sherman McCoy is consumed by a world of riotous male chest-thumping, craven social climbing and professional envy – the atmosphere is one of sweaty, vertiginous, psychic insecurity. Yet he is a 'master of the universe', a pedigree model of what used to constitute the thoroughbred blood-lines of the Wall Street establishment – a WASP from Yale ensconced at a Wall Street power-house. His most indefatigable foe lives a social galaxy away, a ghetto preacher in the heart of Harlem. Yet the heart of Reverend Bacon is more rotted even than McCoy's. His manipulations of the emotions of black oppression are as clever and self-interested as the bond traders' derivatives dealings. The Wall Street incubus is everywhere. Even the liberal philanthropists who fund Bacon's 'charities' write papers on 'The

Quantitative Aspects of Ethical Behavior in a Capital Intensive Corporation'. They think of their donations as 'steam control', an investment in social peace in a city so stressed by class and racial resentment it's about to explode.

Bonfire performs a meticulous autopsy of urban politics – including a telling insight into Wall Street's marginalization, just a decade after Felix Rohatyn and the Municipal Assistance Corporation ('Big Mac') empowered the Street to dictate the city's future. But it is an autopsy. No one can now entertain the hope, as legions of anti-money-trust reformers once did, that protest and insurgency can cure the body politic or the diseased state of social intercourse. For Wolfe, the old vocabulary of 'plutocrats' and 'capitalists' is a tired joke, a dead language expressing either simple-minded paranoia or callous manipulation. Above the satire there looms an air of ruination, of a lost city – any hope to the contrary is a sham.[46]

Other People's Money, a play by Jerry Sterner, later made into a movie starring Danny DeVito, deliberately summons up the old Brandeisian indictment of the Street in its title. It is, like *Bonfire*, a comedy, but nonetheless recalls a moment in the history of the Street when politics was more than delusion. 'Larry the Liquidator' buys and sells companies without any regard for what they do, concerned only with how much they can be liquidated for. Like the money-trust people of Brandeis's day, his machinations depend on access to the financial resources of others as well as to the levers of power in Washington. The only thing Larry loves more than money, he candidly admits, is 'other people's money'. But the phrase also refers to the investments of anonymous shareholders (Larry calls them 'stuckholders') in New England Cable and Wire, a firm whose money is not being carefully cultivated by its family management and whom Larry promises to champion in a proxy fight for control. Larry is rather folksy in an up-from-the-outer-boroughs sort of way (like so many corporate raiders of the Reagan era), and not without a certain humor and rough charm. His argot is the decade's colorful Street slang, full of references to 'poison pills', 'greenmail', 'golden parachutes', and 'gunslingers'. He is allowed to make a convincing case, an appeal to self-interest which somehow sounds right and just. Although the firm survives his raid, and Larry himself undergoes a partial conversion experience (at least in the Hollywood version), we are far from the crusading spirit of the progressive-era jurist.[47]

Gordon Gekko is not funny like 'Larry the Liquidator', but he is a memorable parodic invention. The fact that Oliver Stone, creator of *Wall Street*, loosely modeled his protagonist's bloodthirstiness and candor ('Greed is good') on Ivan Boesky forms a prima facie case for the director's political intentions. This would be cinematic muckraking, and was originally entitled 'Greed'. Gekko is loathsome in ways familiar to generations of Americans who'd never run across a corporate raider and wouldn't have known the difference between an LBO and a PhD. He's pure parasite, leeching off the productive enterprise of others, embodying a moral antimony in which the Street had found itself trapped for generations. 'I create nothing. I own,' he boasts to his young protégé. He's as pitiless as the most heartless mortgage-forecloser in the depths of the Depression. Merciless when it comes to dealing with his opponents, he orders his chief aide, 'the terminator', to 'rip their fucking throats out. Stuff them in your garbage compactor.' Furthermore, he's a sleaze in his personal life, something conveyed less by anything he says than by the sleekness, theatricality and exhibitionism of his furniture and premium-priced contemporary art collection.

But Gordon is also something new. He is the lowest form of Street life. He lacks what Stone's father – who had worked on Wall Street for years – and others from what was now thought of as the old guard, were purported to carry with them: a sense of trusteeship, a commitment to fair dealing, even latent signs of a social conscience. Precisely such a bygone character shows up in the movie, but no longer has what it takes to stand up to the likes of Gekko.

And yet . . . there is something irresistible about Gordon. It is not merely the devastating combination of decisiveness, animalism, and sexual allure. It is also his astonishing power to persuade. Gekko is unscrupulous beyond compare, but he succeeds not initially through skullduggery. He triumphs in the same way that the Wall Street upstarts of this gilded decade first did, by a mesmerizing invocation of shareholder value as a form of global liberationist theology. He's not a destroyer but a savior, not only of companies but of 'that other malfunctioning corporation called the United States of America'. It is to *Wall Street*'s credit that the charismatic grotesque who personifies the era's deepest temptation retains his pull even as he repels.[48]

Perhaps this ambivalence provides a clue about why the political reaction to Wall Street's transgressions was different this time. The rootedness of anti-establishment, free-market revanchism went deeper than anyone then knew. Not even panic, fraud, and cultural revulsion were enough to elicit the sort of opposition that had been customary and more or less continuous since Jacksonian days. This is not to say there were no political complaints, threats of retaliation, punitive measures – there were.

Milken and Boesky, whose prosecution first made Rudy Guiliani a hot political prospect, were not the only ones sent to jail. Charles Keating, for example, who ran the most infamous S&L, Lincoln Savings and Loan, and who sunk two thirds of the bank's six billion dollars of depositors' money in junk bonds, was imprisoned for a decade. Meanwhile, the political influence he'd purchased in Washington to keep the regulators at bay sullied the career of five Senators, most seriously Alan Cranston of California and Dennis DeConcini of Arizona. The revulsion produced by these and other scandals showed up at the 1988 Democratic Party convention in Atlanta: the delegates' most popular button read 'Die Yuppie Scum'. This was a red herring in so far as 'yuppie' elitism and self-regard were associated as much with the McGovern wing of the Democratic Party as with the Wall Street movers and shakers among the Republicans. Nonetheless, it registered the intensity of the class friction brought on by the Reagan bacchanalia. Journalists like Thomas Edsall of the *Washington Post* reported on growing class inequalities and forecast a political backlash. There were some faint murmurings from mainstream presidential candidates like Richard Gephardt and the Democrats' ultimate standard-bearer, Michael Dukakis, about the 'politics of privilege' and 'monopoly games'. There were more forceful and sustained denunciations on the margins from Jesse Jackson and Ralph Nader. Although the balls were as lavish as anything staged by the Reagans, the new President, George H. W. Bush, included a few words about rejecting the greed and excessive materialism of the past in his inaugural address, invoking instead 'a thousand points of light' for those excluded from Reagan's America. All in all, though, this was pretty thin political gruel.[49]

When Kevin Phillips published *The Politics of Rich and Poor* in 1990 it caused a stir: a Republican apostate, famous for his strategic discovery of Nixon's 'silent majority', was denouncing the Reagan revolution as a 'triumph of upper-class America'. The air was filling up with talk about Wall Street corporate raiders, Gekko types whose favorite sports were asset-stripping and down-sizing. Phillips was convinced that Wall Street had gone too far.

Phillips thought he sensed a movement against the 'oligarchy' that could be traced back to the original Populists. How could this not happen? Homelessness, declining wages, gross and growing inequalities in the distribution of income and wealth, the explosion of a contingent, deeply insecure labor force, a population of the working poor numbering in tens of millions, industrial ghost towns, the decimation of the species of middle managers by Wall Street's predatory henchmen – on and on the litany went. Massachusetts Governor and presidential candidate Michael Dukakis blew his chance to capitalize on all this simmering disgust with a Wall Street-driven economy. But Phillips was convinced the 1990s would be a 'watershed decade'.[50]

It was some watershed. The 'new era' of the dot.com and *Dow 36,000*, of the day-trader and the twenty-thousand-foot suburban housoleum, was not what Phillips had in mind. But that is where the country was headed.

16

Shareholder Nation

It was late July 2003. Although the United States had shocked and awed the Saddam Hussein regime of Iraq into extinction just a few months before, acts of terrorism, in and beyond Iraq, showed no sign of letting up. If anything, the American occupation had exacerbated the problem it was supposedly designed to solve. However, a remedy so bizarre it seemed like satire was incubating within the Pentagon. Retired Rear Admiral John Poindexter – who first won notoriety as a central player in the Iran–Contra scandal during the second Reagan administration – announced that starting in October, the Defense Advanced Research Projects Agency would run a futures market in terrorism. People would be invited to speculate on the likelihood of death and destruction around the globe. In its original incarnation, it was to be open to the first thousand members of the public who applied to participate. This populist version of *el casino macabre* was soon modified so that only insiders, recognized 'experts' from government, business, and academia, would be allowed to place their bets on what mayhem seemed most likely and where. A residual queasiness about the whole proposition led Poindexter and his conferees to leave open the possibility of banning the most distasteful speculations, like wagering on assassinations. And profiteering on bad news – making a killing, so to speak – was to be controlled by keeping individual trades in the $100 range. These caveats aside, the idea was to produce a collective forecast of terrorism that would supplement the normal channels of intelligence gathering and so contribute to the government's overall capacity to short-circuit terrorist plots before they erupted.

Business Week found the notion of speculating on terror 'intriguing'. Almost no one else did. One day after it became public, a storm of political opposition from both sides of the aisle killed the idea of an online trading bazaar in terrorism's future before it got off the ground. Congressmen were appalled and the Pentagon did a quick about-face.

Still, it is an idea worth pondering. Mature adults charged with weighty responsibilities for the nation's security had concocted the plan. Perhaps they felt a perverse attraction to the notion of profiting from human misfortune. After all, what else had long motivated bearish speculations on the stock market but this sense that calamity could pay off? A century and a half earlier, Herman Melville's seductive confidence man had used his own thoughts about the malevolent instincts of the bear to win the confidence of his young 'mark' on the riverboat *Fidele*. The whole history of the Street since then is fair warning against underestimating the depth of this peculiar form of financial Schadenfreude. But despite this, it is unlikely that Pentagon strategists evolved the notion of a 'Policy Analysis Market' in order to turn a quick profit.

What is more probable and also more alarming is that they found the idea alluring because of its apparent rationality. Trading in terrorism futures was merely an extrapolation of the logic of the market. It conformed to what might be called the Wall Streeting of the American mind, a memorable psychological transformation that began in the Reagan years and culminated in the 1990s. Its hyper-rationalism was reminiscent of that 'crackpot realism' of the 1950s, when Dr Strangelove think-tankers talked about 'winnable' nuclear wars in which 'only' scores of millions would die. Back then, confidence in technocratic and managerial fixes for all social dilemmas enjoyed its heyday. Fifty years later, that social-engineering mystique had been supplanted by a messianic faith in the free market. Belief in the market as the supreme conveyor of the truth had gone so far that an idea like this one could wend its way through the bureaucracy of a government institution without anyone bothering to challenge its moral insanity.

Coming as it did on the heels of the most gargantuan financial frauds ever witnessed on the Street, it is an even more remarkable happening. No one worried about the possibility of 'insider trading' or, even more frightening, of schemes to foment terrorism in order to reap a speculative windfall. Nor was it considered just how this odd 'market' would be regulated – a subdivision of the SEC perhaps, in charge of coups, sabotage, and assassinations? And yet the country was still living through an apparently endless saga of Wall Street chicanery. Scandal after scandal severely undermined the credibility of leading financial and corporate institutions. They showed the SEC to be virtually clueless and lacking the will to police even the most flagrant forms of conflict of interest. All this seemed to offer incontrovertible proof that the recent national infatuation with the Street and the free market was a case of misplaced affection. Moreover, the speculative bubble upon which confidence in free-market theology rested had burst two years before Poindexter's brainstorm. None of this, however, made a difference to those for whom conviction about the virtues of the free market had long since taken on the character of unchallengeable dogma.

What the proposition for a futures market in terrorism embodied, however short-lived and grotesque its expression, was the coming together of free-market utopianism and imperial hubris. During the 1990s, Wall Street had won renown for both. It was triumphant. It promised to turn America into a shareholder nation, a land of enterprising players, everyone free to do or die. At the same time, it felt emboldened to dictate to the rest of the world how it ought to organize its economic affairs. It was persuasive enough to survive even in the teeth of economic reversal, felonious fiance, and imperial miscalculation.[1]

Dreaming about the democratic promise of the stock market went back a long way. Indeed, that was the secret of the ambivalence Americans had always felt about Wall Street. Confidence men had roamed the Street since Andrew Jackson's day just because there were always those of little means and grandiose ambitions who could be convinced that the Street was the fast lane to work-free wealth. Every market bubble from the 1830s onward had encouraged this delusion. And every financial craze had, temporarily, extended the social reach of the market into the ranks of the middling classes, mainly in the cities. Still, mass fascination with and even admiration for Wall Street during the nineteenth century was largely a spectator sport. To the degree that average people held a favorable opinion of what went on there, it was more a matter of wishful thinking, hero-worshipping, and vicarious thrill-seeking than it was a practical question of money-making and real social mobility.

At the turn of the century this situation began to change. The emergence of a sizeable white-collar population of well-paid managers, technical people, and professionals extended the circle of actual and potential market players, even if their 'sporting instincts' operated under tight moral and psychological constraints. The proliferation of magazine and newspaper coverage of the market around this time is one measure of this gradual widening of Wall Street's orbit. Even more fundamentally, the rise of the publicly traded corporation as the economy's dominant institution turned everybody's attention to that anonymous being, the shareholder. Even if those early corporate giants were clearly under the thumb of the great investment banks, the rights of the ordinary shareholder became a subject of academic and eventually political debate. It was then that one first heard talk of 'shareholder democracy'. Some even began to imagine the wide dispersion of stock ownership as the best prophylactic against class antagonism. But 'shareholder democracy' remained largely an academic conceit. And stock ownership plans for the proletariat were more about union-busting than anything else.

Not until the 1920s is it really possible to spy the social possibilities of a 'shareholder nation'. The purchase of liberty bonds during the Great War was a kind of mass tutorial in the fundamentals of investing. While a much smaller percentage of the population participated in the Jazz Age stock-market boom that followed, Wall Street nonetheless entered virgin territory. Moreover, the ideology of a 'people's capitalism' found real traction for the first time in the 1920s. When John Jacob Raskob wrote 'Everybody Ought to Be Rich' just before the Crash, he published the article in *The Ladies' Home Journal*, a telling commentary in itself on the widening appeal of the stock market.

During the Great Depression and for a long time afterwards, such talk was heard no more. It enjoyed a modest revival in the 1950s, but mainly as a form of Cold War propaganda. Just because business ideologues and government officials pointed to the stock market as America's answer to communism didn't mean significant numbers of their fellow citizens were sinking their surplus earnings into the market. Those who did, moreover, acted out of the most conservative impulses, seeking out the safest investment vehicles, to which they entrusted only the most modest sums. Cold War financial patriotism notwithstanding, few seriously conjoined Wall Street either with the cause of human freedom or with visions of a 'new era' economy cut loose from those irritating, cyclical hiccups that always seemed to spoil everyone's fun.

As the millennium drew to a close, however, the country witnessed a phenomenon that might, with some exaggeration, be called the democratization of the Street. There were two seismic shifts in the Street's social and psychic geography. For the first time a vast proportion, roughly half of the American population, participated in the stock market. Many did so only passively through pension funds and other forms of institutional investment. Nonetheless, the extent of popular involvement was much greater than ever before. Secondly, Wall Street's cultural reputation underwent a miraculous transformation. Most of the suspicions that had always shadowed it faded away, and for many people it became a zone of liberation and visionary exaltations – that is, not merely a place where with some luck one might become wealthy. A fusion of mundane material passions and spiritual yearnings, then, came close to turning Wall Street into the apotheosis of the American dream. However much this may have been foreshadowed in the 1920s and at other times, what happened in the 1990s was a kind of cultural revolution.

There were ironic features to this revolution from the start. America's first Gilded Age had given rise to Populism, Progressivism, Socialism and half a dozen other political and cultural assaults on the Street and its transgressions. America's second Gilded Age, that of Ronald Reagan and Michael Milken, was as socially negligent and narcissistic as its predecessor but gave way instead to the 'day trader' and a Wall Street that promised power to the people. That this could happen is evidence that the political and cultural resources once mobilized to resist the power of the Street had withered if not vanished entirely. The Reagan revolution had found a grip on the popular imagination. Still, the triumph of 'shareholder nation' was more than a testament to the persuasive talents of the 'Great Communicator'. Its roots went deeper than that.

There was to begin with the sheer expansion of the mass market for stocks, a process greatly enhanced by the growth of union pension funds. Then there were all those path-breaking overtures by people like Charles Merrill, who for years had labored to marry Wall Street to Main Street. The 'financialization' of the economy in the 1980s helped those labors to bear fruit. It vastly expanded the range of securities to invest in, and by marshalling the most sophisticated mathematical thinking and technological wizardry created a reassuring sense of the market's safety and predictability. Nor can one ignore the influence of ideology, especially the everyday drumbeat of applause for the free market and for a people's capitalism that reverberated from print ads and electronic billboards, from cable TV news and talk radio, from think tanks and mass-media pundits. The persuasiveness of the message was only heightened when wedded to the technological utopianism that greased the information superhighway.

There was an antic, 'irrational exuberance' about all this which was a perfect match for a consumer culture that had long since captured the hearts of most Americans. Wall Street, or its virtual equivalent in cyberspace, became a kind of playground or nationwide casino, a twenty-four-hour-a-day spectacle and part-time diversion for moonlighting truck drivers and bored housewives. But less tangible than all the money, less ephemeral than all the hype, the psychology of 'shareholder nation' drew its energy also from a gathering sense of national empowerment. The boom seemed proof positive that it was indeed again 'morning in America'. Wall Street's triumph was the nation's; and the nation's triumph was Wall Street's.

American victory in the cold war was the bedrock upon which this triumphalism rested. The 'Washington Consensus', as it soon came to be known, translated the country's new status as the earth's sole superpower into a form of global financial overlordship. 'Consensus' was the operative word here, implying that America, and particularly Wall Street, had discovered an incontrovertible truth that eventually everyone would have to subscribe to: there was only one path to economic growth and progress. Anyone, any country, who thought otherwise was a fool, a rogue, a retrograde sentimentalist or all three combined. And Washington was prepared to impose that 'consensual' truth not only through its dominant position at institutions like the IMF and the World Bank, but also through the impersonal but inexorable operations of the capital markets run out of Wall Street.

'Consensus' reigned at home as well. While the rebirth of free-market orthodoxy had been the work of Ronald Reagan's Republicans, Bill Clinton's Democratic administration made it a bipartisan persuasion. Government policy under Clinton rarely failed to minister to the needs and desires of the financial community. This extraordinary if not perfect unity on matters that previously divided the parties no doubt also contributed to America's buoyant self-proclamation as the globe's first 'shareholder nation'. Just a few years later, after the bubble had burst and bombs began to fall, the mood would shift and people grew anxious about corporate unilateralism at home and imperialism abroad. But during the Clinton boom years, Wall Street R'Us seemed rather to reaffirm America's optimism about her special, even providential role in the world.

'Shareholder nation' had a pre-history that really began with Charles Merrill. The founder of Merrill, Lynch, Pierce, Fenner, and Smith, Merrill spent the first half of his life as a fairly conventional investment banker. But he reacted to the Great Depression more radically than most of his peers. He was no political radical, although he did recognize the value of the government's new regulatory supervision of the once closed-off world of the stock exchange. What made him unusual was his conviction that Wall Street's only road back from perdition ran through Main Street USA. Unless the Street took concrete steps to win back the confidence of the public, unless it actively tried to market its wares to the broad middle classes, it would never escape its recent ignominy. By the 1950s his firm was colloquially known as 'We the People' and 'The Thundering Herd' (although both monikers originated as joking references to the ever-lengthening list of the company's partners and were only later associated with the idea of a mass-market brokerage).

Merrill did some drastic things to achieve this. Most dramatically, he eliminated commissions for his salesmen so as to remove any hint of self-interest from brokers' advice. Instead of pitching, they provided information, assuming the role of neutral adviser. The firm issued a flood of free 'educational' materials as if it were starting up a nationwide elementary school for financial beginners. Speakers traveled to Rotary clubs, chambers of commerce, the Kiwanis, women's groups, and other middle-class meeting places across the country. Branches were opened in smaller cities and towns, nurturing financial populism at grassroots level. And instead of bulling particular stocks or industries, Merrill, Lynch, Pierce, Fenner, and Smith was 'bullish on America', a slogan that perfectly captured the mood of post-war national self-confidence. In 1956, the firm opened an information booth in Grand Central Station to broadcast its commitment to 'People's Capitalism'. By allying the stock market with popular optimism about the country's future, 'bullish on America' was a foretaste of a time, still far off, when it would seem natural to link people's well-being with that of the Street.[2]

'The Thundering Herd' was a pathfinder, but it was not alone. The NYSE echoed Merrill, launching public-relations efforts in the 1950s that pivoted around the mass appeal to 'own your own share of America', and included pamphlets with worthy-sounding titles like 'Investors' Primer', 'Understanding the Exchange', and 'The Public be Served'. Magazines for the urban middle class began writing more frequently about doings on the exchange. Financial advice columns and books approached stocks with caution but gave the subject more space. In 1954 Walter Winchell started offering stock tips on his Sunday-night broadcasts. During the 'go-go' years in the 1960s, popular enthusiasm for the market registered in the commercial success of books like Adam Smith's, and in the appearance of new board games. *Venture, The World of Wall Street* and others invited players to engage in pretend proxy fights, in one-on-one duels for corporate control, in assembling their own conglomerates and disassembling those of their rivals. There was even a Saturday-morning cartoon show for kids with a segment called *Walking on Wall Street*, starring 'Lester the Investor'. Compared to Europe and Japan, the American marketplace was awash in popular interest: the percentage of stockholders in the US was three or four times what it was abroad.[3]

But the air went out of the market in 1970 and such financial playfulness evaporated alongside it. The Street's everyday business slacked off so considerably that in 1975 the Exchange took a radical measure to win back the people. It ended the reign of fixed commissions first established nearly two hundred years before under the buttonwood tree. Brokers were now free to charge whatever the market would bear – at the moment, this would mean not very much at all. Commission rates dropped precipitously, by forty to fifty per cent, as brokers competed for what business remained. Just as the sunnier years of the mid-century had contributed to a small democratization of Wall Street, the gloomier 1970s also forced it to open up to the mass market, for different reasons. Thus the deregulation of commissions provided the chance for Charles Schwab to revolutionize retail investing by appealing to average folk, eliminating third-party advice, and providing a twenty-four-hour phone service. However it was ultimately not so much those public effusions – Merrill's ubiquitous sloganeering, Smith's antic bestseller, the Exchange's historic about-face – that best account for the embryonic emergence of 'shareholder nation'. Instead, it was a process more silent and invisible – history's little joke.[4]

*

Just as FDR, that 'traitor to his class', had always insisted, he was out to save capitalism, not bury it. Without the New Deal, who can say what might have issued out of the Great Depression. Certainly its existence helped make possible two developments vital to the future of 'shareholder nation'. The first was a regime of Keynesian management premised on sustaining mass purchasing power. It was responsible for that 'great compression' of national income distribution which made the 'American standard of living' the envy of the world. It left not only the middle classes but broad stretches of working-class America with the wherewithal to put some money aside. Secondly, the New Deal provided a friendly political environment for the unionization of the country's industrial heartland. Unions and collective bargaining eventually meant pensions, and even corporations that remained union-free did so in part by offering pension plans to their workers before they organized to get one on their own. Pensions meant the accumulation of huge pools of liquid capital looking for long-term investment outlets. This explosion of institutional investing would revolutionize Wall Street and implicate vast numbers of ordinary Americans in the peregrinations of the stock market.

Mutual funds had been around for some time, but even Merrill failed to appreciate their potential. As early as the mid-1960s, mutual funds accounted for a quarter of the value of all transactions on the NYSE. There were 340 mutual funds in 1982; by 1998, there were 3,513. Together with pension funds run by corporations and unions, they helped transform the investment landscape. The numbers are telling. When the 1960s ended, institutional investors were already responsible for seventy per cent of the Exchange's trades. In 1974, the Employee Retirement Income Security Act established standards for employer-operated pension funds, further helping to enlarge the 'shareholder nation'. The 401(k) provision in particular, by encouraging the shift from 'defined benefit' to 'defined contribution' plans in which the future pensioner was 'empowered' to move in and out of various securities, opened wide the floodgates of retirement money headed for the stock market. In 1984, approximately 7.5 million people participated. About thirty-four million people had 401(k) plans with assets of $1.7 trillion by the year 2000. At the turn of the millennium, union-managed pension funds accounted for $400 billion, and a trillion dollars moved through the treasuries of public-employee pension funds. This endowed the market's institutional players with enormous leverage over day-to-day and longer-term movements on the exchange. By the year 2000, the biggest institutional investors owned sixty per cent of the country's thousand largest corporations.

Even more portentously, it registered how far and wide the market had managed to descend into the ranks of the middling classes. By the century's end, half of all American families owned stock, up from ten per cent in 1960, with most of the rise occurring after 1980. And a third of American households owned mutual funds. At the end of the 1990s, well over a quarter of all wealth was held in the form of stock, more than any other single asset. More was invested in institutional funds between 1991 and 1994 than in all the years since 1939. And the biggest share of that capital was deposited in pension plans.

True, most of this money was managed by banks and brokerages. Its ostensible beneficiaries were therefore at best interested onlookers; at worst they turned out to be the unwitting victims of Wall Street frauds and fiduciary recklessness that surfaced when the dot.com bubble imploded. Even if they weren't fleeced, there is no doubt that a great proportion of those pension-fund stakeholders and mutual-fund investors only rarely bothered to manage their portfolios actively, and in that sense could hardly be considered market players. Nonetheless, their futures, the futures of their children, their material dreams about homes, college, weddings, vacations, medical emergencies, and retirement were now intertwined directly and intimately with Wall Street in a way never seen before. Indeed, these homely motivations further removed the taint of avarice that had always discolored the market.[5]

Moral queasiness was one taboo that had inhibited mass participation in the market, and fear was another. The Street's age-old specter, magnified by the Great Depression, was uncertainty, that lack of control which scared away many a potential investor. During the 1980s and 90s, however, the 'science of investing' seemed to take great strides. As PhDs in maths, physics, and computer science took jobs on the Street, talk of hedge ratios and deltas, beta measurements, linear-programming models, partial differential and stochastic differential equations, even on rarer occasions fractals and multifractals, became commonplace on the trading floor. Elite schools like MIT and Princeton established whole departments of what they dubbed 'Financial Engineering'. The application of advanced mathematics to the otherwise random happenstance of the market acted like a sedative, transforming the way many people thought about risk and return. One observer commented that these innovations 'have added a measure of science to the art of corporate finance'. Converting investment decisions into mathematical formulas conveyed a sense of exactitude. It encouraged a new image of the investor as a rational actor, a master of uncertainty no longer at the mercy of chance. It laid the groundwork for whole new species of securities that could be marketed to managers of institutional funds charged with exercising a certain fiduciary care. It prompted new 'risk-controlling' techniques like index funds and portfolio insurance.[6]

Advanced algebra and calculus reassured some segments of the middle class and helped extend the social reach of the market. Others, however, were just as easily put off by the pretense to special knowledge available only to the highly trained. After all, the new Wall Street was in some ways a folk market where people still managed their own portfolios, acted on rumor, and kept no precise measurement of how they were doing. Naturally enough, they gravitated toward their own set of folk gurus.

The charisma of Warren Buffett of Berkshire Hathaway, the 'Oracle of Omaha', and Peter Lynch, who managed the Magellan Fund of Fidelity Investments, was entirely homespun. Their track records as investors were very good, especially Buffett's – that didn't hurt. It helped account for those annual, revival meeting-like pilgrimages to Omaha to hear the oracle's pronouncements. But the revivalist aura that attracted multitudes to follow the investment advice of Buffett and Lynch was also composed of something less tangible yet closer to the heart of 'shareholder nation'. They were not only plainly spoken and plainly dressed, but were champions of what many people saw as common sense when it came to deciding where to park their money. Look for value and long-term growth, for solid year-in and year-out performance. Stay away from fancy and sophisticated securities or exotic, hyped up stock promotions, speculative vehicles whose roadworthiness no one knew. Trust your instincts, not those scholastic, effete 'experts' Lynch advised. By stripping away the inscrutability which always seemed to surround Wall Street – never more so than in the 1980s with its proliferation of whole new vocabularies to describe what it had invented – Buffett made people feel comfortable there in a moral as well as in a practical sense (even though this particular financial Paul Bunyan was a wily Wall Street veteran from the 1950s). The

Street could be a place where the old verities about hard work and a good product still paid off, and where plain folks could venture forth without leaving their valuables at home. Moreover, the down-home rhetoric that made these men so appealing suggests that 'shareholder nation' was nurtured as much by intangible as material incentives. Millions of ordinary people would feel at ease near Wall Street only when it seemed hospitable to the most cherished values of the heartland.[7]

Buffett's secularized version of the Protestant work ethic was one, but probably not the most important, of several potent folk beliefs that together persuaded millions of Wall Street's democratic potential. 'Shareholder nation' as a cultural conviction came to life out of the fusion of three indigenous ideological traditions: the work ethic, the spirit of insurgent individualism, and the magic of technological transcendence.

The survival of a nineteenth-century egalitarian work ethic made people enormously fond of Warren Buffett. The 'Oracle of Omaha' was hardly shy about publicizing his disdain for LBO speculators like Boone Pickens: 'They aren't creating value – they are transferring it from society to shareholders.' He would even on occasion take pot-shots at the super-rich, rhetorical reminders of the last century's veneration of the producer. Public-relations efforts by certain Wall Street firms – Smith Barney most memorably – to the tune of 'we make money the old-fashioned way; we earn it', struck a resonant chord among people who craved to cash in on the Exchange but wanted to be reassured you could do that without moral, not to mention financial hazard. It was satisfying to know that the people's stock market eschewed the profligacy of yesteryear and respected instead those Calvinist precepts that still had traction in many parts of the country. Financial populism of this kind drew nourishment from middle America where old-fashioned morality – that wealth, even if accumulated through the stock market, ought somehow to be traceable to honest labor – lived on despite the contradictory lure of consumer culture. Indeed, the cultures of work and play merged in the image of the Internet entrepreneur and Wall Street workaholic, devilishly hard workers who were at the same time hip to the latest in consumer cool.[8]

If down-home Calvinism was grounded in a certain self-restraint, Wall Street's new ideological populism also rested on a contrary instinct. In the 1960s, it might have been called 'do your own thing' and ignore the powers that be. But it went right back to the eighteenth century and the bumptious individualism which made a legend out of people like Ethan Allen's Green Mountain Boys. For generations it had accounted for the antipathy toward government interference so deeply ingrained in American political culture. Later on, its animus was directed against bureaucratic life-forms wherever they cropped up, in business, in higher education, and elsewhere. This nose-thumbing posture was characteristic of the Michael Milken gang in the 80s. But as much as they worked to portray themselves as rebels with a cause, their Wall Street remained a charmed circle of privileged insiders.

A distinctive feature of the 1990s boom years was that a great many more people began to think of the market as a place that welcomed, empowered, and informed outsiders. The stock market, in this ideological phantasm, became the medium in which one discovered freedom and truth: the freedom to determine your own fortune and fate; the truth that resided in the inexorable and all-knowing operations of the unencumbered marketplace.

Wall Street's version of liberation theology emanated from many quarters. Warren Buffett and Peter Lynch were hardly the only ones heaping populist scorn on the old guard's alleged expertise, for example. The online *Motley Fool Investment Guide* played that game mercilessly. It did so not on behalf of that old-time work ethic, but in the spirit of anarchic free-market rebelliousness. The Gardner brothers, David and Tim, who founded the website as a place to offer stock-market advice and swap information, denounced 'an exclusive ruling class of financial professionals', and 'elite clergy' living in their 'marbled mansions'. The brothers anointed themselves 'fools' to bait Wall Street's notorious snobbishness when it came to the small investor. But the Web, they predicted, would turn that world upside-down.[9]

The *Motley Fool* was a kind of financial form of *épater le bourgeoisie*, more extreme than most, but not out of synch with the times. Thomas Frank's book, *One Market Under God*, catalogues the wackiest forms of this financial bohemianism. Guru of business 'excellence' Tom Peters, for example, proposed that corporations appoint a CDO, that is, a 'chief destruction officer', to institutionalize the revolution against fat-cat bureaucrats. Conservative ideologue George Gilder, who had been expatiating on the moral superiority of the free market since his 1981 bestseller, *Wealth and Poverty*, waxed messianic about the dot.coms. They represented a kind of technological insurgency of the lower orders – 'immigrants and outcasts, street toughs and science wonks, nerds and boffins, the bearded and the beer-bellied, the tacky and the uptight . . . the born again and the born yesterday' – that would trample underfoot the snobs, plutocrats, and bureaucrats standing in the way of progress.[10]

Wall Street, some pundits declared, had been overrun by the people, as the Bastille and the St Peter and St Paul fortress in St Petersburg had been in earlier revolutions. In *Newsweek*, the economist Robert Samuelson announced that 'the Market R'Us', meaning that the stock exchange had become the preferred medium of the popular will, a post-industrial version of the New England town meeting. Journalist Joseph Nocera published *A Piece of the Action: How the Middle Class Joined the Money Class*, in which he described America's new 'financial democracy'. *Fortune* magazine pronounced that 'What we have here is nothing short of a revolution. Power that for generations lay with a few thousand white males on a small island in New York City is now being seized by Everyman and Everywoman.' Lucent Technologies, a high-tech Wunderkind, caught the spirit and adopted the era's rebel cry, 'born to be wild'. Day traders traveling down the information superhighway saw themselves as freedom-loving guerillas, brash, fearless types who refused to defer to the men in pinstripe suits. One such character compared himself to a 'ninja': 'the way they hide out, they're in black and they can sit there and you can't even hear them breathe.' An ad for the online company E*Trade mocked brokers as useless parasites. A language of transgression, playful insouciance, and militant self-expression captured the imagination of the business world and of young Wall Street in particular.[11]

The whole country, some enthusiasts believed, was in the process of becoming a 'free agent nation', and access to the global stock market would play a vital role in that transition. This was the late twentieth century's version of Horace Greeley's 'Go West Young Man, Go West'. In the ante-bellum years, the lure of free soil beyond the zone of settlement not only promised social mobility for the adventurous, but even more precious, the possibility of self-sufficiency. Now it seemed average folk again had that chance to become homesteaders on the market's virtual landscape, where they could stake out their claim to freedom: freedom from workaday tedium, from material want, from the deference to employers and government. An industrial engineer in New York credited his involvement in the market with a miraculous change in his thinking: 'It gave me a feeling of control over my life I never had before.' Suzie Vasillov, owner of a houseware store and stock-market player, spoke for shareholder nation: 'And whether you're a mommy or the owner of a tony house wares shop, we're all businesspeople. I think it's a great thing that's happened to the country.'[12]

Even the ancient curse of sexual subordination might be exorcised on the Street. *Working Girl*, a movie from the late 1980s, trained its camera on the road ahead. It showed Wall Street as a route out of the working class, and even more stunning, challenged the gender taboos that had always marked off the Street as strictly male turf. The film's heroine, a Staten Island secretary working in a Wall Street firm, suffers both from 'big swinging dick' misogyny and from the blue-collar blues that result from being looked down on by Ivy League 'masters of the universe'. Her triumph over Reaganaut Wall Street dramatically prefigures the excitement about the Street's liberating potential during the next decade. And although the Street's essential maleness remained intact during the 1990s, women for the first time found themselves in positions of real power and high visibility. Long confined to behind-the-scene roles as stock analysts, they entered the limelight when the analyst's job itself emerged from obscurity. Mary Meeker of Morgan Stanley Dean Witter and Co. was the subject of a glowing profile in *The New Yorker*, made the cover of *Fortune*, and was a featured speaker at the annual summit of the world's financial elite in Davos, Switzerland. Now multitudes of hungry investors looked to the oracular pronouncements of the stock analyst – to buy, to sell, to hold – to guide them through the chaos of dot.com mania. By comparison with the rest of the corporate world, Wall Street seemed liberated.[13]

Praise for the democratic promise of the stock market became ubiquitous and unrestrained. Newspapers and magazines, not to mention the electronic media, similarly proclaimed the market as the latest form of the vox populi. Even in the 1980s, the growing audience for Louis Rukeyeser's show *Wall Street Week* on public television was a straw in the wind, signaling swelling popular interest in the market. Soon enough CNBC, CNN-FN, and Bloomberg would more fully exploit the potential for investment news and advice, running real-time stock quotes along the bottom of the screen beginning in 1996.

The subliminal message was that if you were wired to the right sources, you could beat the market. Financial news plus sports accounted for half the editorial content of many newspapers. Wall Street bred its own media stars, people like Abby Joseph Cohen of Goldman Sachs, who issued warnings against what she called 'FUDD' – 'fear, uncertainty, doubt, despair.' By the 1990s, the overwhelming presence of stock-market news on TV and radio, the proliferation of talk shows and cable channels where market analysts became video celebrities, the birth of new magazines like *Fast Company*, *Smart Money*, and others, and the inundation of the airwaves by commercials for brokerages and online trading websites were all evidence that many people were listening.[14]

Media pundits like Thomas Friedman in the *New York Times* extolled the blind wisdom of what he dubbed the 'electronic herd', those international investors and speculators who roamed from nation to nation, guided only by the mathematical truths of the market, emancipating economies from the dead hand of tradition. This was the 'golden strait-jacket', a 'godsend for both developed and developing countries', which unerringly pointed out the 'one road' to economic growth. Democratic Party writer Daniel Gross applauded his party for empowering 'the monied interests of the 1990s – the mass of individual investors'. Even the discreet world of philanthropy felt the impact of pop finance. Three Wall Street newcomers founded the Robin Hood Fund as an 'anti-establishment' charity and staged 'guerilla benefits' that attracted celebrities like Gwyneth Paltrow and Robin Williams. The idea was to apply a 'stock picker's mentality' to backing poverty programs, where only the fittest charities survived.[15]

Alan Greenspan at first ran up the yellow flag, cautioning the naifs rushing to take advantage of the dot.com boom that they might be suffering from a bout of 'irrational exuberance'. However, the Fed chairman soon backed off, and began issuing blue-skies assurances that this was a new-age economy with limitless potential. In part this reflected fear that his own words might chill the confidence of the stock market, but Greenspan was also a disciple of Ayn Rand and her philosophical defense of unimpeded capitalism, which he pronounced 'the superlatively moral system'. Bestsellers like *Dow 36,000* by James Glassman and Kevin A. Hassett (and other equally exuberant prognostications, like Harry S. Dent's *The Roaring 2000s: Building the Wealth and Life Style You Desire in the Greatest Boom in History*) turned the black-spectacled guru's somber optimism into pure hallucination. According to Glassman, the market embodied America; like Coke or the flag, it mirrored the people's desires, and like them was unstoppable. [16]

Greenspan's concern about the growing intimacy between the country's mass-consumption-based economy and the fortunes of the Street was telling. At the watering holes of the rich and famous, like the Hamptons, the connection was transparent. People there were openly edgy: what if the bubble burst? 'If the market goes, how in the world will I pay for that enormous house? The cars? The lessons? The clubs? So people bravely party on . . . It's like that other Long Island party that Gatsby threw in the 20s, waiting to end badly.' Life in the Hamptons was abnormal by any measure. These were the sort of people who booked $5,000 per night hotel rooms, who read *House and Garden*'s special issue on 'It's All About Lux', who down in Texas were prepared to pay half a million dollars for souped-up recreational vehicles, who felt lost without a retinue of personal trainers, nutritionists, jewelers, and massage therapists trailing after them. The Battery Garage down near Wall Street parked on average 1,500 Jaguars and Porsches a day in 1994. In Silicon Valley, IPO multi-millionaires queued up on a six-month waiting list to get their new Porsche. [17]

But more and more average people also predicated their spending plans on the leverage their assets in the stock market provided. Home building and buying, car purchases, vacation get-aways, consumer electronics, air travel, and consumer durables in general stayed afloat atop the bubble. The percentage of individual wealth invested in the market leapt from twelve to twenty-six per cent during the 1990s. People wore wristwatches that beeped when IBM stock hit its owner's price threshold. A Florida dentist confessed to tracking his investments between patients, sometimes between X-rays and fillings. For a while, investing via the Internet proved as great a distraction from work as computer-generated pornography. Exterior shots of the New York Stock Exchange became a standard background for advertisements, from National Public Radio to Lexmark laser printers. The congregation that worshiped at the Intel altar during the dot.com boom included John Lee, who fantasized about his 'dream house' complete with bar and wooded lot; Fred Runkel, who more modestly hoped for enough to make a down payment on a home; Jon

Maakestad and Bev Turbin, who longed for a cabin in the Wisconsin woods; and Dave Fox, a sales auditor from Mountain View, California who was 'thinking maybe college tuition for my child'. *Business Week* announced that the Depression generation and the World War II generation had been supplanted by 'the Bull Market generation'; long live the 'People of the Bull'.[18]

More important than consumer durables, however, was the cultural impact of the romance of the market. Not since the 1920s had popular and consumer culture found the Street to be such alluring terrain. The world of finance, which had always conjured up images of the greatest gravity, underwent a face-lift and now seemed a playful place, funny and even gay. Michael Jordan showed up in a sneaker commercial dressed as a busy Wall Street executive: 'Give me the Nikkei close and the Detroit score,' the superstar demanded. The Street began to seem more informal, an environment in which blue jeans and sweatpants were not proscribed, where brokers listened to rock 'n' roll and smoked dope. Dress codes were rewritten as pinstripes were traded in for polo shirts, wingtips for Weejuns. Marc Andresson, the geek at the University of Illinois who invented the Netscape browser and became a multi-millionaire when the Netscape IPO ended its first day of trading worth more than Boise Cascade, Bethlehem Steel, and Owen-Corning Glass, posed for magazine photos barefoot and dressed in jeans.[19]

Wall Street, of all unlikely places, emerged as a haven of 'authenticity', a perpetual craving of consumer culture. David Owen, a *New Yorker* writer, confessed to his own love affair with CNBC. He'd become a compulsive watcher not so much for the money he might or might not make, but for its 'companionship': he identified with the on-screen reporters who dressed informally, 'kidded around', and whom he could imagine hanging out with after-hours in a bar like the one on *Cheers*.[20]

Day trading particularly invited all sorts of people who might not otherwise have ventured anywhere near the Street to over-indulge. David Denby, a movie critic, wrote about the addiction to the market that cost him his financial security, his marriage, and very nearly his sanity. Denby wrote in the long tradition of Wall Street confessional memoirs in which lost souls, full of remorse, cautioned others against following them down the 'street of torment'. But those tales carried with them an exoticism, a kind of satanic bewitchment lacking in Denby's. So many people entered the ranks of the day trader that they came to seem entirely ordinary, consumed not by moral qualms but by normal consumer anxieties about being left out and left behind. To be sure, their world was risky, but not morally; rather it supplied the same sort of thrills, titillation, and lightning-like action that popular culture provided in movies, on TV, in the video arcade. *Newsweek* called it a 'blood sport': it can hardly be a coincidence that the country fell head-over-heels in love with casino gambling during the same decade in which the arcane hieroglyphics of the stock market became the idiom of millions. A Connecticut billboard touting OTB summed up the connection: 'Like the Stock Market, Only Faster.'[21]

Wall Street's embrace by consumer culture took many forms. After a long hiatus, cartoonists rediscovered the Street, but this time as a kind of electronic amusement park where the *genus Americanus* came to play, perhaps to make fools of themselves but not to do any harm. *New Yorker* sketches made fun of refugees from the 1960s now working as stockbrokers, decked out in Armani suits but still wearing ponytails. One rather befuddled-looking character sits before his computer monitor and confides to his co-worker that he fears he's 'lost touch with the Warren Buffett in me'. In another, two street beggars compete for alms, but passers-by donate only to the cheery-looking fellow whose sign says 'Spare a dime?.com', ignoring the woeful-looking one with the traditional placard. A *New York* magazine sketch included a trendy-looking twentysomething uttering the newest version of a very old line: 'Care to come up and see my portfolio sometime?'[22]

Investment clubs for school kids and octogenarian ladies and everyone in between sprouted like weeds. They were as much pastimes as financial undertakings. By 1990, there were about 7,000 officially registered clubs with probably three times that number organized on a more informal basis. At the height of the bubble there were 30,000 clubs meeting regularly. More than a third were all-female; the most famous one, organized by a group of women in Beardstown, Ohio, authored the *Beardstown Ladies' Common Sense Investment Guide* which flew off bookstore shelves due to the ladies' reputation for successful trading. (Later it turned out the club's books had been cooked, although innocently.)[23]

Games, some still made out of cardboard and plastic, but most from microchips, treated the market like any other pop-culture simulation of gladiatorial mayhem. There were computer games for kids of all ages, even including one for pre-schoolers who could try out their budding financial savvy on *The Money Machine*. High schools introduced investment teams into the curriculum; already by the late 1980s, 350,000 students were playing *The Stock Market Game* in class and competing in tournaments that went on for weeks. At the St Agnes School in Arlington, Massachusetts, seventh-graders formed teams called 'The Wizards of Wall Street', 'The Money Machine', and 'Stocks R'Us'. Summer camps added playing the market to their menu of daily activities. Mothers who thought teaching their children about the market would be empowering could buy *Wow the Dow*, a kiddies' guide published by Simon and Schuster. One thirteen-year-old bar mitzvah boy was rewarded with a starter stock portfolio – his parents knew he'd consider it 'cool'. When the Four Seasons Hotel in Boston set up a Dollar and Sense Investment Camp, a local magazine editorialized that, 'If kids get hooked on saving and investing, America's future could be free of dependence on foreign capital . . . and the nation closer to a balanced budget.' [24]

Hollywood found the Street an increasingly popular dramatic locale. In addition to *Working Girl*, movies like *Pretty Woman*, *Boiler Room*, and *Family Man* were box-office successes, although those three took a dimmer view of the Street. Lesser-known pictures like *Pi* (1998), *Corporate Affairs* (1990), and *The Associate* (1996) toyed with the Street's ravenous appetite for exploiting scientific genius, its bloodthirstiness, and its genetic preference for white males. Just after the boom ended, television producers even situated a couple of sexy sitcoms on the Street (bearing the rather uninspired titles *Bull* and *The Street*). They featured glistening young male and female Wall Street sharks living in a permanent state of self-absorbed hyper-drive, too cartoonish to be taken seriously, too serious to be amusing. These shows fell flat almost immediately, perhaps in part because their time had come and gone. But as Fox television executives acknowledged, their time would never have come at all without the broad popularization of the Street.[25]

A sub-genre of commercial fiction involving the Street poured forth near the end of the decade with much greater success. Stephen Frey authored a series of Wall Street mass-market potboilers – *The Takeover*, *The Vulture Fund*, *The Inner Sanctum*, *The Insider*, *The Trust Fund*, and *The Day Trader* – whose titles suggested the stew of mystery, romance, and action-packed thrills that readers could expect to find inside. Other novels melded the derring-do of a James Bond spy thriller with the semi-incomprehensible intrigues of a dot.com IPO. While such scenarios might once have pivoted around the self-interested machinations of a basically unlikable financier, in these stories such figures underwent character transplants. In Frey's *Trust Fund* – advertised by its publisher as 'Grisham meets Ludlum on Wall Street' – the Wall Street mogul is an ascetic workaholic whose enemies are those addicted to high living and lazing about. In *The First Billion* by Christopher Reich, the financier is reincarnated as a freedom fighter, a knight of democracy engaged in hand-to-hand combat with the remnants of the 'evil empire', Russian oligarchs who really have more in common with J. P. Morgan and the Mafia than Lenin. Here Wall Street levitates into sacred space, a glorious embodiment of American ideals and power that makes even the most brutalized Russian tycoon blanch. Tyler Cain, 'a brilliant young investment banker at the top of his game', defends Western civilization against alien terrorists in *War on Wall Street*. All in all, the Street entered fully into popular culture, supplying the sense of adventure, the compulsion to be up-to-date, the thrill-a-minute emotional fixes on which the world of mass consumption was predicated.[26]

Fever dreams like this were of course nothing new in the history of the Street. What was different about the 1990s was the way visions of El Dorado were interwoven with the merry informality of consumer culture. The magazines of the 1980s, like *Manhattan Inc.*, adopted the viewpoint of the awed or appalled observer. The glossy new publications of the 1990s, like *Fast Company* and *Smart Money*, spoke directly to an audience they assumed was itself knee-deep in the market. Wall Street, once a symbol of aristocracy, inequity, and oppression, now promised to overthrow itself and to have a lot of fun doing so. In the post-industrial age, where knowledge rather than breeding or connections was king, the Street was reborn as a vessel of revolution. It would not only destroy the old elitism, but also free Everyman from the immemorial dependencies of wage labor and career creep. Oceans of rhetoric, some of it trying to sell a product, but a good deal in praise of an ideal, made the case that times had changed. Wall Street, as the quintessential expression of the free market, stepped forward as a twenty-first-century utopia – like the antithetical communist dystopias of the previous century, it was evangelical, prophetic, and confident that it was the pathway to universal well-being.

*

Marxism had grounded its messianic expectations, in part, on the irresistible evolution of technological progress. A similar techno-utopianism had infused American culture since the days of Ben Franklin. Every major inventive breakthrough – the railroad, the telegraph, electric power, the automobile, radio, air travel – inspired reveries about a new age of universal well-being and emancipation. Microchip technology unleashed the newest version of that hope. Never before, however, had Wall Street been so deeply implicated in fostering the future. Even though J. P. Morgan provided the financial foundation for technically innovative firms like General Electric and AT&T, the underlying science and technology were already in place, their commercial applications already proven. As the twentieth century drew to a close, however, Wall Street developed an unprecedented intimacy with the scientists and technicians who worked at the cutting edge of the 'next big thing'. Consequently, the Street absorbed the atmosphere of social enthusiasm that enveloped the introduction of these new discoveries.

Internet technology promised to do more than make obscure young men and women instantly wealthy. It was itself a means of empowerment for Everyman, a port key into a new world of instant and universal access. It would not only ramp up business transactions to warp speed but would banish the very category of outsider by making the interior workings of the market transparent. Wall Street's kinship with the human promise of scientific breakthrough was a potent element in its reincarnation as a great emancipator.

The Street had got off to a technological false start in the 1980s. Bio-technology was hot. Venture capitalists hooked up with molecular biologists and found the Street increasingly eager to finance start-up firms with glorious visions of cancer cures and other medical miracles dancing before their eyes. Expectations like these invited speculative overtures at early stages in the life-cycle of such firms. After all, the optimism so common among cutting-edge scientists meshed well with the can-do booming of the future that came naturally to Wall Street. A scientist interviewed in *Forbes* magazine described Interferon – a family of proteins once thought to be a cancer panacea and Wall Street's first wonder drug – as 'a substance you rub on stockbrokers'. At first cautious, by the early 1980s Wall Street houses became itchier to bring these embryonic companies to market. There was a series of initial public offerings (IPOs) soaked up by thirsty investors who were also true believers in the medical revolution that seemed just around the corner. Soon enough it was Wall Street setting the research agenda at top biology labs; in fact, Wall Street invented the phrase 'biotech'. A few of these firms, like Genentech, proved commercially durable, but in general everyone had underestimated the gap separating the science of molecular biology and genetics from the technical means of its application, and the difficulty of converting product prototypes to mass production and marketing.[27]

By mid-decade the biotech craze had cooled on the Street. But it might be seen as a dress rehearsal for what lay ahead. All the essential elements – frontier science, extraordinary social promise, premature commercial confidence, oceans of hype, and speculative over-reaching – reappeared ten years later, this time attached to the millenarian vibrations of cyberspace. The microchip revolution was much closer to technological and commercial application, further removed from basic science, than the biotechnology discoveries of the previous decade. But again, thanks to the previous decade's 'financialization' of the economy, Wall Street was positioned to be the harbinger rather than the Johnnie-come-lately beneficiary of the 'next big thing'. Again, Wall Street played the role of midwife, bringing to market 'firms' so frail they scarcely existed . . . except in virtual reality. But for as long as the boom lasted, they seemed very tangible indeed, throwing off windfall profits not just to their Silicon Valley progenitors and their financial godfathers on Wall Street, but to a broader investing public, who tracked their advent and progress with mesmeric fascination on their computer monitors at home.[28]

It was a case of double your pleasure: not only did new Internet firms return lavishly to their early investors, but the very technology they embodied made it possible, at least in theory, for millions more to play the game and come out ahead. Indeed, the very nerdiness of the best-known pathfinders of this post-industrial frontier – people like Bill Gates – seems to confirm, in their body language and their tone-deaf way of dressing, that outsiders, barbarians if you will, had finally stormed the gates: now everyone could rush through.

And beyond that – if one were to believe the most ecstatic prophecies to which this hyper-reality gave rise – information technology would launch the whole economy into interstellar orbit, freeing it from the gravitational pull that for so long had tethered it to the ups and downs of the business cycle. Because the boom was so intimately associated with breakthroughs in a technology that few understood, it carried with it the air of progress and inevitability that for centuries had hovered over the far frontiers of science. George Gilder was especially given to these techno-incantations of the limitless future. His high-priced newsletter told his subscribers why 'the Law of the Telecom' would catapult the right stocks into outer space and clued them in to 'why the bandwidth revolution is inevitable'. Gilder's infatuation with cyberspace was extreme but not unique. The otherwise lugubrious Alan Greenspan again led the chorus celebrating the earth-rending implications of the computerized new economy. In the summer of 1997, he withdrew his cautionary words about 'irrational exuberance' issued just a half year before. 'Something special has happened to the American economy,' the Fed chairman assured everyone, and *Business Week*'s cover story that summer proclaimed 'Alan Greenspan's Brave New World'.[29]

A chorus of academics and media pundits soon echoed this 'new era' invocation. Some credited the baby boom, others the low rate of inflation, globalization, the down-sizing of the 1980s, or the rise of the service sector. But virtually everybody singled out the high-tech sector and the Internet particularly for special praise. The World Wide Web was the future; it conveyed mastery; it was an intimate, deeply personal technology, unlike super-conductive alloys or nanotechnology; it wasn't so much a technology as a myth. One got a tactile feel for its impact on the redesigned trading floor of the NYSE which 'utilizes reflexive surfaces, curvilinear geometry, new materials, and studied ergonomics to evoke a powerful sense of both the present and the future of a Stock Exchange fusing technology and place'.[30]

Air-borne enthusiasm like this swept away even the most sober-minded media. So the *Wall Street Journal* could gush about the Netscape IPO which launched the Internet stock bubble – 'It took General Dynamics Corporation 43 years to become a corporation worth today's $2.7 billion in the stock market. It took Netscape Communications Corporation about a minute' – even while remaining stunned that this could happen to a company that reported no profits and was giving its product away free. Priceline.com, set up to sell empty airline seats online, burst on the scene with an initial capitalization greater than the combined value of Delta, US Airways, and United Airlines. Well over half the high-tech investment funds that cropped up almost every day were powered by these 'new era' fantasies. They were part of 'a virtuous cycle' in which high-tech productivity justified expectations of high profits, which in turn made the astronomical rise in security prices justifiable, which in turn fueled new investment leading to ever higher plateaux of productivity, and on and on. This 'virtuous cycle' seemed to suspend the conventional laws of financial physics and made previous ways of valuing securities look old-fashioned. After all, the Dow went from 2,588 in January 1991 to 11,302 in January 2000; the NASDAQ zoomed from 414 to 5,250 during the same period. When the Dow topped 10,000 in the early spring of 1999, ten times what it had been in 1972, the *Wall Street Journal* acknowledged that the 'values are dizzying', but reassured its readers that 'they also reflect the economy's rare strength.'[31]

Moreover, these new enterprises girdled the globe and reached terrain once cordoned off from the marketplace. Thomas Friedman's Panglossian read of globalization was based in part on his conviction that it carried with it the far frontier of technological progress. In *The Lexus and the Olive Tree*, the *New York Times* columnist in part predicated what he described as the 'democratization of finance' on the advent of the Internet and the way it cracked open the vaults of capital once monopolized by white-shoe Wall Street. Only the Web permitted the 'electronic herd' to migrate from one 'emerging market' to another, feeding on the choicest resources. As John Chambers, president of Cisco Systems, said:

> The Internet will change everything. The Industrial Revolution brought people together with machines . . . and the Internet revolution will bring people together with knowledge and information in virtual companies . . . It will promote globalization at an incredible pace. But instead of happening over a hundred years . . . it will happen over seven years.

The marriage of money and knowledge via technology even made its impact felt where once knowledge was pursued for its own sake. Major research universities, which had already begun scenting the possibilities during the biotechnology boomlet of the 1980s, began spinning off academic discoveries into their own for-profit operations, or found ingenious ways to collaborate with high-tech entrepreneurs, in the hope they might attract the eye of some Wall Street money man. The Johns Hopkins Medical School, for example, set up its own internal venture-capital fund to bankroll commercially promising studies. Research protocols, like those assuring the openness of all discoveries to fellow researchers, were tweaked so as to make them more compatible with the secrecy the business and financial world preferred. By the late 1990s, the SEC was conducting investigations on academic researchers suspected of insider trading. No one could know where this early 'corporatization' of higher education might ultimately lead. Still, it testified to the power exerted by the era's financialization of science and knowledge more generally. 'Shareholder nation' premised its future on a techno-dream that everybody who had a computer could share. [32]

Taken together, the work ethic, the spirit of insurgent individualism, and the magic of technological transcendence were a potent compound. Nonetheless, contradictions soon emerged in the new relationship between the market and Everyman. For example, those whom David Brooks nicknamed 'bobos in paradise', combined a haut-bourgeois standard of living with a bohemian disdain for 'bourgeois materialism'. They were a living contradiction. For 'bobos', many of whom amassed their fortunes in the dot.com stock-market boom, the trick was to adopt a style of living that cost a great deal but still proved their individualism, their concern for the environment, their sensitivity to those less fortunate than they, their repugnance for anything that smacked of hierarchy or status-seeking. So they leveled out the pecking order of command and obey at their sleek new Internet firms, and talked endlessly about consensual decision-making. And they dressed in designer blue jeans or ghetto chic, rode to ~~l~~ ~~vers rather~~ than Jaguars or Mercedes, ~~adopted~~ a kind of peasant earthiness as the guiding aesthetic of their housoleums. They practiced a politics of style, a faux politics. It removed the social issues generated by an unchained free market and a regnant Wall Street – growing inequalities at home, the economic retrogression and political subordination of the global South, the degradation of air, water, and land masses everywhere, the precarious state of social security – from public life and turned them into matters of consumer behaviour. [33]

Forecasts like Friedman's that Wall Street and free trade would lift the rest of the world out of the darkness of the past were belied by the collapse of the 'Asian Tigers' (Thailand, Indonesia, Malaysia, etc.) as currency speculators fled those economies in 1997. More telling, those same tigers had only managed to roar because they had for a long time ignored the prescriptions of free-market therapists, and instead relied on tight trade and currency controls, state subsidies, and other forms of managed mercantilism to get to where they were before the 'electronic herd' lost its appetite for their wares. These 'developing countries' were doing precisely what the United States had done when it was a developing country and had erected steep tariff walls and provided lavish state subsidies for railroads and other vital enterprise. When the Thai bhat was dumped by currency speculators, the British finance minister uttered a less sanguine view of Friedman's 'electronic herd': 'They hunt in packs; they seek out wounded currencies; they savage their prey.' As for the global South, much of it slogged through the 1980s and 90s burdened by negative rates of economic growth (as in parts of Africa and Latin America) or if positive, still well below the levels achieved during the post-war era when free-market orthodoxy was less rigidly applied. An economy like Chile's, ministered to by free-market advisers like Milton Friedman, outperformed many of its continental cousins, but with thousands of its citizens disappearing forever into unknown dungeons or dropped out of airplanes, it was hardly an exemplar of freedom and democracy.[34]

At home in the USA, the news was better, but still not as advertised. During the last years of the boom, living levels generally rose, even among low-income households where declining real wages had been the norm for more than two decades. Unemployment reached a thirty-year low, and public amenities across the country flourished even as the Federal government further withdrew from its responsibilities for public welfare. New York in particular helped fund a makeover of its midtown and other neighborhoods leaving the grunginess of the 1970s a dimming memory. Million-dollar townhouses transformed Chicago's Lake Michigan shoreline, and seaside towns around San Diego like Del Mar and La Jolla experienced their own social makeover. Moreover, no matter how many biotech and Internet start-ups failed, there was no denying the scientific and technological innovation that Wall Street helped finance.[35]

But this was far from the 'Everyman's economy' hyped by the Street's gurus. The gap between the richest and the rest grew even more quickly than it had in the 1980s to truly stupendous proportions, unmatched anywhere else in the world. *Wealth and Democracy*, Kevin Phillips' most recent installment in his saga of plutocracy and equality in America, included a statistical encyclopedia of mounting

the people notwithstanding. One dollar, one vote was, after all, a for-mula for plutocracy.[39]

Both the domestic and foreign policy of the Clinton administration pursued the objectives coveted by Wall Street's biggest interests. This may seem counter-intuitive in light of the fury with which the Republican right wing went after the President. But when it came to issues vital to Wall Street and its corporate partners, little separated the two parties. On the domestic side, financial deregulation climaxed with the repeal of the Glass–Steagall Act in 1999, which eliminated the already weak barriers separating commercial from investment banking. A Republican-controlled Congress cut the capital gains tax. By the end of the 1990s, Federal Reserve policy was being fine-tuned to keep the bubble afloat. Earlier in the decade Treasury Secretary Rubin, a former currency arbitrageur at Goldman Sachs and a true believer in the 'virtuous cycle' linking the health of the securities mar-kets to that of the economy, allegedly informed the new President that the success of his administration depended on a handful of bond traders and that balancing the budget was essential to keep them happy. Confirmation of that advice was supplied by a Goldman Sachs economist who observed that 'rarely, if ever, can so much power have been wielded by such a small number of institutions outside the direct democratic process.'[40]

Long Term Capital Management, the brainchild of three Nobel lau-reates and John Merriweather, trading chief of Salomon Brothers from the days of *Liar's Poker*, was a huge, overly leveraged international hedge fund that operated virtually free of any government regulation. Its advanced mathematics was supposed to immunize it against risk. But when it threatened to go belly-up in 1998, the Clinton adminis-tration rushed in to save it, fearful of the financial ramifications of let-ting it die. Kevin Phillips decried this new regime of 'financial mercantilism' under which the government rushed in to staunch every outbreak of financial blood-letting, whether it was the holdings of Wall Street banks in the Mexican peso or LTCM. Phillips spied a new international ruling elite consisting of central bankers, securities firms, top hedge funds, Treasury bureaucrats, and international economic agencies operating under American supervision. Financial commenta-tor James Grant characterized the government behavior that originat-ed with the Federal Resolution Trust Corporation at the end of the 1980s as 'the socialization of credit risk', and warned that it seriously warped the healthy metabolism of the business cycle. As a matter of fact, of the trillion dollars a day in currency trades in the late 1990s, only two to three per cent involved trade in real goods and services. For the first time in history, the FIRE sector of the economy moved ahead of manufacturing in national income and GDP.[41]

Abroad, Robert Rubin, in cooperation with the IMF and the World Bank, insisted that the rest of the world conform to the 'Washington Consensus'. No matter the particular state of economic development any country found itself in, it was advised to open itself up to the river of capital and trade goods flowing out of the United States and the West. Again and again the IMF and the World Bank, as well as Washington itself, subjected recalcitrant countries to severe financial penalties unless they relaxed their trade and investment barriers, deregulated and privatized their economies, and imposed budgetary austerity. Policies deemed 'bad' by this self-appointed global elite might include food subsidies, unemployment, health or retirement benefits, capital controls, taxes on business, virtually anything that might impede the flow of international capital. Hugo Chavez, the newly elected president of Venezuela in 1998, who swept into office on a wave of populist anger directed at both US corporations and the country's home-grown super-rich, nonetheless felt compelled to pay a cap-in-hand visit to Wall Street to assure the powers that be that he was prepared to impose 'fiscal discipline', to devalue the Bolívar, and whatever else they felt necessary. Socialist Ricardo Lagos, Chilean presidential candidate, made sure his campaign train ran through the offices of David Rockefeller, George Soros, and Steve Forbes. MIT economist Rudiger Dornbusch candidly described the IMF as 'a tool of the US to pursue its policy off-shore'. Dissenting international currency speculator, George Soros, might believe that 'it behoves the authorities to design a system that does not reward speculation', but Treasury Secretary Robert Rubin was sure that would spoil the system and dry up capital liquidity. It was a 'consensus' of the elect: either you subscribed to the dictates of the international capital markets or you suffered the consequences. This was about as far from anyone's dream of financial democracy as one could imagine.[42]

Despite these and other omens that all was not right in paradise, the dream kept its hold on the public imagination. Only when the bubble burst in 2000 and Wall Street again proved its capacity for outrageous corruption did the mood shift. Even then the earth failed to move. Congressmen denounced the banditry, but faith in the deregulated marketplace ran so deep that the legislative consequences turned out to be relatively toothless. The Bush administration, whose commitments to corporate America and laissez-faire were perhaps even more absolute than Reagan's, worked to bury proposals for serious reform. Lewis Lapham in *Harper's* magazine characterized the Bush agenda as an 'act of class warfare . . . not the angry poor sacking the mansions of the rich, but the aggrieved rich burning down the huts of the presumptuous and trouble-making poor.'

After the multi-billion-dollar scandals at Enron, WorldCom and other top-rank firms, which implicated virtually the entire Wall Street banking establishment, the Sarbanes–Oxley bill made only modest demands for greater openness and honesty in financial reporting. This timidity followed in the wake of unprecedented looting: insiders making off with the accumulated assets of pension-holders and mutual-fund shareholders; book-cooking by top management designed to prop up share prices and so cash in on stock options; whole corporations that turned out to be the reincarnations of Charles Ponzi's original brainstorm. Corporate insiders from the top twenty-five bankrupted companies made off with $3.3 billion in stock sales and bonuses as their firms went belly-up.[43]

Admittedly, the Attorney General of New York State, Elliot Spitzer, constructed the foundations of a bright political future by prosecuting the Street's major miscreants. He forced them to cough up major fines and to promise in the future to re-erect the 'Chinese wall', long since breached, that was supposed to separate the objective advice of the stock analyst from the hard-sell securities traders working for the same firm. Spitzer, however, was practically alone among officialdom. That political culture which once depised the Street as usurers, monopolists, con men, aristocrats, and sinners was a dimming memory. The Democratic Party, which had kept those metaphors breathing, could no longer summon up the old-time religion, having largely surrendered to 'shareholder nation' and the more tangible throw-weight of big-money politics. This monetization of democracy infected the whole system.

Past confrontations with the Street – particularly during the Progressive Era and the New Deal – had depended, in part, on the willingness of elites to risk ostracism from their social milieu. As the century drew to a close, however, there were few visible signs of dissent – *pace* George Soros – from the country's business and financial elite. Felix Rohatyn did issue regular jeremiads in the *New York Review of Books*. As an ex-board member of the Alvin Ailey Dance Company, he weighed in against Karol Armitage's *Predator's Ball* ballet, letting it be known he didn't care for Michael Milken and didn't consider his story good dance material. But for most of the decade, he was virtually alone, since in elite financial circles the free-market consensus went unchallenged. Little of the sense of social restraint, trusteeship, or political noblesse oblige that had sometimes diluted and chastened the commercial avidity of past business elites had survived the Reagan revolution. Instead, these circles acted openly as partisans of the country's dominant corporations.[44]

Furthermore, the success of those earlier encounters with the power of the Street had rested not only on disaffected elites but on the political mobilization of millions of ordinary citizens. At the most elementary level, the labor movement, once the single most important mass organization capable of mounting effective resistance to the power of business and finance, was by the 1990s a shadow of its former self, the unionized percentage of the private-sector labor force dropping into the single digits. This was arguably the deepest victory of the Reagan revolution: its 'financialization' of the economy, its gutting of the industrial heartland, had eviscerated the main social foundation of resistance. At the same time, the ascendancy of the Democratic Leadership Council as the kingmaker within the Democratic Party affirmed the party's conversion to free-market orthodoxy and the vacating of its New Deal social conscience. Moreover, treating the market as society's only communal gathering place, yet one whose very reason for being was the pursuit of individual self-interest, insidiously debilitated the instinct for collective action. The political faculties of millions had atrophied. Refinery workers, stevedores, and crane operators in industrial towns like Bayonne, New Jersey might give vent to a bit of old-fashioned blue-collar resentment when multi-millionaire Jon S. Corzine, one time head of Goldman Sachs, ran for the Senate. But Corzine won easily; the very impulse to find solutions to common dilemmas in the public arena seemed sapped of energy, at least on issues of wealth and democracy. [45]

The political weightlessness of the opposition was made even more ephemeral by a wider social condition one academic pundit summed up as 'bowling alone'. Not so long ago, people's everyday lives filled up with multiple vehicles of formal and informal collective activity, from homely neighborhood associations and bowling leagues to trade unions and political organizations. Now people tended to bowl alone, whether on Wall Street or elsewhere. One effect of that condition was to further incapacitate the social imagination. During the 1980s, the in-your-face extravagance of Wall Street's latest generation of upstarts was still shocking enough to produce a literature about their 'lying', 'thievery', 'barbarism', 'greed', 'vanities', and 'predations'. It was a cynical assessment and politically indifferent about what it observed, but it left its footprint.

Even though there was plenty of the same gilded arrogance on view in the 1990s, observers failed to depict it with the same caustic relish. Maureen Dowd quipped in the *New York Times* that 'the 90s are the 80s without the moral disgust'. Michael Lewis went from excoriating his Wall Street compatriots in *Liar's Poker* to lauding the revolutionary struggle of 'market values' against 'aristocratic values' in a *New York Times Magazine* article in 1997, and from there to anointing Wall Street's denizens as heroic freedom fighters after the horrific attack on the World Trade Center on September 11, 2001. For some this was a less bizarre association than it might seem. People could become intoxicated with American global pre-eminence, which was in turn bound up with Wall Street's overlordship. A widely appearing ad for Fidelity Investments' online trading operation conveyed a taste of this with its stark sketch of the intersection of 'Wall Street' and 'Power Street'. A financial and insurance manager for an Ohio car dealership who traded for himself on the Internet made the identification of his own financial empowerment and the nation's even clearer: 'We are the strongest nation in the world. It makes me feel good from where I come from to be able to participate in that.'[46]

The *New Yorker* magazine published an ensemble of essays at the end of the decade to take the measure of this 'New Gilded Age'. While each piece was expertly crafted, the book as a whole utterly failed to capture the yawning social divide, the political corruption, and the moral dissonance which lay at the heart of Mark Twain's baptism of the first Gilded Age. There were no essays about gated communities or the nation's exploding servant caste, or about the recent transformation of poverty into an experience of underpaid work rather than unemployment. The book itself was a sealed-off universe, a perfect embodiment of gilded insularity and profound public indifference. Perhaps that was because the reality of 'shareholder nation' – those millions of families squirreling away their savings in mutual funds, those thousands of itinerant day traders riding the range in virtual reality – gripped enough people that it effaced the outlandish misbehavior of Wall Street's super-rich. [47]

Now and then dissenting voices could be heard. Hollywood, otherwise a bastion of consumer culture, still harbored its dislike for Wall Street. The movie version of *American Psycho* turned the bodacious gore and the numbing high-style inventory of the original novel into a pungent satire; its protagonist, a deeply dissociated Wall Streeter specializing in 'murders and executions', combines a snotty narcissism with a lethal mania that together paint a picture of the Street as a habitat for the depraved. *Family Man* starred Nicolas Cage as an utterly loathsome financial shark, a caricature of the Street's macho preening, narcotic vanities, and anomic cruelty. He was truly 'bowling alone' until given a miraculous chance to relive his life: to choose between his present existence as a hip, filthy-rich sociopath and one that left him stranded in a desert of suburban tackiness, banality and, yes, bowling leagues, but redeemed by the love of wife, children, and neighbors, who still bowled together. The old cautionary tale of Wall Street as a moral sinkhole remained alive and well and overflowing with sentimentality. *Pretty Woman* pivoted around the same theme, but this time the choice was between two forms of prostitution: one practiced by a Wall Street wheeler and dealer, the other by a woman of easy virtue but with a heart of gold (both 'screw people for money', the cold-blooded Richard Gere tells the surprisingly wholesome Julia Roberts). Viewers are never in doubt about where true virtue and emotional health can be found, and it's not on Wall Street.

Another film, *Boiler Room*, revisited the world of Melville's confidence man. Online investing had vastly expanded the capacity to run confidence games en masse. In one case, a pimp whose day job was managing an escort service used his off-hours to fleece thousands of wired victims. In another the two men running an Internet penny-stock fraud were shot in the head by a person or persons unknown, and in one instance a confidence man from cyberspace found himself hanging by his heels out the ninth-floor window of an office building, left there by rival stock promoters. In the movie, however, the tele-

phone is still the weapon of choice. But here the story of high-testos-
terone young men, trained in emotional thuggery and motivational
overkill – they've memorized all Gordon Gekko's lines from *Wall
Street* – scamming the citizens of 'shareholder nation' is really a back-
handed legitimating of the Street. The confidence racket is run out on
Long Island, not on the Street; the twin towers of the World Trade
Center are still faintly visible many miles away, as if to emphasize the
differences between this criminal world and the more sanitary and
above board one in Manhattan.[48]

Amidst all the euphoria about globalization and how it promised to
one day liberate humankind from poverty, Po Bronson published
Bombardiers. The novel was a hilarious satire of the stressed-out
world of the Wall Street bond trader. Its characters are ridden with
neurotic compulsions. They are almost ludicrously competitive. And
they're ready to gull their customers into the most precarious investments without a scintilla of remorse. They prate about freedom while
panting after every disaster as a potential source of booty, and see the
government as one gigantic slush-fund. For these hyped-up salesmen,
'democracy is an obsolete form of management.' The 'new era' is 'a
propaganda economy, an advice economy, a possibility economy, a
rumor economy – an economy of tall tales, fish stories, and oral folklore'. But they really outdo themselves, entering fully into the antic
utopianism of the moment, when they concoct schemes to securitize
whole nations – in particular the Dominican Republic. They decide to
charter it as a Delaware corporation and auction it off as IPO,
bundling its bad debts to the IMF, the World Bank, and the United
States into a corporate shell whose bonds can then be dumped on an
unsuspecting public, in a kind of crazed rendition of 'shareholder
democracy' and 'dollar diplomacy' for the new millennium. In an eerie
presentiment of John Poindexter's futures market in terrorism, our
heroes foresee investment banks and military contractors foreclosing
on whole countries. Coyote Jack, head of the sales force, wants to put
capitalism to work in the Dominican Republic, 'turn it around, and
then sell it. We'll make a killing . . . In a few years the world is going
to thank us for getting rid of government.'[49]

Where *Bombardiers* reveled in the lunatic logic of the 'Washington
Consensus', John Le Carré's *Single and Single* tracked the blood-
thirstiness of the vulpine global financier. This was the 'Washington
Consensus' at ground zero, as the novel's corporate protagonist

roamed the earth, scavenging the 'emerging markets' of Eastern Europe, Russia, and elsewhere. Uninhibited by law or custom, it privatized, looted, or murdered as circumstances demanded, all the while hooked up to a white-shoe London firm that provided its cover. It was a kind of *House of All Nations* for the age of global laissez-faire.[50]

Running against the grain of those superhero Wall Street potboilers, a few works of fiction biopsied the psychological and moral afflictions that the universal fixation on the Street could catalyze. Jonathan Franzen's award-winning novel *The Corrections* deployed the Street's favorite euphemism for its inherently erratic behavior as the controlling metaphor for Wall Street's deep penetration into the intimacies of family dysfunction. The lives of the novel's central characters not only vibrated with the boom, their psychic instability mirrored the market's manic depression. *Moral Hazard*, a post-crash novel published in 2002 by Kate Jennings, gave off a faint aroma of the high moral seriousness that in the late nineteenth century colored virtually all the fiction about Wall Street. Its two unheroic protagonists are both refugees, of a sort, from the 1960s, now working on the Street and suffering from acute cases of existential ambivalence. Attracted by its energy and maverick atmosphere, they are at the same time appalled by its self-absorption, its delusional capacity to buy into its own hype, and the official hypocrisy which sanctions its peccadilloes. They are rather bleak reminders that once upon a time people believed in something other than 'one market under God'.[51]

The prophets of globalization also confronted a gathering chorus of political criticism near the end of the decade. But this happened outside the formal political system. Giant demonstrations at the meetings of the World Trade Organization in Seattle in 1999 brought together trade unionists, environmentalists, and political activists in the first violent political clashes with the police since the 1960s. While the protesters came laden with many grievances and a long list of enemies, the captains of international finance were chief among them. Each subsequent gathering of the WTO or of the World Bank attracted its own Greek chorus of accusatory censure.

Defenders of free-market globalization like Thomas Friedman dismissed the demonstrators as benighted Luddites, hapless reactionaries standing in the path of progress and bound to be run over and left as roadkill by the 'electronic herd'. However, as they kept on gathering in Washington, Prague, Milan, and Cancun, and as the main engines of the global economy began to stutter and stall, even the annual get-together of the world's financial, business, and political elites in Davos, Switzerland began to feel less sanguine about the future. Eventually there were defections from within the temple. Nobel prize-winning economist Joseph Stiglitz and other esteemed economists, including Jeffrey Sachs, once the architect of free-market shock treatment for 'liberated' Eastern Europe, noisily left the World Bank, disgusted with the rigidity and self-evident failures of the 'Washington Consensus'. One-time conservative intellectuals like the British theorist John Gray, who once applauded globalization, ended up burying it – in column inches at least. Nonetheless, when the century ended, Wall Street's ideological, political, and cultural influence penetrated more deeply into the fiber of the nation than ever before.

Perhaps without a true systemic economic crisis, one threatening everyone and not merely the country's peak financial institutions, the Street may continue to embody that ever-renewable American optimism underpinning 'shareholder nation'. However, such a calamity would ignite incalculable political upheaval as well. Should that happen, no one can know where it would lead. The United States was lucky in the 1930s. Wall Street's defeat was a victory for the New Deal, not fascism. Now, however, the context is rather different. Admiral Poindexter's folly is more than a reminder that crackpot realism is still with us. For it comes amidst gathering thunderclouds of worldwide economic disturbance and a presumptive American foreign policy whose blunt use of the mailed fist promises carnage and chaos into the indefinite future. The triumphalism of the Clinton years, linked so intimately to Wall Street and the bubble economy, was by comparison a basically peaceable affair; at least the 'Washington Consensus' did not heavily rely on military means to impose its will. The triumphalism of the new millennium, which rests on high-tech weaponry and asserts its unilateral will even in the teeth of opposition from its co-partners in capitalist globalization, arouses the most dangerous political emotions. Those who can dream of a futures market in terrorism may one day wake up to a nightmare.

Notes

Introduction

Daniel Drew, quoted by Clifford Browder, *The Money Game in Old New York: Daniel Drew and His Times* (Lexington, 1986), p. 277.

CHAPTER 1 Revolution and Counter-Revolution

1 Alexander Hamilton, 'Observations on Certain Documents Contained in #s 5 & 6 of "The History of the United States for the Year 1796" in which Charges of Speculation Against Alexander Hamilton, Late Secretary of the Treasury, is Fully Refuted by Himself' (Philadelphia, 1797).

2 John Steele Gordon, *The Great Game: The Emergence of Wall Street as a World Power, 1653–2000* (New York, 1999), pp. 40–43; Charles R. Geisst, *Wall Street: A History* (New York, 1997); Stanley Elkins and Eric McKittrick, *The Age of Federalism: The Early American Republic, 1788–1800* (New York, 1993), p. 273; Cathy Mason, 'Public Vices, Private Benefit: William Duer and His Circle, 1776–1792', in William Pencak and Conrad Edick Wright, eds., *New York and the Rise of American Capitalism: Economic Development and the Social and Political History of an American State, 1780–1870* (New York, 1989).

3 Hamilton quoted by Charles A. Beard, *An Economic Interpretation of the Constitution of the United States* (New York, 1914), p. 113; Gordon, *The Great Game*, pp. 42–43; 'shopkeepers . . .' quoted in Elkins and McKittrick, *Age of Federalism*, p. 278; Jefferson quoted by Gordon, *The Great Game*, p. 44.

4 Jefferson quoted by Gordon, *The Great Game*, p. 21; Robert M. Sharp, *The Lore and Legends of Wall Street* (New York, 1989), p. 16.

5 Gordon, *The Great Game*, p. 25; Maud Wilder Godwin, Alice Carrington Royce, Ruth Putnam, and Eva Palmer Brownell, eds., *Historic New York: Being the Second Series of the Half Moon Papers* (New York, 1897), pp. 79–80, 82, 92.

6 Abram Wakeman, *Historical Reminiscences of Lower Wall Street and Vicinity* (New York, 1914), pp. 10–12, 21; Frederick L. Collins, *Moneytown: The*

Story of Manhattan's Toe: That Golden Mile which lies between the Battery and the Fields (New York, 1946); Maud Wilder Godwin *et al.*, *Historic New York*, pp. 99, 108, 110; Cadwallader Colden quoted by Stuart Bruchey, *The Roots of American Economic Growth 1607–1861: An Essay in Social Causation* (New York, 1965), pp. 194–95; Frederick Trevor Hill, The Story of a Street (New York, 1908).

7 Gary B. Nash, *The Urban Crucible: The Northern Seaports and the Origins of the American Revolution* (Cambridge, Mass., 1986), p. 205; Christoval de Villalon quoted in Stanley Nelson Passy, 'The Imagination of Wall Street' (University of Dallas, Ph.D. dissertation, 1987), p. 36; *Oxford English Dictionary*; Sharp, Lore and Legends, p. 16.

8 Passy, 'Imagination of Wall Street', p. 149; Daniel Defoe quoted by Peter Eisenstadt, 'How the Buttonwood Tree Grew: The Making of a New York Stock Exchange Legend', *Prospects*, 1994, pp. 75–98. A recent novel by David Liss, *A Conspiracy of Paper* (New York, 2000) provides a fascinating description of the anti-Semitism that pervaded the London financial district in the eighteenth century.

9 Defoe and Pope poems quoted by Charles Mackay, *Memoirs of Extraordinary Popular Delusions and the Madness of Crowds* (London, 1852).

10 Cotton Mather quoted by Wayne Westbrook, *Wall Street in the American Novel* (New York, 1980), p. 8; Anonymous poet quoted by Herbert E. Sloan, *Principle and Interest: Thomas Jefferson and the Problem of Debt* (New York, 1995), p. 110.

11 Ann Fabian, *Card Sharps, Dream Books, and Bucket Shops: Gambling in 19th Century America* (Ithaca, 1996), p. 159.

12 Beard, *Economic Interpretation*. Beard's book is more complex and nuanced than that. It has also been subject to a withering criticism that has exposed its various inadequacies, including its economic reductionism. Its publication in 1914 and the controversy it ignited is itself evidence of the cultural weightiness of Wall Street in the political and historical imagination of Progressive-era America, when similar anxiety about an overbearing financial aristocracy was a chronic feature of public life. Whatever its deficiencies – and there was once a cottage industry devoted to pointing them out – Beard's thesis contains a kernel of truth worth pondering.

13 Washington quoted by Stuart Bruchey, *Roots of American Economic Growth*, p. 111; Alexander Hamilton, 'Report on Manufactures' in Morton J. Frisch, ed., *Collected Writings and Speeches of Alexander Hamilton* (Washington DC); Alexander Hamilton to George Washington, August 18, 1792, in Samuel McKee, Jr., *Alexander Hamilton: Papers on Public Credit, Commerce, and Finance* (New York, 1934).

14 Mason, 'Public Vices, Private Benefit'; Alexander Hamilton, 'First Report on the Public Credit', January 14, 1790 in McKee, *Alexander Hamilton*; Alexander Hamilton, 'Second Report on the Public Credit', January 16, 1795 in McKee, *Alexander Hamilton*; Charles Sellers, *The Market Revolution: Jacksonian America 1816–46* (New York, 1991), p. 32; Vernon Louis Parrington, *Main Currents in American Thought: An Interpretation of*

Literature from the Beginnings to 1920, volume 1 (New York, 1927–30), p. 304; Edward J. Perkins, *American Public Finance and Financial Services 1790–1815* (Columbus, Ohio, 1994).

15 George Washington quoted by Mason, 'Public Vices, Private Benefit'; George Washington to Alexander Hamilton, July 29, 1792 in McKee, *Alexander Hamilton*.

16 Alexander Hamilton quoted by Sloan, *Principle and Interest*, p. 138; Elkins and McKittrick, *Age of Federalism*, p. 116, 123.

17 Poem in *New York Gazette* quoted by Gordon, *Great Game*, p. 38.

18 Excerpt of poem quoted by Karen Weyler, '"A Speculating Spirit": Trade, Speculation, and Gambling in Early American Fiction', *Early American Literature*, 1996, vol. 31/3, pp. 207–42; see this article also for references to *Dorval; or The Speculator*, to Philip Freneau 's 'Reign of the Speculators', and to Benjamin Rush's quoted remarks.

19 Sloan, *Principle and Interest*, pp. 142–43, 163; Gordon, *Great Game*, p. 12.

20 Thomas Jefferson to Thomas Jefferson Smith, February 21, 1825, in Saul Pandover, ed., *The Complete Jefferson* (New York, 1943); Jefferson quoted by Bruchey, *Roots of American Economic Growth*, p. 116.

21 Thomas Jefferson, 'The Anas, 1791–1806' in Merrill Peterson, ed., *Thomas Jefferson Writings* (New York, 1984).

22 John Adams quoted by Parrington, *Main Currents*, p. 314; Light-Horse Harry Lee quoted by Sloan, *Principle and Interest*, p. 143; see also Elkins and McKittrick, *Age of Federalism*, pp. 243–44.

23 Elkins and McKittrick, *Age of Federalism*, p. 271; Nathan Miller, *The Enterprise of a Free People: Aspects of Economic Development in New York State during the Canal Period, 1792–1838* (Ithaca, 1962), pp. 77–78; James Jackson and James Madison quoted by Elkins and McKittrick, *Age of Federalism*, p. 141 and p. 145.

24 Drew R. McCoy, *The Elusive Republic: Political Economy in Jeffersonian America* (Charlotte, North Carolina, 1980), pp. 12, 15–16, 21; see also Elkins and McKittrick, *Age of Federalism*; Bruchey, *Roots of American Economic Growth*, p. 121.

25 Thomas Jefferson to the President of the United States (George Washington), May 23, 1792, in Peterson, *Writings*, p. 986; patriot quoted by Eisenstadt, 'How the Buttonwood Tree Grew'.

26 Alexander Hamilton to Robert Morris, April 30, 1781 in Frisch, *Collected Writings*; Hamilton, 'First Report on the Public Credit' in McKee, *Papers on Public Credit*; Hamilton quoted by Gary J. Kornblith and John M. Murrin, 'The Dilemmas of Ruling Elites in Revolutionary America', in Steve Fraser and Gary Gerstle eds., *Ruling America: Wealth and Power in a Democracy* (Cambridge, Mass., 2005).

27 Jefferson, 'The Anas', in Peterson, *Writings*; Parrington, *Main Currents*, vol. 2, p. 17.

28 Madison quoted by Elkins and McKittrick, *Age of Federalism*, p. 243; Jefferson quoted by Elkins and McKittrick, *Age of Federalism*, p. 243; Sloan, *Principle and Interest*, p. 183; Madison quoted by Elkins and McKittrick, *Age*

of Federalism, p. 244; Philadelphia citizen quoted by Elkins and McKittrick, *Age of Federalism*, p. 460; Kevin Phillips, *Wealth and Democracy: A Political History of the American Rich* (New York, 2002), p. 18.

29 Jefferson quoted by Elkins and McKittrick, *Age of Federalism*, p. 301.

30 Robert R. Livingston quoted by Elkins and McKittrick, *Age of Federalism*, p. 174; Jean Curtis Webber, 'The Capital of Capitalism' in *American Heritage*, 1972, vol. 24/1.

31 Marvin Gelfand, 'The Street' in *American Heritage*, 1987, vol. 38/7; Frederick Trevor Hill, *The Story of a Street*; see also Robert Sobel, *The Big Board: A History of the New York Stock Market* (New York, 1965).

32 Gordon, *Great Game*, pp. 28–29, 37; Elkins and McKittrick, *Age of Federalism*, pp. 137–38, 243–44, 273, 278–80.

33 Eisenstadt, 'How the Buttonwood Tree Grew'.

34 Robert E. Wright, *The Wealth of Nations Rediscovered: Integrationist Expansion in American Financial Markets, 1780–1850* (New York, 2002); Elkins and McKittrick, *Age of Federalism*, pp. 80–82.

CHAPTER 2 Monsters, Aristocrats, and Confidence Men

1 Johnannes D. Bergmann, 'The Original Confidence Man', *American Quarterly*, Fall 1969, vol. xxi/3; Hans Bergmann, 'Peter Funk: Tales of Exchange' in *God in the Street: New York Writing From Penny Press to Melville* (Philadelphia, 1995).

2 Joyce Appleby, *Inheriting the Revolution: The First Generation of Americans* (Cambridge, Mass., 2000).

3 Herbert E. Sloan, *Principle and Interest: Thomas Jefferson and the Problem of Debt* (New York, 1995); Charles R. Geisst, *Wall Street: A History* (New York, 1997).

4 Dana L. Thomas, *The Plungers and the Peacocks: An Update of the Classic History of the Stock Market* (New York, 1967), p. 25; John W. Francis, *Old New York: Or Reminiscences of the Past Sixty Years* (New York, 1865), p. xx.

5 Edward G. Burrows and Mike Wallace, *Gotham: A History of New York City to 1898* (New York, 1999), pp. 336, 756; Margaret G. Myers, *The New York Money Market: Origins and Development – volume 1* (New York, 1931), pp. 16–18 (also includes illustration).

6 Burrows and Wallace, *Gotham*, pp. 333–34, 340.

7 Kenneth D. Ackerman, *The Gold Ring: Jim Fisk, Jay Gould, and Black Friday, 1869* (New York, 1988), p. 19; Charles Sellers, *The Market Revolution: Jacksonian America 1815–46* (New York, 1991), pp. 59,68; 'Constitution of the New York Stock and Exchange Board, 1817, and Proceedings of the Board', Archives of the New York Stock Exchange; Burrows and Wallace, *Gotham*, pp. 333–34, 444; Vincent P. Carosso, *Investment Banking in America: A History* (Cambridge, Mass., 1970), pp. 1–2.

8 James K. Medberry, *Men and Mysteries of Wall Street* (New York, 1870), pp. 287–88; Murray N. Rothbard, *The Panic of 1819: Reaction and Policies* (New York, 1962); Sellers, *Market Revolution*, pp. 64–65, 138; Burrows and Wallace, *Gotham*, p. 444; William Charvat, *The Profession of Authorship in*

America, 1800–1870, see chapter 4, 'American Romanticism and the Depression of 1837' (New York, 1968).

9 Sloan, *Principles and Interest*, pp. 206, 210; Jefferson quoted by Sellers, *Market Revolution*, p. 133; see also Jefferson to Nathaniel Macon, January 12, 1819 in Merrill Peterson, ed., *Thomas Jefferson Writings* (New York, 1984); John Adams quoted by Bray Hammond in *Banks and Politics in America: From the Revolution to the Civil War* (Princeton, 1957), p. 36; Senator Benton quoted by Sellers, *Market Revolution*, p. 138; Mead (no first name), *Wall Street: or, Ten Minutes Before Three* in New York Historical Society, Special Collections (New York, 1819).

10 Abram C. Dayton, *The Last Days of Knickerbocker Life in New York* (New York, 1882); see also Douglas T. Miller, *Jacksonian Aristocracy: Class and Democracy in New York 1830–60* (New York, 1967), p. 73.

11 Nathan Miller, *The Enterprise of a Free People: Aspects of Economic Development in New York State during the Canal Period, 1792–1838* (Ithaca, 1962), pp. 88–89, 110; Sellers, *Market Revolution*, p. 44.

12 Miller, *Enterprise of a Free People*, pp. 92–94, 96, 100; Hammond, *Banks and Politics*, p. 353; Edward Pessen, *Jacksonian America: Society, Personality, and Politics* (Homewood, Illinois, 1969), pp. 128–31; Stuart Bruchey, *The Roots of American Economic Growth 1607–1861: An Essay in Social Causation* (New York, 1965), p. 131; Burrows and Wallace, *Gotham*, p. 445; John Steele Gordon, *The Great Game: The Emergence of Wall Street as a World Power, 1653–2000* (New York, 1999), pp. 56–57).

13 Kevin Phillips, *Wealth and Democracy; A Political History of the American Rich* (New York, 2002), p. 234.

14 Carosso, *Investment Banking*, p. 4; Medberry, *Men and Mysteries*, p. 298; James L. Huston, *Securing the Fruits of Labor: The American Conception of Wealth Distribution 1765–1900* (Baton Rouge, 1998), p. 100; Pessen, *Jacksonian America*, p. 125; Bruchey, *Roots of American Economic Growth*, p. 131; Sellers, *Market Revolution*, p. 44.

15 Vernon Louis Parrington, *Main Currents in American Thought: An Interpretation of American Literature from the Beginnings to 1920*, vol. 2 (New York, 1927–30), p. 147; Miller, *Enterprise of a Free People*, p. 77; John Davis Haeger, 'Eastern Money and the Urban Frontier: Chicago 1833–42', *Journal of Illinois State Historical Society*, 1971, vol. 6/3; Gordon, *Great Game*, p. 67.

16 Charles Dickens, *American Notes and Pictures From Italy* (London, 1957), p. 82; Charles Dickens, *Martin Chuzzlewit* (New York, 1965), pp. 316–17, 376–77; H. Bruce Franklin, 'Introduction' in Herman Melville, *The Confidence-Man: His Masquerade* (New York, 1967).

17 Pessen, *Jacksonian America*, pp. 29, 31; Marvin Meyers, *The Jacksonian Persuasion: Politics and Belief* (Stanford, 1957), pp. 126–27; Frederick Jackson, *A Week in Wall Street by One Who Knows* (New York, reprinted 1969, originally published 1841), pp. 43–45.

18 Jeremiah Church quoted by Meyers, *Jacksonian Persuasion*, p. 138; see Arthur Schlesinger, Jr., *The Age of Jackson* (Boston, 1945) for discussion of

Maysville veto; Edward K. Spann, *The New Metropolis: New York City 1840–57* (New York, 1981), p. 305; Geisst, *Wall Street*; Sellers, *Market Revolution*, p. 353; George Francis Train, *Young America in Wall Street* (New York, 1968 reprint, originally published in 1857) is a highly melodramatic account, in the form of extended letters, of the 1857 panic which Train depicted as a mass delirium.

19 Gordon, *Great Game*, p. 64; John Steele Gordon, *The Scarlet Woman of Wall Street: Jay Gould, Jim Fisk, Cornelius Vanderbilt, The Erie Railway Wars, and the Birth of Wall Street* (New York, 1988), p. 14. Gordon is quoting William Worthington Fowler, *Ten Years in Wall Street* (Hartford, Conn., 1870) which was perhaps the country's first best-seller about Wall Street; Carosso, *Investment Banking*, p. 4; Burrows and Wallace, *Gotham*, pp. 567–69; Robert Sobel, *The Big Board: A History of the New York Stock Market* (Glencoe, Illinois, 1965); Pessen, *Jacksonian America*, p. 134.

20 William Worthington Fowler, *Ten Years in Wall Street: Or Revelations of Inside Life and Experience on 'Change'* (New York, 1870, reprinted 1971), pp. 20, 30, 36; Burrows and Wallace, *Gotham*, p. 584; British traveler quoted by Spann, *The New Metropolis*, pp. 3–4, see also pp. 283, 296–97; Oliver Wendell Holmes quoted by Sobel, *The Big Board* and see *Financial History Magazine*, Spring, 2000.

21 Walt Whitman, *New York Dissected*, edited by Emory Holloway and Ralph Adimari (New York, 1936), pp. 120, 128–29; John H. Hewitt, 'Mr Downing and his Oyster House: The Life and Good Works of an African–American Entrepreneur', *American Visions*, June/July, 1994, vol. 9/3.

22 Burrows and Wallace, *Gotham*, pp. 598, 601; Philip Hone quoted by Edward Pessen, 'Business Elites of Antebellum New York City' in *An Emerging Independent American Economy, 1817–75* (New York, 1980); Lois Severini, 'The Architecture of Finance: Wall Street 1825–62', Ph.D. dissertation (New York University, 1981), pp. 88, 96, 139, 158; *New York Daily Mirror*, June 27, 1840; Alexander McCay quoted by Severini, *The Architecture*, p. 231; Miller, *Jacksonian Aristocracy*, pp. 160–61; Oliver W. Larkin, *Art and Life in America* (New York, 1960), p. 156; Spann, *The New Metropolis*, p. 412.

23 President Jackson quoted by Hammond, *Banks and Politics*, pp. 430–31; President Jackson's Farewell Address, March 4, 1837 in Francis Newton Thope, *The Statesmanship of Andrew Jackson* (New York, 1904); Martin Van Buren quoted by Meyers, *Jacksonian Persuasion*, pp. 156–57, 161; see also, Sellers, *Market Revolution*; see also Schlesinger, *Age of Jackson*, p. 121. While some historians have argued that Wall Street was an active ally of Jackson and Vice President Van Buren in their war against the Bank as part of a devious plot to undermine the financial supremacy of Philadelphia, little hard evidence supports this claim.

24 Meyers, *Jacksonian Persuasion*.

25 John Dennis Hagen, 'Eastern Financiers and Institutional Change: The Origins of the New York Life Insurance and Trust Company and Ohio Life Insurance and Trust Company', *Journal of Economic History*, 1979, vol. 39/1; Emerson quoted by Patricia O'Toole, *Money and Morals* (New York,

1998), p. 93; Charvat, *Profession of Authorship*, chapter 4.

26 Washington Irving quoted by Hammond, *Banks and Politics*, p. 438; Washington Irving quoted by Parrington, *Main Currents* (vol. 2), pp. 204, 208–10.

27 Noah Webster quoted by Joseph Dorfman, *The Economic Mind in American Civilization 1606–1865*, vol. 2 (New York, 1946), p. 606; Michael Chevalier, *Society, Manners, and Politics in the United States: Letters on North America*, John William Ward, ed. (Glouster, Mass., 1967), p. 69.

28 Pessen, *Jacksonian America*, p. 143; Ralph Waldo Emerson, *The Conduct of Life*, pp. 93, 100–01, 122–23; Samuel Rezneck, 'The Social History of an American Depression, 1837–43', *New York Historical Society Quarterly*; Lazer Ziff, *Literary Democracy: The Declaration of Cultural Independence in America* (New York, 1982), p. 17; Edward K. Spann, *Ideals and Politics: New York Intellectuals and Liberal Democracy 1820–60* (Buffalo, New York, 1972), pp. 26, 98; Richard Hildreth, 'Hopes and Hints As to the Future' in *Theory of Politics: An Inquiry into the Foundations of Governments and the Causes of Progress of Political Revolutions*.

29 Stanley Nelson Passy, 'The Imagination of Wall Street', Ph.D. dissertation (University of Dallas, 1987), p. 51; Ann Fabian, *Card Sharps, Dream Books, and Bucket Shops: Gambling in 19th Century America* (Ithaca, 1990), pp. 6–7, 44, 61.

30 Channing quoted by Thomas C. Cochran and William Miller, *The Age of Enterprise: A Social History of Industrial America* (New York, 1942), p. 68; Fabian, *Card Sharps*, p. 55, 167; Karen Halttunen, *Confidence Men and Painted Women: A Study of Middle Class Culture in America, 1830–1870* (New Haven, 1982), pp. 7, 17, 20; Fowler, *Ten Years in Wall Street*, p. 117.

31 Dickens quoted by Paul Goodman, 'Ethics and Enterprise: The Values of a Boston Elite, 1800–1860', *American Quarterly*, Fall, 1966, vol. 18; George Frederickson, *The Inner Civil War: Northern Intellectuals and the Crisis of the Union* (New York, 1965), pp. 28, 32.

32 Nathaniel Hawthorne, *The House of Seven Gables* (New York, 1960); Theodore Parker, 'Social Classes in a Republic', edited by Samuel A. Eliot (American Unitarian Association, Boston).

33 Meyers, *Jacksonian Persuasion*, pp. 59, 74, 80–81, 84; James Fenimore Cooper, *The American Democrat: Or Hints on the Social and Civic Relations of the United States of America* (New York, 1969, originally published 1838), pp. 113, 132, 155; James Fenimore Cooper, *Home as Found* (New York, 1961, originally published 1838); Cooper quoted by Spann, *Ideals and Politics*, p. 81; Parrington, *Main Currents*, pp. 223–24, 231.

34 Richard K. Cralle, editor, *Reports and Public Letters of John C. Calhoun* (New York), Speech in Senate on 'Report of the Secretary of the Treasury', July 21,1841; see also Calhoun 'Speech on Independent Treasury Bill', March 22, 1938; 'Speculation and Trade', *Southern Quarterly Review*, February, 1857; 'Wealth of the North and the South' by George Fitzhugh in *De Bows Review*, November, 1857; 'The Times Are Out of Joint', *De Bows Review*, December, 1857; Spann, *The New Metropolis*, pp. 17–18; Claude Reherd

Flory, 'Economic Criticism in American Fiction 1792–1900', Ph.D. dissertation (University of Pennsylvania, 1936), p. 105; Louisville Courier quoted by James L. Huston, *The Panic of 1857 and the Coming of the Civil War* (Baton Rouge, 1987), p. 16.

35 Peabody quoted by Muriel Hidy, *George Peabody: Merchant and Financier 1829–54* (New York, 1978 reprint, originally a Ph.D. dissertation, Radcliffe College, 1939), p. 274; 'Speculation and Trade', *Southern Quarterly Review*, February, 1857; Alfred D. Chandler, 'Patterns of American Railroad Finance, 1830–50, *Business History Review*, 1954, vol. 28; Sven Beckert, 'The Making of New York City's Bourgeoisie, 1850–1886', Ph.D. dissertation, Columbia University, 1994, p. 16; Bruchey, *Roots of American Economic Growth*; Carosso, *Investment Banking*, p. 3; Speech of the Honorable J. H. Hammond, delivered at Bornwell Court, October 29, 1858.

36 Governor McNutt quoted by Sobel, *The Big Board*, pp. 63–64; Silas Wright quoted by Burrows and Wallace, *Gotham*, p. 614; John Quincy Adams to George Jay, September 13, 1814, *The Writings of Quincy Adams,* Worthington Chauncey Ford, editor (New York, 1913); Asa Greene, *The Perils of Pearl Street: A Taste of the Dangers of Wall Street by a Late Merchant* (New York, 1834), p. 169; Frederick Jackson, *A Week in Wall Street*, pp. 5–6, 9, 19; Fowler, *Ten Years on Wall Street*, p. 42; Charles R. Geisst, *Wall Street From Its Beginnings to the Fall of Enron* (New York, 2004), pp. 42–43; David Black, *The King of Fifth Avenue: The Fortunes of August Belmont* (New York, 1981), pp. 36, 39, 44–45.

37 Leggett quoted by Meyers, *Jacksonian Persuasion*, pp. 199–200; Richard Hofstadter, 'William Leggett, Spokesman of Jacksonian Democracy', *Political Science Quarterly*, December, 1943, vol. LVIII/4; see also Sean Wilentz, *Chants Democratic: New York City and the Rise of the American Working Class 1788–1860* (New York, 1984), pp. 165, 238, 240–41; Joseph L. Blau, editor, *Social Theories of Jacksonian Democracy: Representative Writings of the Period 1825–1850* (New York, 1947), pp. 199–202; Dorfman, *Economic Mind*, pp. 653, 678–79; Sellers, *Market Revolution*, p. 342; William M. Gouge, *A Short History of Paper Money and Banking in the United States Including an Account of Provincial and Continental Paper Money to which is Prefixed an Inquiry into the Principles of the System with Considerations of Its Effects on Morals and Happiness* (Philadelphia, 1833), pp. 3–4, 31, 77, 91, 94, 97.

38 Charles Frederick Briggs, *The Adventures of Harry Franco: A Tale of the Great Panic* (New York, 1969, originally published 1839).

39 Asa Greene, *Perils of Pearl Street*; Thomas Bender, *New York Intellect: A History of Intellectual Life in New York City from 1750 to the Beginnings of our own Times* (New York, 1987), pp. 162–63.

40 Briggs, *Adventures of Harry Franco*; Greene, *Perils of Pearl Street*; 'Speculation and Trade', *Southern Quarterly Review*, February, 1857; Richard Kimball, *Undercurrents of Wall Street* (New York, 1862), pp. 144–46, 252–53, 255, 257–58, 331–32; Clifford Browder, *The Money Game in Old New York: Daniel Drew and His Times* (Lexington, Kentucky, 1986), pp. 57, 61; Fowler, *Ten Years in Wall Street*, pp. 34, 131.

41 George Foster quoted by David S. Reynolds, *Beneath the American Renaissance: The Subversive Imagination in the Age of Emerson and Melville* (New York, 1988), p. 295; George G. Foster, *New York By Gaslight and Other Urban Sketches* (Berkeley, California, 1990, originally published 1850), pp. 131, 220–21, 226–27; Peter Eisenstadt, 'How the Buttonwood Tree Grew: The Making of a New York Stock Exchange Legend'.

42 Emily Stipes Watts, *The Businessman in American Literature* (Athens, Georgia, 1982), pp. 35–37; Halttunen, *Confidence Men*.

43 Black, *King of Fifth Avenue*, pp. 79–80; Marvin Gelfand, 'The Street', *American Heritage*, November, 1987, vol. 38/7; *New York Herald*, April 12, 1836, January 1, 1836, January 16, 1836, January 21, 1836, July 22, 1836, April 15, 1836, June 10, 1836, June 23, 1836.

44 Herman Melville, *Moby Dick or The Whale* (New York, 1992), pp. 516–18.

45 Irving Adler, 'Equity, Law, and Bartleby', *Science and Society*, Winter, 1987–88, vol. 51/4; Michael T. Gilmore, *American Romanticism and the Marketplace* (Chicago, 1985), pp. 140–41; Reynolds, *Beneath the American Renaissance*, p. 295; Robert Shulman, *Social Criticism and 19th Century American Fictions* (U. Missouri Press, 1987), see Chapter 1, 'Divided Society, Divided Selves: Bartleby, the Scrivener: A Story of Wall Street and the Market Society'; John H. Randall, Jr., 'Bartleby versus Wall Street: New York in the 1850s', *New York Public Library Bulletin*, 1975; Barbara Foley, 'From Wall Street to Astor Place: Historicizing Melville's Bartleby', *American Literature*, March 2000, vol. 72/1; Herman Melville, 'Bartleby, the Scrivener: A Story of Wall Street', in *The Great Short Works of Herman Melville*, Werner Berthoff, editor (New York, 1969).

46 Herman Melville, *The Confidence-Man*, pp. 67–71.

CHAPTER 3 From Confidence Man to Colossus

1 *Harpers Weekly*, September 25, 1869; *The Nation*, November 18, 1869, both in *Documents in American Civilization: Popular Culture and Industrialism 1865–1900*, Henry Nash Smith, ed. (New York, 1967), pp. 96–100; Clifford Browder, *The Money Game in Old New York: Daniel Drew and His Times* (Lexington, Kentucky, 1986), p. 215; Sigmund Diamond, *The Reputation of the American Businessman* (Cambridge, Mass., 1955), pp. 55, 61–62, 69, 72.

2 Samuel Rezneck, 'The Influence of Depression Upon American Opinion 1857–59', *Journal of Economic History*, May, 1942, vol. II/1; Ron Chernow, *The House of Morgan: An American Banking Dynasty and the Rise of Modern Finance* (New York, 1990), p. 10; Stuart Bruchey, *The Roots of American Economic Growth 1607–1861: An Essay in Social Causation* (New York, 1965), p. 152; Thomas C. Cochran and William Miller, *The Age of Enterprise: A Social History of Industrial America* (New York, 1942), pp. 83–85.

3 David Black, *The King of Fifth Avenue: The Fortunes of August Belmont* (New York, 1981), pp. 166–67; Edward G. Burrows and Mike Wallace, *Gotham: A History of New York City to 1898* (New York, 1999), pp. 843–46; Engels quoted by Burrows and Wallace, *Gotham*, p. 844; James L.

Huston, *The Panic of 1857 and the Coming of the Civil War* (Baton Rouge, 1987); Charles P. Kindleberger, *Manias, Panics, and Crashes: A History of Financial Crises* (New York, 1978), p. 115.

4 *New Orleans Crescent* quoted by Burrows and Wallace, *Gotham*, p. 844; George Fitzhugh, 'Wealth of the North and the South', *De Bows Review*, November, 1857; 'The Times are out of Joint', *De Bows Review*, December, 1857.

5 Horace Greeley quoted by Burrows and Wallace, *Gotham*, p. 846; Black, *King of Fifth Avenue*, pp. 166–67; Rezneck, 'The Influence of Depression . . .'; President Buchanan quoted by Huston, *The Panic of 1857*, p. 114; *Frank Leslie's Illustrated Newspaper*, September 12, 14, and 19, 1857, October 3, 10, 17, and 24, 1857.

6 Burrows and Wallace, *Gotham*, pp. 850–51; Sven Beckert, 'The Making of New York City's Bourgeoisie, 1850–1886', Ph.D. dissertation (Columbia University, 1994), pp. 79–80; Mayor Wood quoted by Edward K. Spann, *The New Metropolis: New York City 1840–57* (New York, 1981), p. 395; *Frank Leslie's Illustrated Newspaper*, October 3, 17 and 24, 1857, November 14, 1857; Rezneck, 'The Influence of Depression . . .'; Huston, *The Panic of 1857*; Alfred D. Chandler, Jr., 'Henry Varnum Poor: Philosopher of Management, 1812–1895' in William Miller, ed., *Men in Business: Essays in the History of Entrepreneurship* (Cambridge, Mass., 1952).

7 *New York Ledger*, July 27, 1850, May 23, 1857, October 17 and 24, 1857, November 21, 1857.

8 George Francis Train, *Young America in Wall Street* (New York, 1968 reprint, originally published 1857), pp. x–xi.

9 Beckert, 'The Making of New York City's Bourgeosie', pp. 4, 7, 9, 15–16, 56–57; Spann, *New Metropolis*, p. 412; Alfred D. Chandler, 'Patterns of American Railroad Finance, 1830–50', *Business History Review*, 1954, vol. 28.

10 Spann, *New Metropolis*, p. 205; Lloyd Morris, *Incredible New York: High Life and Low Life of the Last 100 Years* (New York, 1975 reprint, originally published 1951), pp. 19–20; *New York Daily Mirror*, June, 27, 1840; Lois Severini, 'The Architecture of Finance: Wall Street 1825–62', Ph.D. dissertation (New York University, 1981).

11 *New York Sun* quoted by Black, *King of Fifth Avenue* (front-matter); Frank Luther Mott, *A History of American Magazines, 1741–1850* (Cambridge, Mass., 1939); Beckert, 'The Making of the New York City Bourgeoisie', p. 225; Douglas T. Miller, *Jacksonian Aristocracy: Class and Democracy in New York 1830–60* (New York, 1967), pp. 160–61, 168, 169.

12 Marvin Meyers, *The Jacksonian Persuasion: Politics and Belief* (Stanford, 1957), p. 200; John Steele Gordon, *The Scarlet Woman of Wall Street: Jay Gould, Jim Fisk, Cornelius Vanderbilt, The Erie Railway Wars, and the Birth of Wall Street* (New York, 1988), pp. 47, 49; Edith Wharton, *A Backward Glance* (New York, 1934); William Worthington Fowler, *Ten Years in Wall Street: Or Revelations of Inside Life and Experience on 'Change'* (New York, 1971 reprint, originally published 1870), p. 42; 'One of the Upper Ten

Thousand' illustration in Carl Bode, editor, *Documents in American Civilization: American Life in the 1840s* (New York, 1967).

13 George Foster, *New York by Gaslight and Other Urban Sketches* (Berkeley, 1990 reprint, originally published 1850), pp. 222–23, 225–26; Francis J. Grund, *Aristocracy in America: From the Sketch Book of a German Nobleman* (New York, 1959 reprint, originally published 1839), pp. x, 21, 45–46, 60, 87, 92; Harriet Martineau, *Society in America* (edited and abridged by Seymour Martin Lipset, New York, 1962), pp. 14–17.

14 'The Lone Tree in Wall Street', *The Living Age*, June 16, 1860.

15 Daniel Drew quoted by Kathleen Odean, *High Steppers, Fallen Angels, and Lollipops: Wall Street Slang* (New York, 1988), p. 179; Fowler, *Ten Years*, pp. 36, 117; Henry Clews, *28 Years in Wall Street* (New York, 1888), pp. 8–9.

16 Senator Washburn quoted by Kenneth Stampp, *And The War Came* (New York, 1962), p. 142 – see also pp. 9–10, 124–29.

17 Jean Curtis Webber, 'The Capital of Capitalism', *American Heritage*, 1972, vol. 24/1; Robert P. Sharkey, *Money, Class, and Party: An Economic Study of the Civil War and Reconstruction* (Baltimore, 1959), p. 277; Vincent P. Carosso, *Investment Banking in America: A History* (Cambridge, Mass., 1975), pp. 13–16; President Lincoln quoted by Dana L. Thomas, *The Plungers and the Peacocks: An Update of the Classic History of the Stock Market* (New York, 1967), p. 33, see also pp. 31–32; Irving Katz, *August Belmont: A Political Biography* (New York, 1968), pp. 143–45; Black, *King of Fifth Avenue*, p. 257; Edward Everett quoted by Black, *King of Fifth Avenue*, p. 258; Jay Cooke quoted by Kenneth D. Ackerman, *The Gold Ring: Jim Fisk, Jay Gould, and Black Friday* (New York, 1988), p. 46; G. S. Baritt, *Lincoln and the Economics of the American Dream* (Nashville, 1978), p. 71; *Frank Leslie's Illustrated Newspaper*, May 7, 1864; Burrows and Wallace, *Gotham*, pp. 900–01.

18 E. C. Steadman quoted by Gordon, *Scarlet Woman*, p. 116; *Frank Leslie's Illustrated Newspaper*, May 7, 1864; 'Wall Street in War Time', *Harpers New Monthly*, December, 1864–May, 1865.

19 Charles T. Harris, *Memoirs of Manhattan in the 60s and 70s* (New York, 1928); James K. Medbery, *Men and Mysteries of Wall Street* (New York, reprinted 1968 originally published 1870), p. 247; Gordon, *Scarlet Woman*, p. 113–14; *Tribune* quoted in Burrows and Wallace, *Gotham*, p. 871, see also pp. 878–79; 'Wall Street in War Time', *Harpers New Monthly*, December, 1864 – May, 1865; Observer (James K. Medbery) quoted by Maury Klein, *The Life and Legend of Jay Gould* (Baltimore, 1986), p. 70.

20 Drew quoted by Burrows and Wallace, *Gotham*, p. 900.

21 Medbery, *Men and Mysteries*, pp. 10–11, 194–95, 196–97; John Steele Gordon, *The Great Game: The Emergence of Wall Street as a World Power, 1653–2000* (New York, 1999), p. 109; 'Pan in Wall Street', *Atlantic Monthly*, January, 1867; Medbery quoted by Edward Chancellor, *Devil Take the Hindmost: A History of Financial Speculation* (New York, 1999), p. 152.

22 Walt Whitman, *Democratic Vistas*, Mark Van Doren, editor (New York, 1945), pp. 400–01.

23 Daniel Webster quoted by Thomas Kessner, *Capital City: New York City and the Men Behind America's Rise to Economic Dominance, 1860-1900* (New York, 2003), p. 74; Junius Henry Browne, *Great Metropolis: A Mirror of New York* (New York, 1975 reprint, originally published 1869), p. 49; *New York Herald* quoted by Kessner, *Capital City*, p. 203.

24 Bruchey, *Roots of American Economic Growth*, p. 152; Beckert, 'The Making of New York City's Bourgeoisie', p. 208; Cochran and Miller, *Age of Enterprise*, p. 133; Sean Dennis Cashman, *America in the Gilded Age: From the Death of Lincoln to the Rise of Teddy Roosevelt* (New York, 1988), p. 29.

25 Chernow, *House of Morgan*, p. 35; Stuart H. Holbrook, *The Age of Moguls* (New York, 1953), pp. 51–52; Thomas, *Plungers and Peacocks*, pp. 35–36; Jay Cooke quoted by Ellis Paxson Oberholtzer, *Jay Cooke: Financier of the Civil War*, vol. 2 (Philadelphia, 1907), pp. 142 and 355; Kessner, *Capital City*, p. 33; Actually, most of the government's war bonds ended up in the hands of wealthy individuals and financial institutions who realized a windfall later on when interest was paid in gold rather than in depreciating greenbacks – see Eric Foner, *Reconstruction: America's Unfinished Revolution* (New York, 1988), p. 22.

26 Kessner, *Capital City*, p. 50; Foner, *Reconstruction*, p. 568.

27 Charles Francis Adams and Henry Adams, *Chapters of Erie* (Ithaca, 1956 reprint, originally published as a book in 1886 by Henry Holt), pp. 95–96, 98.

28 Ackerman, *The Gold Ring*, p. 30; New York Historical Society Exhibit on Board Games, 2001.

29 Washington Fowler, *Ten Years in Wall Street*; Matthew Hale Smith, *Bulls and Bears of New York, with the Crisis of 1873 and the Cause* (Freeport, New York, 1972 reprint originally published 1873), p. 555, and quoted by David Andrew Zimmerman, 'Frenzied Fictions: The Writing of Panic in the American Marketplace, 1873–1913', Ph.D. dissertation, University of California, 2000, pp. 33–34, and p. 22.

30 John D. McCabe, *Great Fortunes and How They Were Made* (New York, 1870); McCabe quoted in Dixon Wecter, *The Saga of American Society: A Record of Social Aspiration 1607–1937* (New York, 1937), pp. 197–98.

31 Holbrook, *Age of Moguls*, pp. 7, 22–23, 34; Ackerman, *The Gold Ring*, p. 12; Gordon, *Scarlet Woman*, p. 62; Vernon Louis Parrington, *Main Currents in American Thought*, vol. 3: *The Beginnings of Critical Realism in American Thought* (New York, 1927–30), p. 11; On Jim Fisk see Frederick L. Collins, *Moneytown: The Story of Manhattan's Toe: that Golden Mile which lies between the Battery and the Fields* (New York, 1946).

32 Fowler, *Ten Years*, p. 124, 167; Chernow, *House of Morgan*, p. 7; Medberry, *Men and Mysteries of Wall Street*, p. 157; Barroom poem quoted by W. A. Swanberg, *Jim Fisk: The Career of an Improbable Rascal* (New York, 1959); Gordon, *Scarlet Woman*, p. 91, 206 309, 318, 332, 337; Russell Sage quoted by Gordon, *Scarlet Woman*, p. 84; *New York Times* quoted by Gordon, *Scarlet* Woman, pp. 374–75; London observer quoted by Wecter, *Saga*, p.

142; *New York Herald quoted by* H. W. Brands, *Masters of Enterprise* (New York, 1999), p. 25.

33 George Wheeler, *Pierpont Morgan and Friends: The Anatomy of a Myth* (New York, 1973), p. 110.

34 Gordon, *Scarlet Woman*, pp. 277, 309, 332, 337, 374–75; Swanberg, *Jim Fisk*, pp. 127–28, 199, 279; Sigmund Diamond, *The Reputation of the American Businessman* (Cambridge, Mass., 1955), p. 66; Adams, *Chapters of Erie*, p. 10; Henry Nash Smith, editor, *Documents in American Civilization: Popular Culture and Industrialism 1865–1900* (New York, 1967), pp. 86, 88; *New York Herald*, January 5, 1877; Black, *King of Fifth Avenue*, p. 365; Theodore P. Greene, *American Heroes: The Changing Models of Success in American Magazines* (New York, 1970), p. 110.

35 Greene, *American Heroes*, p. 112; Browne, *Great Metropolis*, p. 337; Holbrook, *Age of Moguls;* Black, *King of Fifth Avenue*, pp. 36, 44–45, 410–12; Brands, *Masters of Enterprise*, p. 16; Edward Chancellor, *Devil Take the Hindmost: A History of Financial Speculation* (New York, 1999), pp. 167–68; Boyden Sparkes and Samuel Taylor Moore, *The Witch of Wall Street: Hettie Green* (New York, 1935), including quote from fellow Wall Streeter, p. 229; Stanton quoted by Ackerman, *The Gold Ring*, p. 261; Morris, *Incredible New York*, p. 129; *National Police Gazette*, January 1, 1880, carried an account of a Christmas party on Wall Street that resembles nothing more than a frat party.

36 Browder, *The Money Game*, pp. 277, 280–85; Bouck White, *The Book of Daniel Drew: The Inside Story of the First Great Wall Street Speculator* (Larchmont, New York, 1965 reprint, originally published 1910 as *A Glimpse of the Fisk–Gould–Tweed Regime from the Inside*), pp. vii–viii.

37 Fowler, *Ten Years*, p. 482; Holbrook, *Age of Moguls*, pp. 22–23, 34, 41, 43, 46; Webber, 'The Capital of Capitalism'; Gordon, *Scarlet Woman*, pp. 231–33, 309, 318–19; Swanberg, *Jim Fisk*, pp. 7–8, 26, 169, 171; Henry Adams quoted by Chancellor, *Devil Take the Hindmost*, p. 177.

38 Richard Hofstadter, *The American Political Tradition and the Men Who Made It* (New York, 1948), p. 164.

CHAPTER 4 Wall Streeet in Coventry

1 All books quoted by Maury Klein, *The Life and Legend of Jay Gould* (Baltimore, 1986); David Samuels, 'The Confidence Man', *The New Yorker*, April 26–May 3, 1999.

2 *New York Times* quoted by Klein, *Life and Legend*, p. 483; *New York World* quoted by Klein, *Life and Legend*, p. 484.

3 James R. Keene quoted by Edward Chancellor, *Devil Take the Hindmost: A History of Financial Speculation* (New York, 1999), p. 178; *New York Times* quoted by Klein, *Life and Legend*, p. 3; Klein, *Life and Legend*, pp. 217, 477; Samuels, 'The Confidence Man'; Edwin P. Hoyt, *The Goulds: A Social History* (New York, 1969), pp. 65, 86, 119.

4 Klein, *Life and Legend*, pp. 491–93.

5 Richard Ohmann, *Selling Culture: Magazines, Markets, and Class at the Turn*

of the Century (New York, 1996), p. 55; Fritz Redlich, 'The Business Leader as a 'Daimonic' Figure' in Fritz Redlich, *Steeped in Two Cultures: A Selection of Essays* (New York, 1971); Donald Meyer, *The Positive Thinkers: A Study of the American Quest for Health, Wealth, and Personal Power from Mary Baker Eddy to Norman Vincent Peale* (New York, 1965), p. 131.

6 Ohmann, *Selling Culture*, p. 49–50; George Wheeler, *Pierpont Morgan and Friends: The Anatomy of a Myth* (New York, 1973), p. 161; Sean Dennis Cashman, *America in the Gilded Age: From the Death of Lincoln to the Rise of Teddy Roosevelt* (New York, 1988), pp. 29, 31, 37.

7 The richest account of the Erie Railway wars is John Steele Gordon, *The Scarlet Woman of Wall Street: Jay Gould, Jim Fisk, Cornelius Vanderbilt, the Erie Railway Wars, and the Birth of Wall Street* (New York, 1988); see also W. A. Swanberg, *Jim Fisk: The Career of an Improbable Rascal* (New York, 1959).

8 Thomas Kessner, *Capital City: New York City and the Men Behind America's Rise to Economic Dominance, 1860–1900* (New York, 2003), p. 115; David Andrew Zimmerman, 'Frenzied Fictions: The Writing of Panic in the American Marketplace 1873–1913', Ph.D. dissertation, University of California at Berkeley, 2000, p. 22; journalist observer quoted by Chancellor, *Devil Take the Hindmost*, p. 169; Stewart H. Holbrook, *The Age of Moguls* (New York, 1983), pp. 39–41; The best account of the gold ring is Kenneth D. Ackerman, *The Gold Ring: Jim Fisk, Jay Gould, and Black Friday, 1869* (New York, 1988); *London Times* quoted by Gordon, *Scarlet Woman*, p. 277; Ulysses S. Grant to George S. Boutwell, September, 12, 1869 in *The Papers of Ulysses S. Grant*, John Y. Simon, editor (Carbondale, Illinois, 1998); Frederick L. Collins, *Moneytown: The Story of Manhattan's Toe: that Golden Mile which lies between the Battery and the Fields* (New York, 1946).

9 Thomas C. Cochran and William Miller, *The Age of Enterprise: A Social History of Industrial America* (New York, 1942), p. 132; Wallace D. Farnham, 'The Weakened Spring of Government: A Study in 19th Century American History', *American Historical Review*, 1963, vol. 68/3; Holbrook, *Age of Moguls*, pp. 53–54; Cashman, *America in the Gilded Age*, pp. 31–32, 199–200; Chancellor, *Devil Take the Hindmost*, pp. 175, 184.

10 Ohio Congressman quoted by Cochran and Miller, *Age of Enterprise*, p. 158 – see also pp. 78, 81, 134; Wheeler, *Pierpont Morgan*, p. 149; Congressman Banks quoted by Ellis Paxson Oberhaltzer, *Jay Cooke: Financier of the Civil War*, vol. 2 (Philadelphia, 1907), p. 322 – see also pp. 224–25, 233–34, 238, 240, 243, 295, 301, 309; John Steele Gordon, *The Great Game: The Emergence of Wall Street as a World Power 1653–2000* (New York, 1999), p. 143; Chancellor, *Devil Take the Hindmost*, pp. 175, 184; Gould quoted by Kevin Phillips, *Wealth and Democracy: A Political History of the American Rich* (New York, 2002), p. 322.

11 Henry Adams, 'The New York Gold Conspiracy' in Charles Francis Adams and Henry Adams, *Chapters of Erie* (Ithaca, 1956 reprint originally published New York, 1886); Ackerman, *The Gold Ring*, pp. 275–78; Swanberg, *Jim Fisk*, p. 168; 'Gold Panic Investigation', March 1, 1870, House Committee on

Banking and Currency, Report #31, 41st Congress, Second Session, pp. 7, 8, 18, 19, 132 – for Fisk's testimony about Grant see p. 177; Kessner, *Capital City*, pp. 141, 148; *Fraser's magazine* quoted by Gordon, *Scarlet Woman*, p. 165; *New York Herald* quoted by Gordon, *Scarlet Woman*, p. 183; Henry Clews, *28 Years in Wall Street* (New York, 1888), p. 327; 'Report of the Select Committee of the Senate in Relation to Members Receiving Money from Railway Companies', Document #52, March 10, 1869, State Senate of New York, 92nd Session.

12 Oberhaltzer, *Jay Cooke*, pp. 77, 84. *New York Herald*, October 24, 1867; A popular tale recounted how Cooke had once chastised the young Head Cashier of his New York bank for being seen in public on Sunday driving a four-in-hand in Central Park, instructing him that not only had he desecrated the Sabbath, but that 'Credit is a tender plant. Nothing so affects it as such a stupid display as a "four-in-hand" . . . God sees if men do not.'

13 Alexander Dana Noyes quoted by Ron Chernow, *The House of Morgan: An American Banking Dynasty and the Rise of Modern Finance* (New York, 1990), p. 37; Holbrook, *Age of Moguls*, pp. 53–54; Oberhaltzer, *Jay Cooke*, pp. 423–25; Sven Beckert, 'The Making of New York City's Bourgeoisie 1850–86', Ph.D. dissertation (Columbia University, 1995), pp. 300–04; Vincent P. Carosso, *Investment Banking in America: A History* (Cambridge, Mass., 1970), pp. 25–26; Broker quoted by Chancellor, *Devil Take the Hindmost*, p. 186; Eric Foner, *Reconstruction: America's Unfinished Revolution* (New York, 1988), p. 512; Kessner, *Capital City*, p. 161.

14 Walt Whitman quoted by Walter Fuller Taylor, *The Economic Novel in America* (New York, 1964), p. 37; Jan W. Dietrichson, *The Image of Money in the American Novel of the Gilded Age* (New York, 1969); Mark Twain and Charles Dudley Warner, *The Gilded Age: A Tale of Today* (New York, 1994), p. 193.

15 Henry Adams quoted by Richard Hofstadter, *The American Political Tradition and the Men Who Made It* (New York, 1948), p. 172; Charles Francis Adams and Henry Adams, *Chapters of Erie* (Ithaca, 1956, originally published in New York, 1886), pp. 3, 8, 10, 33, 95, 98.

16 Beckert, 'The Making of New York City's Bourgeoisie', pp. 233–34; *Nation* editorial quoted by White, *The Book of Daniel Drew: The Inside Story of the First Great Wall Street Speculator* (Larchmont, NY, 1965 reprint, originally published 1910), p. 349; Vernon Louis Parrington, *Main Currents in American Thought*, volume 3, *The Beginnings of Critical Realism in America* (New York, 1927–30), pp. 161–65.

17 Morton Keller, *The Art and Politics of Thomas Nast* (New York, 1968); *Thomas Nast: Cartoons and Illustrations with Text by Thomas Nast St. Hill* (New York, 1974), plate 85; Tweed for president cartoon cited in Swanberg, *Jim Fisk*; 'On to Washington' , 'Out of the Ruins', and 'Dead Men Tell No Tales' cartoons in Thomas Nast Cartoons, New York Public Library Collection, Prints Division; 'This Street is Closed for Repairs' cartoon cited by C. Van Woodward, 'The Lowest Ebb', *American Heritage*, 1957, vol. 8.

18 Klein, *Life and Legend*, p. 374 contains reproductions of several of these Keppler cartoons; Keller, *Art and Politics*; Richard Samuel West, *Satire on*

Stone: *The Political Cartoons of Joseph Keppler* (Champaign-Urbana, 1988), p. 237.

19 *Harper's Weekly*, October 16, 1869 and October 9 and 11, 1873; *New York Times*, March 21, 1877; *New York Times* quoted by Edwin P. Hoyt, *The Goulds: A Social History* (New York, 1969), p. 117.

20 Joseph Choate quoted by Calvin Tomkins, *Merchants and Masterpieces: The Story of the Metropolitan Museum of Art* (New York, 1989), pp. 23–24.

21 *New York Times* quoted by Bouck White, *The Book of Daniel Drew*, pp. 386–87; Godkin quoted by Holbrook, *Age of Moguls*, p. 47; *The Nation*, September 23 and 30, 1869, October 7, 1869, January 1, 1872, November 11, 1872.

22 Swanberg, *Jim Fisk*; Henry Adams quoted by Chancellor, *Devil Take the Hindmost*, p. 177.

23 *The Nation*, January 1 and 11, 1872, September 15 and 25, 1873, October 2 and 9, 1873, November 6, 1873; Beckert, 'The Making of the New York City Bourgeoisie', p. 323, 335; Song quoted by Robert M. Sharp, *The Lore and Legends of Wall Street* (Homewood, Illinois, 1989), p. 125.

24 T. A. Bland, *Esau; or, The Banker's Victim* (Boston, 1892); Robert P. Sharkey, *Money, Class, and Party: An Economic Study of the Civil War and Reconstruction* (Baltimore, 1959), p. 92; Parrington, *Main Currents*, pp. 108–10; Theodore Saloutos, *Farmer Movements in the South 1865–1933* (Lincoln, Nebraska, 1960), pp. 49–50; Congressman Reagan quoted by Cashman, *America in the Gilded Age*, p. 56; Ignatius Donnelly quoted by Walter Benn Michaels, *The Gold Standard and the Logic of Naturalism: American Literature at the Turn of the Century* (Berkeley, 1987), p. 144.

25 *Chicago Daily News* quoted by Holbrook, *Age of Moguls*, p. 93; *Frank Leslie's Illustrated*, March 15, 1873 and May 17, 1873; see also 'The Rascals of Wall Street', *Scribner's Monthly*, November, 1872, vol. 5/1; Sigmund Diamond, *The Reputation of American Businessmen* (Cambridge, Mass., 1955), p. 60; *National Police Gazette*, November 18, 1879.

26 *Albany Evening Times* quoted by Ackerman, *The Gold Ring*, p. 79; *Springfield Republican* quoted by Klein, *Life and Legend*, p. 125; Henry Nash Smith, editor, *Documents in American Civilization: Popular Culture and Industrialism 1865–1900* (New York, 1967), pp. 86–87; Frederick L. Collins, *Moneytown: The Story of Manhattan's Toe: that Golden Mile which lies between the Battery and the Fields* (New York, 1946).

27 Ackerman, *The Gold Ring*, pp. 265–66; Frank A. Munsey, *The Boy Broker: Among the Kings of Wall Street* (New York, 1888); *New York Ledger*, November 1 and 15, 1873; Diamond, *Reputation of American Businessmen*, pp. 58–59; James W. Buel, 'The Rich' in Henry Nash Smith, ed., *Mysteries and Miseries of America's Great Cities* (1883), *Documents*, pp. 150–57; New York Historical Society, 'Games' Exhibition, 2001.

28 *Frank Leslie's Illustrated*, October 25, 1873; *New York Herald* quoted by Swanberg, *Jim Fisk*, p. 282.

29 Irwin G. Wylie, *The Self-Made Man in America: The Myth of Rags to Riches* (Glencoe, 1954), pp. 56, 65.

30 Sinclair Lewis quoted by Richard Huber, *The American Idea of Success* (New York, 1971), p. 26; Louis B. Wright, 'Franklin's Legacy to the Gilded Age', *Virginia Quarterly*, Spring, 1946, vol. 22/2; William G. McLaughlin, *The Meaning of Henry Ward Beecher: An Essay on the Shifting Values of Mid-Victorian America 1840–70* (New York, 1970), pp. 6, 25, 100, 246; Henry Ward Beecher, *Lectures to Young Men on Various Important* Subjects (New York, 1860); Henry Nash Smith, *Democracy and the Novel: Popular Resistance to Classic American Writers* (New York, 1978), p. 82.

31 Wylie, *Self-Made Man*, p. 68; Beecher quoted by Wayne Westbrook, *Wall Street in the American Novel* (New York, 1980), p. 39; Beecher quoted by Swanberg, *Jim Fisk*, p. 113; Beecher quoted by Wylie, *Self-Made Man*, p. 70; William Van Doren quoted by Wylie, *Self-Made*, p. 71 – see also p. 77; *The Nation*, October 10, 1876; Henry Ward Beecher, 'The Deceitfulness of Riches', quoted by David Mark Wheeler, 'Perceptions of Money and Wealth on Gilded Age Stages: A Study of Four Long Run Productions in New York City', Ph.D. dissertation (University of Oregon, 1986), p. 62; Beckert, 'Making of the New York City Bourgeoisie', p. 216.

32 C. H. Hamlin quoted by Cedric B. Cowing, *Populists, Plungers, and Progressives: A Social History of Stock and Commodity Speculation 1890–1930* (Princeton, 1965), p. 26; Henry Ward Beecher, *Lectures to Young Men*, pp. 76–77; Wylie, *Self-Made Man*, p. 79.

33 Washington Gladden, 'Three Dangers' in *Applied Christianity and Moral Aspects of Social Questions* (New York, 1976 reprint, originally published 1886) pp. 203–05.

34 Wheeler, 'Perceptions of Money and Wealth', including pp. 228–30, 232, 242, 253–54.

35 Taylor, *Economic Novel*, pp. 63–67; Claude Reherd Flory, 'Economic Criticism in American Fiction 1792–1900', Ph.D. dissertation (University of Pennsylvania, 1936), p. 106; Henry Nash Smith, 'The Search for a Capitalist Hero: Businessmen in American Fiction' in Earl F. Chait, ed., *The Business Establishment* (New York, 1964); Lorne Fienberg, *A Cuckoo in the Nest of Culture: Changing Perceptions of the Businessman in the American Novel, 1865–1914* (New York, 1988), pp. 93–97; Frank Lee Benedict, 'A Year and a Day', *Peterson's*, May, 1873; 'The Bankrupt's Wife', *Harper's Monthly*, February, 1868; 'Wall Street and the Merchant of Venice', *The Literary World*, February 19, 1887; Richard B. Kimball, *Undercurrents of Wall Street: A Romance of Business* (New York, 1862).

36 Josiah G. Holland, *Sevenoaks: A Story of Today* (Saddle River, New Jersey 1968 reprint, originally published in New York, 1875), pp. 333–35.

37 Dietrichson, *Image of Money*, p. 336; J. W. De Forest, *Honest John Vane* (State College, Pennsylvania, 1960 reprint, originally published as a book 1875 and first serialized in *The Atlantic*, 1873), pp. 84, 124, 159.

38 Twain and Warner, *The Gilded Age*; Twain quoted by Taylor, *Economic Novel in America*, p. 126 – see also pp. 130–31; Twain quoted by Phillips, *Wealth and Democracy*, p. 240; Chancellor, *Devil Take the Hindmost*, p. 170; Mark Twain, *The Man That Corrupted Hadleyburg*, in *Selected Shorter*

Writings of Mark Twain, Walter Blair, editor (Boston, 1962).

39 Walter Benn Michaels, 'Dreiser's Financier: The Man of Business as a Man of Letters', in Eric J. Sundquist, editor, *American Realism: New Essays* (Baltimore, 1982); Daniel Aaron, *Men of Good Hope: A Story of American Progressives* (New York, 1951), pp. 172, 186–88; Michael Oriard, *Sporting with the Gods; The Rhetoric of Play and Game in American Culture* (New York, 1991), pp. 200–02; Silas Lapham quoted by Michael Spindler, *American Literature and Social Change: William Dean Howells to Arthur Miller* (Bloomington, Indiana, 1983), p. 53; William Dean Howells, *The Rise of Silas Lapham* (New York, 1971).

40 William Dean Howells, 'The Vanderbilts', in *Documents in American Civilization*, p. 84; William Dean Howells, *A Hazard of New Fortunes* (New York, 1965), pp. 167, 191, 194, 226–27; Oriard, *Sporting with the Gods*, p. 202; Basil March quoted by Aaron, *Men of Good Hope*, p. 186.

CHAPTER 5 The Engine Room of Corporate Capitalism

1 David Black, *King of Fifth Avenue: The Fortunes of August Belmont* (New York, 1981), p. 26; Ron Chernow, *The House of Morgan: An American Banking Dynasty and the Rise of Modern Finance* (New York, 1990), p. 20.

2 Poem, remarks of *New York World, New York Tribune, Harper's Weekly*, Reverend William Wilkinson all quoted by Sigmund Diamond, *The Reputation of the American Businessman* (Cambridge, Mass., 1955), chapter on J. P. Morgan; Jean Strouse, *Morgan: American Financier* (New York, 2000), p. 15; Pope Pius X quoted by Dixon Wecter, *The Saga of American Society: A Record of Social Aspiration 1607–1937* (New York, 1937), p. 124; *New York Times*, April 10, 11, 12, 1913.

3 Mark Twain, *The Tragedy of Pudd'head Wilson* (New York, 1894), p. 98; James Livingston, *Origins of the Federal Reserve System: Money, Class, and Corporate Capitalism 1890–1913* (Ithaca, 1986), p. 31.

4 William Vanderbilt quoted by Sven Beckert, *The Monied Metropolis: New York City and the Consolidation of the American Bourgeoisie 1850–1896* (New York, 2001), p. 232.

5 Edward G. Burrows and Mike Wallace, *Gotham: A History of New York City to 1898* (New York, 1999), pp. 1041–43; Samuel Rezneck, 'Patterns of Thought and Action in an American Depression, 1882–86', *American Historical Review*, January, 1956; 'The Wall Street Troubles', *Chautauquen*, October, 1883 – July, 1884, vol. 4; Henry Clews, *28 years in Wall Street* (New York, 1888), chapter 26; George Wheeler, *Pierpont Morgan and Friends: The Anatomy of a Myth* (New York, 1973), p. 161.

6 Burrows and Wallace, *Gotham*, p. 1186; Sean Dennis Cashman, *America in the Gilded Age: From the Death of Lincoln to the Rise of Teddy Roosevelt* (New York, 1988), p. 222; Thomas R. Navin and Marian V. Sears, 'The Rise of the Market for Industrial Securities, 1887–1902', *Business History Review*, 1955, vol. 29; Strouse, *Morgan*, p. 320; Livingston, *Origins of Federal Reserve*, p. 72; Thomas Kessner, *Capital City: New York City and the Men Behind America's Rise to Economic Dominance, 1860–1900* (New York,

2003), pp. 274–75; M. H. Dunlop, *Gilded City: Scandal and Sensation in Turn-of-the-Century New York* (New York, 2000), p. 20.

7 *Harper's Weekly*, September 2, 1893.

8 Navin and Sears, 'The Rise of the Market for Industrial Securities'.

9 Beckert, *Monied Metropolis*, p. 263.

10 Kessner, *Capital City*, pp. 221, 224; Beckert, *Monied Metropolis*, p. 210; Wheeler, *Pierpont Morgan*, p. 138; Vincent P. Carosso, *Investment Banking in America: A History* (Cambridge, Mass., 1970), pp. 33, 36, 38; Burrows and Wallace, *Gotham*, pp. 1044–45; George Roberts quoted by Wheeler, *Pierpont Morgan*, p. 178.

11 Kessner, *Capital City*, p. 287; Cashman, *America in the Gilded Age*, p. 41; Carosso, *Investment Banking*, p. 38.

12 Maury Klein, *The Life and Legend of E.H. Harriman* (Chapel Hill, North Carolina, 2000), pp. 61, 117, 208; Stephen Birmingham, *Our Crowd: The Great Jewish Families of New York* (New York, 1967), pp. 160, 169, and Schiff to Morgan quoted by Birmingham, p. 209; Mark Smith, *Toward Rational Exuberance: The Evolution of the Modern Stock Market* (New York, 2001), p. 39; Howard Schutz, 'Giants in Collision: The Northern Pacific Panic of 1901', *American History Illustrated*, 1968, vol. 21/5; Frederick Lewis Allen, *The Lords of Creation* (New York, 1935), chapter 2.

13 Livingston, *Origins of the Federal Reserve*, pp. 51, 58; Navin and Sears, 'The Rise of the Market for Industrial Securities'; 'Final Report of the United States Industrial Commission', Vol. xix (Washington DC, Government Printing Office, 1902), pp. 616–19; Thomas C. Cochran and William Miller, *The Age of Enterprise: A Social History of Industrial America* (New York, 1942), pp. 192–93.

14 Carosso, *Investment Banking*, pp. 47–50, 140–44.

15 Kessner, *Capital City*, pp. 290, 299; George E. Mowry, *The Era of Theodore Roosevelt and the Birth of Modern America, 1900–12* (New York, 1958), pp. 7–8; Navin and Sears, 'The Rise of the Market for Industrial Securities'; Strouse, *Morgan*, p. 395; Livingston, *Origins of Federal Reserve*, p. 56.

16 Burrows and Wallace, *Gotham*, pp. 1045–46; Kim Phillips-Fein, 'Free Markets, "Potential Competition" and Investors' Rights: The Merger Movement and Late Nineteenth Century Economic Thought', unpublished ms. on the rise of the publicly traded corporation in possession of author; Kessner, *Capital City*, p. 299; Henry Clews, 'Wall Street's Wild Speculation: 1900–04', *Cosmopolitan*, August, 1904, vol. xxxvii; Navin and Sears, 'The Rise of the Market for Industrial Securities'; Cochran and Miller, *Age of Enterprise*, p. 189; Carosso, *Investment Banking*, pp. 79, 85.

17 Chernow, *House of Morgan*, p. 68; Barry E. Supple, 'A Business Elite: German–Jewish Financiers in 19th Century New York', *Business History Review*, Summer, 1957, vol. xxxi, #2; Garet Garrett, *Where the Money Grows* (New York, 1911), p. 49; Kessner, *Capital City*, p. 308.

18 Sven Beckert, 'The Making of New York City's Bourgeoisie, 1850–86', Ph.D. dissertation (Columbia University, 1995), p. 323.

19 Beckert, *Monied Metropolis*, pp. 234, 309; Beckert, 'The Making of New

York City's Bourgeoisie', p. 354; David T. Burbank, *Reign of the Rabble: The St. Louis General Strike of 1877* (New York, 1966), p. 6; Robert V. Bruce, *1877: Year of Violence* (Indianapolis, 1959), pp. 225, 310, 313; Nelson W. Aldrich, *Old Money: The Mythology of America's Upper Class* (New York, 1988).

20 Beckert, *Monied Metropolis*, p. 202.

21 Whitney quoted by Richard Hofstadter, *The American Political Tradition and the Men Who Made It* (New York, 1948), p. 181; Burrows and Wallace, *Gotham*, p. 1204; Cashman, *America in the Gilded Age*, p. 224; Strouse, *Morgan*, pp. 299, 350–53; Wheeler, *Pierpont Morgan*, p. 45; Grover Cleveland, 'The Bond Issues' in *Presidential Problems* (New York, 1904).

22 Robert H. Wiebe, 'The House of Morgan and the Executive, 1905–13', *American Historical Review*, October, 1959, vol. 65.

23 Assistant Treasury Secretary quoted by Strouse, *Morgan*, p. 359; William Allen White quoted by Cochran and Miller, *Age of Enterprise*, p. 163; Livingston, *Origins of Federal Reserve*, pp. 66, 90–92, 96–97, 100, 111, 125; Allen, *Lords of Creation*.

24 Wiebe, 'House of Morgan'; *Wall Street Journal* quoted by Robert H. Wiebe, *Businessmen and Reform: A Study of the Progressive Movement* (New York, 1968), p. 195 – see also pp. 80–81; Strouse, *Morgan*, p. 542.

25 Mine workers song and George Baer quoted by Strouse, *Morgan*, p. 449 – see also cartoon, 'Hold on Boys'.

26 Roosevelt quoted by John Steele Gordon, 'The Magnitude of J. P. Morgan', *American Heritage*, July–August, 1989; Jean Strouse, 'The Brilliant Bailout', *The New Yorker*, November 23, 1998; Bernard Berenson quoted by Strouse, *Morgan*, p. 589 – see also pp. 582, 589.

27 Strouse, *Morgan*, p. 595; Richard N. Sheldon, 'Introduction' in Arthur Schlesinger, Jr. and Roger Bruns, editors, *Congress Investigates: A Documented History 1792–1974*, The Pujo Committee, 1912 (New York, 1975), p. 2251; James Dill quoted by Livingston, *Origins of Federal Reserve*, p. 226.

28 Matthew Josephson, *The President Makers* (New York, 1938), p. 101; Emily S. Rosenberg, *Financial Missionaries to the World: The Politics and Culture of Dollar Diplomacy, 1900–1930* (Cambridge, Mass., 1999), pp. 43, 48, 56, 63, 65; Strouse, *Morgan*, pp. 460–61, 613–15.

29 Aldrich, *Old Money*, p. 26.

30 Chernow, *House of Morgan*, pp. 14, 48–51; Godkin quoted by Wecter, *Saga of American Society*, p. 109.

31 Colonel Mapleson quoted by Lloyd Morris, *Incredible New York: High Life and Low Life of the Last 100 Years* (New York, 1975 reprint, originally published 1951), p. 192; Critic quoted by Burrows and Wallace, *Gotham*, p. 1074; Jack W. Rudolph, 'Launching the Met', *American History Illustrated*, October, 1983, vol. xviii/6.

32 Burrows and Wallace, *Gotham*, pp. 1074–76; Frick quoted by Morris, *Incredible New York*, p. 207.

33 Ward McAllister, 'The World of Fashion' in *Documents in American*

Civilization: Popular Culture and Industrialism 1865–1900 (New York, 1967); Wecter, *Saga of American Society*, pp. 212–15.

34 Chernow, *House of Morgan*, pp. 47–51; DePeyster quoted by Burrows and Wallace, *Gotham*, p. 1083 – see also pp. 1076, 1081–82; Strouse, 'Brilliant Bailout'; Michele H. Bogart, 'In Search of a United Front: American Architectural Sculpture at the Turn of the Century', *Winterhur Portfolio*, 1984; Calvin Tomkins, *Merchants and Masterpieces: The Story of the Metropolitan Museum of Art* (New York, 1989) pp. 22–24, 61, 73–75, 82, 92, 186; Beckert, *Monied Metropolis*, p. 271; Daniel M. Fox, *Engines of Culture: Philanthropy and Art Museums* (State Historical Society of Wisconsin, 1963), pp. 37–41; Allen, *Lords of Creation*; Aldrich, *Old Money*, pp. 58, 63.

35 Beckert, 'The Making of the New York City Bourgeoisie', pp. 354, 358; Chauncey Depew quoted by Beckert, *Monied Metropolis*, p. 212 – see also, pp. 238, 243, 247, 271, 309; Burrows and Wallace, *Gotham*, p. 1062.

36 Frederic Cople Jaher, 'Style and Status: High Society in Late 19th Century New York', in Frederic Cople Jaher, ed., *The Rich, the Well-Born, and the Powerful* (Champaign-Urbana, 1973); David C. Hammack, *Power and Society: Greater New York at the Turn of the Century* (New York, 1982), pp. 36, 41, 46, 50–51, 57, 59, 71.

37 Wharton quoted by Strouse, *Morgan*, p. 225.

38 Black, *King of Fifth Avenue*; Livingston, *Origins of Federal Reserve*, p. 47; Aldrich, *Old Money*, pp. 27, 37.

CHAPTER 6 The Great Satan

1 Edward Bellamy, *Looking Backward, 2000–1887* (New York, 1960); Ignatius Donnelly, *Caesar's Column: A Story of the 20th Century* (Cambridge, Mass., 1960).

2 Cedric B. Cowing, *Populists, Plungers, and Progressives: A Social History of Stock and Commodity Speculation 1890–1930* (Princeton, 1965), p. 8.

3 Robert P. Sharkey, *Money, Class, and Party: An Economic Study of the Civil War and Reconstruction* (Baltimore, 1959), pp. 92, 126, 287; Theodore Saloutos, *Farmer Movements in the South 1865–1933* (Lincoln, Nebraska, 1960), p. 49; Sean Dennis Cashman, *America in the Gilded Age: From the Death of Lincoln to the Rise of Teddy Roosevelt* (New York, 1988), p. 37; Chester McArthur Destler, *American Radicalism, 1865–1901: Essays and Documents* (Menasha, Wisconsin, 1946), pp. 3, 77, 54.

4 Destler, *American Radicalism*, p. 66; Laurence Goodwyn, *Democratic Promise: The Populist Movement in America* (New York, 1976), pp. xvii, 115–17, 361; Robert C. McMath, Jr, *American Populism: A Social History 1877–1898* (New York, 1993), p. 46.

5 Goodwyn, *Democratic Promise*, pp. 150–53; Bruce Palmer, *Man Over Money: The Southern Populist Critique of American Capitalism* (Chapel Hill, 1980), p. 106.

6 North Carolina insurgent and Texas editor quoted by Palmer, *Man Over Money*, p. 16 – see also p. 14; T. R. Frentz quoted by Robert Wiebe,

Businessmen and Reform: A Study of the Progressive Movement (New York, 1968), p. 12; James H. Davis quoted by Normon Pollack, editor, *The Populist Mind* (New York, 1967), p. 220.

7 'Wall Street's Interest in Gold', *The American*, July 3, 1897; Sven Beckert, *The Monied Metropolis: New York City and the Consolidation of the American Bourgeoisie 1850–1896* (New York, 2001).

8 Honorable William P. Fishback, 'Railway Financeering as a Fine Art', *Arena*, June, 1897, vol. 17; Ann Fabian, *Card Sharps, Dream Books, and Bucket Shops: Gambling in 19th Century America* (Ithaca, 1990), p. 179; Palmer, *Man Over Money*, p. 14; Michael Kazin, *The Populist Persuasion: An American History* (Ithaca, 1995), pp. 31–32, 35, 44; Terence Powderly quoted by Thomas E. Watson, *The People's Party Campaign Book: Not a Revolt; It is a Revolution* (New York, 1975 reprint, originally published 1892), p. 135 – see also pp. 207–08; James B. Weaver, 'A Call to Action' in Pollack, *The Populist Mind*, p. 131; Henry Demarest Lloyd quoted by Pollack, *Populist Mind*, pp. 406, 414–15; George McKenna, editor, *American Populism* (New York, 1974), pp. 96, 110–11.

9 William H. Harvey, *Coin's Financial School*, edited by Richard Hofstadter (Cambridge, Mass., 1963, originally published 1894), pp. 30–31, 93, 233–34; Richard Hofstadter, 'Free Silver and the Mind of 'Coin' Harvey' in Richard Hofstadter, *The Paranoid Style in American Politics and Other Essays* (Cambridge, Mass., 1952), pp. 242, 245, 270; Palmer, *Man Over Money*; Saloutos, *Farmer Movements*, p. 139.

10 Watson, *People's Party Campaign Book*, pp. 8, 12.

11 Destler, *American Radicalism*, pp. 17, 19, 27; Goodwyn, *Democratic Promise*, p. 230.

12 Stump orator quoted by Pollack, *Populist Mind*, p. 222; Alabama congressman quoted by Pollack, *Populist Mind*, p. 229; Governor Nugent quoted by Pollack, *Populist Mind*, pp. 286–87; Lloyd quoted by Destler, *American Radicalism*, p. 219.

13 Weaver, 'A Call to Action', p. 131; Watson, *People's Party Campaign Book*, pp. 19–23.

14 Cashman, *America in the Gilded Age*, p. 202.

15 Cowing, *Populists, Plungers, and Progressives*, p. 18; Watson, *People's Party Campaign Book,* p. 111; Senator Allen quoted by Hofstadter, 'Free Silver and the Mind of "Coin" Harvey'.

16 William A. Peffer, *The Farmer's Side: His Troubles and Their Remedy* (1891) in Pollack, *Populist Mind*, pp. 98–105.

17 Edward G. Burrows and Mike Wallace, *Gotham: A History of New York City to 1898* (New York, 1999), pp. 1204–05); George Wheeler, *Pierpont Morgan and Friends: The Anatomy of a Myth* (New York, 1973), p. 45; Bryan quoted by Martin S. Fridson, *It Was A Very Good Year: Extraordinary Moments in Stock Market History* (New York, 1998); Bryan's 'Cross of Gold Speech' in McKenna, *American Populism*, pp. 137–38; Tom Watson, 'Wall Street: Conspiracies against the American Nation', *New York World Sunday Magazine*, October 10, 1896.

18 Robert H. Walker, 'The Poet and the Robber Baron', *American Quarterly*, 1961, vol. 13/4; Robert M. Sharp, *The Lore and Legends of Wall Street* (Homewood, Illinois, 1989), p. 125.

19 Claude Reherd Flory, 'Economic Criticism in American Fiction 1792–1900', Ph.D. dissertation (University of Pennsylvania, 1936); Peffer, *The Farmer's Side*, p. 105.

20 Harvey, *Coin's Financial School*; Henry George quoted by John L. Thomas, *Alternative America: Henry George, Edward Bellamy, Henry Demarest Lloyd and the Adversary Tradition* (Cambridge, Mass., 1983), pp. 128–29.

21 *New York World*, January 1, 1888; Lloyd quoted by Daniel Aaron, *Men of Good Hope: A Story of American Progressives* (New York, 1951), p. 151; John Clark Ridpath, 'The True Inwardness of Wall Street', *The Arena*, 1898, vol. 19; Fishback, 'Railway Financeering'.

22 *Sioux Falls Daily Argus* quoted by Sigmund Diamond, *The Reputation of the American Businessman* (Cambridge, Mass., 1955), p. 89; Watson, *People's Campaign Book*, p. 219; Watson, 'Wall Street Conspiracies Against the Nation'; Pollack, *Populist Mind*, pp. 32–36.

23 Donnelly, *Caesar's Column*; William Harvey, *A Tale of Two Nations* (1894) in Hofstadter, editor, *Coin's Financial School*, pp. 58–59.

24 Pollack, *Populist Mind*, pp. 32–36, 229; Peffer, *The Farmer's Side*; Watson, 'Wall Street Conspiracies Against the Nation'; 'In the Mirror of the Present', *The Arena*, October, 1905; Ridpath, 'The True Inwardness of Wall Street'.

25 B. O. Flowers, 'Frederick Opper: A Cartoonist of Democracy', *The Arena*, June, 1905, vol. 33/187.

26 Watson, *People's Campaign Book*, p. 219; Alabama congressman Milford W. Howard, 'The American Plutocracy' in Pollack, *Populist Mind*, pp. 234–35; *Platte County Argus*, June 4, 1896 in Pollack, *Populist Mind*; 'In the Mirror of the Present', *The Arena*, October, 1905; Jean Strouse, *Morgan: American Financier* (New York, 2000), p. 324; Aaron, *Men of Good Hope*, pp. 147–48; Henry Demarest Lloyd, *Wealth Against Commonwealth*, excerpted in Pollack, *Populist Mind*, pp. 499–518; Thomas, *Alternative America*, p. 141; Donnelly, *Caesar's Column*; Ridpath, 'The True Inwardness of Wall Street'.

27 Pollack, *Populist Mind*, pp. 10–11; Watson, *People's Campaign Book*, p. 222; 'In the Mirror of the Present', *The Arena*, October, 1905; Thomas, *Alternative America*, pp. 309–12; Jackson Lears, *No Place of Grace: Anti-modernism and the Transformation of American Culture* (New York, 1981).

28 Thomas, *Alternative America*, p. 141; Kazin, *Populist Persuasion*, pp. 31–32; Howard, 'The American Plutocracy' in Pollack, *Populist Mind*, pp. 234–35; see also pp. 508–09; Ridpath, 'The True Inwardness of Wall Street'; Walter Benn Michaels, *The Gold Standard and the Logic of Naturalism: American Literature at the Turn of the Century* (Berkeley, 1987), p. 144; McKenna, *American Populism*, pp. 126–27.

29 Donnelly, *Caesar's Column*; Richard Hofstadter, *The Age of Reform* (New York, 1955), pp. 74–76; Hofstadter, *Paranoid Style*, p. 8; Ridpath, 'The True Inwardness of Wall Street'; William Harvey, *Tale of Two Nations* cited in Hofstadter, editor, *Coin's Financial School*, pp. 58–59.

30 Harvey, *Tale of Two Nations* in Hofstadster, ed., *Coin's Financial School*, pp. 58–59; Stanley Lemars, 'The Cuban Crisis of 1895–98: Newspapers and Nativism', *Missouri Historical Review*, 1965, vol. 60/1; Weaver, 'A Call to Action'; Hofstadter, *Age of Reform*, p. 77–79; Hofstadter, *Paranoid Style*, p. 267.

31 Donnelly, *Caesar's Column*, pp. 262–63; Destler, *American Radicalism*, p. 246.

32 Hofstadter, *Paranoid Style*; William Jennings Bryan quoted by *Chicago Tribune*, October 28, 1896, cited in Edward Herbert Mazur, *Minyans for a Prairie City: The Politics of Chicago Jewry 1850–1940* (New York, 1990).

33 John Higham, 'Anti-Semitism in the Gilded Age: A Reinterpretation', *Mississippi Valley Historical Review*, 1957, vol. 43/4; Oscar Handlin, 'American Views of the Jews at the Opening of the 20th Century', Publication of the American Jewish Historical Society, 1950–51, vol. 40; Lemars, 'The Cuban Crisis'; William Randolph Hearst quoted by David Nasaw, *The Chief: The Life of William Randolph Hearst* (Boston, 2000), p. 180; Strouse, *Morgan*, p. 350; Donnelly, *Caesar's Column*, p. 15; Hofstadter, *Age of Reform*, pp. 78–79; Professor Pal. Sylvanus, 'Tit for Tat: A Satirical Universal History of How Mr. Solomon Moses is Persecuting His Old Persecutors, Including a New Monetary System and School of Modern Philosophy', in *Anti-Semitism in America, 1878–1938* (New York, 1977); Cartoon 'Shylock's Bank' cited in Destler, *American Radicalism*, p. 27; 'Eish Dodt So?' cartoon cited in Louis Filler, *The Muckrakers* (University Park, 1976); Gordon Clark quoted by Michael N. Dobkowski, *The Tarnished Dream: The Basis of American Anti-Semitism* (Westport, 1979), p. 182; Watson, *People's Party Campaign Book*, p. 12; David Emmons, 'Morton Frewen and the Populist Revolt', *Annals of Wyoming*, 1963, vol. 35/2; Mary Elizabeth Lease quoted by Mazur, *Minyans for a Prairie City*.

CHAPTER 7 Wall Street and the Decline of Western Civilization

1 Marvin Gelfand, 'The Street', *American Heritage*, November, 1987, vol. 38/7; Ferdinand Lundberg, *America's Sixty Families* (New York, 1938), p. 80.

2 *North American Review*, June, 1906; Edith Wharton, *The House of Mirth* (New York, 1964).

3 Henry Adams quoted by Michael N. Dobkowski, *The Tarnished Dream: The Basis of American Anti-Semitism* (Westport, 1979), p. 122.

4 Henry Adams quoted by Dobkowski, *Tarnished Dream*, p. 125.

5 Brooks Adams quoted by Dobkowski, *Tarnished Dream*, p. 126.

6 Oliver Wendell Holmes quoted by Dobkowski, *Tarnished Dream*, p. 79; John Higham, 'Anti-Semitism in the Gilded Age: A Reinterpretation', *Mississippi Valley Historical Review*, 1957, vol. 43/4; Barry E. Supple, 'A Business Elite: German–Jewish Financiers in 19th Century New York', *Business History Review*, Summer, 1957, vol. xxxi/2; *New York Times*, June 19 and 20, 1877; Richard Hofstadter, *The Age of Reform* (New York, 1955), p. 92; Oscar Handlin, 'American Views of the Jew at the Opening of the 20th Century', Publication of the American Jewish Historical Society, 1950–51, vol. 40; Dobkowski, *Tarnished Dream*, pp. 116–17.

7 Jackson Lears, *No Place of Grace: Antimodernism and the Transformation of American Culture 1880–1920* (New York, 1981); Henry Adams quoted by Richard Huber, *The American Idea of Success* (New York, 1971), p. 413.

8 Matthew Josephson, *The President Makers* (New York, 1940), pp. 8, 18; Arthur T. Hadley quoted by B. Mark Smith, *Toward Rational Exuberance: The Evolution of the Modern Stock Market* (New York, 2001), p. 16; Henry Adams quoted by Thomas Beer, *The Mauve Decade: American Life at the End of the 19th Century* (Garden City, 1926), pp. 200–01; Henry Adams quoted by Nelson W. Aldrich, *Old Money: The Mythology of America's Upper Class* (New York, 1988), p. 46.

9 Edith Wharton, *A Backward Glance* (New York, 1934) , p. 176.

10 Henry James, *The American Scene* (New York, 1946, originally published 1907), pp. 78, 80, 83, 84, 159–61.

11 James' 'Passionate Pilgrim' quoted by Jan W. Dietrichson, *The Image of Money in the American Novel of the Gilded Age* (New York, 1969), p. 157, and Count Valentin from *The American* quoted p. 159; Henry James, *The American* (New York, 1960, originally published 1877); see also Lorne Fienberg, *A Cuckoo in the Nest of Culture: Changing Perceptions of the Businessman in the American Novel, 1865–1914* (New York, 1988).

12 Henry James, *The Ivory Tower* (New York, 2004, originally published 1917), p. 217; see also Henry James, *The Outcry* (New York, 2002, originally published 1911) which enjoyed great success as a comic treatment of a fabulously wealthy American tycoon, with a striking resemblance to Morgan, who is on an art collecting expedition to England.

13 Wharton, *Backward Glance*, pp. 9–10.

14 Edith Wharton, *The Age of Innocence* (New York, 1940, originally published 1920); David Black, *The King of Fifth Avenue: The Fortunes of August Belmont* (New York, 1981), p. 660.

15 Wharton, *House of Mirth*, p. 128; Walter Benn Michaels, *The Gold Standard and the Logic of Naturalism: American Literature at the Turn of the Century* (Berkeley, 1987), pp. 225–29, 240.

16 Edith Wharton, *The Custom of the Country* (New York, 1941, originally published 1913), pp. 73–74.

17 Wharton, *Custom of the Country*, p. 119.

18 Ralph Marvell quoted by Elizabeth Ammons, *Edith Wharton's Argument with America* (Athens, Georgia, 1980), p. 108; Wharton, *Custom of the Country*, p. 280.

19 Wharton, *Custom of the Country*, p. 364.

20 Wharton, *Custom of the Country*, pp. 537–38.

21 Wharton, *Custom of the Country*, p. 574; Ammons, *Edith Wharton*, p. 121.

22 Brooks Adams, *Law of Civilization and Decay* (Freeport, NY, 1971 reprint, originally published 1896), pp. 303, 313; Daniel Aaron, *Men of Good Hope: A Story of American Progressives* (New York, 1951), pp. 259–60.

23 Henry Adams quoted by Josephson, *The President Makers*, p. 8; Brooks Adams quoted by Josephson, *The President Makers*, p. 61; Henry Adams quoted by Jean Strouse, *Morgan: American Banker* (New York, 2000),

p. 412; Brooks Adams quoted by Aaron, *Men of Good Hope*, p. 273.

24 Henry Cabot Lodge, *Early Memories* (New York, 1913).

25 Roosevelt quoted by Edwin G. Burrows and Mike Wallace, *Gotham: A History of New York City to 1898* (New York, 1999), p. 1102; Josephson, *The President Makers*, p. 40; Thomas Kessner, *Capital City: New York City and the Men Behind America's Rise to Economic Dominance, 1860–1900* (New York, 2003), p. 258; Roosevelt quoted by Charles Beard, 'Introduction' in Brooks Adams, *Law of Civilization and Decay*; Strouse, *Morgan*, p. 438.

26 Aaron, *Men of Good Hope*, pp. 250–52, 254; Theodore Roosevelt to Henry Cabot Lodge, November 14, 1906 in *Letters of Theodore Roosevelt: Selections from the Correspondence of Theodore Roosevelt and Henry Cabot Lodge 1884–1918* (New York, 1925); Henry Cabot Lodge, 'A Frontier Town' in *Frontier Town and Other Essays* (New York, 1906); Roosevelt quoted by Lears, *No Place of Grace*, p. 116.

27 Henry Adams quoted by Strouse, *Morgan*, p. 405; John Brisbane Walker quoted by Sean Dennis Cashman, *America in the Gilded Age: From the Death of Lincoln to the Rise of Teddy Roosevelt* (New York, 1988), p. 50.

CHAPTER 8 Wall Streeet is Dead! Long Live Wall Street!

1 Frank Norris, *The Pit: A Story of Chicago*, edited and with an introduction by Joseph R. McElrath, Jr. and Gwendolyn Jones (New York, 1994); 'Pit' – Parker Brothers 'Frenzied Trading Game' (in author's possession).

2 Martin J. Sklar, *The Corporate Reconstruction of American Capitalism 1890–1916: The Market, the Law, and Politics* (New York, 1988).

3 Michele H. Bogart, 'In Search of a United Front: American Architectural Sculpture at the Turn of the Century', *Winterthur Portfolio*, 1984, vol. 19.

4 Ann Fabian, *Card Sharps, Dream Books, and Bucket Shops: Gambling in 19th Century America* (Ithaca, 1990), pp. 188, 191, 195; Cedric B. Cowing, *Populists, Plungers, and Progressives: A Social History of Stock and Commodity Speculation 1890–1930* (Princeton, 1965), pp. 28–30; Edwin Lefevre, 'Gambling in Bucket Shops', *Harper's Weekly*, May 11, 1901; the estimate of the number of stock holders comes from Vincent P. Carosso, *Investment Banking in America: A History* (Cambridge, Mass., 1970), p. 85.

5 Jackson Lears, 'What if History was a Gambler?' in Karen Haltunnen and Lewis Perry, editors, *Moral Problems in American Life: New Perspectives in Cultural History* (Ithaca, 1998); Walter Benn Michaels, *The Gold Standard and the Logic of Naturalism: American Literature at the Turn of the Century* (Berkeley, 1987), pp. 225–27.

6 Cowing, *Populists, Plungers, and Progressives*, pp. 8–11, 15.

7 Andrew Carnegie quoted by Irwin G. Wylie, *The Self-Made Man in America: The Myth of Rags to Riches* (Glencoe, Illinois, 1954), p. 78; Andrew Carnegie quoted by Thomas Kessner, *Capital City: New York City and the Men Behind America's Rise to Economic Dominance, 1860–1900* , p. 165; Edwin Lefevre, 'The American Gambling Spirit', *Harper's Weekly*, May 3, 1903; 'The Vanderbilts' in Henry Nash Smith, editor, *Documents in American Civilization: Popular Culture and Industrialism 1865–1900* (New York, 1967), p. 88.

8 Charles A. Conant, 'Wall Street and the Country', *The Atlantic Monthly*, February, 1904, vol. xciii; 'A Wall Street View of our Declining Faith', *The Literary Digest*, February 2, 1907, vol. 34; Matthew Schneirov, *The Dream of a New Social Order: Popular Magazines in America*, (New York, 1994), pp. 111, 240.

9 James Livingston, *Origins of the Federal Reserve System: Money, Class, and Corporate Capitalism 1890–1913* (Ithaca, 1986), pp. 58–62, 136–39; Charles A. Conant, *Wall Street and the Country: A Study of Recent Financial Tendencies* (New York, 1968 reprint, originally published 1904).

10 Chicago Conference on Trusts, September 13–16, 1899; W. G. Nicholas, 'Wall Street as a Manufacturing Center', *Appleton's Magazine*, September, 1907, vol. 10; *Final Report of the United States Industrial Commission*, vol. xix (Washington D.C., Government Printing Office, 1902), pp. 616–19.

11 Jean Strouse, *Morgan: American Financier* (New York, 2000), pp. 320, 322; *Harper's Weekly*, September 21, 1907.

12 Richard Ohmann, *Selling Culture: Magazines, Markets, and Class at the Turn of the Century* (New York, 1996), p. 60; Livingston, *Origins of the Federal Reserve*, p. 62.

13 Carosso, *Investment Banking*, pp. 92–94.

14 James Bryce, *The American Commonwealth* (New York, 1888), pp. 518, 519, 524.

15 Michael Peter Gagne, 'Wall Street: A Symbol of American Culture', Ph.D. dissertation (University of Hawaii, 1996).

16 *Harper's Weekly*, May 13, 1893, September 2, 1893, August 29, 1899, September 2, 1899, September 16, 1899, September 30, 1899, November 11, 1899; Gagne, 'Wall Street', p. 332; Arthur N. Gleason, 'The Investor's Viewpoint', third of three part series in *American Review of Reviews*, August–October, 1912; John Bates Clark quoted by Kim Phillips-Fein, 'Free Markets, 'Potential Competition' and Investor's Rights: The Merger Movement and Late Nineteenth Century Economic Thought' (unpublished ms. in author's possession); Testimony of F. B. Thurber, Hearings Before the Industrial Commission on the Subject of Trusts and Industrial Combinations (Government Printing Office, Washington, D.C., 1899), p. 7.

17 Henry Clews, *Twenty-Eight Years in Wall Street* (New York, 1888), pp. 15, 18.

18 Cowling, *Populists, Plungers, and Progressives*, p. 35; Brooks McNamara, *Day of Jubilee: The Great Age of Public Celebrations in New York 1788–1909* (New Brunswick, 1997), p. 174.

19 James Bryce quoted by Walter Isaacson and Evan Thomas, *The Wise Men: Six Friends and the World They Made* (New York, 1986), p. 41; Ron Chernow, *The House of Morgan: An American Banking Dynasty and the Rise of Modern Finance* (New York, 1990), pp. 64–65.

20 *New York Times* quoted by Dixon Wecter, *The Saga of American Society: A Record of Social Aspiration 1607–1937* (New York, 1937), p. 349 – see also pp. 368–69, 371, 407; *New York Times* quoted by Stephen Birmingham, *Our Crowd: The Great Jewish Families of New York* (New York, 1967), p. 325; Edwin G. Burrows and Mike Wallace, *Gotham: A History of New York City*

to *1898* (New York, 1999), pp. 1072–73; Henry James quoted by M. H. Dunlop, *Gilded City: Scandal and Sensation in Turn-of-the-Century New York* (New York, 2000) p. 2 – see also p. 114; Lloyd Morris, *Incredible New York: High Life and Low Life of the Last 100 Years* (New York 1975 reprint, originally published 1951), pp. 204–07; Sean Dennis Cashman, *America in the Gilded Age: From the Death of Lincoln to the Rise of Teddy Roosevelt* (New York, 1988), p. 53; Stewart H. Holbrook, *The Age of the Moguls* (New York, 1953), pp. 154–55; Wecter, *Saga*, pp. 368–69, 371; Frederick Lewis Allen, *The Lords of Creation* (New York, 1935).

21 Kessner, *Capital City*, pp. 305–06; Noyes quoted by Cashman, *America in the Gilded Age*, p. 81; *World's Work* map cited in George E. Mowry, *The Era of Theodore Roosevelt and the Birth of Modern America 1900–12* (New York, 1958), p. 7.

22 Dunne quoted by Cashman, *America in the Gilded Age*, p. 83.

23 *Current Opinion*, February, 1913, vol. LIV; Morgan quoted by Allen, *Lords of Creation*, p. 95.

24 John Steele Gordon, 'The Magnitude of J. P. Morgan', *American Heritage*, July/August, 1989; *New York World* quoted by Maury Klein, *The Life and Legend of E. H. Harriman* (Chapel Hill, 2000), p. 241; Morgan quoted by Wecter, *Saga*, p. 124.

25 Henry Adams quoted by Matthew Josephson, *The President Makers* (New York, 1938), p. 8.

26 Lincoln Steffens, *The Autobiography of Lincoln Steffens* (New York, 1931), pp. 181–82, 188–89; On Scott Joplin's 'Wall Street Rag' see Edward A. Berlin, *King of Ragtime: Scott Joplin and His Era* (New York, 1994), p. 186.

27 *Bookman*, December, 1900, vol. 14.

28 Edward G. Riggs, 'Wall Street', *Munsey's Magazine*, January, 1894.

29 Klein, *Life and Legend of E. H. Harriman*, pp. 33, 61, 117–18, 208, 211.

30 *New York Sun* quoted by Ron Chernow, *The Death of the Banker: The Decline and Fall of Great Financial Dynasties and the Triumph of the Small Investor* (New York, 1997), p. 19; Theodore P. Greene, *American Heroes: The Changing Models of Success in American Magazines* (New York, 1970), pp. 100, 102, 104–05, 107–08, 109, 112, 124; *Munsey's Magazine*, April, 1892, vol. III; Holbrook, *Age of Moguls*, p. 100; B. C. Forbes quoted by Strouse, *Morgan*, p. ix.

31 Rockefeller quoted by Alan Tractenberg, *The Incorporation of America: Culture and Society in the Gilded Age* (New York, 1982), p. 86.

32 Lorne Fienberg, *A Cuckoo in the Nest of Culture: Changing Perspectives on the Businessman in the American Novel, 1865–1914* (New York, 1988); Vernon Louis Parrington, *Main Currents in American Thought*, volume 3: *The Beginnings of Critical Realism* (New York, 1927–30) pp. 182–88; Michael Oriard, *Sporting with the Gods: The Rhetoric of Play and Game in American Culture* (New York, 1991), pp. 204–08.

33 Frank Norris, *The Pit*; Norris quoted by Michael Spindler, *American Literature and Social Change: William Dean Howells to Arthur Miller* (Bloomington, 1983), p. 46.

34 Norris quoted by Walter Fuller Taylor, *The Economic Novel in America* (New York, 1964), p. 303.

35 Arun Mukharjee, *The Gospel of Wealth in the American Novel: The Rhetoric of Dreiser and Some of his Contemporaries* (London, 1987), p. 204.

36 Norris, *The Pit*, pp. 291–92 – see also McElrath and Jones, 'Introduction'.

37 William Graham Sumner quoted by Richard Hofstadter, *Social Darwinism in American Thought* (Boston, 1992), p. 58.

38 Theodore Dreiser, *The Financier* (New York, 1967), pp. 8–9.

39 Michaels, *The Gold Standard*, p. 83; David W. Noble, 'Dreiser and Veblen and the Literature of Cultural Change' in Joseph J. Kwiat and Mary C. Turpie, editors, *Studies in American Culture: Dominant Ideas and Image* (Minneapolis, 1960), p. 147; Dreiser quoted by Spindler, *American Literature*, p. 43.

40 Charles Edward Russell, *Lawless Wealth: The Origins of Some Great American Fortunes* (New York, 1908), pp. 39–43; Oriard, *Sporting with the Gods*, pp. 214–15, and Dreiser quoted on p. 216.

41 Dreiser, *The Financier*; Theodore Dreiser, *The Titan* (New York, 1965); Walter Benn Michaels, 'Dreiser' Financier: The Man of Business as a Man of Letters' in Eirc J. Sundquist, editor, *American Realism: New Essays* (Baltimore, 1982).

42 Dreiser, *The Titan*, pp. 397, 398.

43 Oriard, *Sporting with the Gods*, p. 217.

CHAPTER 9 Other People's Money

1 Morgan quoted by Jean Strouse, *Morgan: American Financier* (New York, 2000), pp. 434–35 – see also p. 438 quoting Hanna; *The World*, September 7, 8, 14, 1901; Ferdinand Lundberg, *America's Sixty Families* (New York, 1938), pp. 59, 66; *New York Times*, September 7, 8, 9, 11, 12, 13, 14, 15, 1901; *New York Daily Tribune*, September 8; George E. Mowry, *The Era of Theodore Roosevelt and the Birth of Modern America 1900–1912* (New York, 1962), p. 106; Thomas Kessner, *Capital City: New York City and the Men Behind America's Rise to Economic Dominance, 1860–1900* (New York, 2003), p. 314.

2 John Hay quoted by Sven Beckert, 'The Making of New York City's Bourgeoisie, 1850–1886', Ph.D. dissertation (Columbia University, 1995), p. 387.

3 Strouse, *Morgan*, pp. 437–38; Vincent P. Carosso, *Investment Banking in America: A History* (New York, 1970), p. 110.

4 Morgan quoted by Stephen Birmingham, *Our Crowd: The Great Jewish Families of New York* (New York, 1967), p. 203; Robert H. Wiebe, 'The House of Morgan and the Executive, 1905–13', *American Historical Review*, October 1959, vol. 65; Mowry, *The Era of Theodore Roosevelt*, pp. 130–31; Morgan quoted by Strouse, *Morgan*, p. 440 – see also p. 441.

5 Strouse, *Morgan*, p. 438; Theodore Roosevelt to Henry Cabot Lodge, November 14, 1906 in *Letters of Theodore Roosevelt: Selections from the Correspondence of Theodore Roosevelt and Henry Cabot Lodge, 1884–1918*

(New York, 1925); William H. Harbaugh, editor, *The Writings of Theodore Roosevelt* (New York, 1967), pp. 86, 423–32; Mowry, *Era of Theodore Roosevelt*, p. 132.

6 Strouse, *Morgan*, p. 574; Harbaugh, *Writings of Theodore Roosevelt*, pp. 100–01, 104, 107; Roosevelt to Lodge, September 30, 1902, Lodge to Roosevelt, October 11, 1902, Roosevelt to Lodge, October 17, 1902 in *Selections from Correspondence*.

7 Roosevelt quoted by Mowry, *Era of Theodore Roosevelt*, p. 98; Roosevelt quoted by Dixon Wecter, *The Saga of American Society: A Record of Social Aspiration 1607–1937* (New York, 1937), p. 109; Morgan quoted in Frederick Lewis Allen, *Lords of Creation* (New York, 1935), p. 160.

8 Wiebe, 'The House of Morgan'; Roosevelt to Lodge, May 27, 1903, Lodge to Roosevelt, June 2, 1903, Roosevelt to Lodge, September 3, 1903 in *Selections From Correspondence*.

9 Robert H. Wiebe, *Businessmen and Reform: A Study of the Progressive Movement* (New York, 1968), pp. 85, 87.

10 Wiebe, 'The House of Morgan'; Richard Hofstadter, *The Age of Reform* (New York, 1955), pp. 236–37; Wiebe, *Businessmen and Reform*, pp. 80–81; Strouse, *Morgan*, p. 542; 'The Meaning of the Times', Address by Albert Beveridge, January 1, 1908 in Albert Beveridge, *The Meaning of the Times and Other Speeches* (Freeport, New York, 1968).

11 Daniel Aaron, *Men of Good Hope: A Story of American Progressives* (New York, 1951), pp. 250–52, 254; Theodore P. Greene, *American Heroes: The Changing Models of Success in American Magazines* (New York, 1970), p. 192; Wiebe, *Businessmen and Reform*, pp. 85–87.

12 Mowry, *Era of Theodore Roosevelt*, p. 206; Eugene L. Huddleston, 'The Generals Up on Wall Street: Ray Stannard Baker and the Railroads', *Railroad History Bulletin*, no. 145.

13 Mowry, *Era of Theodore Roosevelt*, pp. 206–07.

14 Louis D. Brandeis, *Other People's Money and How the Bankers Use It*, edited with an introduction by Melvin I. Urofsky (New York, 1995) – Frank Vanderlip quoted p. 28 of Introduction.

15 Brandeis, *Other People's Money*; Vincent P. Carosso, 'The Wall Street Money Trust from Pujo through Medina', *Business History Review*, Winter 1973, vol. XLVII/4.

16 Carosso, *Investment Banking*, pp. 137–52; Arthur M. Schlesinger, Jr. and Roger Bruns, editors, *Congress Investigates: A Documented History, 1792–1974*, vol. 3 (New York, 1975), p. 2261.

17 Carosso, 'The Wall Street Money Trust'; Brandeis, *Other People's Money*, pp. 55, 62–67, 122, 125.

18 Brandeis, *Other People's Money*, pp. 62–63, 116–17.

19 Cedric B. Cowing, *Populists, Plungers, and Progressives: A Social History of Stock and Commodity Speculation 1890–1930* (Princeton, 1965), p. 53; Schlesinger and Bruns, *Congress Investigates*, pp. 2264–65, 2267–68, 2295–98, 2343.

20 Schlesinger and Bruns, *Congress Investigates*, p. 2316 – see also p. 2261.

21 Schlesinger and Bruns, *Congress Investigates*, p. 2265; George Reynolds quoted by *Current Opinion*, February, 1913, vol. LIV; Birmingham, *Our Crowd*, p. 315.

22 Carosso, 'The Wall Street Money Trust'; Brandeis, *Other People's Money*, pp. 55–57, 71–73, 89, 97, 139.

23 John Moody quoted by Urofsky, editor, *Other People's Money*, p. 17; Schlesinger and Bruns, *Congress Investigates*, pp. 2261–63.

24 'The Bank Investigation: What It Might Reveal', *The Bankers Magazine*, June, 1912; 'The "Money Trust" Inquiry', *The Nation*, December 19, 1912; *American Review of Reviews*, February, 1913; *Current Opinion*, February 1913, vol. LIV; 'That Elusive Bogey – The Money Trust', *Current Literature*, March 1912, vol. LII; *The Baltimore American*, and cartoon quoted in *Current Opinion*, February 1913, vol. LIV; *Collier's* quoted in 'That Elusive Bogey – The Money Trust', *Current Literature*, March 1912, Vol. LII.

25 David Mark Chalmers, *The Social and Political Ideas of the Muckrakers* (New York, 1964), p. 11; Louis Filler, *The Muckrakers* (University Park, 1976), p. 317; W. G. Nicholas, 'Wall Street as a Manufacturing Center', *Applelton's Magazine*, September 1907, vol. 10; Arthur N. Gleason, 'The Investor's Viewpoint', *American Review of Reviews*, September, 1912.

26 Chalmers, *Social and Political Ideas*, p. 68; Huddleston, 'The Generals Up in Wall Street'; Ray Stannard Baker, 'The Railroad Rate', *McClure's*, November 1905, vol. xxvi.

27 Chalmers, *Social and Political Ideas*, p. 44; Charles Edward Russell, *Lawless Wealth: The Origins of Some Great American Fortunes* (New York, 1908); *New York Evening Journal*, October 23, 1907; 'The Great Uprising in New York City', *Arena*, January 1906.

28 Gabriel Kolko, *Main Currents in American History* (New York, 1976); Robert La Follette, speech to Periodical Publishers Association in Philadelphia, February 2, 1912 in Robert La Follette, *Autobiography* (Madison, 1968); Carosso, *Investment Banking*, pp. 82–83; Birmingham, *Our Crowd*, p. 332.

29 Garet Garrett, *Where the Money Grows* (New York, 1911).

30 Chalmers, *Social and Political Ideas*, pp. 53, 57–58; Filler, *Muckrakers*, pp. 176, 179–82; *New York Times*, April 4, 1905 review of 'A Case of Frenzied Finance'; Stewart Holbrook, *The Age of the Moguls* (New York, 1988), pp. 173–74.

31 Lawson quoted by Filler, *Muckrakers*, p. 190; Russell, *Lawless Wealth*, pp. 188–95; 'In the Mirror of the Present', 'Great Insurance Companies as Fountainheads of Political and Commercial Corruption', *Arena*, October, 1905.

32 Carosso, *Investment Banking*, pp. 115, 131–32; Russell, *Lawless Wealth*, pp. 188, 192, 195; *Arena*, April 1, 1906; Chalmers, *Social and Political Ideas*, pp. 59–60, 83; Filler, *Muckrakers*, pp. 193–97; 'Great Insurance Companies', *Arena*.

33 Ridgway quoted by Chalmers, *Social and Political Ideas*, p. 61 – see also pp. 63–65.

34 *The Autobiography of Lincoln Steffens* (New York, 1931), chapter 32, 'Wall Street Again'.

35 Greene, *American Heroes*, pp. 165, 192, 218, 232, 242–43; Matthew Schneirov, *The Dream of a New Social Order: Popular Magazines in America, 1893–1914* (New York, 1994), p. 208; Wiebe, *Businessmen and Reform*, p. 18.

36 W. G. Nicholas, 'Hazing in Wall Street', *Appleton's Magazine*, October, 1907, vol. 10; 'In the Mirror of Wall Street', *Arena*, October 1905; Mowry, *Era of Theodore Roosevelt*, pp. 7–10; Chicago Conference on Trusts, September 13–16, 1899, Testimony by J.W. Jenks; *Final Report of the Industrial Commission, vol. xix* (Government Printing Office, Washington, D.C., 1902).

37 Traubel quoted by Sigmund Diamond, *The Reputation of the American Businessman* (Cambridge, Mass., 1955), p. 91, observer quoted pp. 100–01.

38 Brandeis, *Other People's Money*, pp. 68–69, 109–11,114; Albert W. Atwood, 'The Borrower and the "Money Trust"', *American Review of Reviews*, August, 1912; *Engineering News quoted by* Thomas C. Cochran and William Miller, *The Age of Enterprise: A Social History of Industrial America* (New York, 1942), p. 199 – see also pp. 188–89, 192–93.

39 John Bates Clark quoted by Kim Phillips-Fein, 'Free Markets, "Potential Competition" and Investors' Rights: The Merger Movement and Late Nineteenth Century Economic Thought' (unpublished manuscript in possession of author); Cowing, *Populists, Plungers, and Progressives*, p. 40; Chicago Conference on Trusts, testimony of J.W. Jenks and W. Bourke Cookman; *Final Report of Industrial Commission*, pp. 13, 616–19; Robert T. Handy, editor, *The Social Gospel in America 1870–1920* (New York, 1966), p. 195; Strouse, *Morgan*, pp. 428–29; John Bates Clark, *The Control of Trusts: An Argument in Favor of Curbing the Power of Monopoly by a Natural Method* (New York, 1905), pp 11, 22–23; Jeremy Jenks, *The Trust Problem* (New York, 1909) p. 126.

40 Russell, *Lawless Wealth*, pp. 14–17, 18, 32, 38, 54, 70, 255, 278–79.

41 Finley Peter Dunne, *Mr. Dooley's Opinions* (New York, 1901), pp. 189–90, 191–92.

42 Arun Mukharjee, *The Gospel of Wealth in the American Novel: The Rhetoric of Dreiser and Some of His Contemporaries* (London, 1987), pp. 211–15.

43 *New York Times*, January 24 and 25, 1911; Nelson W. Aldrich, *Old Money: The Mythology of the American Upper Class* (New York, 1988), pp. 3, 24; Chalmers, *Social and Political Ideas*, pp. 82–83; David Graham Phillips, *The Deluge* (Johnson Reprint Corporation, 1969, originally published 1905), pp. 174, 391.

44 Burt L. Standish, 'Frank Merriwell in the Market or The Wolves of Wall Street' and 'Frank Merriwell's Fight for Fortune, or Putting the Wolves to Rest', *Tip Top Weekly*, January 4, 1908, nos. 611 and 612.

45 Upton Sinclair, *The Moneychangers* (Gregg Press, New Jersey, 1968 reprint, originally published 1908); John Steele Gordon, 'The Magnitude of J. P. Morgan', *American Heritage*, July/August, 1989; Jean Strouse, 'The Brilliant Bailout', *New Yorker*, November 23, 1998; Upton Sinclair, *The Brass Check*:

A Study of American Journalism (self-published, 1920), pp. 80–83.

46 Wiebe, *Businessmen and Reform*, p. 70; James Hill quoted by Cochran and Miller, *Age of Enterprise*, p. 189.

47 Kevin Brownlaw, *Behind the Mask of Innocence* (New York, 1990), pp. 436, 439–40; D. W. Griffith, 'Corner in Wheat', 1909; other films of the era featuring Wall Street include: 'The Spirit of the Conqueror; or, The Napoleon of Labor' (Phoenix Film Co., 1914), 'Fighting Odds' (Goldwyn Pix Corp., 1917), 'Wolves of the Street' (Art-O-Graf Film Co., 1920) – I want to thank Steve Ross for bringing descriptions of these films to my attention; Frederick Opper, 'The Cave of Despair', cartoon appearing in *Arena*, April, 1905, vol. 33/185; 'The Central Bank: Why Should Uncle Sam Establish One, When Uncle Pierpont is Already on the Job', cartoon appearing in *Puck*, February 2, 1910; *Denver Daily News* cartoon in *Arena*, February, 1908; Broadway musical song quoted by Wecter, *Saga*, p. 123; 'Commerce' displayed at New York Historical Society, Exhibition of Popular Board Games, 2001.

48 'The People and the Trusts', three part series in *American Review of Reviews*, August, September, October, 1912.

49 Woodrow Wilson quoted by John Milton Cooper, Jr, *The Warrior and the Priest: Woodrow Wilson and Theodore Roosevelt* (Cambridge, Mass., 1983) pp. 180, 192.

50 Woodrow Wilson, 'Address to the Commercial Club of Chicago', March 14, 1908 in *The Political Thought of Woodrow Wilson – American Heritage Series* (New York, 1965); Woodrow Wilson, 'The Banker and the Nation', Address to the Annual Convention of the American Bankers' Association, September 30, 1908 in *Selected Literary and Political Papers and Addresses of Woodrow Wilson*, vol. 1 (New York, 1925); Richard Hofstadter, *The Age of Reform* (New York, 1955), pp. 236–37, 253; Woodrow Wilson quoted by Richard Hofstadter, 'Woodrow Wilson: The Conservative as Liberal' in Richard Hofstadter, *The American Political Tradition* (New York, 1948), p. 238.

51 Woodrow Wilson, *The New Freedom* (New York, 1913), p. 177; Melvyn Urofsky, 'Introduction' in Brandeis, *Other People's Money* – see also p. 49 for Wilson on the 'money monopoly' as 'the greatest question of all . . .'; Wilson quoted by Richard Hofstadter, *The Paranoid Style in American Politics and Other Essays* (Cambridge, Mass., 1952), p. 208; Walter Lippman quoted by Strouse, *Morgan*, p. 622; Woodrow Wilson, acceptance speech, Democratic Party convention, August 7, 1912 in Schlesinger and Bruns, *Congress Investigates*; Woodrow Wilson, Address to the Jackson Day Dinner, January 8, 1912 in Woodrow Wilson, *A Day of Dedication: The Essential Writings and Speeches of Woodrow Wilson*, edited by Albert Fried (New York, 1965); Hofstadter, *American Political Tradition*, p. 254.

52 Wilson quoted by *Current Opinion*, February 1913, vol. LIV.

53 Sean Dennis Cashman, *America in the Gilded Age: From the Death of Lincoln to the Rise of Teddy Roosevelt* (New York, 1988), p. 82; Brandeis, *Other People's Money*, pp. 27, 33, 68–69, 70–71; Cochran and Miller, *Age of Enterprise*, p. 193.

54 Paolo E. Coletta, 'Bryan at Baltimore, 1912: Wilson's Warwick', *Nebraska History*, Summer 1976, vol. 57/2; David Nasaw, *The Chief: The Life of William Randolph Hearst* (Boston, 2000), p. 180; 'The War Between Democracy and Plutocracy', *Arena*, June 1908.

55 Carosso, *Investment Banking*, p. 131; Hofstadter, *Age of Reform*, p. 232; La Follette quoted by Strouse, *Morgan*, p. 616; Robert La Follette, 'The Undermining of Democracy' in *American Populism*, edited with an introduction by George McKenna (New York, 1974); Robert La Follette, speech to Periodical Publishers Association, February 2, 1912 in Robert La Follette, *Autobiography* (Madison, 1968).

56 Charles A. Madison, 'Robert M La Follette: The Radical in Politics' in *American Radicals: Some Problems and Personalities*, Harvey Goldberg, editor (New York, 1957); Amos R. Pinchot, *History of the Progressive Party, 1912–1916* (New York, 1958); Albert J. Beveridge, 'Pass the Prosperity Around', speech to Progressive National Convention, 1912.

57 Sigmund Diamond, *The Reputation of the American Businessman* (Cambridge, Mass., 1955), pp. 87–88; Woodrow Wilson, 'Curbing Trusts and Monopolies', Special Address to Congress, January 20, 1914 in *Political Thought of Woodrow Wilson*; Woodrow Wilson, 'Address Before Congress on National Currency and Banking', June 23, 1913 in *The New Democracy: Presidential Messages, Addresses and Other Papers (1913–17)*, Ray Stannard Baker, editor (New York, 1926); Martin J. Sklar, *The Corporate Reconstruction of American Capitalism 1890–1910* (New York, 1988), pp. 358–59.

58 Wilson quoted by Jordan A. Schwarz, *The Speculator: Bernard M. Baruch in Washington, 1917–1965* (Chapel Hill, 1981), p. 39; Urofsky, 'Introduction', *Other People's Money*, p. 28; Arthur S. Link, *Woodrow Wilson and the Progressive Era, 1910–17* (New York, 1954), pp. 50, 70–73; Carter Glass quoted by Schlesinger and Bruns, *Congress Investigates*, p. 2271; Wiebe, *Businessmen and Reform*, p. 137; Hofstadter, *Age of Reform*, p. 253; 'William Gibbs McAdoo', *American National Biography*, pp. 40–41.

59 Carosso, 'The Wall Street Money Trust'; Urofsky, 'Introduction', *Other People's Money*, pp. 30–31; Link, *Woodrow Wilson and the Progressive Era*, pp. 70–77; Woodrow Wilson, Address to Congress on Trusts and Monopolies, January 20, 1914 in Fried, *Day of Dedication*; Sklar, *Corporate Reconstruction*, pp. 350, 358–59, 423; James Livingston, *Origins of the Federal Reserve System: Money, Class, and Corporate Capitalism, 1890–1913* (Ithaca, 1986), p. 226.

CHAPTER 10 War and Peace on Wall Street

1 John Steele Gordon, *The Great Game: The Emergence of Wall Street as a World Power, 1653–2000* (New York, 1999), pp. 209–12; S. Marshall Kempner, *Inside Wall Street, 1920–42* (New York, 1973), pp. 77–78; Frederick Lewis Allen, *Only Yesterday: An Informal History of the 1920s* (New York, 1931), pp. 43–44, 62–64; John Brooks, *Once in Golconda: A True Drama of Wall Street, 1920–38* (New York, 1969), pp. 1–3, 9; *New*

York Sun, September 17 and 18, 1920; *New York Times*, September 17 and 19, 1920.

2 Thorstein Veblen, *The Theory of the Leisure Class: An Economic Study of Institutions*, edited and Introduction by C,. Wright Mills (New York; originally published 1899), pp. 21, 35, 41, 71, 76, 120–21, 136–38, 140–48, 154–55, 162; Thorstein Veblen, *Absentee Ownership and Business Enterprise in Recent Times: The Case of America* (New York, 1923), pp. 211, 216–17, 227–28, 232–33, 332, 339, 340–41, 347, 353.

3 Edward Bellamy, *Looking Backward: 2000–1887* with a 'Foreword' by Erich Fromm (New York, 1960, originally published 1888), pp. 53–54; 'Foreword', p. v.

4 David Mark Chalmers, *The Social and Political Ideas of the Muckrakers* (New York, 1964), p. 99; Upton Sinclair, *The Brass Check: A Study of American Journalism* (self-published, 1920).

5 Oscar Wilde quoted by Kathleen Odean, *High Steppers, Fallen Angels, and Lollipops: Wall Street Slang* (New York, 1988), p. 190; H. G. Wells quoted by David Colbert, *Eyewitness to Wall Street: 400 Years of Dreamers, Schemers, Busts and Booms* (New York, 2001), pp. 84–86; David Graham Phillips, *The Deluge* (Johnson Reprint Corp., 1969, originally published 1905), pp. 434–35.

6 Daniel Aaron, *Writers on the Left: Episodes in American Literary Communism* (New York, 1961) p. 20; 'Having Their Fling' Art Young cartoon in Walter Kalaidjian, *American Culture Between the Wars: Revisionary Modernism and Post Modern Critique* (New York, 1993), p. 26; Richard Fitzgerald, *Art and Politics: Cartoonists of the Masses and Liberator* (Westport, 1973), pp. 13–14, 50, 59, 70, 148; 'Evolution', Art Young cartoon, *The Masses*, September 1911, p. 4; 'The Master Class' Barnett Braverman cartoon, *The Masses, December1912*, p. 7; 'That Wonderful Directing Mind', Art Young cartoon, *The Masses, August 1913*, p. 3; 'The Masses' in Stephen Haas and Milton Kaplan, *The Ungentlemanly Art: A History of American Political* Cartoons (New York, 1968) in Print Division of the New York Public Library; Leslie Fishbein, 'The Culture of Contradiction: The Greenwich Village Rebellion' in Rick Beard and Leslie Cohen Berlowitz, editors, *Greenwich Village: Culture and Counter-Culture* (New Brunswick, 1993); Daniel Aaron, 'Disturbers of the Peace: Radicals in Greenwich Village, 1920–30' in Beard and Berlowitz, *Greenwich Village*.

7 Jack London, *The Iron Heel* (New York, 1957, originally published 1907), pp. 4, 6, 53, 57, 65–71, 83, 94, 109–10, 256, 279.

8 Jack London, *Burning Daylight* (New York, 1910), pp. 155, 157–58, 160.

9 Sigmund Diamond, *The Reputation of the American Businessman* (Cambridge, Mass., 1955), pp. 84, 86; Chalmers, *Social and Political Ideas*, pp. 99–100; Ira Kipnis, *The American Socialist Movement, 1897–1912* (New York, 1952), pp. 40, 63, 222, 223, 313; Nick Salvatore, *Eugene V. Debs: Citizen and Socialist* (Champaign-Urbana, 1982), p. 193; Thomas J. Morgan testimony, Chicago Conference on Trusts: Speeches, Debates, Resolutions; List of Delegates, September 13–16, 1899 (Civic Federation of Chicago).

10 Diamond, *Reputation of the American Businessman*, pp. 85–86.

11 Edwin G. Burrows and Mike Wallace, *Gotham: A History of New York City to 1898* (New York, 1999), p. 1097.

12 On 'The Bank Defaulter' see M. Keith Booker, *Film and the American Left: A Research Guide* (Westport, 1999); 'Spirit of the Conqueror; Or, The Napoleon of Labor' (Phoenix Film Co., 1914); 'Wall Street Tragedy' (1916); 'Destiny' (1919); 'Wolves of the Street', Art-O-Graf Film Co. (1920) – these and other films are cited in the American Film Institute Catalog: .

13 *Appeal to Reason* quoted by George E. Mowry, *The Era of Theodore Roosevelt and the Birth of Modern America, 1900–12* (New York, 1958), p. 9; Eugene V. Debs, 'Arouse Ye Slaves', March 10, 1906 in John Graham, editor, *Yours For the Revolution: The Appeal to Reason 1895–1922* (Lincoln, 1990); *Appeal to Reason*, April 21, 1917, Socialist Party Resolution on the War, in Graham, *Yours for the Revolution*; Fitzgerald, *Art and Politics*, p. 70.

14 Woodrow Wilson quoted by Arthur S. Link, *Woodrow Wilson and the Progressive Era, 1910–17* (New York, 1954), p. 76 – see also p. 77; Woodrow Wilson Address to Congress on Trusts and Monopolies, January 20, 1914 in Albert Fried, editor, *A Day of Dedication: The Essential Writings and Speeches of Woodrow Wilson* (New York, 1965); Woodrow Wilson quoted by Jordan A. Schwarz, *The Speculator: Bernard M. Baruch in Washington, 1917–1965* (Chapel Hill, 1981), p. 41.

15 Kevin Phillips. *Wealth and Democracy: A Political History of the American Rich* (New York, 2002), pp. 54–55; Vincent P. Carosso, *Investment Banking: A History* (Cambridge, Mass., 1970), pp. 195, 200–01; Stock market observer quoted by Martin S. Fridson, *It Was A Very Good Year: Extraordinary Moments in Stock Market History* (New York, 1998), p. 40; Robert Irving Warshaw, *The Story of Wall Street* (Greenberg Publishers, Inc., 1929), p. 322; Alexander Dana Noyes, *The War Period of American Finance, 1908–1925* (New York, 1926), pp. 54–55, 88; Cedric B. Cowling, *Populists, Plungers, and Progressives: A Social History of Stock and Commodity Speculation, 1890–1936* (Princeton, 1965), pp. 70–75.

16 Carosso, *Investment Banking*, pp. 200–01, 205, 210, 216, 222–23; Noyes, *War Period American Finance*, pp. 7, 88, 102, 106; William Jennings Bryan quoted by Fridson, *It Was A Very Good Year*, p. 31 – see also p. 40; Stephen Birmingham, *Our Crowd: The Great Jewish Families of New York* (New York, 1967), p. 317; Emily S. Rosenberg, *Financial Missionaries to the World: The Politics and Culture of Dollar Diplomacy, 1900–1930* (Cambridge, Mass., 1999), p. 80; Schwarz, *The Speculator*, pp. 41–42.

17 Marvin Gelfand, 'The Street', *American Heritage*, November 1987, vol. 38, #7; B. Mark Smith, *Toward Rational Exuberance: The Evolution of the Modern Stock Market* (New York, 2001), pp. 64–65; Cowling, *Populists, Plungers, and Progressives*, pp. 76–77; 'Bernard Mannes Baruch', *American National Biography*; Alvin Johnson quoted by Schwarz, *The Speculator*, p. 88.

18 Carosso, *Investment Banking*, pp. 224–26; Rosenberg, *Financial Missionaries*, p. 80; Thomas C. Cochran and William Miller, *The Age of*

Enterprise: A Social History of Industrial America (New York, 1942), p. 302;
Noyes, *War Period*, pp. 88, 183–85, 187; Colbert, *Eyewitness*, p. 110; Smith,
Toward Rational Exuberance, p. 66; Cowing, *Populists, Plungers, and
Progressives*, pp. 95–98; Louis Guenther, 'Pirates of Promotion', *World's
Work*, October 1918–March, 1919; 'Minutes: Committee on the Library of
the New York Stock Exchange', June 18, 1918, February 4, 1919, Archives of
the New York Stock Exchange.

19 *Saturday Evening Post* quoted by Theodore P. Greene, *American Heroes: The
Changing Models of Success in American Magazines* (New York, 1970), p.
299; Schwarz, *The Speculator*, p. 44.

20 Nelson W. Aldrich, Jr, *Old Money: The Mythology of America's Upper Class*
(New York, 1988), pp. 173–79.

21 Biographical sketches of Winthrop Aldrich, James Forrestal, Averell
Harriman, Robert Lovett, Dwight Morrow, Robert Patterson, Henry Stimson,
and James Paul Warburg in *American National Biography*; Walter Isaacson
and Evan Thomas, *The Wise Men: Six Friends and the World They Made*
(New York, 1986), pp. 91, 108.

22 Stephen L. Harris, *Duty, Honor, Privilege: New York's Silk Stocking
Regiment and the Breaking of the Hindenburg Line* (Washington, DC, 2001),
pp. 295, 338.

23 *The World*, April 16, 1903; *The World*, October 3, 4, 14, 16, 18, 19, 20, 23,
1908; Clyde Pierce, *The Roosevelt Panama Libel Case: A Study of a
Controversial Episode in the Career of Theodore Roosevelt, Father of the
Panama Canal* (New York, 1959); United States Congress, House Committee
on Foreign Affairs, *The Story of Panama: Hearing on the Rainey Resolution
before the Committee of Foreign Affairs of the House of Representatives*
(Government Printing Office, Washington, DC, 1913).

24 Bryan quoted by Rosenberg, *Financial Missionaries*, p. 78 – see also pp. 43,
46, 56, 78–79, 86; General Butler quoted in Chalmers Johnson, *The Sorrows
of Empire: Militarism, Secrecy, and the End of the Republic* (New York,
2004), p. 169; 'The Magnet' cartoon in Jean Strouse, *Morgan: American
Financier* (New York, 2000); 'Mr Morgan's Moving Pictures' cartoon, *Review
of Reviews*, March 1912; Donald Meyer, *The Positive Thinkers: A Study of
the American Quest for Health, Wealth, and Personal Power from Mary Baker
Eddy to Norman Vincent Peale* (New York, 1965), p. 146.

25 Carosso, *Investment Banking*, pp. 222–23, Gordon, *The Great Game*, pp.
202, 208; Cochran and Miller, *Age of Enterprise*, pp. 298–300; Noyes, *War
Period*, pp. 7, 88, 106; Ferdinand Lundberg, *America's Sixty Families* (New
York, 1938), pp. 143, 148.

26 Upton Sinclair, 'Imprisonment of Debs is Part of a Conspiracy Against Your
Liberties' in *Appeal to Reason*, May 20, 1920; *Appeal to Reason*, August 2,
1919; David Nasaw, *The Chief: The Life of William Randolph Hearst*
(Boston, 2000), p. 244; Tom Watson quoted by James Weinstein, *The Decline
of Socialism in America, 1912–1925* (New York, 1967), p. 138; George
Norris, *Fighting Liberal: The Autobiography of George W. Norris* (New York,
1945), pp. 195–96; Charles A. Collman, *The War Plotters of Wall Street: The*

Most Remarkable Wall Street Stories Ever Written (The Fatherland
Corporation, 1915).
27 Schwarz, *The Speculator*, p. 116; Noyes, *War Period*, p. 437.

CHAPTER 11 A Season in Utopia

1 Tom Shactman, *The Day America Crashed* (New York, 1979), pp. 211–13;
Jerry M. Fisher, *The Pacesetter: The Untold Story of Carl G. Fisher* (Fort
Bragg, California, 1998), pp. 251, 276, 310; Records of the Montauk Manor
can be found in the Montauk Public Library.
2 *The International Jew* (Dearborn, 1922), originally a series of articles pub-
lished in the *Dearborn Independent* between 1920 and 1922 under the title
'The Jewish Question' – see particularly articles published on June 12, 1920,
September 4, 1920, October 2, 1920, November 13, 1920, November 20,
1920, December 4, 1920, February 19, 1921, June 25, 1921, July 2, 1921,
July 23, 1921; Albert Lee, *Henry Ford and the Jews* (New York, 1980), pp. 7,
8, 14, 16, 45, 47, 49, 59; Leo P. Ribuffo, 'Henry Ford and the "International
Jew"', *American Jewish History*, June 1980, vol. LXIX; David L. Lewis,
'Henry Ford's Anti-Semitism and Its Repercussions', *Michigan Journal of
History*, January 1984, vol. 24; Edmund Wilson, *American Jitters: A Year of
the Slump* (New York, 1932), p. 79; Michael N. Dobkowski, *The Tarnished
Dream: The Basis of American Anti-Semitism*, (Westport, 1979), pp.
196–200.
3 Baruch quoted by Jordan A. Schwarz, *The Speculator: Bernard M. Baruch in
Washington, 1917–1965* (Chapel Hill, 1981), p. 132.
4 Morrow quoted by Stephen A. Shuker, 'Dwight Whitney Morrow', *American
National Biography*; Gordon Thomas and Max Morgan-Witts, *The Day the
Bubble Burst: A Social History of the Wall Street Crash of 1929* (New York,
1979), p. 26; Frederick Lewis Allen, *Only Yesterday: An Informal History of
the 1920s* (New York, 1931), p. 152.
5 Ferdinand Lundberg, *America's Sixty Families* (New York, 1938), pp. 174,
184; Biographical sketch of Willard Dickerman Straight, *American National
Biography*; Kai Bird, *The Chairman: John J. McCloy – The Making of an
American Establishment* (New York, 1992), pp. 19, 63, 58–59, 69, 70–71;
Walter Isaacson and Evan Thomas, *The Wise Men: Six Friends and the World
They Made – Acheson, Bohlen, Harriman, Kennan, Lovett, and McCloy* (New
York, 1986), pp. 71, 112.
6 Larry G. Gerber, 'Henry Lewis Stimson', *American National Biography*; Emily
S. Rosenberg, *Financial Missionaries to the World: The Politics and Culture of
Dollar Diplomacy* (Cambridge, Mass., 1999), pp. 208, 217.
7 Frederick Lewis Allen, *Lords of Creation* (New York, 1935), p. 316; Bird,
The Chairman, p. 70–71; M. R. Werner, *Privileged Characters* (New York,
1933), pp. 454–55, 463, 466, 468.
8 Stuart Chase quoted by Allen, *Only Yesterday*, p. 160.
9 William Allen White, *A Puritan in Babylon: The Story of Calvin Coolidge*
(New York, 1938), pp. 259, 264, 289.
10 Allen, *Only Yesterday*, pp. 118–29; Harding quoted by Rolf Lunden,

Business and Religion in the American 1920s (Westport, 1988), pp. 19, 21.

11 Thomas and Morgan-Witts, *The Day the Bubble Burst*, p. 134; Shactman, *The Day America Crashed*, pp. 128–29; David Burner, *Herbert Hoover: A Public Life* (New York, 1979), p. 199, 245–46.

12 William Allen White quoted by Shactman, *The Day America Crashed*, p. 66 – see also pp. 63–64; Coolidge quoted by White, *A Puritan in Babylon*, pp. 253 – see also pp. 289, 293.

13 George Norris quoted by John Steele Gordon, *The Great Game: The Emergence of Wall Street as a World Power 1653–2000* (New York, 1999), p. 224; Harvey O'Connor, *Mellon's Millions: The Biography of a Fortune* (New York, 1933), pp. 111, 122, 242–43, 301; Nora McMullen quoted by O'Connor, *Mellon's Millions*, pp. 113–14; Harding quoted by O'Connor, *Mellon's Millions*, p. 123; White, *A Puritan in Babylon*, pp. 300, 333, 335.

14 Kevin Phillips, *Wealth and Democracy: A Political History of the American Rich* (New York, 2002), p. 62; Kevin Phillips, *The Politics of Rich and Poor* (New York, 1990), p. 96.

15 White, *A Puritan in Babylon*, pp. 347–48; Allen, *Only Yesterday*, pp. 157–60.

16 Robert Minor, 'The Throne of Wall Street', *The Liberator*, January, 1923 vol. 5/2; Robert Minor, 'The Throne of the World' (n.d.).

17 *Nation* quoted by Rosenberg, *Financial Missionaries*, p. 129; Robert La Follette, 'Why Farmers Should Vote for the Progressive Ticket', 1924 campaign pamphlet of Progressive Party; Cedric B. Cowling, *Populists, Plungers, and Progressives: A Social History of Stock and Commodity Speculation 1890–1936* (Princeton, 1965), pp. 129, 133, 138; James Weinstein, *The Decline of Socialism in America, 1912–25* (New York, 1967), p. 293.

18 Joseph Stagg Lawrence, *Wall Street and Washington* (Princeton, 1929), pp. 1–3, 7–8, 14, 137, 140, 144–45; John Brooks, *Once in Golconda: A True Drama of Wall Street, 1920–38* (New York, 1969), p. 108.

19 Shactman, *The Day America Crashed*, pp. 35–36; Proctor Hansl, *Years of Plunder* (self-published, 1935, New York Public Library), p. 131.

20 Frederick Lewis Allen, *Since Yesterday: The 1930s in America –September 3, 1929–September 3, 1939* (New York, 1940), p. 14; White, *Puritan in Babylon*, pp. 319.

21 Thomas and Morgan-Witts, *The Day the Bubble Burst*, p. 234.

22 Gordon, *Great Game*, p. 226; Allen, *Since Yesterday*.

23 John Kenneth Galbraith, *The Great Crash 1929* (Boston, 1997, originally published 1954), pp. 11–15; Allen, *Only Yesterday*; Samuel L. Hayes III, *Wall Street and Regulation* (Cambridge, Mass., 1987), pp. 12, 15; Brooks, *Once in Golconda*, p. 42; Harold Bierman, Jr., *The Great Myths of 1929 and the Lessons to be Learned* (Westport, 1991), p. 63; Charles R. Geisst, *Wall Street: A History* (New York, 1997); Vincent P. Carosso, *Investment Banking in America: A History* (Cambridge, 1970), pp. 240, 243–44, 249–50; John Steele Gordon, 'The Farthest Fall (capitalist Samuel Insull)', *American Heritage*, July-August, 1997, vol. 4, #8; Michael L. Lawson and Frederick S. Voss, 'The Great Crash', catalog for National Portrait Gallery Exhibition:

October 24, 1979–April 20, 1980; Cecil B. DeMille quoted by Neal Gabler, *An Empire of Their Own: How the Jews Invented Hollywood* (New York, 1988), p. 132 – see also pp. 41–43, 116–17, 134–35; Colin Shindler, *Hollywood in Crisis: Cinema and American Society, 1929–39* (New York, 1996), pp. 5, 7; 'The Motion Picture Industry as a Basis for Bond Financing', Halsey, Stuart Co. prospectus in Tino Balio, ed., *The American Film Industry* (Madison, 1976); Amanda Smith, editor, *Hostage of Fortune: The Letters of Joseph P. Kennedy* (New York, 2000), editor's introduction.

24 Galbraith, *Great Crash*, pp. 53–54, 60–66; Allen, *Only Yesterday*, pp. 271–72.

25 Observer of stock market as sport quoted by Brooks, *Once in Golconda*, p. 72; 'The Great Crash' catalogue; Edward Chancellor, *Devil Take the Hindmost: A History of Financial Speculation* (New York, 1999), p. 202; Shactman, *Day America Crashed*, p. 43; Galbraith, *Great Crash*, pp. 20–21; Proctor Hansl, *Years of Plunder* (self-published, n.d., New York Public Library).

26 Robert Sobel, *The Great Bull Market: Wall Street in the 1920s* (New York, 1968), pp. 17–20.

27 William Z. Ripley, *Main Street and Wall Street* (Boston, 1927), p. 116.

28 Thomas and Morgan-Witts, *Day the Bubble Burst*, pp. 73; Cowling, *Populists, Plungers, and Progressives*, pp. 119–23; Chancellor, *Devil Take the Hindmost*, p. 204.

29 *Harper's* Weekly quoted by Thomas and Morgan-Witts, *Day the Bubble Burst*, p. 191 – see also pp. 189–91; Allen, *Only Yesterday*, chapter 12; Werner, *Privileged Characters*, p. 478; Charles Merz, 'Bull Market', *Harper's Monthly*, April 1929, vol. 158; Chancellor, *Devil Take the Hindmost*, p. 200; Edmund Wilson quoted by Marvin Gelfand, 'The Street', *American Heritage*, November 1987, vol. 38/7.

30 'Smith's First Investment: A Dramatization of a Typical Investment Transaction Made Through the New York Stock Exchange', 1922; 'The Stock Market: Its Relation to the Building of Proper Manhood', 1923; 'The Stock Exchange as a Moral Force', 1923 all in Minutes of the 'Committee on Library', Archives of the New York Stock Exchange. The Exchange was so delighted with Laurence Stagg's book on *Wall Street and Washington*, that they ordered two hundred copies from Princeton University Press and by the mid-1930s employed Stagg as an adviser; Carosso, *Investment Banking*, pp. 249–51; Cowling, *Populists, Plungers, and Progressives*, p. 183; Merz, 'Bull Market'; Thomas and Morgan-Witts, *Day the Bubble Burst*, p. 249.

31 Ibid., p. 258; Brooks, *Once in Golconda*, pp. 74, 78; Frederick Opper, 'Simple Simon in Wall Street', cartoon, *New York American*, November 1928; Dougal Rodger, 'Inexperienced Snake-Charmers Beware', cartoon, *San Francisco Bulletin*, January 1929; 'The Golden Stairs', cartoon in *Literary Digest* cited by Kathleen Odean, *High Steppers, Fallen Angels, and Lollipops: Wall Street Slang* (New York, 1988), p. 175; *New Yorker* cartoon, September 10, 1927; Allen, *Only Yesterday*, pp. 178–80; Rolf Lunden, 'The Protestant Church and the Business Spirit of the 1920s' in Rab Kroes and Alassandro

Partell, editors, *Social Change and New Modes of Expression: The United States, 1910–30* (Amsterdam, 1986); Lunden, *Business and Religion*, pp. 33, 39.

32 Italian newspaper quoted by Thomas and Morgan-Witts, *Day the Bubble Burst*, p. 189 – see also p. 258; Malcolm Cowley, *Exile's Return: A Literary Odyssey of the 1920s* (New York, 1969, originally published 1951), p. 81; Charles R. Geisst, *Wall Street: From Its Beginnings to the Fall of Enron* (New York, 2004), p. 186.

33 Thomas and Morgan-Witts, *Day the Bubble Burst*, pp. 70, 78, 134; Werner, *Privileged Characters*, chapter 7, 'The Pied Pipers of Wall Street' which is drawn from Congressional testimony given to the 'Pecora Committee' which began its hearings in 1932 under Hoover and continued for several more years under Roosevelt, see particularly pp. 445–48; Odean, *High Steppers*, p. 131.

34 Max Weber quoted by Daniel Bell, *The Cultural Contradictions of Capitalism* (New York, 1996, originally published 1976), pp. 290–91.

35 Merz, 'Bull Market'; Warren I. Susman, *Culture as History: The Transformation of American Society in the Twentieth Century* (New York, 1984, originally published 1973); Brooks, *Once in Golconda*, pp. 72–74; 'Playing the Stock Market', *Christian Century*, February 21, 1929; Michael Oriard, *Sporting with the Gods: The Rhetoric of Play and Game in American Culture* (New York, 1991), p. 351.

36 Edward N. Warren, *Shakespeare in Wall Street* (Boston, 1929).

37 Lawson and Voss, 'The Great Crash'; Claud Cockburn, *In Time of Trouble: An Autobiography* (London, 1956), p. 160; Daniel Colbert, *Eyewitness to Wall Street: 400 Years of Dreamers, Schemers, Busts, and Booms* (New York, 2001), p. 119; Chancellor, *Devil Take the Hindmost*, p. 203; Thomas and Morgan-Witts, *Day the Bubble Burst*, p. 5; Brooks, *Once in Golconda*, p. 81; Odean, *High Steppers*, p. 6; Fredric Smoler, 'Wall Street Jokes Vintage 1929: Gallows Humor from the First October Catastrophe', *American Heritage*, July–August, 1988.

38 White, *Puritan in Babylon*, p. 346; Shactman, *Day America Crashed*, p. 104.

39 Thomas and Morgan-Witts, *Day the Bubble Burst*, p. 67; Stanley Nelson Passy, 'The Imagination of Wall Street', Ph.D. dissertation (University of Dallas, 1987), p. 127; Cowling, *Populists, Plungers, and Progressives*, p. 156; Mayor Walker quoted by Chancellor, *Devil Take the Hindmost*, p. 215.

40 Cowling, *Populists, Plungers, and Progressives*, pp. 178, 180, 183; Carosso, *Investment Banking*, p. 251.

41 Brooks, *Once in Golconda*, p. 90; Edgar Laurence Smith, 'Speculation and Investment', *The Atlantic Monthly*, October, 1925; B. Mark Smith, *Towards Rational Exuberance: The Evolution of the Modern Stock Market* (New York, 2001), p. 79; Benjamin Graham, *The Intelligent Investor* (New York, 1973), pp. 315–21, and quoted in Chancellor, *Devil Take the Hindmost*, p. 196.

42 Congressman O'Connor quoted by Cowling, *Populists, Plungers, and Progressives*, p. 190; Irving Fisher quoted by Galbraith, *Great Crash*, p. 70; Thomas Lamont quoted by Thomas and Morgan-Witts, *Day the Bubble Burst*, p. 345; Shactman, *Day America Crashed*, p. 18.

43 Cockburn, *Time of Trouble*, pp. 149–50.

44 Thomas and Morgan-Witts, *Day the Bubble Burst*, p. 25; Bernie Abbott, *Changing New York: The Complete WPA Project* (New York, 1997 reprint).

45 William Z. Ripley, *Main Street and Wall Street* (New York, 1927), pp. 38, 76, 84, 91, 128.

46 Thomas and Morgan-Witts, *Day the Bubble Burst*, p. 282; Lawson and Voss, 'The Great Crash', Allen, *Only Yesterday*, p. 322; 'Playing the Stock Market', *Christian Century*, February 21, 1929, vol. 46; Paul Warburg quoted by Sobel, *Great Bull Market*, p. 126; John Foster Dulles quoted by Cowling, *Populists, Plungers, and Progressives*, p. 168 – see also p. 172.

47 Garet Garrett, 'Business' in Harold E. Stearns, editor, *Civilization in the United States: An Inquiry by Thirty Americans* (Westport, 1971, originally published 1922); Thorstein Veblen, *Absentee Ownership and the Business Enterprise in Recent Times: The Case of America* (New York, 1923) p. 361.

48 'The Rake's Progress' and 'Morgan über Alles' cartoons in Richard Fitzgerald, *Art and Politics: Cartoonists of The Masses and Liberator* (Westport, 1973); Salter Brown, 'Hesperides, or The Plunger Plunges', *Broom: An International Magazine of the Arts*, November, 1923, vol. 5/4; Daniel Aaron, 'Disturbers of the Peace: Radicals in Greenwich Village, 1920–30', in Rick Beard and Leslie Cohen Berlowitz, eds., *Greenwich Village: Culture and Counter-Culture* (New Brunswick, 1993); John Dos Passos, *Manhattan Transfer* (Boston, 1953, originally published 1925).

49 Malcolm Cowley, *Exile's Return: A Literary Odyssey of the 1920s* (New York, 1969), pp. 83, 207–08, 215, 227.

50 Nelson W. Aldrich, Jr., *Old Money: The Mythology of America's Upper Class* (New York, 1988), p. 187; F. Scott Fitzgerald, 'Babylon Revisited', in *Babylon Revisited and Other Stories* (New York, 1960); David Andrew Zimmerman, 'Frenzied Fictions: The Writing of Panic in the American Marketplace, 1873–1913', Ph.D. dissertation (University of California at Berkeley, 2000), pp. 293–96; F. Scott Fitzgerald, *The Great Gatsby* (New York, 1925).

51 Lunden, *Business and Religion*, pp. 33, 38, 39.

52 Congressman George S. Graham quoted by Carosso, *Investment Banking*, p. 252; 'Playing the Stock Market', *Christian Century*, February 21, 1929.

53 'Extravagance', 1919, 'The Plunger', 1920, 'The Blasphemer', 1921, 'The Silent Partner', 1923, all cited in American Film Institute Catalog.

54 Vachel Lindsay, 'Bryan, Bryan, Bryan', in *Collected Poems* (New York, 1927).

CHAPTER 12 Who's Afraid of the Big Bad Wolf?

1 Steven Watts, *The Magic Kingdom: Walt Disney and the American Way of Life* (Boston, 1997), pp. 77–78, 100; Kathy Merlock Jackson, *Walt Disney: A Bio-Bibliography* (Westport, 1993), p. 21.

2 Harold Bierman, Jr., *The Great Myths of 1929 and the Lessons to be Learned* (Westport, 1991); Robert Sobel, *The Great Bull Market: Wall Street in the 1920s* (New York, 1968), pp. 147, 155–59; B. Mark Smith, *Towards Rational Exuberance: The Evolution of the Modern Stock Market* (New York, 2001), p. 114.

3 Edward Chancellor, *Devil Take the Hindmost: A History of Financial Speculation* (New York, 1999), p. 217; John Kenneth Galbraith, *The Great Crash 1929* (Boston, 1997), p. 100; William Manchester, *The Last Lion: Winston Spencer Churchill – Visions of Glory, 1874–1932* (Boston, 1983), pp. 826–27.

4 Fitzgerald quoted by Chancellor, *Devil Take the Hindmost*, p. 217.

5 Thomas K. McCraw, *Prophets of Regulation: Charles Francis Adams, Louis D. Brandeis, James M. Landis, Alfred E. Kahn* (Cambridge, Mass., 1984), p. 169; A Newton Plummer, *The Great American Swindle Inc.* (self-published, 1932), p. 12.

6 Gordon Thomas and Max Morgan-Witts, *The Day the Bubble Burst: A Social History of the Wall Street Crash of 1929* (New York, 1979), pp. 366, 389, 399; David Colbert, *Eyewitness to Wall Street: 400 Years of Dreamers, Schemers, Busts, and Booms* (New York, 2001), p. 136; Claud Cockburn, *In Time of Trouble: An Autobiography* (London, 1956), pp. 179–80; Mayor Walker quoted by Galbraith, *The Great Crash 1929* (Boston, 1997), p. 115; *New York Herald Tribune*, October 24, and 25, 1929; *New York Sunday News*, November 10, 1929; Jimmy Walker quoted by Thomas and Morgan-Witts, *Day the Bubble Burst*; Tom Shactman, *The Day America Crashed* (New York, 1979), p. 279 – see also, pp. 281–82.

7 Shactman, *Day America Crashed*, pp. 159, 238–39; John Brooks, *Once in Golconda: A True Drama of Wall Street, 1920–38* (New York, 1969), pp. 61, 129; Galbraith, *The Great Crash*.

8 John D. Rockefeller quoted by Susan Winslow, *Brother, Can You Spare a Dime? America from the Wall Street Crash to Pearl Harbor – An Illustrated Documentary* (Paddington Press Ltd., 1976); Eddie Cantor quoted by Michael L. Lawson and Frederick S. Voss, 'The Great Crash', catalog, National Portrait Gallery, Exhibition: October 21, 1979–April 20, 1980, Museum of the City of New York archives, MCNY PA, Wall Street, 1901; Cockburn, *Time of Trouble*, p. 177; Frederick Lewis Allen, *Since Yesterday: The 1930s in America – September 3, 1929–September 3, 1939* (New York, 1940), p. 27; 'The Chimneys Are Still Smoking', cartoon by Fred O. Siebel, *Richmond Times-Dispatch*, November 7, 1929.

9 Eyewitness quoted by Brooks, *Once in Golconda*, p. 119; Edmund Wilson, *The Thirties: From Notebooks and Diaries of the Period* (New York, 1980), p. 65–66; Will Rogers quoted by Thomas and Morgan-Witts, *Day Bubble Burst*, p. xiii; James Burkhart Gilbert, *Writers and Partisans: A History of Literary Radicalism in America* (New York, 1968), p. 93.

10 Brooks, *Once in Golconda*, p. 122.

11 Ben Smith quoted by B. Mark Smith, *Towards Rational Exuberance*, p. 136 – see also p. 79; Thomas and Morgan-Witts, *Day the Bubble Burst*, p. 20; Shactman, *Day America Crashed*, p. 52; Brooks, *Once in Golconda*, p. 78.

12 John Dos Passos, *The Big Money* (Boston, 1946, originally published 1936), pp. 523–28; Franklin Delano Roosevelt, *Looking Forward* (New York, 1973 reprint, originally published 1933), p. 149; FDR quoted by John Steele

Gordon, 'The Farthest Fall (capitalist Samuel Insull)', *American Heritage*, July-August, 1997, vol. 4/8; Lawson and Voss, 'The Great Crash'.

13 John Lloyd Parker, *Unmasking Wall Street* (Boston, 1932), chapter 7; Sobel, *Great Bull Market*, pp. 85–87.

14 George W. Johnson, 'The Average American and the Depression', *Baltimore Sun*, February, 1932 in Daniel Aaron and Robert Bendiner, editors, *The Strenuous Decade: A Social and Intellectual Reconsideration of the 1930s* (New York, 1970); John Dewey, 'The Collapse of the Romance', *New Republic*, April 27, 1932, in Aaron and Bendiner, *Strenuous Decade*; Virgil Jordan, 'The Era of Mad Illusions', *North American Review*, January 1930, vol. cccxxix, in Aaron and Bendiner, *Strenuous Decade*; Pare Lorentz, 'A Young Man Goes to Work', *Scribners*', February, 1931, vol. 89.

15 Plumer, *Great American Swindle Inc.*; Proctor Hansl, *Years of Plunder* (New York, 1935); Parker, *Unmasking Wall Street*.

16 Herbert Hoover, *The Memoirs of Herbert Hoover: The Great Depression, 1929–41* (New York, 1952) excerpted in Arthur M. Schlesinger, Jr and Roger Bruns, editors, *Congress Investigates: A Documented History, 1792–1974, vol. 4* (New York, 1975), p. 2608–09; James Rorty quoted by David P. Peeler, *Hope Among Us Yet: Social Criticism and Social Solace in Depression America* (Athens, Georgia, 1987), p. 29; Gilbert Seldes, *The Years of the Locust: America 1929–32* (Boston, 1933), *passim*; *New Masses*, December 1929, quoted by Dan Hausdorff, 'Magazine Humor and the Depression Years', *New York Folklore Quarterly*, 1964, vol. 20, #3; Lewis Corey, *The Crisis of the Middle Class* (New York, 1935), pp. 20–21; Loren Baritz, *The Good Life: The Meaning of Success for the American Middle Class* (New York, 1989), p. 109.

17 Will Rogers quoted by Kathleen Odean, *High Steppers, Fallen Angels, and Lollipops: Wall Street Slang* (New York, 1988), p. 126 – other Will Rogers witticisms about the Street may be found in Steven K. Gragent, ed., *Will Rogers' Weekly Articles*, vol. 4: *The Hoover Years 1929–31* (Stillwater, 1981); Eddie Cantor quoted by Colin Shindler, *Hollywood in Crisis: Cinema and American Society 1929–39* (New York, 1996), p. 11; Cartoons in Fredric Smoler, 'Wall Street Jokes – Vintage 1929', *American Heritage*, July-August 1988; Hausdorff, 'Magazine Humor'; joke about promoter and St Peter quoted by Bierman, *Great Myths*, p. 15; William Floyd, *The People Vs. Wall Street* (New York, 1930); Mercer Ellington with Stanley Dance, *Duke Ellington in Person: An Intimate Memoir* (Boston, 1978), p. 47; Harold Gray, *Little Orphan Annie*, vol. 1931, edited and introduction by Rick Marschall (Fantagraphic Books); Richard M. Huber, *The American Idea of Success* (New York, 1971), p. 391.

18 'Clancy in Wall Street', 1930 and 'Big Executive', 1933 in American Film Institute Catalog; 'The Toast of New York', 1937, was based on the apocryphal hoax *Book of Daniel Drew* by Bouck White, published in 1910 as well as on Matthew Josephson's *Robber Barons: The Great American Capitalists, 1861–1901*; Lary May, *The Big Tomorrow: Hollywood and the Politics of the American Way* (Chicago, 2000), pp. 273–75.

19 Dos Passos, *The Big Money.*
20 F. Scott Fitzgerald, *Babylon Revisited and Other Stories* (New York, 1960).
21 Galbraith, *The Great Crash*, pp. 153–54; Schlesinger and Bruns, *Congress Investigates*, p. 2563; M. R. Werner, *Privileged Characters* (New York, 1933), p. 478; Edmund Wilson, 'Sunshine Charlie' in Edmund Wilson, *The American Earthquake: A Documentary of the Twenties and Thirties* (New York, 1958); 'Big Bankers' Gambling Mania', *Literary Digest*, March 11, 1933; Vincent P. Carosso, *Investment Banking in America: A History* (Cambridge, Mass., 1970), pp. 330–34.
22 Galbraith, *The Great Crash*, pp. 147–51; Schlesinger and Bruns, *Congress Investigates*, p. 2572; Wiggins' dismissive attitude about the Senate investigation was mirrored in Robert Winsome, 'Wall Street's Reply to the Senate Investigation', *Literary Digest*, July 22, 1933; Werner, *Privileged Characters*, p. 486.
23 Carosso, *Investment Banking*, pp. 300, 319, 326, 329, 334–35, 341, 345–47; Schlesinger and Bruns, *Congress Investigates*, pp. 2566, 2570, and testimony of Otto Kahn before the Pecora Committee, pp. 2686–92; Brooks, *Once in Golconda*, pp. 51–52, 190; Roosevelt quoted by Brooks, *Once in Golconda*, p. 156.
24 Katie Louchhelm, editor, *The Making of the New Deal: The Insiders Speak* (Cambridge, Mass. 1983), pp. 130–39; McCraw, *Prophets*, p. 196; Brooks, *Once in Golconda*, p. 273, 287.
25 Michael Denning, *The Cultural Front: The Laboring of American Culture in the Twentieth Century* (New York, 1996), p. 173; Ferdinand Lundberg, *America's Sixty Families* (New York, 1938), pp. 3, 34, 36, 149, 150, 173–74, 408–09, 415–16.
26 Shindler, *Hollywood in Crisis, passim.*; Frank Capra, *The Name Above the Line: An Autobiography* (New York, 1971), pp. 237, 243; May, *Big Tomorrow*, pp. 273–75; Andrew Bergman, *We're in the Money: Depression America and Its Films* (New York, 1971), p. 135; M. Keith Booker, *Films and the American Left: A Research Guide* (Westport, 1999); Archibald MacLeish, *Panic: A Play in Verse* (Boston, 1935); Denning, *Cultural Front*, p. xv; *Gropper: 50 Years of Drawing 1921–71*, including cartoon 'Monopolies', 1933, and 'Capitalist Cartoon', 1933; Charles R. Geisst, *100 Years of Wall Street* (New York, 2000), p. 35.
27 Will Rogers quoted by May, *Big Tomorrow*, p. 27; Wilson, 'Sunshine Charley', p. 487; Brooks, *Once in Golconda*, pp. 180–82; Thomas and Morgan-Witts, *Day the Bubble Burst*, pp. 417–18.
28 Clarence Dillon lampoon quoted by *The Mirror of Wall Street: Anonymous With Drawings by Hugo Gellert* (New York, 1933); 'Dinner at Eight', 1933; Morgan quoted by Dixon Wecter, *The Saga of American Society : A Record of Social Aspiration 1607–1937* (New York, 1937), p. 141; 'Feast of Pure Reason' painting by Jack Levine in Patricia Hills, *Social Concern and Urban Realism: American Painting of the 1930s*, catalog for exhibition at Boston University Art Gallery, 1983; Huber, *American Idea of Success*, p. 391; Nathaniel West, *A Cool Million: On the Dismantling of Lemuel Pitkin* (New York, 1934).

29 Christina Stead, *House of All Nations* (New York, 1938), pp. 18, 23, 27.

30 Archibald MacLeish, 'To the Young Men of Wall Street', *Saturday Review of Literature*, January 16, 1932; Heywood Broun quoted by Carosso, *Investment Banking*, p. 330; Walter Lippman quoted by Nelson W. Aldrich, *Old Money: The Mythology of America's Upper Class* (New York, 1988), pp. 36–37.

CHAPTER 13 Evicted from the Temple

1 FDR quoted by Jordan A. Schwarz, *Liberal: Adolph Berle and the Vision of an American Era* (New York, 1987), p. 108.

2 Milo Reno quoted by John L. Shover, *Cornbelt Rebellion: The Farmers' Holiday Association* (Champaign-Urbana, 1965), p. 36 – see also p. 86.

3 Ibid. pp. 60–63, 67, 96.

4 *New York Times*, January 10, 1935; Alan Brinkley, *Voices of Protest: Huey Long, Father Coughlin, and the Great Depression* (New York, 1982), pp. 40, 41, 55, 71, 117; Hodding Carter, 'How Come Huey Long?', *New Republic*, February 13, 1935.

5 Father Charles E. Coughlin, 'Internationalism', 'Prosperity', 'By the Sweat of Thy Brow', 'Come Follow Me', 'The Next War', 'A Sandy Fondation', 'The God of Gold', 'Quo Vadis? Whither Goest Thou', radio sermons in *Father Coughlin's Radio Sermons Complete, October 1930–April 1931* (Baltimore, 1931), and *Father Coughlin's Radio Discourses –1931–32* (Radio League of the Little Flower, 1932), and *Money! Questions and Answers* (Royal Oak, Michigan, 1936), and 'Driving Out the Money-Changers', radio broadcast, April 18, 1933; Coughlin quoted by David H. Bennett, *Demagogues in the Depression: American Radicals and the Union Party, 1932–36* (New Brunswick, 1969), pp. 40, 192, 230 - see also pp. 11, 47, 50, 75, 78.

6 Seymour Martin Lipset and Earl Raab, *The Politics of Unreason: Right Wing Extremism in America, 1790–1970* (New York, 1970), pp. 170–71, 182–83; Gerald L. K. Smith quoted by Bennett, *Demagogues*, p. 11 – see also pp. 279–80; William Dudley Pelley Christmas card quoted by Leo P. Ribuffo, *The Old Christian Right: The Protestant Far Right From the Great Depression to the Cold War* (Philadelphia, 1983), p. 60 – see also pp. 59, 147, 155, 158.

7 Reverend Charles E. Coughlin, *Money! Questions and Answers* (Royal Oak, Michigan, 1936); Father Coughlin, *Sixteen Radio Lectures –1938 Series* (self-published, 1938); George Q. Flynn, *American Catholicism and the Roosevelt Presidency 1932–36* (Lexington, Kentucky, 1968), p. 203; Bennett, *Demagogues*, p. 63.

8 FDR Inaugural Address in Franklin Delano Roosevelt, *Looking Forward* (New York, 1933), pp. 263, 265 – see also pp. 23–25, 27 32 44–45, 148–49, 223, 234–35; Russell De Buhite and David W. Levy, editors, *FDR's Fireside Chats* (Norman, Oklahoma, 1992), 'fireside chats' on March 12, 1933, October 22, 1933, September 30, 1934.

9 Arthur M. Schlesinger, Jr., and Roger Bruns, editors, *Congress Investigates: A Documented History 1792–1974*, vol. IV (New York, 1975), 'The Pecora

Wall Street Exposé', pp. 2563, 2566, 2570, 2571, 2572, and *passim*, and 'The Nye Munitions Committee, 1934', pp. 2737, 2757–59 (the formal name of the Pecora investigation was 'United States Senate, Stock Exchange Practices: Hearings Before the Committee on Banking and Currency', and the name of the Nye Committee was 'United States Senate, Munitions Industry: Hearings Before the Special Committee Investigating the Munitions Industry'; Senator Peter Norbeck quoted by Schlesinger and Bruns, *Congress Investigates*, pp. 2600–01; Ferdinand Pecora, *Wall Street Under Oath: The Story of Our Modern Money Changers* (New York, 1939); Vincent P. Carosso, *Investment Banking in America: A History* (Cambridge, Mass., 1970), pp. 337–349; Donald Ritchie, 'The Legislative Impact of the Pecora Investigation', *Capital Studies*, 1977, vol. 5/2; 'Big Bankers' Gambling Mania', *Literary Digest*, March 11, 1933; N.R. Danielion, 'The Stock Market and the Public', *Atlantic Monthly*, October 1933, no. 152.

10 Herbert Agar and Allen Tate, editors, *Who Owns America: A New Declaration of Independence* (Boston, 1936), see particularly, Lyle H. Lanier, 'Big Business in the Property State', Allen Tate, 'Notes on Liberty and Property', and Herbert Agar, 'But Can It Be Done?'

11 Charles Beard and *Time* magazine quoted by Schwarz, *Liberal*, pp. 60–61– see also pp. 53, 56, 62, 68; Adolph A. Berle and Gardiner C. Means, *The Modern Corporation and Private Property* (New York, 1932), pp. 7, 8, 33–34, 46, 65, 70–72, 74–75, 115, 244–45, 250–51, 293, 312.

12 John T. Flynn, 'Regulating the Speculators', *The New Republic*, February 21, 1934; 'Gambling vs. Social Planning', *New Republic*, August 2, 1933; *Main Street, Not Wall Street, Brotherhood of Railroad Trainmen: A Reply to the Railroads Demands for a Wage Reduction*', 1938; *Culture and Crisis* quoted by Michael Denning, *The Cultural Front: The Laboring of American Culture in the Twentieth Century* (New York, 1996), p. xvi; Edmund Wilson, *The Thirties: From Notebooks and Diaries of the Period* (New York, 1980); Daniel Aaron, *Writers on the Left: Episodes in American Literary Communism* (New York, 1961), p. 197.

13 Alvin Hansen, *Fiscal Policies and Business Cycles* (New York, 1941); Stuart Chase, 'Shadow Over Wall Street', *Harper's*, March 1940, vol. CLXXX; Alan Brinkley, *The End of Reform: New Deal Liberalism in Recession and War* (New York, 1995), p. 134.

14 B. Mark Smith, *Towards Rational Exuberance: The Evolution of the Modern Stock Market* (New York, 2001), p. 125; Steven Fraser, *Labor Will Rule: Sidney Hillman and the Rise of American Labor* (New York, 1991), chapter 9; John Maynard Keynes, *The General Theory of Employment, Interest, and Money* (London, 1973), pp. 154, 155, 157, 159, 160–61, 162–63; Benjamin Ginsburg, 'Wall Street Under the New Deal', *North American Review*, Spring 1938, vol. CCXLV; Elliot A. Rosen, *Hoover, Roosevelt, and the Brains Trust* (New York, 1977), pp. 22, 143, 245.

15 Alan Brinkley, 'Thomas Gardiner Corcoran', biographical sketch in *American National Biography*; L. A. Powe, Jr, 'William Douglas', biographical sketch in *American National Biography*; Pecora quoted by Schlesinger and Bruns,

Congress Investigates, pp. 2578; Carosso, *Investment Banking,* pp. 362, 368–69, 376.

16 Carosso, *Investment Banking,* pp. 380–81; Joseph Kennedy quoted by Kenneth Davis, *The New Deal Years 1933–37* (New York, 1979), p. 370 – see also pp. 366–67, 369; Amanda Smith, editor, *Hostage of Fortune: The Letters of Joseph P. Kennedy* (New York, 2000), pp. 108, 122, 129, 138; Charles R. Geisst, *Wall Street: From Its Beginnings to the Fall of Enron* (New York, 2004), pp. 235–36; James Allen, editor, *Democracy and Finance: The Addresses and Public Statements of William O. Douglas* (New Haven, 1940), pp. 7, 8, 9, 11, 16, 63–72, 79, and 'Bond Club' Address, March 24, 1937, pp. 37–39, 43–44; Katie Louchhelm, editor, *The Making of the New Deal: The Insiders Speak* (Cambridge, Mass., 1983), p. 143; *Nation* quoted by John Brooks, *Once in Golconda: A True Drama of Wall Street, 1920–38* (New York, 1969), p. 273; Vincent Carosso, 'Washington and Wall Street: The New Deal and Investment Bankers, 1933–40', Winter 1970, vol. XLI/4; 'Wall Street at the Wailing Wall', *Nation,* October 25, 1933; John T. Flynn, 'The Marines Land in Wall Street', *Harper's Monthly,* July 1934, CLXIX; Bernard Flexner, 'The Fight on the Securities Act', *Atlantic Monthly,* February 1934, vol. CLIII.

17 Ferdinand Lundberg, *America's Sixty Families* (New York, 1938), pp. 452 – see also pp. 461–63; Brinkley, 'Thomas Gardiner Corcoran'; FDR quoted by Nelson W. Aldrich, *Old Money: The Mythology of America's Upper Class* (New York, 1988), p. 234.

18 Roosevelt, *Looking Forward,* pp. 44–45, 236; Roosevelt quoted by Kevin Phillips, *Wealth and Democracy: A Political History of the American Rich* (New York, 2002), p. 71.

19 Franklin Delano Roosevelt campaign address, Wichita, Kansas, October 13, 1936, campaign address, Chicago, October 14, 1936, campaign address, Cleveland, October 16, 1936, campaign address, Boston, October 21, 1936, radio address to Business Men, October 23, 1936, campaign address, New York City, October 31, 1936 – all in *Public Papers and Addresses of Franklin Delano Roosevelt, vol. 5 –The People Approve* (New York, 1938); Roosevelt quoted by Brinkley, *End of Reform,* p. 56; Robert Jackson quoted by Brinkley, *End of Reform,* p. 58.

20 Henry Havemeyer quoted by Samuel L. Hayes, III, *Wall Street and Regulation* (Cambridge, Mass., 1987), p. 5.

21 Richard Whitney quoted by Brooks, *Once in Golconda,* p. 143; Schlesinger and Bruns, *Congress Investigates,* pp. 2576, 2721; Robert Winsome, 'Wall Street's Reply to the Senate Investigation', *Literary Digest,* July 22, 1933; Davis, *New Deal Years,* pp. 366, 371; Allen, *Democracy and Finance,* pp. 63–72; Cedric B. Cowling, *Populists, Plungers, and Progressives: A Social History of Stock and Commodity Speculation 1890–1936* (Princeton, 1965), pp. 233, 242; Flynn, 'The Marines Land in Wall Street'.

22 Brooks, *Once in Golconda,* p. 220; Smith quoted by E. Digby Baltzell, *The Protestant Establishment: Aristocracy and Caste in America* (New York, 1964), p. 245; American Liberty League quoted by Pecora, *Wall Street Under*

Oath, p. 297; John W. Davis quoted by Thurman Arnold, *The Folklore of Capitalism* (New Haven, 1937), p. 190; Colin Shindler, *Hollywood in Crisis: Cinema and American Society 1929–39* (New York, 1996), p. 64; David Laurence quoted by Frederick Lewis Allen, *Since Yesterday: The 1930s in America – September 3, 1929–September 3, 1939* (New York, 1940), p. 310; Herbert Hoover, 'The Bank Panic and the Relief Administration Reform', December 16, 1935, and 'Are Our National Problems Being Solved', April 4, 1936, in *Herbert Hoover: Addresses Upon the American Road, 1933–38* (New York, 1938); James H. Madison, 'Wendell Lewis Wilkie' biographical sketch, *American National Biography*.

23 Baltzell, *Protestant Establishment*, p. 253; Walter Isaacson and Evan Thomas, *The Wise Men: Six Friends and the World They Made – Acheson, Bohlen, Harriman, Kennan, Lovett, and McCloy* (New York, 1986), p. 113; Kai Bird, *The Chairman: John J. McCloy –The Making of an American Establishment* (New York, 1992), pp. 102–03; Brooks, *Once in Golconda*, pp. 198–200.

24 Carosso, *Investment Banking*, pp. 301; Otto Kahn quoted by Pecora, *Wall Street Under Oath*, p. 53; Cowling, *Populists, Plungers, and Progressives*, pp. 254–55; Brooks, *Once in Golconda*, pp. 199–200; James J. Lorence, 'James Paul Warburg', *American National Biography*.

25 Russell Leffingwell quoted by Geisst, *Wall Street*, p. 231; Baltzell, *Protestant Establishment*, pp. 246–48; Smith, *Toward Rational Exuberance*, p. 124; Records of the Committee on Publicity (1935–41), Archives of the New York Stock Exchange.

26 Brooks, *Once in Golconda*, p. 212.

27 'Washington Over Wall Street', *Fortune*, June 1937; vol. xv; Henry Luce quoted by Diana B. Henriques, *The White Sharks of Wall Street: Thomas Mellon Evans and the Original Corporate Raiders* (New York, 2000), p. 51; Allen, *Since Yesterday*, pp. 274–75.

28 Warren I. Susman, *Culture as History: The Transformation of American Society in the Twentieth Century* (New York, 1973), p. 162; Alan Axelrod, *Everything I Know About Business I Learned From Monopoly* (Philadelphia, 2002).

CHAPTER 14 The Long Goodbye

1 Henry James quoted by Jane Mulvagh and Mark A. Weber, *Newport Houses* (New York, 1989), p. 9; Thomas Gannon, *Newport Mansions: The Gilded Age* (Little Compton, Rhode Island, 1992), pp. 5, 18.

2 'Letter from a Blighted Area: Wall Street', *Fortune*, November 1941, vol. 24, #5.

3 'Wall Street and Public Relations', *Commercial and Financial Chronicle*, November 4, 1948; 'Wall Street', *The New Yorker*, 1946; *New York Review of Books*, December 12, 2002; *Journal of Commerce* cited in 'Wall Street's Other Boom', *Fortune*, October, 1946.

4 Weston Smith speech to Investment Association of New York in 'Wall Street and Public Relations'; Charles Merrill quoted by David Colbert, *Eyewitness*

to Wall Street: Four Hundred Years of Dreamers, Schemers, Busts, and Booms (New York, 2001), pp. 160–64; Edwin J. Perkins, *Wall Street to Main Street: Charles Merrill and Middle Class Investors* (New York, 1999), p. 176 – see also pp. 9, 12, 142, 148–49, 157–58, 171; Peter L. Bernstein, *Capital Ideas: The Improbable Origins of Modern Wall Street* (New York, 1992), pp. 41–43, 91; B. Mark Smith, *Toward Rational Exuberance: The Evolution of the Modern Stock Market* (New York, 2001), pp. 134, 140, 144; C. Wright Mills, *The Power Elite* (New York, 2000), p. 121; Kevin Phillips, *Wealth and Democracy: A Political History of the American Rich* (New York, 2002), pp. 77, 78, 362; *Fortune* and *Barron's* quoted by Martin S. Fridson, *It Was A Very Good Year: Extraordinary Moments in Stock Market History* (New York, 1998), pp. 137, 140; Robert M. Sharp, *The Lore and Legends of Wall Street* (Homewood, Illinois, 1989), p. 183.

5 John P. Marquand, *Point of No Return* (Chicago, 1985).

6 Louis Auchincloss, *The Embezzler*, pp. 7, 13.

7 Louis Auchincloss, 'Reflections on Wall Street', *Architectural Digest*, November 1987.

8 Loren Baritz, *The Good Life: The Meaning of Success for the American Middle Class* (New York, 1989), pp 212 and passim.

9 Cameron Hawley, *Cash McCall* (Boston, 1955); Robert Kovesh, 'Businessmen in Fiction: The Capitalist and Executive in American Novels', Amos Tuck School of Business Administration, Dartmouth College, April 1955.

10 Cartoons in Robert Mankoff, editor, *The New Yorker Book of Business Cartoons* (Princeton, 1998).

11 *Force of Evil,* directed by Abraham Polonsky, 1948; Eric Cherman and Martin Rubin, *The Director's Event: Interviews with Five American Film-Makers* (New York, 1970).

12 *Business Week*, July 26, 1947; Joshua B. Freeman, *Working Class New York: Life and Labor Since World War II* (New York, 2000), pp. 50–51.

13 Henry Ford quoted by Kai Bird, *The Chairman: John J. McCloy –The Making of an American Establishment* (New York, 1992), p. 436.

14 'White shark' quoted by Diana B. Henriques, *The White Sharks of Wall Street: Thomas Mellon Evans and the Original Corporate Raiders* (New York, 2000), p. 96 – see also, pp. 14–15, 17, 213; Phillips, *Wealth and Democracy*, p. 76; Robert Sobel, *The Big Board: A History of the New York Stock Market* (New York, 1965), p. 331.

15 Robert Brenner, *The Boom and the Bubble: The United States in the World Economy* (New York, 2002), p. 194; John Brooks, *The Go-Go Years* (New York, 1973), pp. 106–07, 154; Daniel Bell, *The End of Ideology: On the Exhaustion of Political Ideas in the 1950s* (Cambridge, Mass., 2000), chapter 2.

16 *Executive Suite*, 1953, starred William Holden, Barbara Stanwyck, Walter Pidgeon, Paul Douglas, and Frederic March.

17 Elisabeth A. Fones-Wolf, *Selling Free Enterprise: The Business Assault on Labor and Liberalism 1945–60* (Champaign-Urbana, 1994), passim.; Harriman quoted by Eric Hobsbawm, *The Age of Extremes: A History of the World, 1914–1991* (New York, 1995), p. 273.

18 William Whyte quoted by Henriques, *White Sharks*, p. 213; Mills, *Power Elite*, p. 121 and passim.; Richard Pells, *The Liberal Mind in a Conservative Age: American Intellectuals in the 1940s and 1950s* (New York, 1985), pp. 147, 165, 185; Richard Polenberg, *One Nation Divisible: Class, Race, and Ethnicity in the United States Since 1938* (New York, 1980), pp. 102–04; Herbert McClosky and John Zoller, *The American Ethos: Public Attitudes Toward Capitalism and Democracy* (Cambridge, Mass., 1984); E Digby Baltzell, *The Protestant Establishment: Aristocracy and Caste in America* (New York, 1964), pp. 318–19.

19 Brooks, *The Go-Go Years*, pp. 11, 154, 173, 180 357; Babson quoted by Colbert, *Eyewitness*, pp. 197–98 – see also pp. 184–85; Henriques, *White Sharks*, pp. 213–14, 247, 251; Bell, *End of Ideology*, chapter 2; 'New Men of Wall Street', *Economist*, November 6, 1965.

20 Perkins, *Wall Street to Main Street*, pp. 148–49, 157–58, 202; Colbert, *Eyewitness*, pp. 160–62.

21 'Women in the Dough', *American Magazine*, March 1948; Sylvia Porter, 'How About Your Lazy Money?', *Good Housekeeping*, February 1950; Shodie Nichols, 'Stock Market Guide for Women', *Good Housekeeping*, June 1955; 'Share Ownership in the United States', Summary and Conclusions of a Brooking Institution report, June 30, 1952; 'New York Stock Exchange – Statement on Exchange Advertising', September 15, 1964; 'Gentleman's Adviser: Financial Security on the Installment Plan', *Esquire*, October, 1961; Michael Peter Gagne, 'Wall Street: Symbol of American Culture', Ph.D. dissertation, University of Hawaii, 1996, p. 164; Kathleen Odean, *High Steppers, Fallen Angels, and Lollipops: Wall Street Slang* (New York, 1988), p. 52; 'Oral History of Ruddick Lawrence, vice-president of public relations, New York Stock Exchange', archives of the New York Stock Exchange – I want to thank Janice Traflet for bringing this material to my attention.

22 John A. Prestbot, editor, *The Market's Measure* (New York, 1999), p. 73.

23 Ibid. p. 33; Bernstein, *Capital Ideas*, pp. 9, 41–43; Smith, *Rational Exuberance*, pp. 174, 179; T. A. Wise and George J.W. Goodman, 'Powerful Men Downtown', *Fortune*, February, 1960.

24 Merrill quoted by Perkins, *Wall Street to Main Street*, p. 221; Gabriel Kolko, *Wealth and Power in America* (New York, 1962), pp. 50, 53, 54; 'Annual Report to the New Stock Exchange', 1952, p. 16, NYSE archives; Robert J. Shiller, *Irrational Exuberance* (New York, 2000), p. 109; 'Remarks Upon Signing a Bill Amending the Securities Act', August 20, 1964, *Public Papers of the President – Lyndon Baines Johnson, 1963–64*; Irving Olds quoted by Gagne, 'Wall Street', p. 136; Sobel, *The Big Board: A History of the New York Stock Market* (New York, 1965), p. 339.

25 Truman quoted by Edward Chancellor, *Devil Take the Hindmost: A History of Financial Speculation* (New York, 1999), p. 234; Truman quoted by Fones-Wolf, *Selling Free Enterprise*, p. 49; Truman quoted by Charles R. Geisst, *Wall Street: A History* (New York, 1997), p. 245; President Truman, 'Address at Dinner of Better Business Bureau', June 6, 1950, *Public Papers of the President – Harry S. Truman*, p. 700.

26 Henry A. Wallace, *The Century of the Common Man*, edited by Russell Lord (New York, 1943).

27 Peter Viereck, 'The Revolt Against the Elite' in Daniel Bell, editor, *The Radical Right* (New York, 1962, originally published 1955; David Potter, *People of Plenty: Economic Abundance and the American Character* (Chicago, 1954); David Riesman with Nathan Glazer and Reuel Denney, *The Lonely Crowd: A Study of the Changing American Character* (New Haven, 1961, originally published 1949).

28 John Judis, *The Paradox of American Democracy: Elites, Special Interests, and the Betrayal of Public Trust* (New York, 2000), p. 76.

29 Riesman quoted by Mills, *Power Elite*, p. 243; Pells, *Liberal Mind*, pp. 147, 165, 185; Polenberg, *One Nation Divisible*, pp. 102, 104; Godfrey Hodgson, *America in Our Time* (New York, 1976), pp. 77, 81; Riesman, *Lonely Crowd*.

30 David Riesman and Nathan Glazer, 'The Intellectuals and the Discontented Classes' in Bell, *Radical Right*; Riesman, *Lonely Crowd*, pp. 20–21, 34–35, 45; Polenberg, *One Nation Divisible*, p. 104.

31 Riesman quoted by Polenberg, *One Nation Divisible*, p. 104; Riesman quoted by Mills, *Power Elite*, p. 243; Viereck, 'The Revolt Against the Elite'; Riesman, *Lonely Crowd*; Pells, *Liberal Mind*, passim.

32 Richard H. Rovere, *The American Establishment and Other Reports, Opinions, and Speculations* (New York, 1962); Hodgson, *America in Our Time*, p. 112.

33 Mills, *Power Elite*, pp. 16, 20, 53, 69, 121–23, 125–26, 147–48, 170, 232, 235, 277, 283, 289–90.

34 Baltzell, *Protestant Establishment*, passim.

35 Mills, *Power Elite*, pp. 91–93, 302, 304, 315–17.

36 Mills, *Power Elite*, pp. 84, 91–93; Walter Isaacson and Evan Thomas, *The Wise Men: Six Friends and the World They Made – Acheson, Bohlen, Harriman, Kennan, Lovett, McCloy* (New York, 1986), p. 106, 109; Louis Auchincloss, *I Come as a Thief* (Boston, 1972); Patricia Kane, 'Lawyers at the Top: The Fiction of Louis Auchincloss', *Critique*, 1964–65, vol. 2/2; Nelson W. Aldrich, *Old Money: The Mythology of America's Upper Class* (New York, 1988), pp. 63, 105; Baltzell, *Protestant Establishment*; Jackson Lears, 'Revitalizing the Rich: The Managerial Revolution and the Fiction of Elite Decline' in Steve Fraser and Gary Gerstle, editors, *Ruling America: Wealth and Power in a Democracy* (Cambridge, Mass., 2005).

37 Potter, *People of Plenty*; Brooks, *Go-Go Years*, pp. 106, 111, 113, 210; Smith, *Toward Rational Exuberance*, p. 214; 'Saul Steps Out', *Manhattan Inc.*, October, 1985; Saul Steinberg quoted by Henriques, *White Sharks*, p. 263.

38 Haynes Johnson, *Sleepwalking Through History: America in the Reagan Years* (New York, 1992), p. 449; Daniel Yergin, *Shattered Peace: The Origins of the Cold War and the National Security State* (Boston, 1978), pp. 306–07; Hobsbawm, *Age of Extremes*, pp. 258, 275.

39 I. F. Stone, *Business As Usual: The First Year of Defense* (New York, 1941),

p. 135; Irving Bernstein, *Promises Kept: John F. Kennedy's New Frontier* (New York, 1991), pp. 127–28; Arthur Schlesinger Jr quoted by Isaacson and Thomas, *Wise Men*, p. 128 – see also pp. 32, 109, 112, and *passim*; John B. Judis, 'Twilight of the Gods', *Wilson Quarterly*, Autumn, 1991; Max Holland, 'The Rise and Fall of the American Establishment', *Wilson Quarterly*, Autumn, 1991; Hodgson, *America in Our Time*, p. 112 and *passim*; Philip H. Burch, Jr, *Elites in American History: The New Deal to the Carter Administration* (New York, 1980), pp. 75–76, 79–80, 82–86, 98–101; Franz Schurman, *The Logic of World Power: An Inquiry into the Origins, Currents, and Contradictions of World Politics* (New York, 1974), p. 48.

40 Galbraith quoted by Bird, *The Chairman*, p. 19, and World Bank director quoted by Bird, *The Chairman*, p. 289, and McCloy quoted by Bird, *The Chairman*, p. 297 – see also pp. 108, 110, 131, 230, 233, 273, 285, 288, 291, 297–98; Stone, *Business As Usual*, p. 135; Judis, *Paradox of American Democracy*, p. 72.

41 Isaacson and Thomas, *Wise Men*, *passim*; Yergin, *Shattered Peace*, pp. 306–07, 312, 328.

42 Leffingwell quoted by Yergin, *Shattered Peace*, p. 310; Isaacson and Thomas, *Wise Men*, pp. 404–07, 414, 429, 433, and *passim*; Judis, 'Twilight of the Gods'.

43 Brooks, *Go-Go Years*, pp. 111, 216–17; *New York Magazine* quoted by Bird, *The Chairman*, pp. 619–20; Judis, 'Twilight of the Gods'.

44 Senator Taft quoted by Bird, *The Chairman*, p. 389 and Senator McCarthy quoted by Bird, *The Chairman*, p. 415 – see also pp. 280, 386, 389–90; Senator McCarthy quoted by David M. Oshinsky, *A Conspiracy So Immense: The World of Joe McCarthy* (New York, 1983), pp. 108–09 – see also p. 105; Paul Nitze quoted by Isaacson and Thomas, *Wise Men*, p. 564 – see also pp. 425, 428, 466, 570; Senator McCarthy quoted by Polenberg, *One Nation Divisible*, p. 125; Dean Acheson, *Present at the Creation* (New York, 1969), chapter 39 – 'The Attack of the Primitives Begins', and pp. 366, 369, 370.

45 Henriques, *White Sharks*, pp. 159, 162–63; 'Communists Penetrate Wall Street', *Commercial and Financial Chronicle*, November 6, 1947.

46 Mills, *Power Elite*, pp. 43–45; Viereck, 'The Revolt Against the Elite'; Riesman and Glazer, 'The Intellectuals and the Discontented Classes'; Schurman, *Logic of World Power*, pp. 7, 48, 58, and *passim*.

CHAPTER 15 The Return of the Repressed

1 *New York Times*, August 25, 1967; David Colbert, *Eyewitness to Wall Street: 400 Years of Dreamers, Schemers, Busts, and Booms* (New York, 2001), pp. 178–79.

2 John Brooks, *The Go-Go Years* (New York, 1973), pp. 8–11.

3 'Adam Smith' (George Goodman), *The Money Game* (New York, 1967); Colbert, *Eyewitness*, pp. 184–85; B. Mark Smith, *Toward Rational Exuberance: The Evolution of the Modern Stock Market* (New York, 2001), p. 214.

4 William Gaddis, *JR* (New York, 1975).

5 E. L. Doctorow, *Ragtime* (New York, 1976).

6 '10cc', *Wall Street Shuffle*, 1974.

7 Daniel Bell, *The Cultural Contradictions of Capitalism* (New York, 1996, originally published 1976), pp. xvi, 77, 84, 98, 291, 306, and passim.; Michael Oriard, *Sporting with the Gods: The Rhetoric of Play and Game in American Culture* (New York, 1991), p. 349.

8 Brooks, *Go-Go Years*, p. 106; John B. Judis, 'Twilight of the Gods', *Wilson Quarterly*, Autumn, 1991; John B. Judis, *The Paradox of American Democracy: Elites, Special Interests, and the Betrayal of Public Trust* (New York, 2000), passim; Nixon quoted by Edward Chancellor, *Devil Take the Hindmost: A History of Financial Speculation* (New York, 1999), p. 234.

9 Judis, 'Twilight of the Gods'; Kai Bird, *The Chairman: John J. McCloy – The Making of an American Establishment* (New York, 1992), pp. 619–20; Max Holland, 'The Rise and Fall of the American Establishment', *Wilson Quarterly*, Autumn 1991; John L. Boies, *Buying for Armageddon: Business, Society, and Military Spending Since the Cuban Missile Crisis* (New Brunswick, 1994), p. 126; Kevin Phillips, *Wealth and Democracy: A Political History of the American Rich* (New York, 2002), p. 86.

10 Brooks, *Go-Go Years*, pp. 1–4, 173, 210, 270–71.

11 Peter L. Bernstein, *Capital Ideas: The Improbable Origins of Modern Wall Street* (New York, 1992), pp. 2–3; Phillips, *Wealth and Democracy*, pp. 83–88; Susan Strange, *Casino Capitalism* (London, 1986), p. 4; Haynes Johnson, *Sleepwalking Through History: America in the Reagan Years* (New York, 1992), p. 118.

12 Smith, *Toward Rational Exuberance*, p. 233; Phillips, *Wealth and Democracy*, pp. 83–88; Judis, *Paradox of American Democracy*, passim.; Robert Brenner, *The Boom and the Bubble: The United States in the World Economy* (New York, 2000), passim.; Bluestone and Harrison quoted by Jefferson Cowie and Joseph Heathcott, editors, *Beyond the Ruins: The Meanings of De-Industrialization* (Ithaca, 2003), p. 6.

13 Brenner, *Boom and Bubble*, pp. 42, 48–49, 50–51, 54, 58, 91–92, and passim; Strange, *Casino Capitalism*, pp. 172–73.

14 Johnson, *Sleepwalking Through History*, pp. 20–21, 94; Diana Vreeland quoted by Phillips, *Wealth and Democracy*, p. 333.

15 Walter Werner and Steven Smith, *Wall Street*, quoted by Phillips, *Wealth and Democracy*, p. 347 – see also pp. 334–35; Milton Friedman quoted by Chancellor, *Devil Take the Hindmost*, pp. 241–43.

16 Judis, *Paradox of American Democracy*, p. 158 and passim; Phillips, *Wealth and Democracy*, pp. 230–32.

17 Connie Bruck, *The Predators' Ball: The Inside Story of Drexel Burnham and the Rise of the Junk Bond Raiders* (New York, 1988), pp. 153, 171, 185, and passim.

18 Judis, *Paradox of American Democracy*, p. 129 and passim; Bruck, *Predators' Ball*, pp. 185–86, 249, 261–62 and chapter 9.

19 Milken admirer quoted by Bruck, *Predators' Ball*, p. 84 – see also pp. 19, 84–85, 93, 95, 270; Oriard, *Sporting with the Gods*, pp. 351–52; Phillips,

Wealth and Democracy, p. 366; Ken Auletta, *Greed and Glory on Wall Street: The Fall of the House of Lehman* (New York, 1986).

20 Donald Regan quoted by Kevin Phillips, *The Politics of Rich and Poor: Wealth and the American Electorate in the Reagan Aftermath* (New York, 1990), p. 66; Johnson, *Sleepwalking in America*, pp. 110, 186, 229; Colbert, *Eyewitness*, p. 247; Michael Lewis, *Liar's Poker: Rising Through the Wreckage on Wall Street* (New York, 1989), pp. 113, 138, 173, and *passim*; Judis, *Paradox of American Democracy*, p. 129; Herbert McClosky and John Zaller, *The American Ethos: Public Attitudes Toward Capitalism and Democracy* (Cambridge, Mass., 1984), p. 141; Chancellor, *Devil Take the Hindmost*, pp. 250, 271.

21 Michael Thomas, *Manhattan Inc*, March 1985 and December 1985; Grand dame quoted in 'A New Opulence Triumphs in Capital', *New York Times*, January 22, 1981; *New York Times Magazine* quoted by Johnson, *Sleepwalking in America*, p. 196.

22 *Newsweek*, September 15, 1980; Jerry Falwell quoted by Johnson, *Sleepwalking in America*, p. 198 – see also p. 199.

23 *Manhattan Inc*, September 1984, April 1985, September 1987, among many other issues.

24 Chancellor, *Devil Take the Hindmost*, pp. 254, 261, 264; Phillips, *Wealth and Democracy*, p. 356; Phillips, *Politics of Rich and Poor*, p. 211; *Institutional Investor* and *Forbes* quoted by Bruck, *Predators' Ball*, p. 270; Michael M. Thomas, 'The Eyes Still Have It', *Manhattan Inc*, April 1985; Michael Thomas, 'Deals', *Manhattan Inc*, March 1985; David Remnick, *Manhattan Inc*, April 1985; Barry Rehfeld, 'The Liquidator', *Manhattan Inc*, September 1985; John Taylor, 'Baby Tycoon', *Manhattan Inc*, November 1985; Michael Thomas, 'The New Tycoonery', *Manhattan Inc*, December 1985; 'Corporate Culture', *Manhattan Inc*, February 1986; Ron Rosenbaum, 'Society's Dissidents', *Manhattan Inc*, April 1986; Hope Lampert, 'Society Steps Out', *Manhattan Inc*, October 1985; Brad Gooch, 'The New Gilded Age', *Manhattan Inc*, October 1986; Paul Cowan, 'The Merger Maestro', *Esquire*, May 1984; Jesse Kornblath, 'The Working Rich: The Real Slaves of New York', *New York Magazine*, November 24, 1986; 'Making it by Doing Good', *New York Times*, July 3, 1983; Auletta, *Greed and Glory on Wall Street*.

25 Ron Rosenbaum, 'The Frantic Screaming Voice of the Rich and Famous', *Manhattan Inc*, January 1986.

26 Oriard, *Sporting with the Gods*, pp. 322–23, 326, 349–51.

27 Revisionist biographies of the era include: Maury Klein, *The Life and Legend of Jay Gould* (Baltimore, 1986), Lloyd J. Mercer, *E. H. Harriman: Master Railroader* (Boston, 1985) and Ron Chernow, *The House of Morgan: An American Banking Dynasty and the Rise of Big Business* (New York, 1990). The trend would continue through the 1990s with new biographies of Morgan by Jean Strouse, of John D. Rockefeller by Ron Chernow, of Harriman by Maury Klein, and in histories of Wall Street and big business by John Steele Gordon, Thomas Kessner, and Charles Geisst among others.

28 Johnson, *Sleepwalking Through History*, pp. 195, 215, 225–26; Lewis, *Liar's Poker, passim*; interview with Richard Leone, March 22, 1999; *Manhattan Inc*, July 1985.

29 Johnson, *Sleepwalking Through History*, p. 239; Ray M. Adler, 'The Kingdom of Wish: Oliver Stone's Problem with History', *Fides et Historia*, Summer 1993, vol. 25/2; Tracy Corrigan, 'Junk Bond Ballet', *Times of London*, October 21, 1996; Anna Kisselgoff, 'Crossroads of Art and Life Where Rap Meets Ballet', *Dance Review*, October 18, 1996; Christopher Reardon, '80s Excess Raised to an Esthetic', *New York Times*, October 13, 1996; Kathleen Odean, *High Steppers, Fallen Angels, and Lollipops: Wall Street Slang* (New York, 1988); Kathleen Odean, 'Bear Hugs and Bo Dereks on Wall Street' in Christopher Ricks and Leonard Michaels, eds., *The State of the Language* (Berkeley, 1990); *Art News*, March 1989, vol. 88.

30 Johnson, *Sleepwalking Through History*, p. 124; Michael Thomas, 'Deals', *Manhattan Inc*, March 1985; Brad Gooch, 'The New Gilded Age', *Manhattan Inc* , October 1986; Lewis Lapham, 'The Dilemma of Money and Class in America', *Manhattan Inc*.

31 Brenner, *Boom and Bubble*, p. 87; Phillips, *Wealth and Democracy*, pp. xiii, 92, 150–51, 220; *Business Week* quoted by Phillips, *Politics of Rich and Poor*, p. 201 – see also p. 16.

32 Chancellor, *Devil Take the Hindmost*, p. 261; Phillips, *Wealth and Democracy*, p. 95.

33 'Death march' comment quoted by Bruck, *Predators' Ball*, p. 245; Lewis, *Liar's Poker*; preview of the film, *Wall Street*, in *Manhattan Inc*, June 1987.

34 President Reagan quoted by Brenner, *Boom and Bubble*, p. 84.

35 Johnson, *Sleepwalking Through History*, pp. 184–86.

36 Bruck, *Predators' Ball*, pp. 244–45, 259–60; Colbert, *Eyewitness*, p. 253.

37 James Grant quoted by Phillips, *Wealth and Democracy*, p. 95 – see also pp. 95–98.

38 Phillips variously calls this the 'financialization of the economy', 'the collectivization of financial risk' (which of course have different if related meanings) in *Wealth and Democracy* – see p. 93; Joseph Schumpeter, *The Theory of Economic Development* (New York, 1961), p. 126.

39 Brenner, *Boom and Bubble*, pp. 81, 86, 88; Phillips, *Wealth and Democracy*, pp. 95–98, 322; Phillips, *Politics of Rich and Poor*, p. 70, 171–72, 174.

40 Strange, *Casino Capitalism*, p. 1; Bernstein, *Capital Ideas*, pp. 286, 306; Smith, *Toward Rational Exuberance*, p. 273; Colbert, *Eyewitness*, p. 289; Johnson, *Sleepwalking Through History*, pp. 380–81; Brenner, *Boom and Bubble*, p. 85.

41 Brenner, *Boom and Bubble*, p. 374; Felix Rohatyn quoted by Bruck, *Predators' Ball*, p. 141 – see also p. 267; Phillips, *Wealth and Democracy*, p. 72.

42 Colbert, *Eyewitness*, p. 235; John Oliver Wilson, 'The Junk Bond King of Wall Street: A Discourse in Business Ethics' in Richard M. Coughlin, ed., *Morality, Rationality, and Efficiency: New Perspectives on Socio-Economics* (New York, 1991); Johnson, *Sleepwalking Through History*, pp. 431–33.

43 Bruck, *Predators' Ball*, pp. 261–62; Phillips, *Politics of Rich and Poor*, pp.

70–72; Oriard, *Sporting with the Gods*, p. 352; Patricia O'Toole, *Money and Morals in America: A History* (New York, 1998), pp. 301–02.

44 *Economist*, May 9, 1992; Louis Auchincloss, *Diary of a Yuppie* (New York, 1986); Paul Lyons, 'Yuppie: A Contemporary American Keyword', *Socialist Review*, 1989, vol. 19/1; Edward Bennett Williams quoted by Johnson, *Sleepwalking Through History*, p. 227; Wall Street joke quoted by Odean, 'Bear Hugs and Bo Dereks'; *Time* headline quoted by Wilson, 'The Junk Bond King'.

45 Bruck, *Predators' Ball*; Auletta, *Greed and Glory*; Lewis, *Liar's Poker*; Bryan Burrough and John Helyar, *Barbarians at the Gate: The Fall of RJR Nabisco* (New York, 1989); Donna Sammons Carpenter and John Feloni, *The Fall of the House of Hutton* (New York, 1989); James B. Stewart, *Den of Thieves* (New York, 1991); George Anders, *Merchants of Debt: KKR and the Mortgaging of American Business* (New York, 1992); Bret Easton Ellis, *American Psycho* (New York, 1991); Tom Wolfe, *Bonfire of the Vanities* (New York, 1987); Kurt Eichenwald's *Serpent on the Rock* (New York, 1995) about the scandal at Prudential-Bache wasn't published until the middle of the next decade, but its title gives off the same odor of brimstone.

46 Wolfe, *Bonfire*, pp. 56, 137; *New Republic*, November 23, 1987; Linda McDowell, 'Fictional Money (or Greed Isn't So Good in the 1990s)' in John Hassard and Ruth Holliday, editors, *Organization/Representation: Work and Organization in Popular Culture* (London, 1998).

47 Jerry Sterner, *Other People's Money: The Ultimate Seduction* (New York, 1989).

48 Phillip Lopate, 'Hollywood Looks at the Business Office', *New Labor Forum*, Fall/Winter 2001, no. 9; Jack Boozer, Jr, 'Wall Street: The Commodification of Perception', *Journal of Popular Film and Television*, 1989, vol. 17; Ray M. Anker, 'The Kingdom of Wish: Oliver Stone's Problem with History', *Fides et Historica*, Summer 1993, vol. 25/2.

49 Colbert, *Eyewitness*, pp. 247, 253; Phillips, *Politics of Rich and Poor*, pp. 50, 72; 'Die Yuppie Scum' quoted by Lyons, 'Yuppie: A Contemporary American Keyword'; Johnson, *Sleepwalking Through History*, pp. 431–33, 442.

50 Phillips, *Politics of Rich and Poor* , pp. xvii, xviii, xxiii.

CHAPTER 16 Shareholder Nation

1 *Seattle Post-Intelligencer*, July 30, 2003; *Business Week*, August 25, 2003.

2 Charles Merrill quoted by Thomas Frank, *One Market Under God: Extreme Capitalism, Market Populism, and the End of Economic Democracy* (New York, 2000), p. 104; Edward J. Perkins, *Wall Street to Main Street: Charles Merrill and Middle Class Investors* (New York, 1999), pp. 9, 58, 148–49, 157–58, 202, 221–22, 234, and *passim*; B. Mark Smith, *Toward Rational Exuberance: The Evolution of the Modern Stock Market* (New York, 2001), p. 142.

3 Michael Peter Gagne, 'Wall Street: Symbol of American Culture', Ph.D. dissertation (University of Hawaii, 1996), p. 164; Smith, *Toward Rational Exuberance*, p. 142; Martin S. Fridson, *It Was a Very Good Year:*

Extraordinary Moments in Stock Market History (New York, 1998), pp. 148–49; 'Venture: Fascinating Game of Finance and Big Business', 3M Company, 1970; 'The World of Wall Street: A Fast Moving Investment Game', NBC At Home Entertainment/Hasbro, 1969; 'Stock and Bonds: The Game of Investment', 3M Company, 1964; Pierre Van Goethem, *The Americanization of World Business: Wall Street and the Superiority of American Enterprise* (New York, 1972), pp. 7, 14, 19; 'Women in the Dough', *American Magazine*, March 1948; Sylvia Porter, 'How About your Lazy Money?', *Good Housekeeping*, February 1950; Shodie Nichols, 'Stock Market Guide for Women', *Good Housekeeping*, June 1955; 'Gentleman's Adviser: Financial Security on the Installment Plan', *Esquire*, October 1961; 'New York Stock Exchange Statement on Exchange Advertising', September 15, 1964, New York Stock Exchange Archives.

4 Smith, *Toward Rational Exuberance*, pp. 232–33; David Colbert, *Eyewitness to Wall Street: Four Hundred Years of Dreamers, Schemers, Busts, and Booms* (New York, 2001), p. 295.

5 Perkins, Wall *Street to Main Street*, p. 232; John Brooks, *The Go-Go Years* (New York, 1973), p. 101; Robert J. Shiller, *Irrational Exuberance* (New York, 2000), p. 35; Peter L. Bernstein, *Capital Ideas: The Improbable Origins of Modern Wall Street* (New York, 1992), p. 9; Smith, *Toward Rational Exuberance*, pp. 216, 231–32, 266; Colbert, *Eyewitness*, p. 288; *USA Today*, March 30, 1999; Roger E. Alcaly, 'How to Think About the Stock Market', *New York Review of Books*, June 25, 1998; Frank, *One Market*, p. 120; *New York Times*, March 19, 2001.

6 Observer quoted by Bernstein, *Capital Ideas*, p. 7 – see also pp. 227, 249, and *passim*; Colbert, *Eyewitness*, pp. 318–21; Gary Taubes, 'Wall Street Smarts', *Discover*, October 1998; Benoit B. Mandelbrot, 'A Multifractal Walk Down Wall Street', *Scientific American*, February 1999.

7 Frank, *One Market*, pp. 112–18; Bernstein, *Capital Ideas*, p. 303; Colbert, *Eyewitness*, pp. 296–300.

8 Buffett quoted by Frank, *One Market*, p. 118 – see also p. 135 and *passim*; Colbert, *Eyewitness*, pp. 296–300.

9 *Motley Fool* quoted by Frank, *One Market*, pp. 148–49; Haynes Johnson, *The Best of Times: The Boom and Bust Years of America Before Everything Changed* (New York, 2002), p. 476.

10 George Gilder quoted by Frank, *One Market*, p. 80 – see also p. 245 and *passim*; Larissa MacFarquhar, 'The Gilder Effect' in David Remnick, editor, *The New Gilded Age: The New Yorker Looks at the Culture of Affluence* (New York, 2000).

11 Frank, *One Market*, pp. 29, 80–81, 88–90, 93, 124; *Fortune*, October 11, 1999; Lucent Technologies slogan quoted by David Brooks, *Bobos in Paradise: The New Upper Class and How They Got There* (New York, 2000), pp. 110–11; Day trader quoted by Matthew Klam, 'Riding the Mo in the Lime Green Glow', *New York Times Sunday Magazine*, November 21, 1999.

12 Brooks, *Bobos in Paradise*, pp. 110–11; Frank, *One Market*, pp. 203–04; Klam, 'Riding the Mo in the Lime Green Glow'; Ron Chernow, 'Hard

Charging Bulls and Red Flags', *New York Times*, September 2, 1998; Chris Smith, 'How the Stock Market Swallowed New York', *New York Magazine* (October 3, 1998).

13 *Working Girl* (1988); Johnson, *Best of Times*, p. 405.

14 Abby Joseph Cohen quoted by Shiller, *Irrational Exuberance*, p. 74 – see also p. 72; Smith, *Toward Rational Exuberance*, p. 255.

15 Thomas L. Friedman, *The Lexus and the Olive Tree: Understanding Globalization* (New York, 2000), pp. 103–04, 109, 112–14, 121, and passim; Daniel Gross quoted by Kevin Phillips, *Wealth and Democracy: A Political History of the American Rich* (New York, 2002), p. 361; Shannon Henry, 'A Way to Incubate Young Minds', *Washington Post*, November 30, 2000; Meryl Gordon, 'The Green Team', *New York Magazine*, June 12, 2000; 'What Makes Us Different', Robin Hood Foundation pamphlet.

16 John Cassidy, 'Pricking the Bubble', *New Yorker*, August 17, 1998; John Cassidy, 'The Fountainhead' in Remnick, *New Gilded Age*; Frank, *One Market*, p. 154; Shiller, *Irrational Exuberance*, pp. 28, 30.

17 'The Summer of Wretched Excess', *Business Week*, August 3, 1998; John B. Judis, *The Paradox of American Democracy: Elites, Special Interests, and the Betrayal of Public Trust* (New York, 2000), pp. 250–51; Johnson, *Best of Times*, p. 22; *Wall Street Journal*, April 23, 1999; Gagne, 'Wall Street: A Symbol of American Culture', p. 172.

18 Phillips, *Wealth and Democracy*, p. 141; 'Stunning Stock Action Pervades U.S. Culture', *USA Today*, March 30, 1999; 'Some Abandon Water Cooler for Internet Stock Trading', *New York Times*, May 29, 1999; 'New Breed of Investors, All Beguiled by the Web', *New York Times*, May 16, 1999; Chernow, 'Hard Charging Bulls'; 'People of the Bull', *Business Week*, April 12, 1999; Colbert, *Eyewitness*, p. 302.

19 Linda McDowell, 'Fictional Money (or Greed Isn't So Good in the 1990s)' in John Hassard and Ruth Halliday, eds., *Organization/Representation: Work and Organization in Popular Culture* (London, 1998); Michael Jordan commercial quoted by Friedman, *Lexus and Olive Tree*, p. 14; Robin Goldwyn, 'Running with the Bulls in a Fashion Sense anyway', *Barron's*, October 19, 1998; 'Fashion: In the office It's Anything Goes – Casual Friday Was One Thing, But This . . .', *Wall Street Journal*, August 26, 1999; Johnson, *Best of Times*, p. 21.

20 David Owen quoted by Colbert, *Eyewitness*, p. 325.

21 Ibid., pp. 355–57; David Denby, 'The Quarter of Living Dangerously' in Remnick, *New Gilded Age*; *Newsweek*, January 11, 1999; *New York Times*, April 14, 1999; Connecticut billboard quoted by Shiller, *Irrational Exuberance*, p. 42.

22 Robert Mankoff, editor, *The New Yorker Book of Business Cartoons* (New York, 1998), p. 65; *New Yorker*, April 23 and 30, 2001; *New York* cartoon in Smith, 'How the Stock Market Swallowed New York'.

23 Jane Bryant Quinn, 'Investment Clubs: What Makes Them Work?', *Good Housekeeping*, September 1997; Barzou Daragahi, 'How to Start an On-Line Stock Club', *Money.Com*, August 1999; Grace W. Weinstein, 'Club Clout',

Ms., September, 1989; Bernard Rashco, 'Investor Illiteracy', *American Prospect*, March/April 1999; Smith, 'How the Stock Market Swallowed New York'.

24 Gagne, 'Wall Street: Symbol of American Culture', pp. 168–70; Jean Sherman Chatzky, 'Money Talk', *Money Magazine*, May 1998; Amy Dickinson, 'Kids and the Dow', *Time*, October 30, 2000; 'Turning Kids Into Investors', *US News and World Report*, October 17, 1988.

25 Plot summaries of *Pi*, *Corporate Affairs*, and *The Associate* from http.//us.imdb.com/plot; Johnson, *Best of Times*, p. 471; *New York Times*, December 11, 2000.

26 Stephen Frey, *Trust Fund* (New York, 2001); Christopher Reich, *The First Billion* (New York, 2002); Peter Sense, *War on Wall Street* (New York, 2001).

27 Scientist interviewed by *Forbes* quoted by Robert Teitelman, *Gene Dreams: Wall Street, Academia, and the Rise of Biotechnology* (New York, 1989), p. 27 – see also pp. 4, 12–13, 186, and *passim*.

28 Ibid. pp. 186, 206–07, and *passim*.

29 George Gilder quoted by Frank, *One Market*, p. 355 – see also pp. 148–49, 356; 'Alan Greenspan's Brave New World', *Business Week*, July 14, 1997; Robert Brenner, *The Boom and the Bubble: The United States in the World Economy* (New York, 2002), pp. 171–73, 177.

30 Phillips, *Wealth and Democracy*, p. 99; Shiller, *Irrational Exuberance*, p. 20 and passim.; 'Asymptote: Rashid and Couture – New York Stock Exchange Trading Floor Operations Center', pamphlet, 1999.

31 *Wall Street Journal* quoted by Colbert, *Eyewitness*, p. 327; Johnson, *Best of Times*, p. 478; William D. Nordhaus, 'The Story of the Bubble', *New York Review of Books*, January 15, 2004; Charles C. Mann, 'The Old New Thing', *American Prospect*, March 11, 2002; Greenspan's 'virtuous cycle' quoted by Brenner, *Boom and Bubble*, p. 177; 'Ordinary People Share Extraordinary Faith, Reap Rich Rewards', *Wall Street Journal*, March 30, 1999.

32 John Chambers quoted by Friedman, *Lexus and Olive Tree*, p. 140 – see also pp. 53–57, 103–04, 109, 112–14; Eyal Press and Jennifer Washburn, 'The Kept University', *Atlantic Monthly*, March 2000; Teitelman, *Gene Dreams*, p. 14, and *passim*.

33 Brooks, *Bobos in Paradise*; Phillips, *Wealth and Democracy*, p. 357.

34 British finance minister quoted by Barbara Garson, *Money Makes the World Go Around: One Investor Tracks Her Cash Through the Global Economy From Brooklyn to Bangkok and Back* (New York, 2001), p. 287.

35 *Wall Street Journal*, March 30, 1999; Judis, *Paradox of American Democracy*, pp. 228–29.

36 *Wall Street Journal* quoted by Phillips, *Wealth and Democracy*, p. 142 – see also pp. 103, 106, 108, 110, 142, 151; Chuck Collins *et al.*, *The Perils of the Growing American Wealth Gap* (United for a Fair Economy, Boston, 1999); Lawrence Mishel, *The State of Working America* (Ithaca, 1998), p. 271; Frank, *One Market*, p. 97; Johnson, *Best of Times*, p. 476; *Newsweek*, January 11, 1999; *New York Times*, April 23, 1999; *Wall Street Journal*, March 30, 1999.

37 Frank, *One Market*; Patricia Cayo Sexton, 'Con Games and Gamblers on Wall Street', *Dissent*, Winter 1999; Edward Chancellor, *Devil Take the Hindmost: A History of Financial Speculation* (New York, 1999), p. 346; Brenner, *Boom and Bubble*, pp. 219–22, 224–25.

38 Garson, *Money Makes the World Go Around*, pp. 192–93, 202–04, and *passim*; Brenner, *Boom and Bubble*, pp. 164, 171–72; Albert J. Dunlap with Bob Adelman, *Mean Business: How I Save Bad Companies and Make Good Companies Great* (New York, 1996).

39 Teitelman, *Gene Dreams*, p. 197, and *passim*; Larissa MacFarquhar, 'The Connector', in Remnick, *New Gilded Age*; Cassidy, 'The Fountainhead'; Frank, *One Market*, p. 97.

40 Shiller, *Irrational Exuberance*, p. 24; Robin Blackburn, 'The Enron Debacle and the Pension Crisis', *New Left Review*, March/April 2002, vol. 14; Brenner, *Boom and Bubble*, pp. 165–70; Gavyn Davies quoted by Phillips, *Wealth and Democracy*, p. 230 – see also pp. 217, 353; Chancellor, *Devil Take the Hindmost*, p. 250.

41 James Grant quoted by Phillips, *Wealth and Democracy*, p. 95 – see also pp. 103, 104, 106, 138; Kevin Phillips, 'Fat City', *Time*, September 26, 1994 (this is an excerpt from Phillips' book, *Arrogant Capital: Washington, Wall Street, and the Frustration of American Politics*); Brenner, *Boom and Bubble*, pp. 171–73; *New York Times*, October 23, 1998; Chancellor, *Devil Take the Hindmost*, pp. 340–44, 346; Colbert, *Eyewitness*, pp. 320–21.

42 Mark Wallace, 'Wooing Wall Street', *Latin Finances*, n.d., #104; 'Whistle Stops on Wall Street', *New York Times*, March 8, 1999; Rudiger Dornbusch quoted by Phillips, *Wealth and Democracy*, p. 230; George Soros quoted by Sexton, 'Con Games and Gamblers on Wall Street'.

43 Lewis Lapham quoted by Phillips, *Wealth and Democracy*, p. 405; Blackburn, 'The Enron Debacle'; Nordhaus, 'The Story of the Bubble'.

44 Judis, *Paradox of American Democracy*, *passim*; Christopher Reardon, ''80s Excess Raised to an Esthetic', *New York Times*, October 13, 1996.

45 *New York Times*, March 28, 2000 and June 1, 2000.

46 Robert Putnam, *Bowling Alone: The Collapse and Revival of American Community* (New York, 2000); Maureen Dowd quoted by Johnson, *Best of Times*, p. 450; Frank, *One Market*, p. 68; *Wall Street Journal*, May 6, 1999; Michael Lewis, 'Why You', *New York Times Magazine*, September 23, 2001; Michael Lewis, 'Faking It', *New York Times Magazine*, July 15, 2001.

47 Remnick, *New Gilded Age*.

48 *Family Man* (2000); *Pretty Woman* (1990); *Boiler Room* (2000); *American Psycho* (2000); *New York Times*, November 2, 1999 and August 23, 1999; Colbert, *Eyewitness*, p. 330.

49 Po Bronson, *Bombardiers* (New York, 1995), pp. 153, 223.

50 John Le Carre, *Single and Single* (New York, 1999).

51 Jonathan Franzen, *The Corrections* (New York, 2001); Kate Jennings, *Moral Hazard* (New York, 2002).

Index